Richard DiLello

Without You

The Tragic Story of Badfinger

DAN MATOVINA

Frances Glover Books

Frances Glover Books
San Mateo, California

Lyric Reproductions (All rights reserved)

Estate of Peter William Ham (PRS)
All rights administered by
Bug Music (ASCAP)

I've Been There Once Before
Catherine Cares
The Clown Of The Party
Sille Veb
It Doesn't Really Matter
Helping Hand
Ringside
No More

Estate of Tom Evans (PRS)
All rights administered by
Bug Music (ASCAP)

Uncle C
Over You

Apple Publishing Ltd. (PRS)
All rights administered by
Warner Bros. Music Corp. (ASCAP)

Beautiful And Blue
Carry On Til Tomorrow
Crimson Ship
Midnight Caller
Perfection
Sing For The Song
Name Of The Game
Take It All
Apple Of My Eye
Day After Day
Baby Blue
The Winner
Blind Owl
Timeless

Warner Bros Music Corp (ASCAP)
All rights administered by
Warner Bros. Music Corp. (ASCAP)

Lonely You
Just A Chance
Meanwhile Back At The Ranch
Keep Believing

Publisher: Frances Glover Books
Graphic Arts and Design: Irene Imfeld, Dan Matovina, Jan Camp
Cover Design: Dan Matovina, Mark Perkins, Chris Charles
Cover Photograph: Richard DiLello
Back Cover Photographs: Tom Hanley

Manufactured in the United States of America
Printed and bound by Consolidated Printers

ISBN 0-9657122-2-2 paperback second edition
ISBN 0-9657122-1-4 paperback first edition
ISBN 0-9657122-0-6 hardback limited edition (1000)
Library of Congress Catalog Card Number: 97-75125

Dedicated to the memory of my father, Mark R. Matovina;

& my grandmother, Frances Glover.

And to my mother, Barbara Matovina;

my brother and sisters, Michael, Lorraine, Christine, and Noreen,

my aunt, Sally Glover, and my cousin, Joe Kirschner –

Thank you for your support and faith.

I couldn't have done this without you. . . .

CONTENTS

1 The Road To Swansea 1

2 Apple Of Their Eye 31

3 If You Want It, Here It Is 61

4 Success, It Had To Be 83

5 Take It All 113

6 Money For Fun 155

7 Where Do We Go From Here? 199

8 Got To Get Out Of Here 233

9 Take Your Seat By The Ringside 275

10 Back on the Airwaves 301

11 Over You 343

Afterword 395

Bibliography & Discography 419

Iveys Live 425

Badfinger Live 429

Iveys/Badfinger Studio Sessions 432

Photo Credits 434

Index 436

Fab 208 (Roger Brown)

Badfinger

Mike Gibbins, Joey Molland, Pete Ham, Tom Evans

Preface

I Can't Live, If Living Is Without You
I Can't Live, I Can't Give Anymore . . . .

These immortal words first gained prominence when Harry Nilsson sang them on his recording of the exquisite ballad, "Without You," a Number One charting single throughout the world during the year 1972. After further decades of continuing airplay and countless cover versions, including Mariah Carey's smash hit in 1994, few have known the irony of these poignantly sad lyrics written by Tom Evans, formerly of the rock group known as Badfinger.

Tom's co-author for "Without You" was his fellow bandmate, Pete Ham. Pete was a musical artist of immense talent; a man whose adept compositions conveyed a rare communicative depth of expression; a man with a uniquely soulful voice; and a distinctively melodic guitar player to boot. In fact, Pete Ham has often been compared to Paul McCartney, John Lennon, *and* George Harrison. And most impressively, Pete's first four compositions to be released as singles, "No Matter What," "Day After Day," "Baby Blue," and the co-written "Without You," all became major worldwide hits. Besides, Pete Ham was known as a tremendous person. Everyone who knew Pete liked him – or loved him – a lot.

At the age of twenty-seven, he took his own life.

For almost a decade afterwards, Tom Evans, the enigmatic and emotional bass player of Badfinger, struggled to deal with his best friend's suicide. Tom was an intense man who poured his heart into everything he did. He continued a music career, though fits of depression haunted his every waking minute. Eventually, in a moment of greatly determined passion and sadness, Tom fulfilled the prophecy of "Without You," killing himself in exactly the same manner as Pete Ham.

What prompted such horrific decisions by these two very talented young men?

This book attempts to answer that question, and to clear up some of the myths and mysteries which have long surrounded Badfinger, the very first act to sign with The Beatles' Apple Records. For example, what kept this group from becoming hugely successful, after they seemed so well-poised to breakout in 1973? They'd had a solid track record for three years running. They'd recently signed a multi-million dollar contract with Warner Brothers Records. One more hit could have vaulted them into Superstar status. Instead, they rapidly descended into oblivion. And sadly, the shams and decadence which encircled their domain have continued on, well after the deaths of Pete and Tom. . . .

Badfinger's story basically begins in the early 60s, in the city of Swansea, South Wales. As a group called The Iveys, the band members were brought to London during the year 1966. Their manager, Bill Collins, got them rolling, but they soon began to struggle under his tentative and inexperienced hands. In 1968, the Beatles' trusted roadie, Mal Evans, stepped up to help. Then the Beatles wanted them. Next came a deal with Apple Records and a hit 45, "Come And Get It," written by Paul McCartney! The group's lives seemed to be moving merrily along....

But with their waters stirred, the sharks soon started to arrive. A new business manager and the presence of a girl caused friction to the band's overall unity. Their core disintegrated. And Pete Ham, the sensitive backbone of Badfinger, became despondent.

Pete trusted like few others have. He cherished the values of "loyalty," "peace," and "respect for one's fellow man," but balked heavily at the concepts of "cruelty," "deceit," and "manipulation." Pete Ham could not bear to lash out at other human beings, and very rarely ever did so. He desired that harmony and love dominate his domain. But the pressures of Pete's life muddled his mind and his susceptible nature became overwhelmed. On an early April morning in 1975, he committed suicide, leaving behind a note that revealed untold private anguish.

Sadly, fellow bandmate, Tom Evans, could not escape his guilt and grieving over Pete Ham's death, and throughout the years, he became more and more vulnerable to exploitation and intimidation from people associated with the music business; many of them the same people who'd made Pete Ham's life so miserable. Tom succumbed to his burden in November of 1983.

After Tom died, Badfinger's legacy began a marked downward spiral, despite the occasional efforts of group member Joey Molland to resurrect some sort of Badfinger "presence." For years there were virtually no Badfinger records available, just the beat-up old albums and 45s of the past.

Then came a revelation. During the year 1987, *Goldmine,* a prominent U.S. magazine oriented to record collecting, conducted a poll. They asked their readers a series of questions regarding the exploding market of CD reissues. Though glutted with Beatles, Stones, and numerous "vintage" series product, the public was still clamoring, as loads of unissued classics remained secured in record company vaults. In March of 1988, the poll results came out. Amongst the categories was *CD You Would Most Liked To See Released.* The winner was *Straight Up,* by Badfinger!

Goldmine editor Jeff Tamarkin was genuinely surprised, "Our readership at the time was about thirty thousand and we got one of our best responses for that poll. Nearly fifteen percent of the respondents named it among their ten most desired CD reissues. It even beat out albums like John Lennon's *Plastic Ono Band* and The Beach Boys' *Pet Sounds*!"

Badfinger's *Straight Up,* first issued in December of 1971, originally spawned two major hits, "Day After Day" and "Baby Blue," almost reaching "gold" status, before being withdrawn from the marketplace in 1975. Over the next two decades, dog-eared copies were ardently purchased and sold. Before its CD reissue in 1993, a mint copy of the album could be exchanged for $100 or more. An enormous price considering the amount of records once generated.

Somehow this album, once condemned in *Rolling Stone* magazine, and disputed by the group members, prospered over the years. When the initial CD reissue came out in 1993, *ICE Magazine* listed it as their readers' second favorite CD reissue of that year; it even beat out the Beatles' *Red & Blue* albums. A few years later, DCC Compact Classics honored *Straight Up* by releasing a newly-remastered "gold" disc, soon citing it as one of their fastest and best selling titles ever. Yet interestingly, if you were to talk to most hard-core Badfinger fans, you would find that for many it is not even their favorite album! That auspicious prize belongs to *Wish You Were Here,* a Warner Brothers LP out for a mere *seven weeks* before its deletion from the world marketplace.

Badfinger's standing certainly is a confusing one. On the one hand, they've long had a cult following who religiously collect everything they've touched. Another large segment of music listeners acknowledge them as one "terrific" band. Then there are those that do respect Badfinger's work, but temper their enthusiasm, citing them as essentially "inconsequential pop." Finally, there's the cranky lot who describe Badfinger as "shameless Beatle-copyists," sacrilegious to have even attempted music similar to rock'n'roll's "true messiahs."

The truth is, Badfinger's talents and chemistry were extraordinary. Be it Pete Ham's warm melancholia, Joey Molland's punchy rock'n'roll grit, Tom Evans' edgy high harmonies, or Mike Gibbin's tasteful drumming; these and many other elements added up to a very special group indeed. Badfinger's early 70s singles "Day After Day," "No Matter What," "Come And Get It," and "Baby Blue," have all stood the test of time. "Without You" remains one of the most enduring ballad standards of the twentieth century. And Badfinger's three albums, *No Dice, Straight Up,* and *Wish You Were Here,* are, more often than not, hailed as "classics."

This biography will reveal many of the darker music business aspects the Badfinger members faced. This is an industry which often traps artists into an unholy web, chews them up, and then spits on them, before unceremoniously spewing them out. As you will see, this sometimes prompts the weaker ones to recycle the same injustices, as their desperation grows with each mounting disappointment. . . .

The following must be clear. This book was not endorsed by longtime Badfinger member Joey Molland. He was asked several times to contribute and declined, always indicating he and his wife, Kathie, would put their own story together. All quoted material from Joey is from taped interviews I conducted with him in 1977 and 1978, plus numerous magazine, radio, and private interviews done by other individuals over the years. Information from his wife, Kathie Molland, came from my various discussions with her during 1977 through 1980, my observance of a 1993 videotaped interview conducted by Gary Katz, and a 1999 taped interview she did with TV director Michael MacNamara. Both Joey and Kathie publically claimed they did not read the first edition of this book, and will not do so.

Former Badfinger manager – though he'd prefer to be called "musical mentor" – Bill Collins, was interviewed by myself, Dan Matovina, and Kent Gray (who assisted with this book). Bill, and his wife, Anne, have always been gracious hosts at their home in England. Bill desired not to be taped, but we were told we were free to use the relevant information he gave us. Bill indicated he was okay with utilization of previous interviews he had done for various magazines, a 1987 Welsh BBC-TV documentary, and a 1999 VH-1 TV program. Bill kept detailed diaries of his life with The Iveys and Badfinger. He did disclose parts of them to us, for requested verification of important points and dates.

As of the year 2000, Bill and Anne are still busy working on a "revolutionary" musical notation and teaching project. Bill said he would have gone through his diaries more meticulously, but it would be very time-consuming, and he stated his own project needs to take priority in his life. Bill desires greatly to do his own autobiography. He also wants it clear he is *not* to be construed as endorsing of this biography – or anyone else's viewpoints – regarding The Iveys and Badfinger, as he is sometimes disputing of what others may say concerning him and past events.

Ex-Badfinger member Mike Gibbins graciously gave countless interviews over a three month period during the year 1992. Later, he stated he was interested in writing his own book. He was encouraged to offer any corrections of any discrepancies he felt were present in the first edition of this book. He only brought up one issue, and that was addressed in this second edition.

As it was, hundreds of other people contributed to making this book happen. I very gratefully thank Martin Ace, Grace Ades, Danny Aharoni, Mark Anders, Roy Anderson, Peter Asher, Neil Aspinall, the Atkin family, Keith Badman, Sigmund Balaban, Glenn A. Baker, Ken Barnes, Gerry Beckley, Nicky Bell, Tony Bell, Barbara Bennett, Pete Bennett, Ivy Beresford-Cooke, Carola Beresford-Cooke, Mike Berry, Alan and William Bevan, Al Biaggi, Robert Bishop, Scott Bledsoe, Gerhard Bohrer, Donnie Bott, Tim Boyle, Tony Bramwell, Tom Brennan, Brian Breeze, Maybellene Breeze, Peter Brock, Harold Bronson, Larry Brown, Peter Brown, Dixie Butz, Charlie Calello, Jan Camp, Lenny Campanero, Junior Campbell, Brian Capocciama, Flemming Erik Carlson, Phil Carson, Mike Chaplain, Chris Charles, Chris Charlesworth, Vincent Chieffo, Lou Christie, Rick Clark, Mark Clarke, Pete Clarke, Michael Clemens, Brian Coffey, Phillippe Colinge, Anne Collins, Bill Collins, David Collins, Tommy Corker, Steve Craiter, Bill Cran, Charlie Crane, Tony Crane, Terry Custins, Jan Dahl, George Daly, Trish Daniels, Susan Danis, Malcolm Davies, Andy Davis, James Davis III, Spencer

Davis, Ron Decker, Anne Denvir, Rob Dickens, Richard Dilello, Dave DiMartino, Peter Doggett, Steve Donahue, Terry Doran, Tim Douglas-Jones, Dave Duffield, Molly Duncan, Stuart Duncan, Renete Dung, Richard Duryea, Dave Edmunds, Geoff Emerick, Cindy England, Barrie Evans, David Evans, Jan Evans, Lily Evans, Marianne Evans, May Evans, Stephen Evans, Brian Fagnano, Andy Fairweather-Lowe, Paul Farmer, Ian Ferguson, Michael Fischer, Dean Ford, Paul Foss, David Franklin, Jackie Friend, Tony Friend, John Fruen, Ron Furmanek, P.S. Gardner, Greg Gehring, Gaynor Gibbins, Anthony Gliozzo, Lynn Goldie, Mark Goldstein, James Gomez, Rob Gooch, Alan Gorrie, Peter Granet, Kent Gray, Beryl Green, Probyn Gregory, Phil Griffiths, Ron Griffiths, Johnny Gustafson, Jeff Hale, David Hall, John Ham, Maureen Ham, Petera Ham, Tom Hanley, Kenny Harck, David Harding, Steve Harmon, Bruce Hastell, Liz Hays, Anne Herriot, Peter Hogan, Bill Holdship, Plum Hollis, Michael Holm, Gary Hopkins, Brenda Hornberg, Bob Humphrys, Colin Hurford, Scott Hurowitz, Mike Hurst, Hiroyuki Imaizomi, Bill Inglot, Jeff Iverson, Alwyne Jackson, Bob Jackson, Christine Jackson, Colin James, Keith James, Pete James, Alwyne Jenkins, David Jenkins, Clive John, Pete Johnson, Colin Jones, Mickey Jones, Vivien Jones, Nick Kanaar, Reed Kailing, Gary Katz, Tony Kaye, Geoff Kebbell, Rick Kellogg, Kenny Kerner, Bill King, Tony King, Billy Kinsley, Joe Kirschner, Peter Koch, Kiyoyuki Kohsaka, Al Kooper, Jack Koshick, Glen Kulkoski, Mike Kulkoski, Chris Lambert, Charles Lane, Jonathan Lea, Dick Leahy, Gary Leeds, Mike Lefebvre, Spencer Leigh, Deke Leonard, Irwin Levine, Mark Leviton, Jeff Levy, Stuart Levy, Mark Lewisohn, Sandy Linzer, Jackie Lomax, Cliff Lorimer, John Luneau, Richard Lush, Michael MacNamara, Janet Macoska, Sam Magdoff, Gene Mahon, Christopher Makris, David Malloy, Rick Manore, Ken Mansfield, Pierre Marchand, Rose Marino, Barry Marshall, George Martin, the Matovina family, Piers McBride, Bernadette McDaid, Phil McDonald, Kevin McElligott, Bob Merlis, Terry Messal, Sean McAnally (Siever), Harold Montgomery, Vyvan Morris, Willie Morrissey, Paul Mozian, Jo Murphy, Sujata Murthy, Gerald Neal, Jeremy Neech, Eric Nielsen, Beverly Newman, Paul Nyman, Richard Ogden, Mike O'Donnell, Anthony O'Grady, Jack Oliver, Randall Packer, May Pang, Thierry Pannatier, Mark Perkins, Bob Pettersen, Brad Petrella, Barry Plummer, Terry Porter, Stan Poses, Paul Power, Robert Press, Billy Preston, Bill Price, Parke Puterbaugh, Peter Radomski, Ian Ralfini, Bruce Rawlings, Jonathan Rayner-James, Mike Read, Gill Reed, Pat Recob, Wes Reynolds, Rod Roach, Anne Roche, Linda Roles, Mike Romanowski, Jean Ross, Jeff Ross, Russ Roth, Jeff Rougvie, Mickey Rudin, Lisa Rugo, Todd Rundgren, Leon Russell, Willie Russell, John Ryan, Les Saville, Dave Schulps, Tom Schultheiss, Bud Scoppa, Jane Scott, Harold Seider, Chrissie Shannon, Ken Sharp, Glenn Sherba, Shepard Sherbell, Alex Shliminoff, Jerry Shirley, Mark

Shurilla, Ed Silvers, Brian Slater, Maureen Slater, Phil Smee, Joe Smith, Mike Smith, Edwin Sneidman, Mike Snowden, Ruth Stavrinou, Al Steckler, Mike Stewart, Mike Stock, Jeff Tamarkin, Joe Tansin, Derek Taylor, Chris Thomas, Jim Tirabasi, Ken Topolsky, Grover Trask, Wayne Christian Treiber, Beverley Tucker, Colin Tucker, Jeff Vaughan, Peter Vaughan, Tony Visconti, Chris von Sneidern, John Walker-Williams, John Weathers, Chris Welch, Jeff Weiss, Ken Whaley, David Wild, Taff Williams, Terry Williams, John Wilson, Paul Wilson, Muff Winwood, Bill Winter, Richie Wise, Al Wodtke, Travis Woodard, Harry Wright, and Martin Wyatt.

There were also people who assisted me that passed away before the initial publication of this book. Conrad Atkin was a huge supporter and his family always provided me with a place to stay in Swansea. He died in 1992, as did Abbey Road engineer Mike Jarrett. Harry Nilsson died in 1993, Nicky Hopkins in 1994, Denny Cordell in 1995, Roger Evans in 1996, Derek Taylor in 1997. Tom's mother, May Evans, died in 1998.

My pursuit of the facts was fervent, and for the record, these people declined interviews: Paul McCartney, George Harrison, Ringo Starr, Stan Polley, Allen Klein, Jeff Franklin, Ray Davies, Pete Townshend, John Cass, Hank Medress, Ardith Polley, Laurie Montgomery, Roy Thomas-Baker, Steve Wax, Donnie Ienner, Mavis Smith, Bill Oakes, Peter Howard, Peter Wiggins, Sam Mendelson, Tony Orlando, Mickey Rudin, Bob Marcucci, and Rey Reneri. There were other individuals I could not locate.

I found out these people were deceased at the time I had tried to reach them: Catherine Ham, William Ham, Irene Bevan (Ham), Thomas Evans Sr., Walter Hofer, Ron Kass, Peter Wood, Tim Hardin, Tony Beresford-Cooke, Sylvia Collins, Terry Harvey, Len Golove, and Bob Lewis.

A special note of gratitude to Travis Woodard and Kent Gray, two friends who gave much needed support toward my accomplishing the completion of this book. Bob Pettersen, who had the faith, and got this project off the ground. And, Gerhard Bohrer, who kept this book alive into the new millenium.

Lastly, a special thanks to the people of South Wales. They have been uniformly wonderful to me on all of my visits there. That is where Badfinger's Pete Ham and Mike Gibbins were born. . . .

INTRODUCTION

AS ONE OF FOUR British provinces, Wales, is best-known for its breathtaking wildwood flowers, sparkling blue lakes, and dry-stone, decaying, grey castles. Towering cliffs range over the many tree-lined glens, while slow-moving sheep often gravitate onto the multitude of twisting, integrated highways. The people of this fertile land have long been heralded as simple folk, renowned for their hospitality and charm. Yet for many in Great Britain, the Welsh are "second class," the target of scathing political and social jokes. As Conrad Atkin, former editor of The South Wales Evening Post described, "We more or less live in caves. We are the 'Polish' of Great Britain."

The population generally falls into two camps. There's the deeply-rooted nationalists, many of whom are reclusive and follow strict cultural traditions (some still articulating the distinctive Welsh vernacular), and their more plentiful English-speaking counterparts; who often wear their free-and-easy nature well on their sleeves. One common theme of both – their commitment to a brutal hard day's work. This derives from Wales' lengthy history of coal, slate, and copper mining, strenuous farm laboring, and rugged boat and dock activities (many of which have long since disappeared).

Along with their rugged living, the Welsh face legendary "elemental" problems, as native musical hipster, Spencer Davis, contends, "It rains so hard there it can blow inside your coat! But while you have that persistent bleakness and cold, you also have the beautiful ocean bays which, when sunlit, are literally *jewels* set in the coastline."

The natives are quite proud of their stunning landscapes, yet it is not enough to stem their need to "while away" the more mundane aspects of their lives. Besides the drinking of ale, "song and verse" are quite popular as past times. In fact, it's not at all unusual for a Welsh person to suddenly break into a tune. As Con Atkin stated, "You could be on a bus with one going in front, another one going in back, two are whistling in the middle, *and it's bloody hell in there!*"

Known for their group-oriented folk singing, the Welsh culture also has a distinguished legacy of individual artistic contributors. Influential writer/poet

Dylan Thomas (pictured below) comes to mind, as do renowned actors Anthony Hopkins, Ray Milland, and Richard Burton. From the musical side they've given us soulful crooner Tom Jones, sweet-voiced Mary Hopkin, gravel-toned Bonnie Tyler, gifted guitarist Dave Edmunds, balladeer supreme Shirley Bassey, and veteran rock'n'roll drummer Terry Williams . . . its obviously been a rich source of entertainers.

Today if one was to travel Wales' windy roads, they just might come across the south-coastal city of Swansea, a kilometer off the M4 motorway. Often referred to as "Swansea town," it's actually quite large, laced with fancy restaurants, bustling shopping malls, and thick, slow-moving traffic. The pubs are filled with workers playing darts and cribbage. And the city, which long had little crime, has since become prey to rampant vandalism; a fallout of Britain's crumbling economic structure.

While visiting there in 1992, I came across John Ham's Sound Studio Ltd., a prominent music "equipment and repair" shop on Mansel Street. The store was filled with eager customers who casually browsed the varied merchandise. Proprietor John observed them all through plaintive blue eyes, answering each of their questions carefully and respectfully.

I watched him tend to a few of the younger ones, knowing he'd probably encountered such enthusiasm a thousand times over. But as I watched, I couldn't help but wonder if these teenagers reminded him of his own younger brother, who had the same hope-filled dreams and buoyant aspirations, many years ago. . . .

1

The Road To Swansea

Peter William Ham was born in the "Townhill" district of Swansea on April 27, 1947. One of the roughest areas of the city at the time, this smallish tract of homes is comprised mainly of city-owned council estates sitting high atop a wide-ranging hillside. William Ham, Pete's father, grew up in Swansea. He left school at age fourteen and subsequently worked a variety of labor-oriented jobs, most of his work centering on the very busy dock area. Catherine Ham, Pete's mother, was first employed at a tinplate factory. She became a full-time housewife after the birth of her and William's first child, Bernard John, in 1937. After John came a daughter, Irene. Pete was the last child born into the Ham family.

Pete was an energetic youth and never seemed to lack for his share of childhood trauma. His mate, Robert Bishop, recalled a couple of times when Pete almost drowned. Once, Pete was barely pulled out of a strong coastal undercurrent in time by some strangers. On another occasion, his makeshift raft disintegrated over a local pond, with Robert's father making the valiant rescue. According to Bishop, "Pete Ham was a great friend, my best friend as a kid. We played, hung out, did everything together. I do remember, though, he did have a lot of mood swings; one minute laughing and joking, the next minute sulking. When he got upset he'd run home and lock himself in his room . . . and that radio would be playing."

Music *was* Pete Ham's passion. His father was a big-band fan and it carried over to Pete, but even more so to his brother, John. Many neighbors of the Ham family recall John standing in front of the house practicing the trumpet for hours on end. Pete himself began to play the mouth organ as early as four years of age. His impromptu playing at the Gors Junior School playground would often draw lots of children to watch. His inseparable friend, Alwyne Jackson, recalls, "Pete was okay at schoolwork, and he could put his hand to anything, but he was always into music first. I remember him running straight from school to go and buy records, and then running home to listen to them. And once he picked up the guitar you could tell he could really play. Even as a youngster I could. Everybody could. . . ."

The first guitar Pete practiced on was a Hofner semi-acoustic which he got during the Christmas of 1959. He began to teach himself the rudiments of the

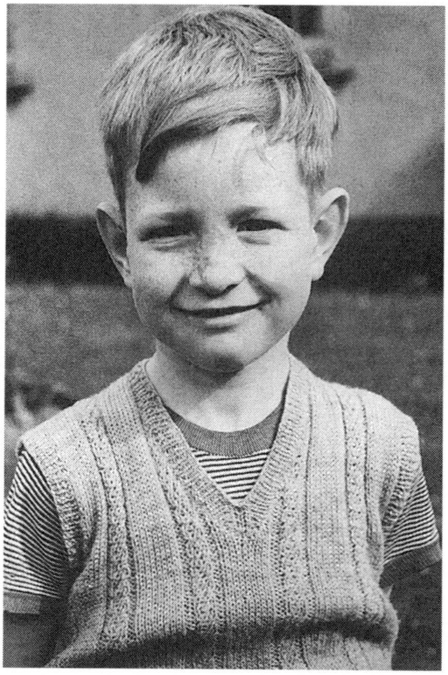

instrument, showing an uncompromising dedication. A Townhill youth club soon became a haven for him. In 1961 a local teacher, Brian Coffey (designated club leader), quickly noticed the youngster's drive and talent. Pete was in a woodwork group there and decided to build a guitar as his main project. To his dismay, as the guitar was nearing completion, the base split. "Peter was bitterly disappointed," remembers Coffey, "I hated to see him so distressed. So I lent him some money to buy a guitar. And Peter repaid me completely; a pound a month."

Pete became totally committed to his newly-bought Fentoweil guitar. Neighbors remember him practicing for hours on end. He soon gathered up some friends to play as a group. David Franklin also played guitar, while mate Roy Anderson got himself a drum; one big, fat snare. An amp came courtesy of Coffey. Anderson recalls, "I remember the first time we played, it was in Pete's house, with his parents right in the next room. Noise levels had to be greatly considered."

The group eventually settled into the Franklin family garage and focused on songs by the Shadows, "I still have that album today," says Anderson, "with the songs we played marked off. We were solely instrumental, no bass player, and we spent hours trying to get a repertoire we felt was presentable. This was before The Beatles and there wasn't a huge music scene yet, but we drew a lot of attention. When we began to rehearse at the Townhill youth club, people would stop and listen."

The band's first semi-professional gig was quite memorable, but not for the reason the boys had hoped. As Anderson explains, "Pete came up to me at the bus stop one afternoon and he excitedly told me, 'We're playing tonight. Some groups

(far left) Pete: ages 7 & 14
(right) The Panthers:
David Franklin,
Roy Anderson,
Pete Ham,
1963

dropped out of a booking at Bryn Hall and my brother got us in.' So alarm bells go off everywhere in my head. For one thing we weren't that good yet, and secondly, the Bryn Hall was notorious for its 'punch-ups'!

"Well, Peter persuaded me it was the right thing to do and we did it. But it was a disaster! We come on, no bass player, no singer, and halfway through our first number Pete's strap breaks, forcing him to play while holding the guitar up. Then the amplifier started making all kinds of noise and the crowd got real restless. Halfway through the manager comes up and says, 'Boys, for your own safety, let me pay you for the evening, and go home!' "

Discouraged, but determined, the fledgling group carried on; christening themselves The Panthers, adding vocals to their sound, and eventually picking up a bass player, John Horrel. Brian Coffey provided a crew-bus for transport, and they would play anywhere they could; youth clubs, pavilions, even the local hospital Cefncoed, a mental home!

Pete and Roy spent many hours discussing music. One week they decided to go on a caravan holiday at Port Eynon on the Gower Coast in South Wales. But their plans to enjoy the sun and beach were dampened by a continual downpour. They sat around, biding their time with Pete's guitar, a little conversation, and a radio. Suddenly a live Beatles concert came over the air . . . "We were listening to the show, just enjoying it," recalled Roy, "And as usual the screaming was unbelievable. And I remember Peter just turned to me and said, 'When I hear that screaming I get shivers, it makes me think of my future.' "

During the late 1950s and early 1960s Swansea had been burgeoning with talented jazz and blues groups. Swansea native Spencer Davis remembers, "There were pub venues like the Glanmor Jazz Club where the jazzers would play, such as John Ham and his bands. And besides jazz and blues, a lot of pop-country music, like Hank Williams tunes, was performed. I played a lot of solo guitar spots and a bit of harmonica. We were 'beatniks' and we'd all hang out."

But John Ham's music of choice was not Pete's staple. "No, he wasn't a jazzer," said John, "but I helped break the ground for him. There was no musician in the family before that really. Pete became more interested in the rock and pop scene."

The Welsh jazz environment quickly became overshadowed when the new rock'n'roll and rhythm & blues sounds really hit big in the early 60s. The jazzers derisively termed these newcomers as "three-chord-charlies," but John respected Pete's sincerity. A local Bingo hall in Townhill, called The Tower, started to book some of these rock-oriented bands in 1962. Pete and his friends began to see other groups in action and were duly impressed. "Pete and I would get up to the front of the stage and watch all evening," stated Roy Anderson. "Our favorite had to be The Fireflies. Their look and their playing were very professional. We were quite taken."

When David Franklin couldn't put in ample practice time after beginning a D.J. position at The Tower, the group intensely began searching for a new guitarist. Finally they came across one; a charismatic lad with swooning good looks. His name: David "Dai" Jenkins. Dai was an apprentice auto mechanic who worked with John Horrel.

Dai was told about Horrel's and Pete Ham's band, and he eventually became their rhythm guitarist. Dai's brother, Alwyne, would often drive him to rehearsals. Alwyne started to help with the group's bookings and eventually became their unofficial manager and "road crew." Alwyne explained, "I drove all their equipment around using the youth club's van and my car. Then we got a hold of an old Bedford. The door was always falling off though. We'd end up in these big arguments at the service station. . . ."

The group's name changed often: from The Panthers, to The Black Velvets, and then to the Wild Ones. "The band went through a stage of not playing much," Alwyne remembered, "just a park or a pavilion . . . I think they played a talent contest as The Wild Ones. They'd play in the Rock & Fountain Pub. That was one of the roughest pubs in Swansea."

By this time, Pete was well into the technical end of the group's equipment. He was an apprentice electrical engineer and had begun a residency at a T.V. and radio repair shop owned by Jack George. Co-worker Les Saville remembers, "I joined installing car radios and Pete did a lot of the technical stuff, like fixing T.V.'s. He didn't drive, so I used to take him to all the places to do the work, and we became quite close. Pete was a mod with wavy hair and I was a rocker with greased-back

The Black Velvets: Roy, Dai, John, Pete
The Wild Ones: Dai, Terry, Pete, Ron

hair and a black jacket; it caused quite a stir. But we got along great. I was into recording and I had a cherished mono Vortexian tape recorder that I was always talking about. Pete used to kid me and say, 'When I'm famous I'm going to get you something, another Vortexian!' "

Using his expanding knowledge, Pete built a public address system for his band, adapting an old army RAF. He was always repairing his and the group's guitars and amps. Alwyne Jenkins helped with the carpentry. A few growing pains came with the territory. One time a gig came up at the Embassy Ballroom in Swansea, which was now putting on a Free Night once a week, drawing capacity crowds. Four scheduled groups would pull out their most danceable repertoire. "Peter was really excited about this," said Roy, "and although we had the chance to use good equipment, used by the prior group, he insisted that we use a homemade amplifier he had just built. We weren't well-rehearsed and by the third or fourth number the speaker 'blew.' I can remember people showing their great discontent at the end of each number."

Soon after, a talent contest in Abercrave led to a third place finish, leaving Pete "devastated," according to Roy. "I don't think I ever saw him quite so depressed as he was over that. I think he was beginning to get impatient with our progress."

Roy Anderson soon quit as he saw the group going nowhere – but Pete remained determined. Terry Gleason was brought in as a new drummer. He was older; a capable musician who loved cabaret. Bassist John Horrel was also soon replaced, as Pete had targeted an impressive young player who fronted another local band, The Jaguars. His name: Ron Griffiths.

Ronald Llewellyn Griffiths was born in Swansea on October 2, 1946. He first sang in his school's choir and developed a good ear for harmony before picking up the bass guitar, due to the influences of The Ventures and The Shadows. "The Jaguars were my first band," Ron remembers. "We just started off as an instrumental group and we progressed to having a lead singer and doing harmonies. This was when the Beatles first broke big."

"One time we were doing a gig at the Dolphin, some wedding reception, and Pete and Alwyne Jenkins came and stared at me like vultures. They had obviously planned to approach me, 'cause at the end of this absolutely awful gig, they came up and asked if I'd like to join their group. I went to one of their rehearsals and was really taken with Pete's playing and his attitude. He was playing bluesy stuff with seventh chords, quite whizzo for those days! I decided to join."

With Ron's inclusion, the band felt a new name was in order. They were dissatisfied with The Wild Ones, a name they'd gotten from the newspapers after the famous riots in Brighton between the mods and rockers. Now they wanted something more representative of their sound. But they were constantly running up against bands with names similar to the ones they'd thought of. Finally, they wrote down more potential monikers on pieces of paper and looked them over. Ron had thrown in The Iveys after noticing Ivey Place, a small street in Swansea. "We liked the song 'Poison Ivy' and admired the Hollies," stated Dai, "It had a number of things going for it."

The handle stuck. With a new line-up, the band felt recharged. Their first gig as The Iveys took place at a talent contest at the Bon-y-Maen Rugby Club. They came in third place, performing a harmony version of "If I Loved You" from the musical *Carousel*.

Throughout the fall and winter of '64, and onward into the next year, the group played in and around Swansea. When they got paid it was nominal. As Alwyne recalls: "The amount of money paid in those days would go to expenses – way above and beyond. The van kept taking a lot of money; it was either the gear box would go, the back axle; we'd always need parts. Because Dai was a mechanic we'd do the repair ourselves, but then there were the amplifiers and guitars. We'd always need bits and pieces . . . the cost was unbelievable."

By now Swansea was the haven of rock'n'roll in South Wales. The only comparable city was Cardiff, but Swansea was special. Conrad Atkin, a Swansea native, had taken on the job as deputy editor for the local *Herald Of Wales* newspaper in 1963, after returning from the newspaper trade in London. Atkin had found his "sleepy little town" transformed into a raging musical mecca, eventually to have over 360 bands in a twenty-mile radius. "I decided to start a column called *Beaterama* using the pseudonym 'Gary Radd,' " Atkin stated. "I had some musical contacts from my days in London and I made a weekly report on the 'happenings' about town."

The *Beaterama* column became the bible for the growing rock'n'roll crowd, as Swansea was soon flooded by an onslaught of neighboring and local talent. In smaller outlying towns everything was pretty much shut down by eight p.m. Often the best these bands could hope for was a youth gig, which meant the transformation of their local school's hallway at six p.m., with the "kids" as their audience! But Swansea had the overall sights and sounds to draw all of the fans and musicians together. "I had a residency at Disks A Go Go in Cardiff," relates rocker Dave Edmunds. "And though that was my homebase, Swansea always seemed more hip. They had better overall musicians and better venues. They also had an agent who liked my band."

That agent was Vernie Ley. His company, Ritz Entertainments, ran one of the top clubs, The Ritz, in nearby Skewen. Besides Ley, hep cat "Schmoo" (a.k.a. Maurice Levenson) accommodated by allowing rock'n'roll into his prestigious Glanmor Jazz Club. Agent Duke McKay booked the Tivoli; David Scott, the Glen.

One oft-noted aspect about this music scene was that the local acts were exceedingly congenial. Andy Fairweather-Lowe of Amen Corner fame remembers, "I lived in Cardiff and their scene was very insular; people didn't mix. But if we went to Swansea everybody knew everybody, everybody talked to everybody, everybody helped everybody, you had a general openness." "That's right," agreed Swansea-born drummer Terry Williams. "The bands from outside were always made welcome. We'd go out of our way to make them feel so. And we had places we could invite them to."

The most prominent after-hours hangout was The Orient, an Indian restaurant near the City Center. Deke Leonard, a veteran of the scene and eventual guitarist for Man, fondly recalls, "It was like most Indian restaurants of the time – flock wallpaper, heavy linen tablecloths, massive cutlery, flaming hot curry – but they had this waiter called Singh, who was a real character. The bands loved him, though I think he loved their money even better."

Outside of this late-night hangout it wasn't at all unusual to see six or seven vans parked tightly together to discourage "thieves of the night." Many of the transports were converted ambulances or hearses splattered with girls' names or graffiti. The restaurant would be packed with musicians and scenesters discussing gigs, guitars, and all manner of gossip. The out-of-town acts could usually be found hobnobbing as well. Vyvan "Spiv" Morris, a local guitarist recalls, "All of the big bands came down and talked with us. The Who, The Hollies, Manfred Mann, even Van Morrison and his surly crew – who fought over tables all night. It was buzzing!"

Other clubs included the mod hangout, Macabre, a ghoulish restaurant with cobwebs and coffin-lid tables, and Maxie's Nightspot, a split-level lounge with all-night jamming in its Cellar Club.

The Iveys fell right in with these "goings on," but often they had to struggle to receive prominent attention. The Meteorites, The Jets, and The Corncrackers stood out, but the two acts which eventually shone brightest were The Bystanders and

The Eyes Of Blue. What gave them each an edge was their vocal prowess, as the former reproduced the Four Seasons and Beach Boys sound quite well, while the latter were exceedingly versatile in many styles. Ron Griffiths: "To me Eyes Of Blue were the supreme band around Swansea. It was a six-man band, and all of them sang well. Richie Francis was an incredibly good bass player, a real innovator, and Taff Williams should've become a millionaire for his guitar playing."

The band also featured Gary Pickford Hopkins and Wyndham Rees on lead vocals, Phil Ryan on keyboards, and John Weathers on drums. In the mid 60s they were probably the most-likely-to-succeed local act while the Iveys were still considered "formative" and "growing."

In the early months of 1965, Iveys drummer Terry Gleason took on a job that required occasional evening shifts and it put the band in the position of having to turn down gigs. By March they gave him the ultimatum he had to alter his schedule or leave. "Terry tried quite a few times to change jobs," said Iveys manager Alwyne Jenkins, "but he finally gave up and was let go. There weren't any hard feelings though, and he filled in while the band searched for a replacement."

The Iveys advertised in the papers with no luck. Local beatnik businessman Schmoo then suggested a buddy of his, Mike "Mickey" Gibbins. Ron remembers his first meeting with Mike, "My father ran me over to his house on the back of a motor scooter. I turned up on his doorstep and Mike thought I looked like some brainy kid because I had a Swansea University scarf on. Mike was like a greaser. He was sporting a great big ginger quiff, the Teddy Boy hairstyle."

Michael George Gibbins was a Swansea native, born on March 12, 1949, to a large family that included six sisters. Known to bang on anything he could, his father decided to buy him a drum kit at age fourteen. He trained in the military style for a year before joining his first group, The Planet. Later, he moved on to a group called Club Four, or Club Foot, as Mike fondly recalls, and finally to The Misfits. Now, just past his sixteenth birthday, he was eager to step up further.

Dai remembered Mike's audition with The Iveys: "Mike was a heavier drummer than Terry and he had more presentation. He had the driving beat of the modern scene." Alwyne Jenkins adds, "He really was quite vibrant. It lifted the band." Mike was welcomed in and progress was swift. On May 1, 1965 the Beaterama column decided to feature the band:

> *Swansea's Iveys did not hit the headlines when they came onto the scene a few months ago, but today their name adds up to a refreshing well-balanced sound that has given them a big following and high-listed name with local promoters. . . .*

The Iveys, 1965: Dai, Pete, Mike, Ron

> *Their biggest advantage over many of the local outfits is their excellent equipment. Amplifiers and their P.A. system are treated with respect and are continually being overhauled to maintain perfect performance . . . Another advantage is their ability to play anywhere. They have the sound control which many groups lack and you will find them happy on a big dance hall stage or small private function dais. . . .*
>
> *Of all the groups that have recently taken a chance on being popular, the Iveys have led from the start . . . Follow their religion of a well-balanced-sound-with-a-well-groomed-look and their success story will be yours.*

The Iveys had clearly stepped up. Pylot Promotions and, eventually, Jayvee Entertainments, took them on. The band was put into opening slots for top touring acts as they played the area: The Moody Blues, The Yardbirds, The Spencer Davis Group, LuLu and the Luvvers, P.J. Proby, and many others. The Who were particularly friendly, allowing The Iveys use of their massive equipment. But Keith Moon, Dai recalls, "was quite difficult to make sense of."

"Moonie" was able to make sense of one thing though, Jets drummer Beau Adams, who made a big impression on everyone who came through. "When Keith Moon saw Beau Adams, it blew his brains!," recalled *Beaterama* columnist Con Atkin. "Beau was the first drummer in Britain to take the skin off the bass drum, the first to turn his cymbals upside down. And he was powerful!" Terry Williams, later an acclaimed drummer for Rockpile and Dire Straits, agreed. "Beau Adams was a huge inspiration to me and many others. He was phenomenal." But Adams career ended prematurely as he gave up rock'n'roll completely in the mid-60s and moved to Australia. "A complete waste," says Williams today.

A lot of South Wales talent stagnated as there were no record companies, few entrepreneurs, and little impetus to broaden the scene. "We needed a few Brian Epsteins," said Atkin. "A lot of the musicians lacked the confidence to step out, though a few tried." The Welsh musicians were all semi-pro, as the commissions paid too modestly to go full-time. Only one local entrepreneur ever set to make a record, Tony Wyn-David paid for and released a Bystanders 45, "That's The End" b/w "This Time" on his own Pylot Records in 1966.

By the mid-sixties, many of the bands from London, Manchester, Liverpool, and other U.K. locales were largely writing their own material, but the Swansea musicians continued to pride themselves on live covers of B-sides, album tracks, and older rarities. Martin Ace, later of the Man band, recalls, "The people passing through would always be amazed at our knowledge, especially of the American artists."

Surprisingly, few of the Swansea area bands ever tried to translate their musical inspirations into their own unique vision. Many simply focused on having a good time playing out. But Martin Ace recognized a difference in the Iveys. "They always dressed in the same clothes and they wouldn't smoke dope. There seemed to be a distinct career-mindedness about them."

Pete Ham's girlfriend of the time, Maybellene, agreed, "Music meant everything to them, especially Peter. I'd always get mad because I'd feel left out. One time we had this big quarrel and at the end it was like, 'It's over! I'm not going to speak to you again!' Later that night I decided to go to his gig and throw this pig tail in his face while he was playing. See, Pete's nickname was 'Piggy,' we all used to call him that. So I came down and threw it in his face. Pete bends down, picks it up, and continues playing, using the pig tail as his pick! Nothing threw him. He was so easygoing. We got back together the next night."

Nicknames were fairly common on the scene, as Conrad Atkin stated, "Lots of people in Wales have nicknames because so many have the same surname: Williams, Evans, Jenkins . . . The Jets Tony Hollis was called "Plum," because of his shape; John Weathers of The Eyes Of Blue was referred to as "Pugwash," after a cartoon pirate with horn-rimmed glasses. There was the immortal "Spew," a quiet bank worker who played a mean boogie woogie piano. Martin Ace was "The Bass." There were many more. . . ."

The Welsh music scene was also characteristic for its unbridled close-knit camaraderie. Bystanders guitarist, Clive John: "Everyone would watch each others' gigs, encourage one another, very little one-upmanship. If your guitar got pinched, someone would lend you one. Or if a band member got sick, a replacement was

The Jets, clockwise from upper left: Plum Hollis, Deke Leonard Beau Adams, Martin Ace

easy to find. The attitude was, 'We're all here, we're all in bands, and we're rockin'' That's what we wanted to do."

One evening, The Iveys became the beneficiary of this solidarity. The band was finishing up a set at the Tivoli and, little did they know, they had been tagged for a "punch-up." As the end neared, someone leapt on the stage and started brushing up to Dai. Alwyne Jenkins remembers, "Dai started scuffling with this fellow, so I jumped in. Before I knew it, the whole hall had erupted in pandemonium. I can remember literally being thrown off the balcony twice! Finally all these groups showed up; The Eyes Of Blue, The Jets, The Corncrackers – all just to help us. Apparently the word had gotten back. It was like a rallying call."

Not long after, The Iveys had a chance to return the favor. Vyvan "Spiv" Morris of the Liquid Umbrella remembers, "We had a gig with The Iveys and Pellinera, this great colored band from London. It was at the Regal Ammanford Ballroom, a nice hall, but bands used to turn down the gig because they knew there'd be a fight. My band was on stage, The Iveys were on one side, and the Pellinera were on the other side looking down from the balcony. I had my shades on and this guy steps from the crowd and pulls them off. So I jumped off and grabbed my glasses back. A few moments later this gang comes strolling through looking like something out of *West Side Story.* They started pounding me and our road manager. They grabbed the mic from my hand and hit me in the head and face.

"Well, by now, Pellinera had leapt from the balcony and all hell had broken loose. I knew my jaw was broken so I curled up in a ball to protect my face. The

The Ritz, March 31, 1966: Phil Ryan, Steve Winwood, Pete Ham, Ron Griffiths, Gary Hopkins, John Weathers, Taff Williams, Wyndham Rees

floor was very slippery like a gymnasium. Guys started kicking me. I was sliding around like a bowling ball. Then Pete, who certainly was a pacifist if I ever saw one, came over and somehow got all these guys off of me. I can see him now, pulling me up and saying, 'Are you okay?' Then this guy comes over and hits him really hard from behind with a chair. And Pete, well he just turned around, and *clocked* him one!"

On March 11, 1966, The Iveys were again playing Ammanford's Regal Ballroom when they attracted the attention of a man who was soon to change their lives. "We got on and started to do our set," recalls Ron, "and about halfway through this band starts walking through the hall. This elderly chap, who was behind them, stops in his tracks and gives us a stare. We'd never had an old fellow look at us before. At the end of the night, this chap came up to Alwyne and told him, 'I thought they played and sang with a lot of soul. I think you've got something there.' I became quite embarrassed because he put his arm around me and said *'You've got a fucking great voice son.'* "

That "old fellow" was William Daniel Collins, better known as Bill Collins. He was born in 1913 in Birkenhead, England, which is part of the Merseyside; just across a bay from Liverpool. As a pianist with various dance bands in the 30s, his musical career was interrupted by World War II. During that time he engineered masts for war ships, yet still found time to play in various situations. By the early 50s he was restoring motor vehicles. His son, Lewis, became interested in music and Bill encouraged him to pursue his dream. Bill even had Lew playing drums in various versions of Bill's dance band, as early as age thirteen. Lewis eventually joined the rock group, The Mojos, in 1963. They had one major U.K. hit in 1964 with "Everything's Alright."

Bill often drove The Mojos around. He also had a brief stint as road manager for The Kinks. By 1966, Lewis Collins had quit The Mojos to pursue a hairdressing career, but Bill continued to help with the band's roadwork. Though Bill was supportive of them, he told several people his main purpose for traveling with The Mojos now, was to find a group which *he* could manage and mold.

Alwyne Jenkins recalls Collins' enthusiasm at seeing The Iveys that fateful day, "We all went into our mini bus and had a chat together. Collins was saying how interested he was. It was obvious he'd been taken." Collins stayed in touch. "Letters. I had tons of letters," adds Alwyne, "Bill was tremendous at writing them. He could write a forty-page letter; have-pen-will-travel."

Collins eventually traveled back to Wales to tape one of The Iveys performances on June 7, 1966, at a workingmen's club in Neath. He placed a mic directly in front of the P.A. and – despite a gravely unbalanced recording – was able to capture the essence of their act, which at the time was heavily rhythm & blues oriented. The Iveys were being closely studied, and though the band was intrigued, they were still dubious. "We couldn't see it," said Ron. "Very few of us from this neck of the woods really think they're God's gift to the music industry. We're pretty down-home people. We just enjoyed what we were doing."

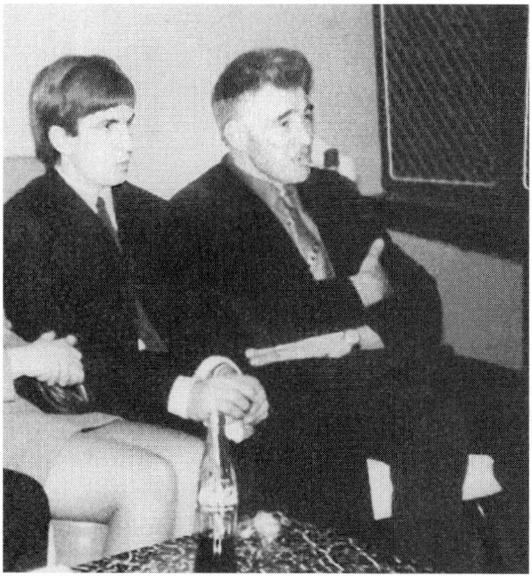

Alwyne Jenkins, Bill Collins, 1966

However, Collins believed and an opening came. "The Mojos were part of the Harold Davidson agency run by this impresario called Robert Wace," said Ron. "The Kinks and Small Faces were part of Wace's stable, as was this chap David Garrick. Garrick had a chart song going with his cover of the Stones' 'Lady Jane' and needed a touring band. So Bill told us Garrick was holding auditions. He said, 'Do you want to come up to London for a weekend, see the town, do the audition and have a laugh at the same time?' And that's what we did, we made a long weekend of it."

It was June of 1966 and The Iveys now had a regular Monday slot going at The Glen in Llanelli. They were being booked exclusively by Jayvee Entertainments, the largest agency in Swansea. They agreed on accepting the offer by Collins and set off on what must have seemed like an adventure. Alwyne recalls, "We left on a Friday morning and Pete, who had just gotten his driving license, said, 'I've gotta have a turn at the wheel.' I said, 'Okay Pete, but be careful.' Well, he was so excited about going to London that it was no more than five minutes when sirens hit and Pete was stopped for speeding. But he just brushed it off . . . like it never happened!"

Ron picks up, "We spent that night at Bill's house in London. We had a few drinks with The Mojos and chatted. The next day we went and did this audition at a rehearsal place in the West End. There had been a few bands in before us who'd done their thing, trying to impress this Garrick bloke. We did a few harmony numbers, and we'd worked out 'Lady Jane.' Garrick did a bundle on us. He didn't even come up with the closing line, 'I'll let you know.' He decided there and then, 'These are my boys!' "

Collins began his plan to take over The Iveys. He wanted to move them into his rented London home. But first he had to address their careers: Pete in electronics, Ron with the gas company, Dai as an auto mechanic, and Mike in design graphics. Alwyne relates, "Bill set up for all the parents to meet at the Swansea Castle Hotel. He put his cards on the table. The biggest problem to address was the boys' apprenticeships. I think David was finishing his up in a few months, Ron wasn't far off, and I think Mickey was fed up with his."

Pete was now working for his brother John, who had taken over Jack George's T.V. and electronics business. John Ham recalls, "Collins was obviously offering the band things which they got very excited about. Peter said 'Look, you know I'm going to finish the apprenticeship, but if I don't have a go at this now I'll never have a go.' So I said 'Well fair enough, if that's what you want to do. You're not going to be of any use here if you are going to regret staying.' There was no animosity. I knew that if he'd made his mind up, he probably wouldn't be of any use to me as an employee. But I didn't go for Collins. He was like the oldest teenager in the country. The guy was a romantic, living in the clouds. And I'd tell him so."

Collins explained how he addressed the parents: "I said 'I can promise you what Churchill promised us during the war years. I can promise you blood, sweat

The Iveys with David Garrick, Seven Club, Shrewsbury, England, July 8, 1966

and tears, but that's about all I can promise you. But if the boys follow my guidance, I'm sure we'll learn to write songs and record them properly. They've got all the studio techniques that are required . . . It might take a while, and we've got to live very cheaply because I've got no money – no savings – but it should be a load of fun for them.' "

Bill's sales pitch worked. On July 8th, The Iveys packed up their belongings and drove to their first fully-professional date with David Garrick, at the Seven Club in Shrewsbury, England. After two more gigs in different cities, they went straight over to their new home, which was situated in the section of London known as Golders Green. A part of the northeast portion, Golders Green is a fairly well-to-do area with plenty of greenery, a beautiful park, and a bustling shopping locale. The Iveys' new quarters were on Park Avenue, a small road, just off one of the main drags, not too far from Abbey Road Studios. Ron recalls, "I liked the house, it was fabulous, but being a 'band' house, it was a bit filthy inside. That was the first thing that struck me. But Golders Green itself, and the surroundings, I loved."

The Iveys were initially put onto camp beds, first in a downstairs lounge (followed by the attic), while the Mojos and Dave Duffield (the Kinks' road

Cavalier Club, London, July 21, 1966:
Mike Gibbins, Ron Griffiths, Pete Ham, Dai Jenkins

manager) each had an individual room. Bill's son, Lewis Collins, also was on the premises from time to time. Lew's former band, The Mojos, were now suffering a severe career downslide. The arrival of The Iveys didn't help. Beverley Ellis, a local girl, recalls, "It was difficult for the Mojos. Here they were, a relatively successful group and Bill moves another band in. It was very crowded."

Many people came over to introduce themselves. Vivien Levensen was one of the local crowd and a good friend of Beverley's. She recalls, "There was an immediate buzz about The Iveys. They were fresh and unaffected – in awe of everything. They were very warm people. We were all quite taken."

On July 14, 1966, the group substituted for The Kinks, who had been scheduled for a headlining gig in Margate, England. Guitarist Dave Davies had become ill and The Kinks manager, Robert Wace, had asked The Iveys to save the day. They played for over two thousand people and went over extremely favorably. Then, on July 21, 1966, the band played their first solo London gig at the Cavalier Club in Golders Green; Ron performing on his metallic-blue Precision bass; Dai, his prized Telecaster; Pete, his cherished white Strat; while Mike pounded on a pearl-blue Premier drum set. The show went well.

Despite getting these bookings, the group immediately had to hustle for their lives. "We weren't paid a retainer by Garrick," said Ron, "so if he didn't work, we didn't work." Collins allotted each member £2/10s a week for spending money.

Eventually Collins revealed his master plan. He felt the best opportunities for the Iveys would come from developing songwriting skills. Before their arrival, Bill had deadened the walls of a small downstairs room, making it more conducive to

rehearsing and recording. He'd supplied it with a Revox "sound-on-sound" tape machine, a stand-up piano, and a few microphones.

On August 2, 1966, Bill wrote a song and recorded it in order to inspire his new band in that direction. He called the group together and played them his demo. To his displeasure, however, the group laughed wholeheartedly. Bill responded, "Well, as soon as you can do better, then you can laugh," and he stormed off. The following evening he was awakened by timid tapping on his bedroom door; Pete had written and recorded a song. Bill said he was elated – his plan had worked!*

Mike recounted, "Bill Collins said 'Write songs, write songs, write songs.' And we did. He stuck in his two-pennies-worth and showed us how to go about it. He was like a football coach, he kept on us." Pete led the way early in writing tunes, as Beverley Ellis recalled, "Pete spent more time in the studio than anyone. He'd push himself to try and complete a song every time."

Bill encouraged the band members to learn the piano, as he felt it broadened their potential for songwriting ideas. Most of the early demos are Pete alone, playing piano or guitar, with maybe a bass line thrown on by Ron. Mike was concentrating on improving as a drummer and didn't attempt to write songs at first; as he was also just learning to play the guitar and piano. Ron contributed a

* According to Ron Griffiths, Pete had actually shown an earlier inclination to compose. Pete had written a song back in Wales called "You Know." "That was a flash of things to come," said Ron. "It wasn't your average three-chord trick. It had a guitar intro with a vibrato pedal. It was a Zombies-type number." Pete's mate, Les Saville, recorded a band performance of it on his Vortexian, but indicated the tape has long since disappeared.

few, but Dai was nearly non-existent on the songwriting front. He found the London nightlife a lot more enticing of his spare time.

Bill was a very eager mentor, often putting in suggestions, or throwing out a few chords or progressions. Mike recalls, "He'd tell you the transcriptions, the dominant notes, and all the rest of it." Bill even attempted to write with "his boys" at times, but the age gap proved a deterrent according to Dai, "Bill was often trying to add a piano bit on Pete's songs, but it usually came off old-fashioned sounding. We'd try and make him feel a part of it."

A listen to some of these early demos exhibits examples of Bill's insistent prodding. He can be heard playing, directing, and even singing his own vocal riffs on a few numbers. One song Bill helped with was "Turn On Your Loving Mood." Ron explains, "Bill gave me some lyrics. I composed the melody and the chorus line. But overall, Bill was not a strong influence on the songs themselves. It was mainly his encouragement that benefited us. In fact, if he liked something too much, we were reluctant to use it."

One example was a Pete Ham song called "Memories." Bill just loved this highly dramatic ballad, but according to Ron, the group thought Bill's wild enthusiasm was not the best sign. It only made it to the "solo" demo stage. But a tune which everyone liked was "Man Without A Heart," another theatrical Merseybeat-type ballad by Pete; one of his very first songwriting efforts. His original demo portrays him struggling to play the piano chords, but overshadowing is a highly inspired vocal performance. {Man Without A Heart – Pete demo} One of the group's versions is sung by Dai, who'd asked Pete if he could sing the lead vocal.

The Revox "sound-on-sound" tape machine was quite cumbersome to use. It has two recording heads, and as you record, you bounce back and forth from one tape head to the other. Unfortunately, each bounce tends to cause a noticeable loss in sound quality. Despite the restrictive nature of the process, The Iveys' demos are generally quite listenable today – especially when Pete took control.

On September 3, 1966, The Iveys went to Swansea to attend the wedding of their former manager Alwyne Jenkins, and to perform that evening at the Glen. They excitedly played some of their demos for friends and family. They were very enthusiastic. Outer Limits guitarist Barrie Evans recalled, "It was a new thing. It was like steps up the rung of a ladder. You could see they had a desire to believe it was gonna happen. Pete was very optimistic."

A petite, young lady with dark hair, Beverley Ellis, had captured the eye of Pete Ham. They started dating formally in October of 1966. "Pete had a gentle nature and I admired his determination," she says. "He really, really wanted to make it in the music business, but he wasn't going to step on anyone to do it." Beverley lived near the band and her entire family took an immediate liking to Pete. He was the beneficiary of an occasional home-cooked meal, courtesy of Mrs. Ellis, as were the other Iveys from time to time.

The Iveys gigged sporadically that fall, twice visiting Liverpool twice, including one gig at the Cavern Club. Beatles manager Brian Epstein caught their act in Finchley. Soon after, another set of dates backing David Garrick was booked for November. The tour was to start out in Ireland, where Garrick was quite popular. He was a trained singer, specializing in dramatic ballads and tin-pan-alley pop. The Iveys eventually flew into Dublin with great anticipation. "We thought we'd hit the big time," says Dai. "We were booked into a nice hotel and we played at a huge club. We clicked real well with David."

Garrick was pleased, but trouble began as the band headed out the next day. "We were driving to Cork in a van," continues Dai, "going through villages and small towns. Boys and girls were running alongside photographing us and taking the flyers we had. Finally we arrived in Cork. We had military jackets on, with white flared trousers, and all the boys and girls were there with little scissors – snipping away at our hair, our buttons – anything to get a souvenir. It was like a dream come true!

"We went on for our spot, 'cause we used to do our own set first, and I got pulled off the stage by some girls. We went over extremely well, too well, and Garrick was acting depressed. Bill said to me, 'You had better say something to him.' So I went

The Iveys, 1966

up to him and I said, 'I'm sorry. It's nothing to do with us.' But you could see by his face he was down."

As the tour went on, the egocentric Garrick couldn't handle the split attention. "Musically and as a personality he didn't cut it for everyone," reveals Ron. Adds Dai, "Garrick used to put this theatrical stuff in his eyes to make him cry when he did certain numbers. He also dyed his hair, which wasn't normal in those days."

As it turned out, even when Garrick did get the attention he wanted, he couldn't win. "He got hit with an obscenity charge," laughs Mike, "His shirt was ripped off and he was bare from the waist up. That was a crazy day. But he couldn't handle all the screaming for Dai. Dai was Elvis Presley to the rest of us. The girls loved him. So we had to part ways with Garrick."

It wasn't long before The Iveys' London home turned into a haven for notorious pranks. The Kinks road manager, Dave Duffield, had a stage item stored at the house. The Iveys used it to their advantage. Beverley relates, "The Kinks had this coffin. They'd used it for their appearance on Top Of The Pops, to promote their single 'Dead End Street.' The boys put Mike in a sheet and made him up with white make-up and powder and stuck him in the coffin. They dressed up in suits and carried him to a Wimpy Bar, which is like a McDonalds for that time. They took Mike out, put him on a table, ordered four hamburgers, ate them, put Mike back in the coffin, and carried him out . . . much to the astonishment of the customers!"

The band members spared no one. Duffield recalls one morning, "I had been asleep for like two days after a long tour with The Kinks. I remember waking and smelling something awful. Then I recall seeing four heads, one above the other, peering into the room, like some children's cartoon. I didn't know what was going on. I finally trudged into the kitchen and when I came back with my tea, I saw these legs sticking out from under my bed. It looked like a dead body! They had stuffed shirts and rotten potatoes into a pair of old pants. . . ."

The band was eventually introduced to The Kinks. Leader Ray Davies took an immediate liking to Pete. Beverley recalls, "Ray started to hang out at the house. One time Pete and Ray were spending a long time talking about music and Ray found that his brother was missing. Everyone was looking for Dave Davies. No one could find him. Then someone opened a closet and there he was, just staring into space . . . He was an odd character."

Some of The Iveys' demos were played for Ray and he was impressed. "Bill arranged that we should audition at the Cavalier Club one afternoon," recalls Dai, "and Ray Davies came along. He was interested in taking groups over at the time, doing production work, branching out. It was a showcase just for him."

The head Kinks man claimed he wanted to produce the band, when interviewed by *Melody Maker* in early December. In the article he complimented The Iveys' writing abilities. On January 15, 1967, Davies did produce some demos for the group in a four-track studio on Old Kent Road. The Iveys recorded three songs in one day. "Taxi," by Pete, is a catchy, mod-influenced song. Said Ron Griffiths, "Ray was quite enthusiastic about that one. He gave it a Kinks sort of mix . . . a lovely 'doong' on the bass, and a clang of the guitar. It was beautiful." {Taxi} Ron's "I Believe In You Girl," an Impressions-styled sing-along, was also recorded, as was Pete's "Sausage And Eggs." The latter describes the travails of the band's struggling pop careers: *"We're just small-time entertainers, hoping for big-time luck."* Ron, Pete, and Dai each sing a verse of this amusing lark.

The Kinks connection had been a newsworthy item back in Swansea. The *Beaterama* section in the *Herald Of Wales* soon reported *"Kink Ray Davies has taken over as A&R man for Swansea's Iveys, who are planning a release of two originals written by lead guitarist 'Piggy' Ham . . . The group are gradually becoming one of the 'In' outfits of the club circuit up North and there is talk that they will soon take the success trail similar to the Spencer Davis Group climb."*

The success premonition was essentially accurate, but Ray Davies' enthusiasm was soon to wane. Mike remembered that Davies was ". . . kind of busy. I don't think he was really into it from the word go. But he did give us some of his time."

With Davies close involvement, Bill had decided it was time to document an agreement between him and the band. On December 8, 1966, Collins had a management agreement signed by the group making him exclusive handler of all their business affairs. Collins was to receive 20% of their net receipts. In other words, Collins would get the same share of profits that each group member would get. But another clause stated he was free to deduct any expenses he incurred in his duties as "manager." It was a five-year deal.

The Iveys began 1967 playing whatever gigs they could while continuing to create home demos. Things were rapidly changing on the homefront. The Mojos were beginning to break up. Their drummer, Aynsley Dunbar, had quit and moved out. Vocalist Stuart James was now losing interest, as was guitarist Nicky Crouch. It turned out their quiet bass player, Deke Vernon, "had the most rapport with us," claims Dai. Unfortunately for him, he also became the recipient of another one of The Iveys' morbid jokes.

Beverley relates the incident: "The boys were really into ghoulish humor. They loved scary movies and this chap was a very nervous person, terrified of ghosts. So one day the boys rigged up his entire bedroom. He came home from a gig, very tired, and fell into bed. After a while, someone started scratching the wall behind his closet with a drumstick. He turns on a light. As soon as he did the boys pulled a stuffed sock attached to a thread across the floor. That really got to him.

"He was trying to get out, but they had locked the door. Then they started playing this tape just outside his window. It was a voice saying, 'Jeremiah, Je-re–miiiii–ah,' very few people knew that was his real name. He was absolutely terrified. He ran to the balcony and someone dropped a shirt rigged with a light bulb right in his face. He went absolutely crazy. He was screaming. He ran back to the door, which was unlocked by now, flew down the stairs, and ran off down the road – with nothing on but his underwear!"

As the Mojos left, the Iveys began to take over their individual rooms. Meanwhile, Bill Collins had been discouraging calls and visits from friends, especially girls. Vivien Levenson relates, "Bill intimidated me a lot. He didn't want girls around the house. One time he said, 'I'd appreciate if you didn't come around here anymore.' Later Pete asked me why I wasn't visiting and I told him. Pete said, 'Please, come round here anytime you want, you're always welcome.' "

Pete's friend in Wales, Les Saville, recalls, "I would call and call and I never got through to Peter once. Collins would always say, 'They're busy 'rehearsing' or 'recording.' Pete told me the phone was in Bill's room and Pete would never get the message. I felt so excluded. Our friendship thinned."

The less-intimidated did come around, but Bill was wary of newcomers. Said Duffield, "Bill was always trying to keep their friends away. He especially didn't like girlfriends because he was concerned they might influence them." Beverley adds, "Pete would occasionally try to talk with Bill about it. I remember Pete coming down to meet me from work one day and he said, 'You know, I had a nice talk with Bill and I think we got somewhere. He really understands how I feel.' Then we'd come in the house and from the way Bill behaved, it was as if they'd never talked. Pete would be hurt. Remember he was just a teenager and Bill was a 'father figure' to him. But Pete would never say a bad word about Bill; though you could tell he was let down."

Despite inconsistent work, The Iveys were able to maintain their existence and remain enthusiastic throughout the first half of 1967. They survived on a lot of rolls and a lot of soup, often sustaining their energy through sheer determination and youthful vigor. They continued to impress audiences and traveled several times to Wales for mini-tours. Fellow musicians from the area were supportive, but the generation gap with manager Bill led to a lot of "shop talk," as Collins was an easy target for the young crowd. For example, he had an everpresent pipe and a demonstrative nature, which often led to hilarious mimicry from Dai.

Eyes Of Blue drummer John Weathers: "There wasn't really any strong animosity from the bands toward Bill. We were young, wild musicians and, to us, he seemed like a 'stick-in-the-mud,' too old and too straight." Said the Dream's Martin Ace, "We thought Bill Collins was odd, mainly because he was so old. I might say, 'I saw "Piggy" last night . . .' and Bill would always cut in, ' "*Peter,*" as we call him.' Gary Pickford-Hopkins, of The Eyes Of Blue, added: "Collins would often shout *'I will be the next Brian Epstein and they will be the next Beatles! Four musicians who sing and write!'* "

Bill's boasting was legendary. But behind the scenes his actions were perceived by others to be reticent. He claims he was just being careful of not making the wrong move for the boys; others saw it as fear of failure. As it was, producer Mike Smith of CBS Records had been showing keen interest in The Iveys since early 1967, as had John Schroeder of Pye. Both were kept at bay. Reportedly Decca Records had an interest in the band. And Philips Records allegedly made a deal proposal, but, according to Dai, Bill told them "The offer is too low."

Bill doesn't remember Philips, but he said that very early on he had brought some Iveys demos over to Aberbach Music, a music publishing company of sorts which had earlier signed The Mojos. Franklyn Boyd worked there and he listened to the demos, allegedly telling Bill, "These are good songs. That group has something. Stick with them, and work with them, as you have been. Let The Mojos go."

Despite these encouraging prospects, the Iveys desperately needed gigs to survive. Booking agents Tim Boyle and Sue Wing helped immeasurably as they provided most of The Iveys' London shows through their employment at Terry Oates Productions, or through other business associations. Both became very close to the band as well. "Sue Wing was a great friend to our band," says Mike, "She was our cheerleader."

On March 15, 1967, Bill Collins bumped into The Beatles' roadie, Mal Evans, in London. Bill knew Mal from Liverpool, from Bill's days of doing roadie work for The Mojos in the early '60s. Mal offered to bring Bill to a Beatles recording session. They both went down to the studio and encountered a very crowded scene. George Harrison's "Within You Without You" was being tracked with a large group of Indian musicians. Bill Collins watched the proceedings in fascination. Suddenly, Paul McCartney caught his eye. Bill knew Paul, as Lewis Collins had been a close friend of Paul's brother, Mike, from as far back as their days together at a hairdressing school in Liverpool. Bill knew Paul and Mike's dad, Jim McCartney, from back in the dance bands of the 30s and 40s around Liverpool. Paul greeted Bill and asked him how he was doing. Bill proceeded to excitedly tell Paul about The Iveys, and how he expected his young band to break someday. Paul offered that he would be quite interested in hearing them. Bill contemplated and moved on.

Throughout that spring and into the summer of 1967, The Iveys melded into the swinging London scene, sometimes playing a number of the more fashionable night spots. But without consistent work, the band occasionally had to hit the "bread line." Mike was known for flipping a coin just to decide whether to buy food or cigarettes, "Cigarettes always won out," he laughs. The group did have an apple tree in back. Added Mike, "We used to stew (the apples), boil them, anything you could imagine."

Dai Jenkins, 1967

Pete continued to immerse himself in the recording of demos; always making himself available to help the others with their songs. Yet a problem was developing within the band. "Dai wasn't into the songwriting thing whatsoever," claims Ron. "If we weren't playing gigs or rehearsing, Mike, Pete, and myself would be working on demos. But Dai would be out with whomever he was having his evil way with at the time!" Dai acknowledges, "I was more for the good life – going out and having a drink. I just didn't have it in me to write songs. I'd try and knock out a riff, but nothing of consequence ever came. Bill would get on me about being out late or carrying on with too many women. He was always telling me I should be spending more time practicing. I was a bit of a renegade."

Agent Sue Wing had developed a crush on Dai and they began to go out. Dai's brother, Alwyne, recalls: "Bill Collins had originally requested Dai ask Sue Wing out because she was very important in the London music field involving booking agents. After her and Dai had courted for some time, Bill wanted them to stop. But by then, Dai had fallen for her."

Dai confirms, "She began taking a lot of my time. I was taking the group van to go to the other side of London. Since I usually drove the group around I thought of its use as a perk, but possibly it was resented. Things started to sour. I got moved from the middle of the stage to one side. Small arguments broke out.

"I'd been writing my brother and telling him what was going on. Then we had a gig at the Glanmor Jazz Club in Swansea. My brother was there and he set upon Bill verbally as to why I was being distanced in the band. Well, Alwyne and him had a right old argument. I got in between them just before it came to fisticuffs. Bill thanked me, but after a few gigs no one was speaking to me. Later at the house I went up to Bill and I said, 'So that's it then Bill, isn't it?' And he said, 'Yeah, that's it.' "

Mike remembers, "The rest of the group figured there was more to it. This wasn't my thought at the time. Dave was my best friend out of everybody in the band. When they decided to get rid of him it almost broke my heart." Beverley recalls, "Pete took it very hard. It was sad, but it was a natural progression for the band. Dai was a lovely guy, but basically they felt he wasn't committed."

Before Dai quit, he'd agreed to wait until a replacement was found. The band first advertised in London with no luck. Then they had to go up to Liverpool to fulfill a few dates. During a night off, they decided to check out the local talent. "We got a list of about four different bands that were playing locally," Ron recalled. "So we just did a quick whistle-stop tour of them all. We ended up at [The Mardi Gras]. That's where we saw [Them] Calderstones. That's where we saw Tommy."

Tom Evans was born in Liverpool on June 5, 1947. He was named after his father, Thomas, a bricklayer, who had been royally commended during World War II. Tom's family lived with his grandmother in a converted air-raid shelter until he was three years old. He spent the remainder of his youth at the modest Knowsley Village Estates, a post-war development of adjoining brick homes.

Tom's aunt, Grace, recalls, "I was about ten years older than Tom. As a child I just adored him. He was a very mischievous lad, lots of jokes and laughs, yet at the same time very troubled. I remember one night we had to sleep in the same bed together, and he bit me while I was asleep. He dreamed he was a dog and I was a bone! And he had these glasses. He'd always hide them – literally dig a hole and bury them! He had a lazy eye, too. He'd rarely look you straight on when he talked."

Music was very popular with the entire Evans family. Tom's aunt, Grace, once entertained professionally as "Pearl Scott," and Tom's younger brother, David, sang harmonies with Tom. Tom's mother, May, played accordion, and his grandfather played banjo and mandolin. Tom was very close to his grandfather, as May explained, "My dad loved children. He'd toss Tommy around and play with him all the time. He was a big inspiration to Tommy with his music.

Tom Evans, 1953

"One day, when Tommy was about nine years old, we were coming down for a visit with my father, and Tommy was saying, 'Oh, I'd like to learn this Everly Brothers song.' His favorite was the Everly Brothers – he was in their fan club. Well, on that day my father had fallen asleep with the teapot on. The flame had blown out on the gas stove and my sister came in and found him dead. We got there and Tommy came running in looking for him saying, 'Where's my grand-dad? *Where's my grand-dad!?*' "

The trauma of this event seemed to take its toll on Tommy. His mother, May, indicated he was a very sad child who would often lock himself in his room. "Tommy was in a world of his own. He'd be upstairs with wires and string going through his entire room. And he would say, 'Don't go in there mum, *please*!' He was inventing his 'electric trumpet!' "

One childhood friend of Tommy's was British playwright Willy Russell, world renowned for writing *Blood Brothers,* the screen-adapted *Educating Rita,* and the long running musical *John, Paul, George, Ringo . . . & Bert,* amongst many other works. He recalls, "I first knew Tommy Evans at around age five or six. At nine years of age I got a record player. He didn't have one, so he'd come to my house a lot. He was a total Everly Brothers freak while I became a total Buddy Holly freak. We spent lots and lots of time together. I felt extremely close to Tommy. But one day he came over when friends were around and he put me down real heavily. I was upset and had nothing to do with him for about a year. It went from intense friendship to intense hurt. But one day, a year or so later, he just turned up . . . and we took up our friendship again. But from then on, I was aware there was this other side to him.

"When we were about fourteen, I met this guy who lived on our estate. He was very odd. He wore his hair forward, with black corduroys – he looked like a Martian to us. He told me about The Cavern and I became intrigued. I told Tommy that we'd have to go and check this place out. So we went down and we were just overwhelmed. We'd been in big theaters before, but to be in a club amongst all that cheap perfume and sweatiness – just ten feet away from the band playing – it was mind-boggling. We'd been listening to Radio Luxembourg and American Forces Radio for some time, and knew all the rhythm & blues artists, but the last thing we expected was to hear 'that' down in Liverpool.

"After watching some Shadows-clone band, we were finally going to leave, and out came The Beatles. We didn't know anything about them and we were kidding about their name. They were all dressed in black with Vox AC30 amps, the likes of which we'd never seen before, so we decided to watch their first number. They blasted into 'Some Other Guy' and we were lost – lost forever. It was a moment of great significance. We both knew it. We never had to discuss it. We went out and bought our first guitars. . . .

Them Calderstones, 1966

"Within four weeks Tommy was playing chords and lead lines and I was still struggling. He was showing a much greater talent for music than me. One time Tom and his 'mob' were going to play this party and I tagged along as this sort of glorified roadie. I saw Tommy playing and singing, and that was it, I knew right then he had it. Part of me was so elated, and part of me was just as equally depressed – monumentally depressed. It was as if I had missed the boat in life. And there was Tommy – sailing away. . . ."

After Tom's first group, The Inbeatweens, broke apart, he then formed the unusually-named band, Them Calderstones. They specialized in Tamla-Motown, and essentially could be termed a "mod" group. Evans appearance with them at the club Mardi Gras on July 23, 1967 certainly made an impression with The Iveys. Ron remembered, "Tom was playing guitar, he was upfront, the little lad in the middle singing most of the material. He seemed to fit the bill image-wise. We thought he looked the part. We went up at the end, when they were packing their gear up, and introduced ourselves."

Tom Evans confirmed, "We were playing a gig when these long-haired weirdies walked in. You couldn't miss them – blokes in Liverpool were wearing their hair all short and moddy at the time. They dragged me on one side and asked if I was interested in songwriting, and offered me a place in the group." In another interview, Tom added, "I had a career in engineering at the time and found the prospects of turning professional – living on seven pounds a week in London, with people I didn't know – pretty slim. But nevertheless, I agreed to go down there and hear these songs they had written. I listened to their songs and spent an evening fiddling with this Revox tape recorder, laying down one of my songs. They liked the outcome and I liked their songs. So I went back to Liverpool and thought about it."

Tom's mother remembers that Bill Collins was really after Tom to join. "Tommy had first told me he said, 'No,' because he felt loyal to his group. Then me and my husband went on holiday one weekend and when we got home we found coffee stains all over the living room table. On it was a note. It said, 'Sorry mom, I've gone professional.' I went down to London and saw Bill Collins there, with his short trousers and his pipe. He told me, 'Look, I've gone to the factory where Tommy worked and if he doesn't make it here they'll take him back.' I was dubious, but I was happy for Tommy."

Tom's first Revox demo was "Good Times Together." It's a happy-go-lucky tune and, for one so inexperienced, Tom showed a good ear for harmony and backing vocal arrangements. Tom really took to making demos, as he had frequently dabbled with songwriting ideas from an early age.

Though the other Iveys were quick to take to Tom's musical abilities, they were slow to comprehend his complex personality. Bill Collins related an early incident which portended his and Tom's future relationship. The band had left one of their gigs by the back door. As their van passed in front, a group of girls on the sidewalk flirted by pulling up their skirts and showing off their legs. The band was waving back. Tom told Bill to pull over. Bill replied "You didn't join this group to go pulling birds – this is professional!" As Bill drove off he said Tom became livid. He turned to Bill and said under his breath, "I'm gonna get you, Collins." Bill was shocked. His Welsh boys had been the epitome of respect and decorum. He knew he was now in for a few battles.

The Iveys, August 31, 1967, Adams Beach, Merthyr Tydfil

Beverley explains, "Bill was initially pleased and then he realized how strong Tom was. Before, Bill had been making all the decisions without question. He realized it wasn't going to be as easy." Ron found it difficult to connect with Tom. Pete was also treading lightly. Mike recalls, "As soon as Tom moved in he was complaining. He was from Liverpool and we were Welsh. He said that he couldn't relate to anybody. My thinking was, 'Just tag along, man. This is a band.' "

Tom had a wry wit and he would tease his new mates about their Welsh heritage. He would say that all Welsh "lived in mines," and they only came up to watch rugby – wearing leeks and daffodils, that Wales was so backwards, there were "sheep walking in the streets." As it turned out, the band had some gigs scheduled in Wales and Tom was visiting there for the first time. As Ron said, "We were driving out of Merthyr when we had to stop, because there were sheep all over the road . . . We were mortified. And Tom never let us forget it!"

On October 6, 1967, the group was heading back to London, after a gig in South Wales, when they experienced a devastating roadway accident. It happened around five in the morning, about ten days prior to a scheduled four-week engagement at two separate clubs in Cologne, Germany. The road was slick from rain. Pete hit the brakes too hard while approaching a traffic light. The van hit a lamp post and burst apart. Mike's drums tumbled down the road.

Mike recalls, "I was in the middle front seat and I saw that we were going to hit the lamp post. The seat wasn't bolted down. I didn't know that and I held on to it when I saw we were going to hit. The seat popped up and I hit an iron crossbar. My bottom jaw came up and snapped out five of my front teeth instantly. I went semi-out, and the first thing I saw was a policeman poking his head in the window saying 'Anybody dead?' Fucking idiot, right? Like somebody was going to say 'Yep, me.' "

Ron picks up, "I'd seen it coming and I was lucky; I had grabbed a side post. I hurt my little finger. Bill broke most of his ribs and Tom was in total shock. Pete was hurt too, but he didn't realize it at the time."

Beverley remembers getting a phone call from Pete, "He said, 'I've been in a terrible crash.' I said, 'Are you okay?' and he said, 'Mike's been hurt real bad, he's lost a lot of teeth.' He was really devastated and I said, 'Who was driving? Was it bloody Bill?,' cause Bill wasn't the best driver, and Pete said, 'No, it was me.' He said, 'Please come, I need you, I need you here.'

"I came over and he was so upset about Mike. I put my arms around him and he just gasped, he couldn't move. His collarbone was broken and he was in terrible pain. But he was only concerned about Mike. He felt Mike's pain more than Mike did. Pete never forgave himself for that."

Mike was to go without his teeth for quite awhile, but eventually he did get the extravagant bridgework done. In the meantime, the Iveys performed their German engagements – doing so wrapped in tape, splints, and bandages. Mike recalled, "I used to tie up Pete's arm every night before we went on so he wouldn't be in pain. We had to perform, otherwise the band would have folded. We were broke."

Upon their arrival in Germany the group found out their wages were not being paid until the end of each week, and they quickly ran out of money

At times the band and Bill Collins had to subsist on lukewarm tea made in the bathroom sink. Tom considered the situation intolerable. This was not what he anticipated when he had given up his engineering career months earlier; finding himself in a foreign country in bandages and virtual starvation. Bill says Tom complained constantly. All Bill could offer was that he might look back on these times as the "good old days." Tom Evans was more than doubtful. . . .

The band's fortunes picked up once they returned to London. On November, 18, 1967, a young publishing promo agent named Mike Berry came across The Iveys as they were playing The Flamingo Club in London. "I was just stunned," he says. "They were a brilliant pop group. I asked who wrote two or three of the songs I'd heard. I couldn't believe it when they told me they were original tunes. I gave them my card and a week later we had a meeting at their home."

Berry was then working for the music publishing company Sparta Music Ltd. He brought his boss Hal Shaper with him. "We heard some of their demos and we became passionate in our interest. But Collins didn't want them to sign. They were living in abject poverty eating porridge and toast. I wanted to at least get them a preliminary agreement so they could eat, but nothing was done. Hal Shaper would have signed them there and then. . . ."

Berry kept in touch. He and Tom Evans would hang together at the local clubs. "Tom was one of the greatest I ever met in this business. He was funny. He was cheeky. He was ambitious. He was what rock'n'roll was all about. I remember buying him his drinks all the time, because he didn't have any money. But I didn't care, because I *believed* in him so much."

Tom Evans

2

APPLE OF THEIR EYE

IT WAS JANUARY OF 1968, with flower-power in full swing, and Britain's primo musical weekly, *Melody Maker,* enthusiastically heralding the Beatles' new "artistic brainchild":

> *APPLE . . . an effort, backed with the financial resources, prestige and communicative powers of the Beatles to change the status quo; its purpose is to open the way for artistic fulfillment to writers, musicians, singers, painters, who hitherto have not been able to find acceptance in the commercial world.*

Whether the young Iveys read this or not, it's doubtful they accepted the announcement with any great anticipation, for this was the "Beatles," and to expect any involvement with them, on any level at all, was certainly too overwhelming to imagine. For Pete, though, anything was possible. He had previously written Beverley while in Cologne; expressing his total faith, "Pete had a conviction that they would somehow make it," she said.

The band's stage act improved from their steady work in Germany. They constantly worked at renewing their repertoire, often distinguishing their cover material with unique vocal arrangements. The blend of Tom's coarse exuberance, Pete's sweet tenor, and Ron's soulful flexibility gave the group a very captivating choral presence. For example, their three-part harmony reproducing the Hollies' cover of "Just One Look" was superbly tight, while their Burdon-like interpretation of the Animals' "Don't Let Me Be Misunderstood" was equally inspiring, with intense high harmonies balanced by Pete's sharp wah-wah guitar. The Iveys could pull off any type of music with aplomb. But, with no records out, the band could only get away with playing original songs on occasion. They *needed* a recording contract.

Throughout the past year, the psychedelic drug influence had been sweeping many rock musicians into its fold. Few of the bands from The Iveys' home of South Wales could escape its unrelenting tug. . . .

The Eyes of Blue, after winning a *Melody Maker* talent contest in mid-1966, released two ordinary pop singles on Deram Records. Now they were entering the

Eyes Of Blue, above
The Bystanders, right

new year with the LP *Crossroads Of Time,* a spinning collage of bluesy, soulful character. Ahead of its time in many respects, it somewhat predated progressive rock with its many classical riffs and choir-vocal arrangements.

The Bystanders, led by Roy Orbison sound-alike Vic Oakley, put out numerous pop 45's on Pye Records. But even with their showy vocal abilities, the band never dented the U.K. charts. By mid-1968, they'd embraced the awakening drug culture with full force, as the newly-formed, wild-and-weird, family of "Man."

Amen Corner (Andy Fairweather-Lowe's group from Cardiff) *did* have considerable U.K. success, peaking with the 1968 Number One hit "(If Paradise Is) Half As Nice." They were the most successful Welsh rock band of the 60s, but the group was promoted as a London act. Fairweather-Lowe recalls, "There was a stigma; a good soul band *had* to come from London."

Another Welsh native, Dave Edmunds, received an enthusiastic BBC radio listener response to his live, souped-up version of Russian composer Aram Khachaturian's "Sabre Dance." This led to a recording deal for his band, Love Sculpture and the song became a U.K. radio hit. Edmunds, quite the chameleon at the time, played blues, rockabilly, psychedelia, "whatever was hip," he stated.

Amen Corner, above
Love Sculpture, right

The Iveys, themselves, had touched on a broad base of styles. But even with their many excursions into raucous soul, heavy blues, and bouncy Motown, their own writing tended toward melodically-oriented pop songs. They usually avoided "progressive" influences. If anything, a good majority of their compositions were either light-hearted themes with lyrics inspired by active imaginations (genies, spider women), or what would be considered meaningful events in the lives of a teenager or young adult: i.e., trying to get up in the morning, being late for a date, or drinking punch with your girlfriend.

Everyone in the group were now composing. Ron focusing heavily on his "soul" and "mod" leanings; Tom on harmony and aggressive pop; and Mike, just learning piano, was writing simple two- or three-chord romps. Pete composed in many different styles, always retaining his keen sense of melody. Pete once said, "Song-writing is one of the greatest pleasures of my life. I get in the mood usually at night, between eleven p.m. and five-in-the-morning."

Pete's late nights were legendary. The familiar red bulb installed outside 7 Park Avenue's sound-proofed room is well-etched into many people's memories. Beverley recalls, "Pete felt he had to go into that studio every night to justify it. Sometimes after a gig he would be in the van tapping out a beat or humming a song. Then he'd go straight in and work all night. In the morning he'd pop out with something for you to hear."

One early song of Pete's is "Take Good Care Of My Baby," a soulful backbeat ballad inspired by the Bee Gees' "To Love Somebody." "Pete wrote that just after they came back from Germany," says Beverley. {Take Good Care Of My Baby - Iveys demo} "He also wrote a tune while over there called 'Weep Baby.' He had been kind of miserable, missing me, and he had an argument with the boys. They were kind of like, 'Oh, come on, there's plenty of girls here,' – that kind of thing – and he wrote, 'They just don't realize how much I care.' "

Another composition of Pete's was "I've Been There Once Before." Beverley explains, "Peter often had extremely vivid dreams – he would say that sometimes when he slept it was like seeing a movie or a film. He wrote this song about a dream. A short time later a flying accident did happen at an air display. It was so similar to the dream it just shattered him."

I had a sleep last night that scared me
Upon a strange and distant shore
And though I feel inside it can't be
I know that I've been there before
A supersonic flying delta
A flying fortress at its side
Spectators flee in holy terror
As they watch the two collide

Beverley adds, "Another time Pete had a dream about a cricket match in which a stand collapsed killing and injuring many people, and, sure enough, a similar incident happened a short time later."

Pete seemed to have a heightened sensitivity. That characteristic, plus his friendly, accommodating nature, led many people to approach him with their problems. His willingness to advise was portrayed in many of his demos: "(Call on Me) For My Sympathy," "Stop Waiting For The Sun To Shine," "Think Twice," and "You Didn't Know Each Other Very Well," the latter, a moody narrative, in which Pete carefully advises a warring couple.

One of Pete's musician friends from Swansea, Barrie Evans, explains how Pete's benevolence especially helped him. "My girlfriend and I had broken up and we found out she had become pregnant. I was only eighteen at the time and found the whole situation just overwhelming. Pete offered to let me stay at their house in Golders Green while things were being sorted out. I ended up there for about a month. I was very confused and depressed, but Pete was always there – supportive, ready to talk, and extremely patient. He really got me through it."

Though Pete had a head start in concentrated songcraft, Tom Evans was quickly advancing. His punchy "Fresh" was a red-hot cross between Motown and Stax, while his chorus from "I Am Myself" proved quite stirring. Tom's titles revealed the many themes of his life. For example: "I Feel Bad Today," "Dancing Girls," and "A Simple Song," a standard blues riff to which Tom adds his hair-raising call for attention:

If I've gone into the background
And you ain't listening anymore
Listen to this
'WAAAAHHHOOOWWWWWWW!'
Just woke you up for sure

Beverley: "We used to tremble in our shoes with Tom. He could fill up a room. Yet, very often he was quiet and withdrawn. Pete was confused by this."

Tentatively, Tom and Pete did start to write together. The dynamics of their divergent personalities led to some early creative sparks, such as one gem of a song, "She Came Out Of The Cold," a kind of Walker Brothers pastiche. {She Came Out Of The Cold - Iveys demo} Still, many of Pete and Tom's collaborations struggled toward fruition; their partnership needed time. Beverley related, "Pete was a little bit in awe of Tom and his streetwise experience. Likewise, Tom noticed Pete could get on better with people than he could. If you're a friendly, easygoing person, as Pete was, people stop and listen to you more, not only what you say, but what you do. With Tom, you had to get used to his moods, and eventually, the relationship would kind of rise above it."

By this time, Mike Gibbins was playing rudimentary piano and guitar on his solo demos, which sometimes included his drumming. Pete strongly supported Mike's efforts and would take time to add guitar bits. Said Bev, "If Mike wrote anything, Pete would be on a high for days. It affected him that much."

Mike's early tunes often had little form, plowing on endlessly, but he stayed within himself. His gift for catchiness was apparent. The songs corralled his moods; happy-go-lucky, hyperactive, and fanciful: "Tomorrow Never Comes," "Sitting Down, Wasting Time," "Dreaming", and "My Head's Like Lead," the latter sung in a droning monotone, not too unlike Pink Floyd's enigmatic Syd Barrett.

Ron Griffiths eventually started to write less than Mike, but his complexity was far more advanced. His "Mr. Strangeways" and "Tube Train" captured the sound and spirit of the Creation or Who at their mid-60s best. Chockfull of falsetto vocal arrangements, and psychedelic breaks, they both are enormous fun, albeit copycat blueprints.

Overall, most of the demos are very listenable, even when certain aspects are a bit off-center, such as a quirkiness in the writing, or an instrument which sounds cheesy. The group, with input from Bill, would come to a consensus on a song, arrange it, and then record a group demo, eventually cutting off a sampling to a compilation reel. Utilizing about six to ten demos at a time, they would have reel-to-reel copies made for interested parties. Collins encouraged a mix of writers and styles. As Tom once said, "We were always believing in the policy of writing our own songs and not getting into the trends that were going down in England. We were just saying 'If we can write our own hit song, we can make it.'"

The Iveys spent January of 1968 gigging and recording demos at home. Interest continued from many fronts. Warm Records producer Mike Hurst (of Manfred Mann and Cat Stevens fame) was curious, as were other talent scouts. Collins claimed he wasn't yet convinced to pull any triggers.

Bill was continually keeping his eye on, not just the business side, but the personal side of The Iveys as well. Bill was said to peep in keyholes and creep around doorways. It became quite comical to the group when his pipe smoke could be seen snaking its way around the corner. Iveys housemate Dave Duffield recalls, "Bill Collins used to hang around and try and listen. Like if you were talking in the kitchen, he'd make a piece of toast, and cut it into three or four sections. He'd leave a few there to retrieve, so he could keep coming back in." Beverley adds, "If he found out there had been some meeting without him, he'd invite someone who was there into his bedroom for a chat. And he'd turn on the charm."

Bill was a proud man, well-acknowledged as a talented woodworker, mechanic, and clever music theorist, but to many his attitudes were manipulative. A close friend of the group said, "Any experience he had, that you hadn't, he held over you. Any experience that you had, that he hadn't, wasn't important."

One of his most prominent features was to bely his age through physical exploits, such as standing on his head, or lifting heavy equipment. Beverley recalls, "One time Bill was in a major feud with his son, Lew, and he came over to my parent's house to leave a message for me, because he didn't know where Lew was. So my mother asks Bill, 'Would you like a cup of tea and a sandwich?' And Bill says, 'Yes, thank you.' When my mother came back into the living room with the tea and sandwich, Bill threw himself on the floor and started doing push-ups.

Bill's on the ground huffing and puffing and grunting. Meanwhile, my mother is standing there holding her tray. My father walks in from work. He stands in front of Bill and waits. Bill finally gets up and he's got this big smile on his face. My dad looks at him and says, '*Oh!* Is *that* all you can do?'"

Beatles' roadie and best friend, Mal Evans, had long been itching to do something other than his standard cajoling and "gofer" act for the Fab Four. The new Apple organization lended him his window of opportunity. One day, Bill Collins contacted Mal, telling him of a gig his young Iveys were playing at the Marquee club in London. Mal went down to check it out, bringing Apple Record's potential new A&R head, Peter Asher. The date was January 25, 1968. Ron Griffiths recalls, "We had just finished our regular 'wind-up-the-audience-and-have-a-laugh-with-them' stint when this giant bloke came up at the end with Bill. We recognized him because we'd seen pictures in the magazines from years gone by. We were thrilled to bits because that was the nearest we'd got to the Beatles at that time.

"Mal found out we did our own material and he came by a few days later to listen. We were up 'til all hours of the morning playing our demos and he was most impressed. He couldn't get over the variety of songs. We were pouring drinks and he started to pass a joint around. He was the first person to ever make it available to us. I didn't enjoy it. Pete was a little wary. But Tom certainly got into it."

Bill gave Mal a reel of Iveys demos, and Mal brought them to Apple's new publishing offices on Baker Street. He immediately began to play them for anybody who'd listen. Apple was just getting their record company end together. Mike Berry, who had wanted to sign The Iveys to music publisher Sparta Music the year before, was now working for the new Apple Music Ltd. He recalls, "I remember telling my Apple publishing partner, Terry Doran, that The Iveys were going to be our first signing. I [had given] Paul McCartney my personal Iveys demo tape, but Paul said he didn't see anything in it. I'd planned to get him another one in the near future."

The Iveys' popularity was growing. A small contingent of fans began to appear regularly at certain venues. Early in 1968, Stella Jones, Sylvia Collins, Joyce Leather, and Ossie Lane, of Reading, began an Iveys fan club, giving out membership cards and a fact sheet. Pete was enthused by this, but easily embarrassed by any demonstrative attention. Beverley recalls when someone approached Pete at a Golders Green shop, praising him to the sky. "His face turned red," she says. "He downplayed it, but I could see it really excited him."

During February and March of '68, the Iveys made two separate excursions to Wales. During the latter trip Beverley accompanied Pete. They spent a lot of time at his parent's house. Beverley explains, "Pete loved his family. He got along great with his sister Irene, and he really looked up to his brother John. And John's wife, Maureen, she was the model of what he wanted, someone who was supportive and

Catherine Ham, Pete Ham

patient. Their daughter Julie – he just adored her. But Pete was especially close to his mother. He was her baby and she was always very concerned for him. He'd hide some of the things he did, because he didn't want to upset her. His dad was really funny too, always joking and laughing. And Pete was the consummate son, always attentive and giving."

But Pete claimed he did have his moments of rebellion as a young teen. He was once quoted as saying, "I've changed a great deal. I used to be vicious to my parents just because they objected to me going full-time with a group. Now I can see that all they wanted was the best for me. And we get on great."

Pete decided it was now time to give his mother a gift of appreciation. "Pete couldn't always just go and say things directly," says Beverley, "but he could do it through a song." Pete recorded himself playing drums, a steady beat for three minutes, layering it with guitars and vocals. The tune was entitled "Catherine Cares."

No matter what I got I just complained
She'd give her last to see me smile
And try to keep me dressed in style
But I had this ambition in my brain
So I walked out and left her there
Without a thought, without a care.
Catherine cares . . .
I know that I was selfish to you mom
Please forgive me

Pete gave his mother a copy of the song. "She was absolutely thrilled," says Bev, "and quite embarrassed. She didn't know what to say. Pete just wanted to tell her, 'I've grown up now and I realize what you were trying to say and trying to do all these years.' He just wanted to say, 'Thank you.' "

One afternoon, Pete and Beverley were alone in the front room of his parents' house. Bev was seated on the sofa. She recalls, "Pete told me he wanted to get married. I was absolutely thrilled. See, at this time it was not the 'in' thing for a pop star to be married. The Beatles were keeping their relationships real quiet. He was aware of that. But Pete felt it would be okay if one member got married. He knew he had very little money, but he had confidence the group would take off. We planned for sometime the following year."

The next day Pete and Beverley took the bus to the train station. "Pete wrote me later and said that he had decided to walk the couple of miles back to his home. It had taken him awhile and apparently his niece, Julie, who was about five at the time, had told everyone, 'We must organize a search party!' She just idolized him. If he sat down and crossed his legs, she would cross her legs. If he picked up something to read, she would pick up something to read. And Pete thought she was such a beautiful child – and such fun! A tremendous sense of humor."

Pete and Julie even concocted a secret code which they would use in letters. "Pete used to think her mind was so wonderful," says Beverley. "He wrote a song called 'Island.' If you could escape into a child's mind – how simple and peaceful it is – to see things through a child's eyes. The song wasn't necessarily about an island, but that special place inside a child's head."

Back in Golders Green, Pete and Beverley decided to keep their marriage plans basically to themselves, only telling a few relatives and close friends. Meanwhile, relationships had gotten hot and heavy around the band's home. Ron was now involved with a girl named Maureen, whom he'd met the year before in Hemel-Hampstead. He would have her down to Park Avenue or go up to her place for weekends. The situation became quite serious when Maureen became pregnant. By June of 1968, she and Ron were married. Mike had a girlfriend named Gaynor, who had known Mike and Pete from Swansea and since moved to London. She would often visit Golders Green. Her sister, Gill, liked Tommy, and they dated from time to time. The house was getting crowded.

Springtime of '68 saw the group picking up sporadic gigs. One was at London's Marquee club, in support of the Scottish band, Marmalade. Group member Junior Campbell was impressed by The Iveys. They asked him if he'd like to come over to hear some of their original songs. Campbell recalls, "I was only nineteen at the time, just learning to write as they were. I remember we sat down and the very first thing they played me on the acoustic guitar was a song called 'Bittersweet Adieu.'

Ron Griffiths marries Maureen, June, 1968

I thought it was a great song. My band was working with a record producer at the time, Mike Smith, who worked for CBS Records. I mentioned the Iveys. He set up a recording session for them at a four-track studio on Denmark St. called Regent Sound. He asked me to show up. I went there basically encouraging them. They did 'Bittersweet Adieu,' but it didn't come out anywhere near its potential. That was a shame. I thought they had a lot of great songs."

Autobiographical in nature, "Bittersweet Adieu" sounds a lot like what Marmalade were doing at the time. For the studio demo, Ron sings lead, and Pete added some nice guitar fills, but the version is meandering and undeveloped. A revamp would be needed. Two other tunes recorded, "Angelique" and "Hi Fli," (later retitled "Looking For My Baby") didn't exactly sound like potential hits either.

It's not known if these demos had any business effect, but the experience did give the band an emotional lift. Working with Mike Smith had been encouraging. Luckily, there were even better developments around the corner.

Mal Evans had continued to receive reels of Iveys demos from Bill Collins over the past few months. On May 6, 1968 he brought a fourth set of songs into Apple. Peter Asher, who was now Apple's head of A&R, remembers Mal's excitement, "He was talking very enthusiastically about The Iveys. This was unusual. Normally Mal didn't express very strong opinions about anything." Derek Taylor, the label's publicist, said that he was quite taken. "The Iveys had an extremely melodic, professional, coherent sound. It stood out amongst all the other tapes that were coming in. And it sounded like a record, which was the best test."

Paul McCartney was equally impressed. He gave Mike Berry a call, "Paul said to me, 'Have you heard the new Iveys tape? It's fucking great!' I told him, 'That's the sign of a good publisher, Paul. To see it before anyone else does.'"

Word got back there was serious interest from Apple. Beverley recalls, "Apparently Paul McCartney had mentioned that he particularly liked the song 'Knocking Down Our Home.' {Knocking Down Our Home - Pete demo on reel #4} Pete was saying, *'He really liked it? He really liked it?!'* I can't tell you how thrilled he was."

At this point, Collins was pretty much assured The Iveys would be offered a publishing contract. As it was, the key to any Apple deal was The Beatles. In theory, any signings had to be approved by all of them. But, with each Beatle going in different directions, it wasn't easy to get something finalized. Most of the early Apple signings were actually rooted in one specific individual's interest. McCartney sought Mary Hopkin and succeeded. George Harrison wanted Jackie Lomax, 'No problem.' Peter Asher *had* to have James Taylor, and he secured him. Label president Ron Kass lobbied for his first love, The Modern Jazz Quartet. It seemed all the top dogs got their one hot ticket. "But John Lennon was scathing about everybody," says Asher. "He would say, 'Who needs James Taylor or The Iveys when you have true artists like Yoko Ono?' "

Though the Apple staff was impressed by the new Iveys tape, they weren't in agreement regarding a recording deal. McCartney mentioned nothing yet struck him as a surefire 45 hit. But Mal Evans wasn't about to give up. On May 21, 1968, Mal brought yet another set of Iveys demos to Apple. Peter Asher recalls, "We would normally have a meeting every week or two, which I would be in charge of, and whomever else was available. There'd be some quorum of the Beatles; a couple, or all four, if you were extremely lucky. We had this meeting, and Mal made an extremely impassioned speech about how much he liked The Iveys and believed in them. Paul admired them. George and John liked the new tapes. And we all liked Mal. So there was no hesitation. They became Mal's baby."

Bill and The Iveys were told it was now a matter of paperwork. They were going to be signed to both Apple Records and Apple Music Publishing. The group was stunned. "We were euphoric," says Ron. "Everyone was going crazy. But we didn't have any funds to have a party, so we just ran down to the local pub."

The group continued to do shows – two weeks of gigs in Italy, sporadic engagements around Wales, a set at The Cavern in Liverpool – before the recording contract was finally signed and secured on July 23, 1968. It called for a three-year term, with two one-year options. Bill recalls discussing it with George Harrison. "He said, 'Tell you what Bill, you're not going to get ripped off like we were getting ripped off in our day. With us you get five percent and you don't pay for production costs.' I thought that was a fantastic deal. I didn't negotiate this, I'm no businessman. That's what he wanted to do."

In actuality, the royalty was four percent of retail for the first 100,000 records sold, and five percent thereafter. A minimum of twelve songs per calendar year was required.

The very evening of the very day The Iveys were documented as signing their recording contract, they were put into Trident Studios with Tony Visconti. Denny Cordell, owner of the Regal-Zonophone record label, had originally been slated to produce. "John Lennon was always keen on me to do something for Apple," Cordell remembered, "and he asked me to work with The Iveys." As it turned out, Cordell did end up overseeing a few sessions before shuffling the entire project over to Visconti. Visconti's arrangements on Cordell's Move recordings had led to some early production opportunities with Strawbs and Tyrannosaurus Rex.

Visconti initially focused on two songs, "Daddy's A Millionaire" and "No Escaping Your Love." The former is a Ham/Evans composition based on a groovy rock riff, a salty story of a young, encumbered, rich girl. The latter is an Evans number. Tom's demo had been full of improvised melody and exhibited some potential, but the band drove home the new recording with every cliché they could muster. Unfortunately, they weren't Freddie and the Dreamers, and this wasn't 1964.

At one of the early recording sessions, Mike and Ron sat down for a break. "McCartney came into the room," recalls Ron. "Mike and I were sitting on the studio floor having a cigarette, drinking a cup of coffee, and Paul walked over to the grand piano and said, 'Hey lads, come over and have a listen to this. This is going to be our next single.' He sat down and gave us a full concert rendition of 'Hey Jude.' He didn't hold back at all. This is just after he wrote it. It hadn't been recorded yet. We were gob-smacked!"

On July 26, 1968, the group were documented working on a Pete Ham composition called "I'm In Love." It's a choppy song based on a traditional jazz feel. Not really commercial, but the freshness of the new number had struck the lads' fancy. The recording featured an obnoxious, Cockney-inflected, call-and-response section. Tony Visconti recalls, "We were at Trident Studios mixing the song and I'm looking down at the desk. The Iveys were all around me in a circle, looking down intensely at the board. The spoken track was very loud, but I wasn't up to that bit yet, so I just let it go by. We looked up after a run-through and fell down in our tracks, because right in front of us was standing Paul McCartney. He said, 'Excuse me, I thought the lads were here,' meaning the Beatles. He said 'We must be recording at Abbey Road. I was under the impression we were recording here.' We didn't know what to say. I had never met him before, and here's McCartney standing two feet away from my face! So I just said, 'What do you think so far?' And he said, 'It's really good except that spoken bit is very loud.' Defensively I said, 'We're not up to that bit yet!' I sort of snapped at him. He said, 'Oh, excuse me – I'm sorry.' *Great!* Within two seconds I've *leveled* a Beatle!"

The Apple signing had rejuvenated the band. Pre-production meetings were being held. Visconti recalls, "They would come around to my apartment in Earls

Court and play me songs on an acoustic guitar or piano. And Collins would always be lurking around. He used to make suggestions that I thought were a bit dated. I thought, 'He's a bit old to be doing this.'"

Visconti was more than pleased when he settled in on the group's talents. "I thought they were amazing. Even in my living room, I could hear the vocal inflections and the sonority, the timbre of their voices was incredible; I was almost frightened by it. And Pete Ham was a phenomenal guitarist."

As a late summer Revox recording of an Iveys' gig shows, their stage act was quite strong. They covered "Long Tall Sally," "Purple Haze," "Walk Away Renee," and performed dynamic versions of Ira Gershwin's "Summertime," and John Mayall and The Bluesbreakers' "Crawling Up A Hill." Pete's playing is clearly confident. As Mike said, "Pete was the nearest guitar player to Clapton I'd heard. He played 'slowhand,' it was all kind of smooth and melodic." At this performance, The Iveys played some of the songs they'd recently recorded, possibly in anticipation of their release. But, as it turned out, any records from the band were still a ways off.

At the time of inking their record deal, The Iveys were also assured they'd be contracted to Apple's publishing arm – Apple Music. But one of the division's managing directors, Mike Berry, says his difficulty with getting Iveys business done was the last straw in his decision to leave the company that summer. "From the time I had joined Apple in January of '68, I had been frustrated. I remember I lost out on signing one writer because a Beatle was never around to get anything approved. One of his songs that I really wanted went Top Five. Finally, we had this meeting between The Beatles and everyone from all the departments. McCartney chaired the meeting. We all agreed we had to get more communication going on all levels. It was decided that Derek Taylor would be a go-between coordinator for everyone to help get things done. The next day I wanted to talk to Derek about getting something going for The Iveys and I was told he had gone to Los Angeles. I said, 'This place is not working.' I got disillusioned and left." But Berry remained supportive of The Iveys. "I was hired back at Sparta Music as a director. I was still around, rooting for them."

At this point, The Iveys' recordings weren't proving to be the potential singles Apple were hoping for. Pete Townshend of The Who presented a number he felt appropriate for the band; "Mary Anne With The Shaky Hands," a number off his own group's third album, *The Who Sell Out*. Ron Griffiths recalls Bill Collins arriving with an acetate, "He told us this had come to Apple as a suggestion, 'Maybe the Iveys would like to do this.' I remember somehow it was suggested I sing it. We heard it, but Pete was being a rock against it: 'It's going to be one of ours! The first one is going to be one of ours!' It didn't matter a tots to me. I had thought, 'Well, lets do it.' But he wouldn't have it. He said, 'If we're going to have a hit record, it's going to be our material.' It became a democratic decision."

The composition was turned down. Bill had succeeded in impressing on Pete the importance of the band showcasing their own writing abilities. This motivation fed Pete intensely. He believed in the group. Jack Oliver, recently hired into Apple's publishing department, remembered, "We could tell they had great potential because they wrote good songs, and they had a good sound. I think everyone knew something was gonna come, but we didn't know when."

Finally a song was picked to be recorded for a single. It was a Tom Evans composition, "Maybe Tomorrow," a tune from one of the first Iveys demo reels submitted to Apple. Bill Collins recalled, "Tom wrote this in 1967, when he first joined us. He was about eighteen at the time and this is what he wanted to do most – highly emotional songs." The group went into Trident Studios on August 9, 1968. Visconti explains, "They gave me what they'd worked out and I wanted to put orchestra on top of it. I wrote the parts, played them on the piano, and asked if they liked it. I think they were so much in awe they were going to get violins they basically just said, 'Great. Go ahead as it is.'"

At completion, "Maybe Tomorrow" was brought over to Apple, along with a new recording of "Daddy's A Millionaire." The reaction was positive, though some had doubts. Tom Evans remembered, as "Maybe Tomorrow" was played over and over, a familiar gentleman came down the stairs, having overheard the tune. "I think you've got a hit there," he said, and with that, disappeared into a back room. It was a nice compliment to dwell upon, and it gave the boys a shot in the arm. After all, the fleeting face had had just a bit of success behind him, having written a pretty decent ballad himself – "Yesterday."

Eventually it was confirmed. "Maybe Tomorrow" was to be the worldwide debut 45 for The Iveys. Beverley recalls Pete's reaction, "He was thrilled, especially for Tom. I think if it had been his song and Tom would've said, 'Well, you're the lucky one,' it would've taken the joy out of it. This was a group success. His day would come."

Tom was "walking on air" with McCartney personally telling him it was a surefire hit. A date was set for U.K. release and a promotional film was made of the band lipsyncing the song while dressed in suits.

September '68, The Iveys' hard work continued: recording, rehearsals, live performances, and more demos. Pete was a whirlwind of composing as he consistently came up with quality melodic numbers. "Beverley" was a standout, a gentle song of reassurance and love. For now, Pete and Beverley's idea of marriage had been put on hold, though plans were still occasionally being discussed. Pete had even asked Beverley's parents about a three room attic flat they were converting for rental, but the cross-section of band activities and newly-found excitement consumed Pete's life. Beverley patiently stood by.

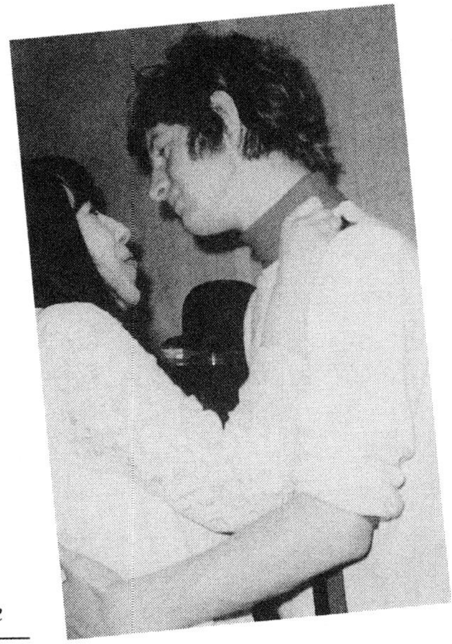

Beverley and Pete

More recognition for the band came in October of 1968: press at home, a photo in the prestigious U.S. magazine *Life*, a ten-minute feature for the Welsh TV show *Etcetera, Etcetera*, which included footage of the band recording, playing, getting haircuts, jollying around . . . The group appeared relaxed and at ease.

By early fall Apple Records had resituated their company into an impressive white-fronted building on Savile Row. The label had garnered two international 45 successes – the Beatles' "Hey Jude" and Mary Hopkin's "Those Were The Days." The Iveys were to be the company's fifth single release. Apple's publishing arm was also now in full swing. McCartney wanted the group to write a song for Mary Hopkin, though it's not known if they ever submitted one, and the Everly Brothers, who allegedly liked some of their songs. But the formality of signing The Iveys to Apple Music had been held up for some reason.

Finally, on October 31, 1968, the band's publishing contract was secured. Apple Music was to split with the group the publisher share of The Iveys songs they utilized. The Iveys would keep their entire writer's share. The term was for three years, with two one-year options. This was as good a deal as The Iveys could have expected.

Prior to the two Apple deals, Bill Collins and the band members had verbally discussed a group agreement regarding song publishing. Back on December 5, 1967, just after music publisher Hal Shaper had shown interest in The Iveys songs, Bill documented in his diary that he met with the band in their home studio and *"thrashed out details of songwriting team."* Two days later Bill wrote of further *"discussions with the boys."* But no specific points were revealed. His diary also shows he met with various administrators over the next month, but no written contracts were sorted out. Explained Bill, "When Tom came in, he took over Dai

Jenkin's position of [the partnership] agreement mutatis mutandis, the good with the bad. After Tom had been with us for about a year, I made this proposal; they all accepted it. It wasn't written down, but it was understood; a verbal agreement."

Bill stated he'd suggested that the songwriter or songwriters of any Iveys material would get 25% of the publishing income off the top, and the other 75% would then be split between all the group members and himself. Bill added he felt he was being more than fair, because he probably should have gotten an "even" five-way split for each song, as he did for the "partnership" agreement.

Ron Griffiths recalled the circumstances somewhat differently. He said Bill came up with a songwriting proposal just after the band knew they were going to sign the *Apple* contracts. And that when Bill came up to them with this proposal, Ron recalls a diagram was drawn up with a pie-shaped graph on it, and 50% was allotted to the songwriter, or songwriters, with the remaining 50% split amongst the five of them. He says he can still visualize it today. Griffiths has no idea what has happened to the paper. He also said the group was naive to music publishing or what it really meant; that they simply trusted Bill with the business issues, so they agreed to it.

Bill did have the group sign a contract around this time, one insuring that all Iveys income be directed to him. That way he could continue to deduct group expenses and balance their books, which he kept with painstaking detail – even down to their purchase of a single "fag" (cigarette).

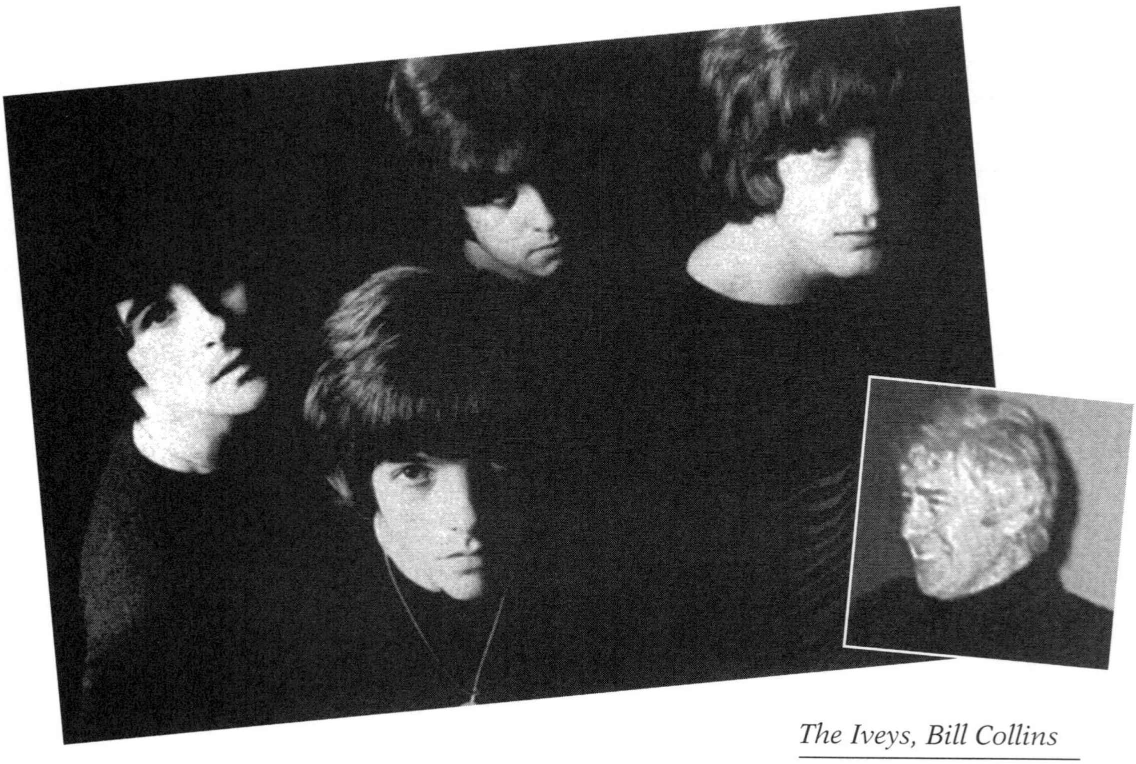

The Iveys, Bill Collins

The "Maybe Tomorrow" single was released in Britain in late November of 1968. The first review came from the prestigious *Melody Maker,* and, despite some compliments, it portended the band's eventual stigmatization in Britain, "*. . . Lead singer sounds like John Lennon." New Musical Express* was more enthusiastic, giving credit to the emotional singing and *"fine orchestral backing."* Back in Swansea, the *Beaterama* column was ecstatic: *"first class," "tremendous," "a very good melody,"* yet they also noted, *"A good promotion campaign is also essential."* Would the Iveys get one?

In a letter dated November 28, 1968, Derek Taylor wrote to England's *Disc & Music Echo* pleading for write-ups on the group. This was the magazine's reply to Taylor: *"Your letter today requesting space for the Iveys strikes me as a fantastic impertinence, coming after your refusal to allow us to interview Mary Hopkin. Okay, I understand she is busy recording but she has to eat, and she has to sleep, and no one is actively recording in a studio 24 hours a day nonstop. So your claim that she is unavailable for a 10-minute chat is indefensible. Own up – which paper launched Mary Hopkin with a colour picture and features? It wasn't* Woman's Own *you know."*

Derek Taylor recalled the difficulties in promoting the Iveys. "Mary Hopkin was easy to get press for, because she was a girl, and there weren't a lot of girl singers then. Also, she had an obvious hit, a *huge* hit. She was pretty, young, Welsh. Twiggy had discovered her. McCartney was awed. What was done for The Iveys was really treading water; keeping them happy with a cup of tea or a drink, and making sure Bill Collins got access to whatever he was asking for. With "Maybe Tomorrow" we had confidence, but a lot was going on at the time. *Get Back* was going to start at Twickenham in early January."

Disc & Music Echo eventually recanted and ran an article on the group. But the piece concentrated on The Iveys' problems, and it contained a little dig at Apple by Tom Evans: *"The business definitely seems to be blocking all that Apple are trying to do and we are the ones who are suffering because we're really the guinea pigs – the first group Apple have launched . . . The un-cooperation of The Beatles and Mary Hopkin is not helping either. I think Apple thought it would be a snowball for everyone that followed. Instead they are having to slog."*

The British press was now relentless in trying to find chinks in The Beatles' armor. Simultaneously, *Melody Maker* ran another piece entitled, "Has Apple Gone Rotten?" Derek Taylor's comments showed him forced into a defensive stance: *"We have been criticized for inefficiency and, I agree, if you're looking for a paradox, you'll find it here in abundance . . . But if you're looking for help, you'll find that, too. And if you're looking for sense, truth, and a friendly face . . . You'll find that too. . . . With the pressures that are on us, it's not that we haven't achieved all our aims; it's a miracle that anything gets done at all."*

BBC radio stations did air "Maybe Tomorrow," but few English consumers bit. By mid-December it became obvious the single was not going to chart in Britain. All the band could do now was wait for the American and European releases, and continue to record their songs.

In December of 1968, Ron Griffiths' son, Jason, was born. It was a brand new responsibility for Ron. With the pressure of being a poor London musician, and an eager-to-please husband, his ability to contribute to the group was becoming hampered. The distractions played differently around the house. Mal Evans was still around – a jolly old friend and engaging influence. He helped Ron by buying a high-chair and a few other needed sundries. He even took the band to a few Beatles recording sessions. But he also introduced them to marijuana, and not long after, something stronger, LSD. Ron and Pete were wary, but the others embraced the drug's oblique philosophy. "Mal gave us our first acid," said Mike. "He called it Strawberry Fields Forever." Mike was quite comfortable with its effect. And Tom was quoted in December as saying, "I know where I'm going now. Acid taught me that." Even Bill Collins took to its lure. Marijuana had usually sent Bill scurrying to bed for a nap. Acid became his new guru, as he was alleged to have told people, "If you haven't considered it on LSD, you *haven't* considered it."

Yet even though the Iveys disdained drugged-out musical trends, they made one obvious attempt with a song called "I've Been Waiting." This was, as Tom put it, "our attempt to be contemporary and jam a bit." It's 60s-psychedelia personified: a rapid-fire guitar riff, distant compressed vocals, and a huge, bounding bass line accented by monstrous piano octaving. Ron remembers the recording engineer, Glyn Johns, "who was very unenthusiastic. We'd wanted to capture some of our onstage sound, which was much fatter than a lot of our recordings, but he'd been working with The Stones, The Kinks, and he had just done Led Zeppelin's first album. His attitude was, 'Who are *these* guys?'"

"I've Been Waiting" ended up very murky-sounding, though some of Griffiths' fine bass work does step out. Visconti had been high on Ron's playing and, according to Collins, he did offer session opportunities. But Bill did not want to distract his young men from their current goals, or mess with the group's potential mystique. He claimed if he had let Ron work on other projects, it would have opened the door for Pete, Tom, and Mike to do the same, thus jeopardizing the unity of the "team." Ron said he was never told about the offers.

By this time, the failure of "Maybe Tomorrow" as a single in the U.K. had greatly disappointed the band. Apple had started to murmur about wanting a new 45, but the label wasn't convinced to release any of the group's other recorded tracks as an A-side. Mal Evans, now listed as an Apple co-Managing Director, decided to take the bull by the horns. He brought The Iveys into the studio himself.

Mal had witnessed numerous Beatles sessions and, as such, marginally knew his way around. The Iveys threw together an arrangement for the most commercial song they thought they had and presented it to him. He approved. Everyone filed into Morgan Studios on December 21, 1968, for a quick go-round. Out of it came "Storm In A Teacup," whose title Bill Collins says he'd thrown Tom's way. Despite a bouncy beat and an interesting double-speed solo, the song doesn't hold up, partly because Tom sings it in an overly aggressive manner. It was rejected as the band's next single.

On December 23, 1968, Apple Records held their first employee Christmas party, during which the company celebrated the releasing of an Italian four-disc Apple package. It included the "Maybe Tomorrow" single, 45s by Jackie Lomax and Mary Hopkin, and a seven-inch Beatles interview disc. The Iveys mingled with the Apple staff and played a short set. Several congratulatory telegrams were sent back to their Park Avenue home.

Before splitting for the holidays, the group and some of their friends got together to have a party. By now the boys had developed into a close-knit clan, and the social scene at 7 Park Avenue was a highlight for everyone. Pete loved to get everyone involved in an activity. He said around this time, "I like parties, but when I say that I mean the old-fashioned kind. The kind where people go to have a good time, not just to roll up a joint and have a big smoking scene. What I like is a real knees-up . . . a time when people really enjoy themselves without the aid of artificial things." Pete inspired his friends to record a geriatric version of "The Twelve Days Of Christmas." Every British accent imaginable is included in this

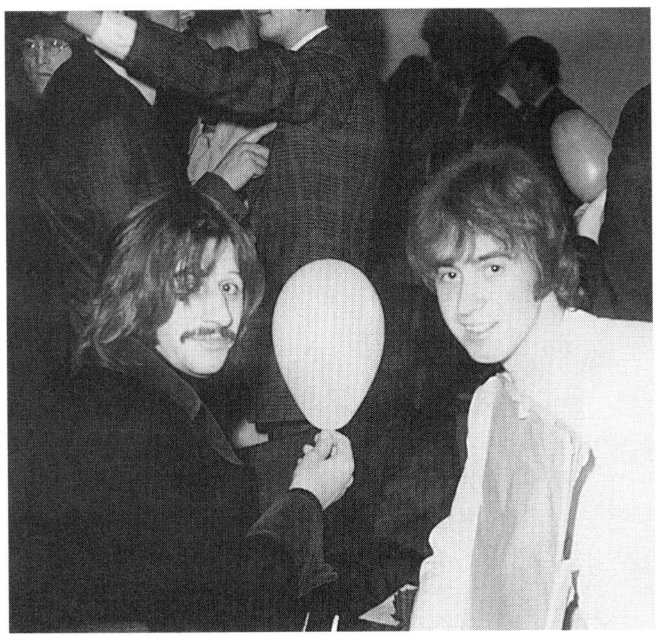

Apple Christmas party, December 1968

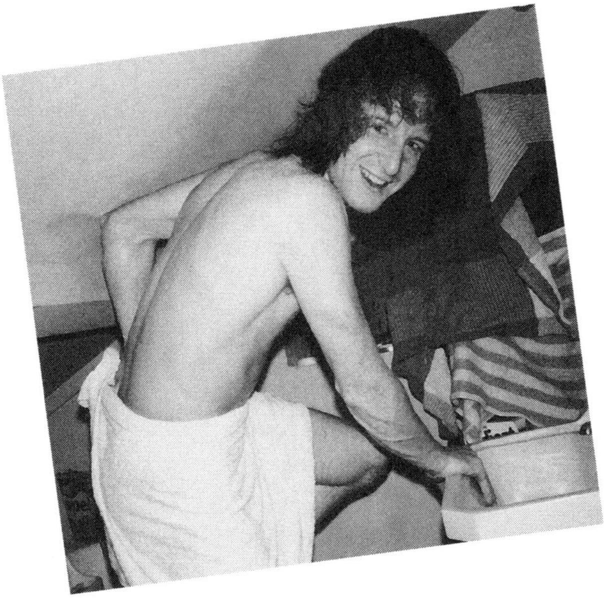

Pete Ham, 7 Park Avenue

Pythonesque romp, which includes lines like "Seven hearing aids," "Five iron lungs," and "A guide dog in a wheelchair." Acetates were given out.

Pete's gracious nature was obvious to all his friends, but there was a depth to his feelings that many failed to see. Pete's songs were his best way of communicating, though many didn't realize that at the time. A revealing composition by Pete is "The Clown Of The Party." {Clown Of The Party – Iveys demo} Its the tale of a misunderstood man who's reaching the bottom of his despair:

Everybody seems to like him, so they say
Like the way he makes them laugh
But beneath that smiling mask he wears a frown
Knows he really doesn't want to be a clown . . .
In his heart he wants to cry

Another early Pete demo, "I'm A Joker," suggests further private quandaries:

I'm a joker, just a joker
But it isn't me, that they really see
Cause inside, is where I hide, all my secrets

"Pete would do anything to cheer other people up," said Beverley. "But deep inside he was often feeling his own pain." By now, Beverley had developed a strong intuition regarding Pete's moods. "I could tell if something was really bothering him. He had his habits and patterns. He would either disappear very quickly into the studio, or he would sit in this great big chair that I had gotten him. It was in his room and he would sit and stare into the fireplace."

Pete sometimes broke out of his depressions by playing outrageous practical jokes. Mike's girlfriend of the time, Gaynor, recalls, "You'd be watching telly and suddenly you'd hear somebody falling down the stairs. You'd rush out and Pete would be lying there with ketchup on him. That's the kind of thing he'd do to wake people up.

"One particular incident sticks in my mind. I came down the stairs one morning and looked over towards the recording room and the door was open. There was a shadow on the wall. It looked like a person hanging. . . ." Beverley picks up, "I heard Gaynor screaming and I came flying down the stairs. When I first saw that shadow, I have to admit I thought it was Tommy. I was in shock. . . ."

Pete eventually stepped out and pointed to the clothing he had stuffed with rags. For him it was just a bit of black humor, but for everyone else who saw it, it was something they'd never, ever, forget.

Pete traveled to his hometown of Swansea for the Christmas holidays and proudly played some of the demos he'd worked on the past year. To make some extra money, Pete's brother, John, let him work in his shop. The Iveys were hurting financially. The band didn't get advances for day-to-day living. Live performances were their only means of survival. They'd often turned to the Arthur Howes Agency for help.

The band was booked to do a four-week tour in February with Marmalade, Mike Quinn, Lucas & The Mike Cotton Sound, Joe Cocker & The Grease Band, and Gene Pitney. As the new Apple act they felt they needed some classy stage attire. Ron remembers, "We went out and got the most metallic looking material we could find. We had someone stitch up these bomber jackets with big shoulders. We were probably five or so years ahead of our time. We thought they were great because they would have really shone up under the lights of a concert tour. And Paul McCartney said 'No. We're not having that. You're going to go on there wearing suits.' We were sickened, because we thought the jackets were great."

On January 4, 1969, the Iveys appeared on *The Lulu Show,* a T.V. program named after, and hosted by, the red-haired, female, Scottish singer. The group's outdated attire, and tightly-knit renditions of "Maybe Tomorrow" and "Daddy's A Millionaire," left them in an unmemorable position, especially when compared to the starring act: Jimi Hendrix. Mike recalled, "Here we were in suits as The Iveys, and Hendrix is on doing Cream songs – on fucking heroin!"

The month brought more home recordings, and lots of rehearsals in the band's matchbox-sized room. There was no ventilation and the cigarette smoke was always thick. The concentration of sweaty musicians often made the heat unbearable. Sometimes, after each run-through, they'd *have* to open the door. The room needed improved soundproofing, as the floor had never been worked on. But Collins required time to tackle such a project.

"Maybe Tomorrow" was about to get its shot in the U.S. The single was beginning to take off in European markets, such as Germany (Top Five) and Holland (#1!). But the real barometer would be America. Capitol Records sent a glowing letter to Apple on January 23rd, 1969, *". . . our field men received a very strong reaction at the Top Forty radio station level. Because of this reaction we went into an immediate rush release situation and in the first few days of our effort the results have been phenomenal."* The letter went on to state that Capitol predicted a million-selling 45, and that field orders exceeded 250,000 copies.

Ken Mansfield, then U.S. Manager of Apple Records, remembers the great enthusiasm, "I felt very strong about the single. We were riding on the success of "Hey Jude" and "Those Were The Days" and I felt the association, the label name, the song itself . . . I thought we had a sure hit." *Billboard* reviewed it on January 25, 1969 and placed it in their Special Merit Spotlight: *"The Beatles' label comes up with another powerful entry and discovery in this solid sounding new group. Easy beat rhythm ballad is delivered in a top emotional reading that will pull it through to a high spot on the Hot 100."* The group and Collins were ecstatic. Enthusiasm ran high at Apple.

But expectations quickly faded. In a letter to Apple on February 12th, Capitol stated: *"We do have a hit, but in all honesty the sales have not reflected the fantastic air play and radio station reaction to this record. We still have our sights set on a Top Ten record and at this time this is a very realistic goal."*

The Iveys were now starting their British tour playing brief, yet well-received, sets of original tunes and their better rehearsed covers. Along the way they became acquainted with one of Marmalade's roadies, Ian "Fergie" Ferguson. He recalls, "Pete and Tommy mentioned to me that Bill Collins could no longer handle it alone. I worked for a different group in Scotland at the time. But I liked The Iveys, so I took up their offer. I moved into their house in Golders Green."

A week before the 45 "Maybe Tomorrow" was set for British release, the group moved into Olympic Studios to record "Beautiful And Blue." This was Tom Evans's sad and lonely ballad of a suicidal teenage girl who feels misunderstood by the harsh outside world.

She feels so unhappy
She no longer cares for life
Has these thoughts of ending all her strife . . .
The world doesn't know her
It's so hard and cold and cruel. . . .

"Maybe Tomorrow" sheet music

Tom's up-and-down nature had clearly manifested now and battle lines were being drawn. Mike wasn't too sympathetic to Tom's fits of despair. And Tom's active rock'n'roll lifestyle wasn't coinciding with Ron's responsibility as a married man. Bill Collins wanted his former teens to listen, behave, and grow artistically, not complain or disagree with his sentiments. Pete was treading carefully around Tom's fluctuating disposition. But Tom was determined to be his own man; to stand up, and wake the crowd. He was also battling internal demons. . . .

Sessions throughout the latter part of '68 yielded other Iveys tracks. "Dear Angie," by Ron Griffiths, was a song about his wife, Maureen, ". . . who was my girlfriend at the time." The recording features Pete's cocktail-guitar lines. "Those licks by Pete were jazzy," said Ron. "Pete's brother was a big influence there." Also thrown in were some silvery shuddering strings. "We were lucky because Visconti fooled the eight-man string section into another take. It sounded like sixteen players, otherwise they would have been paid double on that!"

Another set of sessions yielded "Angelique," a Tom Evans song which portrays his Everly Brothers harmony influence, and "Yesterday Ain't Coming Back," a nostalgic crooner by Pete and Tom. The latter was somewhat embarrassing, as Ron notes, "We were short on the budget for a horn section, so Pete suggested a comb-and-paper brass section." The result – a blaring swash of phony, canned trumpets, plus the added bonus of swirling harps, tinkling piano, and cavernously deep bass vocals!

Pete's "Knocking Down Our Home" was a music hall type number inspired by the destruction of some high-rise flats in his hometown of Swansea. "This was a style of music I was hearing as a kid," he later commented, "It stayed with me." The band's recording is replete with trumpets, clarinets, and woodwinds. The piano part was played by Bill, who fondly recalls that Mal (who was producing the track) heard Bill playing it after Pete had a few difficult run-throughs. Mal asked Bill to record the part, which he did, as Pete watched over Bill's shoulder encouraging him on. According to Ron Griffiths, Bill became quite steamed up at his difficulty in successfully performing a particular passage.

Clearly, a touch of old-school vaudeville was now showing in a chunk of The Iveys compositions: "Knocking Down Our Home," "Dear Angie," "Yesterday Ain't Coming Back," "Angelique" – any of these could've been perceived as reworked Rudy Vallee or George Formby standards. Collins was enamored with this style, the group members liked to write it, and Visconti could go to town with ideas. His style of production was orientated toward ornate arrangements, using any manner of obscure or unusual instruments. He recalls, "In those days it was like 'How many instruments can you find?' Sergeant Pepper's was out, the Beatles influence was there. We were all going for it." But, did it best suit the Iveys?

The group had occasionally been taking breaks from the tour to finish up their album. Mal Evans had full control now, as Tony Visconti had been let go, much to his chagrin. "It took me completely by surprise," he said. "I remember Mal being around at a lot of our sessions. I loved the man – he was such a nice guy – but I questioned his qualifications. I was crushed. I loved working with the band."

The LP was mastered after The Iveys finished their tour in March. Then word came from America: the single had stalled, achieving its best chart position at #67 in *Billboard*'s March 15th issue. The group did not take the news well, especially Tom. "I hit bottom," he said in a 1969 interview, "That period depressed me more than I can say. We thought it would happen. We came to Apple and it was the big pop star thing. I began to think maybe we weren't good enough."

The mumblings amongst Apple employees were that, maybe, the Iveys just hadn't delivered the goods. But Ron Griffiths felt "Maybe Tomorrow" could've done better, "The production lacked presence, and the timing, at least in Britain, left it squashed with a mass of Christmas releases." Pete was also brought down, blaming himself and the band, "We were stupid," he stated, "thinking it would happen. We needed to work harder." But Apple's "house hippie" and promotion man Richard DiLello, writer of the acclaimed book on Apple, *The Longest Cocktail Party*, disputes Pete's comment. "I would visit them at the house in Golders Green and they used to get up, shake the cobwebs out, and be in that studio practicing all day and night. They had a great work ethic."

Prior to their tour, the band had done a half dozen BBC radio shows, most of them taped at the Maida Vale studios. Mike recalled the typical set-up, "We'd go down, go to a canteen, have a cup of tea, a scabby meal, and wait. We'd watch the other bands and wait and wait. Then we'd go on. Sometimes it'd be live over the air." At this time though, very little of the daytime BBC music programs were actually live. Bands were usually recorded for later airing, and sometimes, even given a quick pass at overdubbing. Because it was radio, the artists and groups had the opportunity to augment their sound with additional musicians. The Iveys once used Ron's brother, Phil, on additional guitar. Another time, the song "Maybe Tomorrow" received classical backing from the Northern Dance Orchestra, a BBC "house ensemble" available for whomever wanted to utilize them.

The Iveys sounded spectacular over the transistor airwaves. From Motown to Stax, Beatles to Hollies, Creedence Clearwater to The Lovin' Spoonful, or even the few originals they did, the band clearly had it together. They often came to life in a way their recordings only hinted at. Aretha Franklin, one of Pete's favorite singers, had her smash "Respect" interpreted several times. The Iveys chunky version was quite driving. And a cover of Traffic's "You Can All Join In" gave each member a chance to show off their pipes. The Everly Brothers' "When Will I Be

Loved" got a huge overhaul featuring The Iveys own brand of uniquely imaginative harmonies. This *was* a rock band: aggressive, distorted, and exuberant. "Birthday," "Revolution," "River Deep, Mountain High," even a four-piece version of "Maybe Tomorrow;" were all spontaneous and bristling Their studio recordings were often featherlight in comparison. {Maybe Tomorrow – BBC radio taping}

Home recordings continued and Pete was incessant. "I'm Alone" was a Elvis ballad-cop, while "Monday Morning Blues" was his 50s-style rockabilly rave-up, with humorous lyrics. Tom also chipped in with the promising "I'm Too Shy." Still, the band needed a commercial song, as 45s reigned supreme on the marketplace. The group desperately worked up something in hopes of pleasing Apple.

Ron recalls, "Apple had turned down all our submissions, so we finally thought, 'Right, we'll just give you something so bubblegum, so sickly sweet, and so contrived, you'll *have* to go for it.' So the four of us put together "Give It A Try." My major contribution was the 'weee-oooo's' in the Walt Disney section." The recording was quickly rejected and Apple became concerned. Jack Oliver: "They kept bringing in songs and we kept waiting for the something we thought could be the big hit."

Apple was now at a chaotic peak. The Beatles were in turmoil following the *Let It Be* fiasco, and press scrutiny was in full swing. James Taylor, Mary Hopkin, and Jackie Lomax had all fallen below sales expectations. Getting a new Iveys single approved would not be an easy task. Peter Asher remembers, "Ron Kass was in position to be official word, but all the Beatles had the power to veto him. Everyone who was involved got a bit of say; there was no formalized system."

Throughout 1969, Derek Taylor held court in the Apple press office. Bill Collins was a regular fixture. Mike Gibbins: "There was so much going on. Fucking Hells Angels everywhere. The whole press office was on acid. I used to walk around tripping on my head, watching Derek make up stories for the newspaper people walking in. Bill Collins drove Derek up the wall. I think Derek respected him as a 'pusher.' But he used to tell Bill to shut up, because once Bill starts talking, he doesn't shut up."

Derek Taylor remembers Collins with fondness, "Bill would be down every day. If he didn't come in it would be like 'Where is he?' He'd take me down in his red van to Waterloo station where we'd have a few drinks and I'd catch the train home. It was extremely sociable. He was nice, maybe too nice. But what he lacked in ruthlessness, he made up in persistence. His optimism used to keep us all going. He used to say, 'They will make it, Derek' and, clutching the left hand side of his chest, he would exclaim, *'I feel it here, you know.'* "

The Iveys – as talented as they were – were still having a rough time of it in the studio. Producers Tony Visconti and Mal Evans had been friendly and eager-to-please – one, a gifted arranger; the other, encouraging and full of optimism – but

The Iveys at Apple offices, Savile Row, London, 1969

very few tracks had convincingly touched on the band's potential. Finally, Pete presented a gentle, swaying ballad called "Walk Out In The Rain." The band went in and laid it down quickly. This became, perhaps, their finest moment to date. Graceful, sweet, every note in place, its mood well captured the essence of Pete Ham's warm and kindly nature. The group's abilities were finally beginning to shine through.

In mid-1969, the Iveys went off to Belgium and Holland to play a few mini-tours. Upon their return, they discovered their "loving" Savile Row environment had undergone a huge and drastic overhaul. Allen Klein, a former accountant from New York, had taken over the reins of the entire Apple Corporation. Three of The Beatles had wanted him to take over their business affairs. By majority he was voted in, with McCartney losing out.

The first assignment Allen Klein took on was to try and reorganize the mini-conglomeration into a feasible and profitable venture. Klein immediately cut a swath through the entire Apple hierarchy, and the impact was felt by everyone, right down to the tea boys. Jack Oliver remembers it well, "When Klein came in he canned Ron Kass. He canned a lot of people. The Beatles put out a list and said, 'These people can not be fired.' It was Derek [Taylor], Peter Brown, myself, Neil Aspinall, and a few more . . . We had built up this company where you could be very artistic and free, a lot of good creative ideas flowed and exchanged. People had fun working there. They didn't just put in their eight hours. They were there all the time. Klein brought his people in and turned it into an accounting office."

The effect was stunning and would forever change the Apple mystique. Peter Asher left willingly in June, while Derek Taylor and a few other survivors waited awhile longer. "I was pretty much miserable in those days," Derek commented. But oddly it was *he* that recommended Klein to The Beatles, though not without stern warning. No one at Apple could have expected such an iron hand, but it certainly pleased John Lennon, who Klein especially catered to. Yet, how would his presence affect the Iveys?

The release date for the *Maybe Tomorrow* LP was nearing. The single had done well in some European markets and Japan. Many of these countries were eager to have the album out. A July 4, 1969 release was set for Britain, Japan, and many European countries, while the U.S. had targeted July 14, 1969. A photo session had been shot for the LP's front cover, using the natural surroundings of Golders Green. The band were fitted with suits for the layout on back. Atmospheric pictures of the Swansea rock scene were also taken, but eventually left out. The planned U.S. cover was different – a framed picture of a young girl accompanied by individual band member pictures. The song order varied too, with "Maybe Tomorrow" leading off the American album.

Early in '69, the band had recorded one of Pete Ham's punchier compositions, "See Saw Granpa." A session piano player had been brought in, none other than Nicky Hopkins. The song was cut live; singing and all. Another track was mixed at this time, "Sali Bloo." Both have merits. "Sali Bloo" showcases Ron's rhythm'n'blues heart, while "See Saw Granpa" is an energetic, 50s-style rock'n'roll thumper. "Fisherman" and "Think About The Good Times" were two additional tracks on the LP.

The producer credits are a bit hazy because Mal Evans did get involved in mixing some of Visconti's recordings, and he did get the production byline for most of the album. But, as an example, for "Fisherman," Visconti alleges he did the bulk of the work. It's a Tom Evans composition, sort of an Irish sea-chantey with cornball effects: seagulls, ocean waves, low octave harmonies, and squelchy boots in the sand. It was yet another "send-up" by the boys.

By this time, mid-1969, the group had tired of less-than-serious approaches to recording. Tom later recalled McCartney's reaction to their silly, spoken voices on "I'm In Love." "Paul said, 'You know, I really don't think you should leave that on there. In ten years time you're going to listen to that and say, 'Did I do that?' " And regret it Tom did, as he later expressed great disdain for the song.

Maybe Tomorrow LP, 1969

The Iveys LP certainly was an unusual grab-bag. But it was recorded during the period of the Beatles' *White Album,* and with that era's influence of freedom of expression, plus Bill Collins' encouragement to be open to all forms of music, the group couldn't help but explore their individuality. As Tom said, "That was our trip. We were trying everything and we believed in what we did." But as Mike points out, "We never worked those songs out live. That's why it doesn't sound like a band."

Apparently, Apple didn't think so either. Just days before the LP's scheduled release in America and Britain, the long-awaited album was held back. The Iveys' hard work and dedication had been stripped. It all seemed for naught. And for what reason? Was this a cost-cutting jolt by the new regime? Was there a legal problem – as Apple's Jack Oliver vaguely remembered? Or was this a protective move designed to rescue the band from a potential sales disaster and critical backwash?

Tony Bramwell, part of Apple Records promotion department, recalled the postponement to be a Klein maneuver. "I think he put the stops on it, because he was saying, 'We're not going to issue any more records until I sort out this mess.' Apple really wasn't a mess as far as we were concerned. But a lot of things stopped. I think a Billy Preston single got held up, along with a Mary Hopkin record."

In the U.S., Apple Records manager Ken Mansfield says The Iveys album never even got shipped. "I didn't even get to *hear* it. We weren't involved in that decision. A lot of things came down with no explanation." Klein had let go of the U.K. label head Ron Kass, who was very high on The Iveys.

Somehow, an Apple EP of various artists, sponsored by *Walls Ice Cream,* did come out on July 18, 1969, in England. It included The Iveys' "Storm In A Teacup," a number they'd hoped to forget. This bizarre set was not a favorite of Derek Taylor's, as he stated in an interview with *Record Collector* magazine, *"I didn't like that at all. It shows what happens when everyone gets too busy to pay attention to details. I went to meet a vulgar man at Walls with a big cigar; we had never dealt with people like him before, and all my snobbery reared up! By that time it was too late to stop it."* This EP is now a pricey collector's item, one of the rarest legitimate releases by the Apple label. But what happened to The Iveys LP?

As it turned out, the album *did* get out in a handful of foreign markets. Some had demanded it, based on the single success of "Maybe Tomorrow." Britain pressed a few copies before it was pulled, while Japan, Germany, and Italy each delivered LP's to their stores, following it with a single, "Dear Angie." The 45's B-side, "No Escaping Your Love," was dug out from the band's earliest recording session. This single made it out in a handful of other European countries as well.

Jack Oliver recalls how foreign markets worked at Apple. "'Maybe Tomorrow' was quite successful in a lot of European countries, and they wanted a follow-up single. What we'd do was have a meeting, which normally included at least one Beatle, and we'd try to think of a suitable song. They often went with our suggestions, which I think 'Dear Angie' was. But if they felt something else was better, we'd trust them. They knew their market better than we did."

Oddly enough, Ron Griffiths claims he was not even *aware* of his song becoming a single, until years down the road. At this time, he was quite dejected. In fact, just weeks before The Iveys' recordings were due to come out, *Disc & Music Echo* had quoted Ron and Tom regarding their worries in a July 5th issue:

> *"We do feel a bit neglected," said Ron Griffiths. "We keep writing songs for a new single and submitting them to Apple, but the Beatles keep sending them back saying they're not good enough."*
>
> *"Mind you," adds Tom Evans, "we've had a lot of things most groups could not expect. The Beatles bought all our gear for us, all the equipment and a group van, and we've had all kinds of concessions . . . all we need now is a hit single, or even just a new single, hit or not, and we'll be happy!*
>
> *"We're going to keep on writing, and we're determined to come up with something the Beatles like. At first we were adamant about not recording anything but one of our own songs, but now we'd record anything, so long as it was good. . . ."*

The interview turned out to be an unplanned plea for help – and a Godsend. Because, despite small odds that any of the Beatles would ever peruse this tiny back-page column, Mr. James Paul McCartney apparently did.

3

If You Want It, Here It Is

THE IVEYS WERE continually hungry. Debts were piling. Tom recalled the difficult times, "Getting so much for a gig, and thinking it was the big time, then watching it have to stretch because we had to pay the rent and the expenses and the travel, that was hard." Mike commented too, "I wasn't eating. Not eating depresses me. Being broke depresses me. And I had both." But Pete was not about to let up. "Pete would not want to dwell on things too much." recalls Beverley, "He'd think, 'This didn't work out but the next thing will.' He was absolutely convinced, 'It will happen. It will happen if we work hard enough.' "

Ron Griffiths' stress was doubly magnified. He had a family to support and a household that was not in unanimous approval of his new-found responsibilities. He explained, "They were getting more and more stuck on dope and things. When I was around the house, I'd naturally want to spend more time with my wife and child. Tommy used to play the hi-fi late at night, in the wee small hours, waking my baby up, making life difficult for Maureen and me. The atmosphere started to put a wedge between me and Maureen. I was strained; torn between trying to keep the lads in the band happy and keeping my wife content. I didn't have any money to get our own flat. It affected my personality. I became quiet and withdrawn."

Beverley recalled that Pete was disturbed. Ron was his dear friend, but he couldn't dictate Tom's actions or Ron's response. He knew the Iveys needed to be a focused unit or their dreams could be shattered.

On July 23, 1969, the Iveys had returned from a gig when Bill Collins picked up the mail. Amongst the various bits of correspondence was a letter distinctly marked with the Apple trademark. The sender: Paul McCartney. Without giving details, Paul asked if he might meet the band on the 29th for some important business. The boys were perplexed and excited. A confab with Paul seemed almost incomprehensible. Ron recalled, "We were running around like scalded cats, '*Paul McCartney's coming here*?!' " Beverley adds, "They were very nervous, especially Pete. Meeting this idol who'd been praising him was so much to bear."

Meanwhile, Ron's relationship with the rest of the group was reaching a crisis point. Beverley's diary shows that on the July 28, 1969, there was a

Ron Griffiths

meeting to discuss Ron Griffiths' future. Ron recalled, "Principally it was Tommy convincing the others that I wasn't one of the boys, I wasn't smoking pot; all that sort of stuff. It was 'Ron's married, maybe we better get him out now if we're going to have a chance.' "

The following afternoon, McCartney met with the band at EMI studios. Ron recalls, "He told us he had seen the article in *Disc & Music Echo* and was surprised to read that we felt neglected at Apple. He said, 'Look. I've been asked to do the score for this film, *The Magic Christian,* which I'm not particularly wanting to do. I'm quite prepared to let you have a song I've written as a single release.' "

According to Bill Collins, Pete stood up from his chair and said, "I thought we were supposed to do our own material? We've been told not to do covers!" McCartney raised his eyebrow and looked over at Bill. Collins took Pete off to the side and said, "Look, this is an opportunity here, Peter," and Pete quickly acknowledged it.

Beverley recalls, "Pete had really psyched himself up for this meeting. It was a spontaneous reaction, I think. Part of him felt that it was a knock when Paul offered the song, after all the hours, but another part was flattered because this really great person obviously thought they were capable of doing one of his songs justice. McCartney was good in how he put it, that it would be a springboard for them."

Paul went on to play his demo of the song "Come And Get It." Then he told the band he'd also been asked to do other songs for the film, and might want to give them the opportunity. This was right in the midst of the Beatles recording *Abbey Road,* a project Paul had wanted to give his all. But he was willing to allow some time to help The Iveys.

McCartney had previously completed his demo of "Come And Get It" on July 24, 1969. He talked about it in his interview with Mark Lewisohn for the book *The Beatles Recording Sessions*:

I did a demo of "'Come And Get It" for Badfinger which took about 20 minutes, it was before a Beatles session. Phil McDonald was there and I got in – I always used to get in early because I lived just around the corner – and all the equipment was set up from the day before so I ran in and said, "Just do this, Phil, go on, it'll only take twenty minutes" and I threw it away. I mean it's really nice.

I said to Badfinger, "Look, lads, don't vary, this is good, just copy this down to the letter. It's perhaps a little bit undignified for you, a little bit lacking in integrity to have to copy someone's work that rigidly, but this is the hit sound. Do it like this and we're all right, we've got a hit. No one will know anyway. And if they do say anything say, 'Yes, Paul did the arrangement, big deal, it's not unheard of.' "

Paul told the band he would audition each of them for the lead vocal and left a copy of the demo for them to practice to. Then on August 2, 1969, he took the group into Abbey Road Studios. The first order of business was laying down the basic track. Paul gathered the group around a piano and began to discuss the arrangement. Suddenly John and Yoko appeared. Tom recalled, "They were kind of walking through and Lennon stopped and looked over at Paul, bowed his head, and said, 'Oh wise one, oh sage, show us the light.' The next thing I knew he walked out the door. I thought, "Wait a minute, that was John Lennon!"

The group carried on, "Paul tuned my drums and got them sounding all Beatley," said Mike. "He said, 'Simplicity is the way to go.' " Pete added, "He showed us a lot. Because if we'd done 'Come And Get It' like that we wouldn't have been happy with it. The rough edges, we would've said, 'Oh, lets put something over that to cover it up.' He said, 'No, that's all it needs.' Like bass, drums, and piano . . . he was right, that's all it needed." The group rehearsed the song and McCartney reminded Ron not to snazzy up the bass lines.

Eventually, the track was laid down, at a slightly faster tempo than the original demo. Paul congratulated them on a take well-done, noting Mike's drum fills which do a lot to lift the track, then gently ribbing Ron for his little bass run-off at the tail.

Now they were ready for the vocals. "Paul asked each of us to sing a verse," said Ron, "Pete was too 'muggy.' I tried and he said it was a bit nasal, sounded like Reg Presley of the Troggs. Then Tom gave it a shot."

Evans stepped up and the "magic" hit. It was a perfect song for Tom's rich, Liverpudlian pipes. Much of the Iveys material had put Tom in a less natural vocal range, and he tended to overcompensate with histrionic emotion. But "Come And Get It" fit him like a warm glove. He was controlled, confident, and believable.

Paul finished the session by adding an important tambourine overdub. Ron sang a low vocal harmony, and within three hours, "Come And Get It" was complete. Everyone was quite pleased. As Tom said, "Paul had told us that if he didn't think our version was as good as his original demo, he'd put it out himself. Of course that challenge really made us work hard in the studio."

The group and McCartney traveled to Apple to play the track. Various people strolled into the room to hear it. Enthusiasm ran high, and then George Harrison walked by. Pete recalled the story to several friends over the years, "Paul had asked him to come in, and George listened to the song, but he didn't say anything. He just sat there. Then he pulled out a lump of hash, placed it on the table and said, 'Smoke this. And *then* go see what you can do!' "

McCartney now felt confident in giving the band his go-ahead to write songs for the film. He had been commissioned to work on *The Magic Christian* by himself. Paul had to convince the movie company, Commonwealth United Films, that The Iveys could handle the chore. He played "Come And Get It," which the company loved. They gave approval, as long as Paul oversaw The Iveys work.

The film was a comedy starring Peter Sellers, Ringo Starr, Raquel Welch, and a host of other famous stars in various cameo roles. The group needed to see the segments that required music. Tom spoke of their first assignment, "We saw the opening of the film and Paul gave us his impression, mentioning a 'Simon and Garfunkel' type of style. Pete and I went back and wrote 'Carry On Til Tomorrow,' which we were pleased with. Paul liked the song and brought us into Abbey Road Studios. He gave us leeway, added a few ideas, and produced it. He was very free in his approach."

Pete laid down a stinging guitar break, Ron contributed counterpoint bass, and the Iveys blended their charismatic voices towards the heavens. The hard work and long hours were paying off. This was a solid, well-produced track they could proudly call their own. Mike: "This was a test of our strengths, our potential. We only saw rough cuts. It was difficult for us to imagine the total finished film."

The words to "Carry On Til Tomorrow," and its traditional-folk mood, were inspired by the film's opening title sequence, in which a downcast Ringo is rescued from his miserable life by Peter Sellers; a wealthy man looking for someone to mentor. It showed an increasing depth to Pete and Tom's collaborations:

In younger days I told myself
My life would be my own
And I'd leave the place where sunshine never shone
For my life's too short for waiting
When I see the rising sun
Then I know again that I must carry on

McCartney had hired George Martin to do the string arrangement, and Martin came up with it over the course of one weekend (according to Bill Collins). After it was recorded, the group waited for McCartney to finish some work on the *Abbey*

Road album. Meanwhile, the situation with Ron continued to deteriorate. "Tom kept ribbing me about being the 'odd-man-out.' " said Ron. "My wife was not encouraging me to fight. Tommy and Bill became convinced I was going to hold them back." In a bad stroke of luck, Ron had become seriously ill with the chicken pox, highly unusual for his age. But the group had more sessions coming up with McCartney, so they had to continue on without their skillful bassist.

Tom Evans, in a 1983 interview with Australian journalist Glenn A. Baker, recalled another Iveys session with McCartney, on September 18, 1969, "There's a disco scene in the *Magic Christian* film where they had 'Respect' by Aretha Franklin playing and we had to cover that with our song. We really didn't know what to do, do a 'soul' thing or whatever. Well the time came for the recording and we didn't have a song together. We had a bit of a soul thing together. McCartney comes in and says, 'Well, what've you got?' And we said, 'We don't really know.' So he said, 'Well, what do you know that's really exciting?' I said, 'Well, I can do "Long Tall Sally" in G,' And he goes, 'G, okay!' "

"So we started to make up a song similar to 'Long Tall Sally' in G. We just did the backing track. When it came time to do the vocal I was just floundering over it. He started to sing with me and we both kind of made it up. There's a great take of me and him singing it together. I said, 'You've got to use that on the record, please use that on the record.' He said, 'No, you go down and do it properly.' "

The tune was "Rock Of All Ages," and the Iveys again had produced a winner. A superb rocker; its snazzy blocks of rhythm pour over Tom's doubled wailing vocals. McCartney plays the terrific keys, and is rumored to have added a few of the yelps and "woo-yeahs." Of course, bass was needed on the tune and Tom was enlisted to do the chore. Though he'd never properly rehearsed on bass, any guitar player can at least approximate. But Tom was feeling quite insecure. "I was playing the bass, but not very well," he recalled, "And Paul said, 'Just play the one note we're gonna need, be simple.' We learned from that, to extemporize on that idea. . . ."

McCartney was teaching the band the virtues of simplicity and rawness. Now they had a sound from which they could progress.

The Iveys had completed their soundtrack obligations to Commonwealth United, but they still had more studio time booked with McCartney. Pete and Tom were riding high. Their enthusiasm inspired them to write a song about Paul. They came up with "Crimson Ship," a metaphor for McCartney's whirlwind recording lessons. They proudly played it for him and he liked it. He gave the band extended leeway to arrange the tune. Tom explained, "He took us through the stages to where we were doing a lot ourselves. He gave us the confidence."

"Crimson Ship" is packed with references to Paul and The Beatles – most of the lyrics are Tom's – and it's fun picking them out. The first verse is the most telling, as it illustrates The Iveys fervent appreciation of Paul's help:

My life was colored
Painting pictures out of tune
He came from nowhere in a song
It might have been the way I laughed
He made the jokes
Could only show me what was wrong

Ron Griffiths was still absent from the recording sessions, still too sick to contribute, when another song was cut, "Midnight Sun," a song Pete had written and always let Ron sing. But Ron lost the opportunity. "Pete had to sing the lead," recalled Griffiths. "He came back from the session and said, 'Couldn't do it like you, "mush." I murdered it.'"

Ron's illness had placed his position in further doubt. The group had seen they could successfully pull off recording sessions despite his absence. Ron recalls, "They finally said, 'Look, we think perhaps in view of the circumstances, it may be best if we part company.'" Ron did resign – reluctantly, regretfully, and full of sadness – but he saw no options due to the continued antagonism between his wife, Tom, Bill, and himself. Bill Collins said, "It was his own fault. He got the girl pregnant. He put the pressure on himself." Bill denies strongly that he pushed for Ron's release.

Mike Gibbins was devastated. "That was the worst thing that ever happened to our group. To this day I don't know how that happened. I was considered a nothinghead at that point. I wasn't even worth conversing with." Beverley recalls Pete's torment, "Pete was very depressed about it, very sad. He hated to lose a friend. He knew Ron had put so much into it. He would lament, 'The four of us came to London, now there's only two.'"

Ron Griffiths moved his family out of the house and took on a factory job in Hemel Hampstead. Now the group had a dilemma. An album was scheduled. The single was targeted for a December 5, 1969, release in Britain. With a new product, the band would need to find Ron's replacement and re-evaluate their position.

The Iveys had long been concerned with their name. They were often confused with The Ivy League; three studio singers who'd recorded under that moniker in 1965, achieving several U.K. hits. Many times people would ask if they were one and the same. The impending 45 release and line-up change gave The Iveys the impetus to go for something new. Tom remembered, "We were told many times that The Iveys was a stupid name. We had great arguments with people about it. But we stuck to it. Finally we realized the name was a disadvantage." Bill Collins affirmed, "The Iveys were associated with the Merseyside scene and it sounded a bit dated . . . We had to think about the future."

Pete, Tom, Mike
November, 1969

Apple agreed a change was needed. "We used to write out a list," said Tom, "and we'd get it down to ten, then three, and maybe one guy would like it and another wouldn't. Or we'd like it, and the record company wouldn't. So we just said, 'Well, what have you got to offer then?'" The list of names had included Fresh, The Glass Onion, Tendergreen, The Old, and Hyena's Nose! The most character-revealing of all were Paul McCartney's choice, Home, and John Lennon's contribution, Prix (allegedly pronounced Pricks). None could be agreed to. It came down to a time factor. Apple needed to get their packaging and promotion together. The Iveys were left with a one-day deadline or Apple would decide.

Apple's Neil Aspinall remembers, "I was down at a pub with Bill Collins called The Thistle, which was just around the corner from Savile Row. I was asked to suggest something. Badfinger just popped in my head. It was from an old Lennon thing. He was playing the piano and he had a bad finger so he called the piece he was playing 'Bad Finger Boogie' (which evolved into 'With A Little Help From My

Friends'). Somehow that came to me. Bill instantly liked it. He brought it back to the boys and I guess they liked it too. I remember someone suggesting High and Fun, but Badfinger won out."*

The Magic Christian soundtrack album was also being prepped for release. It was to include three Badfinger songs, plus incidental music. Originally, it was scheduled as an Apple Records release, but the last-minute addition of a Thunderclap Newman song prohibited that, because of their contract with another label. The soundtrack album eventually came out on Pye Records in England and Commonwealth United Records in the U.S.

The movie was guaranteed to have good exposure because of its all-star cast. To capitalize on the publicity, it was decided Badfinger's own album would be called *Magic Christian Music*. Since the band had completed only five new tracks since the time of McCartney's involvement, they would have to select older Iveys numbers to fill out the LP. The group was given leeway in choosing songs. Mal Evans got closely involved. The British album was the culmination of their decisions:

SIDE ONE *Come And Get It, Crimson Ship, Dear Angie, Fisherman, Midnight Sun, Beautiful And Blue, Rock Of All Ages*

SIDE TWO *Carry On Til Tomorrow, I'm In Love, Walk Out In The Rain, Angelique, Knocking Down Our Home, Give It A Try, Maybe Tomorrow*

The American LP version dropped two songs, "Angelique" and "Give It A Try." The Iveys tracks selected did benefit from some skillful remixing, courtesy of Geoff Emerick and Phil McDonald, two brilliant engineers well-known for their work on various Beatles albums.

The freshly christened Badfinger now set out to find a new member. Their premier choice was Hamish Stuart, a Scottish guitar player. He was a good singer, easy-going personality, and a solid musician (later known for his work with the Average White Band and Paul McCartney). Stuart *was* interested, but his manager, Peter Wash, told Bill Collins he wanted £10,000 for Stuart's release from Marmalade. The group had to look elsewhere.

Dave Dalby, Danny DeCosta, and Nick Pinkett, were amongst those who auditioned. No one was working out. Finally, Tom Evans made a bold decision. He was willing to switch to bass, which would allow for more possibilities in looking for a new bandmate. Tom may have liked playing the bass – after getting a taste of it with McCartney – but he never publicly stated why he allowed the move. Whatever the reason, when the new member of Badfinger did finally walk through the door, it would lead to a drastic change in the group's chemistry.

---

* As it was, many rumors about the origin of the Badfinger name were perpetuated over the years. The band tended to have fun with it. One popular story was that Pete's crooked "pinky" from a childhood accident inspired it. Another tall tale was that it came from a load of pigeon boxes lined up for a race, one of which said, "H.R. Badfinger." The most common story though, was that "Bad Finger Boogie" was an old song by a blues pianist; close, but Neil Aspinall corrected that.

Born on June 21, 1947, Joseph Charles Molland had grown up in Liverpool as one of six boys. He showed an early penchant for music, teaching himself piano at age seven before picking up one of his brother's guitars in 1958. "The first record I remember hearing was 'Last Train To San Fernando,' by Johnny Duncan & The Bluegrass Boys," said Joey. "I really enjoyed it. After that I heard, 'Blue Suede Shoes' by Elvis Presley. I really started to listen and play, listen and play."

Joey performed at a grammar school talent show and it went well. He was encouraged to jam with some friends. They monikered themselves The Assassins. Joey showed a more marked interest than the others by often walking down to a local corner to bang on his guitar, as the pedestrian traffic rolled by. A local Liverpool drummer named Pete Clarke recalls, "I was one year older than Joey and I was in a band called The Escorts. Someone said to me one day, 'Come and see this kid.' We went down to see him on the corner; it was Penny Lane. He had this rotten guitar with half-inch-high action. He was barring Chuck Berry chords with his forefinger. And he was playing flawless rhythm. I went back to a friend's house and my friend said, 'Well, what did you think?' I said, 'He'll be playing semi-pro in less than a year.'"

The Assassins finally went the way of most teenage combos. By age fifteen, Joey had dropped out of school to get a job with the Pacific Steam Navigation Company as a messenger boy. But music was still a part of his life, though more as a fan. He explained, "I'd never really thought about joining a band because the players were so great, how could I attain that? I'd listen to these records on the radio and I thought they were fantastic. I used to go to the Cavern on me lunch hour and see groups. My favorites were The Roadrunners, The Undertakers, The Nomads . . . these were knockout groups. I saw The Beatles, too.

Joey Molland, circa 1962

"One day I ran into an old friend called Peter Wiggins. He asked me if I still played guitar and I said, 'Yes.' He asked if I had a guitar and I had just bought a Gibson guitar. He said, 'Do you want to play with us?' I said, 'Well, what do you do?' and he said, 'Just Chuck Berry stuff.' So I went and played with them. We called ourselves The Profiles . . . That was my introduction to writing. We made an acetate and there's probably only three that exist."

By 1964, the Liverpool scene had exploded and The Profiles were just one of three or four hundred other bands in town. "We were playing at night and I'd started working in the garage with my dad, brushing the forecourt and that. So I was earning five pounds a week doing that and fifteen pounds a week in the group. The group meant more money for less work, so something inside of me said, 'Right, this is the life' and I went into music full-time."

It was at The Blue Angel club that Joey caught his first career break. "You had to be known at the door to get in. You'd go there after gigs, and people would get up and jam, have a drink and a laugh. I used to get up with them once or twice a week. There was a band there called The Masterminds. I thought they were great. Brian Slater was the rhythm guitarist. He got a job driving a taxi and I took his place."

The Masterminds played a lot of rhythm'n'blues and 50s rock, but it was their covers of an upcoming American singer-songwriter that led to their jump-start. Joey explains, "One night, after The Stones had played at the Empire, they came down to The Blue Angel with their manager, Andrew Loog Oldham. They caught us doing Bob Dylan songs. We were about the only band in England that did them and that knocked Andrew out."

Oldham brought the star-struck teens into Regent Sound Studios in London to cut an Immediate Records single, "She Belongs To Me," a song written by Bob Dylan. "London was magic," said Joey, "It was the first place I'd been where you parked under the ground. We checked into the Madison Hotel and they have these rooms with eight beds! We freaked out to hear ourselves on tape. Then we played *Ready Steady Go* and The Stones showed. It was great."

The single failed to chart though, and hard reality struck. Oldham never became their manager. The group ended up playing Liverpool clubs over the next year-and-a-half, receiving just an occasional out-of-town gig.

In 1966, Kit Lambert, The Who's flamboyant manager, came into Joey's life. A Liverpool band called The Merseybeats was breaking up. Lead singers Billy Kinsley and Tony Crane were looking for a new backing group. Lambert and his partner, Chris Stamp, recruited a five-piece band, choosing three of The Masterminds. "It was a bit of a heavy situation," recalled Joey, "They took myself, Chris Finley, who plays piano, and George Cassidy, who played bass. Then they got two drummers, Kenny Mundy and Kenny Goodless. . . We were christened The Fruit Eating Bears. Billy and Tony were billed as The Merseys."

A single was cut. The A-side, "Sorrow," became a huge British hit. But Joey did not play on it. Instead, session musicians were utilized. The Merseys, and their backing group, were then sent out on several tours. They opened for The Who and traveled to France. Merseys singer Tony Crane recalled, "Joey stood out because he looked about fifteen and resembled Paul McCartney." Partner Billy Kinsley added, "Joey was one of the first rhythm-lead guitarists. You could just put him on stage and you didn't need anyone else."

After a couple of years, The Merseys had run their course. There was a clause in The Fruit Eating Bears contract that they would get to record after it ended. According to Joey, they cut four or five songs, one of which is a Molland tune, "Traffic."

In 1967, Joey did a brief stint with The Crying Shames, a Liverpool band who'd had minor hits in Britain with "Please Stay" and "Come On Back." After that, he went back to his mother's hometown of Newport. "I stayed there," he said, "I was fed up, just fed up. I was thrown out and told to go to Liverpool. I didn't really know what I was going to do. I didn't want to be a garage mechanic or an office worker, so I started putting a band together."

Joey and his friends were hoping for a few gigs in Sweden. They traveled to London to organize. While there, Joey got a call from a friend who told him that Gary Leeds of The Walker Brothers was looking to form a band. Leeds wanted to audition him. Joey: "I told the guys I had to see what this was all about. I took my guitar out of the van and walked all the way to his house, from Marble Arch, through Shepherds Bush, to Chelsea. It was quite a walk. I didn't have any money. I got there and he said, 'Well, look at you.' And I said, 'Yeah, look at me, man.' He said, 'Can you play guitar?' I said, 'Yeah.' He said, 'Can you play guitar like Eric Clapton?' I said, 'Yeah.' I lied through my teeth. I told him, 'I'd like to do it. I can sing. I'm a great singer and everything else. Give me the job. I want it. I need it.' So he gave me the job and a £20 note. It was amazing, Gary always had these fresh £20 notes in his pocket."

Gary Leeds, also known as Gary Walker, had been a member of The Walker Brothers, achieving great fame in Britain. His new group featured himself on drums, Joey Molland on lead guitar, ex-Universals, John Lawson, on bass, and ex-Crying Shame, Charlie Crane, on rhythm guitar. They had an instant record deal and were soon situated in actor Peter Finch's old house in Knightsbridge.

After a few weeks of rehearsals, the band did a British tour in support of The Kinks, The Herd, and several other acts. At one point they recorded a single, "Spooky," which was soon to be a big American hit for the Classics IV. "That was given to us by Roy Orbison's dad," said Gary Walker, "I knew Roy from touring with the Walker Brothers."

Joey: "We (recorded) it at Pye studios. Scott Walker produced it. He was known as a fabulous musician who had perfect pitch. When I did the solo on 'Spooky,' Scott said, 'That was a really great flatted ninth Joey.' It was a real crack-up."

The song came out on Polydor Records. On February 17, 1968, *Melody Maker*'s Chris Welch reviewed the single: *"It's Gary Walker's cover of the American thing. I don't really react to it. I don't see why it was such a hit in the States. A certain amount of atmosphere, but it's success is inexplicable . . . Might be a hit because of Gary's name."* It *was* a hit, but not in Britain. The Japanese, big-time supporters of The Walker Brothers, pushed "Spooky" to number three in their national charts. "They wanted us to tour right away," said Gary Walker. "We only had three weeks to write and record an album."

The band's rhythm guitarist, Charlie Crane (then called Paul Crane) remembers the studio sessions, which were produced by Fritz Fryer of The Four Pennies "It was very much Beatles-influenced. The psychedelia period was influential." Joey added, "We were doing things like sticking screwdrivers in the tape machine and moving the head about to get sounds."

For example, on the song "Magazine Woman," whistling phased distortion coats the entire track. A cover of Leiber & Stoller's "If You Don't Come Back" has a wild flanging sequence, plus a lengthy stretch of squealing guitar feedback.

Crane especially enjoyed the light-hearted song "Market Tavern" (which he claims he and Joey wrote together). "That was where we used to rehearse," he said. "All of the people we talk about in the song actually were in the pub, 144 York Way, just like it says. We used to play bar billiards with them. Maude was the landlady. She'd drink gin constantly; day in, day out. We gave them an acetate to play in their jukebox and they loved it. Simple townies, now megastars in London!"

The band was pleased with the results, but there was barely time to think. At completion the group was immediately flown to Tokyo, Japan, with their new road manager, Brian Slater. The ex-Mastermind had previously helped Joey by giving him places to stay whenever he was in Liverpool. Joey turned him on to the road gig as a favor.

When the group arrived, hundreds of fans were waiting at the airport. The band members were flabbergasted, except for Gary Walker, who had dealt with this before. Said Crane, "We didn't realize how big we were until we got there. They showered us with gifts. We wanted to go to the zoo and they closed the zoo down for us. We wanted to go to a discotheque, so they opened one up, and hired in a crowd!" At one gig, Joey ripped his jeans. "You wouldn't believe it," he said, "Within minutes a woman was sent to sew it up. It was all very organized."

The album, *Gary Walker & The Rain Album #1*, had been rushed out. It became a big hit in Japan, as did a couple of singles from the LP. The group triumphantly returned home. "We came back and the album still hadn't been released in Britain," says Crane, "That was a big letdown."

Gary Walker and The Rain
Charlie Crane, John Lawson, Gary Leeds, Joey Molland, Japan, 1969

The band continued with more U.K. gigs, and it was at De Montfort Hall in Leicester that a tragedy nearly struck. "It was a soundcheck," remembered Crane, "and Joey leaned forward and grabbed the mic. His guitar strings touched the stand. He went purple!" Said road manager Slater, "You could see he was getting a shock. He started to shudder across the stage. I ran to the main power box and ripped all the wires out of the wall." Added Crane, "Brian Slater saved his life. I thought Joey was a goner. His hands were badly burned."

Joey shook it off and continued to play. Dead skin had to be constantly trimmed, but nothing could keep him down. It was Crane who took blame for eventually stopping the band's progress. "It was probably my fault," he says. "I grew tired of staying up til four-in-the-morning. I quite liked daylight. I fell in love and my one thought became my girlfriend."

The group did release one more single in Britain, "Come In You'll Get Pneumonia," a cover of an Easybeats song. Gary Leeds admits, "It was a bit over the top. We used Joe Cocker's back-up singers, Sunny and Sue. The '1812 Overture' is in there. We had no luck with it at all." *Melody Maker* reviewed it on January 11, 1969, indicating, *"This complicated arrangement won't help their popularity problem in Britain."* By May, the group had broken up.

Joey Molland went back to Liverpool and found a rock'n'roll wasteland. He recalled, "The groups had started to disappear, they'd closed The Cavern, The Iron Door's gone, and the clubs were gone. Most of the musicians were now twenty-five. A lot of good players had moved out of the city. It was really weird. I saw Billy Kinsley there and, even for him, there was nothing happening, and he'd had tons of hit records. So we started a band together. We figured the least we'll get out of it is we'll go to Germany for three months and have a really great time."

Joey had been in Liverpool for about six months when he got a phone call. The Iveys were looking for a guitar player. "I didn't want to go, really. I'd seen the Iveys on TV *(The Lulu Show)* and they wore suits and ties. I'd been through that and I wasn't really keen anymore . . . I was into rock'n'roll music."

Unaware of the Apple connection, Joey said his friends were more than eager to point it out. Billy Kinsley: "I was going to go for the job myself, 'cause when Ron Griffiths left I'd thought The Iveys were going to go for a bass player. But I found out they were looking for a guitar player. I told Joey to go down and go for it. I said, 'Hey man, these guys work with The Beatles! It's a great opportunity.' "

The initial suggestion to Joey came from a friend of his named Bob Adcock, who had road managed for Cream. He'd recommended Joey to Bill Collins. Bill was more than happy to try out a fellow Merseyside native. Joey recalls, "I went to their house in Golders Green and they said, 'Do you sing?' and I said 'Yeah,' and I sang 'My Babe,' the Righteous Brothers song. They were much better singers than me, and as far as playing, Pete could play rings around me technically. They asked me if wrote and I said, 'I can do it.' "

"That was a condition to join the band," said Mike Gibbins, "You had to want to write. Joey had the personality and the rest of it. We weren't too crazy about his lead guitar playing, but Pete did that, so we thought 'What the hell.' "

Joey hadn't yet developed a clear style of soloing, but his rhythm playing was quite dynamic. The group was also taken by his charisma and good looks. After a few days of consideration, Joey was accepted. The new Badfinger was set.

Joey Molland

Come and Get It
U.K. ad, 1969

Badfinger's new single, "Come And Get It," was released in Britain on December 5, 1969. Very few preliminary reviews came from the English press, who were now intense in their mockery of The Beatles. Apple promotion man Tony Bramwell recalls the atmosphere, "The whole Apple thing was falling asunder. We hadn't had many records out in a while and the press was all up in arms because of Klein, John and Yoko, Paul and Linda, the drug busts . . . It was one thing after another."

Somehow, out of this cloudy morass, "Come And Get It," exploded into the British Top Ten. It was just too undeniable, too good, and too catchy. Tom recalled, "I couldn't believe anything so simple as that could have taken off. When pop was supposed to be progressing and getting more involved, we came along with this record so basic it's untrue. And we have a big hit with it!"

As the single began its rapid ascension into the Top Five, the film, *The Magic Christian,* premiered in London at the Odeon Kensington Theatre on December 12th, with the Lennons and Starkeys in attendance. A somewhat nervous Badfinger appeared. "We arrived wearing evening dress," recalled Tom. "We felt sure everyone would be formal, but of course, they weren't!" Also attending was Ian "Fergie" Ferguson, the band's roadie, who recalled, "I think Princess Margaret was sitting in the front row and John Lennon came running up and down the aisles with some protest shirt on. It was wild. We had a good time."

The film received mixed reviews, but the music was universally praised. "We were ecstatic," says Jack Oliver, then Apple's managing director. "The band was well-liked and we knew they were very good. They'd just needed the right song to get the ball rolling."

As Christmas neared, the group played a brief set in the basement of 3 Savile Row for the Apple staff. Derek Taylor remembers it well, "It was more or less the launch of Badfinger. They played a few songs. It was obvious Joey was an excellent find. I remember saying, 'Maybe we didn't know what we had?' It was more or less an admission of guilt on our part."

The group had now moved their rehearsals into Apple's basement, as Bill Collins had undertaken a new soundproofing and expansion project at the 7 Park Avenue house. Tommy was now trying to grasp the bass, and Mike needed to adjust to his new rhythm-section partner. Pete was also coalescing with Joey, whom the band found was willing to slip into the lead guitar role. Joey brought a different slant to the group. First of all, his voice was completely different to Ron Griffiths: kind of hoarse, a little fragile, less versatile, at times boomy, but more distinctive and full of character. It gave the harmonies a coarser edge. His guitar work was rambunctious; he had a good ear for melody. Also, his enthusiasm injected a lot of life into the band.

Tommy and Joey latched on early. After all, they were the two Liverpool lads. They roomed together and the jokes carried on. But for Pete and Mike, it was a big change. As Mike says, "It was personalities, they were from Liverpool. Pete and I were Welsh. There's a big difference there. I couldn't relate as well." Beverley remembers, "Joey was totally different than Ron. He had been around and he came in a bit 'pop star-ish.' Joey seemed to bounce through life – everything was going to work out for Joey. Pete would often say, 'This is serious, mate.' "

Joey's facial similarity to Paul McCartney was obvious. It served to draw attention, but not in the way everyone desired. Bill Collins commented in *Disc & Music Echo*, *"Joey bears a striking resemblance to Paul and it's been worrying us. We've had a meeting about it . . . We want people to know Badfinger for their music, not some accidental gimmick like this. Joey may have to change his hair style or something."*

Badfinger's album *Magic Christian Music* was released in Britain on January 9, 1970, just as "Come And Get It" was peaking at #4 in the *Melody Maker* charts. It

Badfinger rehearsal, Apple basement, 1970

received scant English reviews, most noting the LP's Beatle-ish qualities and the McCartney connection. The album jacket proved to be somewhat deceptive though, as Joey's name appeared, even though he didn't play a single note on it. And a song by Ron Griffiths was represented, even though he was no longer in the band. Additionally, no surnames appear. That was an attempt to give a personal touch to the record, something The Iveys had done with the single "Maybe Tomorrow."

McCartney did not take any production credit. This left several songs unmarked and unclear. Derek Taylor believes it was because The Beatles, ". . . didn't want to be seen pushing themselves at the public, partly because they didn't want other people exploiting their relationships. They were always pretty modest about their involvement with the Apple artists."

The LP jacket design, by David King, appears to be inspired by the works of Twentieth century surrealist painters Rene Magritte and Giorgio DeChirico. On the front cover, a large hand has its index finger pointing (Bill Collins), which is then traversed by a nail. Shadows loom, archways stretch, and heads pop out of circular bases. The overall mood is unsettling, including the wide variety of music portrayed within. Yet, with the majority of songs being of superior quality, the good does outweigh the questionable.

As it turned out, Britain didn't take to this album in big numbers. Still, it was a respectable move forward, a marked improvement over the aborted Iveys LP, and a strong building block for the future. America would be next.

Magic Christian Music, *1970*

On January 12, 1970, the "Come And Get It" single was released to the rest of the world. It became an across-the-board smash! Badfinger appeared twice on *Top Of The Pops*, Britain's premier T.V. music show. The excitement they felt was more than apparent on their faces.

A flurry of U.K. gigs were scheduled. The band now needed more help with their stage set-up. A friend of Bill's son named Nicky Bell came to their rescue. "I was an aspiring actor," he said. "I knew Lew Collins from drama college. He got Badfinger to headline our end-of-term party. As soon as I met them, I asked them if they needed any help. My timing was perfect. We got on great."

The group set out playing a variety of U.K. venues, including the Cavern Club in Liverpool. In early February, the band had several shows in Ireland, where the religious and political scenes were in turmoil. Fergie recalls their visit to Belfast, "A company in Britain called Orange Amplifiers had given the band some equipment. Everything they made was bright orange. They wanted to use the promotion 'Apple powered by Orange.' So we decided to try using their stuff. We had this big line-up of orange amps and orange microphones going across stage. Now in Ireland, the color orange is strictly a Protestant color. Catholics won't wear it. Their color is green. So this crowd was making all sorts of angry comments, *'I suppose you think that's fucking funny!' 'Fuck you mate, what's this!?'* We were lucky to get out of there alive!"

Late in March, the Arthur Howes Agency sent the group on a one month jaunt around England with four other acts: comedian Johnny Hackett, the rock group

Satisfaction, female crooner Clodagh Rodgers, and balladeer Gene Pitney (who used an orchestra as backing). "That was a bad match-up," says Fergie. "Badfinger didn't fit in." A few months earlier, Tom had told the English press, "We're aiming at the teenybopper market because we play good pop. We recognize there's a big gap to fill . . ." But the group quickly found the label irritating, as they occasionally had to deal with condescending attitudes. With Joey's entrance, the group felt its musical horizons had already expanded.

During the first three months of 1970, the band had a string of television appearances: Holland, Belgium, Germany, plus The Mama Cass show, *Make Your Own Kind Of Music*, a variety program filmed in Britain. BBC Radio featured the band six times. The group focused on the McCartney-produced tracks. The song "Crimson Ship" was performed and it came off like a Deep Purple jam. They did a smoking version of "Rock Of All Ages," a serviceable "Come And Get It," and a powerful "Midnight Sun." {Midnight Sun – BBC Radio} The unusual choices were Delaney & Bonnie's "Someday" and The Band's "Up On Cripple Creek." Though some may find their playing of those sacrilegious, the group was able to confidently stroke them home through Pete's self-assured licks and the brisk harmonizing of Tom and Joey.

Despite the regular gigs, Bill Collins only felt comfortable moving the group's salaries up to £15 per week, as many debts had to be paid off. Pete was guardedly optimistic, as shown by his interview in the *New Musical Express* issue of February 7, 1970: "We're *a lot more relaxed than we were a few weeks ago, before the record started to happen. The last year has been an edgy one for us, with debts to pay and a lot of worries and doubts about whether we'd ever be able to make it . . .*

Badfinger at the Cavern Club, Liverpool, Feb. 5, 1970

Make Your Own Kind of Music, *Mama Cass show, March 11, 1970*

Having this hit has helped us get ourselves level again, but we're not going to fall into the trap of thinking we're the greatest. We don't want to get so free and easy we end up a one-hit-wonder . . . I think we owe it to ourselves and the public, to think seriously about the future of Badfinger. Certainly, we're determined to try and make our next single one of our own compositions. Writing songs is the group's biggest satisfaction."

Pete continued to compose – whenever the opportunity arose – and he achieved first-rate results. His "Hand In Hand" is a dynamic sing-along preaching love and togetherness, while "Dear Father" is a quiet song of advice depicting Pete's gentle grace. "Live, Love All Of Your Days" is an accomplished distillation of gospel and soul, while "Dawn" portrays a sweeping grasp of pop melody, sounding several years ahead of its time. "Pete really wanted to write a hit," said Mike. "He was aiming for the big single . . . We knew it was coming."

Back in the U.S., the album, *Magic Christian Music,* had been released on February 16, 1970. *Rolling Stone* mag took notice and prominent scribe John Mendelsohn evaluated the platter, obviously stretching for a witty journalistic angle:

> *By way of elucidation, Badfinger is definitely a throwback to those innocent days of the mid-60s before rock and roll replaced the corny show-biz conventions of the straight pop world with its own corny conventions – I mean, it's not at all difficult to imagine these chaps converging on a microphone to shake their hair, grin boyishly in unison and yell "Oooh!" in falsetto harmony, is it?*
>
> *The archetypal Badfinger song and performance is "Maybe Tomorrow" . . . This one contains all the deliberate melodic ornateness, cuddly cuteness, Paulie-*

cum-Bee-Gees orchestration, and embarrassingly mushy words that in various combinations characterize all but one of the remaining cuts, which are notable mostly for how startlingly Beatlish they are performed . . .

Even when they're so unbearably cute that you want to take them off for a minute to clear the air with Led Zeppelin or something, you can't help but be cheered by their presence. Remember the name: Badfinger, from Liverpool. They're gear.

While quality was acknowledged, this kind of light-hearted critiquing would occasionally plague the band throughout their existence. Many people felt compelled to project a certain cynicism. With the group having similarities to a still, fresh-in-the-mind, "Godhead" band, like The Beatles, plus the Apple label connections, there could be no escape. It was a blessing. It was a curse. The key was, "How would the group handle it?" Only time would tell.

"Come And Get It" remained on the *Billboard Top 100* for four months, reaching its highest American position at #7. Its best charting in Britain was at #3 in January. Despite the single's success, the album only sold moderately well. This was a time when progressive, folk, and hard rock styles were beginning to dominate. Badfinger's melodic songs were clearly against the current trends. In fact, most of the successful 60s pop bands were slipping now. Still, *Magic Christian Music* sold well enough to chart in the U.S. for three months, peaking at #55. But amazingly, no other singles were ever issued from the LP.

Apple was moving extra carefully now. Its English offices had become staid and stale. Time clocks were installed; request memos were required; there was to be no more "steak sandwiches on the stairway." The roster of artists had been cut and held. As for The Beatles, they were now well into separate voyages. But while John, George, and Ringo could occasionally be found hanging around the Apple premises, Paul McCartney had long since vanished.

From the time Allen Klein had begun at Apple, Paul showed him total disdain, to the point of serious disregard of Paul's own Apple business obligations. In early 1970, Apple's English managing director was Jack Oliver, then McCartney's most trusted link with the company. Oliver recalls Paul asking him to coordinate his first solo album, without Klein's knowledge, "I went to meet Joseph Lockwood at EMI and it was a real hush-hush thing. Somehow Klein got wind of our meeting and he dragged me into his office. It was sort of frightening. He grilled me for four hours. He'd found out about Paul's album. But I insisted I had nothing to do with it.

"About a year later, Klein called me into his office, threw down this huge stack of legal papers and said, *'Read this!'* I said I couldn't read all that. He pulled out one part and said, *'Read this!'* It was an affidavit from Paul. It explained everything that had gone on and it said I had put his solo album out. I looked at Klein and laughed, and he just had to laugh back. He said, 'You know, you're one of the best goddamn liars I've ever met in my life!' "

Paul's album, *McCartney*, released in April of 1970, turned out to be, primarily, the relaxed home recordings of a happy house-husband, well content to be hidden away from the outside world. Meanwhile, Pete Ham, the young and eager disciple, had been busily laying down his own creations on a mono, sound-on-sound Revox – a more crude undertaking – and the long, dedicated hours had been paying off in royal flushes. Bubbly pop numbers such as "Tulip" and "I'm Only Human" showed Pete in an optimistic frame of mind, while "Little Mary," "Take Me Back," and "John Forgot To Sing" touched more on his gospel and folk influences. The last tune is a tale of a small town's dilemma in which Pete plays piano, with an occasional vocal harmony from Tom. But the *piece de resistance* of all his hard work had to be "No Matter What," a shiny little gem which Pete composed on his Martin acoustic.

The original demo is Pete alone – guitar and vocal – a straight-on rendition. He gingerly sings the song as if he'd finished it at five in the morning, eager to show it off, but respectful in laying it down, so as not to bother a sleeping soul. In his exuberance though, he blithely vamps on a few verses of melodic gibberish, eventually clapping along, before suddenly, he stops, as if to humble his prideful glee. Pete seemed to know, *this* could be the one!

Pete Ham, 1970

4

SUCCESS, IT HAD TO BE

IN MARCH OF 1970, BADFINGER were offered the opportunity to cover yet another "Beatles-written" song as their potential new single – "It Don't Come Easy." They turned it down; Pete again being the most vociferous. He still believed the group could come up with its own hit tune. George Harrison decided to develop a studio arrangement of the song for Ringo Starr. He brought Pete and Tom in as session men. What Pete did has not been verified, but Tom clearly performed backing vocals, as he is distinguishable in the final mix. Interestingly, George sang the track's initial "scratch" lead vocal, lending to the oft-made speculation he had a hand in writing the song. It wasn't until 1971 that Ringo Starr's version went to #4 in the U.S. *Billboard* charts.

Meanwhile, Paul McCartney was now settled on a new course. Thus Mal Evans again had the opportunity to step back into Badfinger's production picture. He had enjoyed his earlier creative run with The Iveys, even though no one at Apple would take him too seriously. "Mal was the gentle giant, a lovable person," says Jack Oliver. "Everybody loved Mal, especially the Beatles, but sure, everyone was a bit dubious about him as a record producer. That always happens when you see someone walk out of the role you're used to seeing them in. But as long as what comes out of the studio sounds good, it really doesn't matter who does it."

The group recorded four songs with Mal on April 18, 1970: a rocker entitled "I Can't Take It," a group jam called "Get Down," an acoustic-based "No Matter What," and "Without You," a Pete/Tom collaboration. The results were rough. The band needed more time to get acclimated. Tom was now trying to master the bass guitar and he was finding it difficult to write songs. But Joey was blossoming with tunes and Mike had built up a solid handful himself.

Meanwhile, Badfinger's household on Park Avenue was getting more subversive. Bill found his "boys" were becoming shrewd in protecting their privacy. His attitudes were being challenged. "Bill was trying to do the same things as when they were eighteen," says Beverley. "They began to rebel in their own ways."

Fergie recalls an incident, "Before I came in, Bill had usually driven them around in his van. Now I was driving, taking them out, hanging with the band, doing things Bill had been doing, and he became very jealous. One day Tommy and I went out and ended up staying overnight in Earls Court. The next morning Tommy said, 'You go back yourself. I'll get a tube in the afternoon.' As soon as I got back, Bill came out into the doorway huffing and puffing and said, *'How dare you keep the fucking van out!'* He was going insane. Pete came down the stairs and had an amazing go at Bill. He said, 'What do you think you're doing, Bill? Leave him alone! They're just enjoying themselves!' That was the first time I ever saw Pete lose his temper like that."

Collins' omnipresent hovering became a signature. Welsh musician Deke Leonard, who was then living in London with the Man band, recalls visiting the Badfinger home, "Bill would try to fall in and act younger. He'd smoke dope, he'd grown his hair long, he had young girls around. He seemed to relish all the social intercourse that was going on."

Fergie agrees, "We'd have company over and Bill would walk in the room with his shirt off and start flexing his muscles, trying to impress the girls. And every time you'd walk past him he'd be in some conversation: 'Well, I did this' and 'I did that' or 'Paul McCartney! He's a friend of mine!'"

Bill had a second-floor bedroom overlooking the front yard. "He used to keep tabs on everything," adds Fergie, "To leave from any of the upstairs rooms you had to pass by his, which was near the staircase, and the floorboards would creak. He would invariably peek out. You knew he was watching. . . ."

While Collins' eccentricities were begrudgingly tolerated by the younger generation; it was his business skills which were more often brought into question. Though he had the ability to charm and the character to tantalize, he wasn't convincing a lot of people he knew how to manage a rock'n'roll act. His honesty wasn't being questioned; the band just hoped he could do what was necessary to further their careers. "They didn't gang up on Bill," says Beverley. "It was mainly Pete who believed that Bill could do everything he said he could. Pete had faith, because he took people by their word. Bill had told the boys, 'I will guide you. I will take you to the top, because I know how to do it. Just follow me.'"

Bill's son, Lewis Collins, was now in the performing arts doing Shakespeare and other sophisticated plays. Lew had dismissed his Mojos' experience as an inconsequential phase. A hairdressing career had also taken a back seat. Despite Bill's strong interest in Lew's career, he could never escape massive conflicts with his son, and for long stretches, they did not speak to each other.

As it was, Tom was the biggest thorn in Bill's life. Joey, Pete, and Mike were too easygoing to be difficult, but Tom was quite willing to grumble. Tom would openly complain about Bill's competence and lengthy soliloquizing, sometimes

Bill Collins

referring to him as "big-headed Bill." Collins was suspicious Tom stole one of his diaries and that he hid a small tape recorder to tape some of Bill's conversations. But Tom acknowledged the position the band had gotten to. Collins was clearly the dominating force, the patriarch of the Badfinger home. There was a respect there – a bond did exist – but, clearly, this was a love/hate relationship.

Tom always had a decent rapport with his father, Thomas Evans, who was noted by all as a sweet and kind man, but they were also a little distant. Tom *needed* attention though, and Bill was the father figure, the authority in his life. Around this time, Tom wrote a song called "Uncle C." Some of its recording was erased, but what's left of this forlorn ballad reveals some illuminating thoughts from the introspective side of Tom Evans:

Uncle C
Don't let us down
Show us your smile
Then you can make it all worthwhile
Cause we're all here together on a fateful boat
That floats so wide on the water
Don't need to tell me that you see no joke
The hope is that you honor

Badfinger needed to step up as far as their gigging. The previous British touring had netted but a small profit. Collins looked to make some moves. By this time, the Apple staff, which basically liked Bill, had more than a few doubts as to how far he could take Badfinger. Suggestions were always being slipped in, like: "Get an attorney," "Find an agent," "Take a look overseas," "Get yourself an American . . . you know the Jewish-Italian type. Let him handle some things." The last thought stemmed from the idea of a tough, American-style, negotiating presence, which had been magnified by Allen Klein's obvious success at getting money into the Beatles' hands. No one at Apple denied Klein's effectiveness at getting what he wanted. They simply disdained the process, and distrusted the results.

Barrie Marshall, who was helping run the Arthur Howes Agency in England, and had assisted The Iveys and Badfinger in getting many of their live dates, was about to embark on a business trip to the U.S. He invited Bill Collins. They flew in together on April 17, 1970. Collins quickly began getting an education. Marshall recalls, "I was doing my things for Arthur Howes, but inbetween we would see various agents, including ATI (American Talent International). They were a booking agency headed by Jeff Franklin and he had ties with a man called Stan Polley. Franklin introduced Bill and I."

Stan Polley was born April 7, 1922, in New York City, and at early points in his life had practiced law, worked in retail shops, and run a garment factory. He was now a music business manager with a number of prominent artists, producers, and songwriters as clients. One of them, singer Lou Christie, had been very popular in

Stan Polley and Lou Christie

Lou Christie, Charlie Calello, Stan Polley

America throughout the early 60s. Christie had signed with Polley through Bob Marcucci, a former manager of Frankie Avalon and Fabian. Marcucci had used Polley as *his* business manager.

Christie recalls how he and Polley hooked up in 1965, "Stan still wasn't very familiar with the music business at the time. He didn't take me on at first. He was watching and learning, watching and learning . . . Finally we got together for a meeting and after listening to a record I'd just finished, Stan stares into my soul and says, 'All you have to do kid, is make music. I'll control everything. I'll take care of this. I'll take care of that. And we'll make millions. Trust me.' A couple years before that I had to fight like hell to get out of contracts with Morris Levy (a notorious music business manipulator) so you can imagine how paranoid I was. So I brought in my attorney for protection on the deal. They had this meeting and it was rather hysterical, because at the end of it my attorney asked if *he* could have a job with Stan! I thought, *'What the hell is going on here!?'* "

Polley did eventually sign Lou Christie, which led to Stan's introduction to Charlie Calello, an established music arranger associated with numerous Top Ten hits, including Frank Sinatra recordings. Calello recalled: "During the mid-60s, I'd arranged and produced a record with Lou Christie called 'Lightning Strikes.' The record was a smash and Stan Polley had called me saying he wanted me to make another record with Lou. I'd seen Stan with Lou and he'd always impressed me as someone who was always walking around with money in his pocket. I said, 'I want $10,000 to do the next record.' This is when producers weren't paid that much. So the next session Stan shows up with a check for $10,000. I cashed the check and Stan's word became good.

"We stayed in touch. I took a job at CBS and I ended up helping Lou Christie get signed to that company. While I was there I began to introduce Stan to friends of mine that were successful in the music business: Sandy Linzer, Al Kooper, and Bob Lewis. Around late 1968 we all formed a company together called Five Arts Management, Inc. Lou Christie was part of this too. The basic premise was we would pay 30% of our income into the company, which we would write off, because we could claim it as a management fee. We would build the company's capital, and Polley would be the majority holder. The rest of us would own less than 10% of the stock. We would use that as an investment in our future. Polley was the 'daddy.' Whenever we had a problem, we would go to Polley, and he would work it out. But eventually it got to the point where all of our money went to Five Arts – every single penny."

Polley delighted many with his theories of communal artisans; essentially, a collection of musicians, composers, producers, etc., who, by banding together, could keep their artistic careers alive during hard times. The basic theory being if one artist out of the pool had a rough time, the overall income would support them, until things got better.

By 1970, Polley's management services covered producer Hank Medress, songwriters Irwin Levine and Larry Brown, plus the aforementioned Five Arts group: Lou Christie, Charlie Calello, disc-jockey Bob Lewis, composer Sandy Linzer, and musician/songwriter Al Kooper. Polley had also been involved with Elektra Films, an animation company run by Jordan Caldwell and Sam Magdoff. But that partnership was winding down, as was Polley's association with Bob Marcucci.

Polley was quite intrigued by Badfinger, a group with connections to The Beatles. To this point, Bill Collins had been having trouble finding any truly interested American agents. But Polley promised Bill he could coordinate a tour through his friend, ATI agent, Jeff Franklin. And Polley said that he, himself, might be interested in running Badfinger's business aspects. He claimed he knew all the ways to shelter taxes and had strong banking connections. Bill was taken, but he mentioned to Polley that Apple's Allen Klein had said he preferred Bill not get involved with any American managers. Polley allegedly told him, "Tell him it's me. Klein used to be *my* accountant."

Bill met many of Polley's clients, a highly impressive group of successful entertainment figures. A few of them raved about Polley. But Bill maintains he was initially suspicious that Polley would want to help Badfinger do an American tour without asking for any money or commissions up front. According to Bill, Polley told him, "Let me prove to you I can do this first. Then we can talk business down the road."

A tentative agreement was made based on Bill's ability to get the group's interest. Before coming to America, Bill had gotten the band to sign a document authorizing him to sign all contracts on their behalf. Though it did give him the ability to represent them with authority, Bill claims he would never have made any truly important decision without first consulting the four group members.

Upon his return to London, Bill discussed the new American connections. Lou Christie was a good name-drop and the idea of touring in the U.S. was astonishing to the band. There were reservations, especially from Mike. "My personal feeling was we weren't ready for it. We hadn't rehearsed enough. I didn't want us to go out for a while because we'd heard about all the rumors that we were actually The Beatles, or Paul McCartney's backing band. I thought we should just let them think that. 'Cause once they'd find out we were just a bunch of kids who were alright – good writers, but not yet a super-duper live group – we'd lose a lot of mystique. But nobody wanted to listen. Everybody laughed at me at the time."

Joey was the most ecstatic, "I was excited because America was the market, America's the source. I'd been into it since I was ten or eleven. I remember staying home from school just to watch Elvis Presley movies. I used to sit on the docks to watch the American cars being shipped in. I loved America."

In mid-May, Badfinger went into Abbey Road Studios with Mal. They re-cut Pete's "No Matter What," Tom's "Believe Me," the group-written, "Get Down," and added Joey's "Photograph." A week later, they went into Trident Studios, to finish up two of the songs. One was "No Matter What." Joey recalled the

Tom Evans, Mal Evans, Trident Studios 1970

Tom, Joey, and Fergie, Trident Studios, 1970

scene, "I made up the guitar solo on my Firebird. It was a slurring solo, doubling up the notes, bending them, and picking them normally . . . I decided to play it on George Harrison's lap steel guitar. You know the one on 'For You Blue.' I really couldn't play it, but everybody liked the way it turned out." Joey later commented on the completion of the song, "We were real happy. It sounded like us, but at the same time it sounded like a record. We were knocked out."

The group brought "No Matter What" and "Believe Me" over to Apple as their proposed single. Mike recalls, "We all believed in it. Mal believed in it. But Apple thought it wasn't a good single."

Despite the disappointment, George Harrison soon appeased the band members by asking them to do session work for his new magnum opus, *All Things Must Pass*. Producer Phil Spector was planning to use lots of acoustic guitars, often played in unison.

Tom, Joey, and Pete ended up performing on the album. Mike was enrolled for percussion duties. "It was me and Alan White," says Mike. "He and I would switch on tambourine, sticks, bells, maracas . . . whatever was needed. Sometimes he wasn't there and I worked alone." The band contributed to five sessions in late May and early June, staying from about two p.m. to midnight each time. The album's all-star backing cast included Billy Preston, Ringo Starr, and Gary Wright, amongst others. Phil Spector used his "wall-of-sound" technique on more than a few numbers.

Joey: "I remember we played on every song. (George) got about twenty three musicians on the album . . . What we'd do is two or three songs a day. 'Watch out now' ('Beware Of Darkness') . . . 'My Sweet Lord.' We played all the rhythm guitars. Phil Spector wasn't really in charge. George was in charge. George would play us a song and we'd learn it right away. . . ."

Pete was more than humble when asked about the work, "Maybe it's because of the feel we have for playing along acoustically . . . very few people in the business know what we have to offer." Harrison was obviously impressed with their talents. In fact, he called on Tom and Pete for two additional sessions later in the month.

At this point, serious considerations to tour the U.S. were being made. Meanwhile, news had come through that Badfinger was being rewarded for the huge success of "Come And Get It," through an invitation to represent Apple at the Capitol Records Convention in Hawaii; to be held in June of 1970. According to Fergie, Badfinger were informed they could take one person with them. "The group decided that I should be the one. When Bill was told he went absolutely bananas! He couldn't handle it."

As it turned out, Badfinger was also to be accompanied by Apple's Mal Evans. Bill claims he was upset, not because of Fergie's invite, but because of Mal's potential presence. He suspected Mal wanted to take the band away from him. The day the group was going to leave, Stan Polley, coincidentally, showed up. A quick breakfast meeting was arranged for all. The American tour and business management prospects were discussed. As everyone was departing, Polley realized Bill was not going to Hawaii with the group. Claimed Bill. "Polley said to me, 'You should be with them' and I said, 'I *should* be with them. There's a ticket for me. There's a hotel room for me. But Mal Evans is taking it; and no one is saying a word about it!"

Polley offered to pay for an airline ticket for Bill to go. Bill accepted; showing up in Hawaii on a different flight. He said he gleefully surprised Mal Evans in the hotel lobby. "I'm sure he wanted to take the band away from me," asserted Bill. "He was *shocked* to see me there."

Later, Bill exploded when it was discovered that four mic stands had been lost in transit. "Bill made a huge issue out of it," says Fergie. "That somehow it was my fault and I shouldn't have been there in the first place. He was just livid."

Eventually, the Badfinger entourage hobnobbed with the convention crowds, and attended a large special gathering. Mike recalls, "Allen Klein was sitting in his lounge chair, talking to everybody, and his balls are hanging out of his Bermuda shorts. Nobody said anything, but *everybody* was smiling."

As the band's performance neared, they found a problem had developed. "The day had started out overcast," says Fergie, "and no one thought they would get sunburned. But when it came time to play, Tom and Joey's shoulders

Pete, Mal, Joey, and Tom, Hawaii, 1970

were so burnt that they couldn't even put their guitar straps on. They played the whole set sitting down!"

The band came back to England convinced they were now ready to tour America. Meanwhile, Collins had made sure to get a couple of things done before leaving; one was to get Joey Molland to sign his personal management contract, which Joey did on May 2, 1970. The other item was a document for Polley, signed on behalf of the group and Bill. It gave Polley authority to set up an American tour and stated that he now had "irrevocable" power to negotiate all contracts – in the name of Badfinger.

Now back in the U.K., Badfinger prepared for their new album. Meanwhile, Bill Collins had been progressively steaming about Mal Evans' advancement as a confidant and producer to his young group. Beverley recalls, "Mal Evans was a big huggy bear. All of the group had a really good relationship with him. He got on especially well with Tom. Mal had done it, he'd met everyone, and Tom didn't have to worry that Mal was after something. So the only reason Mal could have for hanging with the group was that he really *did* like them."

Bill Collins said he's convinced there was a plot for Mal to take his place. Bill figured Tom was initiating this, and that Allen Klein might have been in on it, too. Bill said one night Pete came into his room and told him he should come downstairs, as a meeting was going on with Mal. Pete felt Bill needed to know about it. Bill says when he came downstairs everyone froze and clammed up.

Shortly after, a meeting was held at Apple to discuss Badfinger's new agenda, a "big brouhaha" according to Collins. Attending were Mal Evans, Bill Collins, Derek Taylor, Allen Klein, Tom Evans, Geoff Emerick, and a few other Apple staffers. Bill decided that he would use this forum to make a stirring speech on his own virtuous behalf. He chose his moment, stood up from his chair, and unveiled a string of strong, salient points. Derek Taylor allegedly acknowledged him with kind, supportive words.

According to Bill, Mal was left speechless and "nearly put his foot through the floor," Tom was reduced to a few meek words, and Klein was brought down from his "pomp and circumstance" pedestal. Geoff Emerick was deemed the band's new record producer and Mal was out; essentially eliminated from all of Badfinger's future musical and business affairs.

"Mal Evans never wanted to take over the band," says Mike Gibbins. "That was Bill's paranoia. He just wanted us to do good and Bill was protective of his position. Mal was our buddy. We used to spend time at his house with his wife and children. Mal never wanted Bill out of the picture."

"Mal was a softie, just a great guy," Joey later confirmed, "He just liked to help people. He was concerned about the band to the point where it alienated Bill. And that messed up his relationship with the band."

It was a sad day for the group as a wonderful friend faded from their lives. Mal was still around, but it could never be the same. Bill was satisfied. He later proclaimed how "dangerous" he could be when someone attacked his "castle." He was very proud of his ability to battle the "giants" of the industry. One friend of Badfinger's summed up Bill this way, "You could never get him to watch a rugby match, because when the players huddled around for a scrum, he'd turn the television off. He'd think they were talking about him."

Back in the early 60s, Geoff Emerick, a young man, born and bred in London, decided he wanted to become a record producer. Dissatisfied with what he perceived as the "poor quality" of many records, he thought he could do better. After sending inquiry letters, he found that EMI's Abbey Road Studios were hiring. From 1962 to 1966, Geoff Emerick worked as a tape operator and cutter, which basically meant he set up and ran various machines before, during, and after the

Abbey Road Studios, 1970:
Richard Lush, Geoff Emerick, top
Nicky Bell, Pete Ham, middle
Tom Evans, Joey Molland, bottom

recording sessions. When The Beatles' usual engineer, Norman Smith, turned to record producing, Emerick moved into his chair – having learned a bit through his four years of experience. Emerick's subsequent engineering with The Beatles included work on the albums *Revolver*, *Sgt. Pepper*, and *Abbey Road*; the last two earning him Grammy awards in the United States.

But Emerick's original goal had always been to produce. Just before The Beatles had started on *Abbey Road*, he'd quit his staff position to seek new landscapes. But under the title of "independent engineer" he was convinced to come back and record these swan-song sessions. His work on that album speaks for itself. Now, early in 1970, George Martin was asking Emerick to join his engineering staff at Martin's newly-expanding Air Studios, but Geoff turned it down. The prospect of producing a Badfinger LP was the opportunity he'd been hoping for.

Emerick had engineered some of Badfinger's sessions and he knew the talents they had. He went to a few rehearsals and traveled to Golders Green to hear their demos. "I was immediately impressed in every respect," he says. "They were wonderful writers and their vocal work was so good."

The new album was recorded, mainly, at EMI's Abbey Road Studios, during July and August of 1970. Joey recalled, "We set up the gear in the big studio, the huge one. You can set up all your gear in there and have a P.A. if you want; it's so big. We had little Vox AC30 amps and we set the drums up and just played."

Because the studio was so heavily booked, the sessions generally ran in just three hour stretches. Luckily, Emerick was familiar with the setting and could make aural decisions quickly. The goal of everyone was to represent the band's strengths: good songwriting, lively ensemble playing, and crisp vocal arrangements in a variety of moods and styles. The harder-edged songs came off as a live, inspired rock'n'roll band. One of the best examples is Pete's "I Can't Take It," which was later colored with shrieky "whoo-oo's" and occasional horn riffs. A spontaneous group jam, "Watford John," was written in studio overtime. It features sizzling guitar over a stampeding beat; very loose, sloppy, at times out of tune, but in all the right ways. Joey's "Love Me Do" is a snappy rock-'n'roller with terrific drumming by Mike Gibbins.

Midway through these sessions, an American record store owner named Wayne Treiber came to England on vacation. His wandering led him in front of Apple's offices. He walked in and noticed a picture of Badfinger on the wall. He decided to tell the secretary he was there to do an interview and take pictures. Treiber recalls, "I said to her 'I'm here to meet Badfinger, are they here yet? She became flustered. I suggested she contact their manager. Before I knew it, Bill Collins was down in the group's van. He took me back to Golders Green and I started off by conducting a group interview. By the end, we'd really hit it off.

"When I got back to my hotel there was a message. I rang and was asked by Bill if I wanted to go to Belgium the coming weekend for a one-off performance at the Bilsen Festival. I was very flattered. I ended up going in Bill's place and managing for the weekend. It was really a wild scene. Cat Stevens played, as did Badfinger. They also had a firehouse choir performing and a firehouse band. To top off the evening, Screaming Lord Sutch did his "bananas" set and ended the night by totally destroying the place – after setting *fire* to the stage!"

Treiber spent more time with Badfinger in England, including attendance at a number of Abbey Road recording sessions. "I remember the control room was up above the studio, kind of like an operating room observation deck. We happened to be talking about The Beatles one day when, suddenly, Harrison and Ringo stopped by. They watched the group play for awhile. During a break, Ringo popped down to the studio and he and Mike were in the room together. We were all looking down and no words were being exchanged. Finally the ice was broken and they started talking. George was with us and he brought up that Ringo admired Mike's drumming. Of course, the group said, 'Yeah, and Mike really likes Ringo's playing, too!' It was really funny."

Later in the week, Treiber found himself the brunt of a typical Tom Evans joke. "The band kept sending me out for food," he explains, "and every time I would come back, I'd sit back, light my pipe, and they would start laughing hysterically. I couldn't figure out what was going on. Finally it came out that Tom had been putting hashish in my pipe! But he forgot, you don't inhale with a pipe. He said, '*Bloody hell!* That's a good lot we've wasted!' "

Certainly it was a sign of the times when drugs were so well acknowledged that you weren't "hip" unless you took them, accepted them, or handled their presence. As it was, one of the less hip "songs" the band recorded was a number called "Blodwyn." On first listen it may seem a bit corny, but this Pete Ham composition is actually quite uplifting. The lyrics became controversial down the road, but the basic theme is one of "giving." Pete delivered the vocals with a scratchy workingman's rasp, but not because he desired to. He'd gone to the session with a terrible cold!

Another song recorded was "Better Days," a co-credit of Joey and Tom's, which Joey basically wrote. This mid-tempo number has a very spontaneous feel with pleasing arrangement touches. Joey's songs complemented the others' well. They're fairly simple tunes, but the hooks are effective. Pete, however, had really blossomed as a writer on this album, as Joey acknowledged, "Pete's numbers are great. When I joined the band they were ahead of me in concentrated songwriting. Pete was a good year ahead of me."

Before the recording of this new album, an old friend of the band had moved back into town – Sue Wing. The one-time booking agent and wife of former Iveys member, Dai Jenkins, was now rooming with Mike's girlfriend, Gaynor, in a West Hampstead flat. Sue had separated from Dai in December of 1969. After quitting her job at a Swansea booking agency, she'd finally decided to return to London. Always popular with the Badfinger entourage, they were quite happy to see her again. "She was a friend, friend, friend," says Mike.

A couple of months after her arrival, Gaynor made an unexpected discovery – Sue was now working for a high-class escort service! "I was shocked," says Gaynor, "I was working all day and when I'd get home Sue would always be going out. Sometimes I wouldn't see her until the following day. Finally someone had told me that she was working for one of those "champagne" clubs in the West End. I asked her about it and she said, 'I didn't want you to find out about it. I thought you might hate me.' "

The word spread quickly. It deeply affected Pete. He wrote a song based on the life of a lonely call girl. He titled the tune "Midnight Caller." "I know that meant a lot to him," said Mike. "Sue was kind of a high-class hooker. She'd be with the Prince of Arabia and people like that. They used to give her jewelry."

Pete's song was recorded with ringing acoustics and an outlining piano base. His fragile vocal breaks ever so slightly at times, but the sincerity of the lyric is well-expressed:

Beneath the midnight caller
She thinks of paper green
You never hear them calling her name
They just know where they've been. . .

She's got no saint to follow
She's got no place to go
Too proud to ask an old friend for help
Too proud to let him know. . . .

As impressive as Pete's "Midnight Caller" is, an even better composition may be "We're For The Dark." Essentially a breezy acoustic song, it just soars with imaginative chorus breaks and an intricate chord structure. The arrangement is subtle: Pete strums, Joey picks, Tom prods, while Mike quietly rolls on muted toms. Arranger Harry Robinson added the strings and horns. "I loved that arrangement," said Emerick.

The album was completed quickly, but the rough edges added more than subtracted. Emerick selected a top-drawer mix of songs and showed his ability to merge punchy sounds together in an effective fashion. He and the band got along well. But Emerick also remembers that, "Tom and Pete were very intense in the studio. You could see there was a lot on their minds. Joey and Mike weren't as intense. What troubled me was when the band and Collins played the tracks for people, they would get fifteen different opinions as to what was right or wrong. This happens all the time with bands. The group needed to be encouraged more. They were very sensitive to second-guessing."

Striving for perfection is a great asset, but the Badfinger members varied wildly in this ideal. Their incongruity with each other was continually a factor for them (a set of four complex individuals, each quite different, each motivated by varying concerns, but at this stage, still a fairly fresh-faced bunch, eager to face the world ahead). Perhaps one example where potential was missed was the Ham and Evans collaboration "Without You." The song is a dramatic ballad, immediately striking for its heartfelt lyrics and inspirational melody. But the final results did leave some listeners a bit wanting. The intro and solo come off a bit like rough sketches; and the extended ending is a bit tedious. The overall arrangement is somewhat raw and uninviting. Tom: "I couldn't get myself to sing it with real conviction. When we got to the studio I said, 'I don't like this. It's too corny.' It seemed like such a schmaltzy tune." Tom was still feeling the effects of "Maybe Tomorrow"'s failure. Dramatic ballads were the last thing he wanted to focus on, as he was quoted around this time saying, "I'm driving at getting away from that, getting into content, without being syrupy."

As it turned out, the chorus of "Without You" was sung exactly as Tom had originally conceived it, for the song was simply a pairing of his composition, "I Can't Live," using Pete's verses from an unfinished number of his, "If It's Love."

Beverley diary brings the origins of "Without You" back to 1969: "One night Pete and I were supposed to go out to a party, we hadn't been out in awhile, and Tom asked Pete to listen to something he'd been working on. Pete listened and I could tell he wanted to work on it. I knew if he went out his mind would've been elsewhere. So I said, 'Go ahead in the studio.' He said, 'But I don't want to upset you.' I said, 'Look. I'm smiling. Go ahead, it's okay.' And he said, 'Your lips are smiling, but your eyes are not.' The next day he came up to me very excited and said, 'I've got this new song. I can't wait for you to hear it. I think you'll recognize a part of it.' "

This was the first incarnation of "Without You," featuring Pete's incomplete chorus and slightly different verse lyrics. Pete knew the song was special, but whereas he normally wouldn't toil over a composition, he wasn't about to give up

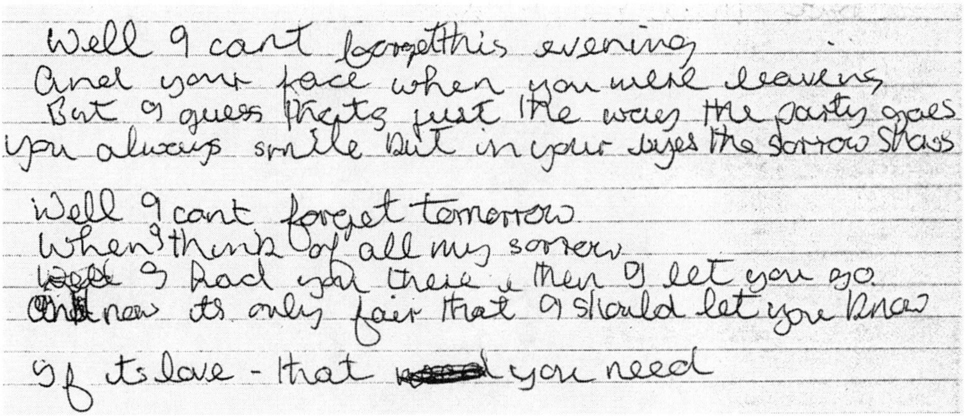

Well I cant forget this evening
And your face when you were leaving
But I guess thats just the way the party goes
You always smile but in your eyes the sorrow shows

Well I cant forget tomorrow
When I think of all my sorrow
I had you there & then I let you go
And now its only fair that I should let you know

If its love - that you need

Original "Without You" verse lyrics, as written by Pete Ham

on this promising tune. Finally one of those strange quirks of fate hit when he realized Tom's song, "I Can't Live," had the perfect chorus. "My song was okay," said Tom. "The verse is a bit like 'Help,' but Pete fell in love with the chorus. He said, 'I'd like to try that bit on a song I have and see what you think.' "

They put it together and the reaction was strong. "A lot of people were very positive about it," says Beverley. "The group did have reservations, but it was such a beautiful song they couldn't *not* use it."

Brian Slater, Joey's friend from Liverpool, lived nearby. He recalls stopping by one day, "As I was walking up the path, Pete knocked on his bedroom window and signaled me to come upstairs. Apparently Tom and him had recently written 'Without You.' Pete played it for me and asked me what I thought. I said, 'It's a monster!'. . . To hear the man pick up his Jumbo guitar and play that song. *That* was a great privilege."

Early in August of 1970, Mike married his Swansea sweetheart, Gaynor. She moved into their Park Avenue home. Midway through the same month, the group submitted their new album to Apple. The group had been rushed in the mixing stage, but they needed to have it reviewed. Apple's releases were now being coordinated by Klein's small staff working out of New York.. The American wing of Apple Records was now headed by Allen Steckler, who had been hired by Klein in the early 60s; initially to look after the Rolling Stones "creative" business aspects. Steckler recalls how his job came about, "I was working A&R and graphic arts for London Records in the U.S., and I was in England doing a lot of record production for the company

Mike and Gaynor get married at Camden Town Hall, 1970

as well. Eventually, London Records accrued artists from British Decca (their parent company) during the British Invasion era. I became a liaison and friend to many of these people. One of them was The Rolling Stones, and their manager, Andrew Oldham. He eventually recommended me to Allen Klein, who was managing their business affairs. I got hired by Klein to work out of his New York office."

"Eventually, I helped with other clients of Klein's as well. When his deal with The Beatles came down, it evolved to where I became heavily involved with Apple. I was doing all the work for the label other than sales; that meant listening to products, getting it to the Beatles, working with artists that were on the label, coordinating the releases between England and America, and making sure that Capitol did what they were asked to do. We eventually had to form our own agency, 41st Floor Associates, out of necessity. We had been telling Capitol to place certain ads and they weren't doing it, so we put together our own in-house agency for the graphics, the ads."

Steckler first met Badfinger at the Emerick sessions in mid-1970. "I was asked by George Harrison to talk to all of the Apple artists, to see if they were happy with Apple, if they wanted to stay with Apple. Harrison had said to me, 'Find out what they want to do. If they want to leave, give them the opportunity to leave.' Badfinger didn't know where they were going at the time. Other than Mal Evans, no one else at Apple in the U.K. was showing any real interest in them; ever since Paul McCartney had dropped out of the picture. Though the company had twenty odd people working there, there were all basically there for The Beatles. It started with The Beatles, it ran through The Beatles, and it ended with The Beatles. If one of The Beatles wanted to do something with one of the artists, fair enough. But if The Beatles were busy being "Beatles," the artists were forgotten about. That is why many of the artists eventually *did* leave Apple.

"When I was seeing Badfinger in England, I heard the finished tracks they'd done with Geoff Emerick. I didn't hear anything I thought could be a single. There were some good songs, but they were not commercial tracks. Badfinger told me they had some tracks in the can they'd done with Mal, but nobody seemed to care for them. So I listened to those tracks and I just loved "No Matter What" and "Believe Me." I said, "That's going to be your next single!"

Steckler's encouragement led to those two tunes inclusion on the new Badfinger LP. Left in the vaults were an unfinished "Get Down," and Joey's "Photograph" (later re-titled as a CD bonus track as "Friends Are Hard To Find)."

One day in August of 1970, New York businessman Stan Polley flew over to London. His client, Lou Christie, was in Europe for a tour, and he came along to a meeting held for Badfinger. "Stan danced around everyone," remembered Christie, "showed off, rented Rolls Royces, wined and dined, and got everyone all psyched up. He explained the whole situation to them. Everyone was *so* taken with this man!" Polley discussed the prospects of becoming Badfinger's business manager, telling them he would again meet with them during their upcoming twelve-week U.S. tour, scheduled to start in late September.

The group felt they would need to get a more versatile stage act together for U.S. audiences. Mike recalls, "We went to Wales and rented a small farm cottage. We set up the drums and amplifiers in a little cowshed, with straw in the bass drum. You could smell the cowshit everywhere. We just hung out for two or three weeks. Got fresh eggs from the chicken coop, bought some meat off a farmer and butchered it. We were getting real down home. That's all we did. We listened to The Band's *Big Pink* album and just generally got stoned out of our brains."

The band was eventually joined by Apple's Richard DiLello and Gene Mahon, the latter the company's chief graphic artist. DiLello had come to take photos for the album's inner jacket design. He explained, "Since I was in publicity and saw the boys a lot, I had said, 'Why don't I do your next album cover? I have an idea for it.' Gene and I pitched the idea. Everyone had said, 'Fine, let's do it.' Gene and I wanted to do a foldout cover. We shot a model back in London, and then we met the group to get some outdoor shots. The inner jacket photo was shot by a stream, late in the day, so the sun haloed their heads." Added Gene Mahon, "Neil Aspinall was a little upset about that. He thought it was not too dissimilar to the spread of *Sgt. Pepper*. But we weren't thinking that way at all."

*Joey Molland, Richard DiLello,
Gene Mahon, Pete Ham,
South Wales, 1970*

The front and back cover of the album turned out to be a young woman dressed as a scantily-clad Middle-Eastern dancer. She seductively stares and points her index finger. "She was a model," said Mahon, "just a professional model, not a fashion model. There are a variety, the ones who will take their clothes off and the ones who won't; and she was *quite* prepared to take hers off."

Film footage was shot by Piers Bedford of Eyeline. It was subsequently edited and used as a U.K. TV promo film for "No Matter What." It shows the group performing in a shed, walking around fields, fetching milk, playing in a stream, and moving off into the sunset. A simplistic venture, but because of the rarity of Badfinger footage, it's treasurable.

The group decided – for their first U.S. tour – they would focus on the new album's material, but it was also agreed, a few cover tunes would be needed. They worked up a medley of older rock'n'roll standards, and arranged versions of Steve Miller's "My Dark Hour" and Dave Mason's "Feelin' Alright." Joey and Tom were the ones who insisted these latter songs necessary. Mike disagreed. Pete was inbetween – he had the strongest faith in their own material – but he also enjoyed the covers, and wanted to do what was best for the group. As it was, Pete was really starting to show a blues and "boogie woogie" influence in his own writing. He had demoed a number of tunes in that vein: "Leaving On A Midnight Train," "Goodbye John Frost," "Blame The Devils," and "Things Are Really Getting Tight," several of which contain his spontaneous soloing throughout.

Pete's hometown friend, Barrie Evans, understood Pete's blues fascination, "Much of what Swansea musicians were involved in was the blues. It seemed to be the beginning point for many of the musicians of that time, guitar players in particular. Blues is derived from emotion. It's very powerful. It's not something that you can sit down and do in a cold way. Pete related to that. His songs are from the heart, an expression of a moment in time. . . ."

Pete Ham

Badfinger flew into Chicago, Illinois on September 23, 1970, full of excitement and anticipation. "We had been all over to other countries," said Mike, "but America was a lot bigger; Americans are a different breed." The group, along with Bill Collins, roadies Ian Ferguson and Nicky Bell, and a driver named Red, were sent off on a refurbished old bus. They traveled to the first of their gigs, starting on September 25th in Grand Forks, North Dakota.

It soon became obvious this wasn't going to be a big-time scene. For one thing, the travel coach was too small for their equipment; much of it had to be stored underneath, which was illegal. The luggage was piled in back.

Initially, the band was overwhelmed just by being in America at all. By their second date in Lincoln, Nebraska, Joey and Tom were ready to pounce at opportunity. "We met these two American girls," said Joey, "sisters I guess, because they were always together. Tommy and I copped on them and we went to their house. It was radical . . . all the smells, the furniture, the TV, everything was different. We spent all our time looking and trying to figure out where the fireplace was. The fridge was so big we couldn't see it! We forgot about the girls."

The group moved through the Northwest and back toward the Central U.S., playing in all sorts of medium-sized towns. Many of the drives were long and at times they had to sleep on the bus. The band had been told to bring their own P.A. system. They had no back-up or technical kit to account for breakdowns. The ATI agency had obviously not wanted to invest much money on an unproven act.

"No Matter What" wasn't released as a single until three weeks into the tour, but the earlier success of "Come And Get It" had sustained the public's curiosity. The ties to Apple and The Beatles proved to be a sore point though. The band expected a little comparison, but the onslaught caught them by surprise. "When we first arrived," said Tom, "people were constantly coming up to us, wanting to shake our hands because we had known The Beatles, and of course, they tried to publicize that fact."

The first U.S. tour, 1970: Tom, Mike, Joey, and Pete

Pete: "The local D.J.s would be the biggest culprits, because they'd say, like three days earlier, that Paul McCartney was going to be there, or that we were discovered by Paul McCartney, or that we were Paul McCartney's backing group. It was insane!" Tom agreed, "We'd get into town and people would be screaming, '*John, John! I see John!*' "

The attention was fun, but as Mike says, "It wasn't so great ducking the jelly beans." These were thrown by fans imitating what had been done to The Beatles in 1964, after George Harrison's statement that he loved "jelly babies."

The loss of identity, the constant questions, the stigma of being called a "junior league" Beatles, all of these struck hard, because the Badfinger members had a lot of pride in their work. The key was, could they sustain the pressure and just stick to the job ahead?

On October 12, 1970, "No Matter What" was officially released in the U.S. After a slow start, the single began to shoot up the *Billboard* and *Cashbox* charts. The 45 was backed with an edited version of "Carry On Til Tomorrow" (which

was originally meant to be the follow-up 45 to "Come And Get It"). In most foreign markets, an edited "Better Days" was the B-side.

The day after its release, the band moved into the state of Minnesota. They were in Minneapolis when Joey Molland's life changed. "I saw this beautiful girl in the crowd, and I thought, 'Who is that beautiful girl? I've got to meet her . . .' We hit it off." The "beautiful girl" was Kathie Wiggins, a Minneapolis native. She had worked at a car rental agency, and was recognizable locally for a T.V. commercial she'd done for Hilex Bleach. Her immediate focus became this cute, Liverpudlian musician. She soon squeezed into the band's bus for the rest of the tour.

The group moved to the Southeast and found themselves playing a number of colleges and universities. They had some very mediocre crowds – at one gig in Georgia only twenty to thirty people showed up. "That was badly advertised," said Nicky Bell, "but one of the people there was Duane Allman. He spent the whole night staring at Pete. After the show he introduced himself and came back to our hotel to jam on acoustic guitars."

At times, the welcome for Badfinger would be enormous, especially when rumors started that a "guest star" would be appearing. Interestingly, despite all the hype and Beatles fanfare, the band would invariably open their sets with an obscure gospel-influenced rocker, Steve Miller's "My Dark Hour." It's very dissimilar to their own material – being rather unmelodic – and the audience rarely reacted with pronounced enthusiasm. It certainly wasn't what people were expecting.

As it was, the group had recently become fascinated by the extensive wave of third-generation rock artists influenced by country, blues, and gospel. The Band, Leon Russell, and Delaney & Bonnie were amongst their big favorites. This was a new sound, and although Badfinger hadn't absorbed it much into their own compositions, they leapt at the chance to glorify it onstage. A prime example was Dave Mason's "Feelin' Alright." Their live version allowed for some nice improvisation, as Pete's guitar locked in with a good blues feel, supplemented by his melodic twists and turns. Tom sang his guts out and Joey took a brief solo spotlight. Despite occasional brilliance, the audiences varied on accepting Badfinger's condescension to a song most suited to typical guitar jamming.

Their sets centered on songs from the new album, *No Dice*, which wasn't released until November 9, 1970, six weeks into the tour. From *Magic Christian Music*, they might perform "Midnight Sun," "Rock Of All Ages," "Come And Get It," and "Crimson Ship." But the last two would be dropped, if the venue did not have a proper piano set-up. Audiences were stunned if the big McCartney-written hit was not played, but the group hated performing it, especially once they realized how "Beatle-fanaticized" so many Americans were.

The band members occasionally drank or got stoned before shows – to both good and bad effect. For example, Joey and Tommy's spontaneous Liverpudlian humor could be fun, but it also could get out of hand, noticeably slowing the pace. They'd laugh and exchange banter, often chiding the audience to respond. They'd also make jokes about Pete: "That's Pete standing over there, he doesn't say much" or, "That's monotone, monosyllabic Peter over there."

Pete often seemed uncomfortable in trying to respond to this or any other light-hearted stage chatter. Most of the time, he would only speak to introduce "Blodwyn," explaining the song politely, "It's an old Welsh custom. You carve an ornamental spoon out of wood and you give it to the girl you love. If she digs it, then she digs you. It's like a proposal of marriage." Then Joey might cut in, "Yeah, then she hits you over the head with it!"

Because of "Blodwyn"'s connotation of a spoon, many people thought the song was about cocaine. "Come and Get It" was also rumored to be about drugs, but in fact, the song was a reference to money. Mike noted at the time, "In the U.S., people read a lot into the lyrics of songs. I think the U.S. record listeners are trying to find psychological help through the music and the musicians." Pete added, "Americans will try and look into you and see what kind of music you do. Say, look into your albums as well as your singles. They really try and get on to what you're doing."

During this tour, the group did get some exposure to cocaine, but it was other drugs that affected them more. "We had everything pushed at us," said Tom. "We'd go into these college towns and everybody would be out of it on mescaline and we'd go, 'Okay, we'll take mescaline.' The whole place was out of it." Joey admitted the dressing room scenes got out of hand. "We had dealers coming in. They'd come in with these bags and they'd pull up their coats to show them to you, 'Well, what do you think of this?' We did take acid at the time, mainly for curiosity reasons, but it really slowed me up."

At one gig in Baton Rouge, Louisiana, the drugs and drinking got out of hand, as roadie Nicky Bell recalls, "Tommy wasn't around for the soundcheck. He'd taken a load of downers, I think half an acid trip, and drank a bottle of whiskey. He was back at the hotel unconscious. I had to carry him from his room to the gig. When I got there I strapped the bass guitar around his neck, and slung him onstage. He ended up with his head in the bass drum! He played most of the set lying down."

All of the group succumbed to occasional lapses due to exhaustion, nervousness, or inebriated states. One of the first things to slip was their harmonies. Tom could get overly aggressive. But when he pulled back, and Joey was attentive, the "magic" was unmistakable. "I Don't Mind," "Blodwyn," "Better Days," "I Can't Take It," "No Matter What," "Believe Me," "We're For The Dark," – all the songs from *No Dice* could sound excellent. "Better Days" *really* came to life. "Believe Me" was outstanding, a good vehicle for guitar solos and an improvised take on the Rolling Stones' "You Can't Always Get What You Want."

As they traveled on their tour bus, Tom encouraged all willing participants to jam on acoustic guitars, bottles, and countless knee-slaps. "There's nothing I like better than to get a guitar out and party and sing songs," said Tom. It was a fun time, but Pete was often more reflective than the others. He would quietly absorb the surrounding scenery. One day he wrote to Beverley, *"This country is obsessed with money and advertising. It seems as if half the people have ten times more than they need and the other half are living in ghettos. The kids are great but seem to be up against a brick wall as far as improving the situation. Unfortunately if no one takes notice of them this country is going to end up split down the middle in violent revolution. I can't see that solving anything. . . ."*

"When Pete got back he was still terribly upset about the ghettos," said Beverley. "He said, 'We should be able to do something for those people. Something must be done!' " Pete did what he knew best. He wrote a song: "Perfection."

There is no real perfection
There'll be no perfect man
Just peace is our connection
Giving all we can

There's no good revolution
Just power changin' hands
There is no straight solution
Except to understand

So listen to my song of life
You don't need a gun or a knife
Successful conversations
Will get you very far

During the second week of November, 1970, Badfinger moved into the state of New York. They had gigs set up with The Rascals, Paul Revere & The Raiders, Mungo Jerry, and even Black Sabbath! A meeting was held on November 16th with Stan Polley , their potential new business manager. The band met more of Polley's clients and were suitably impressed. "Lou Christie and Al Kooper gave us healthy recommendations," said Joey. "Polley had commendations from the New York Police Department on his wall. There were big-time Wall Street accountants involved. He had a Cadillac car . . . It seemed great to me. I was just a hippie."

Collins: "(Polley) told us, 'I know all the tricks. But if you play ball I'll play ball and we'll all get along fine and we'll all finish up millionaires. And in three or four years time you'll be able to retire or do whatever you want to do.' " Added Mike. "You couldn't help but like Polley. He could sell sand to an Arab; he was that good."

Three of the group members were more than ready to sign, but Tom Evans wasn't so sure. "Tommy didn't want to sign," said Joey. "He just didn't have a good feeling about Polley." Despite Tom's reservations, each group member did sign Polley's contract, which is dated November 12, 1970. Tom had told the others he wanted to check out Polley some more. It's not known if Tom felt the specific terms were a problem, but the key point was that Polley was to receive 30% *gross* of Badfinger's applicable income.

At that time, a legitimate "business" manager might get five percent of a client's gross earnings; ten percent if they were extraordinary. Bill claimed at one point Polley told them he was taking 30% of *net* earnings, but the clause clearly states "gross." Collins and Joey Molland also said Polley's logic to the 30% figure was that it was going to be reinvested into an overall Badfinger corporation, from which they would all benefit. According to Charlie Calello, Polley, told each of the Five

Arts members that the 30% he got from Badfinger would be re-invested into *their* kitty. Bill Collins did not have an outside lawyer look over the contract.

The band moved on to do more gigs and Polley was left dwelling how he could get Tom's signature. Badfinger hit the mid-South before coming back to the New York area once again in early December. The group was interviewed there by a DJ at the radio station WMCA, where they discussed their early exposure to the United States. Tom expressed his thoughts on American stereotypes, "I thought we'd get shot off the plane," he said. "In England you get the truck drivers whistling at you for wearing long hair, but here they have guns." Despite his seemingly tongue-in-cheek statement, Tom proved quite sincere when challenged by a call-in listener that Badfinger were only doing this tour for the money.

Mike Gibbins later recalled his own impressions, "Americans were a different breed, like 'What can I do *you* for?' instead of 'What can I do *for* you?' British people aren't so harsh. They say, 'Excuse me' or 'I'm sorry' not 'Fuck you, asshole.' That kind of stuff freaked me out."

The band had been set to play three gigs at a New York City club called Ungano's. For the first one, the press turnout was strong, as the album and single were now doing well. Tom recalled the atmosphere, "We were sitting in the dressing room when George and Patti Harrison walked in. George asked us whether we'd

Badfinger at Ungano's club, New York City, 1970

like him to introduce us onstage. Everybody was sitting around at their tables, looking blase, and when George walked out, it blew them away."

Writer Janis Schacht recalled the scene in *Circus* magazine:

> *Tom, Joey, Pete, and Mike disappeared backstage to prepare for their set, and no sooner had they gone than a hush filled the room. Then the whispering started at the door. "Harrison." "It's George Harrison." "Hey someone just said George Harrison's walked in." . . . all the blase reporters surged forward to shake his hand, to gawk, to get his picture, to get into other people's pictures. The quiet was suddenly transformed to an almost carnival atmosphere.*

Wayne Treiber, the band's American friend, was present, and he remembers the commotion, "Everybody was making a big fuss about George and he said, 'This is the boys' night to shine. All questions are to be directed to Badfinger. I'm here to promote them.' "

Janis Schacht picks up:

> *George and Patti were ushered to a front table, where all eyes remained riveted until the Beatle guitarist rose from his seat and walked onto the stage. There stood George Harrison – a distant idol now unbelievably brought within touching distance – saying, "Hello everybody, thank you for coming tonight.*

Badfinger with George and Patti Harrison at Ungano's

We'd like to have you welcome one of Apple's bands: BADFINGER!" Then he melted back into his seat. For a while, most people watched George Harrison watch Badfinger, then everyone noticed how good Badfinger were – good enough to draw attention away from a former Beatle.

The reviews were sterling. Billboard cited the group's "cheerily irreverent" stage manner and stated "They are certainly a group that lives up to their initial promise and should extend it." They were compared to the Beatles, "warm McCartney-type voice," "the effect is Lennonesque," but in positive terms. There was no doubt the band had gone over well.

Tom later recalled the post-gig scene, "George came back into the dressing room and played us back the show. He had brought a tape recorder and taped the whole gig!" "That was a bit unnerving," said Joey. "He was right in front of us. I was a bit nervous about it, but we played well."

After the group finished the last of three nights at Ungano's, they packed up the next morning and headed off to the next city. Only they forgot one thing – Mike! He recalls, "I went off to get some cigarettes and drinks in a store, and when I got back, the bus was gone! It was a Sunday. There was snow on the ground and I'm in a T-shirt. It was scary. You try walking through the Bowery in the winter with a T-shirt on. I was kind of freaking out. I thought, 'Oh the bus will come back in a minute and pick me up.' It never did.

"I walked all the way to Apple on Broadway street and conned some janitor into letting me use the phone, 'cause I didn't have any money left. Someone got me a limo and it took me all the way to Buffalo [White Plains]. They had driven all the way there and didn't even realize I wasn't on the bus. Apparently somebody had said, 'Is Mike in?' And the roadie said, 'Yeah,' thinking, 'Are the mics in?' Everybody was so stoned in those days."

During an interview on New York's radio station WMCA, the group had been asked about the Beatles connection. DJ Al Bennett told the band, "You get the comparisons to the Beatles, but it doesn't matter, because you write the songs so well and they sound so good." Pete replied, "I think the main reason we get the comparison is we write songs and not so many groups write songs these days. They write a riff and sort of improvise on that riff." Tom added, "It's hip to go on stage, all stoned, and play on one chord. We thought, 'Well, how long's that gonna last?' "

Late in the interview, Tom discussed "Come And Get It," "People said that they thought I was McCartney singing it. Now on 'No Matter What' people are saying that McCartney is singing it. Pete's singing it. So that's two different people singing and they still think it's McCartney singing." Mike added, "A girl thought the eyes of the girl on the *No Dice* cover were McCartney's eyes!"

As with the "Paul is dead" theory, people searched Badfinger's photos and lyrics for clues. One conjecture was a shadow on the *Magic Christian Music*

No Dice *LP cover*

cover symbolized Paul McCartney; others held that Joey was Paul's half brother. And the song "Crimson Ship" allegedly held, even more, clues to McCartney's rumored demise. Despite the band members getting irritated, the commotion did help them get more notice. What was apparent though, was between the lines of analogies and constant comparisons, stood a long list of praise. For example, the reviews of *No Dice* were sterling:

> ROLLING STONE *With their new album* No Dice, *Badfinger has one of the best albums of the year. This time around everything is good: the whole album flows well, Pete Ham sings in his best McCartney-esque voice, their guitarist now plays like Eric Clapton, and the material is all very good: the whole album adds up close to the monster Badfinger may well make in time.*
>
> MELODY MAKER *Badfinger have produced an album that would most certainly have been a best-seller two or three years ago. This is a superb album, with pretty songs full of lyrical awareness, melody, and beat.*
>
> SPRINGFIELD UNION *They're the guys who did "Come And Get It" but that disc didn't do them justice . . . the level of performance on every number is so high it's up to the standard of the Beatles in every department. The guys wrote all the material and Pete Ham, although he isn't in the Lennon-McCartney class quite yet, seems to have the kind of talent for getting it all down on paper that John and Paul had in happier days. If you're going to get one record for Christmas, make it this one. This could be the group of the 70s.*

5

Take It All

Badfinger had numerous road woes down the stretch of their tour. Roadie Nicky Bell was robbed of $1,500 of show receipts in Dayton, Ohio. Another time, the bus broke down. The group had been scheduled to play Augusta, Georgia, but they'd left so late from Ohio, they had virtually no time for error. "Pete was very upset," says Wayne Treiber, who was traveling with them. "He knew their not showing up would be blamed on the band. He hated to disappoint the fans. He couldn't understand the scheduling."

The grind put everyone at wits end. "We felt like zombies," said Joey. "It was really shattering. It got to the point where we were getting on stage and playing numbers purely as a reaction."

Meanwhile, Stan Polley was pleased that the band had taken off. "No Matter What" peaked at #8 on *Billboard,* while *No Dice* climbed to #28; excellent showings for a sophomore group doing music considered way out of date. Polley desperately needed to get Tom Evans secured to his contract.

The tour ended on December 6, 1970. Marianne, then Tom's girlfriend, recalls, "Tom had called me in England to say he wasn't coming back right away. He said, 'I have to check Polley out, see what he's like.'" A few meetings were held in New York. Tom was somehow convinced to sign. Marianne: "It took him about a week to sign. He was suspicious, but he had to sign, because everybody else did. He told me he thought he'd signed his life away really."

For the Christmas season of 1970, the Badfinger members went off to visit their homesteads. Back in Swansea, Pete spent a lot of time with his brother, John, who was still managing a TV and electronics store. John was also leasing a converted church hall, where he'd started to construct a small recording studio. Though in the preliminary stages, it was suitable enough for Pete to work on his first love – songwriting. Pete created several new demos there, including one for his girlfriend, Beverley.

Pete had brought Beverley to Swansea and they began serious discussions about their future. Pete told her that the band's management was insisting the group leave for another tour in March, giving them only two months to get an

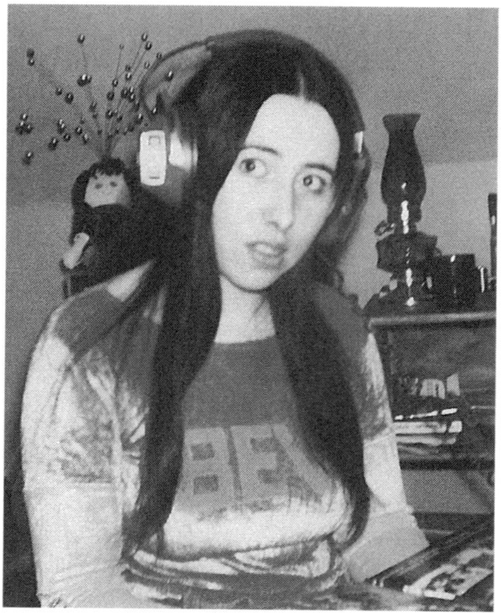

Sille Veb, 1970

album and stage show together. Pete had been away for much of the past year and it had been difficult for Beverley. Pete responded to her frustration by recording a song, which he presented as a Christmas present. The title, "Sille Veb," is a play on her name (Bev Ellis spelled backwards):

Won't be long
I'll be gone
Out on the road
And each song that I sing
Carries the load
Of the one I left behind

After the holidays, the group members reconvened at their Golders Green home. They were presented with several contracts. Stan Polley had come up with the concept of a company called Badfinger Enterprises Inc. (BEI). The group was to put *all* of their income into it, and Polley would manage and consolidate the funds to the group's best advantage. He maintained he could save them on taxes, provide stock options, budget their money, and basically, turn them into millionaires. All they had to do was trust him.

Representing Polley in England was Stan Poses, another American working in the music management field, who was also helping direct singer Melanie's career. Polley titled him as vice-president of BEI. Said Poses, "I was in the middle of just getting involved with Polley, not completely understanding what he was doing, so I was very laid-back at this stage."

Poses had brought over a "BEI stockholders agreement" for Badfinger and Bill Collins to sign. The newly-designed BEI corporation was "authorized" issuance of 200 Common Shares of stock "without par value," meaning the stock had no worth until money started coming in. The contract stipulated that each member of the group, and Bill, would start by owning 19 shares of the stock. This meant that Tom, Pete, Mike, Joey, and Bill together owned 95 shares. Polley would own 105 shares; giving him majority control. He explained that this was all for tax purposes and clearly to the band's advantage.

Five Arts member Lou Christie recalls, "Stan Polley always had these theories, they were instant gratification theories that would somehow turn people's heads. They'd say, 'Wasn't that a fascinating way of putting something together?' or 'This guy is really smart.' Everything he thought about, or how to do a contract, was always unique, to the point that everyone would be dumbfounded!"

The group signed the stockholders agreements on January 2, 1971. By this time they were still on individual budgets of only about £20 a week. They were told if lump sums were desired, they had to explain the need, and Polley would ascertain the availability. Collins was also instructed to send all sums of money earned prior to the BEI agreement to America, and to send any future Apple royalty checks over, as they were then being signed to go to Bill Collins directly.

Charlie Calello, of Polley's Five Arts partnership, recalls that around this time, "Polley came to our group and said, 'I'm changing the structure of this company. I need you to sign these documents.' He was our manager and he represented us, so we trusted him." Songwriter Sandy Linzer, another Five Arts member added,

Stan Polley

"We went along with it, but nobody knew what he was doing. We were young, impressionable, and naive."

Polley had also convinced record producer Hank Medress (ex-Tokens), and songwriters Irwin Levine and Larry Brown, to start yet *another* partnership, entitled Three Dimension Management. Levine and Brown had written Dawn's massive U.S. hits, "Candida" and "Knock Three Times," the latter a *Billboard* #1 in January of 1971. Dawn's lead singer, Tony Orlando, was courted by Polley, but never did sign with him. The Isley Brothers used Polley to help with some legal issues, too.

Badfinger were still blissfully unaware of any potential machinations by Polley. As far as Joey, Pete, Mike, and Bill were concerned, they were well on their way. Tommy, though, remained somewhat suspicious. He just hoped it would all work out. Pete, on the other hand, was clearly ecstatic. Brian Slater recalls, "Pete was very excited when they signed with the manager from New York. He said he had a few big stars on his books. He felt he wouldn't have to worry about money, that this fellow was going to take care of it all."

As the new year began, the group found that the Apple Corporation had further pared down in the U.K. The English press office had closed – both Derek Taylor and Richard DiLello were now gone – but Badfinger still managed to get some media attention. Promotion man Tony Bramwell was hanging on, doing what he could, "I got them on the album spot for *Top Of The Pops*," he says. "They did a few numbers; it seemed to crack open the floodgates for 'No Matter What.' "

The single peaked at #5 in Britain in early January. The group was then rewarded with a flurry of articles in the U.K. music press, with consistent references made to their Beatles connections. The group did their best to defend the constant comparisons:

> MELODY MAKER *Everyone who interviews us wants to talk about the Beatles. Sure, we were influenced by the Beatles, like ten million other groups . . .*
>
> DISC & MUSIC ECHO *When we're arranging something we just put in what we think will sound right – we don't say "Oh, the Beatles would do it like this . . ."*
>
> NEW MUSICAL EXPRESS *Our audience is a strange mixture. In America we seem to be playing to kids who missed the Beatles and we're treated as a substitute band; not that we're complaining . . .*
>
> SOUNDS *All the time we feel we've got to come up with a very high standard, to improve on the Beatles. Of course we know it's impossible . . .*

Despite the press glut, the *No Dice* LP was selling only moderately well in England. Apple Records' British sales were slipping badly now. With many of the employees now gone, the company was on shaky ground. EMI had cut back on distributing the label's records; in fact it was becoming hard to even *find* Apple

Rehearsing:
Pete, Mike, Joey, and Tom

records in many U.K. locales. The group was aware of what was happening, and made several comments to the press. But for now, they needed to focus on creating a solid new album.

Fergie recalls, "Apple had been charging the band for rehearsals in their basement, but it was getting too expensive, so we finally had to get them back in the Park Avenue house." After more than a year, Bill Collins had not yet finished his soundproofing improvements on the band's music room. He finally hired in some outside help. "Bill got it finished," adds Fergie. "It was well-constructed, but he hadn't put in any ventilation. The band couldn't take the heat, so we had to knock holes in the wall and put fans in!"

It turned out the band members were quite happy to work at home again. Joey Molland recalls, "There was always an idea for each other's songs. If someone copped a groove or a riff, we all knew how to jump into it and play that kind of music. We were like springboards bouncing back and forth."

The democratic nature of Badfinger worked well at this stage. Said Beverley, "Pete was always very excited about something he felt added to the group. It wasn't just that he wanted to make it, he wanted the *band* to make it."

Badfinger had been contemplating potential producers for the new album. On the previous tour, when asked about who their choice would be, Tom had said, "We have a pretty good idea of what sound we want, so we just need an engineer – or a spiritual advisor." As it was, Geoff Emerick was again hired. The band had felt comfortable with him; he had given them a lot of freedom on *No Dice*. Geoff knew how to capture Badfinger's strengths and his extra arrangement touches were colorful, without intruding on the essence of the music. With a lot of enthusiasm, Badfinger and Emerick went into Abbey Road studios on January 9, 1971, with almost no time spent on pre-production. Emerick recalls, "Yeah, it was a bit hurried. We did check out going to a more secluded studio in Wales, but I decided against it."

One of the first songs tackled was a group composition called "I'll Be The One," a tune which ably distills some of Badfinger's more intriguing capabilities. Tommy instigated the song's snappy verses, while Joey helped to compose the incredibly catchy chorus line. Pete added some confident guitar phrasing, and Mike pounded out a strong splashy beat. The whole thing ended up like a stompin' country-rock jamboree! But what really stamps it as "Badfinger" is the unmistakable Liverpudlian harmonizing of Joey and Tom. It was pegged as a possible follow-up 45 to "No Matter What," and a mono radio mix was done.

A Tom Evans tune was also tackled early on, "Sing For The Song." It began as a back-to-basics sing-along, but by completion it included "I Am The Walrus" cellos, heavy flanging, piano solos, and a gigantic coda, which featured the group, engineers, neighboring musicians, drinkers from the local pub, the studio's tea boy, "whomever we could find!" says Emerick. This recording carried a lot of tricks Emerick had learned from working with the Fab Four. When you consider it was completed in the same studio, with the same engineers, using the same recording

techniques – plus its obvious inspiration – you get a track about as close to a "Beatles sound" as one could expect.

The lyrics are ambiguous and dark. Partly they seem to be about Tom's difficulties in getting himself ready for the performance of a song:

Words won't come together
And they're very hard to me
Peace of mind is all I have to win
Tuning doesn't matter
Just as long as I can sing
Get myself together for the song

Tom was forever battling major insecurities. His good friend, Brian Slater, remembers him to be extraordinarily deep and sensitive, "Being a road manager, I felt very protective of artistic types. But Tom would frustrate me. He used to give me these funny looks and say, 'You *can't* understand me. You can't know what's going on inside my head.' There was a Liverpool bass guitarist named Johnny Gustafson. He played with the Big Three, Roxy Music, Atomic Rooster, all bass players admired his talent. But Tommy would measure his bass playing against him. I told him, 'There's all levels of playing, Tom. Does it matter that you're not the *best* bass player?' He'd say, 'I'm a fake.' I'd say, 'That's rubbish.' He'd say, 'Well, what's the use in being average?' "

Actually, Tom was proving to be rather effective on the lower end. His work on "Suitcase," a newly-recorded Joey Molland composition, was a real sparkplug to

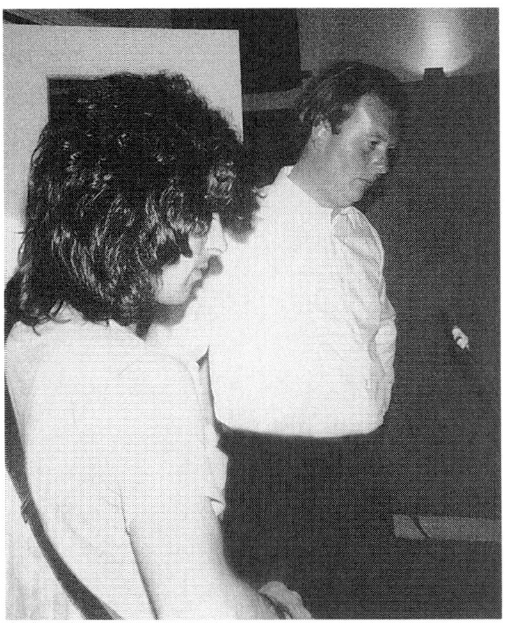

Abbey Road Studios, 1971:
Tom with Geoff Emerick
Pete and Joey (far left)

the song's buzzing guitar and cascading piano. Joey's number had been inspired back during the 1970 British touring. The band had performed it occasionally while in the United States.

"Perfection" was one of Pete's new contributions. He'd demoed it while back in Swansea, filling its chunky rhythm with loads of country-blues riffs. Badfinger's recording ended up faster – very streamlined and very smooth – with Pete's harmonica carrying the song home.

George Harrison had been taking notice of Pete's abilities. Around this time he invited Pete to play some guitar on the backing track for "Try Some Buy Some," a Ronnie Spector single. George later used the recording and dubbed his own vocals on, releasing his version on the album *Living In The Material World*.

By now, the Apple Corporation was mainly being run through its New York offices. A secretary there, May Pang, had befriended the group during their first U.S. tour. She had also gotten to know Joey's new girlfriend from Minnesota, Kathie Wiggins. They both decided to fly over to England sometime in January. May recalls, "I already had a place to stay, but Kathie's coming over was a surprise. I'll never forget Joey's face when we walked through the door at 7 Park Avenue. He was shocked!"

Beverley: "Pete had told us about Kathie. He said, 'Oh, she's probably coming over at some point, you'll really like her.' He was absolutely full of it. He said, 'Oh, it's going to be lovely.' He was really happy that Joey had met somebody. It was another one of the family, and Pete always thought of Badfinger as a family."

Kathie Wiggins

Pete greeted her warmly, as did Beverley and the other girls. But Bill Collins was most displeased at having yet another female guest in the household. Brian Slater was also taken aback, for another reason. "Joey introduced me and Kathie reacted like she didn't want to be bothered at all. Joey didn't say, 'This is a friend of mine, show some respect!' He just left it. That really did me brains in." Another friend of Joey's, Maureen Allen, also greeted Joey, but when Kathie saw them together she put her hand on Joey's shoulder and pulled him away saying, "We're going. *Now*!," leaving Maureen practically in mid-sentence.

Kathie was a strong-willed and serious woman. "No one knew how to take her at first," said Beverley. "I remember she put her modeling pictures up all over the house. We all thought that was strange. No one said anything about them." Gaynor adds, "She was locking herself in Joey's room, sometimes for days. We'd bring her soup and leave it outside her door. We tried everything. We felt sorry for her. We thought she was homesick." Marianne confirmed, "We didn't know what we'd done." Despite Kathie's sulking, Joey was more than pleased to have her around. She soon decided she was going to stay on permanently.

Meanwhile, Tom's girlfriend, Marianne, also moved into the house around this time, as did Fergie's girlfriend from Scotland, Anne. They had a child named Blair, a mischievous, bright, four-year-old. He became a 7 Park Avenue resident as well.

Pete and Beverley's relationship was now reaching a critical stage. They'd been "steady" for over four years. Beverley recalls, "People were always saying things to Pete, that he wasn't being fair to me, that it was time we got married – a lot of teasing. I remember Kathie said something that really affected him. Pete had always said that, for him, getting married meant having a family and being able to provide a proper home. As far as I was concerned, if Pete had to continually go off on these tours, I would have been much happier if I at least had a child to take care of. I could have dealt with not being married right away, but Pete wouldn't want that, not by choice. He had very old-fashioned ideas about how families should be, about how each role should be, that children should be in a secure home-life. He didn't like the idea of wives or girlfriends on the road, at least not as a regular thing. We started to discuss our situation a lot. We were upset, but we didn't yell. We broke our hearts – we cried and cried – finally it was like, 'Well, what should we do?' "

Beverley and Pete decided to put their relationship on hold. Everyone's reaction was, "Oh, it'll last a week," but there wasn't much opportunity to reconcile. A tour was on the horizon and a long-lasting love affair was in jeopardy. "No matter what, we'd still be friends," said Beverley. "We'd been through too much to just walk out of each other's lives."

Throughout the time of their discussions Pete had been working on a song called "Name Of The Game." Lyrically, this tune is quite complex, as it covers a multitude of thoughts and events that were weighing on Pete's mind. Beverley recalls, "The chorus of "Name Of The Game" is about us, our relationship, and what he was going through. He was really agonizing."

Oh, don't refuse me
If you choose me you follow my shame
No, don't confuse me
For I know it's the name of the game

The verses of "Name Of The Game" cover a variety of experiences and topics close to Pete's heart. One important issue to Pete was the environment. "He was very upset about what we were doing to the world," says Beverley, "all the destruction of natural things. Some of his greatest pleasures were to take a walk in the park, work in the garden, or go for a ride in the country. There was a spot at Golders Hill Park where Pete used to sit. It was under a rather large tree. He used to bring bread from the shop and would sit very still. Eventually squirrels would come up and start to feed out of his hand. It was amazing. But one day he got bit! That was the end of that."

Badfinger decided to record "Name Of The Game." They first laid down a foundation of Pete's insistent acoustic rhythm and Mike's solid, simple beat. Ultimately an orchestral arrangement was laid on, which lifts the tension, exploding in each chorus to an abundance of horns and busy strings. The group and Emerick thought *"Single!"* and Apple obliged, tagging it for a May release, as Apple catalog #35.

As the recordings went on, several different studios were being utilized. For their last number at Abbey Road, Badfinger got back into their roots with "No Good At All." This is a balls-out Tom Evans screamer, about as raw and straight ahead as you could get. The group's ease and proficiency at performing in this style was quite apparent. Also conveying this prowess was a similar number called "Baby Please." It was put together at Air Studios. Tom was too sick to attend that day, so Pete, Joey, and Mike decided to jam. Together they came up with an excellent white-hot raver.

Changing pace, Joey contributed "Sweet Tuesday Morning" a featherlight acoustic tune which features beautiful guitar picking. Other completed songs were "Mean Mean Jamima," Joey's plea for a "brown-eyed lady" to "come back home," and Mike's "Loving You," an engaging minor-key waltz.

Near the end of this project, a medley was put together of a Tom Evans song called "Money," and a Joey/Tom composition entitled "Flying." The former is a moody, brooding number which communicates the stranglehold "currency" can have over one's life. It begins quietly, then builds slowly through intelligent vocal interplay and warm orchestration. George Martin was the arranger. Geoff Emerick explained, "I wanted strings to bridge the two songs. We were working in studio #2 at George Martin's Air London, and I went up to George for an arrangement. He turned it down. But then he heard the songs and he told me he'd do it."

The stomach-dipping segue Martin created makes for glorious entrance into the spaced-out sentiments of "Flying." With drugs being so prevalent in the early 1970s, Joey had no qualms about discussing the inspiration of its lyrics, "Generally I write about things going on around me," he said, "or things I can realize myself – like when I was taking acid, I wrote a song called 'Feel Like I'm Flying.' "

Emerick remembers being very pleased with the final results, "There was progression on this record. They were getting tighter and more accomplished as musicians and writers. I was very happy with the project."

The final mixes were completed in one twelve-hour marathon on March 2, 1971, as the band had to leave for their next U.S. tour the following day. The door was left open for a touch-up or two, but Apple first had to wade through the product. Tom had this to say about it in an interview, just days after its completion, "It's more mature than the last record. We didn't make any deliberate attempt to change anything cause we still like the idea of relating our feelings through good songs, not just through good musicianship. It's a hard battle to come through with that idea. You have to be strong in the face of judgment."

During the recordings, Pete had been dealing with the emotional trauma of his break-up with Beverley. Pete was trying to be open to the possibility of a new relationship. One girl who intrigued him was the Apple secretary from New York, May Pang. When she stayed with her friends in London, she would occasionally visit Badfinger's Park Avenue home. Pete, especially, got along with her. "To me it was just friends, everybody hanging out," says May. "We had fun. I enjoyed Pete's company. But I didn't think anything was serious."

One night Pete was toying with a blues riff, and he started to write a tune. He laid down a number of versions, calling the developing song "May Blues." The playful words and carefree bop reflected a burgeoning interest. One recording of it includes what seem like references to John Lennon, as May had recently started to work specifically for John and Yoko in December of 1970. Sings Pete, *"I can't talk about John . . . I can't talk about peace . . . I need all of my song around you. May!"*

May Pang

But Beverley was still on his mind. Their five years together could not be easily dismissed. Mike's wife, Gaynor, especially had picked up on this.

Gaynor usually got up the earliest at the Park Avenue house, and many times, as she came downstairs, Pete would just be creeping out of the recording room after a long night's work on a demo. She recalls, "Pete would always call me in to hear his new song. That was very important to him. We'd talk about music and everyday things. I used to discuss my personal life, but when it came to his, he generally tried to lighten the discussion." Days before the upcoming U.S. tour, Gaynor noticed something quite wrong, "Pete lit a cigarette and stabbed it out on his hand. I couldn't believe it! I said to him, 'What is it, Pete?' And all he would say was, 'Guilt . . . I feel guilty.' I knew it was Bev. But he wouldn't go into it, 'cause Pete didn't like to burden you with his problems. If he was in pain, he'd try and hide it. He'd change the subject. Cause Pete was the 'strong' one, he was there for you."

The second U.S. tour of Badfinger began in Toledo, Ohio, on March 5, 1971. For this go-round the entourage grew, as Mike brought Gaynor, while Joey invited his new girlfriend, Kathie. Fergie brought Anne. They had married just days before the scheduled departure; with the group pitching in to pay her plane fare as a newlyweds gift. Nicky Bell was again on the road crew, while Tim Boyle was hired on as further roadie assistance. Polley assigned BEI vice-president Stan Poses to keep an eye for much of the tour, and Bill Collins was also present, never too shy to throw his two cents in.

A larger bus was chartered this time, driven by Walt, a black, part-time cop who'd carted James Brown and his entourage around for years. Because of the sporadic race-rioting going on, Walt kept a hatchet under his seat. And he wasn't afraid to show it off.

Badfinger didn't have much chance to rehearse up new songs for the tour. "Believe Me" had been dropped, and Joey's "Suitcase" came permanently in its place. The band would often encore with "Sometimes," a new Joey "boogie" as Tom described it, but otherwise, the only changes were dropping "Come And Get It," "Crimson Ship," and "Rock Of All Ages" – unless a longer show was needed. The group was eager to start paring down The Beatles connections.

The gigs started in the South. Then came an early stop in New York. There they met with Polley and Al Kooper, one of Polley's musician-clients. The band had brought along the master tapes of the song "Name Of The Game," which was supposed to be their next single. Kooper was a gifted arranger, so it was hoped he could give the song some extra pizzazz. Mike recalls, "We were in Kooper's apartment and we were dinking around with ideas. At one point Polley suggested it might be a good idea for Kooper to join us as a keyboard player. I liked the idea, but it was overruled. It was Bill Collins and the Fab Four! Bill thought we were the fucking Beatles!"

COPPER

©Shepard Sherbell/SABA

©Shepard Sherbell/SABA

PEPSI

U.S. Tour #2:
Pete, Fergie, Gaynor, Mike, American roadie, Walt, Nicky, Kathie, Joey

Kooper took the multi-tracks away while the group went on to do more shows. Badfinger plowed on with a flurry of performances throughout the Midwest. Midway through April, a single by Ringo Starr came out. The song was "It Don't Come Easy," a number Badfinger had turned down the year before. The Starr 45 rapidly ascended the U.S. charts. Nowhere to be heard, though, was a new Badfinger single from the *No Dice* album.

It would have seemed logical for Apple to capitalize on Badfinger's touring with a new 45, but as Apple promotion man Tony Bramwell recalls, "There weren't many singles out. The label was winding down. We had little input in Britain. The releases were all going through the States by this point." Apple Records' head, Al Steckler, says he remembers feeling there was not another worthy song for a single from *No Dice*. But he also admits being consistently busy with Harrison and Lennon projects at this time, thus Badfinger may have slipped out of priority.

The band continued on, promoting their refreshing pop songs. At times though, they came across more as a mini rock'n'roll revival, with versions of "Johnny B. Goode," "Roll Over Beethoven," and a medley that started with Joey's "Love Me Do," and ended with Little Richard's "Lucille," "Rip It Up," and "Long Tall Sally." Granted, the group played these oldies with great abandon and sincerity – and showcased some terrific lead playing by Pete and Joey – but it was surprising they didn't use

Pete, Richard DiLello, Tom, Mike, Joey

more of their own material to energize the show. This hinted at a lack of confidence in their own compositions, which certainly didn't help their validity. Despite some acclaim, the group's appearances weren't garnering special attention.

Badfinger had been set up to operate on a democratic system. At times, this situation led to a lot of small compromises versus one, inspired, unified direction. Their stage show was a good example. Joey loved 50s rock'n'roll. He greatly encouraged the oldies covers. Tom believed "boogie" was a necessity, and blues were still the rage, so they performed at least two earthy jams every night. Pete liked quiet, melodic songs, so he got an acoustic spotlight, "We're For The Dark," and the bouncy singalong, "Blodwyn." Privately, Mike disagreed with many of the group's decisions.

Despite internal frustrations, the group still enjoyed many good times together on the road. Pete was loosening up now; he was a free and easy bachelor for the first time in years, and he could at least peruse young ladies without unmerciful teasing from his friends. But, as Fergie recalls, "Pete wasn't the type for one-night stands. He would get real involved. Every girl he liked would be very serious to him. He was very susceptible to getting a crush."

May Pang showed up for a few gigs and spent some time with Pete. Then, in one city, Pete came across a picture of an innocent looking lass at a local radio station and became *totally* enraptured. He left his number with a local DJ and asked to have the girl ring him, but when the call came to the band's hotel, Pete wasn't in. They never spoke. Finally, on April 28, 1971, in Wichita, Kansas, Pete's luck changed.

Badfinger played their set that night and were just hanging backstage when Pete caught sight of an attractive young girl sitting quietly in the corner. She was a local lady who had gone to the show rather reluctantly, as her friend had dragged her out that night to see a band she had never heard of. The young woman's name? Dixie.

Dixie, Pete

She recalls, "I was sitting there kind of bored when Peter came over to me. He was kind of surprised – here was a person not really taking it all in at the moment – and I think I was pretty rude to him. I wasn't in the mood to mess with 'these people.' I just wanted to leave. But Pete was so charming and so funny and so handsome that, by the end of the night, I just became infatuated with him. He grabbed my hand like he never wanted to let it go and said, 'Could you come to the West Coast with us?' I thought, 'Well . . . okay . . . I'll go!' I was pretty much a free spirit at the time. I had been house sitting for someone and I just gave the keys to my girlfriend who'd brought me to the concert and said, 'I'm off — to California!' "

Two days later the group was in the Golden State for their West Coast debut at the Pasadena Civic Auditorium, just outside Los Angeles. They had driven straight through, arriving at six in the morning. The roadies were sent out early to hunt down a P.A., as theirs was not in good shape. With a combination of nerves, exhaustion, and what turned out to be another bad P.A., the group did not have a particularly memorable show. "We couldn't hear ourselves at all," said Tom in an interview. "We had all these people here watching us and we got a bit down. It was our first time in L.A., after hearing so much about it." Pete added, "The one thing about this group is we are not very good actors, and when it's bad, everybody knows it. We aren't good at hyping. But when we get it down well, it's real, and everybody digs us for it."

Another show had been scheduled up the California coast. The gig was in San Jose was where future journalist, and future Young Fresh Fellows member, Scott McGaughey saw the band for the first time. "My friend and I couldn't believe we were actually going to see Badfinger there. They were the special guests between Tower of Power and Lee Michaels. This was Tower of Power's home town and they got a rousing reception, but when Badfinger came on they had all kinds of

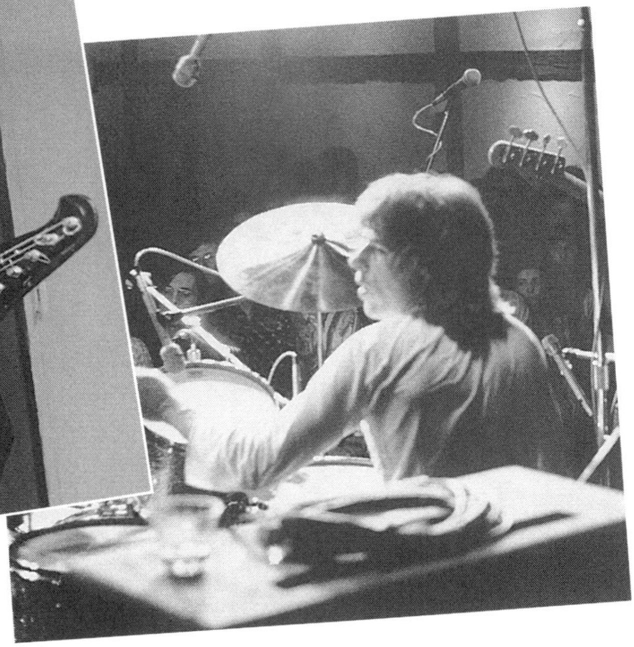

technical problems. For 'We're For The Dark' there was feedback on the acoustic guitar. The crowd started shouting 'Boogie! Boogie!' It was only when they did a rock'n'roll medley that they really got a reception. They were great, but it was a difficult pairing."

One problem for Badfinger was there weren't many similar-styled groups around. This tour saw them matched with the likes of Poco, McKendrie Spring, Leon Russell, The Grassroots, and the Mothers of Invention. Many times they were not the headliners.

Courtesy of Capitol Records, Badfinger were brought back to Los Angeles, and they received full Hollywood treatment. They were taken to Disneyland via limousine and situated at the Hyatt Hotel on the prestigious Sunset Strip. It was an active scene then, with lots of rock'n'roll highlife. Dixie recalls, "Pete wasn't as much into the drugs, so we didn't party a lot with the other people. One night the police decided to make a raid at the hotel and they picked our room to come into. They came in shouting and yelling, with flashlights blaring in our faces, and here it was – this mellow, dark room with a sleeping couple – and *no* drugs!"

Badfinger sat down to do an interview with *Rolling Stone* correspondent Harold Bronson, who was doing a story for the magazine's June 10th issue. This May 3, 1971, discussion led to some key insights into the band's perceptions of their management at the time:

U.S. Tour #2:
Joey, Mike, left
Tom, above
Pete, right

PETE *We're doing this continuous tour so we can afford to take time off to make an album which we'd be completely satisfied with. We'd like to relax, stop work for like three months, writing nice and easily. We tried to get this tour put off for two weeks but we were advised if we pulled . . . we'd be bankrupt.*

TOM *We came to America without a single and we're still playing the same stage act that we played last fall . . . it's really stagnant.*

MIKE *I'd like to go home tomorrow and forget the gigs. After the first gig I felt like that so you can imagine how I feel now. We didn't want to come to America. The album suffered and the stage act suffered.*

PETE *It has to do with financing. You have to be in a position to stop work and take time off to really get it together.*

TOM *The business people tell you "Take this and do that. You can't pull out now 'cause you're gonna use up all you ever did." So you do it. But we're hoping this tour will pay off for five months in England so we can get all our equipment together, get ourselves a stage act together, and be totally satisfied.*

PETE *It's very difficult because it's not as if people are trying to screw us or anything like that. All the people we're associated with are really sincere people.*

When asked what problems "sudden success" created, the band replied as follows:

PETE *Business, it's the big problem. The only really big problem is business. . .*

TOM *It's not so much making money, as our goal is to do what we want to do.*

JOEY *That's what [our business advisors] are supposed to do. Make us money.*

Badfinger flew to the New York area to complete more shows before finishing in Pennsylvania. Then it was back to New York. Stan Polley introduced the band to one of his clients, songwriter Larry Brown, who was then riding a hot streak with partner Irwin Levine. Says Brown, "I played Badfinger a song we'd just written called, 'Tie a Yellow Ribbon Round The Old Oak Tree, and I asked them if they thought it could be successful in their country. They said, 'This could never be a hit in England, nobody ties ribbons around trees for nobody.' They didn't think much of the song. But then, neither did anybody else in New York. Stan Polley told me, 'Forget it, everybody's got an opinion, that's why there's chocolate and vanilla ice cream.' He taught me how to get past those things. His thing was to take over, so you didn't feel the pain of the business experience."

"Tie A Yellow Ribbon Round The Old Oak Tree" *did* become a monster hit, but things were not all that rosy amongst the various Polley camps. Rose Marino* worked as a secretary in his office. She remembers her days there as a "nightmare." "Polley ran his office out of an apartment," she says. "It was in a nice building, but I always had a funny feeling there. This man, Terry Harvey, he was always around, and an old man who used to make up money games like 'Tic Tac Dough.' I had no idea what they were doing. The clients all seemed unhappy. Polley used to bad mouth his wife all the time. Even in front of his children he would say the most horrendous things. And he didn't give Stan Poses any respect at all. He was very secretive, too."

Early in 1971, Charlie Calello of the Five Arts group began to have inklings that something was seriously wrong, "I began to get suspicious because Polley's ego began to get out of whack. He'd bought a Rolls Royce Corniche and I knew it cost $26,000. I found out he'd bought it with company money. He'd given the impression he was already loaded before he met us. He supposedly never took his own salary. But things he was doing, like getting us to sign all kinds of documents, and other behavior, made me suspicious."

Another Polley client, Lou Christie, was now on the career bubble, having to deal with the 60s backlash that stalled or killed many careers around this time. He

---

* Rose Marino later served as executive secretary to Albert Grossman at Bearsville and Clive Davis at Arista. The apartment she referred to was on Park Avenue South near 116th St. in Manhattan. It was owned by Polley's father-in-law, Charlie Levine. Levine had first gained notoriety as the second man to fly across the Atlantic Ocean in 1927, following his friend, Charles Lindbergh. Later Levine became a millionaire who had numerous brushes with the law. Terry Harvey was a former New York City police chief who had been a friend of Polley's father.

needed the strength and support of his manager. "When I was hot, Polley touted me everywhere. He used to carry checks made out to me all around New York and show them off. One time there was a check in my name for $105,000 and he was saying 'Look at this! Lou Christie just got $105,000!' But you turn the check over and of course it says 'Five Arts.'

"Stan was supposed to be taking care of all my accounts. I had a house in Pittsburgh and my roommate, Twyla Herbert, was contacting me all the time and saying, 'Where are the checks? The house payment's due, the gas bill is due, the credit card is due!' I was doing shows in Europe, writing songs, running around just trying to keep my career going and this was crazy. I was gonna lose the house! I couldn't concentrate. *'Where's the money!? Send the money!'* "

Meanwhile, Polley courted Badfinger throughout their stays in New York. He would drive them around, show them the sights, telling them what big stars they would become. He would tell Bill Collins that he loved listening to him talk. Most of Badfinger and Collins were still under his spell.

Late into the tour the group ran into Wayne Treiber, their new American friend. He hooked on for the last ten days of a long journey's haul. "The band were pretty much exhausted by this point," he says. "Their dates were all over the place. A lot of times they had to drive straight through. They didn't get motels, they'd sleep on the bus and pick up food on the road. One time the bus broke down and everybody had to push it off the road. Between the conditions, the booze, and the drugs, they weren't always together onstage. It was live rock'n'roll and it had a life of its own, but it was schizoid compared to their records.

"They threw in 'Rock Of All Ages' once and it was incredible, but they didn't do it at the following shows. I asked Tommy why and he said, 'That's from the old Iveys days, we don't do it anymore.' But they'd do 'Johnny B. Goode' and 'Roll Over Beethoven' every night! I couldn't understand that.

"Another time they went offstage with the audience screaming for a second encore. But none of the group would come out. Finally, Tom appears and starts singing a Little Richard song, all by himself. It was great, he was really getting into it. Then Mike comes out and it's bass and drums. Finally the whole group comes out and is kicking ass. Then they went right into a killer version of The Iveys number, 'Daddy's A Millionaire!' I was shocked!"

Stan Poses, Polley's BEI assistant, stayed on for most of the tour. He recalls the incessant Beatles hype that followed the band, "They couldn't get away from it, but I didn't mind. I do remember that Pete especially hated the comparisons. He did not want to do 'Come And Get It' because everyone said it was the Beatles. I would beg them to do it every night, but they refused absolutely."

Pete was consistently put on the defensive by interviewers regarding The Beatles and Apple. He'd answer as best he could:

U.S. tour #2
Pete Ham's
home movies:

We appreciate being with Apple and what the Beatles have done for us, but it tends to be a bit of a drag when you get to a gig and you're advertised as Paul McCartney's group or that Paul McCartney is appearing on stage with you. . . .

There are a million groups copying Led Zeppelin at the moment and nobody bothers to criticize them for it. We like melodies and songs and we get criticized for it. . . .

Mention the Beatles to any other band in this country and they'll say, "Yeah, we dig what they did, and somewhere they must have influenced us." But it's beginning to become a sore point for us. . . .

The group had numerous influences other than The Beatles, but as Tom put it in later years, "We'd say, The Band, Leon Russell, *anything* but The Beatles. It just

Stan Poses, Kathie Wiggins, Joey Molland, 1971

wasn't the thing to say. I saw all the other bands, but The Beatles had something; vitality, humor, the songs. Looking back, it was an honor."

As the tour progressed, BEI's Stan Poses picked up on the group's personalities. "Pete was very, very quiet. He would hardly open up. But he had this charisma, when you put him on stage, everybody stared at him. He stood right by the mic with his guitar and hardly moved. He'd just bob his head front to back. The rest of the band would jump around and do what they had to do – not Peter. He stayed very still on stage. But he played incredible."

Poses recalls the other band members as, "Pretty nice, more outgoing than Pete. Tommy was crazy, Mike was in his own world, and Joey, well . . . he was always with Kathie. She would sit there and tell him he was the star of the show – not Peter, not Tommy. She'd say, 'Joey should be doing this' and 'Tommy should be doing this' and 'Why does Pete get to do this?' She would start arguments in the band. I could see they were getting irritated."

The band returned to England in mid-May 1971, and soon discovered that "Name Of The Game" had been rejected as a 45 release. The early April single mix by Al Kooper included extra tinkling piano, organ fills, and organ swoops, along with some noticeable reverb and flange effects. Apple had tagged it for a June, 1971 release (with "Suitcase" as the B-side), but the song's power was somewhat diluted by the ambitious new arrangement. Apple's Al Steckler deemed it unworthy for release. Another mix was completed by George Harrison and Phil Spector on April 23, 1971. It, too, was rejected.

The album was also being re-evaluated. Producer Geoff Emerick remembers, "I was getting annoyed, because I knew we'd done some good tracks, and people were hedging on them. It happens often when you present an album at a record company. There's all kinds of opinion and doubt. Bill Collins and the band kept going from this person to that person and he'd say, 'Oh, we played the tapes for so

Badfinger, 1971

and so last night and they said this.' I'm thinking, 'By God, at least have *some* faith in what you're doing.' "

Meanwhile, Emerick was becoming odd man out at the Apple U.K. offices. He was a part of the Apple Studios operation, which was now in its finishing stages. Because he was a good friend of Paul McCartney's, he says he was suspected by Klein of being a spy.

While waiting for a determination on the album's status, a phone call came into Badfinger's Park Avenue home. According to Joey Molland it was John Lennon's chauffeur. "He said, 'John Lennon's doing his new album and he wants to know if a couple of you guys could come down and play a little guitar?' We said, 'Well . . . you know . . . okay, I guess.' I mean who wants to go to John Lennon's house? I mean, 'Who cares?' It was a bit of a scene because, who was it going to be? Was it Pete and Tom? Or Tommy and Joey? Well, I was definitely going. That was it, I was gone. I mean this guy's the greatest writer we've had. It was quite difficult even getting dressed. . . .

"We cruised down to Lennon's place in Surrey. He had a beautiful estate there and his house was very different. Instead of paintings and things he had hammers and screwdrivers hanging on the wall in frames, black carpets everywhere. There was a stepladder where you climbed up and looked through a magnifying glass on the ceiling. It said, 'YES.' We spent about half an hour in a daze looking at all his stuff, the jukebox, the 'Sgt. Pepper' room, his magic stuff. . . .

"Finally, in walks John Lennon and he's really bug-eyed, really gone – *'Hello everybody!'* He was shouting. It was eleven o'clock at night and he'd just gotten out of bed. There was a bunch of people there: Nicky Hopkins, Klaus Voorman, Jim Keltner, Mike Pinder and he was really brusque with us, really almost rude, but not rude. I was just in awe, just ga-ga. Then he sits down on the stool and starts playing, 'Jealous Guy' and I'm so flabbergasted I can't play. He was singing and I'm literally astounded, 'It sounds like John Lennon.'

"So we recorded acoustic guitars on that and John said, 'You can fuck off now if you'd like.' Of course he wasn't being like, 'Fuck off.' It was like, 'Do what you like.' So they started playing 'I Don't Wanna Be A Soldier Mama' and me and Tommy were just hanging out. We just started to play along because we weren't about to move and let somebody throw us out. We didn't play it, we just started this 'doodley-do' kind of Bo Diddley strumming, because the song didn't seem to settle into any particular rhythm. And it ended up on the record. One of the most exciting nights of me life."

During the long U.S. tour, Pete and his girlfriend Dixie had gotten along well, but after the final show, they made no specific plans to stay together. Dixie recalls, "We realized we'd had a lot of fun, but I don't think Pete was ready to say, 'Come home with me.' We had a tearful goodbye, and agreed we'd keep in touch."

Soon after the band's return to England, word came that their album was being rejected, and Geoff Emerick would not be asked to salvage it. Said Bill Collins, "Geoff Emerick gave me the understanding that he was more than an engineer, that he could tell the difference between a good song and a bad song. But he couldn't, as far as I was concerned. I think he put the blame on me, but it wasn't a deliberate move as much as a consensus of the group's opinion and mine."

Joey Molland's memory was that Apple rejected the album because it was "too much like a beat group." Mike Gibbins says he was disappointed in losing it. "A lot of that material could have been done on stage and it would've sounded good. We could've reproduced it to a 'T.' "

Al Steckler: "Really, I wasn't thrilled with Geoff's work. He's a great engineer, but I didn't feel he had the ears to hear something commercial. I felt the group didn't have a real producer."

Steckler presented a new plan. "I told George Harrison about my feelings on the new album and he said, 'What would you like to do?' I said, 'Would you be willing to bring them into the studio?' And he said he would find some time to do it. And he did.' "

"I was made up when George came in," said Joey. "I had moved out of the house by then, and was writing tunes when I came to find out that Pete and George were

George Harrison

already working out new arrangements. I think George wanted to make our music more sophisticated."

The band and Harrison moved into Abbey Road Studios on May 30, 1971. They revamped "Name Of The Game" and, the next day, followed with a brand new version of "Suitcase." "The sound changed," said Joey. "George started all that. Klaus Voorman was there and he played electric piano on it. I just banged on me guitar."

George also initiated working on "I'd Die Babe," another Molland composition. "I was a little nervous about the lyrics," said Joey, "But George said, 'Don't worry about them.' It was kind of a silly song, but he had a lot of ideas for it. He plays some of the guitar on that, the low guitar riff, I think . . . When we were playing the song back in the studio, George was dancing around, and Leon Russell walked in behind him. George turned around and he seemed quite embarrassed. He really admired Leon."

George Harrison was making various impressions with the band members. "Pete just loved working with George," said Beverley. "He felt he learned a lot from him." Tom kept fairly low-key, while Mike found George to be "Aloof, very aloof. He didn't make you feel uncomfortable on purpose. It was just his Hare Krishna godliness. He tried to make us feel relaxed, but it never worked because he was such a mystic – you could never see the real George Harrison underneath all that fucking hair!"

The group had laid down basic tracks for Pete's "Day After Day" and "Name Of The Game." Now came time to flesh out the arrangements. Said Joey, "After we finished the backing track for "Day After Day" we knew we had to do the slide guitars on the front, and do the solos and do the fills. Pete and I were working on the slide and George said, 'Would you mind if I played on this?' I said, 'No man, sure, go ahead.' I mean this man's a Beatle, this man's a hero."

Recording the session that day was Abbey Road engineer Richard Lush. "Pete and George spent hours on that," he recalled. "They were playing their slide parts simultaneously. I remember thinking, 'There's an easier way to do this,' but George really wanted to do it that way."

The group was later monitoring playbacks when a familiar face again popped in – Leon Russell. Said Joey, "He listened to it and said, 'I could play a little piano on this. What do you think?'" Added Lush, "George got really excited. He leaned over to me and said, 'This guy's a genius. He's the best. We're lucky to have him.'"

The recording session was being held in Abbey Road's Studio #2, where the control room looks down onto the performance area. Lush continues, "Leon sat down and all you could see was the lid of this big top hat he was wearing. We ran the song by him and it was almost to the end when George said, 'Why isn't he playing? Are the mics on?,' because the engineer is always the first scapegoat. I assured him the mics were on and George felt sort of embarrassed. He wasn't sure what to say. Finally he comes on the intercom and says, 'Um . . . did you hear the track, Leon?' and Leon says, 'Yeah man, I'm just getting the vibe.' One pass later, the piano track was done." "It was perfect," said Joey. "Just knocks me out when musicians are that good."

Pete, Tom, Abbey Road Studios, 1971

Harrison had also played "Suitcase" for Russell, who then contributed a "carhorn" guitar. "It wasn't our band though," said Joey, "it was George's version of our band. I thought the original "Suitcase" was more of what Badfinger was. At least as I saw it."

When it came time to sing "Suitcase," Joey found his "Beatles nirvana" further eroding. "George came up to me and said, 'We can't have the second verse, the last line, 'Pusher, pusher.' I had written it about the dealers at all the gigs. They come in the dressing room and kind of show their drugs to you. That was 'pusher, pusher, on the run.' It was all about the game we'd been playing, and that was part of the theme of the song.

"Well George said, 'You can't have 'pusher, pusher' in the song.' He was thinking of the song in terms of a single. I was upset and he was right, they probably wouldn't have played it on the radio. Looking back, in 20/20 hindsight, I was being a bit of an asshole. I was a little surprised that George, who represented all that anti-authority, was telling me that I had to change it to get it played on the radio. It kind of alarmed me, so I changed the words to, 'butcher, butcher.' The message was clear."

Joey found his experience with George to be double-edged, "George is a great producer, more brilliant than you can imagine, but I was uptight working with him, mainly because he had his own ideas and I thought the band's ideas were getting altered and changed. We'd had two hits. I thought we deserved more regard for what we had achieved."

During many of the sessions, Joey's girlfriend, Kathie, attended. Said Marianne, "She would sit there all night and Tom would come back and say she was interfering. When they first started working with George she got really made up and wore a long dress. Tom told me, 'She made a complete fool of herself.' He was quite upset about it."

Kathie had no qualms about making her opinions known, and Harrison reportedly wasn't too thrilled to hear them, though Kathie maintains he complimented her a number of times. Said Fergie's wife, Anne, "The other girls didn't want to get involved at all. Kathie wanted to be involved in everything, even the music side of the band, like what to do on an album, the songs, all of it."

Kathie was becoming a stronger and stronger factor to the group. Around this time, Brian Slater came by the band's house for a visit. Just as he entered, his attention was taken. "I saw Kathie screaming up the stairs, *'I've had enough of all this! I want everyone down here right now for a meeting!'* Tom ran outside and said, 'Who the hell does she think she is? I'm not going to a meeting that *she's* called!' He was furious!"

Badfinger continued on with Harrison. He may have brought in a keyboardist to play on "Name Of The Game," as various recollections cite the piano player to be either Gary Wright or Pete Ham. Whoever it was, they laid down a superlative performance. Joey later lamented the lost original, but the new arrangement really brought out the delicate melody and introspective lyrics.

A short time before the recordings had started, Tim Boyle, Badfinger's friend and agent, had found out about a castle that was for lease in the Forest of Dean, South Wales. The place had been built in 1729, near the small town of Clearwell; basically a village with three inns, a spring, and an abandoned iron mine. Several fires had damaged the structure, but in 1954, a gentleman named Mr. Yeats had started reflooring and renovating the building. A few families had lived there, but Mr. Yeats was now looking for a new tenant.

The group had been feeling the pinch of their crowded Golders Green home. For months they had been talking about getting a space in which they could do their own rehearsing and recording. Bill Collins said it was the "hippie-commune era" and the group was into that ideal. With a reasonable rental price at hand, it became a unanimous decision to move into the castle (which was really a replicated version of a "true" one). The plan was to give it a six-month to one-year trial, with the hope the secluded setting might cut down on distractions and spark the band to new, creative heights.

When the group knew they were going to move in, both Mike and Tom had gone out a few days ahead of time to scout out their bedrooms. The castle had two large ones, the rest were much smaller. Tom and Mike laid claim to the biggest ones. "It was magic," says Mike. "I had a fabulous room with a balcony, bat ornaments, and big cathedral-like church windows. It was really cool."

By the time Joey and Kathie arrived they had to take one of the tinier rooms, which infuriated Kathie. "She wasn't happy at all," said Gaynor. "She immediately started locking herself in her room. There was nothing we could do. We had to get on with our lives."

Kathie's distress led her to toss garbage out her bedroom window into the castle gardens, which didn't set too well with the groundskeeper, Mr. Yeats. Joey was forced to collect the remains. "She was throwing moods for days," says Nicky Bell. "There wasn't much Joey could do about it."

Tim Boyle began working on converting the wine cellar into a permanent rehearsal and recording facility. Initially, the band rehearsed on the lawn outside. They could be heard for miles. Many curious townsfolk strolled up their path for a look-see, including one puzzled farmer who traveled countless acres in search of the "mysterious rumblings." As it turned out, the local villagers were quite taken with the castle's new tenants and were quite friendly.

Badfinger at Clearwell Castle

Bill Collins was still living at the Golders Green house in London, so the group could stay there when they had to be in London for business. It was an ideal situation for the band, one which could save them money in the long run.

While Badfinger had been away on their previous U.S. tour, Mike's wife, Gaynor, had called Beverley in England, just to let her know how things were going. Bev recalls, "Gaynor told me that she hadn't been feeling well so she had to get checked by a doctor. It turned out she was pregnant! I was so happy for her." But Beverley had been going through her own devastating personal trial. "I couldn't work, I couldn't function. I had to get away at one point. I ended up spending time in Spain with Sue Wing. She was trying to renew her life after her breakup with Dai Jenkins and we ended up making some friends there." Beverley admits she missed the emotional support Pete had provided. "Pete was such a good person to lean on. He was just as much a support system for me as I was for him. I really missed that."

From the time Pete had come back from the U.S. tour, Beverley hadn't spoken to him much. "I didn't want to complicate his life," she says. "But not too long after they moved into the castle, I did go over to visit them. Pete came up to me and said, 'Bev, would you come and listen to this song I've written?' I said, 'Okay' and he played me 'Day After Day.' I told him I really liked it and he said, 'You know what it's about, don't you?' I said, 'No.' And he said, 'Mike told me.' Apparently Gaynor had talked with Mike about me and he talked to Pete. Well, it took my breath away. I went pale. We just sat on the bed, held each other, and cried."

I remember finding out about you
Everyday my mind is all around you
Looking out of my lonely gloom
Day after day
Bring it home, baby make it soon
I give my love to you

I remember holding you while you sleep
Everyday I feel the tears that you weep
Looking out of my lonely room
Day after day
Bring it home, baby make it soon
I give my love to you

Beverley and Pete, 1971

In mid-July, George Harrison called a meeting and told Badfinger he had to go to New York to help set up a concert for Bangla Desh, "I've got to help Ravi [Shankar],' he told them. "I've got to split." The group waited and a few days later they got a phone call. George told them he would like the band to play at the charity concert. "Within six hours we were on a flight," said Pete. "The whole thing was put together very quickly." Joey later added, "We went to New York on Air India, and I nearly fell out the back on the way. They had these planes, the Constellation, and the back doors are flimsy. I'm riding the plane and I can see the air outside!"

The band arrived on Monday, July 26, 1971 and immediately went off to the Steinway facility on 59th Street to rehearse. At that point it was George, Ringo, Klaus Voorman, Billy Preston, and Badfinger. "We were asked to do what we did on the *All Things Must Pass* album," said Mike. "All I did was shake a tambourine and hit a cowbell now and then. There was no need for me to be there, but it was cool just the same. What I would've liked is to have played the drums. George had asked me if I didn't mind if I didn't play. I said, 'No man, I'm only here for the beer.' He laughed at that."

Joey, Pete, and Tom, Bangla Desh concert, August 1, 1971

Tom Evans: "During the week George was phoning up, trying to get people to come. There was hearsay that Dylan was coming, that Lennon was coming, that 'so-and-so' might be coming. But as the week went on, no one was showing up."

Eventually, other musicians did trickle in: Eric Clapton, Jim Keltner, Leon Russell, Jim Price, Jesse Ed Davis, back-up singers, horn players. George had wanted to recreate his record's big sound. Finally, the day came for a dress rehearsal at Madison Square Garden. "We were just hanging around afterwards, waiting for limos," said Joey, "and this guy walks onstage – acoustic guitar and harmonica. Who's that? The answer my friend is 'blowin' in the wind!' " Tom added, "Dylan went through about twenty or thirty songs and remembered all the words – it was amazing. Everyone was getting cold feet before that. . . From then on it started working. It got really elite, though, because everybody wanted to play with Dylan and a bit of backstabbing began. Klaus was playing bass and Leon said, 'Well, I'll do that.' There were some tense moments."

An afternoon and evening show had been scheduled for August 1, 1971. The day before, George Harrison told Pete he wanted to perform an acoustic duet of "Here Comes The Sun." Pete said in an interview, "George just said he wanted to keep it simple. He told me he used a capo on it and what changes were important. Then I went back to the hotel and listened to the *Abbey Road* tape. We never rehearsed it – no time!"

It seems inconceivable that George would put that much pressure on Pete, but he had the highest regard for Pete's playing abilities. George was soon to use Pete's guitar on "Blindman," a B-side for Ringo's single, "Back Off Boogaloo." Beverley recalls, "Pete was thrilled that someone he admired thought enough of him to do that stage spot at the Bangla Desh concert. It was really a buzz for him."

Pete played with George for each set, performing flawlessly, and Badfinger made their contribution to the hugely successful event. There were rumors that George *did* consider having Badfinger do a song, if some of the musicians hadn't shown, but the story has never been confirmed. Mike Gibbins has stated that at early rehearsals, Pete was singing "My Sweet Lord" with George.

After the event, a post-gig party was held at Unganos, and Badfinger was featured in a short set. "It erupted into a jam session," says Mike. "The Who were there, Phil Spector sang 'Da Do Ron Ron,' Keith Moon played drums and trashed the place. Everybody was there."

When Pete arrived back in England he didn't speak much about his experience onstage with George, as it had been tempered by some ribbing from Joey and Kathie. "They had gotten on Pete about the fact that it was him who got that solo spot with George, not Joey," said Beverley. "Pete told me that he thought Joey was quite pissed about it. Because of that he couldn't enthuse. Pete was very sensitive to accusations of putting himself ahead of the group."

Joey and Pete

Pete Ham responded the best way he knew. "He wrote about it in a song," says Beverley. This was the one arena where Pete could be himself, where he could let his emotions run free, and not impinge on someone else's space. The impassioned tune he wrote was later recorded by the band, "Take It All": {Take It All - Pete demo}

In a way, the sun has shone on me
Makes it easy to make it hard
Take an inch, take a yard, take it all
I don't need it at all. . . .

Any day, the sun will shine on you
Makes it silly to take it bad
Make it good, take it glad, take it all
I don't need it at all
I don't want it at all
No, no, no

Back on January 15, 1971, the front page of the *New York Times* had featured a story on an investigation of possible impropriety by a prominent New York State Supreme Court Justice, Mitchell D. Schweitzer. The investigation had been going on for about a year when a Nathan Voloshen was finally indicted for "influence peddling," which basically means paying people off for favors. Voloshen tied Judge Schweitzer into a series of incidents, dating as far back as 1960, indicating he could be "bought for the right price."

By mid '71 a series of related people had been questioned and Judge Schweitzer could not fully deny his acquaintance with a majority of them, including Voloshen. On July 22, 1971, the New York Times headlines read, "*$25,000 Schweitzer Bribe Alleged By Senate Witness*." The story reported that *another* witness, whose name was withheld for protection, had stepped forward during the investigation to report that, in 1955, he paid the judge $25,000 in order to get a light sentence on a grand larceny charge. The witness stated that the night before he was to be sentenced, a man, "well-connected with organized crime," drove him to a hotel in the Bronx, took his money, and in plain view, handed the money over to Judge Schweitzer in the hotel lobby. He also named the alleged "bagman" – *Stan Polley!*

"The report was on the 11 o'clock news," said Five Arts member Charlie Calello, "and the phones were ringing off the hook. I saw Polley the next day and he denied it, but he was clearly shaken up. He was hoping to go public with our company and this was obviously going to hurt him. I saw Terry Harvey (Polley friend and former police chief) telling him to get himself together. Harvey said, 'Look, these kids are depending on you. This is something from a long time ago. It will go away.' So now I'm thinking, 'Stan may not be all he's pumped up to be.' I mean, if you're a 'bagman' for the Mafia, how high up do you go?"

The news item had come out four days before Badfinger's arrival for the Bangla Desh concert, and follow-up newspaper stories over the next few days revealed further accusations that Polley had, *again*, in 1961, acted as "bagman" in yet *another* $25,000 bribe taken by Justice Schweitzer; this time in return for easy parole conditions for one Michael Raymond. But Polley's name did not appear in a couple of articles written just after Badfinger arrived in town, and all indications are, the band and Bill Collins had no clue of this commotion.

After Badfinger had returned to England from the Bangla Desh concert, they found out George Harrison would not be finishing their album; they needed to get a new producer. While this was being sorted out, they continued to write and rehearse at the castle. Previously, while the band was in New York, Tim Boyle had continued working on tightening up the sound of the castle's reverberant wine cellar. He also procured a 4-track machine. The group had wanted to get an 8-track, but Joey indicated their request had been turned down. Then one day, Stan Polley showed up.

Fergie recalls, "Polley came in this beautiful big limousine that he had picked up in London. He told us he was taking us out to the best restaurant in town. For Clearwell that was basically a small inn. His wife was with him, but for some reason she didn't want to go out with us. She stayed back at the castle with my mother, who was visiting. We went out and Polley talked and talked about money, about how the group was going to become very rich. He was really convincing. He

Badfinger, 1971

said, 'Your money problems are over.' When we got back, my mother came up to me and said, 'Stan Polley's wife was talking to me and she said, "You've got to get the boys away from my husband. He's not good for them." ' I mentioned it to the band, but what could they do?"

Around this time, Pete did purchase an old Jaguar X150. The vehicle needed renovating, but it was still drivable. Pete drove it home one weekend and everyone in Swansea was quite impressed. Coming back to Clearwell, he got caught up in the excitement of the sporty vehicle and had a blow-out at high velocity. But somehow he avoided a collision. He later told Gaynor that at the speed he was going, it was a miracle he survived.

The band members' salaries were supposed to be up to about £50 a week now, but the funds did not get to them consistently. Pete's personal bank account rarely exceeded £10 over the next four and one-half months. But Pete loved being in Clearwell, and he seemed quite happy overall. The wide open spaces made it ideal for visitors. Besides relatives and close acquaintances, the band hosted a number of musicians, including the entire Man band on occasion. Man had released three albums by this point, with songs sometimes up to twenty minutes long. Deke

Leonard, one of the group's lead guitarists, fondly recalls his group's visits with Badfinger. "We used to jam with them whenever we got together. Clearwell was ideal for that, we'd go in the cellar and have a blow. It was a great time.

"One time we came over and the place was full of Ovation guitars. Apparently the band had received them at the Bangla Desh concert. Pete said the Ovation representatives were handing out models to the musicians because the product had just come out. Apparently, Dylan had played one and didn't like it, so he put it down. He wasn't going to take it, so Pete asked if he could have it. Dylan said, 'Sure, go ahead.' I picked up the guitar and I was playing it and Pete said, 'Dylan played that.' I said, 'Really, mate!' I quite liked that. He said, 'Go on, you can have it.'

"The man was generous to a fault. When they lived in London we had visited and it came up in the conversation that my electric piano was on the blink. Pete said, 'Here, take my Hohner piano. Go ahead. Use it as long as you want.' I ended up with it for three years, I think, and Pete never pushed for it back. . . ."

Badfinger spent much of August and September putting together new material. One day they were asked to do a gig in Iceland with the Man band. Iceland was practically virgin territory for established rock acts, as only Led Zeppelin had played there before. On September 17, 1971, Badfinger, Man, and Scotland's Writing On The Wall flew in to the capital city of Reykjavik. Deke Leonard recounts the setting. "The guys were short and ruddy, but the women were tall and Nordic, just beautiful. And it was about a two-to-one ratio of girls to guys. As soon as we arrived they were just strolling up and offering themselves. We go in broom closets, toilets, anywhere we could. The Icelandic blokes were real ratty about it and would want to fight with us. It was an odd place. Beer was illegal, yet spirits weren't! And dogs had not been legalized. There was an underground society of dog owners!"

George Harrison, Pete Ham, official opening of Apple Studios, August, 1971

Deke Leonard

Man drummer Terry Williams recalls the local hospitality. "The mayor of Reykjavik invited everyone to a club and since we couldn't have beer we just said, 'We'll have what's going round.' So they put four bottles of Scotch on the table. I noticed people were a lot drunker there."

Deke continues, "Some Iceland band was playing at the club and during their break they asked if we'd like to jam. We were reluctant, but I finally went up to play. The guitar had a string so loose it was resting on the fretboard. It must have slipped off the saddle or something. Anyway I started playing a solo on this string and it sounded terrible. Only one sound would come out, 'Di-dank, di-dank.' I was taking the piss out of it. I came off-stage and the owner of the guitar started picking on me for making fun of it. I said something like, 'Get real, mate.' He decided he didn't like that, so he started scuffling with me. Somehow we all spilled out into the road and this huge melee formed."

Man bassist Martin Ace picks up: "They have to be the worst fighters in the world. They would put themselves into a boxing stance: fists up, legs spread, Queensbury rules and all, while we would go after them boots, legs, knees, and hands."

Deke finishes, "At one point I was growing tired and I stepped outside the fray to watch. I was looking in and I saw Bill Collins in the middle of this pile. Some chap was going to hit him, so I went in to stop the guy. I started one of those punches that begins in Mississippi, gathers speed in St. Louis, and by the time it gets to New York City, it's really burning. Suddenly this guy ducks, Bill pops up, and 'Wham!' I hit Bill right in the solar plexus! Everyone stopped. They were in stitches, even Pete and Mickey [Mike]. They were trying to hide their laughter. They didn't want Bill to see them."

Later on that night, Deke Leonard and Nicky Bell were returning to the hotel with two "Icelandic birds" when a few of the local men showed up at the entrance. "They were boyfriends of some of the girls we'd had our way with earlier," says Deke, "and they challenged us to a fight. This one fellow with thick, Buddy Holly-type glasses, went into one of those corny fighting stances and Nicky walloped the poor chap right in the kisser. His glasses split in two and fell to the pavement. The guy was stunned. Then he got doused by this waterfall of cold water from a second floor window. I look up, and there's Tommy laughing hysterically – with a metal trash can in his hands!"

Badfinger needed a producer to finish up their album. Al Steckler of Apple recalls, "A friend of mine, Paul Mozian, who had previously worked as Allen Klein's assistant, knew Todd Rundgren. I knew of Todd's reputation as a producer, so I called Mozian and I told him of the situation with Badfinger. He said he would speak to Todd. Then Todd's manager Albert Grossman came into the picture."

Rundgren met with Steckler and Grossman. "I had heard Badfinger's two hits," said Rundgren, "and I liked the songs and the production. I was definitely interested." The band itself was unfamiliar with his work. "None of us knew who he was," said Mike Gibbins. "We'd never heard his records."

At this point, Rundgren had distinguished himself mainly through his solo work, particularly with the song "We Gotta Get You A Woman." He'd also recently helped mix The Band's *Stage Fright* LP. Badfinger loved everything about The Band, in fact they'd attended their London Albert Hall concert just months before, but it's not clear if they were aware Rundgren had worked with them. Todd's memory is that his reputation as a fast worker helped. "I seem to remember that was a factor in getting hired," he says, "I was told that Badfinger had been trying to get an album done for about eight months, and it wasn't getting done to everyone's satisfaction."

Rundgren was eventually hired and flown over to England. Recording engineer Bill Price was present when he met the band. "The Badfinger lads were usually pretty easy-going," said Price, "but when Todd walked in to the studio they pretty much went into shock. He had green and lavender streaked hair, unheard of at the time, and a multi-colored zebra-stripe suit!"

Todd Rundgren began to work at a feverish pace and the band was taken aback. Rundgren recalls, "I had been told by Apple I had carte blanche to finish the album however I wanted. In other words, I could discard, use, or revamp any old material. George Harrison came a few days after we started and handed me tapes. He said, 'Do anything you want with them.' "

Despite the fact they had to bounce from studio to studio, Todd was able to keep the momentum going. Mike: "Todd was the fastest, zippiest producer we ever had. He was bam-o, bam-o. He did a good job with the drum sounds. They didn't sound that good on the tapes George had done and he beefed them up. He came into one studio and told the engineer to take the day off, even the tape operator. The guy was a wizard behind the board. I was really impressed."

Todd Rundgren

But not all was well. Behind the scenes was a growing discontent. "Todd was too intense," said Joey. "For me he was very difficult to work with, very rude." Pete also expressed dissatisfaction at Todd's strong hand, "His ideas restricted a lot of our own creativity. If you start leaning too heavily on a producer he tends to become integrated with the band . . . he'll start wanting to implement his own ideas, which, of course, may not be those of the band."

"They were kind of awestruck," said roadie Fergie. "It was quite a change from Mal and Geoff, where they had a lot of say. The band were all budding producer-types anyway. They would argue and bitch amongst themselves. But they didn't express it directly to Todd."

Todd: "Whatever their opinions were musically, they were probably expressed with greater emphasis before I got there. They had failed to complete a record for nine months, and were probably considerably more docile by the time I came in. There's always a lot of politics involved in making records. And unless something gets really ugly, or there is some particular altercation, I consider it part of doing business. My agenda at the time was the record had to be finished. It wasn't going to be a long, tortuous road. Maybe it got that someone didn't get their two cents in, but this wasn't expressed to my face."

Todd recalls Pete as, "Quiet, the least aggressive in the band. He never had an agenda he was pushing and seemed most open to ideas. Mike was the happy-go-lucky guy. Joey was the most aggressive. But it wasn't a situation of pulling teeth or anything. They usually performed everything within a reasonable amount of takes. They were all good singers. I remember the singing went down quickly."

What is noticeable about the songs Todd produced *is* the very strong vocal performances. He coaxed Tom, Joey, and Pete to the peak of their vocal potential. On "Take It All," Pete and Tom sing brilliantly. The studio version is slower than Pete's original demo, and features keyboards prominently. The use of organ and piano ended up permeating many of the new recordings, possibly a newly-infused influence of The Band's sound.

"Money" was re-cut, but Rundgren kept the earlier Emerick version of "Flying" and continued to bridge the two as a medley. "Todd changed the key," said Joey. "He was obsessed with keeping them together. That's why my voice is sped up higher than I can sing."

"Perfection" was started again from scratch. Pete initially laid down an acoustic guitar. "Pete's tempo was inconsistent," said Joey, "so Todd came up with the idea of percussion overdubs to disguise it." Rundgren even enlisted the help of roadie Nicky Bell, who revealed, "Todd had us get anything we could pick up . . . rattle, scrape, knock . . . everybody was playing on it."

Rundgren's choice of material was generally of a mid-tempo to ballad pacing. The only out-and-out rocker was "Sometimes." Since rock'n'roll was such a large part of Badfinger's current live set, the lack of such songs did leave the band frustrated. "We knew what we wanted to do," said Joey, "but we didn't know how to get it. I was too freaked out at the time. We worked for Todd."

Todd remembers things this way, "I had arrangement suggestions but they seemed to have the material pretty well-rehearsed, so I didn't change much. I thought the songs were well-written, good English-style pop songs. Pete's writing especially had a sensibility, an obvious commercial bent."

He couldn't have been more correct, as the group was soon to find out.

One day, the band was working at Air Studios. Down the hallway, in a different studio from their own, was an American artist named Harry Nilsson. He just happened to be covering one of their songs. "I was shocked to find out Badfinger were there," said Nilsson. "We were just completing our final mix of the song that day. I had someone rush out and get some food and wine. We set up a spread in the control room and then I went in and invited the Badfinger boys over. They were pretty shy. After a while I said, 'I have a surprise for you.' We turned the lights down and played the song full blast. Then we turned the lights up and they were just looking at each other, then at us, back at each other . . . they were stunned!"

Right after hearing it, Pete strolled back to the studio he'd been working in. In the hallway he stopped Fergie in his tracks. Fergie recalls, "Pete's eyes were huge! He said, 'There's some guy down the hall doing one of our songs, and it sounds *amazing*!' "

The song was "Without You," a Tom Evans and Pete Ham composition from the *No Dice* album. Pete later recalled, "As soon as we heard it, we knew that was the way we wanted to do it, but never had the nerve." Tom added, "We were totally paranoid of doing it that way. Nilsson's version really showed what you can do with a song, production-wise, and with a good singer. It blew me away."

Harry Nilsson was still an up-and-coming artist at this time; having had one Top Ten hit with "Everybody's Talkin'." He was more acclaimed as a songwriter, having written "One," a big American hit for Three Dog Night, and other songs, as covered by a variety of artists such as The Monkees, The Turtles, Lulu, and Mary Hopkin. Pete was familiar with him through his solo albums, which Pete quite liked.

Nilsson later explained how he came to cover the song "Without You." "I was at a party in Laurel Canyon in L.A. and me and some friends were all sitting around smoking joints. Around three A.M. someone played this song and it stuck in my mind. The next day I called my friend and said, 'What was that song last night that sounded like a McCartney song?' I hummed the melody, but he didn't know what I was talking about. I couldn't get it out of my head. I was leafing through my Beatle collection and then it came to me, 'It's Grapefruit, that's it! One of those groups the Beatles helped out.' So I told someone and they said, 'No, it couldn't have been them, maybe it was Badfinger.'

"Eventually I found the record and played the song over and over. Then I called Richard Perry, who was supposed to be producing my album, and I said, 'Look, I've found this song. I think it's a number one. You've got to hear it!' He came over and heard it and said, 'God, I think you're right. It's a killer!'

"When we started the album that was the only song we had. We came over to England to record it and I tried it in one key and nearly got hemorrhoids singing it. We changed that and decided that the keyboard part was too busy, too complex. So we replaced Rick Wakeman with Gary Wright and he began, just like you hear it on the record, very simple. It was just right!"

Back at the Rundgren sessions, "Sweet Tuesday Morning" was touched up with organ, Bill Collins on accordion, and plucked acoustic guitars. A new number, "It's Over," was Tom's response to the completion of the band's previous American tour.

Then there was "Baby Blue." Pete had composed the song for Dixie, the girl he'd met on the previous tour. He later explained, "I hadn't seen her for a few months and I thought she was angry for me not writing or calling." Pete's words are basically written as a letter to her:

Guess I got what I deserved
Kept you waiting there too long, my love
All that time without a word
Didn't know you'd think that I'd regret
Or I'd forget
The special love I have for you
My baby blue

A melancholy big-beat ballad, "Baby Blue" is a superb showcase of Badfinger's classic chemistry. As Pete gets ready to sing the song's stirring verse one, ascending and descending guitar lines dance around Mike's Spectorish drumbeat intro. Eventually Tom joins Pete, for some dynamite dual lead vocals. A punchy fuzz-rhythm guitar also finds its perfect foil in Joey's ultra-tight, concise guitar solos. The group *knew* this one was a winner.

The band added more overdubs to "Day After Day" and "Name Of The Game." Todd then took the twelve songs back to New York to be mixed. Badfinger had spent two hard-working weeks with him and were not especially happy to be left out of this important final stage.

Rundgren explains, "I'd had some bad experiences back then, having bands at the final mix. As a producer you get stuck between a rock and a hard place. The drummer hears the drums, the guitar player hears the guitar, they all want their parts louder. When everything turns into a mess, everyone complains. If you have one member that everyone respects, that can be valuable."

But Badfinger didn't have a particular leader, so they stuck with Rundgren's decision. The band next went to Clearwell Castle for a much needed break.

For most of the group and their families, the atmosphere was "paradise." Marianne recalls, "It was away from show business, away from the crazy people. We were like a big family. We played games every night, strolled the grounds, we did things together." Fergie adds, "It was great, there was peace and tranquility, lots of open space – everyone was relaxed and at ease."

The group did record many four-track demos in their makeshift basement studio, which was under continual construction. They also rehearsed for a new tour. Todd finally sent them a copy of the completed album in November. Nicky Bell recalls, "As far as I remember they were pretty knocked out." Beverley remembers Pete was quite happy with Todd's mix. Mike says, "He did a good job." But Joey claims he was discontented. "It doesn't sound like Badfinger at the time. The vocals are there, and he got some nice guitar sounds, but *No Dice* was more real."

For the LP package, the group again requested that Gene Mahon and Richard DiLello do the job. Tom had come up with a title, *Straight Up*. "We wanted to create a David Bailey, early Rolling Stones-type of thing," said DiLello. "The look was 'straight up.' " Gene Mahon explained, "David Bailey was an English fashion photographer who did portraits of personalities during the swinging 60s. My contribution was to say, 'Let's put nothing on but them,' and to make sure the photo would fit inside a square cover."

What they ended up with was a close-up of the band members standing while wearing brown leather and suede jackets. Each member of the group has a blank stare on their face. There's no title on the front. But somehow, the overall effect is striking.

Straight Up LP Cover

Apple Records selected "Day After Day" as the new worldwide single, and in mid-November, they released it in the United States. By December 4, 1971, it had entered the *Billboard* charts and quickly started to climb. On December 13th, *Straight Up* came out. It too, was lapped up by the American Christmas-time buyers. The outlook was good. Meanwhile, Badfinger had an important decision to make. After nearly six months of staying at Clearwell Castle, the band was suddenly given an option. The owner wanted to sell. The castle could be theirs for £30,000.

"It was such a nice place," said Gaynor. "It was definitely considered. There was the outdoor life, the band could unwind, they had their studio they were building there in the basement . . . I had my child there; it was a great place for kids. We had a great time." Mike agrees, "That was the best part of my Badfinger experience, living there, but Joey would tell you different. He hated the joint. And Kathie hated it, too."

"Joey didn't want to stay," says Beverley. "He and Kathie were city-oriented people. I don't think it appealed to them. Pete was very happy there, and Tom was really happy, but without Joey's share, the others didn't think they could afford it."

Failing to get Joey's consent, any plans to purchase the castle were out of the question. It was decided everyone would leave. "What was frustrating," said Marianne in 1995, "is that the price of the castle went way up after we left. In fact, it's worth well over one million pounds today!"

6

Money For Fun

Toward the latter part of December 1971, Badfinger played a sprinkling of dates around the United Kingdom. For the Christmas holidays each member visited their family homes. Tom was upset about having to leave Clearwell. He'd enjoyed the castle; his relationship with Marianne had flourished; he'd grown closer to the band members, roadies, and his friends, especially Tim Boyle. "If there was one person who really understood Tom, it was Tim," said Beverley. Boyle had been doing odds-and-ends for the group since 1967. While living with them at the castle he was known to use his meal allowance to buy extra supplies for the studio he was building, as management was not very forthcoming with funds.

"Bill Collins disliked Tim," said Fergie. "He always perceived him as a threat. But Tim was just a go-getter, an honest guy who liked helping the band." Boyle had once found the group the opportunity of some film soundtrack work, which included composition of the incidental music (something Pete was very interested in doing), but because it was Tim who found it, Collins allegedly vetoed its possibility.

January '72 brought news that "Day After Day" was exploding on the charts worldwide. England's *Melody Maker* made a feature review of its release: *"A song for those troubled in heart and mind. It has a cooling quality and as a love song has strength and optimism. One of those occasional productions that make the business of pop singles worthwhile. And it should make number one."* As it was, the song received minimal U.K. promotion, and it only made it to #10. Yet the group did get to perform it on English TV's *Top Of The Pops* twice, once with Mike wearing a three-foot-long blonde wig!

Late in the month, a scathing review of *Straight Up* appeared in *Rolling Stone* magazine. It didn't set well with the band, but for Joey, there had been a bit of vindication. "What I got from the review was that the band had been fucked with and altered, which I agreed with. At the same time I was brought down a bit." The write-up had been done by Mike Saunders, who had previously raved over *No Dice*. This time Saunders complained, *"The result here is self-consciousness in place of spontaneity, solemnity in place of former exuberance, and a general all-around deadness where infectious energy was once the rule . . . that magic scooby-doo is gone."*

Tim Boyle

Protest letters streamed in to *Rolling Stone*. The magazine printed one from Tim Noe which stated: "Straight Up *isn't disappointing at all and is well worth the year's wait. Everything good about* Magic Christian Music *and* No Dice *is in the album if one will listen, which Mike Saunders obviously didn't do. The quality of the songwriting is the best ever (especially Joey Molland's) and the album has 'magic' beyond the old scooby-doo of rock'n'roll. I've never been more pleased with an album.*"

Saunders, who later played in the punk and parody outfit, Angry Samoans, did have a valid point in that a side of Badfinger had been tailored down. There is not a lot of "rock'n'roll spirit," as he interpreted it. But the majority of people took the album for what it was, an impeccably crafted pop production, and enjoyed it on that level. Interestingly, what Saunders decried the most was his hope that Badfinger would continue to bridge the *"joyous sound of pop-ish rock and roll with a real hard rock sound,"* something he said, *"If anyone does . . . will be a real milestone of an event."* What he is loosely describing is "power-pop," a term coined in the late 70's to characterize the sound of aggressive, guitar-based, pop songs. The term has since been diluted to cover just about *any* material reminiscent of a 60s Beatle-ish sound, but in early 1972, "true" power-pop was nearly non-existent. There were still no records out by the Raspberries, Big Star, or some of the era's other well-known proponents of an occasional "power-pop" blast. Thus Badfinger, with their hit, "No Matter What," may have had the first, easily-defined example of this genre.

With *Straight Up*, the group had essentially created an extension of *No Dice*; a collection of three to four minute tunes using the talents and chemistry of four individuals who had similar musical inspirations. It was Todd Rundgren who made the decision to go with a majority of slower to mid-tempo numbers, and to his credit, he did a phenomenal job of putting an album together.

Today, the LP is described as a "classic," but at the time, reviews were generally guarded. Most of the write-ups cited the Beatles influence in a positive way, but were careful not to portray the band as anything more than decent purveyors of a "good era gone by."

> KANSAS CITY STAR *A thorough listening demonstrates that Badfinger's music is more like a logical extension of the Beatles sound from the days before the plucky lads went through their psychedelic electronic studio tricks . . .*

> CIRCUS *. . . "Day After Day" has the satisfying feeling that used to be achieved when a Paul McCartney track would sneak in between two Lennon cuts . . . in fact the entire album has a Beatle feel . . . This isn't to say the music is bad. In fact, the sound is nourishment for the famished ear, especially the ear that's been starving for something Liverpudlian.*

> STEREO REVIEW *With this album Badfinger grows. The vocals haven't changed much . . . remaining more coarse-grained but almost identical in harmonic texture to those of the early Beatles, but the instrumentals have gone from middle-ground rock to sophisticated rock. . . .*

> SCENE MAGAZINE *It's almost like listening to a before and after "Sgt. Pepper" Beatle album. . . . all of (the songs) employ the same harmonics, dynamics and phrasing (not to mention guitar solos) that the Beatles did years ago. However, for all concerned about conceptual originality, they will have to take a back seat . . . the music is very good . . . If* only *McCartney or Lennon had written some of these songs.*

"Day After Day" did very well in America, reaching #1 on the *Cashbox* sales charts late in January. Eventually it went "gold" (one million sales), peaking on the *Billboard* list at #4. Harry Nilsson's version of "Without You," released around this time, also showed signs of imminent success.

The group started working with Todd Rundgren on a new album in January. The *Straight Up* album was showing rapid signs of financial success, and even though the group felt somewhat constricted under his hand, they did give it another shot. It was a doomed partnership this time around.

The sessions started at Apple Studios on January 17, 1972. Two Joey Molland compositions were concentrated on, "The Winner" and "I Can Love You," though other basics were allegedly cut as well. Todd recalls, "I really liked a lot of the material they played me, but after a few days problems started coming to a head. While we were working, my management and I were simultaneously negotiating

Todd Rundgren

with Apple to try and make sure what happened on the *Straight Up* LP didn't happen again. The songs I had revamped had been credited to George Harrison, including the big hit single, "Day After Day." George had originally said, 'Take the tapes, do anything you want.' I should have had credit and been paid for those tracks. My impression is the band got involved in the new negotiations. It wasn't clear to me, but I think they got the impression I was being greedy in what I was asking for. They should not have been involved. They didn't know the first thing about business. So between our dissatisfaction, Apple's, and the band's, I ended up leaving the project. It's too bad. I thought it could've been a very exciting record."

Todd lasted less than a week. Four studio dates are confirmed in the Apple Studio logs. They show the following week's sessions as being "canceled."

For Joey Molland, the experiences of working with Harrison and Rundgren left a bitter taste. He explained to writer Ken Sharp in 1994, "We had these guys coming in telling us how to play. Actually telling us words to songs. That's the last thing any group needs to be successful. They don't need anybody messing with their music, messing with their words, messing with their people, with their characters; they don't need that. Musicians need their freedom. Once you get successful at what you do, nobody should fuck with you at all. But they do."

In early February, the group went off to do their third U.S. tour. *Straight Up* was selling solidly, but promotion was spotty at best. Badfinger needed to make a strong impression on the road. In preparation, the band worked up three songs from the new album: "Take It All," "Day After Day," and "Sweet Tuesday Morning," besides re-rehearsing the two they previously performed, "Sometimes" and "Suitcase." The latter became *really* extended. Joey explained, "We were practicing 'Suitcase' and we went into this big psychedelic jam. I remember everybody was quite excited by it because it was very outside our pop songs. We were looking to get into that stuff and be a jammy band. That's what we wanted to do."

The tour began on February 3, 1972, with two sets at the Fenway Theater in Boston, Massachusetts. William Kowinski did a massive newspaper write-up of the event and Beatle connections prefaced his every thought: *"There were those who had come not only in response to a hit single or to three moderately successful albums, but for something else, something beyond or buried within the partial but evocative resemblances of Badfinger to the most charismatic group in history . . . With the Beatles gone . . . might there still be a reservoir of magic?. . . I came looking for a Beatle illusion; I left touched and sustained by the reality of Badfinger."*

Kowinski went on to give specific appraisals, even citing the group's engaging personalities from a post-gig interview. But he also pointed out what he perceived as two numbed, unappreciative audiences.

Following their initial Boston gigs, Badfinger played the Paramount Theater in Springfield, Massachusetts. An audience tape of their first set reveals the band sounding a bit loose, but very fresh, as the vocals and playing were exceedingly invigorated. But when the band came to play their new hit, Tom introduced it by mumbling, "We're gonna do 'Day After Day'. . . see how it turns out." They were obviously insecure about performing it. "If we could've gotten away with not doing it, we wouldn't have done it," said Joey. "It's a hell of a song to do with a four-piece group on stage." Mike added, "Because of the production we couldn't go out and reproduce it, or many other songs on the album. We didn't have the piano, the acoustics, or the big-sounding background vocals."

Even though Badfinger's act could have benefited from an additional musician, the group was reluctant to be perceived as the smoothly-produced pop purveyors of *Straight Up*. They wanted to boogie, rock-out, and blues-it-up a little. They still performed "Feelin' Alright," and it had evolved into an even *more* improvisational arrangement, as Pete was really showing his mastery of the wah-wah pedal in an effort to make something fresh out of the restrictive two-chord pattern of the song. Dave Mason's "Only You Know And I Know" had also been added to their set, and

Badfinger, U.S. tour #3, 1972

to their credit, Badfinger exploded for this number. During "We're For The Dark," Joey played his electric guitar leads with a mellow tone, while rapidly soloing over Pete's Martin acoustic. The entire band went acoustic for "Sweet Tuesday Morning," with Mike playing congas. Though generally well-received, Mike felt the latter two songs hurt the show's momentum. "We'd get going and then I'd have to suddenly stop and get warmed up all over again. I thought it wasn't solid-sounding. It was okay, but other artists do an acoustic set and it rocks!"

A few weeks into the tour, Badfinger played F&M College in Pennsylvania, and this time they received a terrible review from a writer who perceived them as *"another group to enter the annals of crappy acid-rock."* Unlike Boston, this scribe was perplexed by the "fanatical" reaction the band got.

Bill Collins said he felt the group had been losing sight of their greatest strengths — their songs: "I didn't like the band doing so much jamming, and the all the covers. That was mostly Tommy's influence. I know that Pete would've done 'Without You' and more songs from the albums. But the band weren't so interested in my suggestions by this time. The "team" was breaking apart."

Badfinger were certainly creating mixed emotions. Scott McGaughey, later of the band Young Fresh Fellows, recalls his second opportunity to view the group in late February. "They opened with Steve Miller's 'My Dark Hour' and did a couple of Dave Mason songs. It was good, but there were so many great songs of their own to play. I don't think they gave themselves enough credit for having fans. They did a fantastic succession of songs from *Straight Up* and then came out to do an encore of 'Johnny B. Goode!' It was like, 'Well that's pretty cool, I guess, but. . . .' "

Another gig led to similar sentiments from the *Chicago Tribune: "The catchiness that makes some of Badfinger's songs a delight was there, but in between were the rest*

– okay. After an acoustic set they continued full force . . . finishing with a long jam and the rock'n'roll finale that everyone seems to be driving into the ground."

Badfinger was feeling the peer pressure of an expanding scene. They were playing with bands such as Grand Funk, King Crimson, The Doors, Canned Heat, Pure Prairie League, Rare Earth, Alice Cooper, War, and Deep Purple. Roadie Nicky Bell recalls, "People were getting into the heavier scenes – metal rock, superstars, super bands. They were as capable of jamming as anyone, but they didn't have the black leather jackets, hair down to their waist, exploding drum kits, smoke machines . . . Their songwriting style wasn't in vogue." Mike adds, "Our albums were considered like twelve potential singles tied together. At that point bands were making albums you'd get high to listen to. People weren't going to smoke a joint and say, 'Yeah, let's go and get the fucking Archies album!' They'd go and get Pink Floyd!"

Despite the fact Badfinger's records bucked the trends, they were obviously coming up in the music business. Badfinger played the Whiskey-A-Go-Go in Los Angeles on February 21, 22, and 23, 1972, each night performing double sets. "These were pretty nerve-racking gigs," said roadie Nicky Bell. "All the industry people were there, and other musician peers of the time. Just before they let people in, Keith Moon gets onstage and starts whacking Mike's drums. He's knocking cymbals all over the place and he tore up the bass drum. Fergie and I just freaked. Luckily his roadie turned up with a new bass drum, minutes before the set."

The group's tension was great. "Their nervousness would manifest in different ways," said Nicky, "Tommy would get fucked up. Joey would be jumpy. Pete would vanish into the toilet. Mike would, as drummers do, be fiddling and tapping away. But they pulled the shows off, they always did."

Phonograph Record Magazine, a strong supporter of melodic rock music, assigned writer Mark Leviton to cover Badfinger and see their Whiskey shows. He prepared a cover story for their May issue. Titled "Badfinger At The Crossroads," the article came off as a bit of a character study and "peek behind the scenes." After a historical rundown, obligatory Beatles comparisons, and a review of the band's stage show, Leviton began to delve into their personal views:

> *Pete Ham feels a lack of control over the basic logistic problems involved in getting the group organized and accounted for, financially and otherwise. For instance, Pete has complaints about equipment. He would like to play certain numbers in the band's live act, which is as much a part of Badfinger as their recordings, but the lack of a suitable piano pickup restricts the amount of slow numbers that can be played with adequate sound . . . therefore they project the image of a powerful rock band much more than Pete might want them to . . . "We're For The Dark" manages to be played at nearly every concert, but the splendid "Take It All" is used sparingly due to poor piano reproduction, and "Without You" is not performed.*

Badfinger, U.S. tour #3, 1972

It was in every venue contract that a piano had to be provided, but many times the band were given shoddy, second-hand set-ups. Without their own, they were at each promoter's mercy. Even when they received a good quality set of keys there was something else to contend with. "We used to have this old microphone that went across all the sections of strings," says Fergie. "It was in five pieces and the object was to get as close to the strings as possible without touching. It was difficult to keep it stable and I remember one time it came down and was touching the strings while Pete was playing. It had happened before, but this time he got mad and just ripped the whole thing out of the piano."

Pete was quoted several times during the year about his frustrations with faulty equipment and the miking of acoustic instruments. But he also defended the band vigorously on a number of occasions when they were criticized as being "boring" or "boogie-heavy."

In the *Phonograph* article, Leviton noted the group's complaints about Rundgren and their hopes to produce themselves in the future. But he especially focused on Pete and Tom's tension over the live act:

> *Evans further expresses his belief that audiences like, and almost demand, some good "boogie" music in the course of an evening's show, and he's more than willing to provide it . . . The strong rock format is partially precipitated by those equipment problems Pete speaks about, but it's also partially due to the group's undeniable fondness for early rock'n'roll.*

> *But after a particularly poor performance in L.A. recently (the sound system was wholly inadequate, hampering severely the group's abilities to hear each other on stage), Pete Ham said angrily,* "Okay, we're not doing 'Feelin' Alright' anymore! Let's stop foolin' ourselves!" *Fooling themselves because the audience barely reacted to the long jam that evening; fooling themselves because Pete's conception of Badfinger is something more than a boogie band.*

Leviton finished the article citing the group's favorable talents and personalities, but he was cautiously optimistic about their future:

> *Badfinger is a schizophrenic aggregation: they live in dual worlds of satisfaction and doubt, and waveringly show signs of change. Everything seems precarious, tentative . . . They would like to stop and examine their position carefully, but they have a paradoxical need to keep moving, to resist slowing down, for hesitation at this time could have serious consequences to their future careers.*

After a few more West Coast gigs, Badfinger flew to New York City, where they were scheduled to play the prestigious Carnegie Hall. They were on a roll. "Day After Day" was a confirmed million-seller, their dates were selling out, and Harry Nilsson's cover of "Without You" had exploded as an international #1 hit! Beverley recalls Pete's reaction, "He thought Nilsson's version of 'Without You' was marvelous, but it was really the fact that both he and Tommy and had written it that made him so proud. It was a 'group' success."

The day before the Carnegie Hall gig, the band were situated at the Loews Midtown Hotel. Unbeknownst to them, one of their Welsh friends was staying there; Gary Pickford-Hopkins. Gary had since left the band Eyes Of Blue. He now sang for the progressive act, Wild Turkey. "My band had just arrived at the hotel when I walked straight into Tom and Mike. They said they were hanging out because they didn't have any money. They said they had tried to get some and couldn't. Glenn Cornick and I ended up taking them out to dinner. 'Day After Day' was Top Five, 'Without You' was #1, and *these* guys were hungry. That really struck me."

Stan Polley and Allen Klein had been expected to attend the Carnegie Hall show. The band was nervous. They knew they'd receive a lot of press coverage. In fact, Apple had acceded to their request to have an English journalist fly over to cover the event. His name was Chris Charlesworth. He was one of *Melody Maker*'s primary feature writers. Charlesworth recalls, "They were like a lot of British bands at the time that were doing better in America and wanted more recognition in their homeland . . . Personally, I liked Badfinger. I didn't think it was a bad thing to have song structures and harmonies like the Beatles. . . ."

As the band prepped for the show, ex-Apple employee Richard DiLello appeared, "I had been asked to photograph them," he says. "They were in a good mood, riding high. That's when I first became aware of Stan Polley. It was obvious he was much different than Bill Collins – he seemed like a very slick businessman. I was told he was very successful in his own right and had taken them on simply because he liked them."

The band nervously waited through opening sets by Michael Gately and Al Kooper. By completion, Allen Klein still hadn't shown; though everyone else in town seemed to be there. Finally – around 11:30 p.m. – Badfinger hit the stage. They started with "Better Days" and "Midnight Sun." Each brought a modest reaction. Next, they did their two acoustic numbers, "Sweet Tuesday Morning"

Badfinger receives gold record for "Day After Day" from Al Steckler, Carnegie Hall, New York, 1972

and "We're For The Dark. Both brought on a very strong ovation. "Feelin' Alright" was then introduced, but it's mention received a barely noticeable whimper from the crowd. The group played it very dynamically, though, and the momentum was now going strongly in their favor. A passionate "Take It All" followed with Pete and Tom singing their guts out. Badfinger finished on a roll.

Afterwards, congratulations were in order. The backstage was jammed; everyone wanted to meet them or greet them. After the fanfare died down, *Melody Maker*'s Chris Charlesworth was left with a dilemma. Though he was attending the gig to do his story on Badfinger, he was also in New York, where he had friends and the possibility of checking other bands. But, he found he could not get out of the sight of Bill Collins. Charlesworth recalls, "It was obvious Collins wanted to keep me in their inner circle, because I got shuffled into a limousine with the group. We ended up driving around for what seemed like ages when someone finally said, '*Hey, we're in the middle of Harlem!*' The driver had gotten completely lost!"

Over the next few weeks, Carnegie Hall reviews trickled out, and they unanimously agreed – Badfinger was a viable act with a lot to offer; now and for the future:

> BILLBOARD ... *Badfinger's collective ability to construct tight and highly stylized pop songs is truly impressive. They place little value on their eclecticism, preferring to move their audience with lovely melodies, pure rhythm, and an enthusiasm that never detracts from that overall precision. What really matters is not how much Pete Ham sings like Paul and plays like George, but how well he can stand on his own, and he passes that test easily.*

> VARIETY ... *It's rock'n'roll that the British combo shined on, with Mike Gibbins' drumming and the vocal breaks and powerful electric guitar work reminiscent of the Beatles. This might not be an accident as the group was presented with a gold record for "Day After Day" . . . The group deserves its plaudits. . . .*

> NEW YORK TIMES ... *Badfinger's musicians play and sing with a bright enthusiasm that has been rare since the demise of the Beatles.*

March 6, 1972 saw the release of a new U.S. single, "Baby Blue" b/w "Flying." Apple exec Al Steckler and recording engineer Eddie Kramer had remixed the A-side. It now featured a loud, heavily-reverberated, snare drum – very unusual for the time. Steckler explained, "I had loved the song, but I didn't think it popped the way it should. I called Todd to see if he would do a single remix, but I can't remember now why he didn't do it. I told the guys I thought it needed to be done and I could do it myself if necessary. They said, 'If you think it makes sense, do it.'"

The single had been scheduled as a March 10, 1972, release in Britain. Oddly, it was never issued there, which shows how much the U.K. end of Apple Records had disintegrated. This was a major blow to the band's momentum in their native country. The rest of the world did receive it though, and it became quite successful. In the United States, the song didn't become quite the smash "Day After Day" was, but eventually it peaked at a very respectable #14 on the *Billboard* charts.

The month of March included gigs throughout the South, the Midwest, and Canada. The band appeared on T.V. and did numerous interviews. They also received news that a headline gig was "theirs for the taking" at Madison Square Garden in New York City. A promoter had mentioned the idea earlier, but now, when presented with the opportunity, the band allegedly turned it down. They didn't feel comfortable playing the almost twenty thousand seat venue.

During their previous tour, the band had also turned down a show with Stevie Wonder scheduled as their opening act. Though the Motown star was on a slight career lull at the time, he was still an "icon" to the group. Pete explained, "We were horrified. There was no way we were going to follow an artist of Stevie's talent onstage. We had no choice but to pull out of the gig."

Surprisingly, some of the group's wishes were apparently being met. When asked in an interview about larger-scale shows, Joey Molland had said the group felt the expansive format of a stadium or arena was not conducive to their stage act; they needed the intimacy of a smaller setting to get their show across. Pete also expressed the same opinion, stating, "Our show is based on the numbers, not the volume."

But after the Madison Square Garden gig was turned down, their booking agent, Jeff Franklin of ATI, was not pleased. ATI was a fairly successful agency at this time and Polley used them almost exclusively for his clients' U.S. bookings. Wayne Treiber called to see if Franklin could fit Badfinger in to play a charity event Treiber was organizing. After verifying the groups' interest, Treiber rang the agency. "Franklin heard me out and put the call on a speaker-phone for everyone in his office to hear. He said, 'I don't give a damn what the band wants to do! They do what I want them to do. If I say "jump," they say "how high?" If I say "Play the fucking men's room at Penn Central Station," they'll ask, "What time?" They aren't going to do *no* fucking benefits for *nobody!*' "

During this tour, Badfinger had a stopover in St. Louis, Missouri. Mike Gibbins recalls, "I had given my hotel room to one of the roadies, 'cause he had a girl he wanted to be alone with. I slept in his room with the other roadies. The next morning they went out early and I went down later to get some breakfast. I told the waitress to bill my room and she said, 'What do you mean? You guys checked out of here two hours ago.' Sure enough, everybody was gone. I didn't know where the next gig was. I had to get in touch with my wife in England, 'cause I didn't have any phone numbers with me! Finally, I reached Polley's office and he arranged a flight in this three-seater plane, with some guy training his son how to fly! I was scared out of my mind!"

Yes, for the second time in his career, Mike had been left behind. But he wasn't being intentionally disregarded by the others. He sometimes actively kept himself out of sight. "Mike would often go and disappear," said roadie Nicky Bell. "We'd have to go looking for him. He'd be out shopping or something."

His sprees became legendary as all the Badfinger roadies recall searching for him at stores and malls. "If he had two pounds in his pocket," said his wife, Gaynor, "he'd go out and buy two T-shirts. Mike was a compulsive shopper." But Mike had additional reasons for venturing out. "He didn't like to be around any arguments," adds Nicky, "so he would stay out of any politics or bitching that might go on with the band. He wouldn't want to get involved. He'd split."

On April 2, 1972, Badfinger were scheduled to play at the Steel Pier in Atlantic City, New Jersey. That morning they ran into a problem. Nicky Bell recalls, "We were in Birmingham, Alabama, at an airport hotel. Fergie and I got up at 5:00 a.m. to put the equipment on a flight. We'd left Bill with the wake-up call for the band. After we finished, we sat down for breakfast at the airport, but by 6:45 no one had shown. The flight was for 7:00 a.m. Bill had overslept, and we missed it. There was tremendous pressure to get there, but there were no more commercial flights until late in the day. So I had to charter two 5-seat Cessnas to fly all the way up the coast. We crowded into these little planes and immediately hit a huge thunderstorm. We were trying to fly side-by-side, but the turbulence was so bad that a gust would hit

Badfinger backstage with Al Steckler, 1972

and the plane next to you would disappear in a split second. We were in shambles by the time we got there."

The band had three sets scheduled that day, but only missed the first. After one of them, Bill Collins had started to chat with a middle-aged divorcee who was accompanying her daughters to see the band. Her name was Beryl Green. She immediately became allured by Bill's engaging English charm. "Bill invited us to the Holiday Inn, brought drinks, and played piano for us." says Beryl. "He took me for a stroll. I was quite taken." Collins requested Beryl stay on for the rest of the tour, which she agreed to. The band members and roadies immediately took to her polite, motherly presence. She soon became Bill's girlfriend, and accepted his request to come live in England after the tour.

After the last tour gig, Collins, the Badfinger members, Stan Polley, and Stan Poses, all met at a New York City office. The date was April 11, 1972. Minutes of the meeting were taken by Stan Poses. They indicated the first order of business was a discussion *"relative to the status of Bill Collins as a full and equal member of 'Badfinger Group.'"* Bill's role with the group had diminished by now. His original management agreement was due to run out later in the year. And although the group knew he was not integral to their future, there was still some loyalty there. Bill was always an active lobbier on his own behalf. It can be surmised that, with everything going well, the feeling was "let things go on as they were." According to the documentation it was agreed that Bill Collins was to remain as a *"full participating partner and will share equally with the other Four (4) members of the 'Badfinger Group.'"* No time limit was revealed.

The next order of business was *"a discussion relative to a division of proceeds, equity and income derived from any songs and/or poems written and/or copyrighted*

Badfinger, 1972

BADFINGER ENTERPRISES, INC.

Minutes of Special Meeting

-of-

Shareholders

(1972)

A apecial meeting of the Shareholders of Badfinger Enterprises, Inc., was held on the 11th day of April, 1972, at 1:00 o'clock in the afternoon, at 116 Central Park South, New York, New York, pursuant to a written waiver of notice signed by all of the Shareholders of the issued and outstanding shares of stock, without par value, of the Corporation.

There were present:

Pamalan Management Inc. by Stanley Polley
Joseph Molland
Peter Ham
Michael Gibbons
Thomas Evans
William Collins

constituting all of the holders of the issued and outstanding shares of stock of the Corporation.

Minutes of April 11, 1972, BEI meeting, as taken by Stan Poses

by any individual member and/or members of the 'Badfinger Group.'" It was also written down that *"a lengthy discussion"* ensued. This was a crucial issue, as it involved a major source of income – music publishing. One part of the potential earnings is performance rights royalties (often referred as "the writer's share"). Back in the Iveys days, Collins and the band verbally discussed some sort of sharing of publishing royalties, which included Bill receiving a part of this income as well. Up to this point, such an agreement had never had been written down in any formalized way; thus leaving it to wide-open interpretation. Now, with "Without You" becoming such a huge hit as a "cover version," a lot of money was to be made for the "writer(s)" through ASCAP income.

On this day, the meeting's minutes showed that everyone agreed to the following:

RESOLVED, that any advances of any kind from any Performing Rights Society, and royalties or publishing moneys will be divided thusly: To the member and/or members of "Badfinger Group" creating such composition, such individual and/or individuals will receive fifty percent (50%) of writer's share. The remaining fifty percent (50%) will be divided in equal shares among all five (5) members of "Badfinger Group."

For this agreement, an important final note was added: "*. . . this division of writer's share will continue until April 11, 1974.*"

Since Pete had, by far, the greatest majority of songwriting success, he seemed to have the most to lose from the stipulation. But, as many people noted, he was not motivated by the money angle and never touted it. When interviewed, he often made the statement that the most important key to Badfinger's success would be their "loyalty" to each other. Yet, at this meeting, someone had made the point to limit the time frame of this agreement, thus showing an awareness of what truly was at stake here.

A few months prior to this meeting, Stan Polley's accounting firm, Sigmund Balaban & Co., had completed a financial statement covering all operations of Badfinger Enterprises Inc. It was for the period of December 8, 1970 through October 31, 1971. Some of the figures listed were as follows:

1. Salaries and Advances to client	*$8,339*	*(Joey Molland)*
	$6,861	*(Mike Gibbins)*
	$6,211	*(Tom Evans)*
	$5,959	*(Pete Ham)*
2. Net corporation profit	*$24,569*	
3. Management commission	*$75,744*	*(Stan Polley)*

Polley's earnings clearly show how unconscionable his contractual agreement to take "30%" of gross receipts was. It's not known if the band members ever saw this rundown, but Bill Collins certainly did, as his handwriting is on one of the copies.

The accusations of Stan Polley having acted as a mafia "bagman" had fizzled out by the end of 1971. The man he allegedly delivered bribes to, Judge Mitchell Schweitzer, had been continuously investigated for over a year now. New evidence had been acquired alleging Schweitzer had secured loans under false pretenses, and then re-loaned the money out at higher interest rates. A list of Schweitzer's past questionable court decisions had also been brought forth, such as his involvement in the famous "Twenty-One" quiz show scandal of the late 1950's.

Despite the constant public scrutiny, Judge Schweitzer was never formally held accountable, as he retired just *days* before his hearing, claiming he couldn't handle the stress and strain of the impending proceedings due to his "acute agitational depression." The allegations regarding Polley were not pursued. But, by April of 1972, a number of Polley's clients were clearly concerned about Polley, especially Lou Christie and Charlie Calello.

Christie had previously been suspicious about being moved to two new labels by Polley – first to Columbia, then to Buddah – back in 1969. He'd only had one big achievement on Buddah, "I'm Gonna Make You Mine." In 1971 he cut a new song, "Lion Sleeps Tonight," with one of Polley's client-producers, Hank Medress. The tune was a natural for Christie and it pointed to big-time success. He recalls, "For some reason, Polley wanted more money from Neil Bogart, [president of Buddah Records]. The word I got was, he wanted more money because of the strength of this song. Bogart refused. The next thing I know, Polley and Hank Medress took the song, erased my voice from the multi-track, and re-recorded Robert John's voice! This was *devastating* to me!"

Robert John's version, on RCA Records, was a huge smash, peaking at #3 in *Billboard* in late March of 1972. Lou Christie's relationship with Polley was now completely strained.

Meanwhile, Charlie Calello had wanted to move on, as his suspicions regarding Polley had mounted over the years. "I went to Polley and told him I wanted out. According to my account I had over $125,000 coming. So I decided the best way for me to get out was to convince Polley my problems were so severe that I *had* to get away. My wife had made a suicide attempt the year before, so he knew I was fighting a poor domestic situation. I had four kids and I was spending a lot of time trying to save my family. Also, I had become a Jehovah's Witness. With a good enough explanation, I thought we could work out a buyout, cause he could see my ship was sinking.

"I talked to him and we set up a deal to sell my house to Larry Brown, who was signed to him. But he put the papers in the Five Arts name, and then worked out some kind of debt I supposedly owed the corporation. Here I was with four kids and he finally says 'You're getting nothing!' "

By mid-year, Calello had to quit the business and get other assistance in resituating his family. Meanwhile, Lou Christie didn't know what to do. "Stan had this incredible way of saying, 'Listen, I have all of your money, I have control of it. You don't have any paper. You don't have anything to get me.' And then he would laugh . . . like it was funny. It was getting scary because this guy is laughing now, and I'm thinking, 'Am I supposed to take this guy seriously?' In the meantime, I've got a concert to do, I've got a record to do, I've got to get back on the charts! I need a record out!

"He used to tell me, 'If anybody tries to get anything from me I'll take their eyeballs out of their head.' That was his famous line. I thought, 'My God! This guy has all of my money and he's threatening me – in his own way. He could wipe me out, he's got control of everything. And I had none of my contracts. He kept all of them in his office.' "

Lou Christie had an apartment in the same building that Polley had his "office" in, but he claimed the proximity never helped him get any special access to his papers. "Everything was made out to his control anyway," said Christie, "so I don't know what difference it would have made."

Christie began plans to relocate to England, and tried to warn some of the other Polley clients before he left. "I talked to Bob Lewis, but he didn't seem to want to talk about it. He actually seemed quite happy with his situation."

Badfinger had little inkling that some of Polley's clients were upset. But they had noticed a few things on their own, such as the inconsistent delivery of their checks. Pete seemed content on the surface. "He totally believed any explanation he was told," says Beverley. "He trusted Stan Polley fully."

Jeff Franklin, of ATI, and Stan Polley, ultimately decided to forego Badfinger's touring ideals. Franklin scheduled them for a glut of large-scale gigs. The band was informed they would *have* to go out for a forty-five-day American tour in June, this time focusing on festivals and larger venues. Most of the dates would be opening for The Faces. Pete had really wanted to take a long break so the band could properly prepare for the next album, but Polley had insisted they go back out on the road.

Right after Badfinger had returned from their previous American tour, Kathie had spoken with Gaynor and told her Mike had been with a groupie. Gaynor recalls, "I was very upset. I really didn't want to hear it. But I was so angry that I confronted Mike. I told him I wanted to go back to Wales. He said, 'Look, I'm sorry. You can either accept it or not. I can't change it.' He didn't want me to go. I was in the living room crying and Pete walked in. I told him what had happened and he put his arm around me. He said, 'You know Mike loves you. He's here with you now, we're here with you now, and we all love you. Don't do anything you might regret. Think about Owen, think about yourself.' He was like a big brother. He really cared."

Gaynor and Mike made up and Pete had bonded even closer to his dear Welsh friend. Gaynor adds, "Pete always made me feel like one of his sisters. He loved to joke around. He'd hide my clothes, or I'd be cooking and ingredients would come up missing; he'd swap salt for sugar, anything to drive me mad. We each had our own cupboards; it was very territorial. One of his favorite pranks was to pinch something from a cupboard and watch us go crazy accusing one another. Then Pete would smile and go, 'Did you try looking . . .' We'd chase him. It was silly stuff, but we laughed anyway.

"Pete and I didn't really party or do drugs as often as the others did. But one time we all took some acid and somehow, me and Pete ended up on the floor of Joey and Kathie's room holding hands. We thought we were going to die. We were in a terrible state. I'll never forget the two of us, walking over to Golders Hill Park, trying to get our heads together. We were there until five in the morning, just holding on to each other. Poor Pete was really scared, and I was petrified. But together we got through it."

During the tour break, Joey and Kathie rented a place called Sunshine Cottage. It was in Hampstead, not far from Golders Green. In order to help with the rent, Pete's former girlfriend, Beverley, was brought in as a roommate. She was an easy-going person. Kathie considered her a friend.

The band was scheduled for an appearance with The Faces on May, 28, 1972. The venue was the London Colosseum and Tom's brother, David, attended with his wife, Jan. David enjoyed seeing his brother's band and was especially keen this time, as it had been so long since Badfinger had been playing in England. Jan Evans has vivid memories. "The band seemed to go down okay performance-wise. After the show we went backstage to congratulate them. I can recall walking past Rod Stewart and his entourage; they had booze, groupies, everyone was having a blast. Then we get to Badfinger's dressing room and they're all arguing. They didn't think they'd gone down too well. You could feel the tension. Suddenly bottles

Gaynor Gibbins

Tom Evans, David Evans, Jan Evans

started getting thrown and it really scared me because I'd recently gotten glass in my eye from a car accident. I remember Tommy yelled, 'I'm going!' and he ran out. David went after him because he was afraid he was going to drive in that state. Marianne and I waited and waited, but they never came back. Finally, we had to leave, but there were no more cabs; we literally had to beg an off-duty one to give us a ride home."

Shortly after, Badfinger played a BBC radio show. The band focused on *Straight Up* material, performing it admirably. Then, Pete and Tom were honored for the success of "Without You," in a special ceremony at Apple (for which Harry Nilsson appeared). Finally, a complete surprise came: Mike was quitting the band!

Just three or four weeks before their American dates, Mike's revelation was a stunner. No one had expected it. Mike had always been "the cheerful one," a jokester known for quick one-liners, "quiet," "easy-going," "a born dreamer." No one knew that deep inside he was actually quite frustrated. He recalls, "Tommy was always on my case. If something was wrong he'd assume the drummer was fucking up. He was looking for perfection. But if I played like a machine, he'd say the 'feel' was wrong. Or he'd go the other direction and say

Harry Nilsson presents Pete and Tom silver discs, Apple Records, June 19, 1972

Mike with Gaynor, and with son, Owen

it was too 'mechanical.' He had so much fucking 'soul,' it wasn't funny. One time he got on me when we were working with Todd Rundgren. He said, 'This is wrong!' and Todd said, 'There's nothing wrong with his drumming. It's fucking great!' I said, 'Yeah. Thanks, man.'

"Pete didn't want me to leave. He said it was stupid, but I was frustrated. I couldn't practice. Bill Collins used to tell me all the time, 'I don't want you to practice! I don't want you playing like Aynsley Dunbar!' I got bored. I couldn't flash out."

Gibbins had proven himself an accomplished studio drummer, whose versatility allowed the Iveys, and then Badfinger, to explore their different musical tastes. *Straight Up* was certainly a consummate album for him. Live, he was an energetic presence, often pushing the material faster, but that was partly due to his own frustration. "I could only do what the songs allowed me to," he said. "A lot of the material was herky-jerky. It wasn't groove-oriented. And I'm a speedy kind of guy."

Gaynor Gibbins, Mike's wife, remembers his quitting as more that "he was itching to try some things on his own. I supported him, but I didn't understand it." Tim Boyle encouraged Mike to record some of his growing inventory of songs. The opportunities to show his wares in a four-man group of writers had limited him. Mike asked Boyle to help him in setting things up.

Meanwhile, Badfinger was now in a terrible jam, no drummer, and about a month until their American tour. They began auditions, but were disappointed. Joey's friend, Bob Adcock, knew of an American drummer named Rob Stawinsky, a member of a band called Sky. Adcock believed in him so much that he reportedly *paid* to fly him over. Stawinsky blew everyone away and that was it – he was in.

Just before leaving for the U.S. tour, Joey and Kathie got married at the Hampstead Registrar's office. Pete shot a bit of the aftermath on his 8mm home movie camera. Joey had proposed to Kathie the year before, but she kept putting Joey off. Finally, she'd agreed and their bond was "official." Kathie Molland was now firmly entrenched in the Badfinger circle.

Badfinger's first date of their fourth U.S. tour was at the Schaefer Music Festival in New York City's Central Park. A reviewer in *Variety* indicated attendance was a bit disappointing, partly due to rainy weather, but the band received a positive critique. Rob Stawinsky was described as their "solid new drummer." Wayne

Joey and Kathie wed, 1972

Treiber showed up, took some pictures, and afterwards introduced Badfinger to some friends of his, an up-and-coming rock act called Shadow. "Pete and Tommy insisted on taking them out to eat," says Treiber. "The kids were blown away. Pete said, 'Look, when you get up there, you can return the favor.' "

Badfinger had been given a tour manager named, Danny Aharoni. He'd been free-lancing for the ATI agency and became acquainted with them during their previous tour, when he was road managing for Dave Mason. Under Aharoni's guidance, the group became more serious. He recalls, "They rarely went on stage under the influence of anything. At least not on this tour. After the gigs they did whatever they wanted, but onstage they stayed pretty sober."

The group found a lot of frustrations in playing outdoor festivals. They had not had a chance to build up any kind of stage show to impress massive audiences. Their sound could get lost. And none of the band members were wild, flashy showmen. When interviewed about the situation, Pete would say, "We're doing it now, just to get to as many people as possible, but I prefer to play to about five thousand or less."

For many of the gigs, Badfinger were second on a bill with Cactus opening, and The Faces, led by Rod Stewart at the time, closing. Stewart and his gang were quite

Badfinger U.S. Tour #4, 1972

rowdy in those days, but Tom had no trouble falling in. Nicky Bell recalls, "That tour was completely wild. Rod Stewart used to announce that there was a party back at the Holiday Inn. If we were lucky, we'd get back before the Faces were done and lock ourselves in our rooms before the onslaught hit. People would come streaming in the hotel; the lobby would be jammed; the lift would be full. When the doors opened, you couldn't move. If you dared open your room door, the party was in there. One time our shower got pulled down, the sink got taken off, lampshades were broken, curtains were torn down – and the hotel manager knocked on the door. People were jumping in drawers, going under beds, hiding in closets, balconies, and Tommy was the only one sitting out there, stoned out of his brain. Even today, you talk to Ronnie Wood, Kenny Jones, and those guys. They still talk about Tommy and all the things that he did."

Tom was forever rambunctious, one time throwing a shark down a hotel's laundry chute. But Nicky Bell was a good match. Nicky got so out of hand he accidentally broke Joey's arm while they were wrestling on a hotel bed. Luckily, Joey was still able to play, but Nicky got a big scare. Another time, Nicky started a mattress fire at the band's hotel after falling asleep near some strobe candles, knocking them over. He recalls, "We were seven or eight stories up, and Fergie and I are on the veranda throwing little cups of water on this huge mattress. Luckily, someone saw the smoke and fire engines showed up. The hotel held the group's guitars as ransom though, until they were paid for the damage. I was sweating that one out."

Pete had been pursuing Dixie throughout this tour. She'd left the previous one midway and he hadn't seen her since. She explains, "We had been keeping in touch with phone calls and letters, but eventually I'd started to see someone and Pete got wind of it. He asked me to join them on the road. He was so convincing. He could write the most beautiful love letters."

The group was now riding the success of their two recent 45's and the *Straight Up* album (which lasted in the charts for thirty-two weeks). As it was, each member of Badfinger was now occasionally suffering from insecurities regarding "fame" and "notoriety." Joey stated he often tended to play it low-key, staying in the background. He said, "I was kind of paranoid. I kind of felt like I was getting away with something amongst all these great musicians and super-talented people. Even the heavyweight record executives intimidated me."

Pete was more of the group's spokesman when it came to public and business relations. Dixie recalls, "Pete was very witty around business people. He seemed to get a lot of respect. They were drawn to him." Nicky Bell agreed, "Business-types always seemed to gravitate to Pete as the backbone of the band. He took it seriously."

Tom Evans with shark, shower cap, holding Marianne

Al Steckler of Apple Records confirms, "Pete was looking to build a career. He was a very serious young man; intelligent, interesting to talk to, a real gentleman. I don't think I ever saw any of the other guys in my office without Pete. Usually he was with Tom. Joey came up occasionally, and Mike, very rarely."

Pete can be heard in a number of the group's radio interviews trying to insert sanity into the chaos, as Tom, Mike, and Joey would more often joke around. "Pete could be totally silly, too," said roadie Nicky Bell, "but business was business, and work was work. He clowned around on his own time." {Interview with Pete on CHUM Radio in Toronto – June 25, 1972} & {Backstage interview with Pete at O'Keefe Center in Toronto – June 25, 1972}

On July 9, 1972, in Pittsburgh, Pennsylvania, Scott McGaughey got to see Badfinger for a third time. He recalls, "Joey had a cast on his arm and was hampered, but they managed to be excellent. There was a piano setup and Pete sat down, introduced 'Take It All,' and the piano went dead. He was totally frustrated. He pushed the bench away, grabbed his guitar, and ripped into this unbelievable version of 'I Can't Take It,' just *screaming* his head off. . . ."

A week later in Tulsa, there were more technical difficulties. Pete kicked down a mic stand. But he didn't rag on the road crew. "He would keep to himself now," says Nicky. "In the very early days, if something didn't go right, he might get heavy with Fergie and I, but it would pass, and he'd always be great. Now, he just wouldn't say much."

Though Pete had Dixie accompanying him, and the band was drawing better than ever, he was still getting ill before some of the gigs. Tour manager Danny Aharoni, "I got close to Pete, but I had to keep a certain distance, too. I saw a lot of pain in him. I took it as artistic sensitivity."

On July 23, 1972, Badfinger flew into New Jersey. They were scheduled to perform for seven straight days on the Steel Pier of Atlantic City. They were supported by some unusual entertainment. "There was a horse on the pier," says Nicky. "The band would play for awhile and then they'd announce this horse was going to jump into the water. Everyone would run over to see it. After he jumped in, everyone would run back to the band. This went on three or four times a day."

All throughout this tour, Stan Polley had been contemplating Badfinger's future. Their Apple Records contract was due to run out in about a year and Polley wanted to use the leverage of their current success to negotiate a new deal. Joey claimed the group was content with Apple; they were willing to sign for basically the same deal. They just wanted a few items in advance – a sixteen-track tape machine and a mixer. "We wanted to build a recording studio for ourselves," said Joey. "It was maybe $100,000 in advances. We'd had four major hits, so it didn't seem like much to ask. We told Polley to request it for us."

Whether Polley ever negotiated with Allen Klein is not known, but Joey claimed they were told by Polley that, ". . . Klein wanted us to sign for nothing. We'd only gotten five percent and he wanted us to get less, and pay for our recording costs, which we hadn't before."

Tony King, then Apple Record's English head of A&R, recalls, "The company was winding down. There were a handful of projects such as Yoko Ono and Lon & Derek Van Eaton, but the days of becoming a major label that serviced other artists was well past. We dealt mainly with Beatle solo albums at that point. Klein was so busy with Beatle-related business that I don't think he had much time for anyone else, including Badfinger. But we were proud of them. They did the label a lot of good. They'd changed it from just being the 'Beatles' label."

Starting back in April, Polley had been in contractual discussions with Clive Davis and CBS Records. Polley also heard that Warner Brothers Records was hot to sign acts. Joe Smith was head of its American wing and he remembers being approached. "Stan Polley came to me; I remember Jeff Franklin somehow being involved. The group had a reputation. There was a direction in the songwriting we liked. Pete Ham was the key. We wanted to be sure he was secure in the band."

Derek Taylor was then employed by Warner Brothers Records as Head of Special Projects. He recalls, "I remember Joe Smith saying, 'I see Badfinger as an "important" signing.' 'Important' meaning 'profitable.' He'd been keeping an eye on them for a long time."

Ed Silvers ran the Warner Brothers music publishing division. He remembers a call from Joe Smith. "Joe asked if I was interested in making a deal that would bring Badfinger into the Warner Communication fold. He was very enthusiastic. We were a very young, aggressive company at that point, very much into pop music. We liked Badfinger as writers. They had the qualifications, they understood songwriting. And I looked up to Polley's lawyer, Walter Hofer. Walter was an icon in the industry."

May Pang was still involved with Apple in the U.S.. When the band told her about the developing situation, she gave them some advice. "I told them the best thing to do was wait. They had told me George Harrison had wanted to speak to them. I told them at least wait until he spoke to them. Even though Apple wasn't functioning as well at the time, Warner Brothers was signing everyone in sight. The band certainly had the credibility to see what other offers might come about."

Apple's Al Steckler recalls, "The first indications I had gotten they might leave was when Collins came in to the office upset one day. I asked him what the matter was and he said, 'I think they're going to go with Warner Brothers.' I said, 'It doesn't make sense to me.' He said, 'Why?' I said, 'We love them here at Apple. We've worked them. We've taken them from where they were and made a real entity of them. We've nurtured them. They're getting paid decent money. We can renegotiate a royalty.' But he said, 'That's not good enough. Polley and Poses believe at Warner Brothers they can get a lot of money.' I said, 'Well, what is a lot of money.' And he gave some figure like three million.' I said, 'Well, exactly what does that mean.' He says, 'Three million for six albums.' I said, 'Well, if you look at that and break it down per album, and you get all the taxes out, and you divide by four, and you take out your share, and Polley and Poses share, you're not really talking about a lot of money per member.' He said, 'Well, it makes sense to me.' Pete and Tom came in later and I went through the same numbers. They said, 'Basically, it's in the hands of Polley now . . .' "

Meanwhile, Badfinger Enterprises Vice-President, Stan Poses, now felt it was time to have a serious talk with the group. He recalls, "I had started to figure out that what Polley had set up didn't make sense. Everything, contract-wise, you name it; he wasn't being a straight-shooter. I invited Pete and Tommy over to my house for dinner. I sat them both down. I said, 'Look, Polley is setting you up for a renegotiation with a major company; you could make a lot of money. But I'm going to fill you in on something, and you've got to trust me. If you don't trust me then what I'm going to tell you is academic: I'm going to leave Stan Polley. I'm not going to be involved with him at all because what he's doing doesn't make any sense business-wise. And you guys will never see a God-damn penny the way he's structured your contracts. He has control of everything.

"Here's what I'd suggest you do. You have meetings coming up with record companies that want you. You don't need Polley, and you don't need a manager for this. You need a lawyer or someone you trust who you can deal with. When you go to the meetings, just tell Polley that you don't want to sign his contracts and you don't want him to manage you. By Tuesday or Wednesday of next week, I'll be gone. If you want advice in a year or two, call me. But it's best we stay clear of each other, that way we avoid a lawsuit."

Stan Poses

Stan Polley, 1972

Poses explained to them why he didn't bring Joey in on the discussion. "I told them the reason I didn't tell Joey was because of Kathie. I said, 'Kathie totally controls Joey. He's beyond talking to, you've got to talk to Kathie about everything.'

"Apparently, they went back to Joey and he spoke to Polley. Because the next day, Polley took them out in his speedboat and his Rolls Royce and heavily schmoozed them. One of his favorite things to do was to drive them past Chemical Bank and say, 'Your money's in there.' I guess he convinced them I was full of shit.

"I asked Pete later what had happened and he said, 'I told Joey because he's one of the band. We had to tell him.' I said, 'Okay, there's nothing I can do about it. I warned you. I'm gone.'"

While Stan Polley continued his wheeling and dealing, the band gigged on, concluding their fourth American tour on August 9, 1972. All throughout, Polley had been touting prospective new record deals to the band members. Marianne recalls that Tom was suspicious of his motives. Before going home, Tom met with Stan privately. Polley now wanted to bring Badfinger into a variety of new business deals (presumably to continue maneuvering his lock on their income). Tom claimed that Polley asked him, "What is it you want?" Tom thought a bit and said, "A midnight blue Porsche with a black leather interior." The next day Tom alleged he went outside his hotel room and sitting in the parking lot was a dark blue Porsche Targa! Tom was flabbergasted! Tom alleged he called Polley and asked, "How am I going to take that with me?" Polley allegedly replied, "Take it on a boat!"

Months later, when the fancy Porsche arrived in England, it caused quite a stir around Park Avenue. Joey Molland claimed he feels Tom manipulated to get the

Porsche, and that he was continuously developing "separate deals" with Polley. "He had his own games going," said Joey. Marianne disagrees, "Tom told me he thought Polley had bought the car just to show he had easy access to money; to give Tom the impression he could get him anything he wanted." Mike says this, "Look, Tommy comes back with a Porsche on a boat, with a New York license plate. Of *course* we questioned it, but whatever it was . . . nobody will ever know."

At the end of the tour, Pete had asked Dixie to come live with him in England. She accepted his invitation and made it over around mid-August. Beverley recalls, "Pete was so excited. When she arrived, I could see she really cared for him. I was so happy for Pete." But Golders Green turned out to be a bit of culture shock. Said Dixie, "I was an independent American girl brought over to live in this crowded house. We had no car and the refrigerator was this tiny little thing, you'd have to go shopping every day. But everybody was so nice that I quickly got used to it. Pete and I did discuss buying a home, but he wasn't sure he could afford it yet."

Pete did get another car though, buying a used Triumph TR-6 to replace his forever broken-down Jaguar. The Mollands purchased an Elan. Tom also had a Mini, which he'd had from the year before. The Mollands commented they thought Tom had swung yet another sweet "deal" with Polley to get it. But according to Marianne, Tom never received any "special" allotments, "Sue Wing bought Tom that car. I think she and Tom had an affair. She always had money. He didn't get the money to buy it. She was still doing her escort thing. She'd get all dressed up and I'd say, 'Where are you going?' and she'd say, 'I'm an actress.' One time she got dressed like a little schoolgirl and she said, 'Oh, that's just the part I'm playing.'"

Also, around this time, Tom Evans announced he was purchasing a house in New Haw, an area in Surrey, just southwest of London. He made a down payment of £4,000 on a £17,000 bungalow. Joey and Kathie claimed to be suspicious that he could get yet another large chunk out of Polley, but Marianne says it wasn't that complicated. "Tom told me he didn't trust Polley and he thought he should get what he could, while he could. He asked for it when he was back in America. It was Tom's money. Why wouldn't Tom have the money for a down payment?" Tom recommended to Pete he buy some property, too, but Pete held off. Despite the warning from Poses, Pete still wasn't allowing himself to believe that Polley was out to rip-off the band, at least not openly.

Tom was continually doing investigations on Polley. He had become quite friendly with Beryl Green, the girlfriend of Bill Collins. Tom asked her if she could do a little snooping for him. Beryl recalls, "Tommy was suspicious. He really wanted to know what was going on. He had come to me during the tour and asked me if I could keep my eyes and ears open. I told Tom I would. I tried to find things out. I stuck to Bill like glue. But he and Stan Polley would often send me out of the room. I'm not sure if Bill was suspicious of me or not, but I

Tom and Marianne at their home in New Haw, Surrey, 1972

had to be careful not to let him think I was meddling. He knew my feelings ran deep for the boys. I had come to regard the whole group and the roadies like they were my children.

"I was concerned about their money myself. Things just didn't seem right. Polley was talking about millions and millions of dollars all the time, but they didn't really have anything to show for it. I did pick up a few things. I can't remember what they were today. I told Tom what I could."

Badfinger had to get going on a new album for Apple. They went to work at Apple Studios, producing themselves (with John Mills doing the engineering). It's not clear how this responsibility came about – though the fact Apple's hierarchy was in transition may have opened the door. Now they had the creative control they'd dreamt about.

Drummer Robbie Stawinsky was not used for these recordings, and why his involvement with Badfinger ended after the tour is unclear. The group recorded with a variety of drummers over a two-week period: Harry Rix, Jeff Sweetingham, and Howard Burkett. On September 11, 1972 Badfinger were documented working on two Joey Molland compositions, "Do You Mind" and "Dreaming." Over the next few weeks they also started on "Rock'n'Roll," "Timeless, "and "Piano Red." A few of these numbers had been written as far back as the Clearwell Castle days; some were basically "roots" interpretations.

Pete's "Piano Red" was a number inspired by an old blues singer. Nicky Bell recalls, "During the previous tour, Pete had met some old guy at a bar called "Red's Grate On The 88." He was playing the piano – he had no teeth – and Pete was blown away with this guy. His name was Piano Red."

Pete's original demo featured slide guitar, but when the band put it together, they dropped the lead. Pete sung it more like a blues "parody." The group claimed they enjoyed it, but the song didn't seem serious enough to be on an album. Or was it? The band's new-found freedom was allowing them to try out numbers which may have been instantly vetoed by most producers. But eventually, intelligent decisions would have to be made.

Late in September, the band was scheduled to do an English TV spot. They were to lipsync to "Without You" and "Day After Day." At this point, Bill and Pete were keen to get Mike back in the fold. Bill Collins asked Mike if he'd do the TV show as a favor. "I was only going to play that one day," states Mike, "but on the way to the studio they tried to get me back in the band. Bill was playing up the image, that the fans wanted the original band. At that point, I just wanted to get the money owed me and get out. I was enjoying playing with my Welsh mates."

A collection of Welsh musicians helped record some of Mike's songs that past summer. Many of the them were Mike's friends: Tommy Riley, Dave Charles, Deke Leonard, Phil Ryan, and Martin Ace. Mike picked out his tunes and they recorded four songs with full, lavish production. One tune, "This Time," has a distinct Harrison-esque edge. Mike claimed to sing only; the drums were allegedly played by Tommy Riley. Martin Ace supervised the proceedings. Three of the four songs cut were augmented with monumental orchestral arrangements, courtesy of Phil Ryan, the ex-Eyes Of Blue keyboardist. These recordings inspired Mike, but he didn't know what to do with them. The studio bill had run to over £2,000. Only rough mixes were ever completed.

Mike had the pressure now, with Pete and Bill wanting him back in the band. He recalls, "I was in an elevator with the two of them, going to this T.V. program, and Rod Argent was in there. I'd known him from earlier tours we'd done over the years. He's been in the Zombies and Argent, and I heard he was putting something together. I was dying to ask him if I could audition. But I bit my tongue. I didn't have the balls with Pete and Bill breathing down my neck."

Acknowledging that Badfinger was an international hit act, with a wide-open future, Mike accepted Pete and Bill's offer to return. "I came back with a different level of acceptance though, it was, 'Nobody fuck with me, or I'm out!' "

It was now October of 1972 and a new record deal had been finalized. Stan Polley and Terry Harvey were flying over with contracts. Polley had gotten the company he wanted: Warner Brothers Records [WB Records]. It was a major label with a number of popular artists of the time: Black Sabbath, Deep Purple, Jethro Tull, The Faces, and ex-Apple artist James Taylor, to name just an assortment. The company was in a tremendous state of expansion. Warner Brothers had two other record divisions – Reprise in the U.S., Raft in the U.K. – but WB Records, headed by Joe Smith, was the biggest money-making machine of all.

The deal Polley, his attorney Walter Hofer, and Joe Smith, negotiated, was basically the following:

1. *Six LP's were due over three years – four more optional over two*
2. *Three 45s (minimum) to be released by the company per year*
3. *Badfinger's LP royalty – 12% of retail in U.S., 8.5% elsewhere*
4. *$225,000 would be advanced per each album delivered*

For the advance aspect, Warner Brothers dictated that they would put $500,000 into an escrow account (basically a "holding" bank account). And for each of the albums delivered, $83,333 could be withdrawn from the account by "Badfinger." Warner Brothers would then pull an additional $141,677 from their *own* bank accounts – making the grand total of $225,000 advanced per album. This was a tremendous enticement. Even if the albums were a huge bomb, a large sum of money was assured of being turned over.

Warner Brothers had also been eager to involve their publishing company, WB Music. They had seen the tremendous success of "Without You," and felt the band offered lucrative songwriting potential. Polley and Hofer negotiated with Ed Silvers and the company's attorney, Len Golove. Together they came up with the following:

Badfinger with Joe Smith, president of Warner Brothers Records,

1. *Same time frame as record deal.*
2. *For the first six LP's, all publishing and performing rights royalties go to WB Music, until $1.4 million is accrued.*
3. *Badfinger then gets 50% of the publishing share and 100% of their writer's share, from there on out*
4. *$100,000 is advanced to the band for each album set of song copyrights delivered.*

The $100,000 publishing advance was similar to the record deal's enticement. This time, $100,000 was designated to be put in another escrow account. As each album's song copyrights were assigned to WB Music, $16,667 could be taken out by "Badfinger" and WB Music would kick in $83,333 from their own accounts, making a grand total of $100,000 advanced per album.

Bill Collins says that while he was in the United States, copies of these contracts had been handed to him. He later recalled the following scenario in a 1987 BBC T.V. documentary. "Polley took me all around New York in a big limo and he said, 'It's probably unnecessary to read this contract – it's three inches thick!' But he said, 'Basically, you've got to understand . . .' and he talked and talked and talked and drummed into my mind that we had a three-million-dollar deal to make six albums in three years. Polley was very pleased. He said, 'It's no good you trying to read through the legalese. I'll explain it in ordinary language. . . .' "

Collins largely trusted Polley, but certain aspects troubled the band. Pete hated the pressure of two LP's due per year. Tom was also wary, but Polley had made it impressive by adding up all figures, telling them, "It's a three million dollar deal! You're millionaires! *Millionaires*!" And basically, that's all they heard.

Joey: "We didn't want to bother with the business stuff. We were hippies. We wanted to be musicians. But when your business manager says you're being offered three million dollars, do you take the deal? Three million dollars!? *You bet your ass*!"

On October 4, 1972, the band signed the WB record deal. Though dated retroactively to September 21, 1972, it was not to take hold until September of the following year, just after the Apple contract was due to run out. Badfinger signed the papers to a Warner Brothers Music publishing deal the same day.

Somewhere around this time, George Harrison called Bill Collins and said he'd like to speak with him. Bill claimed he came down to the studio Harrison was working at and found him quite upset. "Why didn't you come to me before you signed?" George allegedly asked. Bill told him, "Look, we couldn't get a hold of you. Your people weren't doing their job." Bill discussed Klein's negotiations; that Klein had not been forthcoming regarding Badfinger's desire to get their own studio together; that he had wanted to give them lesser royalties than they'd had before; and to have Apple recoup any advances for studio time. Harrison was reportedly very angry to hear these things; of which he claimed to be unaware. After a long discussion, he canceled his recording session for that evening, apparently too upset to go on. Coincidentally, Harrison and the other Beatles ended their relationship with Klein around this time. But it's not known if Badfinger's situation had any direct effect on that decision.

In mid-October, Tom and Pete did some session work for George Harrison. Then the band moved into Morgan Studios in London. Tommy, Pete, and Mike started to toy with the previous tracks. Joey recalled, "I had been off visiting my mother in Shropshire and when I came back, the band was already in the studio. I lost my mind, because they were recording without me. I didn't like that."

The group's self-production came with a set of problems. Without a specific leader, the sessions were undisciplined. The members were exploring individual trips; a lot of indulgent ideas were being tried. An example would be Joey's "Regular." "It was a pub song," explained Joey. "It reminded me of going to pubs, playing in pubs." The track is sung in an inebriated fashion and ends with honky-tonk piano. "Joey drank half a bottle of whiskey to sing that," says Fergie. "He was very drunk."

Mike's "Cowboy," was another light-hearted tune. He recalls, "I wrote that as I was watching a western movie with the sound turned off. I was sympathizing with the cowboys." For the recording, Tom had the idea of using a wobble board. Basically a giant piece of cardboard, once "wobbled," it perfectly replicates the sound of a giant bathroom plunger! "Tommy was making fun of me," added Mike. "That wobble board was made famous by this Australian, Rolf Harris. He'd played it on a song called, "Tie Me Kangaroo Down Sport." Tom thought it was funny. I was disgusted."

For "Timeless," Pete recorded a melodic recorder line. "He couldn't play it that well," says Mike, "so I went down into the studio and as he blew the note, I pressed his stomach in-and-out real fast, so he could get the vibrato. It was hilarious. We couldn't stop laughing." On "Blind Owl," the group brought in Ginger Johnson's African drummers. "One of the guys got violent," says Mike, "We said, 'Nah, don't play it like that.' He said he was going to put a voodoo on us. So we put him in a glass booth and didn't even record his part. He never even knew."

In the past, Badfinger's producers had selected a well-rounded collection of material that fairly represented the different members' talents and the band's unique chemistry. Now, it would be up to them to make these crucial final decisions together. But the group's tight democracy had been crumbling for some time now. Badfinger was no longer just "the four boys" and Bill Collins. Not since a young lady from Minnesota had entered their lives. . . .

Throughout most of the history of The Iveys and Badfinger, the concept had been "everyone will write songs, we'll use the best ones, and we'll all share in the proceeds." However, Pete had clearly gained prominence. With four prolific writers, jealousies were bound to happen. "There was a lot of respect amongst the members," says Fergie, "but it was competitive, too."

Mike remembers that Joey was perturbed at not having gotten any A-sides, and that Tom would sometimes pout when his songs were rejected. "But," he adds, "no one would yell or scream about it. That is, no one except Kathie."

"She used to shout a lot," added Fergie, "And I'm not sure she wouldn't have been more comfortable if we all shouted back. She was forceful. She was loud. She

Kathie Molland

was pushing Joey. He was basically laid-back. But he started to assert himself more and more."

Kathie had constantly been encouraging Joey to step up, though it may not have been just for his sake. Beverley recalls, "She seemed to take on Joey's glory as her own. He was doing things that she really wanted to do. One time back at the Park Avenue house she was sitting in the recording room playing a keyboard, and Pete wanted to go in there to work, but he didn't want to seem pushy. I went in and listened to her bit, came back, listened some more, and I kind of hinted that Pete wanted to do something. But she wouldn't leave. Finally I came in and asked her politely if Pete could come in to do some work. She said, 'No! I'm writing!' "

"Kathie was a wishful Linda McCartney," added Nicky Bell. "If she had her way she would have ended up part of the band – singing, playing tambourine, and co-writing songs."

In a 1999 interview, Kathie claimed to have played tambourine during the *Straight Up* album sessions. "(George Harrison) complimented me. He said I was the only one who could do it right." And she acknowledged her abilities, "I did know my music. I played drums, piano, and guitar, and I had been trained in classical music. . . I was able to converse with anybody on the subject, and I did with George a lot."

Nearly everyone connected with Badfinger at this time noted that Kathie was continuously pushing to be involved in almost *every* facet of the band. Commented Fergie, "Pete just wanted it to be the four guys together, making decisions, working things out. She was really getting to him."

Beverley: "For Pete, it even got to the point that, whenever Joey would say, 'That's nice, Pete, but we can't use that,' Pete would see it as partly Kathie's interference. When Joey had first joined, Pete realized a lot of things he had written would no longer be applicable to the band. But he accepted it, because he was excited by the new prospects with Joey. But after a while, he started erasing a lot of his demos and ideas before he even presented them. He started feeling like they were going to get rejected anyway; that his ideas meant nothing. He was becoming disheartened."

For the prospective new album, Pete had made up a demo reel. Included were a number of ballads: the McCartney-ish "Love Will Be," the epic "You're Such A Good Woman," the quaint "Scarlet Willow," and the poppy "A Lonely Day." All were summarily rejected. "Pete's confidence could be easily shaken," says Beverley. "And now, with Kathie involved, he felt ganged-up on. But he certainly didn't want a confrontation with her."

But it came. One day Kathie went over to the Park Avenue house and got into a heated battle with Pete. "It was really unusual to see Pete in any argument," said Gaynor. "Kathie was the only person I ever saw that could get him that mad. I could

Pete Ham

tell she wanted to kick him, but she knew she couldn't do that, so she went outside and kicked in his car door instead!"

Kathie's boots made a large dent on the driver's side. When she realized what she'd done, she quickly ran home. Beverley, who was still rooming at the Molland's "Sunshine Cottage," remembers Kathie entering in a frenzied state. "She told me what had happened and she said, 'I wonder if I've gone too far this time.' Later on, I saw Pete and he was very angry. It hurt him terribly that she would do that, because he had always been the most supportive of her. There had been many times when people had made comments about Kathie and Pete had said, 'Oh, I'm sure she didn't mean that. Kath's a good lass.' He really stuck up for her. But gradually he couldn't deny the effect she had on him.

"One time Dixie had come back to the Park Avenue house a bit loaded. Pete was furious because he thought Kathie had given her something. But she hadn't, 'cause I was with Kathie the whole time . . . I remember another time he was at Sunshine Cottage and Kathie had a real go at him. He was crushed, absolutely crushed. Many times I was upset, but he didn't want me to get involved."

Though Pete was frustrated, he knew the task at hand. And that was to help Badfinger make an exceptional final album for Apple. But the lack of support of his ideas played on his mind. The "group" ideals, which he'd long held sacred, were now taking a major beating. . . .

After more fiddling about in the studio, the Badfinger members decided to move to a more secluded recording set-up in Kidlington, England, called The Manor. They had hoped the studio's privacy would make them more focused. But they soon found that without an outside producer, it would be no easy task.

Prior to their going there in November of 1972, the band had worked on five of Joey's songs, three of Tom's, two of Pete's, and one of Mike's. The group continued to touch up a majority of these recordings, but they also started some new tracks. One was Joey's "Get Away." Its origin he later explained, "Peter had this thing about working so hard. He worked really hard; he'd play everyday and work everyday and write a song everyday. It wasn't my attitude, basically my attitude was 'I'll play guitar when I fancy and if I write a song when I'm playing it – great! If I don't, I'm not gonna worry about it. Just like the lyrics say, *"You may be right working all night and day. But I know sometimes I've got to get away."* The song is solid, bang-em-up, rock'n'roll. Joey sings terrifically and was recorded playing piano for the first time. Pete also shines, with confident lead guitar.

Tommy had a number called "When I Say," composed after a brief falling out with Marianne. He'd been having trouble writing songs for some time now, partly because he'd been focusing on his bass playing, but he also needed some type of inspiration to create his lyrics. "Tommy told me it was easier for him to write when he was depressed," says Marianne. A riveting ballad, "When I Say" builds from a sparse acoustic opening to an inspired peak of twin lead guitars. Tommy later cited it as one of his favorite personal compositions.

A new song of Pete's was "Apple Of My Eye," his tribute to Apple Corps. Pete had often said he was honored to be with the Beatles' company and expressed his sincerest gratitude:

Oh, I'm sorry but it's time to make a stand
Though we never meant to bite the loving hand
And now the time has come to walk alone
We were the children, now we've overgrown
You're the apple of my eye
You're the apple of my heart

"Pete really felt bad about leaving Apple," says Fergie. "To him it was like family. He took a great personal interest in it. I know he would've been happy to sign with them for less money."

Joey, Pete, Mike, Tom, Manor Studios, Kidlington, England, 1973

The sessions at Manor Studios turned out to be a bit of a circus. Mike: "Our attitude going in was, 'Hey man, we know what we're doing. Leave us alone!' But all we did was eat hash cakes and get stoned!'" Tommy also recalled the setting. "We had a great time there, took a lot of dope and got very loose. But we didn't concentrate enough on the work."

When it got to the mixing stage, the chaos really began. "Put it this way," says Mike. "It was five guys on the faders, every man for himself, every fader for itself. We were hippies. It was 'I don't care. Give me a fader. *I'll turn it up*!' "

The band didn't get the album finished before taking a break for the holidays. Pete was looking forward to the time off, but when he got back to Park Avenue, he found his relationship with Dixie had hit a major crossroad.

Dixie had been getting restless. Pete had been busy and sometimes he came home from sessions in a daze. Dixie had noticed Pete distancing from her and was confused by it. "We had kind of drifted apart," she says. "I didn't know what to attribute it to."

Almost on the spot, it was decided she would return to the United States. Dixie recalls, "When I had first moved to London, Pete and I had settled in pretty well. I got along great with everyone at the house. We were a rather private couple, but that was okay with me, because I wasn't one for the limelight. Pete and I would

Dixie

watch T.V. or listen to music in our room. He'd show me how to make Welsh favorites, like fried tomatoes or watercress sandwiches, all these bizarre things, and of course, tea with sugar and milk. I was just amazed at what they ate.

"Sometimes we'd go for drives in the country, have lunch at little roadside taverns. When we were in Swansea he'd take me to the seashore and show me where he caught mussels on the rocks. In the middle of the night we'd listen to Welsh ponies wander the cobbled streets, just neat stuff like that. Pete could have the best time, be so carefree and such a clown. On the other hand, he had a solemn side to him and a very shy side. He could express himself much better in his letters or through his music.

"Outwardly, he always wanted to seem in control. I couldn't really tell if he was more the person onstage entertaining and involved in all the business hoopla, or if he was really the shy, sensitive Welshman searching for love and stability in his life. I think music may have been number one for him, but I'm not sure he wanted it to be.

"Pete often had a lot of business things on his mind, but he did not discuss them with me. I do know that when they signed with Warner Brothers he felt there was a lot of pressure and it took away some of his creativity. He was a bit panicked. When the band started going off to work, that was the beginning of the end for us. As he was away more, I started to get bored and homesick. Everyone had their own lives and routines to live. I went for a lot of walks, watched T.V., went to the village, but I needed more than that.

"Pete had liked the romanticism of our long-distance relationship. He liked my free-spiritedness, but ultimately he was looking for something more traditional.

When we had gone to visit Wales you could see he loved his family and had great reverence for his mother. When he thought of a family he thought of that kind of stability. He wasn't sure I could take care of myself. He used to say, 'What would you do if I died tomorrow? How would you take care of yourself?' He wasn't sure I could do that.

"At some point, there was an undertone of discontent. We didn't really try to talk it out, because he wouldn't communicate with me very well. I didn't want to second-guess him, I just wanted him to talk to me. But one day we just agreed, 'It's over.' We hadn't really fought or even had a disagreement. It was more like, 'I love you. Goodbye.' I felt it was time to move on."

Beverley recalls, "I didn't see it coming when Pete and Dixie broke up." Added Marianne, "We all liked Dixie very much. Pete really cared for her, but she was getting homesick, and she'd get lonely when Pete was gone. It was sad when she left." Commented Fergie, "Dixie was a gorgeous girl, a free-spirit, a flower-child, no shoes, kind of spacy, easy to fall for because she was really sweet and really cute. But she was the opposite of Pete in many ways. It didn't surprise me when they broke up." Gaynor: "Pete was really down then. I hated to see him suffering. To him it was another failure in his life. Something he thought would go further, hadn't. He seemed to take it very hard."

Pete and Dixie's relationship wasn't the only one winding down at 7 Park Avenue. Beryl Green, girlfriend of Bill Collins, was finding her situation difficult. She relates the circumstances. "Bill was behaving very eccentric. He used to wake me up and make me sit and talk to him all night. He could go days without sleeping and he'd keep me up, too. He used to say that eating and sleeping were 'western decadence.' You'd catch him napping and he'd try and deny it.

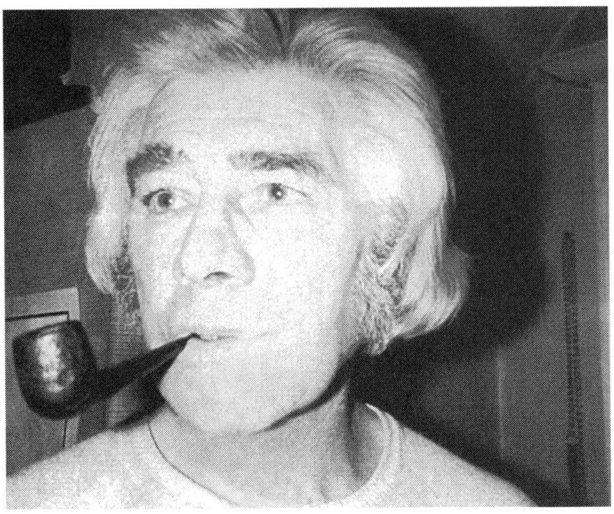

Bill Collins

"We spent most of our time in our bedroom. Bill cut off all the heat to the room. It was very, very cold – bitterly cold. Eventually I got very sick and had to be taken to the hospital in the middle of the night. I got better, but I was stuck. I had no money, I couldn't buy anything. I could only eat what Bill bought and that wasn't much.

"The boys could see something was wrong. I remember Pete saying, 'Bill, you better straighten up.' He knew I was on the verge of leaving. But I wanted to help the boys. They were like sons to me. Tommy wanted me to find things out, but everything regarding money was very secretive. Bill kept his books under lock and key.

"I thought the excitement of the music industry was too much for Bill. He was a very excitable person. He used to work himself up into such a frenzy. He started to tell me that he was 'God.' He used to cut out pictures of Jesus and paste his own face over. . . .

"Bill also told me many times that the only reason he did Badfinger was for his son, Lew, that he was doing it to further Lew's career. That infuriated me. My allegiance shifted to the boys.

"He used to complain about Kathie all the time. He blamed everything on her. But he was so afraid of incurring Joey's wrath that he would never say a lot. Bill was paranoid the boys were going to fire him. He would be very careful in his arguments with them."

The group members went home for the holidays. On Christmas Eve, Tom left a family gathering in Liverpool to meet up with a few friends. Brian Slater recalls, "Tommy had asked me to meet him at a pub in Old Swan. He'd been showing off his [Porsche] all day. Not long after he came back into the pub and said, 'You won't believe this, but I just smashed up the Porsche!'" David Evans, Tom's brother, had been waiting at their parents' home. "Tom had been gone for ages. Finally he came in and said he'd smashed up his car. He said he was playing a tape of John Lennon's *Imagine* album, and when it came to the song, 'Crippled Inside,' he'd crashed into the center junction!"

Pete discussed Polley with his brother, John. Pete mentioned a birthday party for Stan he'd walked in on earlier that year. John Ham recalls, "Pete said the staff was presenting [Polley] with some gifts and when Polley opened up one of the boxes, inside it was a replica of Jesus; a crucifix on a plaque. Pete looked closer and underneath it was an inscription. It said:

IF ONLY HE'D BEEN MANAGED BY STAN POLLEY
THIS NEVER WOULD'VE HAPPENED

7

Where Do We Go From Here?

After the Christmas holidays, Badfinger returned to The Manor Studios to put finishing overdub touches to their album. After New Years Day, they mixed the entire record at Trident and Air Studios. By January 14, 1973, the projected LP was complete, with the following order:

Side One *Get Away, When I Say, Apple Of My Eye, The Winner, Blind Owl, Do You Mind*
Side Two *Piano Red, Cowboy, Regular, I Can Love You, Timeless*

Many of the songs chosen were skewed quite differently from the band's previous pop-rock slant. There were still plenty of cascading melodies to go 'round, but it was obvious the subtle influences of country and "boogie" had infiltrated, along with a touch of the blues. What was quite apparent, too, was the reduction of group-oriented vocals, so much a staple of the band's earlier sound. Now they would often double their own voices, and simply tack on distant answers. "Partly, that was their individualism coming through," said Fergie. "Also, they were being influenced by some of The Band's vocal arranging; call-and-response, that off-key type of blending."

In January, Pete was asked to play guitar for George Harrison (who was working on his *Living In The Material World* album). Badfinger roadie 'Tag' Hall recalls bringing Pete's equipment to Apple for a number of sessions. "I used to sit in the control room and watch," stated Tag. "George had a lot of respect for Pete's talent. They seemed to glide off each other." Apple engineer, Nigel Oliver, also recalls Pete coming in, and has documentation to back it up, "Pete and George got on very well," he said. "They seemed like good friends."

Somehow, Pete was not credited on Harrison's album, so it's not known if his playing was ever utilized in the final mixes. Pete had done a Keith Moon session the previous year, as well as guitar work on a Splinter recording of "Lonely Man," (the version was released as part of a film soundtrack). There was allegedly some sort of

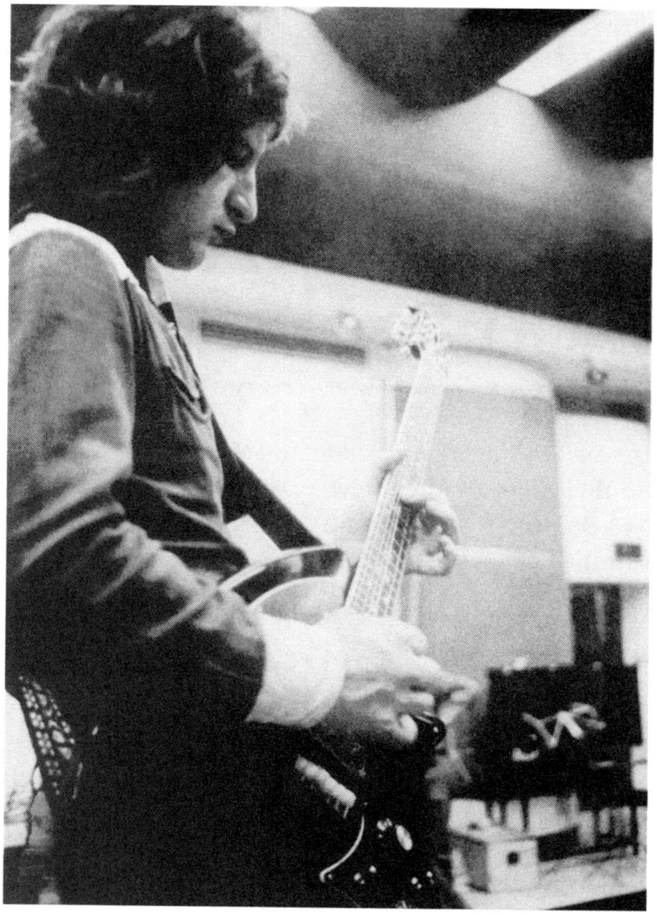

Pete Ham in the studio

Apple contractual issue regarding Pete's receiving credits for outside projects. This was somewhat verified by his appearance on a 1972 album by Gothic Horizon. He was listed, but under the pseudonym "Piggy."

Mid-month the group rushed out to do another American tour. ATI had arranged a five-week jaunt, anticipating the new album's release, but, as it turned out, the LP wasn't going to be ready in time. Pete was upset by the scheduling and related his views on band logistics. "The key to a group's success is not to rush success, but to take it as it comes . . . People in the business tend to take it too fast. What we'd like to do is savor every little change, really savor it and get into it. We'd like to spend more time rehearsing and take longer in the studio. But it's all a matter of time. And there never seems to be enough."

Joey later commented, "The things that normally happen to a band when they make it, and have a few hit records, weren't happening to us. When you have a bit of bread in the kitty it should be spent on the band. You spend it on equipment, lights, and sound. Then the band gets to sounding better and better. You need your manager to get that together."

The tour started off on January 16, 1973. Danny Aharoni, who had spent the previous few months working at Polley's New York BEI headquarters, was again their road manager. Aharoni said he had not enjoyed his stint in Polley's office. "It wasn't the place for me. Too harsh. Full of tough people; insincere, callous. Charlie Levine, who owned the place, was a bitter old man. And Terry Harvey, he was this sort of Runyonesque character – half-drunk all the time – who'd always talk about how he'd finessed the New York D.A. when he worked for the police department. He would tell me how he shook people down, all kinds of things. I hated being around him. And Polley, I couldn't put my finger on. I just didn't trust him."

Early on, Badfinger focused on the Midwest, including a gig at the Aragon Theater in Chicago. Their support that night was the Raspberries, who also championed melodic rock'n'roll. They were considered a strong parallel act, ever since their 1972 hit, "Go All The Way." A lot of journalists were jumping on the Raspberries bandwagon now, but on this night, Badfinger was given the distinct edge. The *Chicago Tribune* said, *"[The Raspberries] play competent variations on a straight pop-rock theme. But the presentation is so formula-bound they come across like a well-starched shirt . . . Badfinger, on the other hand, is a thoroughly enjoyable rock unit whose music is much less of a conspicuous repetition of Beatle-esque sounds than an unashamedly pleasant extension of that genre."*

The reviewer, Jack Hafferkamp, went on to praise Badfinger's new material and performance of a cover tune. He also made note of the Raspberries guitarist Wally Bryson watching admiringly in the wings. Eric Carmen, of the Raspberries, was already a big fan, having been quoted in *Phonograph Magazine* the previous year: *"We played on the bottom of a local bill featuring (Badfinger) and I thought they were just about the best rock'n'roll band I'd ever heard."*

For this tour, Badfinger had thrown in "Timeless" and "Blind Owl" from the upcoming album, plus Joey's "I'd Die Babe" from *Straight Up*. They occasionally performed "Perfection" and "Baby Blue" but didn't feel confident in doing those numbers every night. "I used to beg them to do more original songs," said road manager Aharoni. "I wasn't a big fan of all the long jamming they did."

While on tour, the band got word that Harry Nilsson's version of "Without You" had been nominated for a Grammy, as "Record of the Year." Also, Nilsson himself had been nominated for "Best Male Pop Vocal." Pete was proud, commenting, "Nilsson showed us what can be done with our material. He gave it the treatment and got it to so many people."

Badfinger, Midnight Special, *filmed February 20, 1973*

As it turned out, Nilsson was interested in covering yet *another* Badfinger song for his next album. "But my producer wasn't as high on it," he said, "and it never got done."

As the tour moved on, road manager Danny Aharoni found himself getting to know the band members better. "I especially got on with Pete and Tom," he says. "And when Bill Collins was in reality, he was a most charming guy. But he'd disappear a lot and I couldn't rely on him to get the few things he did done. And Mike, truthfully, I barely remember now. Joey was always with his wife – there was no real spark there. She seemed to be a really disruptive force to the guys in general. It was always, 'Joey should have a more prominent role' or 'Joey should get to do this,' . . . A wife on the road can cause problems, because the other guys may have to watch themselves."

Pete would rarely take advantage of pursuing the always-available groupies. "It wasn't in his character," said Gaynor, "He had high standards." But Tom embraced opportunity, "He was the one for doing those things," says Fergie, "It was that free-spirit kind of thing."

Tom spent a lot of time with a girl named Patsy, whom he'd met on a previous tour. He asked if she'd like to visit him when the band went back to England. When she said "yes," he sent a telegram to Marianne, who was then in Germany.

"Marianne just freaked out," recalls Gaynor. "She came back to London to get her stuff and went straight back to Germany. She was really upset." Fergie explains, "It's one thing to do it behind someone's back, but to bring it home like that. That was Tommy. He was two people, and one of them was a wild partier."

Tom kept to his shenanigans on this tour, but generally stayed in check while onstage. Aharoni recalls, "Tommy gave me some trouble in the beginning. He was full of internal moods and dilemmas. There was one gig where he didn't want to go on. He was having a tantrum. It was in a small town and I had this thing about that. I told him, 'Hey, this is the biggest thing this month for these kids. You owe it to your fans, unless you're deathly sick, to go out and give them a show.' He didn't want to do it. I got pissed, threw him in a gym locker, and slammed the door shut. It's pretty hard to cram someone in a locker, but I did it, and he got so scared he went onstage . . . We came out of it friends. He respected me for believing in what the show was all about. We had a long talk and I got a sense of what he was all about, too."

Tom was forever battling his blue moods. He once said of himself, "I hate walking into strange rooms or crowded offices. I get paranoid because I worry about who's looking at me . . . I feel down sometimes, sure, but I'm not that way all the time . . . I love music, I love the potential, the atmosphere. . . ."

Music *was* Tom's main motivator; the stage his most comfortable medium. "It's me who's got the advantage, me who knows what's next," he once said. Yet, because of Tom's forays into sex, drugs, and alcohol, he could be perceived as a typical, lowbrow, rock'n'roll personality. "But underneath," contends Nicky Bell, "Tommy was a completely different guy. He was actually very down-to-earth, very generous, and very bright. A lot of things he did to keep up the image. People would give Tommy things just to see what he'd do, 'cause they *knew* he'd do it."

Tom's joking could carry a biting edge. He used to dig at Pete about the break-up with Dixie, by deliberately messing up "Baby Blue" lyrics onstage. He would sing different words when it came to the line 'Dixie Dear,' and sometimes Pete would chase him in frustration.

But Tom could get even far more outrageous, as Gaynor recalls, "There was this tall American fellow that came by our hotel and Tom thought he was a 'poser,' which Tom couldn't stand. This chap passed out drunk at some point and Tom cut off his Levi's to the top of his boots and marked them 'LEFT' and 'RIGHT' backwards with a marking pen. Then he lit a piece of paper and started heating up the boots, but he caught the pants' leg on fire instead! He grabbed a fire extinguisher from the hall and started spraying it everywhere; the entire room was filled with foam. It was a huge mess. And the American bloke? He never woke up – not until the next day!"

Tom Evans
(with Nicky Bell, upper left)

Toward the latter stages of the tour, the band found themselves again in New York City. Al Steckler recalls, "Pete came up to my office. He said he wanted me to know he was very upset at leaving Apple. He wanted to thank me for everything I had done for them. He told me what basically clinched for him signing the Warners deal was that Polley had promised the group that while they were on their previous tour, he was going to build houses for their parents. Pete absolutely took him at his word on this. When they had gotten back, Pete found out nothing had happened at all."

Stan Polley again met with the band and their entourage. "He took us to a Hilton Hotel," recalls Gaynor, "and room service brought in some caviar. Later on, he took us to a Japanese restaurant and a gambling casino. I remember the boys all had to round up ties to get in. These were very exclusive places."

Beryl Green, girlfriend of Bill Collins, remembers Polley discussing hopes of purchasing some business for millions of dollars, and his desire to go public with Badfinger Enterprises Inc. The group was quite taken, but suspicions were heightened. Danny Aharoni: "The band members were always asking me to give them the straight account of what was happening. They'd ask me about Polley. They'd say, 'What's going on here?' I was trying to be diplomatic. I'd say, 'Guys, I don't know of anything that's improper, but I gotta agree with you, something doesn't feel right. It was complicated because Polley had just gotten them this new Warner's deal. How do you get rid of a guy whose just gotten you into such a big situation? I didn't have the knowledge to know how to deal with that. Tommy was starting to hint to me about taking over as their personal manager."

Tom and Joey were discussing letting Collins go. They felt that some things weren't progressing as well as they could. Plus, they were frustrated that Collins never seemed to have a clear explanation for what Polley was doing. "Everything was being soft-selled over," says Nicky Bell. "Here's a prominent band, and they have a manager who couldn't provide answers to anything they would ask."

Fergie: "Tommy was the first one to say Bill should be put out; that he wasn't doing his job. He got Joey in as an ally, and Kathie really wanted him out, too. But Pete would always defuse the discussions. There were things Bill did that he didn't like, but when it came to letting him go, Pete would say, 'No, he's an old guy. It would kill him. I can't do that.' "

Possibly Pete agreed to some sort of compromise, because Aharoni clearly recalls being asked to come to England after the tour. "They asked me to become their manager in England. Bill even said to me, 'Yeah, it's okay with me. You can help us and you can still work with other acts, as long as you're there for us.' I think he sensed they were trying to phase him out. But he was trying to hold on in some capacity."

Bill Collins admitted, as long as he was secured in having a financial arrangement, any lessening of his duties was completely tolerable to him. He used to say, and still does, *"I'm not a bloody businessman."* But when it came to the creation of the group and their musical development, Bill has always insisted he was very integral; a major reason for Badfinger's success. He wrote in a 1991 letter:

> *I taught them (the Iveys) music theory, and about different 'tastes' in music. I coached them as songwriters, performers, and recording artists. The mature qualities in their songs reflected our partnership of youth and experience. . . . It was a five-man partnership, a unique situation that no one has seen the likes of before or since. Without my presence, there would be no Iveys story to tell!* I AM THE CENTRAL CHARACTER IN THE IVEYS AND BADFINGER STORY!

On the one hand, Collins' contribution to the group had been important. He had given them their first break by bringing them to London, and his encouragement to work on original songs was a valuable step in their development. Bill also points out, it was *his* Commer van and much of his equipment he put at the group's disposal during the early days, for which he never got any direct compensation.

But, according to most friends and family of the group, being under Collins' wing came with its own set of baggage. "Bill suffocated them," said Nicky Bell. "He would say, 'We're a family; your the boys; I'm the father . . .' When they were teenagers it may have been helpful, but he would not let it go. He continued to talk to them like kids. It was emotional blackmail and it had a big effect on Pete, 'cause Pete was like the oldest son of a family. It was a family without a 'mother,' and Pete felt the responsibility of keeping things together. And whenever things went wrong, he blamed himself. . . ."

The fifth American tour had proven to be a decent one; the band had played well, and most of the shows were received with enthusiasm. But the lack of a 45 and LP diffused a lot of potential interest. By tour's end, no real progress had been made, other than a small profit and a chance to play some new material. What *had* evolved though, were many changes in the Badfinger camp.

Bill, and his girlfriend, Beryl, came to an agreement; they had to split. She left for good during a tour stop in Towson, Maryland. "I couldn't take my situation anymore," she says, "It was hard, because I loved the boys. I tried to help them by finding things out, but I hadn't had much luck, because Bill and Polley kept me out of meetings. The band were very nice. They came to my room and tried to talk me out of leaving."

Roadie Nicky Bell had been working with Badfinger for three years now, and he also felt in dire need of a change. He told everyone he was leaving after the last show. "I was totally burnt out after all the tours," he says, "but the biggest reason

Nicky Bell
Danny Aharoni

I left was I was a frustrated musician. I wanted to try and get my own band together."

Tour manager Danny Aharoni also had a decision to make. The offer to become personal manager for Badfinger was very tempting. "I thought it would be fascinating to live in England for a while and I really liked the guys. But I decided against it. I had been thinking about going to law school and that's what I chose to do."

The group returned to England in late February and immediately received news that Apple had rejected their album. Though a blow, the band agreed they hadn't supplied a very good product. Joey explained, "We tried to be honest, but because of the trips going down, we couldn't produce it ourselves." Apple's Tony King began a search for someone who could salvage it.

Some small-scale dates were played around England. Badfinger was still basically regarded as a lightweight pop act in their native country. Despite three hits there, they still could not headline large-scale gigs. This was an era when "progressive" bands drew the biggest audiences. It irked the group, but it was a difficult situation to overcome, for the English were very quick to typecast. Tom explained at the time, "You've only got one station that plays Top 40 songs. They don't play albums. The general feeling with us was, 'Well, the Beatles already did that.' " Joey added (in a separate interview), "At the time you were either underground or pop . . . we were marked down as a pop group."

Badfinger had yet to release anything that would signify them as a "heavy" band or as having an original sound. They were respected by the English press, but they hadn't come out with an album that showed a new slant on music. That's what the writers were looking to promote.

In March of 1973, the band got word that Harry Nilsson had indeed won the Grammy for "Best Male Pop Vocal," for his performance of "Without You." Though the song did fail to win "Record of The Year," the band was ecstatic. Shortly after, "Without You" received two Ivor Novello Awards (Britain's answer to the Grammys) for "Best Song" and "International Hit of the Year." Apple's Tony King remembers their excitement, "They were very proud of that. To be recognized as something more than just a rock band was thrilling to them. I remember Pete wouldn't show as much as the others. He was a "still-waters-run-deep" type of personality"

Around this time, Pete made a long list of his concerns in one of his songbooks:

> *Songs – push for yourself*
> *Decide whether it's a business or a hobby and run it accordingly*
> *If we decide to go on with it then let's realize what we are deciding –*
> *Any feeling that we are doing it against our will can only lead to bad shows, bad records, and bad vibes*
> *What went down in New York?*
> *Why did we sign with Warners so early?*
> *Why didn't we sign with them on our present strength?*

References were also made to the band's live show and the state of music on the radio – which Pete seemed disillusioned by. It was clear he was dissatisfied in many areas of his life.

The major part of Apple's business operations had, by now, drifted back to the English offices, ever since Klein was put out of the picture. Late in 1972, Apple's English A&R chief, Tony King, finally came up with a prospective producer for the rejuvenation of Badfinger's self-produced recordings – Chris Thomas. Born in 1947, Thomas was a former keyboardist who'd bounced around in several bands before getting hired as a producer's assistant at George Martin's Air Studios, in 1967. Thomas soon encountered the good fortune to actually *play* on the Beatles *White Album*, but record production was always his goal.

By early 1973, Thomas had established himself by producing albums for The Climax Blues Band, Roxy Music, and John Cale. He'd also mixed Pink Floyd's *Dark Side Of The Moon*. But his primary claim to fame was Procol Harum. Their baroque stylings were well-suited to his classical training; perhaps the peak of their partnership being the *Grand Hotel* LP, which he'd completed in late 1972. Tony King played the album for Tom, who liked it. Tom brought it over to Park Avenue for Pete to hear. "Pete really dug it," Tom later said, "We both decided we wanted Chris to do our next album."

Joey, Mike, Pete and Tom at Olympic Studios, 1973

The band and Thomas went into Olympic Studios in early April. They first went through older tapes, and began to overdub on a few songs. Joey's "I Can Love You" had previously ended up heavily reverbed and fuzzy. Thomas did a nice restoration job, though he did leave the lead vocal surprisingly upfront. Joey didn't have the pure warm tone that Pete had when singing ballads, but he could portray a lot of feeling. Joey later said he wrote "I Can Love You" with Rod Stewart in mind, but Stewart allegedly rejected the song, claiming he didn't cover songs previously done by other artists unless they were old standards.

Another song by Joey, "The Winner," was possibly just a remix. The lyrics are puzzling, until Joey gives his explanation, "It's about John Lennon," he says. "I was so angry that here was this man at the top of the world, who could have anything he wanted. It was at this period when all he seemed to be doing was moaning. He just seemed to be angry about everything, and it just pissed me off."

You can drive a car, be a movie star
Any day of the week
You don't have to shout, or walk about
You just have to speak. . . .
Here he comes, that's a winner
Take a look, write a book
You can eat him up for dinner

Producer Chris Thomas remembers being impressed, "Joey's lyrics often had a funny sort of thing going through them, like an irony, which is great. I really enjoyed his words."

Joey's "Get Away," was overdubbed on, whereas a couple of newer tunes by Joey may have been started from scratch. "Icicles" is an dynamic ballad, which begins with a backwards guitar, while "Constitution" completely switches gears – a rocker with a heavy-sounding riff and detuned chords, not too unlike the Beatles' "Helter Skelter."

Mike Gibbins' "Cowboy" was kept from the earlier sessions at The Manor, but Mike feels it ended up a bit of a disaster. "I thought the take I did with my Welsh mates was better," he says. The Badfinger version, which includes an Irish fiddler, has the "wobble-board" rhythm mixed way up front.

For this album, it would have been reasonable to expect Badfinger would feature more instrumental passages, based on their recent live outings, but it only partially turned out that way. "Most of the good playing, especially the drums, was all cut out," says Mike. "On a lot of songs we'd be jamming and jamming, but it was all faded out."

Tom's "Blind Owl," was one track where the momentous build-up is quickly faded after an explosive opening and some engaging rhythmic interplay. Tom later explained the lyrics were mainly about touring woes and personal demons:

Pill-driven skills
Weeping whippoorwills
Too much going round to get high
Days, plays, interviewer's maze
Play the role, sell your soul
Come into yourself
A hero who must never lie {Blind Owl – Tom's initial demo}

One song *did* end up extended: "Timeless." It had been a challenge, as the group hoped to create a powerful climax. "We must have recorded it a half-dozen different ways," said Joey. "We were obsessed." Pete's final guitar solo has brilliant moments, but the song's grinding windstorm finale does go on maybe *too* long. The lyrics are simple and direct. Pete's theme is quite philosophical:

How can we look and not even see?
How can we live and not even be free?
Are we the future?
Are we timeless?

Pete had increasingly been examining his own mortality. Beverley recalls, "The idea of there being nothing after you die frightened Pete. He didn't come from a religious background. But as time went on, he started to contemplate it more and more. When he was a teenager he found it hard to believe in God, because there was so much suffering in the world. He couldn't rationalize it. When you're eighteen you feel invincible and pretty safe in saying, 'There isn't a God,' but as the years go by, things happen and you start to talk more about it with people."

Beverley and Pete had been communicating to a greater extent at this time, but very few of their friends were aware. Beverley explains, "After Dixie had gone back to the states, I did meet with Pete openly at first, but people were gossiping and saying, 'Oh, it's back on again,' so we decided to meet away from everyone. At first we used it as an opportunity to cry on each other's shoulders. I was recovering from a broken relationship, just as he was. Then we started to talk about other things. We talked about our families and personal issues. He would discuss whether someone had said something that hurt him or made him happy. He talked about his concerns for the band, his frustrations over writing material and having it rejected, or getting a lukewarm reception. He had a few songs he really believed in that got dismissed. I would say, 'Don't throw them away, Pete.' I told him to do a solo album some day. He would have liked to do some blues type numbers and some things with his brother, but he was still into the group, *always* what was best for the group.

"He was really down about Kathie pushing and pushing and getting involved. He said she was really getting into their business and money. Pete wasn't interested so much in material things. He just wanted to earn enough money to continue a music career. But Kathie wanted a lot more. She could see it was possible, 'So why not have it?' Pete had trouble understanding her ways. He felt she was influencing Joey to her ways of thinking."

Brian Slater recalls, "Prior to Kathie, Joey Molland was a fun-loving guy who had no responsibility, didn't want any. Everyone liked him, he was good-time, good-laugh Joey. He became very serious and very heavy after Kathie came 'round. She indoctrinated him into a much more mouthy leadership role in the group."

Beverley: "I would see Kathie talk with Joey and he would present the same exact thoughts back to the band word for word. Some of it made sense, but it really bothered the boys, because it was obviously her speaking, not him." Fergie adds, "Kathie may have had some good ideas, but the rest of the band resented her input. Watching her was like the movie 'Spinal Tap'."

Pete had written some lyrics at this time which showed a major pent-up frustration. For one tune, "I've Waited So Long To Be Free," he even uses a four-letter word. Other lyrics show him thinking about relationships, writer's block, and the environment. It was apparent Pete also had a burgeoning interest toward spiritual and philosophical issues, as he had put down words directly relating to God, religion, and afterlife. The following was in one of his songbooks:

. . . when he reached down for a stick on the ground
He saw a tear on the petal of a rose
The rose, it appears, was so happy before
That is, before the grey dust had covered the floor
It knows that it's going where all roses go
To the garden that grows in the sky

On April 21, 1973, Beverley left for Zambia, Africa, where she had been invited by a friend to visit. She was expected to be gone for about two months. By early May, the band and producer Chris Thomas had completed mixing tracks and they presented the rejuvenated album to Apple. Despite Pete's major recent songwriting success, he had ended up with only two songs on the LP. His third recorded track "Piano Red," had been dropped. Joey had five of his eight recorded songs included, and granted, they were all quite solid. In fact, a *very* strong tune of his, "Do You Mind," was left off. Pete had written a lot of songs too, but the issue for him may have been – they were never even recorded.

The album was called *Ass*, Tom's idea of cleverly indicating what he felt was progressively happening to the group, i.e. *"No Dice, Straight Up* your *Ass*." He gave the title to Peter Corriston of AGI Graphics and suggested a design symbolizing money, fame, and the temptations that come with it. Corriston painted a donkey

Ass LP cover

(with headphones on) being beckoned by a giant hand-held carrot. He added a shot of a braying jackass for the inner sleeve. "Peter Corriston came up with that whole idea, the whole painting," said Joey. "We were the donkey being tempted by the golden carrot in the sky."

The cost of redoing the album, including the fee of Chris Thomas, had ended up close to £15,000. Apple had given the band a decent chance to produce a quality new album, nullifying rumors that this was a hastily put together project.

After the previous tour ended, Tom brought Patsy back to England. And though Marianne was the true love of his life, they were estranged now. It was difficult for Marianne's friends to feel congenial toward Patsy. She was a carefree girl, and a more than willing partner to Tom's outrageous inclinations. Tom's mother, May, recalls an incident not long after Patsy arrived at Tom's home in New Haw, Surrey. "Tommy had a big party and the next morning Patsy woke him up and told him she had a terrible toothache and would he take her to a dentist? Tommy said, 'Yeah, after I get up' and he went back to bed. She didn't want to wait, so she took his car out and started to drive away, but she forgot you drive on the other side of the road in England. She crashed into a wall, and all these bricks came apart.

"She came back and told Tom and he went out to look. It was really a mess – bricks were everywhere. He calls up my husband who was a bricklayer and says, 'Would you come down here, dad? Patsy's knocked down a wall. Could you build it up?' My husband was in Liverpool and he said, 'You've got a bloody cheek, Tom!' "

Patsy was eventually taken to a hospital for observation, but quickly released. She stole a stethoscope as a souvenir. Meanwhile, somebody had noticed the car's license plate when she had driven into the wall, and the police traced it as Tom's vehicle. They showed up at his door and he explained about Patsy. They asked where she was, and when Tom went to look for her in the house, he couldn't find her. Meanwhile, the police had noticed the remnants of a party and started to check for drugs.

May Evans picks up. "The police couldn't find Patsy. They didn't see how she could have gotten away without their seeing her. At some point they asked Tommy if Patsy might've taken her life. He said, 'No, no, she's a laugh,' but they dragged the canal behind his property anyway. Eventually they gave up and left. Tommy came back inside and opened up one of his cupboards. Patsy was curled up inside, in a little ball, shivering. Tommy said 'So, how's your toothache, Patsy?' And she said, 'What toothache, Tom?' "

Shortly after, Patsy was deported back to the United States by United Kingdom authorities – on drug possession charges.

Tom and Marianne had known each other for almost five years now. And though their relationship had been stormy at times, they had strong feelings for each other. Tom's infidelities, mood swings, and wild antics made him suspect husband material. But Marianne stuck by him. She was a hard worker who always had good jobs, usually at restaurants, and many times fed Tom by bringing home substantial late-night meals. But Tom had taken advantage of Marianne's willingness to hang without a commitment. The situation regarding Patsy had been a pivotal point. After Patsy left, Tom wrote Marianne, who was now in Germany. Gaynor recalls, "Tom said in his letter he was sorry. He'd made a mistake in bringing Patsy over. He wanted Marianne to come back to get married. She told him, 'No, not until I speak to Gaynor.'

"Tom took me out to the *Bull & Bush* pub and started buying me drinks. He said, 'Marianne's gonna call you and ask if I'm serious about marrying her. Would you tell her 'yes?' He got me drunk. I was terribly giddy. We came back to the house and Marianne called. I said, 'Oh, he loves you, he loves you Marianne, come over, come over to see him. . . .' She said, 'Only if you're telling me the truth, Gay.' I said, 'Yes, yes. Of course he loves you, of course he does, Marianne. In fact . . . *he's here right now*!"

Marianne accepted Tom's proposal and a wedding was hastily arranged. It was held in May of 1973, with many friends in attendance. The reception was at a restaurant in London called *Teddy Bear's Picnic*. Jan Evans, Tom's sister-in-law, recalls how the evening transpired. "It was terribly festive and you could see that Tommy was getting drunker and drunker. I remember that somehow the wedding cake had been forgotten and someone had to run out to get one. We were all waiting and Tommy was getting restless. With Tommy there was always this feeling in any group situation, that excitement was just around the corner. He said, 'I'm gonna jump through that plate glass window.' And because it was Tom saying it, everyone was going 'Hmmmm,' 'cause Tom could do just about anything.

Finally the cake came and we moved out to the balcony. Guitars were being played; it was really getting 'out there.' I remember Tom's dad had his drink spiked, and everyone thought it was Tommy who did it!

"Around midnight, I got startled because Tom's mother screamed. He had jumped over this little three-foot wall, not knowing it was a ten-foot drop to the other side, and he hit his face on a birdbath. There was total chaos. Some people were laughing, others were stunned, some were hysterical. Finally, one of Marianne's Swedish friends drove Tommy to the hospital, but they went the whole way on the wrong side of the road!"

Except for a few chipped teeth, Tom turned out okay. He and Marianne then left for their honeymoon in Greece.

Tom and Marianne's, wedding reception, May 18, 1973

Badfinger had expected the *Ass* album would be released sometime during the summer of 1973. The band also assumed they'd be doing a tour with The Beach Boys in the United States. Instead, they received word from Polley that all touring plans had been canceled. He wanted the band back in the studio to begin work on their first Warner Brothers album. The group was very upset. There would be no support gigs for the impending *Ass* album. They were being given only two weeks to prepare for a new LP. The band was not clear on why this scenario was happening.

A situation had been developing which the group was basically unaware of. When Joey Molland had joined Badfinger he did not sign into the original Apple publishing agreement. In 1970, Apple Music made at least two documented attempts to get Joey to sign the long-term contract. For some reason, he never did At certain stages, Polley had been instructing Bill Collins that he make sure Joey did not sign with them. Joey had been signing over his individual song copyrights to Apple as each album was completed.

When the group turned in their *Ass* album in February of 1973, Apple requested Joey's copyright assignments, just as they had in the past. Bill Collins assured Apple's Tony King there would be no problem. But Joey never did comply.

Polley used this situation as a bargaining chip for negotiations. It was later testified in court, that on May 9, 1973, Polley, and his attorney, Walter Hofer, met with Bernard Brown, head of Apple Music Publishing, and Neil Aspinall, who was now managing director of the Apple Corporation (Allen Klein had left by this time). At this meeting, Polley was documented as stating that Joey Molland's copyrights would be turned over to Apple if:

(a) *the* Ass *album would be released to coincide with Badfinger's planned summer tour*

(b) *the Apple Publishing Agreement and Recording agreement would immediately terminate*

(c) *Badfinger royalties amounting to £20,000, which were past due, would be paid out within a few weeks.*

Polley claimed Bernard Brown verbally approved to these requests on behalf of Apple Publishing. But Neil Aspinall said he could not give final authorization on behalf of Apple Corps., only George Harrison or John Lennon could.

Without the response he desired, Polley's next move was to cancel the summer tour. He instead focused on getting the band to record a new album, presumably so Warner Brothers advance money could be freed up as soon as possible. WB Records president Joe Smith recalls, "Polley was continually representing to me that the band was having financial problems. He was trying to get early advances from us to help with the situation."

The Warners contracts weren't due to kick in until September 1, 1973, but Polley went ahead anyway and set up recording dates. The group had no choice but to follow his orders. Without much incentive, they prepared to go back in.

Living in London at this time was Polley's ex-client Lou Christie. Christie had established himself there, partly because of some current success in the U.K., but mostly because he'd wanted to escape the Polley "net" back home. He recalls, "Polley had stopped giving me my checks at one point. It got so I couldn't even live from week to week. When I'd complain he'd tell me things like, 'You know when you fight me, you'll spend all your time fighting me, and you'll never go further. You'll be too caught up trying to find the answers.' And he was right, so I left.

"I occasionally ran into Badfinger at London pubs. I kept hearing bits and pieces about their problems with Stan, different things. They were such sweet guys. I dreaded to think what was going on. . . ."

Fergie recalls the band members and himself having conversations around this time, relating to their financial future. "I remember us sitting in a car and talking about how nice it would be to have our own houses. In fact, as I recall, Pete was trying to get a home at some point."

Pete's bank records show that on May 24, 1973, a £2,000 debit draft was set against his account. But Pete only had £122 available, so this would have put him deep into the red. The bank would only have issued a debit draft if they felt the money covering it was going to come through. "Pete was so careful," says Beverley. "He would never do something like that unless he was sure the draft was going to be reimbursed. I remember my parents did something like that once, and he was so taken by it, like, 'Boy, what if the money doesn't come through? That would be terrible!' "Six days later, Pete's debit draft *was* canceled. Somehow the money had not materialized.

Beverley remembers different scenarios which might come up whenever the group members would make monetary requests from Polley. "They would often get told things like, 'There's a hold-up' or 'There's a problem in getting money transferred from point A to point B.' Whatever the reason, Pete was more than willing to believe it. Obviously, money would trickle through, they got cars and a few bits of equipment, but they were often frustrated. . . ."

In June of 1973, the band did receive an increase in their monthly salaries to £600 per month. On the surface, Pete seemed content with the financial set-up. He was not showing any outward notion that he believed Polley might be ripping them off. He was upset by some of the creative and touring decisions, but when the other members would criticize or question Polley's integrity, Pete would defend him vigorously. "You would never hear Pete dragging anybody down," says

Gaynor. "He didn't like people to be negative about each other. He always chose to see the best in people."

But Tom said he felt Pete was a little too insistent in his defense. "Pete was the type of guy who, once he put his trust in somebody, he was gonna stick by it and persevere in what he believed in – right or wrong. He wasn't easily led into different ways. He could be very stubborn with his beliefs."

Just before the band was to start recording a new album, a gentleman named Richard Duryea appeared. He was the son of American actor Dan Duryea, and had worked in the music business as a tour coordinator for groups like the Beach Boys, The Faces, and Chicago. Jeff Franklin of ATI had recommended him to Polley, who then sent him to London. Duryea recalls, "I was hired by Polley to keep things going, to babysit the band. Prior to this they had been having trouble getting albums done and he wanted me to keep them working. They had a high demand of records from Warner Brothers, and they had to pay for their studio time. He asked me to do what I could to keep things moving. We discussed a price. I wasn't cheap."

Fergie recalls Duryea's arrival, "The band went out to see him in London and he was living in a prime location in a very nice house. Everyone thought, 'God, this must be expensive!' It was questioned, but Bill said he was a 'rich boy,' that his father was a famous actor. But the band wasn't satisfied. The fact Polley was always in limousines and eating at the fanciest restaurants, all of these things started to get to them. They thought, 'Well, why can't we have some of that?' "

Mike adds, "Duryea was living in a fancy house in a fancy part of London, which was more than I could afford, and we were footing the bill. He was just a gofer for Badfinger Enterprises and I was in the band living in a scumbag house!"

Duryea began by coordinating with Bill Collins, "I tried not to make Collins feel like I was usurping his power," he explains. "But basically Polley told me to take over the reins, because he didn't think Collins could handle things. I used him as much as I could. He was definitely a factor, because he knew the band intimately."

Bill Collins says Duryea checked his accounting records, as Bill was still handling the band's expenses on the English side through deductions and payouts from the Apple royalty checks (which were still being made out to him). "Duryea couldn't find anything wrong," asserted Bill.

The Badfinger members wanted Chris Thomas to produce their first Warners album, and he agreed to it. But Thomas recalls the group were not overly enthusiastic. "They'd wanted to tour off the Apple album," he says. "They didn't want to record. They hadn't had time to prepare. Everyone was kind of mentally exhausted going in."

The sessions began on June 21, 1973. One of the first songs tackled was a Joey Molland composition entitled "Love Is Easy." Joey recalled how it came about, "Every time we'd rehearse I'd try and throw out tunes I was working on just to see how they sounded with bass and drums. The guys would generally get behind them. We were at Olympic Studios and I just started playing a riff I had. Everybody went 'Wow!' and we put it together real quick."

The recording is very loose. Joey's lead vocal sputters, sounding more like a scratch take, and towards the end he runs out of ideas. "I was just going, 'duuuh doo' because I hadn't finished it yet," said Joey.

The rhythm guitars ended up quite indistinct and an oddly distorted guitar solo cuts in-and-out. "That was all intentional," said producer Thomas. Additionally, the snare drum was doubled and augmented with occasional handclaps. Many U.K. pop acts at the time were emphasizing the beat for their glam-disco singles.

Joey felt the song had potential as a British 45. He and Kathie lobbied hard. "Kathie was really pushing then," says Gaynor. "She said it was Joey's turn." Beverley, who had since returned from Africa, recalls. "[Kathie] was absolutely adamant that Joey get the next single. Pete told me the band okayed it, but I don't think it was what he really wanted."

Fergie: "If Joey, Tommy, or Mike had written a dynamite single, Pete would have had no problem putting it out. He would've been ecstatic if Joey had a hit. But I don't think he really felt this was the song to do it."

WB Records in England was approached. Working as managing director at the time was Ron Kass, a former head of Apple Records from the pre-Klein era. Kass had recently been at MGM Records, where he'd once tried to lure Badfinger, but fate brought them back together when he accepted the job at Warners U.K. in 1973. "Love Is Easy" got his go-ahead as a single for the U.K. market.

At some point, the recording contract had been moved up to start on August 1, 1973. "Love Is Easy" was scheduled to come out in September, with a B-side of Mike Gibbins' "My Heart Goes Out," a folk ballad featuring two acoustic guitars. Yet the track gives the sensation a multitude of mandolin-like guitars are playing. Chris Thomas explains, "I put all sorts of tape delays on that." Mike wasn't pleased, "What Chris did sounds nice, but I thought it lost its soul. I originally finger-picked it and I was making noise with the strings. I kind of dug it, but he wouldn't have it."

Mike also found he didn't like the pace Thomas and the others were working. His frustration peaked with Tom's song, "Why Don't We Talk." "Five days to do the

1973 Japanese documentary film

backing track and *two weeks* to do the vocals!," shouted Mike. "Every time I'd come in the studio I'd hear it going round and round. At that point I was listening to the Mahavishnu Orchestra and I wanted to play drums as much and as fast as possible."

Another Evans song, "Where Do We Go From Here," is a mid-tempo pop tune which utilizes electric piano as its main instrument, with a *steel drum* playing the solo. "An experiment of mine," says Thomas. "Unfortunately some of them didn't work out too well."

The group had one more tune recorded. It was written by Tommy and its working title was "Oh Wow." It's a loopy, moody song that features a recurring riff and a bit of an uptempo jam, very reminiscent of the band's live act. It was left in the can, possibly unfinished.

During a five week break in the sessions, Badfinger were filmed at their tiny practice space by a Japanese crew shooting a documentary. The group, and their extended families, ended up being periodically shot over a period of about three weeks. A segment (ultimately made use of) features the band rehearsing a song called "Shine On." Pete is the main focus here, and in a few short minutes you get a chance to view many of his traits: the silly side, the serious side, his soulful ability on guitar, his creative intensity, and, at the end, his deeply-rooted introspection. It's a good capsule view of the man.

"Shine On," is a collaborative song by Pete and Tom, which the band arranged with a country-rock tinge. Oddly enough, The Eagles, who championed that approach in the mid-70s, were recording in the very next room at Olympic Studios. A few of their members were excited to find Badfinger working nearby. They came round a few times to listen and socialize.

While completing the song's lyrics, Pete and Tom had each thrown out verses. Pete came up with the majority of words, but Tom tidied up a few lines. In Pete's songbook, there is a lyric written as, *"Slip and slide and fall into the fantasy."* Tom scribbled out the last half and slotted across the entire top half of the page: "SO I'LL FORGET REALLITTTY." The line stuck.

Prior to this, Tom and Pete had not worked closely together for almost two years. Tom now had bouts of writer's block and lived far across town. Pete's confidence had been declining after the many rejections he'd suffered. Their getting together was almost an act of desperation. "Pete had been panicking that he'd written his last good song," says Fergie. "The others weren't supporting him as much as they used to. They weren't saying, 'Well, let's see what you have and try and change this bit.' They had been getting less and less likely to discuss his ideas."

Mike said he always felt he was quite open with Pete, "He used to come up to me with a rough draft of a song and say, 'How'd you like it?' and sometimes I'd say, 'No, it's bullshit.' He'd just rip it up and scrap it."

Over the years, Pete had written in a lot of styles: torch ballads, blues, show tunes, Motown, even jazz instrumentals. But it wasn't until now that he tackled anything quite like "Matted Spam." The song was earthy in nature and Pete's original demo features a furious rhythm guitar and passionate lead vocal. This may have been his attempt to write a stage-oriented number. But the group recorded it with a clean, syncopated rhythm and a prominent horn arrangement.

Pete's demo of "Matted Spam" also had a section sung to the lyrics of "Day After Day," possibly in tribute to Beverley, who was apparently still on his mind. Pete had been dating several women over the last few months. The one he saw most was a London girl named Zoe. She'd been a casual acquaintance for years, and Pete finally became intrigued enough to see if there was a spark there. She was crazy about him, but he never reached the same sentiments toward her. In some of the Japanese documentary you can see her watching Pete's every move. Pete had been trying to let her down easy and finally he told her it wasn't going to work out. She became very distraught. Pete was devastated to hurt her so badly. He wrote a song for Zoe called "Lonely You."

Pete and Zoe, 1973

When I ask you just to be my friend
I want to lend a hand
But if we get too close it's sure to end
Oh can't you understand
Lonely you – lonely me

The band recorded it with tasteful slide guitar and warm organ pads. Pete added most of the background vocals, with Tom contributing one chilling walk-down line. Thomas recalls, "Tommy used to come up with a lot of their vocal ideas."

During these sessions Joey started off yet another guitar riff, which turned into a number called "Andy Norris." "Andy Norris was the tape operator at Olympic," said Joey. "He was always doing crazy things like standing on a piano. I named it out of affection for him" (The engineer's real name is Andy Morris).

The song is uptempo rock'n'roll. Saxes were planned, but they never made it in. Kathie helped Joey with the lyrics, but she claimed he was reluctant to give her credit. She said Joey relented, after she wouldn't speak to him for three days.

Joey had another number, "Island," on which Mike pounds out some jungle-like drums. It's a slow-paced tune; Pete running off a succinct solo mid-stream. The jam at the tail features Joey's slide guitar which builds to a very satisfying climax. Producer Thomas was impressed, "Their solos were always perfect," he said, "just right for the songs."

As good a composition as Joey's "Island" was, his "Give It Up" may have topped it. Opening with subtle pathos, Joey sings with his electric guitar muted, "I think it starts off being about the band," he said. "The second verse is about the money-hungry people, the young deceivers who play their games." Joey's eventual chorus of "give it up" rides over a colossal wall of buzzing guitars. The background voices blend effectively, cutting off at strategic points. Pile-driving solos find their way through the entire din. Arguably, this was Joey's finest composition to date. Though a departure from the band's usual pop-rock vein, it portrayed a "healthy" progression.

On August 4, 1973, Bill Collins got married. His new wife was a young lady from Canada named Toni. She was twenty-four years old. He was sixty. The Japanese documentary shows the band and others preparing an outdoor tent for the reception, and a few incidents before and after the actual wedding. Everyone gets quite loaded as the night wears down. No one is spared embarrassment.

As the documentary closes, descriptions are made of the group's personalities. Mike is said to have a "good sense of humor," Tom is "quiet," and Pete is "slightly nervous." It's Joey who gets the strangest take from the narrator, as he is called "a spoiled man, who may implicate anyone into his own pace, unnoticeably."

When Joey Molland had first come on board with Badfinger, he was quickly termed a "comedian." Though everyone in the band could get crazy, he was the most often "on." Roadie 'Tag' Hall, who had known the group for years, and been working as a Badfinger roadie since early 1973, recalls, "Joey was a stereotypical Liverpool person. He's the only person I've ever met who could sit for eighteen hours in a recording studio, six days a week, for six straight weeks, tell jokes the whole time, and never repeat himself. A very dry sense of humor." Many recalled Joey's light-hearted take on life, which sometimes carried to extremes. It's alleged Pete became so upset at Joey's constant joking during interviews, he turned to him one time and said, "That's it Joe, I'm not doing any more interviews with you."

Joey had long taken the business side lightly, trusting everyone, as Pete and Mike had. But with Kathie pushing, he began to speak his mind more and more. "Joey started to become the businessman of the band, along with Tom," says Gaynor. "Pete and Mike were always more focused on playing their instruments, writing songs, being musicians." Adds Mike, "Joey was kind of a half-hippie, half-banker. He was quite one or the other." Joey was described as changing mood and opinions at a moment's notice. "A classic Gemini," some said.

In an Apple bio, Joey stated, "Basically, I'm a coward. I don't like making decisions, not unless I have to." But with Kathie's arrival, Joey had become more assertive. Kathie pushed him to be more involved musically, and it was paying off, as he was writing some excellent material and growing as a guitarist. But his close involvement with her was also bringing a certain detachment to his relationships with the other band members and Bill.

Joey Molland
(with Bill Collins above)

Badfinger, 1973

After the Warner Brother's record contract had gone into effect, the group had a meeting with Derek Taylor, then head of their Special Projects Promotion. Badfinger wasn't considered his territory, but he was asked to to write their first press bio, and to meet with them, as a goodwill gesture. Derek recalls, "Joey was much more vocal now. He had stepped up. He had a lot more to say. Pete was very quiet. Tom seemed excited. I was happy for them. I felt they would be successful."

"Derek gave them a great big pep talk," says Fergie, who was there that day. "He said they'd be treated even better than they were at Apple. He said everything was going to be great for them. But the Warner Brothers company was so big; they were just ultimately another act to them."

At that time in 1973, the record industry was basically six multi-national companies; Warner Brothers Communications being amongst the biggest. They had hundreds of artists spread throughout their labels and subsidiaries. But Badfinger did expect special treatment due to their sterling track record. Interestingly, the first Badfinger/Warners single put out in the U.K., "Love Is Easy," *did* have a promo film, but it wasn't Warners who'd financed it. A BBC filmmaker, Tony Beresford-Cooke, used footage he'd shot with his own Bolex camera when the group had recorded at the Manor Studios the year before. He used his own facilities to process and edit the film, with some help from Tony

Bell, Nicky Bell's brother. The film was a series of close-ups of the band with their instruments and studio gear. Previously, Beresford-Cooke had shot the back cover photo for the *Ass* album. He'd also become a good friend of the group. He was especially close with Tom.

Badfinger was now expecting the *Ass* album to be released on September 5, 1973. But the date passed and there was no sign of it. Polley's attorney, Walter Hofer, started threatening lawsuits to Apple and Capitol Records. Nothing happened. Walter Hofer then gave one *final* request to have the album and all of its rights transferred to Warner Brothers. Again this was ignored. When the band was interviewed at this time, Pete was quoted as saying, "I don't know what's going to happen to (the album). But I hope it is put out at some stage. It's horrible to think that there's a part of our lives locked away somewhere."

On October 15, 1973, Capitol (Apple's distributor) gave notice to BEI they were finally going to release *Ass* in America. But Hofer advised them that Polley was now the publisher of Joey's songs and he would not be giving out the "mechanical licenses." Polley had decided he wanted to *stop Ass* from getting out. Hofer also told Apple that they still had royalties overdue to Badfinger, and their continuing failure to pay indicated a crumbling empire, possibly unable to pay out any future revenues.

A few months earlier, Apple attorney David Braun had requested an extension from Polley to pay overdue royalties due Badfinger. He stated that most of Apple's funds were then being restricted by English courts, due to a lawsuit involving Paul McCartney. But Polley had not been agreeable to the proposal, even though Braun assured him Apple could get a loan to pay if necessary. Instead, Polley had begun a new series of strategies.

Dated November 1, 1973, one day after the Apple Publishing contract would be terminated, a contract exists which shows Pete Ham assigning half his gross publishing income go directly into the BEI company. Polley had always pushed it would be beneficial for the group to put more money into the company name – for more protection on taxes, to create assets for BEI going public, and for further utilization towards future investments. Though the band was skeptical by now, allegedly each member went ahead and signed similar papers.

The prior week, the "Love Is Easy" b/w "My Heart Goes Out" 45 had been released in Britain. A *Melody Maker* review cited the A-side as *"great dance music,"* but was unenthusiastic about its chances. *Sounds* gave it a mediocre critique. The BBC radio stations immediately complained about some of the distortion effects. "They wouldn't play it because of the sound of the solo in the middle," said Joey.

The single was "dead-in-the-wool," Badfinger's first out-and-out failure. Noted producer Chris Thomas, "The mix is very inefficient. The drums are too loud. It's a mess. There's some good ideas in there, but they don't come across." Mike concurs, "Would you buy that record? Joey never even finished the words. Yet we recorded it!"

The sessions for the first Warners album were moving slowly. During the previous three months, the group had played intermittent gigs around England. One was performed as a favor to George Harrison. Fergie recalls, "The band used to get a lot of Hare Krishna followers coming to shows because of the connection to George. He had bought this house for British Hare Krishnas, which was about thirty minutes north of London. Badfinger was asked to play for some benefit. The Hare Krishna in Britain was more of a druggy scene, a lot of hangers-on, and it was a madhouse when we got there. The place was packed, but it was totally unorganized and chaotic, just stoned hippies wandering around. The gig was a disaster."

Unbeknownst to Pete at this time, Beverley Ellis was making important plans. She explains, "When I had gone to Africa in April, I had visited a friend of mine, Colin Tucker. I had originally met him because he was roommates with someone I worked with. We'd become good friends. He'd even met Pete a few times. After I had been back in England for awhile, I had gotten a telegram from Colin proposing to get married. I accepted. This was in October. I told people not to tell Pete because it was something I felt I had to do. I didn't want it to be, 'Oh, by the way, Bev's going off to get married.' I wanted to sit down, have a drink, and tell him by myself, because I knew it would affect him a lot.

"It was about the second week of November and I was at my parent's house in Hemel-Hempstead. It was quite late and I got a phone call from Anne (Fergie's wife). She said, 'Could you speak to Pete?' I thought, 'This is strange? If Pete wanted to talk to me he would.' She said, 'I had forgotten about not mentioning your engagement and I told him. I'm sorry, he's in a terrible state.' She said she had been in the kitchen cooking and they were just chatting when she mentioned it.

"Pete came to the phone and he was very upset. He said, 'Why didn't you tell me?' He was very drunk and he started to cry. That was very difficult for me. He wanted to come by, but it was very late. I didn't want him driving in that state, so I told him I'd have to see him the next day.

"The following day I was waiting for him at a pub. Pete came in with a bandage wrapped around his wrist. I was shocked and frightened. He told me he had put his fist through a drink machine at the recording studio. His wrist and his hand had gotten cut. He was very emotional. Knowing I was leaving had opened up a lot of old feelings for him. Remember, from the first time I was in London I had been a part of his life in some capacity or another. It was a mixture of things. He was losing a friend he could confide in. He didn't have a girlfriend then. He was lonely. He was feeling uncertain of his future.

"I decided to extend my leaving a couple of days, just so I could talk to him a bit more. I spent some time with friends; then I was going to focus on Pete before I left. I offered to Anne to let me babysit Blair, to allow her and Fergie to go out. That way I could talk more privately with him at the Park Avenue house.

"By the time I got there, we had done a lot of talking on the phone. We were a bit talked out. Instead, it was more like we went back in time. Pete was acting like we were eighteen again. It was strange because he responded like nothing was happening. I didn't say anything. I just thought, 'That's his way of dealing with it.'

"On the last day, Pete went into the bathroom. I had been in there earlier and taken off my engagement ring. I left it on the sink. Pete came out holding it and tears were in his eyes. He said, 'I think you forgot this.' I said, 'Pete, I have to leave. You'll be in the studio the next few days. I don't think I'll be able to see you again.' That was very difficult for him. He became very sad."

On November 17, 1973, Beverley departed for Africa. On December 7th, in Lusaka, Zambia, she married Colin Tucker.

Toward the latter stages of completing the Warners album, the band finished a song by Pete called "You Had A Dream." It's a pleasant pop tune, though not quite as distinguished as Pete's past work. The track is somewhat salvaged by a forceful ending – a rising guitar over a blitz of compact harmonies. Pete had discussed the song with Beverley, telling her it was partly about him, and partly about her. "Pete told me the line, 'For awhile your dream came true,' was about both of us." After Beverley moved away, he retitled it, "Song For A Lost Friend."

Pete also told Chris Thomas he had an older song he wanted to do. It was highly unusual for Pete to dig into his back catalogue. Beverley recalls, "Just before I was to leave for Africa, Pete told me there would be a song for me on the new album. I asked him how I would know which one it was. He said, 'You'll know it as soon as you hear it.' "

The number was, "I Miss You." Pete had written it for Beverley back in 1968. "Pete and I had a brief break-up at the time," says Beverley. "About a week into it

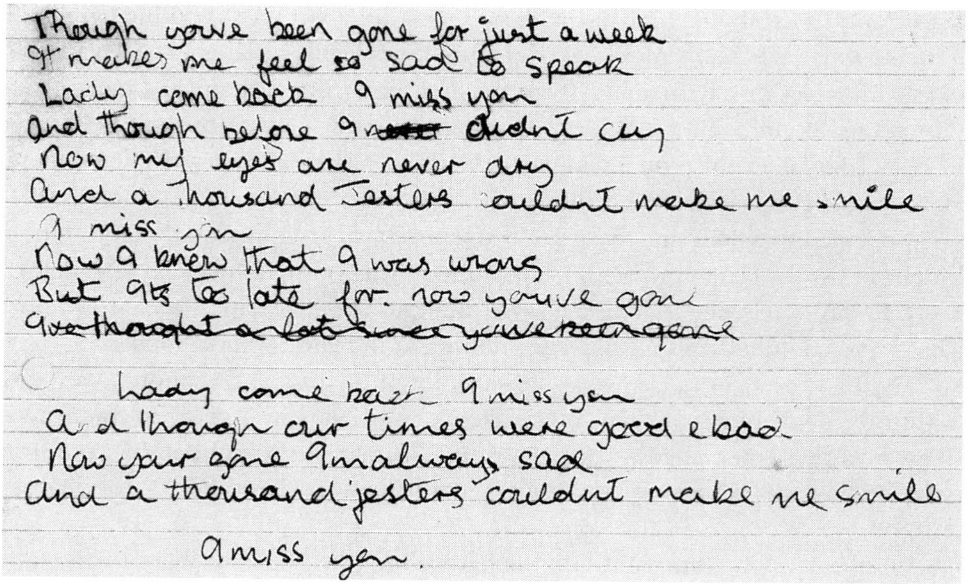
Though you've been gone for just a week
It makes me feel so sad to speak
Lady come back I miss you
And though before I ~~never~~ didn't cry
Now my eyes are never dry
And a thousand Jesters couldn't make me smile
I miss you
Now I knew that I was wrong
But it's too late for now you've gone
~~I've thought a lot since you've been gone~~

Lady come back I miss you
And though our times were good & bad
Now your gone I'm always sad
And a thousand jesters couldn't make me smile

I miss you.

Pete Ham's original lyrics of "I Miss You"

he'd become severely depressed and he wrote 'I Miss You.' " Pete recorded all the instruments for the album version himself.

The first Warner's album was completed by November 22, 1973. It had taken five months, but the actual time spent was more like two to three months, as there had been numerous breaks and one-off gigs. "Everyone was exhausted at the end," says Chris Thomas, "I could tell because the band's interest seemed to wane. When it got to the song order, we were all very tired. We thought the first three songs ("I Miss You," "Shine On," "Love Is Easy,") were the most likely singles at the time. There was some disappointment in how "Lonely You" came out. That may be why it got buried. Pete was the pickiest one. He was more of a perfectionist than the others, but in a good way."

Noticeable about the album is the wide variety of material and arrangements. Many of the tracks sound solo-oriented, sort of like a Badfinger *White Album*. Joey: "That was the first time we had what I thought were weak tracks. Up to that point I had liked everything we did. Also, we were pissed off about the management, and I think it affected the recording adversely."

"They were definitely getting discouraged and depressed," says producer Thomas. "But much of what happening with that album was partly my fault. I was experimenting a lot, trying different approaches from one song to the next. I don't know if it was particularly the right thing to do."

On November 19th, just three days before the first Warner Brothers record was completed, Apple released the band's *Ass* album in the United States. Walter Hofer tried to reach Apple's lawyer, David Braun, but was unsuccessful. He finally got in touch with Capitol Records and told them they should have the record pulled immediately. But Capitol declined any comment. Two days later, Hofer sent a letter to Apple threatening a lawsuit if they did not respond in twenty-four hours. Seven days later Apple's law firm finally did reply: *"Apple Records, Inc. is under no obligation whatsoever to request licenses from Badfinger . . . Accordingly, Apple Records, Inc. shall not delay the release of any such recordings."*

On December 5, 1973, in a New York City district court, Badfinger Enterprises (BEI) sued Apple Records, Apple Publishing, and Capitol Records, for copyright infringement.

December saw a lessening of band activity, but a lot of scrambling was going on behind the scenes. On the same day Polley filed his lawsuit on behalf of BEI, he also filed American copyright registration forms for Joey's songs from *Ass*. Polley had noticed on the American release of the *Ass* album, each of the songs were listed on the label copy as being written by "Badfinger," instead of by the individual writer's names. Polley portrayed this move as a cover-up by Apple in a December 12, 1973 affidavit. The very next day, Polley petitioned for an injunction to recall *Ass* from the marketplace.

A week later, Apple attorney Peter Bierstadt gave a deposition to the court. He said the lawsuit was simply harassment by Polley to gain leverage to get overdue royalties. He added that Polley had no evidence to support his claims and asked why there was no statement from Joey Molland, whose behavior was very much at issue. Joey was flown to New York, and an affidavit from him did appear, notarized by Walter Hofer. It read: *"I confirmed the recording agreement. Although on numerous occasions I have been asked to sign an exclusive publishing agreement with Apple Publishing Ltd., I have refused to do so."* But Joey gave no reason as to why he had refused to sign it, or why he had now assigned his *Ass* material over to Badfinger Music (a new publishing sub-division of BEI) instead of Apple. Additional statements portrayed that he had *willingly* given Badfinger Music his copyrights. Other affidavits from other parties followed, but it would not be until the following months that Apple would fully prepare their responses.

The *Ass* album still had not been released in Britain or Europe and it was off to a slow start in America. It entered the *Billboard* charts on December 15th. Two days later, a single was released, "Apple Of My Eye" b/w "Blind Owl." Neither received

Pete Ham

Sue Wing

much promotional push. But the band was kind of oblivious; Sue Wing, the band's former agent and good friend, had recently been found dead from a drug overdose.

Never really comfortable with her life, Sue had often resorted to drastic measures. "She'd almost overdosed twice before on sleeping pills," says Mike. "She'd phone up, and Gaynor and I would have to go over and fix her up, take her to the hospital." Gaynor adds, "She'd been in good spirits. She was about to go on a trip. It may have been an accident this time."

Pete hadn't dealt much with death before. Now, one of his good friends had apparently taken her own life. Reportedly, he found her passing quite difficult to bear. He needed to talk, he needed to communicate, but his closest friend, Beverley, was gone; and his other friends had their own lives to contend with. His family didn't really know Sue. Pete Ham, pretty much, suffered alone.

8

GOT TO GET OUT OF HERE

WITH THE FIRST BADFINGER album for Warner Brothers Records now ready for release, the publishing company, WB Music, decided it was time to check on the whereabouts of the $100,000 advance they'd given BEI's Walter Hofer for "escrow" placement. On December 3, 1973, a Warner Brothers auditor contacted Hofer as to where the money had been secured. Hofer wrote back that he had "no idea," indicating he had given the check to Stan Polley. The auditor pursued Polley and received no reply. WB Music's, Ed Silvers, then approached both Polley and Hofer, but he, too, was ignored. "I was getting irritated," he commented.

While home for the Christmas holidays, Pete mentioned to his brother, John, he was becoming a bit worn of the band situation, especially of the touring, and often wished he could just go off and write songs. He reportedly had a brief fling with a previous Swansea girlfriend. Upon his return to London, Pete greeted Fergie's wife, Anne, who had just come back from an operation she'd had in Scotland. Fergie had not contacted her there at all, but Pete had called several times. Anne told Pete she appreciated his concern for her health. They started to go out to the local pubs together. "Fergie and I weren't getting along," says Anne, "and Pete would listen to me and talk with me. He was like a big brother."

For the first part of the year, the band rehearsed for an American tour. The debut Warner's album had been scheduled for release on December 28, 1973, but because of *Ass* coming out late it was now being held back. Meanwhile, *Ass* was not doing too well in the United States. The album peaked at #122 in *Billboard*, and then started a rapid decline. There was virtually no promotion going on. The single, "Apple Of My Eye," was an unmitigated disaster, failing to reach the Top 100. The band was discouraged. Nonetheless, there was hope an impending tour and the Warner Brothers LP release would bring everything back to life.

In late January, a *Rolling Stone* review of *Ass* came out. It was encouraging, but showed the "Beatle" comparisons were not about to be let go:

> *The album title is the band's reference to themselves as unwitting followers of some enticing but unrealizable dream. That dream may have been Badfinger's expectations of their place in the Beatles' initial plans for Apple as the nurturer*

of worthy talent, or it may have been the group's fantasy that, by being in close proximity to the Beatles, they could somehow BECOME them. In discarding that dream, they've discovered their own identity as a group, and that discovery gives this album its surprising forcefulness . . . This is a surprisingly inspired album from a group that has never managed to string its scattered hits into a distinguishable identity. . . .

Though Badfinger had a lot of early success, the "Beatle" tag contributed to keeping them from being regarded as a viable musical force. Now, after a long absence from the marketplace, they desperately needed a hit single or some consistent FM airplay to restrengthen their position.

In January of 1974 there were more proceedings regarding the BEI/Apple lawsuit. Apple attorney Peter Bierstadt gave his rebuttal of the depositions of Polley, Hofer, and Molland, stating, *"When one examines Joey Molland's affidavit . . . his omissions are striking."* Bierstadt questioned why Joey would agree he was under the Apple recording agreement, but not the publishing agreement. Bierstadt also discussed the copyright assignments Joey had made to Badfinger Music. They're on American registration forms, with the date listed as January 3, 1973. But the group was in England at the time. Bierstadt also noted Stan Polley's name was signed for by a "J.A.S," a person apparently never identified. The implications were these papers were doctored and thrown together after the fact.

What shows these accusations may have been true is some of Joey's songs listed on the copyright assignments, like "Constitution" and "Icicles," were not even recorded at that time of registration date. Yet songs of his clearly intended for the then proposed *Ass* album, like "Regular" and "Do You Mind," were left off!

Tony King (Apple's English A&R man) and Bernard Brown (head of Apple Publishing) gave testimonial affidavits on January 14, 1974. King stated that Bill Collins had always represented that Joey was subject to the original Apple publishing agreement. Brown added, *"Bill Collins always maintained that the reason Joey Molland never signed . . . was because of a dispute Badfinger was having with Allen Klein . . . and that this technicality would never be used against the Apple companies."*

The presiding New York judge, Arnold Bauman, took the evidence and denied BEI's injunction to have *Ass* stopped in its tracks. In his opinion, he stated the prevailing law in America is *"copyright license may be implied by the conduct of parties."* But despite indications he was going to ultimately favor Apple's side, it would be several months before the lawsuit was fully resolved.

Continually during this time, Ed Silvers, head of WB Music, had been trying to get an answer regarding the $100,000 he had entrusted to *"Badfinger,"* or *"an attorney for Badfinger,"* for escrow holding. In a letter dated January 23, 1974, he informed BEI they *"must correct"* themselves and place the $100,000 in an escrow account. He said their actions were in breach of contract. He also warned that he might terminate the publishing agreement if this wasn't rectified shortly.

Polley ignored the request. Originally, he had spread the $100,000 into five Savings & Loan accounts under the name BEI. But WB Music was not aware of this. On February 6, 1974, Polley withdrew the money from the five accounts. On February 21st, Polley's attorney, Walter Hofer, sent a letter to WB Music claiming the $100,000 was now in a federally insured S&L. On February 27th, WB Music sent a letter requesting more specific details. No reply was ever given to them.

Badfinger's first WB album was finally released in America in mid-February, 1974. It was simply titled *Badfinger*. This was not what the band had intended. Tom originally came up with *For Love Or Money*, which referred to the group's dilemma over having signed the lucrative Warner Brothers contracts. The band was quite surprised when the title was left off. Pete indicated that Warner Brothers was not happy with their idea and took liberties to retitle the record themselves. Pete also said the band got no say in the cover design.

The LP's front cover is a lady wearing horseback riding attire, with a cigarette holder in hand. On the back the group straddles horses. Mike recalls, "All I remember about (the photo session) was this photographer saying, 'You're gonna be a star, man. Just keep on the fucking horse! *And stay in the camera!*' "

Badfinger *LP cover*

The group's sixth U.S. tour began on February 18, 1974. Starting in Texas, the band worked their way up through the Midwest. They did a lot of numbers from the two new albums, but there was still no single from the Warner's LP. Everything was beginning without much of a buzz. The gigs varied in size and quality. Sometimes they played two shows a night; two-hour sets were also done. The venues ranged from extravagant halls to small-scale rock clubs.

Jamming was still an onstage priority with Joey now performing as many solos as Pete. "Suitcase" had become totally free-form, and it could either be interminable, or a great showcase of spectacular energy. "Timeless" was often – endless. But other songs had a tighter scope. "Constitution" and "Blind Owl" were well-constructed, and despite their length, usually received good reactions.

On February 23, 1972, the group played Michigan State University in East Lansing. Former *Creem* magazine editor, Dave DiMartino, was a student there. He recalls, "The show was at The Brewery, about a five hundred capacity bar. There was this degree of awe that a band of their caliber, with four previous big hits, was playing this tiny club. If Brian Auger had been there, that would've been more realistic, not a band everyone had heard of.

"They were having a rough time. It was an awkward show and everything was going wrong with their sound system. I remember they started "Day After Day" and midway through they had to stop. They played an improvised blues tune for quite awhile before they could start up again. I felt sorry for them.

"I went backstage after the show and I went over to Pete Ham. I tried to make some small talk and he was being really nice to me. It wasn't as if he saw some moron hippie guy, he was being very affable. I started to mention some songs of his that had been covered, like "Without You" and "Midnight Caller," and I sort of naively stressed how ironic it was that people were covering his material and getting airplay, and yet here, their albums weren't getting played on the radio, and they were at this small college club, dealing with a screwy record release pattern. The whole tone of the night had been semi-tragic.

"After I said all that Pete looked really dismal, as if I'd thrown a barrel of salt into a gaping wound. I felt like a bonehead. I could see that it ran really deep in him. I was overwhelmed that I could have such an effect on him."

The group toured throughout March, still without a new single. They had not been provided with their own quality sound system; having to rely on house systems or local rentals. Despite these obstacles, the band had some great receptions. On March 4, 1974, in Cleveland, Ohio, they played the Agora nightclub and an attendance record was set. When the band arrived, they had found a 16-track recording set-up was wired into the stage, and they decided to tape the show. Chris Lambert, then a writer for the city's *Scene Magazine*, was

U.S. Tour #6

in attendance with his father. He recalls, "It was announced the gig was going to be recorded for a live album. The band came on, but they ended up doing blues jams for almost forty minutes while they were fixing all these microphones that weren't working. Then they did a really long set with lots of encores. Afterwards we went backstage . . .

"They were drenched in sweat. Pete Ham was by himself sitting in a chair, catching his breath, and we went up to him and introduced ourselves. He shook our hands and I said, 'Pete, this is the highlight of my career so far. I really like your music.' He said, 'Listen, it's my honor that you like our music.' Then he put his arms around me and my dad. He called my dad 'Mr. Lambert' and he said, 'You're the guys who have to go out and work all day. You're the guys who should be put on pedestals. I'm just singing the songs.' That blew us away!"

The band listened to some of the show's recording later that night and were not happy. There had been lots of technical problems and some of the songs were performed sloppily. The vocals of Joey and Tom were wildly inconsistent. It was not taken seriously for a live album at the time.

At a gig in Boston, with Big Star supporting, Pete's frustration climaxed. Student Christopher Makris was in the audience. He recalls, "The band was doing two sets and, during the second set, Joey was acting a little tipsy, a little mouthy. He started bumping into Mike's cymbals, generally being obnoxious and unprofessional. Pete was upset. He started scowling at him and staring at him. Pete stopped the show. They were doing a song and suddenly it was decided that it was going to be the last one. It was obvious to me they were cutting off early."

In early March, the *Ass* LP, and the single "Apple Of My Eye," were finally released in Britain – to little or no fanfare. *Melody Maker* was guardedly optimistic, citing "Timeless" as an exceptional track, but the reviewer wondered if the band were on their way to becoming *"another Apple casualty." New Musical Express* called the album *"deadly dull."* Both were critical of the production, noting the group had remarkable potential which had not been brought out.

At various times throughout the month, Badfinger played dates across Canada. {Hotel interview with Pete and Tom, Toronto, Canada, March 29, 1974} The shows in Vancouver and Edmonton went over well, but there was an inconsistency to their receptions. The group's technical and logistic problems were omnipresent. The stage sound – quite raw. Mike was frustrated, "We could've done what other bands did and gotten a keyboard player, a percussion section, and a few chick singers, but we never did that. It was up to us to go on stage and sound like the records with just four guys." Joey adds, "We never got to rehearse with lights and all that stuff. The general presentation was a bit shabby. All we did was go onstage and play music."

*Cleveland Agora,
March 4, 1974*

*Joey and Pete listen
to Agora tapes*

The band's abilities were such that when they did "click," they could be sensational. "But this tour wasn't going real well," says Fergie. "The band kept to themselves more. They knew the records weren't selling and the record release pattern was fouled up."

It wasn't until late March that a single was finally released by Warner Brothers in the United States. Despite the fact their record contract had said it must be a mutually agreeable decision between the group and the company, WB Records put out "I Miss You" without forewarning the band. "It wasn't our choice," said Joey. "I remember we were all shouting and raging about it. That got played some, so Warner Brothers put it out. From the band's point of view we were always being promoted as Pete Ham's vehicle. There were a lot of other good songs on that record."

Mike says he was unhappy for another reason. "I was disappointed because I imagined that song with a big orchestra, a big thing, but it was a throwaway version. The song was not made use of. Someone could pick that up and do an A-1 version with an orchestra. Then you'd have some dough."

The 45 of "I Miss You" b/w "My Heart Goes Out" turned out to be a complete bomb, not even charting in *Billboard*. The Warner's album also did not do well. It peaked at #161 before dropping off the Top 200 after only five weeks. Because the albums *Ass* and *Badfinger* were released so closely together there, they were sometimes critiqued simultaneously:

> ZOO WORLD *Badfinger seemed, at one time, to be the hope of the future for those who relished the past efforts of the Beatles . . . Apparently, something has shaken them off their confident path . . . These two albums are half-worthy of the Badfinger talent, and it's pretty upsetting. . . .*
>
> PHONOGRAPH *Two Badfinger albums in one month! What more could a fan ask for after a two-year drought? . . . actually, the fans will be asking plenty, and Badfinger have a lot to answer for, because these two mediocre albums are already one of the biggest disappointments of the new year . . .*

Circus described *Ass* as *"a self-explanatory album from a once inspired band,"* while Fusion said *"it has to be put at the bottom of their work."* The *Badfinger* album was lambasted in Rolling Stone, yet Circus called it *"one of their finest albums,"* Disc & Music Echo praised it as *"stunning,"* and Sounds cited it as *"damn good."*

The best shot the band seemed to have to give the Warner's LP life was to release Pete Ham's "Lonely You" as a single. Though the recorded track lacked an instant immediacy their previous hits had, the song obviously had commercial potential. What's really strange is the Warner Brother's record contract had stated that a minimum of three 45's would be released for each year term, starting on September 1, 1973. But, for some reason, WB Records, never released any other singles from the *Badfinger* album!

The group's sixth U.S. tour was due to finish the first week of April, 1974. That same month the Japanese T.V. special was shown in Japan. It turned out to be a half-hour retrospective of the band's history and was dominated by a lengthy scene of Bill Collins' wedding reception. Bill had brought his new wife, Toni, on the tour. She had previously been getting restless and bored at 7 Park Avenue. Fergie recalls, "There was a band that lived down the street called Wild Horses that she kept going down to visit. Bill caught wind of it and became insanely jealous. He went down there one day and she was in bed with someone. He jumped right through a window and started smashing things up. He went mad!"

Collins kept tight reins on Toni during the tour. "He mainly watched her," adds Fergie. "He didn't really have a role to fulfill now. He just talked about himself and tried to show off. He'd say, 'You take the lift. I'm going to run up to the eighth floor!' We'd meet him upstairs and he'd be falling over, beet red. He'd stand on his head, do pushups; the band was getting embarrassed by his behavior."

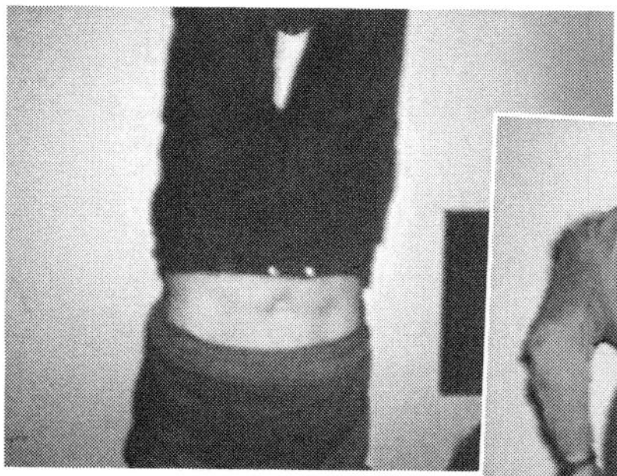
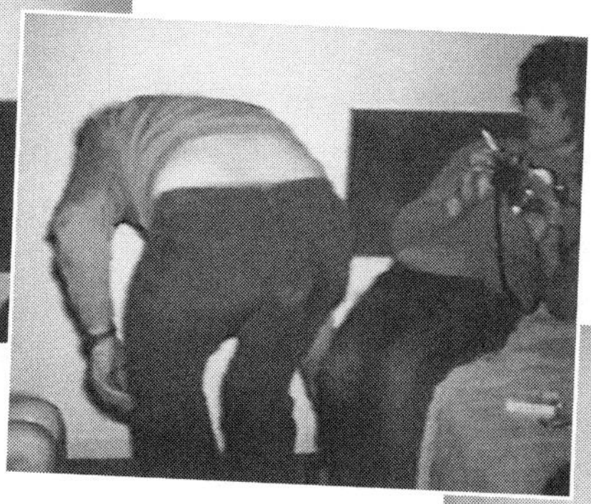

Bill Collins

Bill admits to his stunts without shame. He also recalled his overall role had truly diminished by this point. "I remember one time Joey looked at me and said, 'What is your doing on these tours anyway?' I told him, 'Looking after my share of the partnership!' "

Badfinger had been told they were to go straight from their last touring gig to a recording studio. This was a very upsetting scenario, as they would have preferred to come home, relax, and write for at least a couple of months. But they were given no choice. Their record contract required six albums over the first three years, a hugely demanding pace. "We couldn't possibly deliver it," said Joey. "We were totally goosed in a business sense."

Richard Duryea had booked the band to record at Caribou Ranch, a fairly new recording studio co-owned by Jimmy Guercio, manager of the band, Chicago. It was in a very secluded spot – about sixty miles outside of Denver, Colorado – with horses and plenty of room for guests.

On April 2, 1974, just days before the American tour ended, Marianne, Gaynor, Anne, and the children, flew from England to Boston, Massachusetts, to join the group, so they, too, could enjoy the ranch setting. Fergie initially didn't have the funds to fly Anne and his son, Blair, over; he explains how it was accomplished. "Anne kept saying on the phone that she was really missing everybody. She really wanted to come to America. I went to Tommy to ask him if he could help out. He was my closest mate, he said, 'Try asking Pete.' I thought, 'Well, maybe I will.' But I ended up asking Mike next. He said, 'Why don't you see if Pete can help out?' I thought, 'This is strange.' I went to Pete and asked him if he could help and I'd pay him back. He started to cry. He said he would pay for the tickets."

On April 4, 1974, everyone flew out of Boston to Chicago for the last gig of the tour. Anne recalls, "We got to Chicago and I found out from Kathie that Fergie had been having an affair . . . I'd always wondered why he never called me in Scotland when I had my operation. . . ."

That evening – which was the night before the band's final show – Pete, Bill, Toni, Fergie, and Anne, were gathered in the lounge of a Holiday Inn they were staying at. Fergie recalls, "I remember clearly, a bunch of us were downstairs and I started to sense something going on between Anne and Pete. I found myself getting a bit grumpy and excused myself. Pete's room was just down the hall from mine and around 2:00 a.m. I heard people coming up and I went outside. I saw Pete and Anne holding hands. I flipped out. I said, 'What the hell is going on here!?' Pete was really shaken. He went into his room. Anne and I got into this huge argument. She said she was leaving. She said our marriage was over. I couldn't believe it."

Anne: "I was already mad at Fergie and ready to leave him before he confronted me about Pete. Everyone had known about his affair with that girl except me. I brought it up and he said, 'That's different.' Well, Pete and I had done

Fergie and Anne

nothing. There was no comparison. That was it. I said I was taking Blair and going back to Scotland.

Fergie: "I was freaked out. I never thought my marriage would end like that. I'm not saying I'd been the best husband, or the most faithful, but there was no chance to work anything out. I had to leave right away because of the circumstances."

Anne prepared to go home as word traveled around on what had happened. Pete came into Anne's room. She recalls, "Pete said that he cared for me and didn't want me to go back. I had sensed before that he cared about me, and I had strong feelings for him, but nothing had gone on between us, despite what people may think. I asked him why he hadn't told me about Fergie's affair. He said he wouldn't have wanted me to leave Fergie because of something he'd said or done. He asked me to go to Caribou Ranch with him. I told him I would."

The other band members and their families were quite upset about Fergie. "There was a lot of friction right away," says Anne. "Joey and Kathie would hardly speak to us. And Tommy and Marianne weren't too happy about it either."

Gaynor recalls Pete's anguish, "This wasn't the type of thing Pete would've set out to do. He would not have set out to have something like that happen deliberately. I could see he was suffering. I felt really bad for him."

After the gig, Fergie left for Minneapolis with Joey and Kathie, who were taking a brief stopover there before the recording would start. With Fergie gone, roadie David "Tag" Hall ended up driving the band's equipment by himself to the isolated Caribou Ranch. "I was stunned by the situation with Fergie. I didn't even get to say goodbye. I was totally numb. But when I finally got to Colorado, I thought I'd died and gone to heaven. It was beautiful out there."

The setting was radiant, as winter was coming into spring. The Badfinger entourage were set up in chalets and encouraged to horseback ride and snowmobile. But the stress of having to jump into recording, in addition to Pete's developing relationship with Anne, left a very unsettled vibe.

Chris Thomas was again enlisted to produce. The band had felt the failure with the last album was more to do with their material than his work. Thomas recalls, "I had been in Japan producing the Sadistic Mika Band when I was contacted to work with Badfinger again. It just so happened I had about a five-week break in the recording so I could give them about a month to start on their record. I remember the first night I got there we all met and I was wondering how they were. I asked them, 'Are you really ready to make a new record? Do you have enough material?' They were bringing up problems: they hadn't had a chance to write any songs, they were upset about the tour, their manager. They felt the reason they were in the studio so soon was so the advance could get picked up. Then it was brought up that nobody wanted it to end up like the last album. So I said, 'Look, the way out of all of this is – let's just make a great album, the best you've ever done!' Sure, everybody wants that, but I thought we should make a very conscious effort to succeed. It was a pep talk."

The band jumped into the recording. Thomas encouraged the band members to present any ideas they had. Mike was noodling on the piano, and while doing a practice exercise, he came up with some words. "Chris had asked me what I had and I said, 'I got this.' He said, 'Let's do it.' I thought he was joking." Mike's endeavor became "In The Meantime," a song about "the decadent know-alls and bigheads," relates Gibbins. Thomas made Mike lay the piano track down first. "He was frustrated when we did that," says Thomas. "It was hard work."

Joey also had an unfinished tune, "Some Other Time," and Thomas suggested they create a medley with Mike's tune. "It wasn't any brilliant revelation," says Thomas, "I thought 'Why not try it out?' "

Mike, Pete, Tom, Caribou Ranch, 1974

Stan Polley

Even with things rolling, there were problems that were interfering. "Tom Evans was going nuts," said Richard Duryea. "He was complaining about Polley. He could be real nice, have one drink, and then he'd go off."

Besides Tom, Joey was also not of a good mood at Caribou. "They both were down on Polley," says Mike. "It was 'This guy's shit,' and 'We ain't got no dough,' and 'If he's got it, we ain't ever gonna get it.' "

About a week after the sessions started, Stan Polley showed up. He wanted the band to sign more papers. The animosity was very strong, especially from Tom. At one point, Tom came into his chalet and started smashing up an acoustic guitar. "He threw the pieces into the fireplace and burned them," said Marianne.

Just before Polley had arrived, the band's agreement with him – to put 50% of Badfinger's publishing income directly into BEI accounts – had expired. On a document dated April 15, 1974, the band and Bill Collins now authorized Apple Publishing and Apple Corps Ltd. to pay 100% of Badfinger's future Apple publishing and recording royalties directly to BEI (Badfinger Enterprises).

Also, by this time, the 1972 meeting regarding five parties sharing in the band's publishing and writer income – if technically such agreement was valid – had expired; on April 11, 1974. Court documents from 1985 portray a Polley lawyer alleging that Joey signed a paper in 1974 reaffirming this split to continue. But there has never been any indication anyone else in the band signed such a paper, no document has ever been produced, and no time frame to this alleged agreement was indicated. If there was a legitimate document, was this done for Polley's benefit, or was it a renewal for the band's and Bill Collins' purposes?

Polley's visit to Caribou Ranch certainly had a major effect. "Tom was upset," said Mike. "He couldn't write or play. He was useless. He wasn't around half the time. We'd be doing backing tracks with no bass."

"Tommy actually quit at one point," says Chris Thomas, "but Polley wouldn't give him an airline ticket to leave. So Tommy sat there for three days. He was trying to hold everyone to ransom, but he didn't have any money to leave. He got bored. He finally figured if he was stuck, he might as well play on the record."

Throughout the band's stay in Colorado, Pete was dealing with unsettling treatment over his liaison with Anne Ferguson. "Joey and Kathie were giving him the cold shoulder," says Anne. "And Tommy was teasing him. Some cowboy took me out to go shopping one day, and Tommy started on Pete about it. Another time, one of Pete's songs about an old girlfriend came on the radio and Tommy said, 'It's a good thing Anne isn't hearing that.' Pete was hurt by those things."

Pete unleashed his frustration through a tune he wrote called, "Just A Chance." It comes off as his plea to everyone concerned:

I won't tell you if it's short or long
All I know is that it don't feel wrong
You may say it's not a great romance
All we want from you is just a chance to try
Any way we can
Don't you think we know it has to hurt?
Won't you understand?

The instruments were laid down and another Pete tune, first entitled "No One Knows Me," was recorded. Pete was being very autobiographical. But soon he changed its words to his love for Anne, titling it "Know One Knows." No one recalls why he changed the spelling of the first word.

Other thoughts of Pete's came out in a cassette demo, in which he sang:

Lawyers pricing, temperature's rising, all day long
All I wanted was a sunny afternoon . . .
Nothing to show for the hard work
Nothing to show for the time we've spent

No evidence was found this song was recorded by the band, but another tune of Pete's certainly was, "Meanwhile Back At The Ranch," in which his singing is extremely impassioned:

If only they would let us know
Then we'd know just how far to go
But instead they just tell us no, tell us no

Joey Molland was also getting frustrated. He came up with a song called "Got To Get Out Of Here." Joey sings of a man wanting freedom, not fully sure of what moves to make. "It was unbelievable," he later said. "I couldn't think of anything else. I just wanted to get out."

Joey also wrote, "Love Time," while Mike contributed "You're So Fine." Both said they were love songs written for their wives. Gaynor, Mike's wife, especially enjoyed the ranch setting, despite a startling accident that knocked their son, Owen, out cold. Kathie, meanwhile, had been her typical vocal self. Chris Thomas recalls, "I remember her being around and discussions between the band like, 'Well, is Kathie going to be the manager then?' and stuff like that. But I let the details flow, because I had a job to do."

Anne remembers Kathie approaching her several times at the ranch. "Kathie would say to me, 'This is great! You can work on Pete now!' She said I could have an influence on him, that I should work on changing his attitude. I told her I wasn't interested."

Kathie ended up in some heated arguments with Joey and it led to her saying she was going to leave him. She ran into Pete after one episode and he tried to calm her down, but she was so upset, she threw a jar of peanuts at him. It missed, and instead of hitting Pete, broke a window, right behind his head.

Kathie Molland, Pete Ham, Caribou Ranch, 1974

On April 19, 1974, Kathie went off to California. She had seriously warned Joey she was breaking off. Meanwhile, the band was working long hours – usually mid-day to three in the morning. The actual recording was going well, though the band had lost valuable time over the business arguments and Tom's tantrums. Then, a studio problem arose. "Our engineer suddenly left," says Chris Thomas. "He went to do live sound for the band, Chicago, and the studio didn't have anybody else available. I had to do it myself. Luckily, things were sort of left set up."

Late into the sessions, a letter had been received at the BEI offices in New York, dated April 30, 1974. It stated that WB Music, the publishing arm, was *terminating* their contract with Badfinger. Ed Silvers, then head of WB Music, relates, "I was infuriated with what I interpreted as being ripped off by real sharpies. I wanted to pursue getting the money back, and I was willing to go to court if necessary."

Polley responded by sending Richard Duryea papers at Caribou Ranch, to have the band members sign a new agreement concerning Apple Publishing money, similar to the one they had allegedly signed weeks earlier. It was dated May 1, 1974. Under this new agreement, 50% of the group's publishing income was to now go directly into Badfinger Music (BEI's publishing company), instead of BEI itself. Polley was probably leveraging against the WB publishing termination threat, which could affect how he ultimately held onto the band's overall publishing income in the long run.

Of course, the group members didn't know what was developing with Warner Brothers at this time. Polley had left the ranch a few weeks earlier, but his assistant, Richard Duryea, was there throughout the proceedings.

Possibly other papers were signed. Somehow, Polley was still getting contracts inked, despite the fact Tom, Joey, and Mike, had strong beliefs they were getting ripped off behind the scenes. Kathie also had recently returned from Los Angeles with warnings at hand. But Pete was refusing to openly accede to the others' suspicions. Mike recalls, "Pete was being stubborn. Joey and Tommy were yelling. Guys from Liverpool yell a lot. Welsh people take a back seat. They watch and listen, watch and listen."

Up to this point, Polley may have manipulated what he wanted from the Badfinger members, but it had been a particularly tough year for him regarding his other clients. At one point, songwriting partners Irwin Levine and Larry Brown had procured a large royalty check. Polley wanted a share. Says Levine, "This large sum of money had come in for our song, 'Tie A Yellow Ribbon Round The Old Oak Tree.' My partner, Larry, had gotten suspicious over time. He decided he didn't want it put into the company accounts. It was about $100,000. Stan took us to court to get it. But we beat him. The very next day he took us out to lunch. . . ."

Though they terminated their relationship shortly after, Levine and Brown considered their days with Polley their heyday; a lot of good luck and fond memories. But for ex-client Charlie Calello, the nightmare was far from over in 1974. He recalls, "I had finally decided to come back to New York to pursue the money Polley owed me. I'd worked out what I wanted to get. I walked up to his office and I confronted him. He said, *'Get out! You have no money here!'* Then he pulled a gun on me. My wife had just left me. She had taken off to 'find herself,' that 70s thing. With the trauma of that and Polley pulling a gun on me, I went totally into shock. My ten-year old son had come with me and he had to pull me out of the office. He was saying 'C'mon dad . . . c'mon.' I had a breakdown on the spot."

Polley's gun was no secret to Badfinger. Tom told many people about seeing it, and felt it was a not-so-subtle reminder. Mike and Bill also talked of seeing it, as did Pete. But no one confirmed any specific threats behind it.

Badfinger's final day at Caribou Ranch was May 8, 1974. The recording sessions were to be picked up again at Air Studios in London. That was the place where Chris Thomas was most comfortable. Joey took advantage of the break to fly over to Los Angeles with Kathie. She had previously returned to the Caribou Ranch with interesting news. May Pang, then John Lennon's girlfriend, recalls, "Kathie had called and told me that they didn't have any money and there were problems. I remember telling her at one point she could try talking to Harold Seider, who was a friend of mine. Harold had worked at Apple as legal counsel for Allen Klein. He was now helping John Lennon. Harold was also working as VP of Music Affairs for United Artists Records; he was not out there soliciting work. His only outside job was representing John Lennon."

Kathie related that while visiting in California, she met Harold Seider at the beachfront residence May Pang and John Lennon were staying at. May Pang says she does recall Seider being there with Kathie, on the one day in which Kathie visited. Kathie claims she talked with Seider fairly extensively that day, and several times afterwards.

Joey said in a 1991 interview conducted by Jon Johnson for *Discoveries, "(Kathie and I) saw an attorney and he gave us the goods. This is when it was put to me by people in the music business that Badfinger was getting creamed . . . When I found out about it I wanted to sue our business manager, Stan Polley. I asked the guy, who was a major attorney, if he would represent me . . . He said he would do it if I could get all the other guys to come in with us. He said, 'I don't want to be fighting them as well.' "*

In other interviews, Joey Molland claimed Harold Seider was the attorney he referred to. For some reason, Harold Seider, when approached for verification in 1995 and 1999, continually denies he ever talked to the Mollands and will comment no further. May Pang, who has known Seider for over twenty-five years adds, "Harold never actually told me he did speak to [Joey and Kathie] . . . If Harold had spoken to them, he would not have spoken about Polley specifically. I've known him for over twenty-five years. Harold Seider is not the type to spread rumors or talk about other people in the music business."

In another interview, Joey claimed "The president of United Artists told me that Polley tried to sell Pete as a solo artist." Mike Stewart was president of UA at that time in 1974. He responded in 1994, "I never even *knew* Polley had an association with Badfinger. I only had dealings with Stan Polley in regards to Al Kooper. Badfinger was a big band. I would've remembered something like that." Joey also claimed there were others in the music business who gave him rundowns on Polley, yet he has never publicly named who they were.

For his next move, Joey said he went to Polley to try and see if he could set up a deal to get the band released from Polley's contracts. From the *Discoveries* interview: *"I told (Polley) that we were going to go back to England and close up the business. 'We'll freeze everything, and you're going to have nothing.' Or, we can make a deal, a settlement, where we would give him that money and he would give us all the Warner contracts back and tear up the Badfinger Enterprises contract. And then we'd be back to square one with our four-piece band and our one-piece manager."*

In another interview Joey claimed he came back to England with his plan. "I told the group the deal. The group was a little screwed up now. Peter could not believe we were being ripped off. He just could not believe it. Total faith, could not believe it. Tommy could believe it, but he didn't want to believe it, 'cause he didn't want to make the change. He had a little arrangement there that we didn't know about. Mike didn't care about it. He just liked to get high, everything was cool. I didn't really care. It was my wife who cared."

On May 24, 1974, BEI's Walter Hofer mailed a letter to WB Music refuting their right to terminate the publishing contract. Meanwhile, Ed Silvers had been continuously digging into Polley's background. He relates, "Bright Tunes, a production company with former members of the Tokens, such as Hank Medress, had terrible things to say about their business relationship with Polley. We started to find that his background was highly questionable, and that some of that background was not in the music business."

After everyone had left Caribou Ranch, Bill Collins paid a visit to Polley's New York City office. Bill stated that Tom was constantly on him to try and dig up more info on Polley; what he was really up to regarding Badfinger's business and financing, and that Tom demanded Bill go. Bill acknowledges he was more trusting of Polley at this time, but he claims he did have some suspicions, mostly based on the lack of paperwork he would get from Polley regarding the group's finances, and the paucity of "corporation" meetings that were supposed to be held regularly.

Over a three day period, Bill spent a lot of time sitting and waiting. Polley was claiming to be too busy to see him. Collins said it was BEI vice-president Terry Harvey who finally said to Polley, 'C'mon, the poor guy has been waiting for three days. Why don't you see him?' Bill says he finally got in, but he received no straight answers from Polley. Bill recalls getting to see some paperwork, through BEI's bookkeeper Beverley Newman, but he said it wasn't that informative. Bill also tried to visit with Jeff Franklin of the touring agency ATI, but he was not successful in getting a meeting, though he did see their prominent executive Ira Blacker.

In June, the group and Chris Thomas reconvened at London's Air Studios to finish up the second Warner Brothers album. There was a lot of passion flowing. Joey said he was very disappointed that he hadn't been able to get the group to agree unanimously on getting away from Polley. He began to seriously contemplate leaving the band. His song "Should I Smoke" seemed to relate. It's a brilliant, emotionally-charged number; Joey laying down a magnificent spine-tingling guitar solo to close it out.

Record producer Chris Thomas was working extra hard to make sure a quality album was being generated. His engineer for the Air Studios sessions, Bill Price, relates, "Chris would get specifically involved with the detail of a sound. Before that, many producers would say, 'Oh, just get the best sound you can get.' But Chris was meticulous, hard-working, and would get frustrated if he didn't get what he wanted."

Thomas had found his foil in Price, a tireless engineer. "Bill Price was patient," says Thomas. "I would often say 'I'm not satisfied' and he was quite prepared to work long hours to get what I wanted. For example, Pete had a song called "Know One Knows," which sounded great when I was working on it at Caribou. It was just bass, drums, and one guitar. The plate echo at Caribou Ranch had made it sound fantastic. When I tried it at Air it sounded like a joke. Luckily, I had printed a tambourine with Caribou's plate echo. Bill Price found a broken plate at Air and was able to set it up and transcribe that exact sound. It was amazing!"

Chris Thomas

This finicky approach was too difficult for Mike Gibbins to bear. "I almost got in a fist fight with Chris Thomas, because it was going so slow. He'd say, 'It's not right,' and I'd say, 'It fucking is!' He'd say, 'It's not right. We have to do it again.' He had to pull teeth to get me to sing 'In The Meantime.' I said to him, 'Get someone else to sing it 'cause I'm not a singer.' I wanted him to bury my voice. But he forced it. I give him that. He did try to bring out the best in people."

The hard work approach didn't bother Pete. He was always willing to put in extra takes if necessary. Mike was earlier quoted as saying, "Pete lives and breathes music. He goes into a studio and it gets hot and horrible in there, but he won't come out. He likes it too much."

Pete had a new song called "Dennis," about Anne's son, Blair. Anne recalls how the lyrics had started off, "There was a bubblegum machine at the studio and Blair had taken my purse and cleaned out the change. We were laughing about it. That started the idea." Pete used the metaphor of the mischievous T.V. character, "Dennis the Menace," as he did not want to use Blair's name in the song. There was a reason for that, as Beverley recalls, "After Dixie and Pete broke up in 1972, Pete told me he would never put the name of someone he knew in a song again. It was too painful, the constant reminder. . . ."

Apparently, Pete was proving to have a paternal instinct. "He was like a father to [Blair]," says Anne. "He was very concerned for his feelings. In fact, it was about ten days before Pete and I actually slept in the same cabin at Caribou, because he was so worried about Blair and how he'd react."

The band recorded "Dennis" with an extraordinarily long ending, which was quite hypnotic. After a test mix, Thomas shortened its length, though it was still rather extensive.

Pete also started a tune around this time called "It Doesn't Really Matter." This song had references to Pete and Anne's relationship, and the turmoil he felt surrounding it:

It doesn't really matter how they try
They'll never break up you and I
And though sometimes they'll make you cry
There's nothing they can do

It doesn't really matter how they sneer
For you will always have me near
From day to day, and year to year
There's nothing they can do

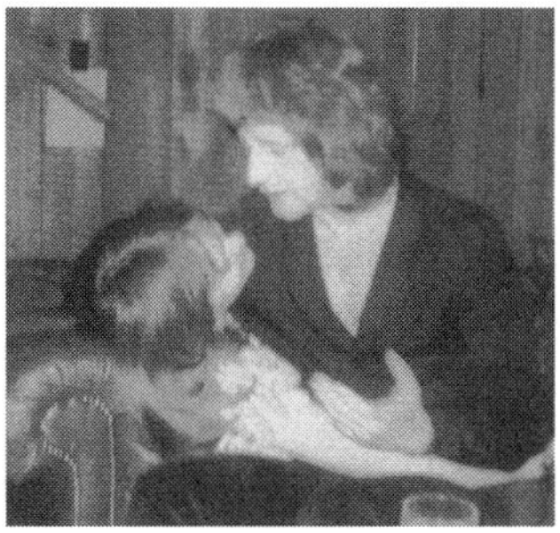

In June of 1974, the attorneys for both sides in the "Badfinger Music vs. Apple, et. al." lawsuit agreed to several resolutions. U.S. District court Judge Arnold Bauman declared a *"stipulation discontinuing action,"* effectively ending the case. Two of the things agreed upon were: *"1. Joey Molland shall personally acknowledge in writing that he is bound by each and every term of . . . (Apple) publishing agreement dated October 31, 1968 . . ."* That was not a surprise, but the second stipulation may have been: *"2. Apple Publishing Ltd. and Apple Corps. Ltd. shall, within two weeks . . . pay all royalties determined to be due under the publishing agreement and the recording agreement. . . ."*

Polley had seemingly gotten what he wanted – to have Apple pressured into paying overdue Badfinger royalties. Meanwhile, the whereabouts of the $100,000 WB Music advance had not been accounted for. Polley later indicated that sometime in July of 1974, he had absorbed it with other unrelated funds as a "certificate of deposit" at a Bank Of California. Interestingly, this "certificate of deposit" was put under the moniker Pamalan Management (named after his children Pam and Alan). Polley titled that as the "parent corporation" of BEI. Other ex-clients remembered Polley funneling their money into Pamalan Management as well.

By mid-month, Badfinger had nearly wrapped up the album. Tom had a song he'd written back in 1972 called "Queen Of Darkness," and there are indications it may have been recorded by the band at this time, but was eventually dropped. A new offering, "King Of The Load," (a song about roadies) "was thrown in at the last moment," snaps Mike, "and laboriously done."

During the latter stages, Thomas hired an orchestral arranger. Her name was Anne Odell, a keyboardist known for jazz gigs and studio work. Thomas says she happened to be working at Air Studios when someone recommended her. She took up his offer. Thomas recalls, "I went through the arrangements with her, in terms of sketching what I wanted. I told her things like french horns here, or a certain type of orchestral line there. The long chord in the front of "In The Meantime" was completely her invention. The whole idea of chords over that arrangement was her's. They were obviously brilliant arrangements."

"In The Meantime/Some Other Time" got the bulk of Odell's input. Another tune receiving her touch was "Know One Knows," on which Mika, a singer with Sadistic Mika Band, recited the chorus lyrics in Japanese, over the guitar solo. A few songs were augmented by the Average White Band's horn section.

By July 24, 1974, Chris Thomas had finished the LP. He presented the final mixes and the group was highly impressed. Almost every song was arranged to the hilt. The orchestration was creative. The band's performances: top-notch. But what especially pleased everyone was the clearer Badfinger identity. The Beatles influences were there, but no longer so obvious you *had* to acknowledge them. "We thought this was going to be the one," said Tom. Added Joey, "We'd finally solidified our ideas." Pete praised it highly in an interview, and Mike says he was elated, because he felt they'd finally made an "album," versus a string of "single attempts." Chris Thomas agreed with them all, "I mean it goes back to that first meeting. We thought, 'We've really pulled it off.' They came across as great songwriters and singers. I thought it was the best album I'd made to that point."

An LP cover was designed in which the group was shown as sailors partying in a Far Eastern bar. Joey explained how it came about. "We'd wanted to call the album *Wish You Were Here* and have a postcard album cover. It was going to be a double album cover with a perforated leaf attached. It would have six postcards on it with the band logo, and they would be detachable. We found some beautiful postcards from a friend of ours; Mike Doud, who used to work for Album Graphics in London. He had a bunch of really nice old postcards, old sepia kinds of things, fat ladies, art deco, it was really nice. The cover was going to be a shot of us at

Wish You Were Here LP cover

Caribou. Warner's said, 'No, we don't want to do this. It costs too much money.' So Mike Doud came up with the idea of the sailors uniforms. The idea was, we were sailors in Hong Kong and it was like, 'having a great time, wish you were here.' "

On August 6, 1974, the group played one confirmed show on BBC's Radio One, for which they performed "No Matter What," "Timeless," "Suitcase," and "Blind Owl." They were eager to do gigs in the U.K., as they'd done very little touring of late. Old friends Tim Boyle and Barrie Marshall were booking agents in London. They offered Badfinger a British tour with the Man band, whom they now managed. Though every Badfinger tour since mid-1970 had been set up through Polley and ATI, the band took some initiative and accepted this offer. Defiance was beginning to take hold.

Bill Collins: "Tommy called me up one day and said, 'Barrie Marshall is managing us now and we're going to do this tour.' I wasn't being consulted on their decisions any more. The "team" had broken apart. I called Polley and he said, 'Let them go ahead. They can't touch me.' He laughed it off."

The group spent the early part of August taking a much-needed break. Pete was the only group member still living at the Park Avenue house. The band members salary checks had increased and Pete was able to be somewhat generous with Anne and her son, Blair. "Pete was different in how he approached our relationship from what he did with Beverley," says Anne. "He bought me things. He wanted to get married and have a baby."

Anne Ferguson

Pete seemed quite determined to make Anne happy, but there was a snag. "I was hoping to get a divorce rather quickly," says Anne, "but Fergie wouldn't have it. We were going to see lawyers about it."

Fergie had taken on a roadie gig for the band, Blue, and was now living in Finchley. "At the time I was still very angry," he says, "A lot of what I was doing was to get back at Anne, not giving in."

In August, Polley's business accountant Sigmund Balaban, sent a letter to London accountants Goldblatt & Co. It stated that Bill Collins had called and asked for the individual account balances for each member and himself. Balaban wrote that he gave Collins the amounts over the phone, minus a few outstanding debts. Goldblatt & Co. were an English firm who had been recommended to Bill, by Polley, to handle the band's English tax issues. They were hired in 1972 and eventually became distributors of the band's salary checks. Balaban also addressed a "developing situation" which involved Polley. . . .

On August 14, 1974, BEI's Richard Duryea had shown up at the Warner Brothers' U.S. offices with tapes of the new Badfinger album, *Wish You Were Here*. However, while WB Records had taken their tapes in, WB Music's Ed Silvers refused their copies outright. He explains, "We were serious about filing a lawsuit, and were told that accepting the tapes may have invalidated our claim of fraud." Two days later BEI's Walter Hofer sent a letter to WB Music stating their refusal of the tapes was "capricious and without explanation."

Though WB Music hadn't yet made a lawsuit filing, they were obviously moving towards litigation. In the meantime, Warner's record division somehow kept abreast their plans to release the new *Wish You Were Here* LP. It's possible they knew what was going on, but hoped these matters would get resolved before an "official" lawsuit was filed. Joe Smith, then WB Records President, claimed in 1993 he couldn't remember the specific circumstances.

Interestingly, numerous ex-Warner Brother Records employees with major staff positions who worked for the company on both sides of the Atlantic during the 1973-75 era, now maintain they have little or no recollection of ever dealing with Badfinger at all. This sampling of comments typifies their overall response: *"I only remember meeting with Badfinger once the whole time they were there . . . Warner's was always struggling because there were so many albums and singles out. It was overwhelming to deal with . . . A lot of acts were signed on impulse and didn't get special attention . . . I don't think there was a general awareness of Badfinger at the company. . . ."*

In late August, Badfinger spent much of their time rehearsing for their British tour with Man. One day they broke off for a meeting with agent Barrie Marshall, who was still working for the Arthur Howes Agency. He recalls, "I had Badfinger come to my office in Islington. The meeting was very emotionally charged. We talked and talked and they said they were totally at the mercy of Stan Polley and they couldn't get away from that position. There was nowhere to maneuver. But Pete Ham was an incredibly loyal person. He still believed in Stan Polley and wouldn't be disloyal to him. He thought their money was being well looked after. Joey and Tommy felt this wasn't the case. They also felt having Bill Collins complicated the situation even more."

Joey recalled later in the meeting, "Before this, Collins had come back from America and told us Warner's was going to cancel the contract. I'd asked Kathie to call one of the Warner's representatives in England to have it confirmed or blown out. They telexed Warner Records in America and they get a telex back saying 'no.' They said, 'The deal is okay. Everything is alright.' Kathie calls at Marshall's office and tells me everything is fine. I came in and told the group, 'That's Kathie on the phone. Warner Brothers has called our house. Everything's fine. It's all bullshit.' Well, Pete stands up and says, *'I don't want Kathie managing the band! I'm leaving.'* He just freaked out!"

Pete had finally hit the roof and Mike wasn't surprised. "Pete had always been pissed off about Kathie running the band. She was just an American girl who came years after he laid the groundwork. 'Why was she getting heard?!' He couldn't take it."

Mike recalls the group's initial reaction, "The attitude was, 'Well, fuck you Pete. If you want to leave, leave.' I mean, 'What else can go wrong?' The group was so fucked up managerial-wise and money-wise it was starting to become every man for himself."

Joey concurs, "Pete was reacting to the 'Yoko Ono-syndrome.' I told him to fuck off. I was pissed off because of what he said about my old lady. Kathie was very straight about the whole situation. She'd say, 'You're getting fucked!' That plain."

Kathie Molland

There seems to have been some confusion regarding the WB Music threat to break the publishing contract. Taking in Joey's scenario, the events regarding the publishing arm had seemingly gotten confused with the record division. Either Collins misunderstood what he was told, or the Mollands misunderstood him. But Bill Collins claims, "I don't remember telling anyone, or even *knowing,* about the Warner contract being canceled, but I do remember [label prez] Joe Smith was getting irritated by calls he was getting from Kathie!"

For now, the main issue was – Badfinger had lost one of their main members. Bill Collins: "Pete came into the house and said, 'I'm not going to be in this band if Kathie is managing it!' He was really angry." Anne adds, "Pete was raging about Kathie. He said he'd had enough. He couldn't take it anymore, of Kathie wanting in on the meetings and the business. He couldn't see an end to it."

Pete stormed off to a local pub and met with Tim Boyle. Boyle indicated that Pete expressed indignation that Joey and Kathie should now be able to take over Badfinger after he'd laid a lot of the groundwork. Pete said he felt his ideal of the "Badfinger" family had been destroyed. Boyle was obviously concerned about the tour he'd booked, but what was more important to him was that Pete do the right thing for himself and the others. He said he urged Pete that if he was going to quit, make *certain* it was what he wanted to do. Pete went home to think.

Though Anne has no such recollection, Kathie has claimed she came over to Pete's house, with Anne present, and pleaded with Pete to change his mind. When he wouldn't budge, Kathie said she used the reverse psychology of 'Well go ahead, we'll do just fine without you!' But Anne says that attitude was quite common, "She used to say that to Pete all the time, that they didn't need him in the group. She was always of the attitude that Joey was the strong one in the band."

Pete stuck to his word and made plans to transition out of Badfinger. Anne recalls, "Pete told me he called Stan Polley and he said to him, 'If you want to go on your own, say enough!' I remember that clearly."

Pete's new aim was to focus on songwriting. He began plans to purchase a cottage in mid-Wales, where he could have more privacy. He went to visit his family and an estate agent was contacted. John Ham: "Pete wasn't real happy touring on a regular basis. He was mostly interested in songwriting at this point. He told me this frequently."

Beverley, Pete's ex-girlfriend, was now happily married and living in Africa. She was kept familiar with a lot of the Badfinger events through Marianne and Gaynor. She recalls, "Marianne had written me and said Pete had left the group. I felt Pete was a wonderful writer and could make it on his own. I wrote him and said, 'Do what you know you can do. You know you can do this.' "

While Pete made his moves, the band needed a replacement as soon as possible. Bill Collins says it was Joey who decided on pursuing a keyboardist. An ad was put out and, at first, no one suitable turned up. Then a gentleman named Bob Jackson came their way. He had just gotten off an American tour with the British group, Ross.

Born on January 6, 1949, in Coventry, England, Jackson was influenced by many of the blues artists, especially Jimmy Smith, but he also loved melodically oriented music as well. His first band, Indian Summer, had an LP out in 1971. His following band started as John Entwistle's backing group, before evolving into Ross, a progressive unit which released two albums. Jackson performed two U.S. tours with them, the latter opening for Eric Clapton in mid-1974. "I decided to quit after that tour," says Jackson. "After I got home, I got a telegram from a friend, asking what I was up to. He'd recommended me to Badfinger for an audition. I'd never heard their albums, but I knew the singles. I didn't know what to expect. I went down to London.

"They had a practice room on Denmark Street in the Tin Pan Alley, a sort of famous street where a lot of the music business was focused at the time. I went into

Bob Jackson

the room and it was Joey, Tom, and Mike. We talked for a little while and they said, 'Alright, let's play something.' It was a bit embarrassing because they said, 'Well, what about this track off this album?' and I kept saying, 'I don't know that one.'

"We ended up jamming. We sang a bit. It was only a half hour or so and the three of them went upstairs, came down, and said, 'Well, it sounds pretty good to us. If you're interested, let's take this further. We have a tour coming up. Would you like to do it?' I said, 'That would be great!' "

Jackson made preparations to transition into Badfinger. But he had noticed something, "I knew the group was originally four members, so obviously I was replacing someone, not adding to it. I had no idea Pete Ham was such an important member. I hadn't realized he had written so many of their popular songs."

Jackson was given a set list to rehearse. His original notes read as follows:

> ***The Winner, Blind Owl, Suitcase, In The Meantime, Some Other Time, Gotta Get Out Of Here, I Don't Mind, Love Is Easy, King Of The Load, Andy Norris, Give It Up, Get Away***

Joey now dominated the picture. Nine of the twelve songs were his. None of Pete Ham's numbers were being used, and *none* of the hits were being played. It looked like a new era for Badfinger.

Badfinger's long overdue Apple royalties were finally scheduled to be released, prompted by the judge's demand in the BEI/Apple lawsuit. In the *Discoveries* interview, Joey Molland recalled, *"We got a letter from Apple, about two weeks after this meeting (where Ham walked out), saying that Apple had sent a check to Bill Collins for what at the time was about $200,000. I called up Bill Collins and told him that I needed some money to buy a four-track tape machine, a Teac. He said, 'I haven't got the money. I sent it to the office.' I told him, 'You know when you send that money to that office, that's the last we'll ever see of it. Why are you doing that?' I called up Neil Aspinall, right the next call, and I said, 'Neil, can you put a hold on that check you sent us? Bill sent it to America and that'll be the last we ever fuckin' see of it.' He said, 'I can't. But if you can get one of the other members of the band to call me, I'll stop the check for you.' "*

Joey got Tom to contact Neil Aspinall. Pete was out of the picture, having quit six days prior, and Mike was usually left out of Joey's business discussions anyway. Aspinall jogs his memory, "What happened was, I knew Polley wanted the royalties under the deal he'd done with the band, but I was told by the band that they wanted the royalties, 'That deal's not on,' or words to that effect. So for Apple it was 'piggy-in-the-middle.' I figured whoever was paid, I was going to get sued. So I told everybody I was going to go to court, which is what I did, it's on the record, to get a direction from the judge."

Aspinall canceled the check. Down the road there was a hearing. "I told the judge, 'Look, this is the position I'm in. I don't want to be in this position. I don't want the money. It's not my money. What should I do?' And he said, 'Give it to me!' "

As it was, Bill Collins had brought the check from Apple to the United States. Stan Polley had spoken to Bill, telling him to fly to Beverly Hills, California (where Polley was then situated) immediately. Under a new agreement the band had signed with Polley – the Apple publishing and record royalties were now supposed to go directly into Badfinger Enterprises Inc. (BEI).

Bill claims he was suspicious that he was asked to "fly" over, but he didn't want to get Polley mad. He also didn't want to get the band mad. He admits he was protecting his position, and "why shouldn't he?" As far as he was concerned, the overall situation had broken down to the point that everyone involved with Badfinger was having to look out for themselves. He said he was thus relieved when he found out the check had been stopped by Joey and Tom.

By mid-September, Pete Ham was in Wales. His brother, John, recalls, "Pete had found this remote country cottage where he was going to build his own home studio and write songs. He seemed quite pleased. Then one day he told me he'd been contacted by someone from Warner Brothers and they said they weren't interested in the Badfinger band if Pete left. They said, 'If he goes, or he goes, or he goes, fine. But if you go, no contract.' Pete was really upset. He felt he owed the rest of the band a living. He was afraid that if the whole thing folded, he'd be to blame."

Legally, Warner Brothers needed two members leaving to break the contract, so it's not known if Pete had been told Warner's had legal grounds to end the record and publishing deals, or they simply told Pete they wouldn't support the band any further. As it was, Pete did come back to London, popping into one of Badfinger's rehearsals. This was about two-and-a-half weeks after he'd quit.

Joey: "Pete said that he wanted to come back in the band, that he wouldn't be stubborn, that he would go along with getting rid of Polley. He was apologizing."

Anne doesn't believe this, "Pete didn't have to crawl on his hands and knees. It was *Pete* who Warner Brothers wanted. Pete told me Warner's wanted him back in the band."

Joey and Pete

It's possible Pete didn't want to admit the true circumstances to the group, and that he did come in a bit sheepish. Bob Jackson recalls, "Pete had turned up and said we sounded great. I hadn't realized he'd had this big loggerhead with Joey. I could see something had gone on between them. He went off to talk with Joey and Tom."

Joey indicated he was not happy by the turn of events. "I told Pete, 'No, I don't want you in the band if you're not gonna be yourself. If you're not going to be Peter Ham there's no point in you being in the band.' Tommy said, 'We should let him in the band. He was a founding member. I said, 'What the fuck for? That guy is gone. This is another guy.' "

Mike: "As far as I was concerned, Pete had lost his temper and wanted back in. Badfinger was The Iveys, who were a Swansea band, of which Pete was the main member. But Joey and Kathie wanted him out."

Bill Collins also claimed Joey was jealous of Pete and wanted control of the band. In his diary, Bill wrote of Pete to be *"very down – Joey doesn't want him in!"*

After a series of meetings and phone conversations between the group members, Pete was accepted back in. Joey said he then began contemplating leaving himself. Meanwhile, Badfinger was now a five-piece with a short time to prepare for an impending support tour for Man. Though Badfinger were a much more known act world-wide than Man, their Welsh partners had an intense live following in the U.K., and were near their peak of popularity there.

The first gig was on September 27, 1974 in Norwich, England. Man had a four-piece line-up: Deke Leonard and Mickey Jones on guitars, Terry Williams on drums, and Ken Whaley on bass. After a few weeks it was apparent to them something wasn't right with Badfinger. "They seemed to not give a fuck," said Leonard. "Mickey Gibbins was out there for a laugh, but the other three guys seemed to have an edge to them. Tommy was drunk a lot of the time. Joey was very detached. Pete was quieter than usual."

"I could see they were depressed," adds Terry Williams. "Pete was keeping a lot in. Tom was being out there. I remember Bill Collins was not to be mentioned. They felt he sold them out without good advice and led them into a trap."

Most of the early dates were in Scotland, Ireland, and Northern England. 'Spiv' Morris – a veteran of Swansea scene – was working as a roadie, M.C., T-shirt seller, and occasional opening act. He recalls one night at a hotel in Manchester, England. "This comedian named Tommy Cooper was sitting in the hotel bar. He was very famous in England and he was Pete's favorite comedian. Pete was in awe. He would never have approached this guy. But someone broke the ice by going up to Cooper

Terry Williams, Ken Whaley, Deke Leonard, Micky Jones, Man, 1974

with a sheet over his head . . . Pete and Cooper had a drink together. Pete didn't normally drink a lot, but he had a glass of whiskey, that was his 'Goodnight Vienna' drink. He and Cooper stayed up the whole night talking."

For Pete this was a pleasant distraction, but he generally wasn't upbeat. "Pete wasn't smiling so much," adds Spiv, "I would sit in hotel rooms with him and he'd play Beatles songs, 'For No One,' 'And Your Bird Can Sing,' 'It's Only Love;' he was to 'himself' . . . I saw him throwing up before some of the gigs . . . This was after he'd done it all. I couldn't believe it. He seemed to think it was all on him . . . On the bus rides everyone would be playing games, limerick games, where whoever guessed the punch line got the 'joint.' Everyone was joining in except Pete. He'd be at the back of the bus, working on a set list."

Pete's sister, Irene, had been a big supporter of her brother over the years. Beverley recalled a good many visits between the two of them. "Irene thought the world of Pete. He confided in her. They used to have a great time together."

Anne remembered herself and Pete going to see Irene at the Queensway Hotel in London, where Irene was then working. "She'd just had a baby and Pete surprised her by saying, 'We're going to have one of those, too!' We'd recently found out I was pregnant. Pete figured he was financially secure now and could handle having a child. He was ecstatic. He really wanted to get married."

But Fergie was still not amicable to a divorce. Anne says Fergie came over to the Park Avenue house one day really angry. "He got verbally abusive to me. When Pete got home that day he said, 'That's it! We're not going to pursue you getting a divorce while you're pregnant.' He was concerned I'd get upset and lose the baby."

Fergie: "I was still angry and I was being stubborn. I knew [our] relationship had deteriorated, but the whole thing was handled wrong. Someone should have sat us down and said, 'Let's not be kids. Let's talk about this.' "

The band picked up with dates in South Wales and Southern England. They were performing three songs from the upcoming *Wish You Were Here* album, but the group would liberally mix their set up on a moments notice. Despite the internal frustrations going on, the shows generally went over well. Man drummer Terry Williams recalls, "Badfinger were incredible. I never saw them do a bad gig." Bassist Ken Whaley agreed, "I was new to Man at the time and I only knew of Badfinger casually. When I saw them play I thought, 'These guys are great!' The songs and harmonies were absolutely brilliant. I thought it was sad they were a support band. They easily deserved a headline tour."

Roadie Spiv Morris: "The Man band and Badfinger would get together for encores and Pete played some mean guitar there. Man were known for their jams and it was nice for Pete, because he could really stretch out. I mean he could put people in the shade."

Mike Gibbins liked the new setup, "With Bob Jackson, I thought we gave Man a run for their money. Bob fit in perfectly. We had a pad sound and the harmonies were improved. We went over a storm in Wales. I was surprised, because Man in Swansea was like what the Grateful Dead are to San Francisco."

Badfinger played the Swansea Top Rank on October 23, 1974. Pete had several days to visit with his family. His brother, John, remembers, "Pete said no one in the band was talking to him. He said Joey Molland's attitude was, 'This band isn't big enough for the both of us.' Pete wasn't taking it too well."

As the tour proceeded, Joey had been hinting at quitting, despite the high expectation for the pending *Wish You Were Here* album. Bob Jackson recalls, "I was just an observer at this point. I never really had been told what was going on with Joey. It was just sort of long faces in one corner, and chatting in another."

The members of Man all recalled a degree of moaning and groaning from Badfinger about management and money issues. Pete's bank records showed no substantial deposits for almost three months. His account dwindled.

Despite the group's worries, there were still lots of good times on the road, as Man and their entourage were long-time mates. "That was actually the most fun I

Badfinger U.K. Tour, 1974
Bob Jackson, upper right
"Tag" Hall, middle right

ever had on the road," says Mike. "Everyone just partied down. It was fabulous. This wasn't a heavy United-States-police-with-their-guns-and-dogs-in-back type of deal. We'd done all kinds of gigs in the U.S., where it was all very impersonal, professional, and cold. This was just a great time."

The last gig of the tour was October 26, 1974 in Southend, England. Bob Jackson, "It was very emotional at the end, particularly between Tommy and Joey. It wasn't made clear to me, but Joey had apparently been planning to leave. At the last gig I can remember being in a street with Joey, Tom, and Mike – Pete wasn't there – and we were all talking about it. And Joey was saying, 'Look man, there's nothing I can do. That's it.' Tommy was saying, 'Look, c'mon, we can get something together here. We can work something out here.' And Joey kept walking down the road saying, 'Well, look, it's my wife. I can not go against my wife.' That's my memory of it, him saying that, walking off down the road."

The day after the tour ended, Steve Craiter, who was living in Philadelphia, Pennsylvania, called Pete Ham at his home in London. Steve had met the band during their U.S. summer tour of 1972. Since that time, Craiter had kept an occasional phone correspondence going with Pete and Tom. Craiter had taped a number of the calls, including a flurry to Pete during the 1974 months of August, September, and October. Pete was eager to get progress reports on the *Wish You Were Here* LP, which was released in the U.S. in mid-October. Craiter's early investigating indicated little effort from the Warner's promotional front. Pete was clearly bothered by what Craiter told him, and by other matters concerning the band, though he often wasn't specific.

At one point, Pete expressed a lot of frustration with Warner Brothers, from as far back as the beginning of the band's involvement. He also indicated a continuing complication regarding communication with the band's management in the U.S. Though Pete sounded rather depressed on one particular night (the day after the tour had ended), he showed a lot of resolve to want to sort things out. He told Steve Craiter, "You can call me anytime, reverse charges, just let me know what's happening . . . Basically all I want is feedback, see what's happening. Then if nothing is happening, I can push . . . I can try and push things on a legal basis from this end." {phone call between Pete Ham and Steve Craiter, October 27, 1974}

Meanwhile, Joey kept to his threat and quit Badfinger on November 4, 1974, as he handed in a notice to Bill Collins. He and Kathie went over to the Park Avenue house to pick up a few things. Joey said in several interviews that Kathie snuck out the group's sixteen-track masters of the 1974 Cleveland Agora show, though he alleged later, she took it from Air Studios.

Joey expressed about his decision: "I left the group because there was no way it could work. We talked and talked and talked about it. I wanted to get away from the managers and there was no way we could reach an agreement on it. It was obvious they weren't going to change the management. We were going to have the same people, the same organization. It was going to be bullshit . . . I couldn't do anything else. Pete was obsessed that my wife wanted to manage the band. Tommy was too. I know for a fact because they'd say things. They resented her. But she was just hip enough or alert enough or paranoid enough – she saw what was going on without the clouds around it."

The day following Joey's resignation, on a letter dated November 5, 1974, WB Music notified Polley that they knew the *Wish You Were Here* album was out, but to be aware, the compositions had not been copyrighted by them, thus hinting at troubles to come. . . .

A week earlier, when the Badfinger tour with Man had ended, road manager Spiv Morris was asked to deliver each musician's individual earnings, "I remember giving out checks and I was getting the same amount as Pete Ham. I remember thinking, 'Pete deserves better than this.'

But, surprisingly, days after the tour ended, Pete *did* get a major lump sum of over £6,000 put into his bank account – by Stan Polley! Marianne says she and Tom had been pushing Pete that he should demand a house down payment; that when Tom had put his foot down to Polley, he had gotten one. Obviously, Polley wanted to keep Pete content. Immediately after Pete had quit, Polley had started to shop a solo deal for Pete, but now that was out the window.

Interestingly, Bill Collins claimed *he* was the one who arranged for Pete to get the £6,000 for the house down payment! He said it came out of money that had

Pete Ham

come in from Apple earlier; which would have been some time before the recent check stopped by Joey and Tom. Bill said, "I remember Polley was upset when he found out I had given Pete the money. He wanted the money."

Later investigation proved Bill's memory was off. He *had* given Pete two installments over the previous months, but they only totalled £2,200. Possibly, Bill never knew Pete received £6,000 from Polley. Bill claimed that, up to that point in time, he had not sent *any* of the Apple publishing and recording royalty checks to Polley! He said he had been continually using the funds to pay band expenses on the U.K. side, and for payment of his own salary.

Pete was very eager to provide privacy for his new family. There were some incidents at the Park Avenue house which had shaken both himself and Anne. One, concerning Bill's wife, Toni, had been especially startling. Toni had an unstable mental background and she had been getting psychiatric treatment before marrying Bill. "One day she flipped out," says Anne. "She went after me with a bread knife. It was over nothing, really. She'd started to get depressed and was acting strange. We'd always gotten along, but she kept slipping. After she went off on me, Pete took me and Blair out of the house. He told Bill we weren't coming back until he got her out."

Bill claims Anne's account of the knife incident is highly exaggerated, but he admits Pete did put Toni into a very tight grasp, as Pete seemed to panic about the situation. Shortly after, Bill sent Toni back to Canada on a plane, to return her to her family; urging them to get her some immediate help. Bill planned to come to Canada later to sort out the details.

Meanwhile, Pete and Anne had been looking for a new home, using the same estate agent Tom and Marianne had procured. They looked in the Surrey area where Tom and Marianne lived. Anne recalls, "We were interested in a house right next door to Tom and Marianne, but there was some question about the land in back, that it didn't belong to the property, and Pete had liked that there was a canal in back. We were with the agent when Pete happened to notice another home on Woodham Lane."

Pete liked the house. It had a garage and three bedrooms. It was about one mile from Tom's. There was a yard and plenty of room for children and pets. Shopping was nearby. It cost £20,000 with furnishings included. Pete put £5,000 down to secure it. He also arranged to have the property surveyed. He then began to investigate what sort of mortgage and loans would finalize the deal.

As it was, the new Badfinger album, *Wish You Were Here*, had gotten off to a promising start in America. There was no single, though "Just A Chance" was planned. The early sales were decent; the critical reaction – phenomenal:

PHONOGRAPH *Badfinger have made the album I always hoped they would – an album that matches the standards of their brilliant Apple singles . . . The album is bursting with hits – or rather tracks that eminently deserve to become hits . . . a sparkling album, easily one of the year' best.*

ROLLING STONE *Wish You Were Here is loaded with songs that are both catchy and electric . . . a wonderful album to play right through. . . .*

CREEM *Badfinger, having the distinctive honor of being better Beatle imitators than the Beatle boobs themselves, decide to forcefeed us with another masterpizza . . . 'Cept it's gotta be pushed. . . .*

Of course, Badfinger would need publicity *and* singles *and* a tour, in order to ensure success. Journalist Ken Barnes raved about the album for a Warner Brothers bio, at one point stating, *"It's the kind of invigorating album that fueled the rock explosions of the mid-60s. . . ."* Though bios are traditionally fluff material, he said in 1994 he was genuinely blown away by the record. "I thought they'd done some excellent tracks before, but that was a great album, still tremendously underrated today."

Despite the press and a promising sales start, the band was in a limbo-like state. Bob Jackson says he was not aware of how the record was doing, and doesn't remember the others discussing it. Bob recalls, "After Joey had quit, the focus was on getting new management. I remember during the Man tour the others had gone to Bill to ask him to assist them in getting some money, to get things they felt they needed. But it didn't happen. Joey and Tom often commented how they felt Bill wasn't looking out for their interest. They said he'd become a 'yes-man' for Polley. The discussions were 'How do we get rid of Polley *and* Collins?'

"I had gone back to Coventry after the tour. In early November I got a call from Tom, 'You've got to come down.' I came down and Bill Collins was at this meeting. He said, 'Polley rang through and said you've got to get your next album together fast. You've got three weeks.' I can remember Tommy saying, 'What do you mean we've only got three weeks? To get it done?' Bill said, 'That's the way it is. We have to do it.' There was this mad panic. I stayed over at Tommy's."

Badfinger was not in a good position to mutiny. Though they did not want to rush into a new recording situation, a refusal would be of great risk. Mike recalls, "We weren't getting paid regularly at this point and we thought, 'What are we doing this for, when we haven't even gotten the money for the last one yet? Our hearts weren't in it. But being a musician it was, 'At least we're doing something, at least we're playing music.'

Actually, the band was only going to get two weeks to *record* the album. Apple Studios was booked for the sessions and in late November, Polley sent over American producers Kenny Kerner and Richie Wise, along with Richard Duryea.

The two producers were then in their early twenties. They'd had great success in 1972 and 1973, including the production of a *Billboard* Number One hit by The Stories, "Brother Louie." Kerner explains how he and Wise had become connected to Polley. "Richie Wise and I had produced the first two Kiss albums for Neil Bogart, the owner of Casablanca Records. He'd refused to pay us and Polley had stepped up and said, 'I'll straighten it out.' Polley came back to us and said, 'I worked it out. You're going to get $75,000.' I said, 'Stan, we're owed $250,000, not $75,000.' He said, 'Look, Bogart's not going to pay that. If we go to court it'll be five years, so take it.' We did, and he took his thirty percent off the top. What we didn't know was he managed Bogart in some capacity. My guess is that he cut a deal and pocketed a lot more. Stan was real slick. He could sell you a piece of shit and you'd be thanking him for it."

Kerner admits he couldn't complain when the call had come to produce Badfinger. "We were giant fans of the band. When it was presented to us we jumped. You don't often get to work with people you really admire. In fact, if someone had said, 'Kenny, I can't pay you to do this,' I'd still have been at the airport taking off for England.' "

The band met Kerner and Wise at their rehearsal space on Denmark Street. Richie Wise says it couldn't have been more than one day that they ran through material. There was no time to truly acclimate. Everyone moved almost directly into Apple's recording studio. "Phil McDonald was the engineer," says Kerner. "Working in the Beatles studio, with a Beatles engineer, and Pete Ham – one of my favorite songwriters – was an incredible honor. I felt like a kid getting away with his hand in the cookie jar."

The group needed new material to record, but "Pete had been having a lot of trouble writing," said Anne. Finally, a new song did come to him, "Keep Believing":

I couldn't wish you any bad
I only miss the many highs we had
Our problems made it hard to talk
Slowing our run down to a walk
I would have liked for things to last
But now the time has floated past
We were the pawns in someone else's game
Keep believing, you can make it now

Pete

Joey

Tom later said Pete's ballad was about Joey. Though Joey and Pete were never truly close friends, Pete perceived Joey as part of the Badfinger "family." "Pete didn't hold any grudges against Joey," says Anne. "He was genuinely concerned with his well-being. Pete cared about everybody."

During the start of this album, the band's friend from the United States, Wayne Treiber, had called Pete at the Park Avenue house. He recalls, "Pete mentioned he felt really bad about Joey's quitting. He alluded to the fact he felt a lot of pressure on himself now. They were starting an album unprepared. He tried to keep the conversation light, but things definitely weren't to his liking."

Joey and Kathie continued to stay in London after Joey had quit, but they did not stay in touch with the band members – except for one brief pop-up visit by Joey to Apple Studios. Kathie has said she and Joey were surviving off a house down payment they'd received from Polley, which they'd gotten just after they'd came from California in June. She claimed they had only been given half of what they'd asked for, and when they'd complained to Polley, he'd said, 'Then send it back!' She also claimed Joey's salary checks were stopped at that time.

Bob Jackson had been asked to present material for the new recording project. "I was really happy," he said, "I'd been in a lot of bands and this was the first time I'd been in a situation where everyone could contribute." Bob was over at Tommy's one evening playing his backlog of tunes. "I had this song 'Turn Around.' I had other songs I had written, more poppy, but Tommy liked that. 'More gutsy,' he said. He liked the feel of it. He didn't want my poppy things."

The band recorded "Turn Around." It was bluesy, heavy, and unlike anything they'd ever tackled before. Bob has a versatile voice, and one of his styles was close to Steve Winwood's, which the producers encouraged. Bob sang on two other songs he helped write, "Passed Fast," and "Moonshine."

The recordings were moving quickly, as little vetoing was going on. Mike had noodled up a sing-along called "Rockin' Machine," ". . . something I wrote on the spot. That was just a joke. I couldn't believe it was used."

The fact the band were given only two weeks to finish an album didn't leave much time for contemplation. Richie Wise recalls leaving virtually all of the arrangement ideas to the group's discretion, with him and Kerner basically giving a 'yea' or 'nay' votes to performances or songs.

At some point the producers made note of needing a single. "I remember those discussions and the band feeling pressure," said recording engineer Phil McDonald, "especially Pete."

Furiously working up ideas on cassettes, Pete finally presented "Lay Me Down." Richie Wise recalls, "We'd heard him working on that in the lounge. We thought that could be the hit."

Late into the sessions, a strange incident happened. Pete was putting down an overdub. "He had this beautiful Martin guitar," says Wise. "And he couldn't get through the whole song without the tuning screwing up. So he kept stopping and retuning. Suddenly he let out this huge 'ARRRGH!' at the top of his lungs. He grabbed the guitar like he was gonna smash it, but then he just threw it across the floor. It smacked up against the front wall."

Producer Kenny Kerner said he had ducked behind the console when he saw Pete wind up. Bob Jackson: "It really struck me as odd, because I'd never seen Pete do anything like that." After the incident, Pete stormed off to a pub. Kerner and Wise caught up with him later. "He was real apologetic," says Wise. "He put his arms around us and said, 'I'm really sorry. I got caught up.' "

One of Pete's surviving songbooks from this time indicated a lot of heavy, introspective lyrics being written, like the accusing "Look What You've Done," the autobiographical "A Portrait Of Someone We Knew," and the harsh "By Order Of The Fuhrer," whose words seem to indicate an intense foreboding:

You will create or get no daily bread
You will cast aside all feeling
You will beg for what is yours
You will not have an opinion
You will sacrifice the ones you love
You will accept all my mistakes
You will pay for all yours

Meanwhile, Tom Evans was openly obsessing about Polley. He wrote two songs specifically relating. One was called "Rock'n'Roll Contract," the other "Hey, Mr. Manager." The latter is a sauntering, bleak-edged pop tune that *clearly* shows his frustration: {Hey, Mr. Manager – rough mix}

Hey Mr. Manager
Your messing up my life
Hey Mr. Manager
Don't think I need that kind of strife . . .
You've got no feeling
You've been dealing
All the wrongs
You're lies are stealing
Lord, I think you should be gone

In "Rock'n'Roll Contract" Tom sings:

Wrapped up in a rock'n'roll contract
Lots of things I had to sign at the time
Man told me not to worry 'bout the business
Just keep on poppin' those hits . . .

And he commiserates over the developments:

You made me your slave
Whatever God gave me
You took to the grave
Now it's gone

On December 10, 1974, a Warner Brothers Music attorney filed for rescission of the Badfinger/WB publishing contract in Los Angeles Superior Court. This action led to a sweeping stop of *Wish You Were Here*'s distribution and promotion. Badfinger didn't know it then, but their business and creative affairs were now near the point of a complete and absolute standstill.

9

Take Your Seat By The Ringside

Wish You Were Here had been off to a promising start in the U.S., having risen to #148 on the *Billboard* charts in just seven weeks, despite no single, no tour, and minimal promotion. But Joe Smith, then president of WB Records, said in 1993, "If we pulled the album, it was because our lawyers told us to do so."

The group continued to record at Apple Studios. Mike had a tune called "Back Again," which the band dressed with a country flavor. A brief instrumental was also done. Bob explains, "We were running out of time and Pete said, 'I've got these chord progressions from my brother, John.'" Pete called the keyboard piece 'Savile Row.' Richie Wise: "That was the title I remember discussing for the album."

But others recalled something different. *Head First* was the title Tom always mentioned. Bob verifies, "One day we went to this little London photo studio on Wardour Street and a photographer put us in the middle of all this foliage, like a jungle, and had us peer out from it. The idea came from Tommy. He wanted the LP cover to be a lion roaring. The idea was the situation we were in, how we were diving in, 'head first.' "

Ten songs were completed by December 14, 1974. The seeds for a good album were there. Pete's guitar work was a highlight. Be it plaintive, rockin', or soulful, he was clearly in stellar form. Bob Jackson also played tastefully, often utilizing the ARP String Ensemble, one of its first uses in England. Mike and Tom did their usual solid job on bass and drums.

But despite there being a number of top-flight songs, the project showed signs of being a rush job. The running time was only about thirty-two minutes. And some of the material was questionable. Richie Wise recalls, "I was naive, twenty-three years old, a kid working with a group I idolized, yet I knew Polley was doing this for an advance. It was obvious Warner Brothers wasn't involved."

On December 16th, after rough mix copies were distributed to the band, Kenny Kerner, Richie Wise, Bill Collins, Richard Duryea, and the group members all gathered for a goodbye dinner. Bob Jackson recalls, "We met at some plush

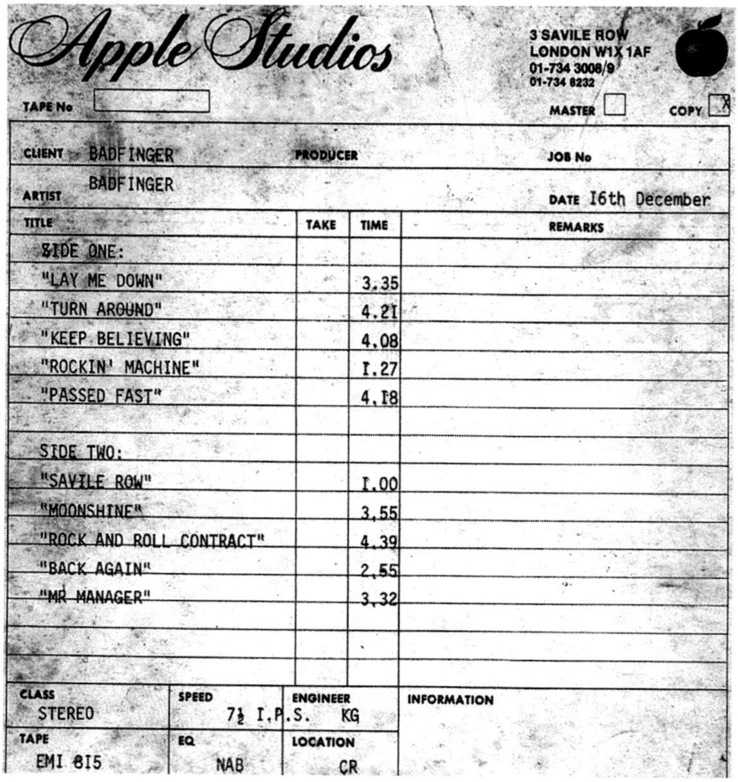

Apple Studios

3 SAVILE ROW
LONDON W1X 1AF
01-734 3008/9
01-734 8232

TAPE No

MASTER ☐ COPY ☒

CLIENT BADFINGER		PRODUCER	JOB No
ARTIST BADFINGER			DATE 16th December
TITLE	TAKE	TIME	REMARKS
SIDE ONE:			
"LAY ME DOWN"		3.35	
"TURN AROUND"		4.21	
"KEEP BELIEVING"		4.08	
"ROCKIN' MACHINE"		1.27	
"PASSED FAST"		4.18	
SIDE TWO:			
"SAVILE ROW"		1.00	
"MOONSHINE"		3.55	
"ROCK AND ROLL CONTRACT"		4.39	
"BACK AGAIN"		2.55	
"MR MANAGER"		3.32	

CLASS	SPEED	ENGINEER	INFORMATION
STEREO	7½ I.P.S.	KG	
TAPE	EQ	LOCATION	
EMI 815	NAB	CR	

Head First
rough mixes

restaurant in London. Richard Duryea presented me with this thick wad of contracts to sign. I'd say about a half-dozen signatures were required. I was told I had to sign them, there and then. Some of the figures were filled in and some weren't. I remember saying, 'But hang on, there's no percentage on this bit.' And Richard Duryea said, 'Oh yeah, that's just a formality, we'll just fill those in later.' I said, 'Well what if I decide not to sign? What happens then?' The guys in the band were saying, 'You're in anyway. You're an equal member as far as we're concerned.' But Bill Collins and Duryea were pressuring me. Finally I said, 'Okay, I'll sign.' So I signed the lot of them.

"Later during the evening, I went into the bathroom and Tommy followed me in. He said, 'I've got them! I've got the contracts!' He had pinched them off the bar counter. I said, 'Well, what do we do now?' He said, 'Let's get rid of them.' So he went into the cubicle as if to flush them down the toilet. Suddenly these footsteps came round and in charged Collins and Duryea. They started pushing on the cubicle door with Tommy. Duryea was yelling, *'Look, don't be like kids. Give me those contracts!'* Tommy let go of the door. They fell in. . . ."

Tom was obviously angry towards Polley, as his lyrics included some caustic diatribes. Bob remembers Tom saying to Duryea (who was going to be leaving with the master tapes), "'Look Richard, tell Stan not to take the words too seriously. Tell him it's just a song.' It hit him that he was biting the hand that fed him, and it could cause a problem. He was worried."

After arriving back in the U.S., Richard Duryea went to WB Records in Los Angeles with the rough mixes. Ed Silvers of WB Music recalls, "Joe Smith was put off when he heard those tapes. He sent them to me and it sounded like the whole thing was thrown together in a hurry. I thought it was an obvious attempt to please contract obligations so that Polley could extract further advances from us. It was depressing. I'd trusted Hofer and he'd really disappointed me. His and Polley's moves had said to me, 'We'll just make all the money we can and screw the band.' "

The holidays were coming up and Pete was planning to take Anne and Blair to visit his family in Swansea. Bill Collins was preparing for a trip to Canada. Bill says he was trying to talk to Pete about a phone bill which was in arrears. Collins claimed he did not have enough funds to pay it. He indicated that per Pete's request, he had taken out a communal phone box he'd installed at the Park Avenue house earlier, and as he feared, the new phone was abused by people for long distance calls, many of them to America. Pete's response was that Bill should simply debit Pete's personal account, as he usually did. But Bill said that because he did not get the Apple money from the last check, he now did not have enough in the "group" checking account to cover the bill.

According to Collins, Pete sometimes became "testy" when these issues were discussed. Bill indicated that, on December 23, 1974, Pete was rushing around for his trip to Swansea, and again avoided a discussion when the phone bill was addressed by Collins.

Stan Polley was now situated in Beverley Hills, California (though the New York office was still in existence). On December 24, 1974, he received the *Head First* rough mixes back from WB Music. Three days later, WB Music requested a legal writ of attachment for the return of $175,969.27 from "Badfinger." A California Superior Court judge reviewed their request and immediately approved $20,000. If WB Music was going to recoup the full amount, they would have to take matters a whole lot further down the road.

In the first week of 1975, the Badfinger members received their monthly salary checks. Pete and Anne were still living at 7 Park Avenue, but Pete was now preparing for the move to Surrey. Anne says he was not working much on music; having told her he'd hit a mental block. At times, over the past years, Pete had played tennis with roadie "Tag" Hall. "On the way to the court we would talk." said Tag. "I knew he was frustrated. I knew things weren't as they should be. Pete was taking his frustrations out on the court."

Carola Beresford-Cooke and her husband, Tony, had been visiting occasionally over the previous two years. She recalls coming over around this time, "We were expecting Pete to be really happy with his new family and everything. But he didn't seem happy. My husband noticed it. Something wasn't right. . . ."

Pete had a lot on his mind. Still, he generally kept upbeat when interacting with Anne, Blair, and their dog, Layla. "Pete was exceptional to us," says Anne. "I would drive Blair to school and Pete would always get up to start the car and warm it up for us. He'd go shopping with me. He'd help me with gardening . . ." Pete thrived on the homelife, but when he'd go out in public, he could become quite discreet. Says Anne, "We went to eat at a restaurant one night, and there was a guitarist playing. He recognized Pete and announced to everybody he was there. He asked if Pete would come onstage and play something. Pete was terribly embarrassed. He never wanted to promote himself like that."

The Badfinger members would occasionally contact each other, usually to discuss the management situation. Barrie Marshall was one potential manager they'd sought. He'd been asked as far back as the Man tour to see if he could talk to Polley and work out a parting of the ways. Marshall recalls, "I finally had a trip to the states and I was able to meet with Polley at the Polo Lounge in the Beverley Hills Hotel. His lawyer Walter Hofer was there, too. I said, 'Look, Badfinger really want out, totally. They want to know where their money is, what's happened to the royalty statements.' Polley was very unforthcoming. He suggested *I* become a manager for him in England, and he'd put *me* on a salary!"

On January 19, 1975, producers Kenny Kerner and Richie Wise were sent by Polley to the Record Plant in Los Angeles to do a new mixdown of the *Head First* multi-tracks. They spent six days on them and the mixes came out mediocre, many not even as good as the earlier roughs. Polley sent these new mixes to WB Records, obviously to portray the band was still acting under contract obligations.

Meanwhile, Pete was moving closer to securing his new home. Pete obtained a £12,800 loan from a building society, using a life insurance policy he'd set up the previous November as collateral. But he still needed another £2,200 to finalize the deal. On January 20th, Pete made arrangements to get a £2,200 "bridging advance" from the National Westminster Bank. A "bridging advance" normally is not granted unless the bank has the legal papers of a coming transaction – usually one involving property – with a firm indication that the bank will be reimbursed. But, by January 30, 1975, Pete's "bridging advance" *still* had not been reimbursed to the bank. Surprisingly, Pete utilized the money he'd received to complete his new home purchase. This left his checking account almost £1,500 overdrawn!

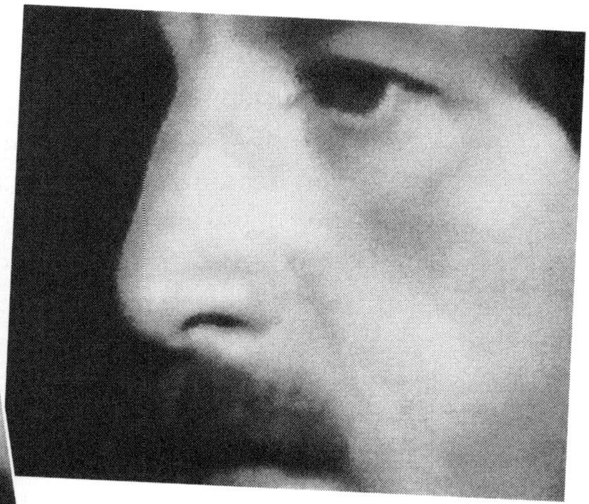

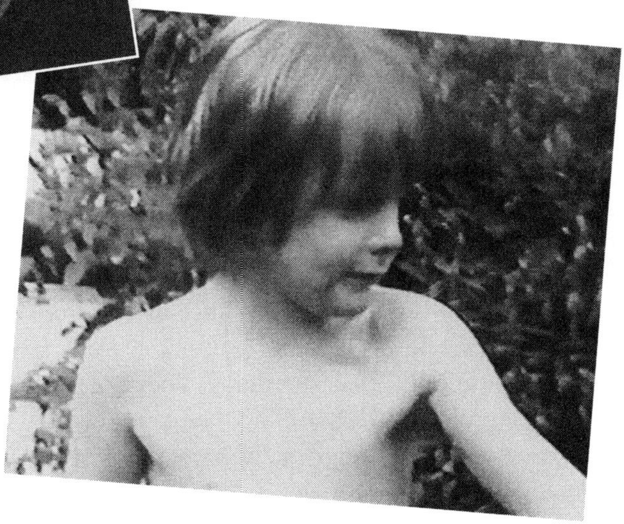

Anne, Pete, and Blair

Come February of 1975, the band's monthly salary checks did arrive. Bob Jackson was quite pleased. He'd received two salary payments now. He was beginning to feel like an official Badfinger member. Bob was staying in Coventry with his girlfriend, eventually planning to move near Pete and Tom.

Jackson remembers coming down to London for occasional band meetings related to business. He recalled the four of them going to WB Records in London one day to meet with Derek Taylor. Derek had become Warner Brothers English managing director in January of 1975. "About halfway through this meeting," recalls Bob, "Derek opens this drawer, pulls out this sheet of paper, and hands it to Tom. No one else seemed to pay much attention, but I noticed Tom turned white as a ghost when he looked at it. I asked him about it later and he said, 'Oh, it's nothing.' But I got a look at it and it was a sheet relating to Alcoholics Anonymous."

Derek Taylor couldn't remember the specific occurrence, but said he had gotten heavily involved in Alcoholics Anonymous starting in December of 1974. He recalled often handing out leaflets around this time. What was discussed at this meeting, though, was not remembered by either Jackson or Taylor.

Late in February, Pete and Anne moved into their new home in Weybridge, Surrey. Pete's checking account was still in the red, yet his bank had been allowing him to write checks and make withdrawals. Pete was getting desperate to pay back the "bridging advance." His phone records show him making weekly calls to the United States; presumably to get the money from Polley. Since Polley had situated in Beverly Hills, California, Pete may not have had a direct number to reach him. Polley was often fronted by a new female assistant, Micki Wood.

The March salary checks arrived early in the month, but weeks after depositing them, the band members were told they had not cleared. Bob recalls, "I remember ringing Pete up and he said no one knew what was happening. We were told "insufficient funds." We were ringing Bill and he said, 'Well, obviously there's a problem. I'll have to talk to Stan about it.'"

Bill Collins had been back in England since the second week of February, after a trip to Canada and Los Angeles. He'd met once with Polley, in Beverley Hills, on his last day there. Bill was now establishing a bond with a new lady friend, Anne Collier, a violinist whom he'd met in November of 1974 at a London recording studio. Bill had begun taking music lessons from her, as he was eager to learn more about orchestral arranging. They got along extremely well.

In March of 1975, the band members received tape copies of the new *Head First* mixes done in Los Angeles. "We were at Pete's house listening to them," says Bob, "and our jaws kind of simultaneously hit the ground. They sounded terrible. Pete said, 'Well, maybe there's something wrong with my tape recorder. Maybe it's the alignment or something.' He rang up to verify if it was the right tape, and it was." (A playing of Pete's tape shows he actually did have a defective copy).

Around this time, the group got the news that *Wish You Were Here*'s distribution and promotion had been shut down by Warner Brothers. The band had hoped the LP would be a take-off point for them. Mike: "We'd worked so hard on that album. It went out with a bullet, and then they pulled it. That was devastating."

Producer Chris Thomas: "We were all completely defeated when it got shelved. You feel like, 'Well, I may as well change my job and open a greengrocer's shop.' I was incredibly disappointed."

Bob says desperation was now beginning to peak. "We'd been looking and looking for help from everywhere. We'd say, 'Look, we're in this terrible situation and we'd really just like to continue our career. We just want to play and carry on.' The managers or agents, or whomever we'd talk to, would say, 'Well, who are you with?' We'd explain the set-up and they'd say, 'Well, it's up to you to get out of that situation. When you do, come back to us.' "

One manager they'd approached was Billy Gaff. He had managed The Faces for years and often showed an interest in taking on Badfinger. He liked them as artists and as people. His biggest client was Rod Stewart, a Warner Brothers artist.

Early in 1975, WB Records president Joe Smith was at Gaff's London office for a meeting. Smith recalls, "Coincidentally, I ran into Pete Ham, who was just walking out. We started out talking about music, for five minutes or so, and then he brought up how it was a bummer dealing with Polley on the business side, and the troubles they were having. I suggested he get some legal help . . . I proceeded to tap dance my way out of there." (In a 1999 interview, Smith said he received a number of "impassioned" letters from Pete around this time, which he no longer has)

Man's Deke Leonard recalls bumping into Pete at the Hammersmith Odeon, a London concert hall. "I was talking to him and his voice kept getting quieter and quieter. I asked him if there was something wrong. He said, 'No, it's alright. I'm okay.' He was talking so low; I could barely hear him."

Pete was feeling enormous pressure. His career was fading; he'd just bought a house; he was in debt, and a new child was due. Seemingly, his salary had been cut off. When he'd tried to strike out on his own months earlier, he'd been told it would essentially end his bandmates opportunities with Warner Brothers, possibly ruining their careers. No matter what option he contemplated; it seemed hopeless. It was hard for him to accept the reality of what was happening.

Musician/Producer Al Kooper sheds some light through his own scenario as a Polley client. "When Stan Polley saw what he perceived as an end to my career, he abandoned me, too. He said, 'I'm not sending you any more money.' Before that, when I had gone into long periods of not assimilating income, Stan would always make it appear he was lending me money, when in fact, it was my *own* money. At the end, when we finally parted ways, with all my contracts in the company names, all my money ended up going to him. And there was absolutely nothing I could do about it."

Polley had undoubtedly received word of the Warner's lawsuit, the withholding of the Apple royalties, the *Wish You Were Here* album being shelved, and the rejected *Head First* album. His Badfinger "well" was rapidly running dry. . . .

Early in April of 1975, Pete Ham started to write songs again. Anne recalls, "For a long time he hadn't been writing, but then he started strumming his guitar around the house." Pete recorded a lot of his ideas onto an inexpensive cassette recorder. Many of his lyrics related to his current woes. One song concerns a villain named Will Parker who carried a "smoking gun," and the innocent Johnny, who "played the game." In the end, "Old Will shot him, just the same."

Pete made a visit to South Wales that same month. He spent part of it helping with construction work at his brother's new home in Swansea. Said John Ham, "Pete was telling me he was setting up a studio at his house. He'd begun to work on the walls and beams, but had run out of money. He said he had a lot of work to do to make it comfortable."

But Pete did not let his brother know how truly desperate his financial situation had become. Anne recalls, "I had suggested he talk to his brother. But Pete said, 'I can't. I can't do it.' His pride was too strong."

John Ham: "I used to beg Pete to bring papers home, so I could look over the group's financial situation. I'm not an expert, but I'm a businessman. I can read a balance sheet. But Pete would always say, 'Oh, it's not the money that we're interested in.'. . . Pete would often be ringing me about some huge recording deal or big tour, and the following week he'd have trouble getting money to fix his car . . . Even after the group had a few hits under their belts, when Pete came home to Swansea, his shoes would have holes in them, his toes would be sticking out. Even when he played gigs he'd use those shoes. I asked him once if they were part of some comedy act or something."

During the first week of April, Roadie "Tag" Hall went to see if the April checks had been sent over, even though the March salary checks were still bouncing. "It was my job to pick them up from Goldblatt & Co. in London," he says. "They never came in. I went back again and again. . . ."

Pete Ham

Meanwhile, Mike Gibbins had taken his family to Wales, as he said he saw the handwriting on the wall. Bob Jackson was in Coventry, ". . . dazed and confused." Tom was fortunate in that Marianne was currently working. She had a job at a restaurant and there was no problem with food or necessities for the time being. But Pete was sinking badly, with several mouths to feed and a new one coming. On April 11, 1975, in a desperation move, he remortgaged a life insurance policy he'd set up the year before – with his mother as the beneficiary – and was granted £2,072. But even with that money, Pete's checking account was *still* in the red.

Barrie Evans, a friend of Pete's, remembered talking with him about the second week of April, "Pete expressed to me he was getting financially stuck. I didn't press him, but he was very concerned. It was scary. You haven't got the money. Where did it all go? There's supposed to be people to take care of this stuff. . . ."

There was another situation few knew about. Pete's ex-girlfriend, Beverley, had recently returned to England from Africa. Beverley was a shoulder to cry on in the past. She recalls, "I had come back from Africa for a visit. My husband was going to meet me in late April. I was staying at my parent's home in Hertfordshire and I went to see Tom and Marianne in Surrey several times . . . I was avoiding seeing Pete at first. Anne and Pete were a couple now and I was concerned about seeing Pete without my husband there. I didn't want to make Anne or my husband uncomfortable. I mean he could've thought, 'Well, my wife goes back to England and there she is seeing her ex-boyfriend.' I didn't want to worry him. I wanted to wait until he came over, too.

"I was over at Tom's and he told me he was worried about Pete. He wanted me to talk to him. I said, 'Look, if I run into Pete and he wants to talk, fine, but I don't want to pursue it.' I'd only had occasional contact with Pete from the time I left, and though I felt we would become good friends again, once I settled back in England, I didn't think it would be fair to Anne for me to initiate a discussion with Pete now.

Beverley said that Tom had mentioned he'd noticed Pete's personality changing. "Tom told me Pete was getting pessimistic about everything, and Pete had always been the one to say, 'It will work out. It will work out in the end.' Tom depended a lot on Pete's strength."

"I was at Tom's one day, and he was going to call Pete. Tom asked me if I wanted to speak to him on the phone. I wouldn't do it. It seems so ridiculous now, and I can't really explain it. Tom was a little surprised. But my impression at the time was maybe he was overreacting about Pete's state of mind. See, it was hard to read Tom sometimes. He said to me, 'Well, what if you're here and Pete happens to come over?' I said, 'That's fine, that's different. It would be a natural occurrence then.' He said, 'Well, when are you coming over here next?' It got kind of comical 'cause he kept asking that all day long. . . ."

Since moving to Weybridge, Pete had been spending a lot of time with Tom. They would have discussions which Pete might keep from Anne. She wasn't surprised by this, "Pete would never discuss things like the band issues with me. There were times I tried to talk to him and he'd say, 'No, it's fine.' He mentioned they couldn't go on tour. I knew there were money problems. I remember one time suggesting we pack up the house and move in with my family in Scotland. But he was so proud. For Pete to turn up on my family's doorstep with no money; that would have been very difficult for him."

On some of Pete's songwriting cassettes you can hear Anne working and Blair playing in the background, as he softly sings and strums. But Anne says Pete didn't really push her to listen. In fact, she says, "He didn't think the songs were any good." One tune, Pete completed was "Helping Hand":

We just need to discover
Some way to soothe the blues away
On my darkest of days
And when I need a helping hand
If you'd talk, oh my love, I wish you'd understand
Wish you'd feel inside my mind
And join in with the things that you'll find

It was typical of Pete to confront through his music, instead of conversation. "Helping Hand" may have been his way of trying to clue Anne in that he wanted to be pushed harder to communicate. Anne admits she hadn't questioned Pete as ardently in the early stages of their relationship, but with a crisis looming, she'd begun stronger and stronger efforts to try and get him to talk about his problems. Beverley admitted it took years for her to get Pete to talk about many topics. Tom also expressed that, despite all the conversations he had with Pete, he never really felt like he could get to the bottom of what Pete was thinking. Mike simply said, "Pete was like my brother, but he never showed his feelings. He was a loner."

By mid-April, Pete's bank account had gone almost £500 in the red. Somehow his bank was still allowing him to pay bills and make withdrawals. He'd been calling to the United States, but nothing was getting resolved. Mike remembers ringing Pete up, "I said to him, 'Why don't you come down to the farmhouse in Wales I'm at and cool out?' He said, 'No, I've got too many things to do at home.' He said he was tearing down a wall."

During the third week of April, Pete did ask Bob Jackson to spend a few days at his home. Bob says he and Pete had been getting along quite well, and he was happy to accept the invitation. Bob recalls, "I was at his house and we talked about a change in the management. I can remember one night (April 19th) Bill Collins came over for dinner. We all sat down and had a meal together. We were sitting across the table having a chat and finally it came up about the hole we were in, and how were we going to climb out of it. Bill was siding with Polley. He said, 'He's on your side really' and 'In time he'll sort it out.' He was defending Polley. So I said, 'Look Bill, basically we need to start afresh and if you're not with us, you're against us, mate. We don't need placating by you, with all due respect to you, but you really ought to bow out.' He got out of his chair, reached across the table, and pulled me up by the collar. A few words were exchanged; then he let go. . . ."

Bill admits to grabbing Bob, but he says he was upset that Bob was there at all, "Bob wasn't a part of Badfinger, as far as I was concerned, Joey had brought him in. I wanted to talk to Pete alone. Bob was in the way."

Collins added that Pete talked about money problems and Bill recalled telling him, 'Pete, I don't know how to get you out of this. This is out of my league. . . ."

Bob continues: "The following night, Pete and I sat up late. We sat across a table chatting and Pete's general mood was gloomy and doomy. I remember saying, 'There is light at the end of the tunnel.' I was being optimistic, and he wasn't arguing against it. He was saying, 'Yeah, you're right . . . but things are so difficult.' I said, 'I know things are difficult, but we're going to come through it.'

"One of the main topics of conversation was Polley. Pete could not see how we were going to get out of the Polley thing. I think he was still unsure about working with Polley, even though we'd been meeting other managers. He was still saying, 'Are we going to work with Polley, or aren't we? And, if so, couldn't we have the money to tour, and carry on?' He was really concerned how the band was going to carry on. With no money we couldn't even get the gear together to do our own tour,

Pete Ham

Pete Ham

and Bill was not helping us. We had all guessed that Bill was looking after Bill. He refused to argue for our corner.

"Pete told me that he thought Bill was a nice guy who had done a good job, but I think he was ready to move on. I think the relationship there was that Pete didn't blame Bill for anything. He was very forgiving."

Anne adds, "Pete knew what Bill's limitations were, but he always had this loyalty to Bill because he helped get them in the door. Pete was like that. He was very, very loyal. But now, even Bill was getting to him, because Pete couldn't get help from anywhere he went."

Bob recalls another time he and Pete went over some music. "Pete had a rented piano and we jammed together a little. We were talking and he was playing his acoustic guitar and he started scat singing and playing back the phrases on the guitar. Then he started doing them together. He was quite amazing really. I said, 'Why don't you do something like that with the band?' He said, 'No, I couldn't do that. I wouldn't feel comfortable.' I said, 'Why, because you'd be making a feature of yourself?' He said, 'Well, kind of, really I couldn't, not in this band.' I thought it was sad that he felt that.

"We went into the garage to hear some of his songs. He kept saying over and over, 'I've got to get this place finished up.' He had recently put a girder in [the living room], where he had knocked a wall out. He played me some ideas; a few songs. There was one mid-tempo thing. I can still remember some of the words today, *'Take me back to the father, take me, take me, take me home.'*"

After a few days, Bob returned to Coventry. Pete went to Tom's house to play four songs he'd recently demoed on his Revox recorder. One, he'd started the previous year; "It Doesn't Really Matter." Another was "Helping Hand." Pete had two additional songs which reflected a deep inner suffering, "No, Don't Let It Go" and "Ringside." For the latter there exists several versions {Ringside – initial cassette demo} :

Take your seat by the ringside
Watch them bidding for your blood
Who will own you tomorrow?
Will you be misunderstood
Take me back to the father
Take me, take me, take me home
For I can't bear to feel the sorrow
Of the evil that you've shown . . .

Why oh why
Did you prove me wrong
When my faith in you was strong
Really strong . . .

The "Ringside" recording Pete brought over to Tom's reveals that Pete had done a version with the ending ad-lib of *"Oh, you let me down, you let me down."* But he recorded over most of it and, instead, laid down a more antiseptic version; doubling the lead vocal. In fact, the whole four-song tape was somewhat numb; possibly Pete was afraid to show Tom the raw edge of his emotions. A prime example was the recording he presented of "No, Don't Let It Go." Pete had changed its lyrics. In an earlier, starker version, then called "No More," he sang:

Drunken days, drunken nights
Someone please turn out the light
I can't face the mirror anymore
Move along, magic gone
Someone else can sing my song
I can't lift my head up off the floor
No, no, no, no more . . .

Empty days, sleepless nights
Have I lost the will to fight?
Someone help me back onto the road
Fight is gone, writing's wrong
I can't even play along
Can't you see behind this old facade? . . .

There's no use in tryin'
When I only end up cryin'
It's a fools game
It's no longer funny
When you're doing it for money
It's a shame, shame
No more, no more . . .

The irony is the sprightly, upbeat music that carries these words. Pete had drifted so far that even when creating one of his typical bright melodies, he still couldn't hide his heavily anguished heart. Now, when faced with playing it for Tom, he'd re-recorded the song with altered lyrics, singing the same themes, but from the perspective of someone advising a friend.

Anne recalls that when Pete came home from playing Tom these demos, "He was really deflated. He said Tommy thought they were hopeless."

Sometime in April of 1975, May Pang flew into London to visit some friends. It had been a few years since she'd seen anyone from Badfinger. She had a phone number for Tom and rang up one day, asking if he and Marianne would like to go to dinner. "I suggested we meet at Apple and Tom said, 'Should we?' He was thrilled to be going over there. When I arrived Pete was there too, and I was so glad to see him. Apple was on St. James street then and Pete and Tom felt strange in the new atmosphere . . . We were leaving and the receptionist, Laurie, said to me, 'God, I didn't even realize that was Pete Ham. He looked so different. . . .'

"We had dinner at a Greek restaurant and we talked about old Apple. They were obviously stressed. They said money wasn't going into their accounts. Pete mentioned an overdraft. Afterwards we went to the club Dingwalls. Pete looked depressed the whole time. At the end of the night I said to Pete, 'Look, if I can help, I will help you. Just tell me what I can do.' We were sitting in the car. He looked me straight in the eye and said, 'Thanks, May.' That was it."

Brian Slater got the urge to call Pete on April 22nd. "I mentioned to Pete that I was going to play tennis and he kind of shyly asked if he might come along. I was delighted. He said he might have some trouble scraping money together for petrol.

Pete Ham

Brian Slater

I thought that was odd. We got together and during our conversations he mentioned he couldn't pay the mortgage on his house and something about his money being squandered in New York. He said he had a meeting scheduled the next day with his accountant in London. . . ."

Pete went over to Tom's later that evening. In several interviews, Tom described an incident in which Marianne asked Pete to keep Tom upstairs. Tom's time frame has varied regarding this story, but logically this would have been when it occurred. Marianne had bought an inflatable dingy for use in the canal in back of their house. She wanted to blow it up and surprise Tom. When Pete and Tom came downstairs from working on demos, Tom was quite taken with his new gift. Tom claimed he said to Pete, 'C'mon, let's go for a ride in this' and they walked over to the canal's edge. Instead of jumping into the dingy though, Pete jumped into the water, and sank below the surface for quite some time. Finally Pete came up and stood dripping on the bank. Tom asked Pete what was wrong and Pete said, "Well, the situation. You know, it isn't very good." Tom replied, "Well, I think everybody knows that. I'm just waiting for you to realize it." It was then Pete allegedly declared, "Well, I think I want to do something about it."

Tom remembered an old friend who had once offered to help them, former BEI vice-president, Stan Poses. Poses had continued to work in the rock management field since he'd broken off his association with Polley in 1972. He'd recently managed The Raspberries, who had just broken up, and was now helping direct the solo career of Eric Carmen.

Poses recalls, "I got a phone call from Tommy and Pete. They told me some of the things that had gone on and would I be interested in managing them. I told them, 'Look, if you want me to help you, there are going to be a couple of conditions. One, if there are any lawsuits with Polley, who has your contracts, or Collins, or any of those people, you will indemnify me from any lawsuit. Second, you have to get back to me after you get all four guys together, and show me that you're all in on this. If you want me to fly to England next week, I will. Or you can fly here to New York, you can stay at my house with me, Michelle, and the kids. So call me back after you discuss it.' "

The next day, Pete went out and made a small payment on his life insurance policy, perused some home building materials, and traveled to see accountants Goldblatt & Co. When Pete got home, Anne noticed he seemed especially bothered. "He was very upset about the Warner's legal action. He tried to get Stan Polley on the phone. He'd been trying for ages and ages." Pete's phone records show calls had been made to America every day of the past week. Anne recalls, "I was getting close to having my baby and Pete was getting quite upset with me needing to go into the hospital soon."

Later that evening, Pete seemed to be in a much better mood. Anne recalls, "Pete was sitting with me on the settee, laughing and talking about names for the baby. One of the names we discussed was Georgina, because he wanted a long name to go with Ham. Pete put his hand on my stomach. The baby was moving about. He was going to go to the hospital with me the next day to have a scan.

"I remember the John Alderson program came on and I was lying down. We were laughing and I tried to get up. Pete was kidding me, 'C'mon fats.' We were both laughing. Then the phone rang . . . Pete came back in the room and he said something about his money being gone. I'm pretty certain he said he'd gotten a call from America. He said he was going out to have a drink with Tom."

Tom came over to pick up Pete. Anne says Pete asked if she wanted anything. She figured he might be coming back after the pub closed. Tom took Pete to the White Hart pub. Anne waited up until 11:00 p.m. before going to bed.

Over the years, Tom did many interviews where he was asked about this particular night. There were minor inconsistencies, but his most comprehensive version was as follows: "I picked up Pete around 10:00 p.m. The English pub closing hours were about 10:30 at the time. We came in and Pete ordered a triple scotch (whiskey). I hadn't even put the Guinness to my lips before he downed his drink and was ordering another. I said, 'Wait a minute, Pete.' He must have had the equivalent of ten scotches before we left.

"When we were there he said, 'I've decided to get away from Polley.' He kept saying he'd seen the light. He said, 'Let's go back and call Poses and tell him it's over.' So we went back to my house and had some wine. It was like a celebration that we had decided to do it, or he had anyway."

Stan Poses recalls getting another call in the States. "It was both Tommy and Peter. I remember Donnie Ienner was in the office with me, when Peter Ham called. They basically said, 'Everybody says 'yes.' I was excited. I started calling agents and was trying to figure out how to put a package together of Eric Carmen and Badfinger touring across the country."

Tom said he and Pete continued to work on some songs before breaking off for the evening. They went downstairs and had a conversation with Marianne. She says Pete seemed worried, but "you could never really tell. Pete didn't show a lot of things. He was the type of person who could drink a lot of liquor, and you wouldn't realize how much he'd had. The strangest thing he'd do was put lit cigarettes out on his hands – and not make a sound."

Pete had been stabbing out cigarettes on his hands more and more over the years. Bob Jackson recalls, "I saw Pete do that a number of times. Once it was at a gathering at Tom's house with a lot of people there. I couldn't believe it. I remember saying to Tom, 'What's that all about, Tom?' and he wouldn't have an answer. It was so strange because Pete wouldn't show any pain. . . ."

Tom stated that Pete seemed especially depressed when he first picked him up that night, but at some point, Pete mentioned some of the things Poses had said to him really opened his eyes about Polley. Tom said this was the first time Pete ever *clearly* acknowledged that he felt he was being taken by Polley. And once Pete started to drink, he rose to unusually good spirits.

Tom brought Pete back home at about 12:30 a.m. He recalled, "We continued to talk about the situation in the car and when we got to Pete's house, he said, 'Don't worry, I know a way out.' He banged on the top of the car and went inside."

Bob Jackson: "Tom told me that when Pete had gotten out of his car, he said, 'I know a way out of this. Goodbye, Tom.' That was very strange to him, because Pete would normally say 'Tada' or 'See you,' not 'Goodbye.' "

Richard Duryea, Polley's BEI assistant, was now staying in Los Angeles (where the time zone is eight hours earlier than in London). He said that he hadn't taken on any tasks for Badfinger or Polley for quite some time. He claims he got a call from Pete Ham on April 23, 1975. "Pete said that he needed money. He sounded drunk. He said that he could not reach Stan (Polley). Well, everyone had trouble reaching Stan. Unless Stan wanted to be reached, you didn't reach him. I was not in a good position to help Pete. I told him I would try to get in touch with Stan and see what I could do. Managers get calls like this all the time. You do the best you can and normally things work out. Usually it's not a life and death situation."

Late into the night, Beverley was sitting up talking with her sister at her parent's home in Hertfordshire. "I remember feeling all day like something terrible was going to happen. My mother had felt the same way. She told me she'd jumped every time the phone rang, thinking it was some kind of bad news involving me. Then, about two in the morning, the phone did ring. I picked it up and no one answered.

"At first I thought the call was from my husband, Colin, because of the delay on long-distance calls from Africa. I kept on saying 'Hello. Hello.' I put the phone down and picked it up again to see if anyone was on the line. Someone was. I could tell, because they hadn't hung up the receiver. I said 'Hello' again, and still there was no answer. Finally I hung up."

On the morning of April 24, 1975, at about 6:55 a.m., Anne arose. She found that Pete was not in bed. "It wasn't unusual," she explained, "because Pete would often go into the garage and work on music throughout the night. Almost always Blair woke up before me, and if Pete wasn't in bed, he would go down, knock on the garage door, and tell Pete he should come up to bed now. But for some reason, I woke up first that day. I came down to the back garage door. It was really stiff and heavy. I couldn't get it open. I called to Pete. He didn't answer. I had to pound on it to get it open. I went in and Pete was in front of me. He had a rope around his neck. I couldn't get it off. I remember screaming in the garden."

Tom recalled, "At 7:00 in the morning I was awakened by a call from Anne. She was screaming for me to come over." Marianne: "She was yelling into the phone, *'It's Pete! It's Pete!'* " Tom left quickly, not really knowing what had happened. When he arrived at Pete's home he couldn't find anyone. He ran through the different rooms and, finally, into the garage. "That's when I saw Pete. I thought, 'That's it for me and rock'n'roll.'"

Tom checked to see if Pete had a pulse. He had none. Tom was in shock, but managed to call the police. By 7:30 a.m. two officers had arrived. The following scene was documented: a rope had been tied to an overhead beam and, at one end, a noose was wrapped around Pete's neck. His body was partially slumped to the floor. Found next to it were a wooden stool and a drummer's stool. Both had been knocked over. Nearby; a half-empty bottle of wine.

A doctor examined Pete's body before it was taken away. Anne then came into the garage. There was one of Pete's songbooks out, but for some reason Anne felt compelled to pick up another one sitting on top of some musical equipment. Anne opened it. The date and time of her discovery – April 24, 1975, at 8:20 a.m.

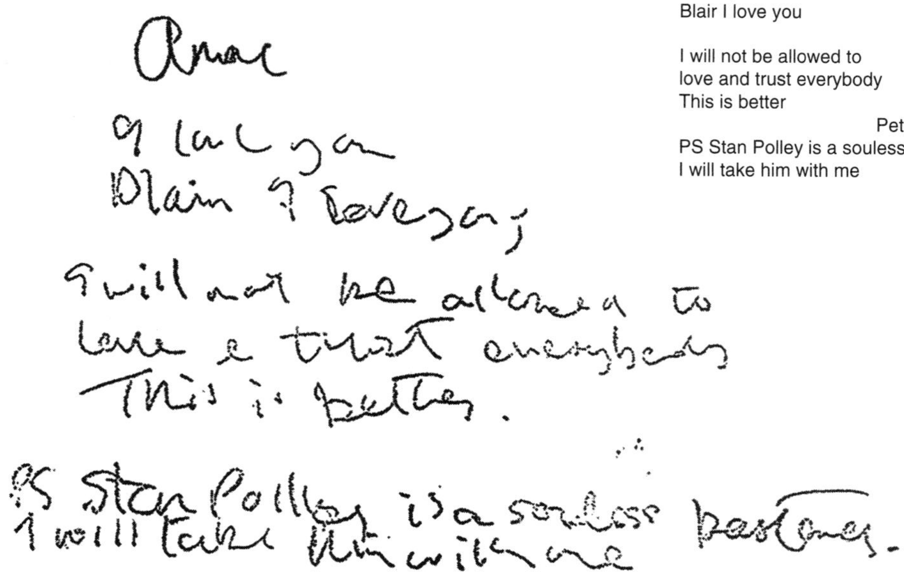

Anne
I love you
Blair I love you

I will not be allowed to
love and trust everybody
This is better

Pete

PS Stan Polley is a souless bastard
I will take him with me

May Pang had been in London on April 23rd, but she left for the states the same morning Pete was found. She explains why she cut her visit short, "I'd told my friends on Wednesday I was leaving on Thursday. They said, 'Why not stay through the weekend?' I had no reason not to, but something had been compelling me to leave. I told them, 'No, no, I've got to go!' I could not explain why. I was gonna call Tom and Pete in the morning and tell them, 'Hey, if you need anything. . .' But I remember thinking, 'Oh, it's too early. Musicians never get up this early.' So I let it go. Right after I landed in New York, I came home and there was a message from Tony King of Apple. I called him back and he said, 'Pete Ham has killed himself!' I could not believe it!"

Bill Collins was at home when he got an urgent telegram from Tommy. Bill says his telephones had recently been turned off due to the overdue accounts he couldn't pay. "I had been thinking about getting in touch with Pete," recalled Bill. "I was planning to tell him he should go solo, even though this would probably break up the band and end my deal . . ." Bill called Tom back from a pay phone and received the terrible news.

Tom had the especially difficult task of contacting Pete's parents and Mike Gibbins. They spread the word around Swansea. Bob Jackson received a telegram from Tom, as he had no working phone. Tom contacted Richard Duryea at his home in Los Angeles, "I was totally surprised," said Duryea. "I called Stan Polley and he said he wanted me to go to England for the inquest. He wasn't emotional about it though."

Joey Molland was in America. "I got a message from a friend who worked at one of the record companies to call Tommy. I called Tommy from an office there and he told me. I had to call back to make sure it wasn't a bad joke."

Stan Poses remembers, "It was Tommy on the phone. I said, 'Well, what are we doing? Are you coming here or should I come over there?' He said, 'You're not going to believe this. I found Pete hanging in the garage. He left a note cursing Stan Polley.' I was blown away. I walked the streets of New York for hours."

Anne stayed at Tom's house, but she needed things from her home. Tom was too shaken to go back. She waited for her brother to arrive from Scotland. Meanwhile, Pete's brother, John, hadn't been reached. He was vacationing in Spain. As it was, Pete's father, William, and one of Pete's cousin's, immediately drove up from Swansea the day Pete died.

The following day, many people were at Pete's house: Bob Jackson, Gaynor Gibbins, Mike Gibbins, and others, each of them in a complete state of shock. But no one had yet contacted Beverley, knowing she would be overwhelmed. It was finally decided Gaynor would be the one to phone her. Beverley recalls, "I had just gone out and bought a birthday card for Pete. My husband was coming over from Africa on Sunday and I anticipated that I'd finally get to see Pete. I was showing the card to my sister when the phone rang. . . ."

Beverley says she became totally numb from the news. Somehow, she made her way over to Pete's house. The talk was disbelieving. Many said Pete had to have been murdered, despite the presence of a suicide note. "It was easier to think that," says Beverley. "We couldn't face the reality of him taking his life, it was too out of character."

Mike: "At the time I could not believe that he would do that. I was crying. I said, *'He did not write this note!'* I was shouting. It did not look like his handwriting. It was all spidery and shit. I said, 'If he wrote this he was either scared, or 'out of his mind' drunk.' " But, as Beverley indicates, "The writing on the note was definitely Pete's, but it was unlike anything I'd ever seen. People wondered if he'd been coerced."

Pete's note was found in an older songwriting book, not the one he was currently using. "I don't know why it wasn't out," says Anne. "Maybe he'd wanted me to discover it later." Beverley added, "Some people wondered if it was actually written then, or maybe another time when he was low."

Beverley's sister, Denise, reminded Beverley of the late night phone call, when no one had answered the phone. Beverley had put it out of her mind, but when her sister brought it up, "I went cold; it was absolutely devastating. Of course, I'll never know if it was Pete. I asked many people if they had called that night. I didn't want to believe that Pete didn't feel he could talk to me . . . It's very hard. . . ."

John Ham finally made it to Pete's home and found a crowd there. He saw a lot of unfamiliar people and became concerned. He shuffled some of them out. He wanted answers. "What Pete did was completely out of character as I knew him," he said, "I hadn't known of any indication leading to this. It didn't ring true. A lot of people were hinting foul play to me."

Anne says she got a phone call from Polley's office, "They were asking if I needed anything. Then Richard Duryea suddenly calls, saying he's come in for the inquest. It struck me as odd that Pete could never get a hold of anyone, then he dies, and they're right over."

John Ham arranged to have Pete's body taken to Wales for cremation. When he got back to Swansea he got a call. "It was a music store operator in London. I knew a lot of people there on the retail side. He told me a fellow had been in trying to sell Pete's Stratocaster. I found out Pete had lent this fellow his guitar after the guy had sold his for rent money. It was one of Pete's nicer ones. I was never able to get it back."

The inquest was held on Monday, April 28, 1975. Richard Duryea was there. "Nobody was very pleasant to me," he says. "They all seemed to put the responsibility on Polley for Pete's suicide." Bob Jackson recalls, "Duryea was too smooth about the whole thing. It was like, 'Don't worry lads. This is unfortunate but we can all tie this up if we all stick together. We can still carry on.' It was too insensitive. Tommy said to him, 'Fuck off! I don't want to talk about it now.' "

Anne and Tom had their previous police statements gone over, as did one of the attending officers at the scene. The autopsy report determined Pete had died from the hanging. The only out-of-the-ordinary aspect was that his lungs were very congested. Pete had written near the end of his life, '*The way that my lung hurts, is making me sad. The way that my lung hurts, is driving me mad.*' But no one related any specific complaints of ill health, though many people noted he looked very worn and very tired his last few months.

Pete's blood alcohol level was three times the legal driving limit for England. How much that would affect his thinking varies by opinion. The time of his death was figured at somewhere between 3:00 and 7:00 a.m.

Slowly the word got out about his suicide. Most of the music papers and major newspapers in England had brief write-ups. Brian Slater says that was how he found out, "I opened up the paper at work. Having just seen Pete made it so hard to take. . . ."

Producer Chris Thomas: "I was told while I was eating at a restaurant. I was shocked. I went right over to see Tommy. I knew it would be especially difficult for him."

There was a service planned in early May at the Morriston Crematorium in Wales, with Pete's ashes to be spread in one of the gardens. No commemorative stone was made, but Pete's name was printed in the crematorium's "Book of Remembrance." And contributions in his name were made by his family, to the "Society For Brain-Damaged and Crippled Children.

On the day of Pete's funeral, a long procession of vehicles traveled to the crematorium. Gaynor recalled watching from the window of a friend's home. The womenfolk stayed behind, the traditional Welsh custom being that only men attend a funeral service. But Kathie Molland – who had flown over from America with Joey – went anyway. She became the only female present.

Bob Jackson recalls, "It was a horrible, horrible day for me. My train was late and I just missed the service. I went over to the Ham family home afterwards and Tommy was quite morose. Mike was saying, 'I'm not going to worry about it.' That was his way of dealing with it. Joey and Kathie were bouncy. Joey said, 'If we do another album we could call it *For Pete's Sake,*' that kind of Liverpool thing. That's just how he dealt with it."

Several people were not happy Kathie had attended the service, as even Pete's mother had decided not to break custom. Anne recalls afterwards, "Kathie stood in Pete's mother and father's living room and announced, 'Well, this puts the icing on the cake. Now we can go after Stan Polley.' I was heavily sedated and I can still remember that. I thought that was a terrible thing to say in front of his parents. They were just devastated."

In the United States, there turned out to be an astonishingly small amount of publicity regarding Pete's death. It appears neither Apple, Capitol, nor Warner Brothers, made any public statements nor sent out any press releases. None of The Beatles said a word. *Billboard* tried to list his death in their "international" section, but a typographical error left out the part that Pete had actually "died!" They never corrected it, and never even reported Pete's death in their domestic news; astounding treatment for a songwriter of four major hit records. In fact, a *Billboard* report, just two weeks after Pete's death, bragged about the lucrative publishing income "Without You" had generated for Apple and The Beatles, without even *mentioning* Pete Ham and Tom Evans as the songwriters!

This period in 1975 was arguably the bleakest time in history for purveyors of pop rock, as three of its leading proponents from the early 70's: Badfinger, Big Star, and The Raspberries, all dissolved nearly simultaneously. Disco and glam rock were the up-and-coming rages, along with syrupy, middle-of-the-road ballads. It was a decidedly uncool time for 60s-pop-influenced rock bands.

Shortly after Pete's death, Apple pulled all of Badfinger's records from the shops. As it was, over the past few months, Apple had been phasing out their record division, publishing division, mastering house, and recording studio. All that was left was Neil Aspinall, a secretary or two, and a board of directors. Badfinger's legacy was rapidly disappearing.

Thankfully, *Rolling Stone* magazine did a column on Pete's death about a month and a half after he died. This let a lot of people know at least *some* of what had happened. Joey quoted the key line from Pete's note which mentioned Polley. Fans and admirers were saddened. Two letters of remembrance were printed in a later issue.

Today, Pete's death retains some mystery, as any suicide generally does. His note certainly revealed his deep-seated beliefs in "love and trust" had been irreparably damaged. And the part about Polley showed a suppressed burning rage; most likely the catalyst which pushed him over the edge. But one still wonders how a man with so much going for him could make the choice that he did.

Professor Edwin S. Shneidman of UCLA University, one of the world's acknowledged experts on suicide, wrote in a 1993 commentary, *"Suicide is caused by psychache . . . It occurs when the psychache (intolerable psychological pain) is deemed by that person to be unbearable . . . reality is introspectively undeniable . . . the individual sees no other possibilities than death."*

Dr. Shneidman also pressed the fact that every individual has different thresholds for enduring psychological pain. Pete appeared to feel his emotions more deeply than the average person. He came off as an optimistic being, but he also made the point once that "reality depresses me." Pete also showed a great willingness to bear the responsibility of any given situation. Possibly, he felt his suicide would help expose Polley, and thus free others from his seemingly inescapable bonds. Of course, no one will ever really know for sure. . . .

Ex-Polley client Lou Christie: "When someone controls you to the extent that Polley did – controlling all your income, then abandoning you – it's very hard to let go of the anger you're left with. How do you keep your career moving? You don't have the luxury of fighting a court battle for four or five years. You can't be a creative and functioning person until you let go of that anger. A lot of artists crumble under bitterness and hate and become self-destructive. It may manifest as drinking, drugs, or maybe something as simple as not being able to get out of bed. In Pete's case, well, it's very sad. . . ."

Ex-Polley client Al Kooper: "It's understandable to me, being in Polley's hands. I've been at the point where I could throw a rope around my neck. The guy had no sensitivity to the human condition. He was like Hannibal Lechter from the Thomas Harris books. Lechter was a psychiatrist, incredibly bright, but he was also a cannibal. He *ate* some of his patients. . . ."

Photographer, filmmaker, and friend, Tony Beresford-Cooke, responded to Pete's death, with a letter, which was published by *Melody Maker* and *Sounds* in late May, 1975: *"The music industry doesn't realize that musicians in its care must be treated with gentleness and sincerity, only then will the music grow and flourish. Musicians are special, sensitive people who give much, and many, like Badfinger, are adrift within a hostile so-called "industry" that seems based solely on money and self-interest. . . ."*

Richard DiLello, the ex-Apple "house hippie," was very upset at the lack of reaction to Pete's death. He made a long angry speech while at a Beatles convention in 1976: *"In the case of Pete Ham everyone was too busy stuffing their own pockets to take time out to ask him how he felt about all this. When everyone looked the other way, Pete Ham went into a garage and strangled himself. The result: we can add one more victim to the list of 'No one waved goodbye. . . .' "*

Though none of the Beatles commented publicly on Pete's death at the time, years later Paul McCartney did, in several interviews: *"It was tragic 'cause Pete Ham was a lovely fellow. He wrote 'Without You,' which was a magnificent song . . . It was sad because he was good. Well, I told everybody he was good . . . It was one of those things where you hear about it and think, 'If only I had called him a week earlier. I wonder if I could have helped to save him?' "*

May Pang was involved with John Lennon at the time Pete died. She discussed his reaction, "I told John and he couldn't believe it. He said, 'How could he go that way?' It wasn't an idea he'd even entertain. He was very apologetic about how he'd acted about Pete. He knew I'd been friendly with the band, but he hadn't really known them or cared to . . . But he did feel bad when Pete died."

George Harrison made this comment to Australian journalist Paul Cashmere in 1996, *"Pete Ham was a lovely fellow; he was a good guitar player and a great singer . . . He wrote 'Without You,' you know, the Harry Nilsson record."* In 1993, when asked to comment on Pete for this book, George relayed through an assistant that "he did like Pete Ham a lot," but did not want to offer anything beyond that to say. Friends of George's have indicated he seems to find the topic of Pete's death difficult, and usually won't discuss it in detail, though he does readily compliment Pete. Ringo has highly commended Pete's talent, but will always point out to those who ask, he "hardly knew the man."

Badfinger roadie, Ian 'Fergie' Ferguson, pays tribute to his one-time friend, "Pete Ham was the thoughtful one in the band, the intelligent one, the sensible one. Pete Ham was someone you could always go to for advice. I have tremendous regrets we hadn't made up before he died. He was like a brother to me. . . ."

Roadie David "Tag" Hall: "Pete Ham was a fantastic person. He was a very gentle person, very even-tempered. He'd get frustrated if things didn't go right, but he'd never snap at you. He liked to joke and laugh – when the time was right – but then he would go deep inside . . . He cared about everybody. As far as I'm concerned he was like a saint. He was always, "What's wrong with 'so-and-so? What's wrong with 'so-and-so?' Pete Ham cared about people. He truly cared. . . ."

Apple's Al Steckler: "Pete Ham's death hit me like John Lennon's and Brian Jones. These were people I had good relationships with, nice people that I liked. In a business full of of sleazes, a lot of "I Me Mine" type of people, to find someone like Pete Ham was truly special. He was obviously not just looking out for himself, but others as well. He was a really good human being. To find out he was dead at such a young age, and the way he died. It was stunning. It was intolerably sad. . . ."

Gaynor Gibbins: "Pete Ham was as good as it gets, an absolutely wonderful man He loved his family, his friends, he was great with kids, a true gentleman. I've never stopped thinking about him. When I think of Pete I think of the guitar being an extension. There was never an acoustic guitar far off. . . ."

Iveys member Ron Griffiths: "I think if Pete had lived, he would've become known as one of our all-time great songwriters. His one great ambition in life was to write an evergreen song, a standard, and he realized that ambition, but never really saw it. I think the saddest thing of all is when people hear 'Without You,' they automatically think of Harry Nilsson. That's deserving, because of his exceptional version, but. . . ."

Man's Deke Leonard: "Pete's ability to write pop standards sets him far apart from any other Welsh musicians. When Pete Ham played you something it was always a good song. Yet he never changed from the days of The Iveys. You wouldn't have a clue he'd written all those hit songs."

Mike Gibbins: "I didn't realize how much talent Pete had until he died. When Paul produced us, when George produced us, they were like, *'You can play?!'* In fact he played as good as George, and he could sing as good as any of them. There's a lot of songs of Pete's that could be big, if someone picked them up."

Joey Molland: "Pete was a great player, very underrated. And a great writer . . . He was in a difficult period, but the guy was more powerful than he understood, because of his writing capabilities. Even if he never wrote another hit in his life, the fact he'd written four or five hit singles in a row, in the business world, made him extremely powerful. And he went and did that. That got me really angry. I wasn't sad. I was angry. . . ."

Anne counters, "I could never feel any sort of anger towards Pete, despite what he did. It could have been easier to accept his death if he was a bastard, but he was such a lovely man, and that's the thing that hurts more than anything else. He was such a genuine and beautiful soul."

Beverley Tucker: "When people related to Pete's words or his music, that just pleased him so much, and when that was taken away, I know it must have been very hard for him . . . But what's difficult for me to understand is, the Pete I knew was so very terrified of death. He had to have been very unbalanced for that fraction in time. . . ."

Bob Jackson: "I think Pete's suicide was a moment of madness, anger, and frustration, all mixed into one. Pete was down, sure, but he seemed very happy with Anne and the kiddie coming along. I'm sure if someone had been there and said, *'Pete, you're an idiot! Stop!!'* He would've said, 'You're right, you're right.' But for that one brief moment in time, you're insane."

Peter William Ham

April 27, 1947 – April 24, 1975

10

BACK ON THE AIRWAVES

ON MAY 2, 1975, Warner Brothers Records sent a letter to Stan Polley in which they threatened to end the Badfinger record contract. They indicated to Polley they could terminate if two members from the original agreement were no longer in the band. As it happened, after Pete's funeral, Joey Molland had continued to stay in a hotel in London, for weeks on end, and this aroused a lot of conjecture. Bob Jackson recalls: "Tom and others were saying, 'How is Joey living in this swish hotel with Kathie, and always with record execs?' There was suspicion he was being bought off by Warners so they could legally end the contract." Marianne concurs, "Joey and Kathie were staying at the Blakes Hotel, which is very expensive. There was no way they could have afforded to stay there as long as they did. . . ."

After Joey quit the band in November of '74, he and Kathie had stayed in England until March 22, 1975. Then they'd moved to Los Angeles, California. Joey said he sold almost everything he had to survive. Joey and Kathie Molland also stated that, during the first six or so months after Joey quit, they were continuously investigating situations regarding Badfinger. At various stages Joey has made mention he met with Stan Polley, Walter Hofer, Joe Smith, and Ed Silvers (who allegedly gave him the rundown on the Warner Brothers lawsuit). Joey also said Stan Polley had continuously been threatening him regarding leaving the band.

While staying at the Blakes Hotel in London, Joey ran into Mark Clarke, an old Liverpool mate and former bass guitarist for Colosseum and Uriah Heep. They talked about getting together for a jam. Says Clarke. "I told Joey, 'It just so happens I've been working with Jerry Shirley.' He'd recently left Humble Pie. So Joey came over and it felt right. We decided to form a group."

That same month, Anne Ferguson had gone back to live in Scotland. At some point, she got a call from Polley's California office. "It was a woman. She asked me if I would send in a letter exonerating Stan Polley from any blame in Pete's death. I refused."

Polley was obviously worried about what effect Pete's suicide would have on him. Al Kooper was still a Polley client at the time. He recalls, "Polley would continually deny the existence of a suicide note. He would yell, *'Where is the paper? They've never produced that paper!'* He said it didn't exist."

Late in May, Pete's brother, John Ham, received a notice from an United States insurance company called Bankers Life Of Iowa. They were requesting information on Pete's death. A life insurance policy for $250,000 had been secured by Polley back on September 1, 1974. The potential beneficiary was Badfinger Enterprises Inc. (BEI). After Pete had died, Polley had contacted the insurance company to try and collect. He initially expressed to them Pete's cause of death as "unknown." John Ham told his lawyer that he knew nothing about this policy. The lawyer sent Bankers Life a death certificate indicating Pete had committed suicide. What became of Polley's claim is unknown. Banker's Life Of Iowa has since been bought out by Principal Financial Group, who, in 1993, said their computer indicated the policy as "no longer active," with no details on the final determination.

Towards the very end of the month, Polley filed a cross-complaint to WB Music's lawsuit. It stated they breached in their duties as a publisher, and they were unnecessarily hurting "Badfinger" through their frivolous litigation. Shortly after, Warner Brothers Records sent a notice instructing *immediate termination* of the Badfinger record contract.

Then on May 31, 1975, the last day of the month, Anne Ferguson gave birth to Pete Ham's daughter, a child she named in his honor – Petera Ham.

Tom Evans had initially appeared quite sturdy in dealing with Pete's death – making the difficult calls, dealing with the families – but it was only a matter of time before the event took its toll. Beverley recalls, "About two weeks after Pete

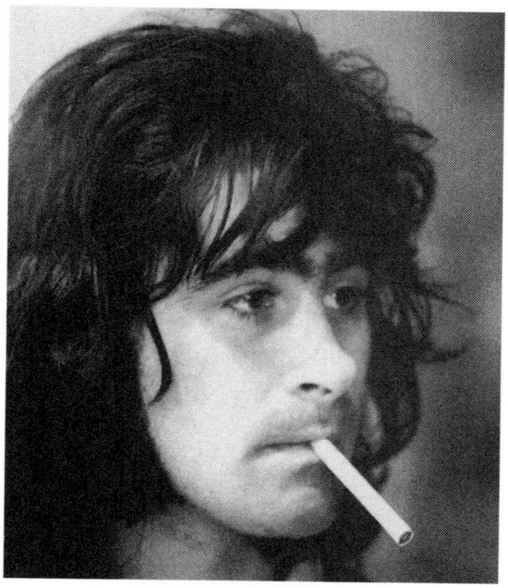

Tom Evans

died, Tom started having lots of trouble. Before that he'd been brilliant. He'd been supporting me. Now he was feeling very lost, as though a part of himself was gone."

Richard DiLello: "I sent Tom a condolence letter and I got back a very disjointed letter from him expressing his pain and confusion over what had happened. He was obviously struggling to pull himself together."

Over the next few months Tom tried to take on regular work. "I was still writing songs," he said in a 1979 interview, "but I'd pretty much given up on the music business. I went to work with a neighbor of mine who was in the pipe-insulation business . . . the guy would introduce me to the other construction workers, tell them I used to be in a famous band . . . Sometimes we'd be working in rich people's homes and there would be a piano, and the guys would try and make me play a tune . . . It was highly embarrassing."

Brian Slater recalls, "I think Tom tried being a taxi driver, but it didn't last. It's very hard after you've lived a transient lifestyle to become "normal." It's only through maturity and time that you can actually put your feet back on the ground and say, 'Okay, that was that and this is this.' "

About mid-year, Bill Collins contacted Bob Jackson about a piece of musical equipment Bob had been given to use with Badfinger. Bob returned it after confirming that Tom definitely had no interest in continuing the band. In August, Mike Gibbins wrote Bob telling him Bill was now attempting to sell all of the Badfinger equipment he had.

Bill Collins strongly denies doing so. He cites it wasn't totally clear at this time whether the group was going to disband. He recalled that one day, the "Badfinger van," which was parked out in front of 7 Park Avenue (and filled with various gear and sound reinforcement equipment) had disappeared. "Tag (Hall) came back with it the very next day," said Bill. "He had taken it down to Tommy's. They had emptied out everything except some speaker cabinets."

At this time, Bill Collins was still responsible with having to pay the band's lease of their two-room rehearsal space on Denmark Street. He put out an ad and was eventually approached by shop owner Malcolm McLaren to let the Sex Pistols take it over. McLaren gave Bill a Fender Rhodes piano and £650 upfront.

The Sex Pistols were just getting off the ground and a couple of the band members ended up housing in the, admitted, two-room squalor. Bill and Anne Collier met with the group and McLaren many times over the next couple years. They saw about a half-dozen of their gigs and had several social sit-downs together. "They were very polite to us; gentlemen," said both. Sex Pistols bassist Glen Matlock later wrote of Bill (who never fails to make a strong impression) in his book, *I Was A Teenage Sex Pistol*, published in 1990.

Meanwhile, Joey Molland's new band had come up with a name: Natural Gas. "It sounds dumb," said drummer Jerry Shirley in a 1976 interview, "But when you think about it, without any bullshit attached, the only meaning was what the group was going to be – a 'natural gas.' "

Mark Clarke's personal manager had taken over the group. The three musicians began rehearsing at Headley Grange, Hampshire, where Led Zeppelin and The Rolling Stones had once recorded. Natural Gas added Rare Bird keyboardist, David Kaffinetti, and cut a studio demo in London. Several labels, including A&M, rejected the music. By September, the band had replaced Kaffinetti with Peter Wood, whose previous gig was with Sutherland Brothers & Quiver.

Joey was on a plane around this time when he met a gentleman named Bill Cameron. "He wasn't a manager," said Joey, "He was a financier. Very, very rich, fifteen million dollars a year the guy made. He said, "I'll back the band! What do you want?" Clarke recalls, "Joey came back to us and said we had to get rid of our current manager because this guy had a lot of money. It was hard. We let the first guy go – which was horrible for me."

Natural Gas was relocated to Los Angeles, California, sometime that fall. Bill Cameron's excitement at being involved with a rock'n'roll group led to great generosity. Clarke states, "He would have $1,000 bills flying around. We had a mansion out in L.A. which he rented. His driver would go to the supermarket and one of us would go with him. We'd fill the limo from the floor to the roof with groceries!"

On September 21, 1975, Bill Collins wrote Bob Jackson stating, *"Stan (Polley) has been in touch with me assuring me he's trying to resolve the situation with Warner by his dealings with Joey."* Over the past few months, Polley had been trying to get something sorted out with Joey, in order to salvage the Badfinger record contract.

On October 2, 1975, Polley sent a letter to Bob, Mike, Tom, and Bill collectively, in which he stated: *"Warner Bros. Records Company has threatened a lawsuit against us if we do not return to them the sum of $250,000 now held in an escrow account. We must put our heads together to see if we have a unified stand to sue Warner Bros. Records, not only for the third album, but also for damages in what we suspect Warner Bros. has done, to wit, inducing Joey Molland to terminate his association with Badfinger. . . ."* Joey later claimed, "I never got any money. Polley lied to them about that. He told them Warner Brothers gave me $60,000, *fuckin' rubbish!"*

By mid-November, Stan Polley and WB Records vice president Ed West had finalized an agreement to officially end the Badfinger record contract. West noted that Badfinger had been paid $165,091, and he acknowledged they were legally entitled to keep that. Polley was also directed to release the $250,000 recording advance he'd been entrusted to put in escrow. Suspiciously, Polley had spread that money over *thirteen* banking institutions.

Meanwhile, in order for Joey to proceed with Natural Gas, he'd been told he *had* to get out of any Badfinger contracts. Joey explained, "I was still signed to all of the contracts that I'd been under with Badfinger . . . So what I did was I got my lawyer to write to Polley saying Joey doesn't want any money, doesn't want anything from you, just give him his release . . . The people financing the Natural Gas band weren't interested if one of the members was signed to another manager. So I signed the paper and gave everything I made up to that point, and got out of the contract."

The release by Joey indicates he gave up all of his rights to any income which was generated by Badfinger – before November 18, 1975 – to BEI. After that date he was to retain his share of future "Badfinger" income, with BEI's 30% gross commission reduced to 20%.

Tom Evans finally decided a music career was too important to abandon. He contacted Bob Jackson late in 1975. They started to talk about doing something together. Tim Boyle connected them with Mickie Most – a high-profile record producer in England – for some session work. Boyle was managing several artists in partnership with Barrie Marshall, including one named John Wilson, who'd just left a band called The Rockits. Jackson recalls, "Tim Boyle said, 'This guy Wilson is with Island Records. He can sing and he writes pop songs. It looks like he might have a new deal with Island. It's iffy, but if you join up, it might cement things."

Tom and Bob met with Wilson and the Rockits drummer, Dave Powell. They were put into the studio in December. Four tracks were cut with producer Muff Winwood, brother of Steve Winwood. Meanwhile, Joey's band, Natural Gas, were getting record label interest. Warner Brothers was said to be one possibility, but Private Stock, a New York based label, had the inside track, because of their close affiliation with the band's lawyer. Some of Private Stock's artists at the time were The Troggs, David Soul, Frankie Valli, and Jose Feliciano.

Former Badfinger producer and Beatles roadie Mal Evans had overseen the recording of a few Natural Gas demos, and was interested in working with them further. He was staying in Los Angeles, spending a lot of time hobnobbing with Ringo Starr and Keith Moon. Mark Clarke visited Mal around the Christmas holidays. At one point Mal, who was heavily into cowboy paraphernalia, showed Clarke a replica of a Winchester rifle. "It shot B-B's," says Clarke. "It wasn't a real one." Clarke noticed Mal seemed rather downcast.

A few days later, Mal was on a conference call with Clarke, Jerry Shirley, Bill Cameron, and the Private Stock president, Larry Uttal. Clarke recalls, "We were starting negotiations with the record company and Mal was asking for a ridiculous amount of money on his behalf. I don't know if he was having financial troubles or what, but I was asked for a "yea" or "nay" vote and I said 'no.' Everyone else did, too. We left it unsettled."

On January 3, 1976, Marianne and Tom had a social gathering at their home in New Haw, Surrey. Later on that evening, they were joined by Bill Collins and his lady friend, Anne Collier, at a pub. Marianne recalls, "Mal Evans' parents and his wife, Lily, came by, too. Mal lived near us and we were good friends with him and his family. He had gone to L.A. to do something with Ringo, fallen for some girl there, and stayed on. He had called us that day. He was quite depressed on the phone. He said to Tom, 'Could you do me a favor and look after Lil?' "

Mal had taken a large amount of valiums and locked himself in a bedroom at his girlfriend's apartment in Los Angeles. Accounts vary, but the most consistent story is that his girlfriend became alarmed Mal was suicidal. She called the police, possibly thinking he was handling a real gun. Mal had the bedroom door barricaded. When the police came, they broke in, and saw the Winchester replica near him, or in his hand. Mal never had a chance. He was shot and killed.

The Mal Evans tragedy was a setback for Natural Gas. Early in 1976, they signed with Private Stock Records, despite the fact they hadn't yet approached many labels. The band's manager, Bill Cameron, was eager to get moving.

Private Stock president Larry Uttal suggested Felix Pappalardi as producer of their first album. Pappalardi was an ex-bass player with Mountain. He had once produced Cream. "Felix was a friend of mine from the road," says Jerry Shirley. "I thought he was a nice guy and would do a good job." But Mark Clarke said he was hesitant, "Our sound was 98% together. We just wanted Felix to record us properly."

Pappalardi was hired. The band then went into L.A.'s Crystal Sound Recording in February; banging out a record in about seventeen days. They relied heavily on the basic tracks, which included fairly busy playing from keyboardist Peter Wood. Joey's material was in his Badfinger-tradition: hook-filled pop, dramatic ballads, and basic rock'n'roll, while Mark Clarke's tunes were similarly styled. The two handled all of the vocal chores; each voice being distinctively different.

When it came time to mix, Pappalardi insisted on no band members presence. "I should have gone," says Clarke. The results were sloppy. Often the vocals sound thin and buried. Joey's guitar tones have little guts. And the keyboards, in many spots, conflict sonically. "The speculation was, it was because of Felix's damaged ears," says Shirley, "The songs just don't jump out at you."

Meanwhile, Tom Evans and Bob Jackson had settled in with their new band, now dubbed The Dodgers. The group spent the early part of 1976 working on new

The Dodgers: John Wilson, Tom Evans, Bob Jackson, Dave Powell

material, eventually cutting thirteen demos in two days. Two studio recordings they had done the previous December were put out as a single by Island Records. Released in March for the U.K. was "Don't Let Me Be Wrong" b/w "Get To You."

Both were solid. The A-side, by John Wilson, has a bursting pre-chorus and catchy refrain, while the B-side, "Get To You," showed off the promising potential of the Evans-Jackson songwriting team. Producer Winwood allowed the vocals to dominate, putting an English-style compression on the mixes, which gave punchy dynamics to rather average sounds. Despite the good effort all-around, the U.K. radio market of 1976 was not geared to this style of tune, not unless the song was an overwhelming standout. It wasn't, and it failed to crack the British charts, even with some radio airplay, a promotional film, and a television spot by the band.

Months later, the same single was released in America. It was well-received by critics; *Pop Top* favorably compared it to Badfinger's best work, while *Phonograph* called it *"impeccable as a pop recording."* Yet, the latter writer, Greg Shaw, admitted it probably wasn't *"distinctive enough to be a hit."* It ended up floating around the lower reaches of the *Billboard Hot 100*.

Natural Gas *LP cover*

The Natural Gas album was released in America near the end of May. Entitled *Natural Gas*, it featured a solid black gatefold cover with a fancy silver insignia. An early review in the L.A. Times call*ed it "quite simply, delightful."* Writer Robert Hilburn was unceasing in his praise, claiming, "*. . . Natural Gas – of all the bands to arrive so far in 1976 – stands the best chance of brightening up the AM (radio) playlists."*

The group got a tremendous break for its initial touring. Jerry Shirley explains, "I knew Peter Frampton and one day he said to me, 'I'm doing a tour for this live album I'm releasing. Would you like to come along?' We said 'yes,' not realizing how big it would be. It was going to be his support tour for the album *Frampton Comes Alive!"*

Natural Gas played throughout the U.S. during July, August, and September, mainly to large-scale audiences straggling into arenas and stadiums to see Frampton and other big name acts which they opened for. The band usually performed for thirty-five minutes, often getting an encore. They would play The Beatles' "Birthday;" the group's way of saluting America's Bicentennial anniversary. The press reaction was remarkably strong. Newspaper writers consistently commented that they were a group to look out for.

Their album received mixed reviews, though. Generally, it was cited for fine material, but many noted the weak production, at times damning it. In *Trouser Press*, Joel Webber lambasted producer Pappalardi for the resulting *"quagmire of equalization and echo that's as thick as a brick."* But Webber ended by saying, *"These guys are too good to be buried by critical indifference, bad hype, or even*

Joey Molland, 1976

Natural Gas: Jerry Shirley, Joey Molland, Mark Clarke, Peter Wood

dismal production. I've been waiting too long for a new band as talented as this to let these things get me down. . . ."

Surprisingly, the album never did chart. There was rumor that, after selling out on an initial LP pressing of 30,000, Private Stock had problems getting new records out. Joey commented that one batch of records had been warped, and when customers came in for exchanges, there was no back stock to replace it. The band was disgusted with the label, who blamed its distributors.

But other problems had been developing which jeopardized the group's future. Initially, everyone had been wildly enthusiastic: all four musicians got along well, they loved the musical freedom, and their respect level for each other was high. But the idyllic atmosphere had been continually waning. Jerry Shirley recalls, "There were certain outside influences that weren't healthy, as in the Bill Cameron situation and Joey's wife. Cameron had come in with no managerial experience, and though he opened his purse strings generously to begin with, it was often misguided in what it was spent on. He could have been putting more on our future, rather than, shall we say, buying shares in Peru."

The cocaine scene revolving around Natural Gas was widely known. There was a reputation around the Sunset Strip in West Hollywood that the drug was easily available if you hung around the group and its manager. Stories abound of the resulting decadence.

After the tour, Shirley, Clarke, and Wood found apartments in New York City. They were quite content to situate there, but Joey wanted to stay in Los Angeles. Joey recalled, "The idea had been that the other three would return to L.A. to rehearse and make the new record. But now they wanted to fly me and all the equipment to New York, and work out of New York. I didn't want to do that."

Both sides remained stubborn. Then feelings came up that Bill Cameron was favoring Joey and giving him more money than the other members. Side arguments formed about Kathie. Shirley recalls, "She thought she was capable of managing the band along with Cameron. She liked to get involved in the group's business and we resented it." Clarke adds, "Kathie was sticking her nose in everything we did. She was always at our meetings and always had something to say. We hadn't been pushing Joey about it at first. We'd been letting it slide, but then it reached a critical point, and the band broke up."

Joey says he was baffled. "It was mystery-conflict time. Somebody says something to somebody else, it all goes round in circles, spins itself up, and maybe explodes. It got to the point where I didn't want to be involved anymore."

Shirley and Clarke agreed the group's camaraderie had been very tight when it was just the four members. They both admitted suspicions that Cameron had been influenced to pursue backing a Joey Molland solo career. Joey did go into a recording studio two weeks after quitting to make solo demos, but nothing came of them. The other Natural Gas members evolved into a band called Magnet (minus Mark Clarke) and they got one more album out on A&M Records.

The Dodgers' second single was released in Britain in June of 1976, "Just Wanna Love You" b/w "Don't Know What You're Doing." The A-side was a John Wilson tune. The B-side was written by Bob Jackson. It was another example of well-constructed melodies and intelligent pop production. But once again, the songs cut against mainstream radio formats and did not break through.

Drummer Dave Powell quit during this stretch and Bob called a friend from his hometown of Coventry to see if he was interested in replacing him. Paul Hooper had played with Bob in his first group, Indian Summer. Hooper took on the gig. Prior to that, Man's Terry Williams filled in as a temporary replacement. The new line-up did a month's tour of England in August. It was only slightly successful though; failing to push the single into the charts.

Over time, the Dodgers continued to develop material. Wilson pushed the hardest in putting forth songs, and Tom did express he felt Wilson was somewhat overbearing in that way, but Wilson claims Tom seemed quite amiable in accepting his attitude. "Tommy would always push for me, even though he was the one with the track record. We'd just pool the songs and he'd say, 'Yeah, that's the best song.'"

Tom and Bob Jackson proved to have a large number of excellent songs written. Tom was writing with a much more upbeat and positive tone than he had in recent years. "I Believe In You" and "Don't Let It Go" are two particular standouts. {I Believe In You – Dodgers demo}

A third British single was put out in the fall. It was another John Wilson tune entitled, "Down." Little promotion was done and it failed to chart in the U.K. Despite the lack of success, a public relations man at the Dodgers label, Island Records, was quite taken with the Dodgers talent. "His name was Clive Banks," says Hooper. "He was a sort of get-up-and-go whiz kid. He was going to leave Island to start his own management and promotions company with a few other chaps. He was really into our stuff and said he was quite keen to take us on and manage us."

Since the group hadn't progressed to an album deal with managers Tim Boyle and Barrie Marshall, they felt they could take a shot by signing with the new Red Shadow Management team. They inked with them in the early fall of 1976.

All along, Tom Evans had been getting along well with his bandmates, but his inconsistent demeanor also kept everyone on edge. Wilson explains, "We all used to comment on Tom's strange behavior. He was full of innuendo, a very taciturn personality. He could be really friendly, a great chap. Then he might turn around and call you a 'cunt.' You'd think, *'What the hell was that?'* A couple of times I nearly got in a punch-up with him and I'm a big guy and he was a little guy!"

Bob recalls, "When Tom would drink he could become sarcastic. He'd say things that people couldn't pick up on. They'd say, 'What? What was that?' and he'd brush it aside. It wasn't always nasty. It was just a little joke at their expense. When he didn't drink, he was polite, a rather quiet person."

Drummer Paul Hooper: "I used to stay at Tom's place when we were working in London and he was often very reflective. I remember he used to get phone calls relating to Pete Ham and Badfinger. I could see it was a great weight on him. I didn't pry. It was up to him if he wanted to discuss those things with me."

Tom had been approached by Stan Polley in mid-1976 to sign a release for all of his past and present Badfinger-related income, in return for £5,000. This was a tremendous enticement due to the fact Tom felt it would be hard to ever get any of his deserved Badfinger royalties through the Polley net. Tom did eventually sign the release, which is dated August 17, 1976. Mike Gibbins signed an identical document, while Bill Collins signed a similar agreement in November. But the lawyers for Pete Ham's estate refused to even acknowledge theirs.

Prior to signing his release, Bill Collins said he received a call from Polley. He said he hadn't spoken to Polley in over a year. Polley invited Bill and his girlfriend, Anne Collier, to visit him in America. Bill said they took up his offer and ended up spending three weeks being wined and dined in both New York City and Los Angeles. They were escorted by some Polley friends for a trip to Mexico. Toward the end of this whirlwind excursion, Polley met Bill at the Polo Lounge of the Beverly Hills Hotel. Bill said he suspected the hospitality was done for a reason, and he asked Polley what it was. He recalled, "Polley asked me, 'How much money is being held for Badfinger in the Apple account?'" (Apple was still holding Badfinger sales and publishing royalties for unresolved claims still pending between Polley, Bill, and the band members). Bill told him "£20,000."

Now, at this time, Polley was presumably getting these releases signed in order to give him a clear path to the band's past, present, and future Apple royalties. Polley allegedly told Bill at this meeting, "When I get the Ham estate signature, and the Apple money gets released, put £15,000 of it in a bank account in both our names. But you take it. I won't touch it."

In Bill's opinion, Polley may have been feeling guilty about what had happened to Badfinger, and was simply being generous to Bill. But one might consider that if the Ham estate was steadfastly refusing to sign a release at this time, and if the money was eventually given to Bill Collins upon settlement (as it currently was contracted to do from Apple), Polley's scenario would allow Polley to get his hands on £15,000, just in case he never got any court-appointed rights to the money. Bill said he refused Polley's offer, his reason being, it wouldn't look good for him to take the £15,000, and secondly, it wouldn't be morally right.

By year's end, Tom and Mike had not been paid for their releases. There was a sense that Polley had shafted them once again. But Bill said he *did* receive £5,000 from Polley, and he highly disputes the fact that Tommy and Mike say they did not get their money. As it was, Polley continued to portray everyone, including Pete's estate, as legally signed off to Badfinger rights – for years to come.

Joey's life was interrupted when his mother died late in 1976. He returned to England with Kathie for the funeral. After the ceremonies, he went down to the visa office in London. He recalled, "They wouldn't give me a visa to return to America. They said, 'You've been there too long and you've been there too many times. We're not going to let you back. You're going to have to wait two years' . . . I had a house in Los Angeles I was renting. I was a regular person there . . . In London I was a derelict. I had nothing going on at all. I went and checked into this cheap hotel because I had no idea how long I was going to be there."

Later, Joey admitted he had actually misplaced his entry visa in Los Angeles and somehow it had been sent to Bill Cameron's office. But Cameron had put it in his briefcase and, unbeknownst to Joey, was traveling all over with it. "This is how spacy it was," said Joey.

Kathie and Joey managed to survive in England for almost three months, during which time Joey cut his hair short and tried to get a record deal. He claimed Swan Song Records came close to biting, but nothing happened. He even had a few visits with Tom Evans and broached the idea of reforming Badfinger. In February, he and Kathie made it back to L.A.

Meanwhile, Tom's wife, Marianne, had given birth to her first child in January of 1977, a son named Stephen. Tom was delighted. Said his mother, May, "Tommy just idolized his son. He said, 'If I was a woman I'd have twenty-two of them!' He thought it was a marvelous experience."

Marianne, Stephen, and Tom

More good news came when the Dodgers new managers announced they had a record deal with Polygram. The group was to start new recordings that spring. They had decided not to use any of the Muff Winwood produced tracks from the previous year.

The Red Shadow management team had a prospective producer in mind. He was a staff engineer from Rockfield Studios, named Pat Moran. He offered a good financial package. Paul Hooper recalls, "We had this meeting and the management team played us a track and said, 'What do you think of this?' It was a recording by this band called Airwaves, who had unlimited studio time at Rockfield. Moran was using this tape to show his production work. I'd done sessions with him and thought he was a nice guy, but I was reluctant." Bob Jackson knew Moran from another band he played with and Bob didn't think, musically, Moran was right for the Dodgers. The Red Shadow team insisted. The album was started with him in charge in early April of 1977.

Off and on during the past year, the Dodgers had been playing gigs and doing mini-tours around England. Tommy's drinking had been an occasional problem. John Wilson recalls, "He was getting too pissed on stage. Me and Bob had this joke going because Tom would sometimes hit a bum note and we'd glance at him. He'd look at his hand and give this expression as if to say it wasn't him. We'd make a joke about his '*Baaad* finger.' "

Drummer Hooper thinks the situation was overblown, "Tommy's drinking wasn't a problem. He became a scapegoat for what wasn't happening. The managers were a little frustrated because we weren't going over that well. They were having great success with their New Wave acts. They were promoting Ian Dury, Boomtown Rats, Elvis Costello . . . you name it and it was happening in a big way. But they decided our problem was Tommy – which it wasn't.

"We had a meeting and everyone was there except Tom. The managers just came right out and said, 'He's gotta go.' We were reluctant. We came back to them and said, 'We can't do it.' But we got worried they were going to drop us. We finally agreed to it."

Bob remembers arguing heartily on Tom's behalf, but to no avail. He recalls the day the band let Tom know, "We all met in a rehearsal room. The rest of the guys tried to keep a front. Paul said, 'Look Tom, there's something we have to say and basically, it's over mate. Sorry, it's not our fault, but this is the way it is.' Tom said, 'Can't you give a dog a bone? Give me a chance.' John said, 'I'm sorry, mate.' Tom argued against it a bit, finished his beer, and said, 'Right. Well that's it then.' And he left.

"I felt terrible. The honorable thing to do would have been to quit myself, but it was hard. We were right in the middle of doing this album. It would've been very hard for me to give that up. I shook his hand, but I was afraid to call him for quite some time."

Hooper adds, "Looking back, I don't know if we were strong to do it, or if we were weak in that we didn't stand up to stop it. It hurt me because I really liked Tom and had great respect for him. I lost a friend there. Tommy didn't want anything to do with me after that."

The Dodgers managers insisted on erasing all of Tom's vocals and bass lines from the partially finished album. It was later completed with Roger Lomas taking Tom's place.

By March of 1977, Joey's partnership with Bill Cameron had broken apart. He recalled, "This is where I'm broke now; totally broke. I had moved to North Hollywood, California. I tried various things. Nothing would happen. I mean, just the cocaine addiction and all that stuff, everybody knew. Nobody was going to deal with me . . . I went to work laying carpets. That kept me alive for about a year, six months or a year. Thirty-five dollars a day."

Tom Evans was also struggling to keep his optimism. The few months after his firing were very hard. Badfinger's former producer, Chris Thomas, had been keeping in touch. "I saw Tommy a lot then. We'd become good mates. He felt all the cards were stacked against him. He was asking me for help at times."

Tom was considering a solo project. He was also spending a lot of time at local pubs, his favorites being the Black Horse and the White Hart. The latter was owned by Jack and Marge Tidbury. Jack Tidbury recalls, "He used to sit at the bar in the mornings and quietly listen to the tapes we'd put on. There was a piano there. Music was going all the time. He'd pop in at any time and have a couple. He listened to the music real intently." Marge Tidbury adds, "Tom used to be the first one in when we opened. He spent many hours talking to our two sons. We all thought the world of him."

Tom was a popular pub patron, despite the fact he could be private and brooding. A local couple named Tony and Jackie Friend had met Tom back when Pete Ham had first moved into the Woking area. Jackie now gave Tom his haircuts. She recalls, "He was a really nice guy; a lot of fun. He had that Liverpool tongue though. He could be wicked like that." Jackie's husband Tony adds, "He was a good mate of mine. We were both into intellectual puzzles and lateral thinking. He would call me at three in the morning and say, *'I've got the answer Tony!'* He was very smart in that way . . . I didn't know for years that he had been in a successful pop band. He never discussed his music."

Tom would sometimes go into a deep shell. Jackie recalls, "He would look so sad and you'd say, 'Are you alright, Tom? What's the matter?' and the shutter would come down. If you questioned him too much he would leave."

Tom was not having much success finding work, and he was beginning to feel the financial pinch at home. "He was worrying a lot," says Marianne. "Money was getting low, even though I was still working. I'd tell him, 'Look, we still have a roof over our head and food on the table. At least we have that.' But he couldn't accept it." He became extremely depressed. "He was resigned to being depressed. He would say, 'You don't know how it is. This runs in my family.' " Tom had also started to make a lot of cryptic comments about Pete Ham.

By the spring of 1977, Joey Molland had pretty well settled into his carpet laying job. Then one day he got a knock at his door. It was a young musician named Kenny Harck. Harck was a drummer from Chicago, Illinois, who had recently relocated to Los Angeles with a few friends. They had come out through a manager's financing, but were struggling to get a complete band together. Harck found out Joey had left Natural Gas and decided to see what he was up to. He recalls, "At that time I was the biggest Badfinger fan in the world. In high school my friends and I were the kind of guys who used to run around with Rod Stewart haircuts and flashy clothes. Bands like the Faces, Badfinger, Humble Pie were the ultimate for us. It was a big deal. That's what prompted me to show up on Joey's doorstep. He took it like any other day."

After a few get-togethers, Harck told his friend, guitarist Joe Tansin, about meeting Molland. They both went over and convinced Joey to jam. Joey was quite impressed, "I thought this guy Joe (Tansin) was really good. He was a really good

Kenny Harck, Joe Tansin

writer, and he had a peculiar, smooth style that I liked." Soon, discussions began of starting a band. The third fellow from Chicago was a lead singer with a strong blues influence. Joey and Tansin were singer-songwriters with a melodic bent. The singer decided to look elsewhere. A bass player was what the new group needed.

Tansin, Harck, and Molland recorded a four-track demo using a bass player named Ray Lester, but they hadn't wanted him in their permanent line-up. Somehow in conversation, Tom Evans name finally came up. Harck had asked Joey what he was doing and Joey didn't know. They'd lost touch. The consensus became to see if Tom might be interested.

Joey called Tom in England and found out he was totally free, but Tom was skeptical. Tom later said, "My first thought was, 'Oh no, not again.' I told Joey the best thing to do was to exchange tapes to see if we were still musically compatible." Tansin recalls, "Tom sent us a tape with vocal and piano demos of 'Lost Inside Your Love' and 'Sail Away.' We loved it and he really liked our tape."

At this time, Kenny Harck was laying a lot of the groundwork. After Joey had joined forces, Harck and Tansin's managers from Chicago were given a chance to see what interest they could generate. But the new band was quickly dissatisfied, and let go of any loyalties. Harck then contacted John Ryan, who had previously produced Rare Earth and Styx. "Ryan knew me and Joe Tansin from Chicago," says Harck. "I got him to agree to produce a demo for us. The plan was to bring Tommy out to record, and see how we all got along."

Money was pitched in to get Tom over to the States. In January of 1978 everyone met. "It started out loose," said Tansin. "We were just having fun. It really clicked. Everybody loved everybody." After a few weeks, a four-song demo package was recorded over one weekend. John Ryan had convinced a very well-respected recording studio named Sound City to give them free time. Ryan was producing with the understanding that if a record deal came of it, he'd get to produce an album. Harck: "I was going, 'We don't need to sign anything,' 'cause even though Joey and Tommy had been in the big band Badfinger, they were being offered something when they didn't have anything going on."

Ryan was impressed and got caught up in the enthusiasm. "To be honest, I was amazed by how fast everything was coming together. Tommy was the guy who really inspired me. When he sang and played there was something special. It took my attention back to the Beatles. He wasn't just a pop singer. There was an obvious depth to him."

The band was happy with the recordings. Tom went to England with the hopes a major record deal could be pulled off. Ryan gave the tapes to his attorney, Michael Rosenfeld, for label shopping.

While waiting back in England, Tom went to pick up Marianne from a dental appointment one day in London. She recalls, "We stopped at a pub. Dave Edmunds (of Rockpile) was in there. We were talking and Tom mentioned that I worked in a restaurant. Edmunds said, 'You mean your wife has to work?' Tom said, "Yeah, it's paying our mortgage.' Edmunds said, 'You mean your house isn't paid off?' Tom told him it wasn't. Edmunds said, 'Aren't you getting your ASCAP royalties for 'Without You?' Tom told him no. Edmunds couldn't believe it. He told Tom how to get his checks directly."

Tom quickly arranged to have his ASCAP writer's share income sent to him. Unwittingly, he had lost thousands of dollars, most of it from airplay of "Without You." As it turned out, ASCAP had been directed at some point to put all of the individual Badfinger income shares in an escrow account, starting back in December of 1975. Before that, Stan Polley had been taking in the band members ASCAP shares. In April of 1977, Pete Ham's trustees had gotten Pete's share freed up for his "estate."

Joey and Mike Gibbins never gave any indication they actively pursued their ASCAP songwriting income around this time. There were no outside covers of their material. Neither one were getting their songs played on the radio to any appreciable degree. Meanwhile, Apple, was continuing to house into escrow Badfinger's 50% of the "publishers" share of Badfinger's song publishing income. Apple was still waiting for a resolution between Collins, the band members, and Polley, before they would release these earnings to them.

Tom was aware the group had made certain financial agreements amongst themselves at various stages of their career. With the details never having been sorted out with lawyers involved, there were miles of potential interpretations, mostly because of the scarcity of solidly-written documents.

Mike Gibbins was now living in Wales and he claims he got a call from Tom. "Tommy said, 'I'll give you three thousand pounds, if you sign away your rights to Badfinger.' I said, 'I know you think I'm a bit stupid, but I'm not that stupid,' I slammed the phone down on him. . . ."

Tom may have realized that Mike, Joey, and Bill might some day try to lay claim to his "performance rights" songwriter income. Obviously, as one of the co-writers of "Without You," Tom was going to be getting a decent annual check from ASCAP for years to come. The 1972 Harry Nilsson version had been re-released in Britain in 1976, and again, was successful as a single. Other cover versions of the song were continuously being put out worldwide.

Tom came back to Los Angeles in April of 1978. The new band needed to start thinking about a name. Kenny Harck recalls, "I had been noticing the whole time that the name Badfinger had been opening a lot of doors. People in the business didn't seem to know much about Pete Ham and that whole situation. They just thought the band had disappeared. It was like, 'Oh yeah, that band sold a lot of records.' I told Joey and Tommy to think about calling it Badfinger. At first they didn't want to do it, but one day they came in and said it was a great idea."

The choice to use the old name created a big change in the band's chemistry. Joe Tansin recalls, "The minute it became Badfinger, Joey and Tommy became more powerful. They began making all the decisions. We were supposed to be a group. Now Kenny and I were being told about things after they'd been decided."

A financial offer came from Capitol Records. Elektra-Asylum's VP, Steve Wax, also showed interest. A less lucrative proposal was made by him, but he used an extra enticement to draw the group in. Joey explained the scenario, "We went down and played the tape and (Wax) stopped it after one-and-a-half songs and said, 'What do you want man?' This is fantastic!'. . . We walked out of there with ten grand in our pockets. In fifteen minutes, man. Ten grand in the bin. Two weeks later we got another ninety!"

Wax had used the argument that the group was less likely to get lost-in-the-shuffle at Elektra, than they might at some of the bigger labels. Some of Elektra's most prominent artists at thet time were The Eagles, Carly Simon, and Jackson Browne. As it turned out, Elektra were not sold on having John Ryan produce Badfinger, despite the fact they loved the demos. At some point, more demos were cut at Sound City, to further assess Ryan. They sounded very close to finished tracks. Nicky Hopkins had come in to play keyboards.

These recordings were not too unlike Badfinger of the Pete Ham era. Everything was upfront and thick. The arrangements weren't too far removed from the old band. But there was enough of a freshness in the sounds and textures to make this Badfinger project sound newly relevant. The songs had an irresistible quality. Joey and Tommy had matured as writers. The future looked very bright indeed.

Kenny Harck said that when the group had gotten their initial advance from Elektra, "Joey and Tommy attacked the money like a couple of sharks. Their idea seemed to be, 'Well, the money's only going to be here so long, so let's spend as much as possible. They started out renting very expensive places to live."

Up to this point, the group had gotten along pretty well and were musically solid. "In rehearsals we'd often sounded like Rockpile," says Harck. "It was very rockin.' Many times it had just *reeked* Liverpool, in the best sense."

There was still loyalty to use John Ryan as producer, but "Ryan didn't have a big reputation at the time," said Joe Tansin. "Until you have a certain amount of credibility, nine times out of ten, the record company will say 'Okay, now let's stick you with someone who has a big name and a big track record.' But if the guy who did the demos did a good job, and everyone likes it, you shouldn't mess with it. Then again, there was always a continuous discussion amongst us about producers."

Harck recalls, "I remember after Tommy had gone back to England the first time, he came back and told us he had played our demo for Paul McCartney and Chris Thomas at some recording studio they were working at in London. Tommy said McCartney liked it and seemed to hint he might be interested in producing us. Joe Tansin and I were out of our minds like, *'Oh wow, how fucking cool!'* It was beyond any dream we could fathom. But Joey and Tommy were like, 'There's no way we're going to do an album with McCartney.' They felt the association with the Beatles had been too much of a hindrance. They blew the whole thing off."

Eventually, the band acceded to the label's wish to dump Ryan. Tansin: "I think Elektra had already made up their minds. At some point we said, 'Fuck it then, we're not going to risk our necks and rock the boat. If you want to get rid of him, give him a couple thousand bucks and send him on his way."

The band had been rehearsing with super-sessionist Nicky Hopkins. He was considering joining the band. Hopkins had gotten to know Joey during the Natural Gas days and he known Tom from off-and-on encounters over the years. "It was really great with Nicky Hopkins," says Harck. "We sounded incredible."

But when John Ryan was let go, Hopkins decided not to commit to Badfinger. Hopkins explained, "I considered their handling of that a bit of a warning sign. I thought it was a slight to John." Hopkins added it was disappointing, because he thought it was a very talented band, and he was definitely ready to give it a go. Hopkins continued on in the music business, contributing to many recordings for various acts, before passing away in 1994.

George Daly was employed as an A&R man at Elektra Records at this time. He recalls, "I wasn't in on Badfinger's signing, but I worked with them on getting their record together. We had a hard time finding a producer for that."

Joe Tansin, "Kenny and I wanted Chris Thomas, but Tommy said he wasn't available. We tried working with Ron Nevison. He sent two of his boys down. But they were ordering us around, so we pulled the plug on that. We were really interested in Roy Thomas-Baker."

Thomas-Baker was exceedingly big in this industry at this time, mainly for his work with Queen, Journey, and the Cars. Molland, Tansin, and George Daly all said he was interested in producing Badfinger, but his commitments took him at least a year forward. Kenny Harck says the group actually *did* meet with Thomas-Baker at one point, and his impression was the producer felt he'd been slighted by Badfinger in the past, and he strongly reprimanded Joey and Tom for it. (Roy Thomas-Baker engineered Badfinger sessions at Trident Studios in 1973. He declined any comment on Badfinger for this book.)

Joey: "We tried to get (Bill) Szymczyk, but we couldn't get him. We tried to get (Glyn) Johns, we couldn't get him." George Daly suggested Bob Ezrin (Kiss, Alice Cooper, Babys) but the band didn't like what they'd heard. Label VP Steve Wax lobbied for Peter Asher, but Asher eventually demurred. Finally, in desperation, Daly mentioned David Malloy. He was an Elektra staff producer whose father

Badfinger rehearsals, 1979

headed the label's Nashville division. Malloy had recently had big success with Eddie Rabbitt and Stella Parton, artists in the country music field. He was willing to produce something from the pop market."

After a huge plug from Daly, and the fact that panic was setting in, David Malloy got the job. Daly recalls, "I really wanted Malloy to get a chance. He's a very sensitive, astute producer, a good song man. We hoped to get that 'old sound,' that cliché." Tansin recalls, "Joey and Tommy seriously wanted to play ball with people and not rock the boat. The company was pumping us in a big way. So we finally just went with their pick, Malloy."

The band went into rehearsals, but by now the band's chemistry had severely deteriorated. Harck recalls, "Joey was smoking pot every twenty minutes. He'd drift off into, 'Let's go smoke another joint and tell more stories.' Joey and Tom were acting like hippies stuck in the Woodstock era. Joe Tansin was writing material as good as they were, but he wasn't being encouraged."

Joe Tansin, "When Malloy came in, his entire focus was Joey and Tommy. There was a lot of ass-kissing. It made me feel small. I thought I deserved a lot more consideration. Kenny and I had knocked on Joey's door. It was our connections that got them off the ground. It was favoritism and it pissed me off.

"I could talk to Tommy. Even if we disagreed, if I came across as honest he would respect it. But I didn't have that kind of rapport with Joey. Partly because of Kathie. I didn't want to go up against *that* force."

Harck says he tried to steer clear of Joey's wife, "The first time I met Kathie we were rehearsing and she was sitting there on an amp making suggestions. She stopped us from playing songs. She wanted to sing and play tambourine in the band. Then she started talking about what we should do, and how we should do it.

Joey and Kathie, 1978

Tom Evans, Joey Molland, Jeff Wald's office, Los Angeles, 1978

I thought, 'What the hell is going on here!?' Eventually it got that whenever there was some meeting, and she happened to be around, she would do all of Joey's talking for him."

The group wanted big-time management and were led to Jeff Wald. He was helping with the careers of Sylvester Stallone, Flip Wilson, and the band, Chicago. Harck recalls, "Wald had been in the tabloids about chasing his wife, Helen Reddy, with a shotgun. Joey and Tommy saw that and said, 'Yep, this is the guy we want.' They were turned on by his power.

"We met him and this guy was the ultimate cliché. He was sitting there with a cigar in his mouth that was bigger than he was. He had the governor of California coming in and out of his office. His favorite thing to say was, 'We'll go into the record company, we'll step on their throats a little, and we'll get more money.' That lit Joey and Tommy up like a Christmas tree."

Tom Evans never publicly commented on Wald, but Harck adds, "Tom seemed intimidated by business types." Marianne agreed, "Tom lacked confidence with business people. Joey could put on a good appearance and he knew all the bullshit to say." Joe Tansin: "It was more that Tom didn't *trust* managers. He just kept a watchful eye."

The group planned to start recording their album early in 1979. They were given a budget that was considered middling for the time. The President of Elektra Records was Joe Smith, who had been head of Warner Brothers Records when Pete Ham was with the band. He commented on their Elektra signing, "To me it was not a serious signing. I was concentrating on black music and country music. Steve Wax had been given latitude to go and sign a few acts. There was not a lot of money involved. If there had been, it would have gotten my attention."

A recording studio was needed. Harck recalls, "We wound up at this rundown house in the San Fernando Valley. It was full of out-of-date equipment. It was basically a demo studio that the record company used to demo new artists. Half the stuff was falling apart." But producer David Malloy didn't think the room was a big factor, "I thought the room sounded fine. The place had a stumbly track record; there had been a few hits recorded there. It was workable within the budget."

The sessions were typical of that era. Harck: "There was a big drug scene going on. I remember every break there would be twenty lines of coke on a mirror which would get snorted. Then someone might go and tune a guitar. Then they'd come back and do more coke. We wouldn't get started until 8:00 at night. At one point I got so sick of the whole thing I just blew the coke off the mirror and put down twenty lines of Coffeemate. These guys were so blitzed they didn't even know the difference."

Things got off to a slow start. Harck: "I was getting pretty hung up on getting a good drum sound. My thought was, 'Well, now that these guys have raped and

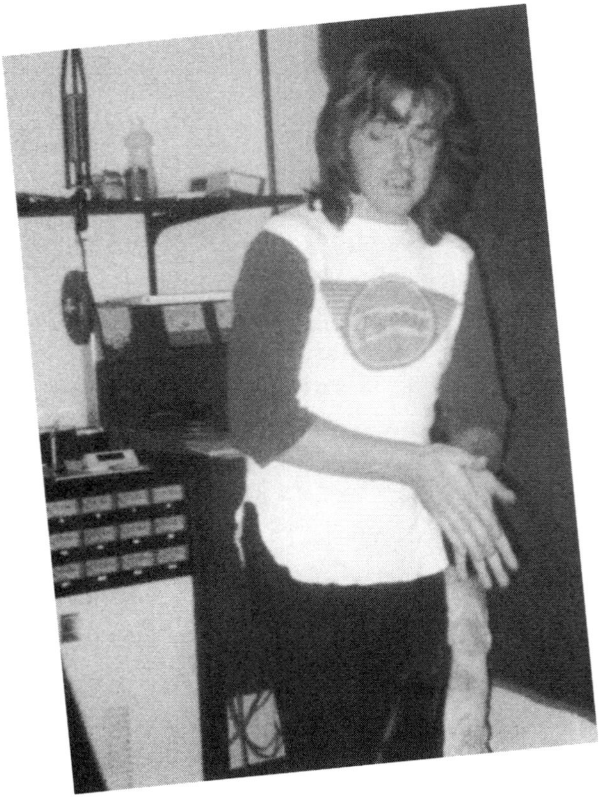

Joey Molland, David Malloy

taken away everything that was good about this band, at least I want to have a good sounding record. I was telling the producer and engineer how to do their job. I imagine there was a lot of complaining about me.' "

One day Harck was sitting out by the studio's backyard pool, "I said to Joe Tansin, 'Look, I can't take this anymore. How can you work with people when you know the truth and every step of the way you're being beaten down by people so high they don't know what's going on.' We discussed that after the album was done we would quit. The next day Joey and Tommy came up to me and said I was fired. I took it quite hard because of all the work I'd put into getting the whole thing together."

Joe Tansin, "Kenny had been making a major, major, deal about the sound of the drums. He was inexperienced in making records, as I was at the time. He went on and on; everyone was getting sick of it. At some point he pushed everyone too far. In the end, a drum sound is not going to make or break a record.

"I was caught in the middle. I agreed with them that he had gotten out of hand, but I resented having my friend tossed out. They had forewarned me and I had said, 'Look, talk to him and see if he'll change.' But they said, 'He's not going to change. He's a pain in the ass, and we're going to get rid of him."

A drummer was now needed. But Joey, Tommy, and Joe Tansin, didn't know many musicians in L.A. Somehow, Mike Gibbins name came up. He was an original member. Joey and Tommy knew his style. It would help solidify calling themselves Badfinger. A call was made to Wales.

After Pete Ham's death in 1975, Mike had jumped into the South Wales rock'n'roll scene. Mike had always been well respected by the musicians there and had no trouble finding people to play with. In 1976, Martin Ace, a former member of the Man band, had asked Mike to play with his group, The Flying Aces. They toured across the U.K. on various occasions, using a double-decker bus to get around. "It was just a hippie band," said Mike, "good fun."

In 1977, Mike had been asked to play with Bonnie Tyler, an up-and-coming gravel-voiced singer from Llanelli, South Wales. Mike ended up recording the drums for her RCA Records album, *It's A Heartache*. The title song became a worldwide smash. Mike did tours across Europe and the U.K. with Tyler, but eventually the situation deteriorated. Almost all of her backing musicians, including Mike, walked after a pay dispute.

In mid-1978, another RCA Records artist named Digby Richards had Mike do the drumming for his album *Whiskey Sundown*. Mike completed other sessions as well. Then the phone call came from L.A. late in the year. Mike was convinced to fly over, despite his anger with Tom months earlier for requesting Mike's Badfinger rights be sold to him. Mike's airline ticket was paid for; he was walking into a record deal; it was a hard offer to turn down.

Because of the delay in getting the new album rolling, Mike was thrown directly into the recording fray, practically off the plane! He recalls, "(Malloy) said my playing sounded too much like 'Day After Day.' I said, 'Well man, that's the band I used to play with.' He said, 'Well, we're trying to do something different.' I said, 'Fuck you.' I made a major enemy with the guy. He told me I couldn't keep time. I said, 'It takes a band to keep time.' He turned the click track on me. I said, 'Turn that fucking thing off. It's getting on my nerves!' But he kept saying, 'You're not keeping time.' I said, 'Look, I just got done doing a platinum album and they didn't give me any hassle. He said, 'Bonnie Tyler, right?' I said, 'Yeah, that's right.' He said, 'She used to be a cabaret singer, didn't she?' That pissed me off!"

It was quickly decided that Mike wasn't going to work out and he was let go. "He was only there for one or two sessions," said Tansin, "I agreed that he wasn't getting it together." Malloy claims to have a very hazy memory of the circumstances, but comments, "If I blew off a drummer it was because I sat down and talked within the group and they were in agreement; because I'm not that type of producer. My big beef with a drummer is tempo. That's the drummer's big gig in life. If he can't do that, what's it for?"

Mike was given some money and sent back home. He groans, "I lost all my sessions in Wales. I couldn't get them back. Joey and Tommy were licking (Malloy's) ass. They had their record deal. They were intimidated. They didn't want to get Malloy upset. It was devastating for me."

Mike Gibbins, 1978

During the spring of 1978, Stan Polley had nearly died. He'd gone in for heart bypass surgery in April. Kathie Molland's sister worked at the hospital he was in and she came by his room, dropping off a card. Al Kooper, Polley's last remaining music client from the time, recalls, "Polley told me Joey Molland sent him a card that said, 'I hope you die!' He said Molland was constantly dogging him." (Kathie Molland has stated the card's message was more along the lines of innuendo).

By year's end, Polley's health had recovered. It was now been nearly four years since the WB Music lawsuit against Badfinger had first been filed. On December 6, 1978, WB Music attorney Vincent Chieffo laid out Warner Brothers final summary in court. His basic argument was that WB Music had the right to terminate the publishing agreement *"due to BEI's repudiation and breach of the escrow provisions."* He went over Badfinger Enterprises' (BEI) actions, step by step, and defended against amounts sought by BEI through a counterclaim.

Polley's lawyer, Michael Clemens, gave his summary the following day. He stated that Badfinger had fulfilled their obligations, and that BEI continually followed the accorded guidelines set forth in the contract language. But interestingly, in looking at the original WB Records contract, the clauses involving the holding of the $100,000 advance had been physically altered on the day the contract was signed. Instead of stating *"the attorney for Badfinger"* could hold the funds in escrow, or store them in a financial institution, it was rewritten in that *"Badfinger"* could hold the money, *"Badfinger"* could deposit it accordingly, and *"Badfinger"* could place it as a certificate of deposit held in escrow by *"the attorney for Badfinger"*?!

Stan Polley had presumably proposed changing this language so that, as a representative of *"Badfinger,"* he could more conceivably confuse the issue and handle the money himself. Walter Hofer was the *"attorney"* WB Music president Ed Silvers expected to take care of such matters, yet Polley was allegedly an *"attorney,"* too. Still, regardless of the possible semantic interpretations, the escrow aspects were fundamentally unchanged, and Polley's arguments appeared weak.

These written-in changes had been initialed, and they show they occurred in the presence of Stan Polley, Ed Silvers, and the four members of Badfinger. There is no indication of any legal representative of WB Music being there.

During these court proceedings, Polley claimed that his later shifting of money from bank to bank was only to obtain higher interest, which Warner Brothers didn't buy. They sensed an embezzlement scheme had been under way, but didn't pursue attacking that angle heavily. Polley's lawyer contended that Warner's *real* reason for the lawsuit was they were dissatisfied with the product the band was presenting to them, and they found the members irresponsible to deal with. Ed Silvers denied that sentiment.

represents and warrants that Badfinger will record and release an average of one (1) LP album during each six (6) month period, commencing November 1, 1973, and that, in any event, at least one (1) LP album will be released in each or any period of eight (8) months.

8. Warner agrees that it will pay to Badfinger the following sums at the times and in the manner set forth below.

(a) $100,000 upon execution of this Agreement, to be paid to ~~the attorney~~ for Badfinger and to be held by ~~him~~ in escrow. ~~Said attorney~~ may place said $100,000 in any federally insured savings and loan association or banking institution. The terms upon which said attorney may release said money are set forth below in sub-paragraph (d).

(b) $83,333.33 upon delivery by Badfinger of the materials set forth in paragraph 5 above relating to the Compositions contained in each of the first five (5) LP albums.

(c) $83,333.34 upon delivery by Badfinger of the materials set forth in paragraph 5 above relating to the Compositions contained in the sixth (6th) LP album.

(d) At the time each payment set forth in sub-paragraphs (b) and (c) above becomes due, one-sixth (1/6) of the $100,000 set forth in sub-paragraph (a) above shall be paid by the attorney for Badfinger to Badfinger and not subject to return to Warner. However, in the event of default by Badfinger during the term of this Agreement, in addition to other legal remedies available to Warner, the attorney for Badfinger shall repay to Warner that remaining portion of the $100,000, including interest thereon. At such time as Badfinger

Portion of Badfinger publishing contract with Warner Brothers Music

On December 8, 1978, Judge Julius Title declared the case settled in chambers. It was agreed that BEI turn over the copyrights for all the songs on the *Wish You Were Here* album to WB Music, and that BEI would pay WB Music back the sum of $42,000 within one week's time. The ownership of the unreleased third album was not addressed. But somehow, Polley had managed to retain approximately *three* album's worth of the original $100,000 publishing advance.

WB Music attorney Vincent Chieffo commented in 1994, "When an artist or band gives their money over to a 'manager,' there is no law that applies. No special law. The manager can put the money into their own account, co-mingle it, do whatever they want with it. While in the case of a lawyer, if he has a client's money, he *has* to have a separate account.

"Some of these rock'n'roll managers are well-meaning, but may get sucked up into economic problems, and the money ends up paying for their personal debts. Others are simply bad people who take money they shouldn't. When Pete Ham killed himself it pretty much validated to Warner Brothers there was an extreme amount of trouble in their situation. . . ."

Ed Silvers recalls being at the final court hearing, "As I left the court room Polley came up to me and started smiling and laying his salesmanship on me. It was all I could do to keep from punching him in the nose."

It was now almost five weeks into the "new" Badfinger recordings, and the group still didn't have all of their basic tracks done. "Malloy finally brought in Andy Newmark," says Tansin. "Now it was down to session men." Andy Newmark was known for having worked with George Harrison and other Warner Brothers artists of the time. Producer David Malloy's background was mainly in the country music field, where sessionmen are commonplace. His recording philosophy came across with these comments. "Joey and Tommy were not studio-quality musicians. It wasn't like session guys who can give you that same great performance every time. We needed a drummer to be on time so their tracks could come together quickly."

As the album started to take shape, it was apparent this was going to be a markedly different sound than the original demo tapes. Songs were being changed in every possible way. The demo of "Sail Away" had opened with a explosion of twin electric guitars and carried along briskly. The new version was featherlight and arid. "The Winner," by Joe Tansin, was totally changed from its original pulsating charge to a pseudo-anthem, which now included airy background vocals, tinny strings, squeaky-clean guitars, and questionable synthesizer fills.

Perhaps the biggest alterations were done to Joey's tunes, "Love Is Gonna Come At Last" and "The Dreamer." The latter was once a stirring power ballad, now sterilized, with strings upfront. "Love Is Gonna Come at Last" originally sounded like a glistening, upbeat, Pete Ham, pop song. The Malloy-produced track comes across as tepid and slowed to its detriment.

Thankfully, Tom's "Lost Inside Your Love" did survive the Malloy transition quite well. Though it would still have to be described as middle-of-the-road-sounding, some positive subtle changes were made.

"Look Out California" was another Tom tune which held up. Tom described its origin, "I wrote it when I knew I was coming over (to America). It was cold and raining in England. California seemed like such a good idea at the time, so much to look forward to." A bristling rocker with an effective chorus hook, the production is decent enough, though the gritty chemistry of Joey and Tommy singing together was not well capitalized on.

There had been many examples of Joey and Tommy magically merging their voices on the earlier Badfinger albums. For this project, the vocals are too often uncomfortable sounding. Sometimes, it's in the way they are blended, their sonic treatments, or the performances themselves, which occasionally are weak. On "Come Down Hard" Joey's strained singing clearly hurts the song. "There was a lot of struggle getting Joey's vocals down," said the recording engineer, Peter Granet. "He was losing his voice a lot."

Another track was "Sympathy," written by Joe Tansin. "It was originally a Motown-styled song," said Kenny Harck. "The Rolling Stones 'Miss You' was big and Malloy decided he wanted to make it a dance thing. Joey's thinking was, 'Yeah, disco is big now, if we can have a hit doing it like that, I'm all for it.' Joe Tansin and I were absolutely sick about it. We'd wanted to recapture the old British rock sound, not the fucking Bee Gees or Donna Summer!"

David Malloy commented, "The thing was, we were making that album at the absolute height of disco. We were making a Badfinger record and the record company promotion people were going, 'Huh?' It was because of the pressure I felt from the record company, and the band not having itself together, that we went for that. Granted, the kick drum *is* ridiculous. For Tommy, disco was the last thing he wanted to know about. But both Tommy and Joey were a little reserved in their opinions around me. They didn't challenge me a lot."

Elektra A&R man George Daly: "The two original Badfinger guys seemed world-weary to me. They were incredibly talented; "naturals." When they would come into my office to play acoustic guitars and sing; they were amazing. But they always seemed to want to 'do the right thing,' instead of just being themselves."

Tom had written into the lyrics of "Look Out California," *"We're tryin' our hardest, just to follow the plan."* But Joe Tansin thinks a lot of paranoia could have been overcome, simply by having the right producer in charge. "David

Tom Evans

Malloy was a mismatch, period. He was a country producer. There was no connection to us at all. The original concept was to sound like the band used to. That's what we did with the demos and everybody loved them. It hadn't needed to change a lot."

The final LP was nine songs. As it turned out, the overall results were such a letdown from the earlier demos, it's somewhat surprising Elektra didn't consider recutting, or at least a new mix here and there. In hindsight, A&R man George Daly admitted, "It sounded flat." Steve Wax would not comment, but label president Joe Smith said, "There were a couple of good-sounding songs, but our pairing of Malloy with Badfinger obviously didn't click."

Throughout these recordings, Joe Tansin had been sulking. He did what he was asked, and mostly listened. He says he had been contemplating leaving throughout the proceedings. "When Kenny had gotten fired he hadn't taken it very well. He was really working on me, seeing if I could get him back in. I felt sorry for him. He was crying. He said, 'Look, why don't you quit and we'll start a new band.' So I thought, 'Okay, we came out here together, we'll do something else together, I don't need this anymore.

"I was at the final session for the album and Joey, Tommy, and I went to a Chinese restaurant next to Capitol Records. Joey and Tommy were drunk out of their minds. They knew I was thinking about leaving and they were getting emotional about it. Tommy put his arm around me and started crying, saying, 'I really want you to be a part of this and Joey does, too.' This really confused me

Tom Evans, Joe Tansin

because I didn't know if they were putting me on or being serious. They said they were going to go back to the studio.

"They finally left and I sat in the restaurant for awhile. I remember walking out to my car thinking, 'I'm either going to go straight and walk into the studio, or I'm going to get in my car and go home.' I got in the car, started it up, and drove away. Looking back, I wished I'd stuck it out. It wasn't a great career move.

Joey and Tommy now needed a band in order to do a support tour for the album. During the final stages of recording, former Escorts, Stealers Wheel, and Apple house drummer, Peter Clarke, commonly known as "Clarkie," had shown up. He recalls, "I had called Joey's house and Kathie told me they were going to need a drummer for the band. She said you may as well ask. It was a funny situation because I had been blown off three times in the past. Mike Gibbins had quit twice in the old band, and both times they'd asked me to join, and he came back. Then Joey told me he'd do something with me after he quit in 1974, but he got that gig with Jerry Shirley.

"I went over to the recording studio and they were doing that "Airwaves" track. Joey was out there in the studio with this huge old mic. He was doing the acoustic guitar. I came out there in the dark and when Joey started playing, I walked around him playing this "legs, hand, and feet" pattern to keep him constant. Someone came over the intercom and said, 'What was that?' I said, 'It's 'legs, hands, and feet.' He said, 'Whatever it is, keep on doing it.' We came back in to listen to the playback and it was me, Joey, and Tom standing side by side. The song was fading out and they just looked at me and said, 'Well, you want to join then?' I said, *'Well, it took you fucking long enough!'* We were hysterical."

Joey and Tom also wanted to add a keyboardist to their line-up. Tony Kaye was being considered. Tony was classically trained. He had gained most of his prominence from the band Yes. He'd also been a key member of Detective and Badger. Kaye had just gotten off the road as part of David Bowie's backing band when he was invited to listen to the new Badfinger album. He was impressed and subsequently jammed a few times. Clarkie recalls, "Joey and Tommy had said at first, 'Well, he doesn't play rock'n'roll piano.' I said, 'We can make him.' "

Tony Kaye signed on for the scheduled tour. The group considered a second onstage guitarist. Former Apple labelmate Jackie Lomax auditioned first. He'd had a few solo albums out, and was looking for something new. He recalls, "I had known Joey casually from the old Liverpool days, and I had crossed paths with Badfinger in Apple's basement. Joey and Tommy rehearsed me, but I don't think my style was what they were looking for."

Pete "Clarkie" Clarke

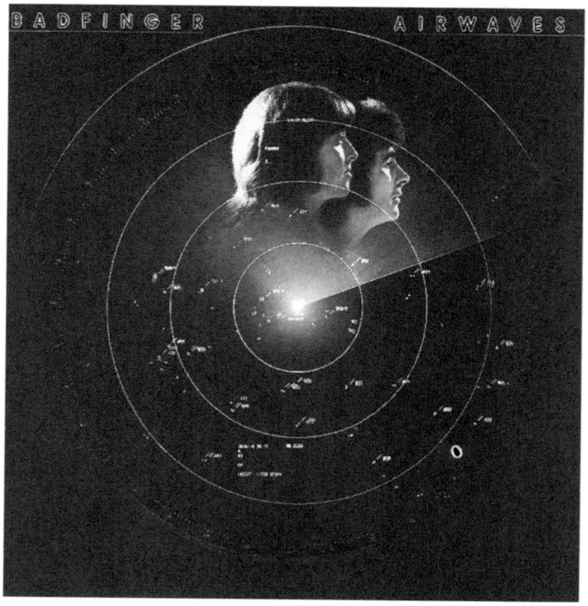

Airwaves *LP cover*

Joey and Tom

The group eventually hired a guitarist named Bob Shell, but they were undecided if it was cluttering up what they really wanted to do: bare-bones, kick-ass, rock'n'roll.

Late in March of 1979, Elektra issued the new Badfinger album. It had a conceptual album cover inspired by the title song, "Airwaves." It featured profiles of Joey and Tom against a giant green radar screen. The back was a green-tinted satellite dish. On the inner sleeve, Joey and Tom wear matching casual jackets. Lyrics were included. Promotional lip-sync videos were also shot. The label pushed Joey's "Love Is Gonna Come At Last" b/w "Sail Away" as the first single in America. In England and Europe they released "Lost Inside Your Love."

When the album came out, there was an eager reception from many old fans and radio programmers. The classic British pop sound was always a well-liked style, even though few could pull it off. Badfinger's mystique had grown since Pete Ham had died. Badfinger's out-of-print albums and singles had become big collector's items.

But once everyone heard the new Badfinger record, the initial hype quickly wore down. This wasn't a true pop-rock explosion. It was mostly "California cool," "sleek and carpeted rock." Despite a few over-the-top reviews from publications like *People*, there was not a lot of overall enthusiasm:

> ROLLING STONE *Badfinger, when faced with the dilemma of pop versus pap, opts for an uneasy commercial compromise that renders even a forceful rocker like 'Sympathy' impotent with a flaccid disco beat. Similarly, such dramatic ballads as 'The Dreamer' and 'Sail Away' are hurt by David Campbell's wimpy string arrangements and the dryly unimaginative production of David Malloy. . . . with no apparent feel for Anglo-American pop.*

> TROUSER PRESS *Guitarist Joey Molland and bassist Tom Evans have made the insidiously pleasant pop album one might have predicted a Pete Ham-less Badfinger would make: high on melody, direct in lyric, but somewhat diffuse in focus. . . good as some of it is, Airwaves doesn't quite hold together as an LP. . .*

> BEATLEFAN *Most of the album consists of nice, pleasant, and sometimes even catchy pop/rock tunes, but there is nothing really striking or memorable about any of it . . . much of the production has a sameness about it which tends to make the songs less distinctive than they should be. . . .*

> NEW MUSICAL EXPRESS *Badfinger have lost their late beat era charm of their old hits and what remains is a rather vapid tunefulness. . . .*

> CREEM *Not that Airwaves is that bad, it just isn't the Badfinger that I came to know and love somewhere a long time ago.*

Despite the backlash, producer David Malloy cherished his experience with Badfinger. "I got a lot out of working with them. Tommy was like one of those Van Gogh type artists, the kind of guy people are quick to misunderstand. He was a true original. I thought some of the criticism for the album was a bit harsh. There were some nice cuts. "Lost Inside Your Love" is a beautiful song. I was proud of that. "Sail Away" was real pretty. But overall, the record was against the flow of the times."

Tom and Joey were initially optimistic about *Airwaves*. But they found themselves having to answer to a lot of disappointment from interviewers. When asked why the album sounded more like California pop, Joey said, "We didn't try to get away from what we sounded like before. We just played the way we play now . . . It's more contemporary, maybe, but the same idea."

Joey has remained supportive of *Airwaves* over the years, and in 1987, when made to address the production again, he said, "I thought David (Malloy) made a great record for us, although he's a country producer. That's why the record's soft and kind of lush-sounding. He got a beautiful sound . . . but it really didn't sound like Badfinger."

Badfinger began their 1979 American tour as a four-piece band. They had done a preliminary performance on the TV show *In Concert,* with their second guitarist, but he was dropped before the first gig. The group decided to focus on rock'n'roll, but they also incorporated a good mix of their older hits and ballads. The set included five tunes from the new album, as well as occasional standards, like "Johnny B. Goode." Tony Kaye proved to be a brilliant live musician. The band performed at a furious pace and he kept up solidly on the piano. Pete Clarke recalls, "Tony would tell you that one of the things written in his touring contract was for two buckets of ice to be offstage, every night. One bucket for each hand. His hands were like balloons afterwards, just throbbing."

Now that Joey had the sole guitar responsibility onstage, he more than rose to the occasion. The looser he played, the more exciting it could be. And Tom sang more consistently in control than he had in a while. The chemistry was exuberant. Tough-to-pull-off numbers like "Without You" and "Baby Blue" came off decently. Yet songs like "Andy Norris," "Get Away," and "Rock Of All Ages" were the heart of a true rock'n'roll explosion.

The band was pleasantly surprised to be playing to many sold-out clubs. Clarkie remembers, "When the tour first opened we were stiff, but it really picked up. When we got to the end, we came to L.A. and you could tell every reviewer came around with a large kitchen knife behind their back ready to carve the band into little pieces. As it turned out there were nine reviews, two were okay, and seven were over the moon!"

*Tony Kaye,
Tom Evans,
Pete Clarke,
Joey Molland,
1979*

The two-set, two-night, sold-out shows at L.A.'s Roxy Theater, were a great culmination for Badfinger. The *L.A. Times* said the band was *"revitalized."* The *Herald Examiner* mentioned they had made *"a miraculous recovery the instant they left the recording studio. . . ."*

Despite the tour success, the album only peaked at #125 in *Billboard*, staying in the charts for just eight weeks. The single stalled at #69. Elektra was disappointed and their decision to have the band record a second album was put on hold.

Tony Kaye recalls, "The tour had gone great. We had done *American Bandstand* and *In Concert*. We were getting along well. But we didn't have proper management."

Joey had said in a *Rolling Stone* article, "This time out we have the business aspect under control. We have no management contract. The only contract we have is to Badfinger." But no one influential was lobbying on their behalf.

A second block of live dates were done in July and August, mostly in the south and western United States. And though the shows were fairly well-received, the impact on record sales was still not apparent. A second American single of Tommy's "Lost Inside Your Love" b/w "Come Down Hard" failed to make much of a chart impression.

Because of their early success with 60s-influenced pop rock, Badfinger was still perceived as a group cutting against the rock'n'roll mainstream. Now they were stuck with a new album that *sounded* like typical late 70s fodder. Bands like The Cars and The Knack had shown that, if you had a well-produced pop-rock song powerful and undeniable enough, you could rule the airwaves, even through an endless sea of disco and middle-of-the-road balladry. But Badfinger, once considered the "heir apparents" to the Beatles throne, had not delivered a new product of any real consequence. Would they get another chance?

Badfinger started to cut demos while waiting to see if their second album option was going to be picked up. But a problem had evolved. Pete Clarke recalls, "Months before I'd joined, I had severely broken my right wrist. And in rehabilitating through playing the drums, I had overcompensated for the weakness in the arm so that my right foot was a little out of coordination. We listened to some studio playbacks and it was weird. It didn't work. Joey and Tommy told me they'd have me do the live gigs, but they might need to hire a studio drummer. I told them I'd quit instead. I figured it was time to stop. They thought I was being nonchalant, but I stayed up day and night for a week wrestling over it."

Clarkie's loss was a blow. The group had wanted to do a quick, minimal overdub, rock'n'roll album while their inspiration was still up. But as they waited, finances were starting to run dry. Marianne recalls, "A lot of cocaine was still going around and Tommy was going out to clubs a lot. The money was going fast."

Badfinger, Roxy Theater, Los Angeles, July, 1979

In September of 1979, Elektra dropped Badfinger. The label had laid off many of the people who'd supported the band. Typical of when this happens, and the act is not entirely successful, they will be let go. Badfinger would have to shop for a new deal. Joey had a friend who knew someone at K-Tel Records, a label known for its reissuing of old hits, often re-recorded versions which allowed for easier rights clearance. Joey recalled, "They had previously been in touch with us, they wanted us to re-record 'Come And Get It.' So we phoned up and said we'd do it for them now. . . They gave us $5,000."

The band used some of the money to record three new demos. They hired drummer Ian Wallace, who'd played with Bob Dylan, and laid down "Three Time Loser," "Because I Love You," and "Rock'n'Roll Contract" (a Tom Evans number previously recorded for the *Head First* album). Tapes were given out.

It was a tough sell. In the first place, comebacks were considered major longshots in the record industry and Badfinger had been given their chance. Joey recalls, "We'd spent all our money. We were broke again. Now when I say broke, I'm talking broke. Rock'n'roll bands don't have savings accounts."

Luckily for Tom and his family, they had sublet their home in England with the option of moving back at any time. Marianne and Stephen returned in the summer of 1979. Tom stayed with Tony Kaye in Los Angeles a while longer, but when the band didn't get much positive feedback regarding the demos, he returned to England that fall, worn-out and rapidly discouraged.

In the late autumn of 1979, a gentleman named Rod Roach entered the White Hart pub in New Haw, Surrey. Rod was a veteran musician, a former guitar player for The Nashville Teens, Saturnalia, and Horse. He'd been coming into the pub for months now. Recently the patrons had told him about a Tom Evans, who had just come back from America. On this particular day, Rod noticed a drunk fellow making a commotion. "There was no way to avoid him," recalls Roach, "He was in the middle of the pub carrying on. I didn't know who he was." No one told Rod that night, but the next day he saw the same fellow crouched at the bar. "He was totally different, quiet and reserved. I started a conversation and found out it was this Tom Evans everyone had been talking about. He came over to jam that night."

It wasn't long before a close friendship developed.The two began to write songs together. "We started recording at Tommy's place," says Rod, "Then I suggested the idea of writing music for commercials and jingles. I set up a four-track recording studio at my home."

Rod and Tom worked on ideas for products such as toothpaste, orange juice, and wine. Rod: "We would sing to each other while drinking in the pub and then we would rush back home to put them down on tape. Then we'd rush back to the pub before closing time for a few drunken rounds of 'Imagine' on the piano, and a quick game of 'let's windup the locals.'"

Tom couldn't resist opportunities for tomfoolery. Rod recalls, "Once I was standing in a pub with Tom and this big, tall fellow was standing nearby with a corduroy jacket. His pocket was partially torn off. I saw Tommy looking at it and I said, 'I know what you're going to do.' No sooner did I say it than Tom ripped the pocket completely off and this chap went berserk. His wife and I were trying to hold him back. The chap whacked his wife clear across the bar, pushed me down, and chased Tom into a driving rainstorm. We looked outside and Tom was rolling around in the mud laughing hysterically. All this fellow could do was stare."

But Tom didn't have to be in a pub to pull one of his many surprises. Rod recalls, "One day, during the height of the punk scene in England, my wife, Tom, and I were walking down the road, when six punks with spiked hair, safety pins, and leather clothing came by, shouting and pushing people out of the way. Tom went up to them – he had a very loud voice – and *screamed* at the top of his lungs! They were all so scared they just pissed off down the road!"

Dick Barton was one of Tom's nearby neighbors. He had been helping Tom get work and was somewhat of a drinking buddy, "The two of them would drink too much," says Marianne. "One time Dick's wife came over to our house crying, because she had been in a fight with him. Tom put his arm around her to console her and Dick came in at that very moment. He said, 'You're having an affair with my wife!' He started chasing Tom with a hatchet!"

Tom escaped by hiding in the local pub's cellar.

By October of 1979, the Apple publishing and sales royalties being held for Badfinger had grown to almost £85,500. During this month, Stan Polley had his lawyer present a "statement of claim" in a London courthouse. Carefully laid out was Polley's representation of the group's contracts. Among the items addressed was Polley's 30% gross commission, and Polley's assertion that all Badfinger earnings were to be funneled through BEI. Also portrayed were the releases signed by Joey, Tom, Mike, and Bill.

In 1975, Joey had signed over to Polley most of his Badfinger income (everything accrued prior to November 18th, 1975) and severed his ties with BEI, for no apparent compensation. But Tom and Mike had not been paid their promised compensation, so Polley's representation of any validity toward their releases was risky. Polley had also been portraying the Ham trustees had signed their release, too, but he now had to acknowledge, they had *not* done so.

On January 4, 1980, a statement of claim was presented by a London lawyer representing Bill Collins. A evaluative listing of the group's contracts was made from the perspective of Collins; the main argument being that Polley's 30% gross commission was *"unconscionable and unenforceable."* Bill's lawyer also represented, from the group's 1972 stockholder's meeting, it had been decided that: *"In respect of any song which was not performed by the group but performed by outside artists . . . 60% of the royalties should go to him (the writer) and 10% to the other four."*

It was a brief statement, in vague language, and it only partially described what the original meeting's minutes had actually indicated. What was interesting was it confirmed that there had never been any "written" contractual agreement between the band and Bill regarding songwriting. Otherwise, Collins would have put one forth. Bill kept a complete account of financial records and important business matters for virtually every day he was involved with the band, in diaries.

Collins was aware "Without You" had earned massive "writers share" royalties over the years, due to its successful cover versions, and would continue to do so in the future. With Tom back in England, Bill was alleged to be pursuing the "Apple money" (as this income, and the other Badfinger holdings were being called). But Bill claims he never personally hassled Tom about his ASCAP rights, that he only fought to contend against Polley. This dispute was only beginning to get truly complicated at this time. Joey, Mike, Pete's estate, and Stan Polley all had a strong interest in how this money was going to be divided.

During the Christmas season of 1978, Tom's mother, May, visited Tom and his family at their home in Surrey. Tom would always have a gathering during the holidays, and he and Marianne would invite many of their friends. May recalls, "We would all be having a great time except Tommy. I would say, 'Why are you so quiet? You're friends want to know why you're not enjoying yourself.' And Tommy would say, 'Mum, Pete is here. He's all around me. I know he's here with me.' Tommy never did get over Pete Ham's death. Never. . . ."

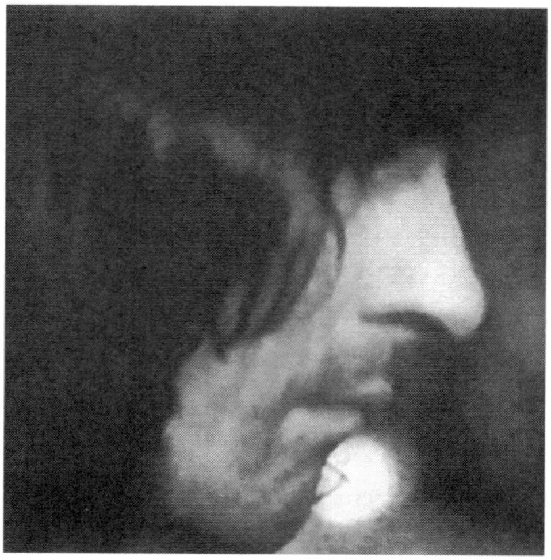

Tom Evans

11

Over You

Early in 1980, there still had been no bites on the new Badfinger demos. Joey was struggling financially, so he went back into the carpet-laying business, but that didn't last long. "I couldn't do it," he said, "Peter Clarke was doing his carpentry now . . . he's coming to my house in an English sports cars, having a good time with a little chicky, and a grand in the pocket . . . He said, 'Do you want to work for me?' I said, 'Right on!'. . . ."

Joey worked with Clarke throughout the first half of 1980. He and Tommy talked occasionally, but the prospects of a new record deal were fading. Luckily, a booking agent who was hoping to get into the management field had gotten one of their demo tapes. He became determined to do something. His name was Scott Hurowitz. "I was working for the Jim Halsey company; at the time the largest country music booking agency in the world. They had opened up a division called Thunderbird Artists, which was just beginning to touch on rock'n'roll. I came across Badfinger through this agency and found out they weren't doing anything. I wanted to try managing, so I called and told them I'd try shopping their tapes. We had a handshake deal."

Hurowitz had a lead on a dawning record label called Radio Records. "They were affiliated with Atlantic Records," he says. "The owners were Rob Walker and Dick Kline. They were located down in Fort Lauderdale, Florida. I sent a tape down and explained the situation. They immediately made an offer. It was a big thing for them to sign Badfinger."

Joey recalled, "Out of the blue, somebody calls and says, 'Hey, I'll give you fifteen thousand dollars.' He says, 'I'll fly you out to Miami, pay all your expenses, you'll make a record.' I said, 'It sounds good to me . . .' " But Tom Evans was reluctant. "Tom and Joey had some catastrophic phone calls," said Rod Roach. "Tom was wary of working with Joey again. He really felt Badfinger was over and this was the wrong thing to do. If there had been something more worthwhile happening he would not have agreed to it."

Badfinger became Radio Records' first signing. Tom had insisted to Joey that Rod Roach be included in on the deal, to which Joey was initially reluctant. Tom also wanted Tony Kaye involved. Kaye had been busy pursuing work as a manager, but he was still itching to play. "I didn't know anything about Radio Records," said Kaye, "but there was a lot of enthusiasm from them. It was a chance to go and make a record." Kaye found the band a drummer, Richard Bryans, purely through the recommendation of a friend.

The new Badfinger met in Key Biscayne, Florida, in October of 1980. Things got off to a bad start. The group was rehearsing and Rod Roach realized Joey was ignoring him. Rod felt unwanted and uninspired. "I had come over because Tommy wanted me to. After a week or so I told Tom I wanted to leave. Tommy got really pissed at Joey and lost it one night. He was smashing glass everywhere. He threw Scott Hurowitz in the pool. He was taking a lot of his frustration out on Scott, instead of Joey, because Joey wasn't staying where we were."

Joey had come to Florida and insisted on a separate setting for Kathie (who was pregnant) and their first child, Joseph. They were put into a different hotel in Miami Beach. "That was something I had to ask for from the record company," says Hurowitz, "and they didn't like it. But the really bad aspect of it was the isolation from the band. Kathie was off doing her personal management on Joey, and it caused continual resentment amongst the guys."

After Rod Roach returned to England, Tom insisted another guitar player be brought in. Tony Kaye called up Glenn Sherba, an L.A. native. "He had a reputation as a crazy heavy-metal player," says Kaye. "I thought he was really good."

Meanwhile, even though Radio Records had hand-picked a producer for the sessions, Joey was continuing to lobby to have the band produce themselves. He recalled, "I'd started to argue with Tommy. Every time we'd made a record we'd had a producer, and we allowed the producer to dominate the proceedings . . . The fact the band let them do it made me angry. I was trying to get Tommy to say, 'Let's produce it ourselves . . . Tommy didn't want to do that. He preferred it the other way."

The producer finally arrived. His name was Jack Richardson, best-known for working with The Guess Who and Alice Cooper. After a few rehearsals, the recording began. "We just blasted through the basic tracks," says Sherba. "We didn't really get a chance to work out the kinks."

Joey and Tom were determined to make a rock'n'roll oriented record. They made a point not to have *any* acoustic guitars. A slew of high-energy songs were laid down: "I Got You," "Passin' Time," "Come On," "Rock'n'Roll Contract," and "Crocadillo," the latter germinating from a wine commercial idea Tommy had co-written with Rod Roach.

Guitarist Glenn Sherba found he was being given a good chunk of the lead guitar role. "I had gone down there thinking it was a session player gig, maybe to do a few tasteful Pete Ham/George Harrison type licks, but Tommy wanted me to go crazy. Joey and I traded off. For example, on 'No More' and 'Rock'n'Roll Contract,' he did the first solo and I did the long outro ones."

Both songs became LP side-ending epics, as Sherba was basically told to "go for it" in each case. "I worked up this solo for 'Rock'n'Roll Contract' and Tommy hated it. He said, 'No, I want *madness!*' So I did four straight takes on four different tracks. I was kicking the amp and rubbing the guitar on the mic stand. He loved it!"

Sherba's solo is quite exciting, but the track goes on rather long, and is lacking in oomph. Molland's "No More" comes off better. It is a Harrison-esque, psychedelic venture, distracted only slightly by its heavy-metalish ending, "I did two leads for that," explains Sherba, "and there was considerable disagreement over which one to use."

Tom's "Too Hung Up On You," was originally an Evans/Roach demo. It became molded from its bouncy pop origins; transforming into a beautiful, deeply-felt ballad with a surprising twist – a blues oriented bridge. "Tom always wanted to try and get a blues element in what we did," said Roach.

There was also the expected pop-rock material recorded, Joey's "Because I Love You" and "Three-Time Loser," plus Tom's "Hold On," a composition from the *Airwaves* days (whose chorus was alleged to be written by Joe Tansin). Despite each tune being of first-rate quality, and quite commercial-sounding, all three ended up below their potential, mainly because of undistinguished production. "Hold On" also suffers from a shockingly strained vocal by Tommy. Sherba recalls, "At one point, Tommy and Joey couldn't sing vocals for two weeks because they got sick with the flu. When we picked back up, it put the pressure on. No matter how good a day it was, we were always behind."

Luckily, most of the album's vocal performances did end up terrific. But, as it turned out, the use of harmonies and background voices was not emphasized on most of the songs. Sherba claims this played more into the minimalist angle Joey and Tommy had wanted to take.

During these recording sessions major conflicts were continually brewing. Radio Records was upset because the band had been refusing to sign a contractual agreement to sign over a portion of their publishing; to go into effect once the recording began. Hurowitz recalls, "The guys had told me they were going to refuse to sign it. When I told the record company they told me 'I better get it signed or else.' I couldn't get the band to do it. I could not control Joey and Tommy and their personal conflicts. Joey's wife, Kathie, she had her problems with Tom. And it seemed like everybody wanted to be the manager."

While recording the song "Rock'n'Roll Contract," Tom had producer Jack Richardson vocalize a menacing script of a manager gloating – using phrases Tom had scratched onto a "fish'n'chips" napkin. Tom also screamed "*I hate you, I hate you, I hate you*," with an effect masking his words. This song, which originated from Tom's frustration with former manager Stan Polley, still carried great weight. Tom had many emotional outbreaks during the group's stay in Florida, and he often directed them toward his new manager, Scott Hurowitz.

Richard Bryans, Tom Evans, Joey Molland, Tony Kaye, Glenn Sherba (on floor)

"Tommy was merciless," says Sherba, "One time Scott was gone for the day and Tommy put yogurt on his bed, cheese in the mouthpiece of his telephone. He jammed it in his hairdryer . . . Another time Tom found a "STOP" sign that had been knocked over and we dragged it back to our villa and set it up so that when Scott opened his door, it would fall over and knock this large plant into the pool. We stood outside his room and yelled 'Fire!'

"But the one incident that really sticks in my mind was when we came out of a session and Tom collapsed to the ground like he'd gone unconscious. Scott starts freaking out and I said 'Oh, just leave him be. At least we know he'll be on time tomorrow.' Scott jumps in his car to get help and Tommy gets on Scott's car hood, and starts *pissing* on the windshield!"

Tom's antics were sometimes part of his penchant for testing one's loyalty. Hurowitz claims he could see that and he somehow managed to retain respect for Tom. Hurowitz also felt Tony Kaye was a true professional. But he had his gripes with Joey. "Out of everyone, for me, Joey was the most rude. Joey, for lack of a better term, expected that he was due what he was receiving, and a lot more. Sort of like, 'I take no responsibility for the past. I'm great and I deserve this.'"

Tom was often upset with Joey and Kathie while in Florida. He mailed Rod Roach a few notes back in England, sometimes scribbling on old napkins or crumpled pieces of paper. "Tom was well out of his skull," says Rod, "He said Joey was being ridiculous, asking for limousines and stuff. . . ."

It was at this album's mixing stage that the project suffered the most. The final results were short of needed finesse, and though the record was an improvement over *Airwaves*, it was still not fully accomplished. The effort was there, most of the rock'n'roll tunes were snappy and did hit home, but the key single-oriented tracks lacked pizzazz. Tom Evans later commented, "Jack Richardson was mixing the album and was running out of studio time. He just kind of rushed through it." Sherba adds, "I'm not even sure Jack Richardson was available for all the mixes. I think he had to leave before it was done. But we were all pretty happy with the album at the time."

Right after the recordings, Tom and his family traveled to Los Angeles. Marianne recalls, "We didn't have much money. We'd been told by some friends in L.A. that we could stay in their guest house. But when we got there they had disappeared. Luckily, Tony Kaye put us up in the Tropicana Hotel in Hollywood. But Tommy was

Marianne Evans with Stephen

very restless. I suggested we take a bus down to the beach one day and he said, 'Only poor people go on the bus!'

"Tommy was easily embarrassed. There were times I'd wanted us to go to visit friends in Germany and he'd say, 'What am I going to tell people? I'm not doing anything. I can't even buy them drinks!' He even turned down going to a good friend's wedding once, because he couldn't face people asking what he was doing."

Though Tom had been getting his ASCAP royalties over the past few years, he was never one to be careful in spending. And despite the fact Marianne worked to support the family, there were constant financial hardships to bear.

After a few weeks in L.A., Tom and Marianne returned to England with their son, Stephen. Then on December 9, 1980, Tom got word that John Lennon had been killed the day before in New York City.

For Tom this was a major event. When he was a teenager he had accidentally bumped into Lennon at the Cavern Club in Liverpool, and gotten a brusque brushoff. The rude retort had stayed with him. But Tom always listened and studied John's music far more than any of the other Beatles.

"When Lennon died it was like someone had chopped off Tom's right arm," said Rod Roach. "It was like his father had been killed. He sat motionless by the radio for days. . . ."

In January of 1981, Scott Hurowitz came to England and spent some time with Tom and his family. Hurowitz was trying to get the Radio album a foreign rights deal. "Tom and I spent a lot of time just hanging at his local pub," he states. "He discussed the friction between himself, Joey, and Kathie. He said it went back to the Pete Ham days. He talked a lot about Pete Ham. He was really affected by his death. . . ."

It was January 17, 1981, when the new Badfinger album was finally released in America. Titled *Say No More,* it featured brightly colored artwork by Peter Max, the well-known poster designer who had come into prominence in the late '60s. On the back jacket was an orange backdrop portraying a small figure running across tiny squares. The front cover proved more intriguing; a profiled man wearing a black coat has his neck tightly wrapped in a red shawl. "We were surprised," says Tony Kaye, "because it looked so much like Tommy, the black hair, that faraway look. It really was him."

A single of "Hold On" b/w "Passin' Time" was released just after the album came out. It entered the *Billboard* charts on February 7, 1981. By mid-March it had reached number 56. "The label was getting really excited," says Hurowitz. "They contacted me and said 'Well, what's the touring situation?' I had to tell them the band didn't want to tour. Tony Kaye, Joey, and Tommy had been in agreement that they didn't want to start out with small club gigs. They wanted to see if the record's

Say No More *LP cover*

momentum could get them a headline tour. Radio Records saw it differently. They thought the band had to do whatever was necessary. They'd spent all this money and they wanted them out touring. They got mad and let up on their promotion."

Because the single had looked like a Top 40 probability, a performance on the American TV show *Solid Gold* had been arranged, which the band eventually did. But the single had started to drop by that point. In April, Radio Records put out "I Got You" b/w "Rock'n'Roll Contract" as a follow-up 45. The band was booked on *The Merv Griffin Show.* As the lipsyncing of their first number began, Joey fell off the stage. Guitarist Glenn Sherba recalls, "We did 'I Got You' to open the program, and we were actually supposed to speak and do another song later in the show. At one point Merv was doing this big build-up for Angie Dickinson and just before the dramatic pause, Joey yelled something off-camera and Merv heard it. He freaked out and said something to the stage manager and canceled us. He was noticeably shaken backstage."

Months later, Radio Records put out "Because I Love You" b/w "Too Hung Up On You" as a third single. But the label had long since dropped any efforts to promote Badfinger. Radio was now in the midst of an explosion with their "Stars On 45" single, a pseudo-Beatles disco medley, and most of their efforts went towards sustaining it. It eventually reached #1 in the *Billboard* charts.

Reviews of the *Say No More* LP proved to be scarce. *Trouser Press* declared Badfinger to be *"back on the right track,"* while *Seventeen* stated, *"good news for anyone who dotes on good-time rock'n'roll." People* magazine praised it, too, but noted with regret, *"Badfinger has forsaken the acoustic guitar that once gave it a*

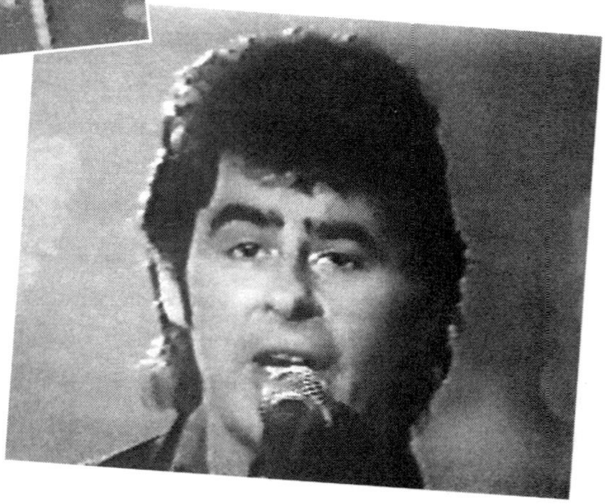

Joey Molland, Tom Evans
Solid Gold TV show, 1981

distinctive folksy anchor . . ." The album did not chart until March 27, 1981, ten weeks after it was released. It hung around for six weeks, eventually peaking at 155.

Hurowitz recalls, "I was so disappointed. I really believed in it. Even if the guys disassociated from me and got somebody else in, I think the project could have been salvaged. Tony Kaye could have gotten them to a number of major managers. I don't know why it didn't happen."

As with the previous LP, any new Badfinger album had the burden of many people knowing Pete Ham was no longer involved. *Airwaves* had generally been perceived as a failure by Joey and Tom to show they could truly deliver a pop album of real consequence without Pete Ham. Thus, many music listeners were even less eager to check out *Say No More*. Joey and Tom had the added disadvantage that this was an era of great skepticism toward rock'n'roll comebacks anyway, mainly because of the then-current enthusiasm for "new-wave," "punk," and "synth-based disco." Many 70s icons were now being *severely* ridiculed.

Yet, if this version of Badfinger had delivered memorable 45s in the group's classic pop single mold, they still had enough enthusiastic radio programmers and old-time fans to jump-start interest. But none of the singles were successful, the group wasn't touring, turmoils were rampant, and the record label was disillusioned by what they perceived as the band's egotistical behavior. The future of Badfinger did not bode well.

During the summer of 1981, Joey took off for Detroit, Michigan, to produce some demos for a band called Straight Up. The group was led by Bob Evans, a self-proclaimed Badfinger fanatic. Joey was paid to spend a weekend overseeing the recording of two tunes. Meanwhile, Joey and Tom were now getting interested in doing *any* kind of a tour. But it wasn't coming together. Tom was in England now, while Tony Kaye was involved in other projects. Communications with manager Hurowitz had become scarce.

Meanwhile, Radio Records was trying to consider whether to even take up their option to do a second Badfinger album. In the fall of '81, Tom flew out to L.A. to meet for band rehearsals. Joey recalled, "I came in with a cassette of songs I made on an acoustic guitar . . . I didn't sing the words really . . . a tune and I sang some words. Tommy came in with this demo with drums and all this stuff. The record company guy came in and gave us a check. He only gave us half the advance . . . I said, 'What's this?' 'Well, that's what they told us to bring.' I said, 'Well, this is no good' and I put me tape away and me guitar and I said, 'I'm going home now. Call me when the rest of the money comes. I'm not going to play.' "

Glenn Sherba recalls, "When I got to rehearsals, Joey had already gone. Our producer, Jack Richardson, had come down and there weren't many songs." Tony Kaye adds, "The record company was upset. They said there better be songs before we'll let you do an album."

For the next few weeks Tom and the others tried keeping it together. Joey found out they were continuing without him and it made him quite upset. He stated, "Everybody was told I left the band. That made me really angry. So I got Joe Tansin and a couple of friends . . . a fellow named Larry Lee and a guy named Bobby Wickland . . . I said, 'This is Badfinger. That band you have isn't Badfinger.' Because I didn't want Tommy Evans and Tony Kaye to be able to go and be Badfinger, no matter what the cost, I did not want that to happen."

Joey went out with his new group within a few weeks of putting it together. Joey's Badfinger did a series of gigs at an amusement park and then focused on small clubs around the South and Southwest for the remainder of the year. Joe Tansin and the other musicians were friends with Tom. For them it was an awkward situation.

Tom was recorded in a phone conversation with old Badfinger friend Steve Craiter around this time. He is trying to be optimistic about his hopes Radio Records would let them do a new album, but he is clearly upset at Joey's going out as Badfinger. He states during the call, "I really just want to bury the name Badfinger . . . I need to clear the legality of it and then bury it . . . for Peter's sake."

Soon after, Radio Records gave indication they were definitely not going to pursue the second album option. "Tom was quite depressed about it," said Tony Kaye. Tom returned to England just before the Christmas holidays.

With Tom back in Surrey, Rod Roach again renewed their working relationship. "I was willing to give Tom a lot of time. I realized he was a very good songwriter and had a unique voice all his own." Rod had noticed Tom got a lot more done when he was sober. He upped his efforts to get Tom's drinking under control. "Marianne knew what I was trying to do," he states, "same as her, trying to get Tom straight in the head. She used to tell me she was worried about his drinking. I'd tell her I was trying."

At some point early in 1982, Rod did get Tom to quit drinking completely. Then things started moving. They were writing more songs, working with other musicians, doing occasional gigs; Tom had more energy and drive. Then a call came out of the blue for Rod. "I was offered this gig playing guitar with two Australian girls who called themselves Cheetah. They were sexy girls in tight leather. It was managed by the same guys who managed AC/DC."

Apparently, a full band was needed and Rod told Tom about the openings. Tom then contacted ex-Badfinger member Bob Jackson. Jackson had done a few things since being forced out of the Dodgers in 1979. He'd recorded an EP with The Scene, done session work with the Searchers, and most recently backed ex-Uriah Heep singer David Byron. Now he was totally available. Tom let him know there were no hard feelings. He simply wanted to know if Bob was interested.

The three musicians auditioned for Cheetah together. Bob Jackson: "We went to some rehearsals and their managers pushed that they wanted a heavy-rock backing band. It was a bit of a scene at first, because we couldn't find a decent drummer to play with. There was talk of making an album."

All three were hired and they did a few warm-up gigs. The management was gearing the band for an industry showcase at the annual MIDEM festival being held in Cannes, France. Rod Roach recalls the day they left. "Tommy had been lying low, behaving himself up to this point, but as soon as we were off to MIDEM he resurrected his old self . . . everyone was in fits of laughter. . . .

"We were onstage performing and Tom apparently got bored with the whole thing. He started singing with the girls. People were noticing, 'Ah, Tom Evans.' The president of CBS came up to Tom afterward and ignored the girls. The girls and their management got extremely pissed off at the attention he was getting.

"Tom ended up getting outrageously drunk. There was some huge student protest going on in the city – bottles were getting thrown and people were chanting – and Tom went right into the middle of it. I was standing there with Bob Jackson and I said, 'Do you think I should go and get him?' and Bob said, 'You must be joking!' We couldn't see him, but we could hear him. He was louder than the demonstration!"

After wandering into a bar, Tom ran into Cheetah's management team, where he had a huge argument with them. Needless to say, he got fired on the spot. "But he didn't care," said Rod, "On the plane trip back he was sitting next to the president of K-Tel Records (who'd released the 1980 "Come And Get It" remake) and Tom was having a good time needling him. 'So you're the guy who gets to play God with

Tom Evans

everybody's music. Well, you seem like a nice guy. You're making bread off of us now. How about giving some of that back?!' After we landed Tom said, 'He survived. It was a test. He's a good guy.' "

But after three months of total sobriety, Tom was once more tightly wrapped to the bottle. It would be difficult for him to ever again escape its relentless tug.

Joey Molland continued to book his "Badfinger" band that winter. Joe Tansin and the other musicians had already dropped out, just before the Christmas of '81, and Joey was now using whomever was available. One of his shows caused an angry letter from John Ramsey to be published in *Trouser Press* magazine: *"When I arrived home in Abilene, Texas for the Christmas holidays I was amazed to learn Badfinger was going to play two nights at a local club . . . I went to a seedy little club wondering why Badfinger, who had recently released an excellent album on a major label, would play here in the first place . . . I shouldn't have wondered. "Badfinger" consisted of Joey Molland and two pickup musicians: a drummer who might still have been in high school and an American bassist who was so unfamiliar with the material he missed notes all night . . . Needless to say, I felt ripped off . . . ."* He finished by asking, *"Does Tom Evans know about this?"*

Tom was indeed aware of Joey's gigging. One day, Tom got a call in England from Mike Gibbins, who was now situated in Detroit, Michigan. Bob Evans (the ex-leader of the Badfinger-inspired band, Straight Up) had caught Mike's ear through some demo tapes he had sent him. Mike decided to come over to the states. Mike touted Bob's work to Tom, and he suggested Tom join them to do their *own* Badfinger tour. Tom was motivated enough that he set off for Detroit, where Bob Evans was based. Mike Gibbins had spent the previous few years doing occasional gigs and sessions around South Wales, often playing with the Martin Ace All-Stars and a country band, Faded Glory.

Bob Evans now had two of his idols in his fold. He claims to have worked on some demos with both of them for a few weeks, all the while scrambling to get shows set up. Tom later said the situation was not well-organized, and there were a few disastrous gigs. Mike and Tom quickly angered. "I was used everywhere I went," says Mike. "It was always people introducing me, 'Hi. This is Mike Gibbins from Badfinger.' They were just using me. People would take me to parties and put me on a pedestal just for their own egos."

With no money to get back to England, Tom soon found himself broke. He contacted an American named John Cass (whom he'd recently met) and asked for a loan to get home. Cass was involved in the printing of advertisements, and reportedly told Tom, "Forget the fare home. I can get something going. Let me handle it."

Bob Jackson recalls getting a phone call in England (which he documented in a journal as happening on May 16, 1982). "Tom says, 'What are you doing, Bob?' I said, 'Not a lot really.' He said, 'Come over to the states. I'm in the states now. When can you get here?' I was like, 'Well Tom, what is this all about?' He basically said, 'I'll explain it when you get here.' At this point I was married and I had a kiddie six weeks old. Tom said, 'Look, I'll put you on with this guy John Cass. He's gonna get us television, he's gonna get us this' . . . but not a lot of detail. Tom was a man of few words in that sense. He kind of assured me the situation would be good. A few days later I agreed to do this supposed six-week tour.

"I fly into Detroit, Michigan and no one's at the airport. I got off the plane and sat there waiting, continuing to drink a bottle of Jack Daniels I'd bought. I was ringing this number Tom had given me and there was no answer. I got tremendously drunk waiting around. Then Mike finally answers the phone. He came and got me, but I was quite ill by now. I became so sick I thought I was dying. I called my wife. It was quite a scene.

"Once I came to my senses, I said, 'Okay, where are we rehearsing?' They said, 'In a garage in back of the house.' I said, 'Who is the guitarist?' They said, 'Some local guy.' I said, 'Okay, so where are the dates?' Tom said, 'Well, the dates aren't in yet. John Cass is going to come down and give them to us.' I was thinking, 'Oh, no!'

"We rehearsed this guitarist and he wasn't good enough. I had to fire him because I didn't know him. Then Cass finally comes down from Milwaukee. He gets into this conversation about the Beatles and what prophets they were. He says, 'They were kind of Christ-like really.' I said, 'Yeah?' He said, 'Actually, I've written a book about it. I keep it in my fridge.' I'm thinking, 'Oh God, we've attracted another fruitcake. And here he is, *managing us!*"

Cass produced an agents contract for everyone to sign. It was for eight weeks, with an additional ten-week option for Cass. It didn't specify a tour itinerary. It mentioned that dates would be forthcoming with a focus on the state of Wisconsin. The lack of specific gigs infuriated Tom and the others. Bob Jackson and Mike refused to sign the papers. Arguments ensued.

As it turned out, Tom had already signed a personal management contract with Cass a week earlier, much to Bob's surprise. "Tom later told me Cass had gotten him heavily coked up so that he didn't know what he'd signed," says Bob. "He was nervous about it. He didn't have a copy."

Cass had arrived in Detroit with a fellow named Alex Shliminoff. Alex recently had met Cass after coming to his house to fix his TV set. Cass introduced Alex to Tom Evans shortly after. Cass invited Alex to go with him to Detroit under the premise of, "I'll drive, and you pay for the hotel room!" Alex was very eager to see Tom again, so he went for the Cass offer. But he developed a *huge* dislike for Cass over the course of the trip. "I quickly realized this guy was total bullshit. After we got to the house where Tommy was staying, Tommy told me he thought Cass was taking him for a ride. I asked him if he'd signed anything yet. He told me he had."

Tom was now over a barrel and Bob Jackson couldn't believe what was happening, "Cass kept pushing that he couldn't get us work unless we signed his agent agreement."

Jackson felt little option for himself other than to go back to England with his head between his legs, or help Mike and Tom, who had nothing going on. Eventually all three signed the eight-week agreement. Alex Shliminoff recalls, "On the way back to the hotel Cass said to me, 'Yeah, I got them. I got them by the balls.' "

Over the next few days, John Cass came to see the band while they rehearsed guitarists. Bob recalls, "Tom had big arguments with Cass. He'd say, 'You better come up with the goods, man.' Cass would say, 'Don't worry. I'll handle my end. You handle yours.'

On June 14, 1982, Tom and the others had the idea to call Joey Molland and see if he'd like to make it an even bigger Badfinger reunion. Mike started out talking to Joey. Tom finally got the nerve at two-thirty in the morning. But Joey would not commit, even though his most recent Badfinger tour had been a disaster. He'd gone out in May with three other musicians and his whole group had been arrested for marijuana possession. They'd spent five days in a Louisiana jail and had their equipment impounded. Somehow they had straggled around for a month afterwards, borrowing equipment along the way.

After spending a few days in Detroit, John Cass finally returned to Milwaukee. Later, he contacted Tom and the others, saying he needed them to get to where he was, so he could get the ball rolling. The band was infuriated, but had little choice. To raise money to get there they ended up playing a few local parties, but were embarrassed and humiliated. By now, a guitarist named Adam Allen had been recruited. On June 22, 1982, they crowded into a van and made their way to Milwaukee.

Bob recalls, "We arrived and Cass says everything's going to be fine. He brings us over to this house with a *For Sale* sign on it. It was completely empty except for a few chairs and one bed. He says, 'You're going to be staying here.' There was no carpeting. It was bare floor boards. We said, 'Whatever! Just get us on the road!' But nothing happened. For the first week we had absolutely nothing going on."

Cass assured them gigs were coming up. Then he started talking about selling his interest to other people. "It was insane," says Bob. "He started talking about wanting my publishing income. It made no sense."

On July 1, 1982, Tony Sgro (whose family's home Bob, Tom, and Mike, had all stayed at in Detroit) came to deliver news that Tom's wife, Marianne, had called, saying she'd signed a lien on Tom's home in England because he owed back taxes. Tom was extremely upset and went out for a drink. Sgro came back later and took the bass and drum set-up the band had apparently borrowed. Says Bob, "Later that night we all met with Cass and had huge arguments. He told us he'd get us a new drum set-up. I told him I was going back to England." Bob had originally gotten a round-trip airline ticket. But Tom didn't have money to go back, so Bob decided to stick it out longer.

On July 5, 1982, the band played the Wisconsin Summerfest. "It wasn't anything fantastic," recalls Bob. "Afterwards Cass wouldn't give the roadies any gas money to get home. He said it was our responsibility. It was ridiculous. We weren't getting paid ourselves! We were getting desperate. I remember literally starving. We were living on a box of saltines and a jar of jam. Then one day Cass sent over one of his cronies with a box. Inside it was a bunch of dog food! It was a sick joke!"

On July 9, 1982, Cass came over with some agents and threw a contract in front of the band. The agents were from Talent Associates. Cass claimed they were prepared to set up a sixteen week tour. Jackson recalls, "We had understood Cass was supposed to be booking us. Now he wanted to get us involved in another contract. We were skeptical, because we'd been totally screwed to this point."

Heavy arguments continued as everyone was reluctant. The new contract again did not lay out specific gigs. Cass kept saying they were missing a good opportunity, *"Don't blow it! Don't blow it!"* he would scream. He became more and more incensed.

The next day Cass took Tom out early. Bob says Tom was gone all day and all night. When Tom came back he was very quiet and would not say what happened. Bob had strong suspicions he had been plied with alcohol and drugs.

That evening the band played a local Milwaukee T.V. program called *Shock Theater*. It was your typical vehicle for a schlocky late night horror movie with a goofy host; in this case a bearded man named Toulouse No-Neck. The band played between commercial breaks and performed nine songs. Considering their circumstances, this proved to be a good performance. The guitarist Adam Allen had definitely done his homework, as he captured all of the Badfinger riffs right on target. Bob and Tom were in good voice. Despite some fooling around, it proves to be worth seeing. Bootleg videos do exist.

One highlight is the stellar performance of Bob Jackson's "I Won't Forget You," his tribute song to Pete Ham. Tom and Bob faced each other to sing the emotional lyrics. Tom often told Bob how much he liked the song. "He really mourned Pete's loss," says Bob. "A lot of times he was off in his own world thinking about it."

After the show, Cass nearly got in a fight with the *Shock Theater* host. He followed the next day with a physical threat to guitarist Adam Allen. Emotions were running rampant. "Tom was pretty much unable to handle it all," said Bob. "I went off for awhile and when I got back Mike came out to meet me at the walkway and he said, 'You better go and sort Tom out.' I went up to the bedroom and Tom was sitting there crying with knotted up sheets in his hands. I said, 'What the hell are you doing?' I shouted at him. I said, *'You idiot! This isn't going to solve anything!'* He took it all in. I could see it was a cry for help."

Shock Theater
July 10, 1982,
Tom Evans,
Mike Gibbins,
Adam Allen,
Bob Jackson

The band's next gig was on July 17, 1982, at a ski resort called Little Switzerland. Again it was poorly organized, with no pay coming. The following evening they played the Eagles club in Milwaukee and had a great reception. But they *still* weren't getting paid. Bob had been promised at least $500 a week. Tom claimed he was promised $1,500 a week.

After this gig, no one even had the gas money to get home. Bob tried calling Cass at three in the morning, using the ruse that a few members of the road crew had been put in jail. "It was the only thing I could think of to try and get him to come." Cass didn't show and they had to literally beg someone for the money. The next day Tom was *very* upset. Cass took him away again, returning Tom twenty-four hours later. Tom wouldn't say what had happened.

The next few days saw more screaming matches, and two of the road crew quit. Cass suggested the band handle the road work themselves. Tom and Bob then went to the Talent Associates office, as they knew they had booked a few of the band's gigs. Bob and Tom explained to them about losing their sound man and lighting operator. Talent Associates said it wasn't their problem, but they'd try to help. Then they launched into their own complaints about Cass, saying he wasn't following through on promotion he'd promised them.

A few days later, another show was done in Milwaukee. Cass got physically threatened when the people who'd brought in the rented P.A. were not paid. The club refused to pay afterwards, claiming the band arrived late, and wouldn't turn down their volume when asked. Things had completely fallen apart.

Cass asked the band to come over to his house to unload the equipment he'd gotten them, and to discuss the money situation. The band was fearful he'd lock up the gear, shut them down, and leave them unpaid, so they refused to come. Cass's girlfriend, Paula, finally arranged to meet Tom and Bob at a bar. "She was manic," said Bob. "She shouted her piece. She offered us $300 to keep us going. We took it to get some money, but it was far from what we were due."

There was one more disastrous gig before Bob contacted Talent Associates to see what other shows had been booked. The band had been waiting for the date of August 2, 1982, because that was the final day Cass had to verify he was picking up the ten week option of his agent contract, which was due to run out on August 9th. Talent Associates indicated there were only five more gigs booked over the next three weeks. Cass had carelessly overlooked his need to set forth the new option in writing. Everyone took advantage to split. Mike Gibbins and Adam Allen went back to Detroit. Bob and Tom decided they would hide from Cass until they could get back to England.

They first went to see Alex Shliminoff, who lived near the house where the band was staying. "I could see they were starving," says Shliminoff. "Tommy felt threatened by Cass. He thought he was Mafia or something. He told me I could be in trouble for helping them."

Jackson recalls, "Cass had been telling Tom he was very well-connected and Tom better not screw him. Tom would say, 'Go on John, send the wet fish. Get it over with.' Apparently, the fish is something the Mafia send you before they kill you. Tom got really scared."

Tom was in a bind. Not only did he not have money for a ticket home, but his relationship with his wife had suffered greatly. Jackson recalls, "Tom had not been keeping in touch with Marianne and she needed money. She'd gone to a social security office at one point and they said she had to prove her husband wasn't with her anymore, just to get some money. It was difficult for her."

Shliminoff recalls one particular evening: "Tommy was saying, 'Why God? Why is everything happening to me?' I said, 'Don't worry Tommy. Don't worry. Would you like to call home?' I took him to my shop and he called his wife from there. He kept saying, 'I will see you. I will see you.' Tears were coming to his eyes. . . ."

Bob and Tom spent the next few days hiding out. John Cass showed up at Shliminoff's TV shop, asking if Alex had seen them. Another time Tom and Bob spent one entire evening with Alex and his family. They played music, sang, and Bob performed magic tricks, "It was the first real fun we had in ages," said Jackson.

On August 5, 1982, Alex and his brother took Tom and Bob to breakfast, and surprised them with an airline ticket for Tom, toys for both their children, and extra money to take with them. Bob and Tom were extremely grateful. "We had to avoid Cass a few more days until we left," recalled Bob. "It was like a movie – *Escape from Milwaukee*. We disguised ourselves. We were nervous right up to the time we got to the airport."

Finally they got on the plane and Bob remembers as they arrived in England, "Tom was a wreck. Marianne wasn't there. He called home and apparently she was out of town. He looked very depressed. I stayed with him a little while longer, bought us some drinks, and tried to cheer him up. In the end, he got in touch with Rod Roach who came to pick him up. Tom was really down then. . . ."

Bob Jackson, Alex Shliminoff, Tom Evans, Amelia Shliminoff, 1982

Tom Evans had come back to England in a state of shock. He was physically and mentally exhausted. His relationship with Marianne had been stressed by his constant departures. His mind was muddled. His musical future – uncertain. But Tom had responsibilities to attend to. He had an ever present mortgage, tax problems, and a young son to think about. He decided to look for a regular job. "Tom was very capable, very intelligent," says Rod Roach, "but he didn't have a specific trade to fall back on. One day he said, 'Fuck all this. I'll get a job as a postman.' He got the forms and the next day a check from ASCAP came in. That was the end of that."

Tom was not aware, but Joey Molland was now in England wanting to pursue the ASCAP shares and Apple royalty holdings for Badfinger. Back in July of 1982, Joey had borrowed money from Philadelphian, Steve Craiter, to get his family to the U.K. They first situated with Joey's relatives in Newport, England, where he was getting chauffeured around by a young musician named Mal Coote. Joey considered starting a group there, but he found prospects for live work dim.

On at least two occasions, Coote drove Joey down to London. A Collins' diary entry confirms Mike and Bill had a rendezvous with Joey, and together left to see Tom. Bob Jackson recalls, "Tom rang me up and said that Bill, Joey, and Mike had all showed up unannounced. They were pushing him to sign papers. He said he tried to reason with them, but they were like, *'You better sign this!'* He said he had to kick them out of his house. He was half-angry, half-surprised. He said, 'How could they do that to me, show up and just gang up on me like that?'"

Bill Collins claims they did *not* present any papers for him to sign.

Rod Roach recalled being at Tom's home several times when Bill Collins had visited. "Things would start out cordially, but as the drinks would flow it would erupt into shouting. Tom could never come out in a business-like way and tell Bill what he felt. He couldn't just say, 'Look Bill, Peter and I wrote 'Without You.' It's our song, the money is being generated by a cover version, not Badfinger's version.' Instead, he would drink, and it would come out argumentative."

The major dispute *was* over "Without You." Though money had built up from radio play of the other Badfinger hits written by Pete Ham, the biggest income flow was the ASCAP shares of this oft-covered Evans/Ham composition. It functioned as a money-making machine due to its universal appeal as a "standard." Joey, Bill, Mike, and Stan Polley all wanted a part of Tom and Pete's "writers share," as certain precedence for this had been discussed years before. Lawyers were being conferred. There was wide dispute over any potential previous agreements.

Tom's mother, May Evans, recalled talking with Tom many times about this issue, "For a long time the discussion between Bill and Tom had been 'Pete Ham's share.' When Tommy started getting his money for 'Without You,' Bill got right into Tom's money."

But Bill Collins asserted that he never pressured Tom about the ASCAP money Tom was receiving; in fact, Bill claimed that they never had any dispute at all!

When Tom and Bob Jackson had been in Milwaukee months earlier, they'd been introduced to Jack Koshick, a local concert promoter who'd just returned after working in New York the previous few years. Koshick had told them he would try and get a legitimate Badfinger tour going. They were completely skeptical, but one day he called them in England. Soon after, he mailed a financial breakdown with tour dates. "It looked legit," says Bob, "and we went for it."

By early October, Bob and Tom were again in Milwaukee. "You can imagine our wives' reactions to us going out there again," says Bob. "Of course, we started out sleeping on Koshick's floor. I mean, we had returned before with our tails between our legs and no money. Now we go back to America, we're on floors again, and we have no band. We got Mike interested. We tried to get Joey, but he said 'No.' "

Reed Kailing was contacted. He was a veteran Wisconsin musician who'd toured extensively with The Grassroots, played Paul McCartney in a version of Beatlemania, and once guested on a John Lennon album. Kailing recalls, "I was asked if I played slide guitar and I told the agent who contacted me I could do vocal and guitar work, but I wasn't that proficient on slide. So I called Donnie Dacus." Dacus had played with the band, Chicago, and recently backed Boz Scaggs.

As it happened, both musicians were recruited because of their multi-talented abilities. Rehearsals began straight away. Numbers from all eras of Badfinger were worked up, including two Joey Molland tunes. "Tom suggested we do 'Suitcase' and that struck me," said Bob Jackson. "I thought, 'Boy, he's being awfully fair after all he's gone through with Joey.' But Tom had said, 'We can knock this together quick. It's a good number.' "

The tour was supposed to start on November 10, 1982. After the first date was canceled, Bob wrote in his journal: "*Tommy pretty depressed . . . Tommy now talking about doing only one week. All-time low morale. . . .*"

Eventually the shows got rolling, but there was a lot of grumbling. Koshick immediately wanted to cut corners. For example, he pushed to have the band sleep in the mid-size RV camper they were traveling in. Kailing says, "It was like going back to the days when you first started and you're compromising your professionalism. Donnie and I fought against him constantly."

The band also found themselves playing some offbeat gigs. Says Kailing, "We had this one show in the middle of Montana where we pull up and they're having target practice against the building. We go in the dressing room and there were bullet holes in the walls. Someone had carved in the door: '*We played here. We*

Tom Evans, Bob Jackson, Reed Kailing, Mike Gibbins, Donnie Dacus, 1982

were a band in red jumpsuits. WARNING: Do not wear jumpsuits in this club!' We're thinking, 'We're gonna be killed!' Then the bar maid asked if we packed guns – you can imagine Tommy hearing this – but it was so late, we figured we'd better stay and fulfill our contract. So we do the gig and they absolutely loved us. We ended up doing three nights instead of two. We were the talk of the town!"

The tour ran on, but problems developed at every turn. Kailing recalls, "One time we were driving, it was about two in the morning, and the RV suddenly dies, 'MMMmmmmmmmmmm.........' like a spaceship that lost its momentum. Here we are in the middle of this two-lane highway, it's pitch black, and all you can hear are chirping crickets. Tommy gets out and starts to open the hood. Then this state trooper shows up. He had a flashlight and he shines it under the hood and says, 'Look, I'll call a tow truck.' Tom says, 'No, it just needs some water.' Everyone starts grumbling, 'Yeah right, Tommy. Let's get the tow truck and get on our way.' Tom asks the policeman, 'Sir, is there any water out there?' We could just barely see the silhouette of some cattails. Tom says, 'Just give me a beer can.' Of course we had plenty of those. So he starts strolling out into the brush. Then we hear, *'AAAAGGHHHH . . . !&*!$*!&*'* Tom had fallen into some water tributary . . .

"He finally comes back and he smells like a swamp. Tom tells the cop to shine his flashlight under the hood, but the cop couldn't take the smell. So Tom grabs the flashlight from him, puts the water in, and I'll be damned if the RV didn't start right up. That was his genius. But we made him take his clothes off. He was naked the whole rest of the way."

There were numerous conflicts between Tom and the band's roadie/driver. Early on an engine blew. Tom accused him of forgetting to check the oil. Bob Jackson recalls, "We hired another van and Tom said to him, 'You better get things right this time!' The chap kept saying, 'It wasn't my fault!' A few days later we're at this motel. It had a canopied room with a glass window, kind of a check-in, check-out. So we're leaving and our driver goes, *'Okay boys! Wagon-time!'* and he sets off. He started toward this room and we said to ourselves, 'Oh, he'll turn the wheel. He's got to turn the . . .' *BAM!!!!* He crashes into the building, tearing the canopy down, the walls, glass was everywhere. Tommy's going crazy. It was quite a scene. The police came and I remember one of them was taking pictures saying, 'This is great! I love it!' . . . They took the roadie away by the scruff of his neck.

"A few days later he gets released from jail . . . We were planning to drop him off in Detroit. We were just about there, it was two in the morning and the van runs out of gas. We had to hike across the highway, carrying our equipment. It was a big hassle. Tom was really angry. We get to some hotel and at the check-out I hear, *'You fucking bastard!'* and *'You English faggot!'* Tom and this guy were rolling on the floor fighting. I had to drag Tommy into his room kicking and screaming and lock the door!"

Reed Kailing, Mike Gibbins, Donnie Dacus, Bob Jackson

Reed Kailing says the whole first leg of the tour was completely haphazard. "We were going from Minneapolis to Indiana to Montana to Illinois. It was as if you took a dart and threw it at a road map. Donnie and I were looking at each other like, 'This is insane!' We had this show where we had to leave Illinois to get to Calgary, Canada and we said, 'That's it! This bus is going back to Milwaukee. We've got to re-think this.' We mutinied. We were all dead tired."

"First thing when we get back I tell Koshick he really needed to find a way to get this thing together. We were going down well. A lot of the promoters really wanted us back. And I was amazed at the devotion of these Badfinger fans. They used to follow us from state to state. It was like a mini-version of the Grateful Dead. We had T-shirts sold out right away. People used to carry the albums around like they were gold. I wanted to see this thing through. That's when Koshick brought Rey Reneri in."

Koshick had known Reneri from New York, having been a business partner there. "Reneri went way back," says Kailing. "I think he road managed Judy Garland at one time, and a lot of rhythm & blues acts. He came in and helped Koshick reroute the tour. He became our road manager."

While things were being sorted out, Tom occasionally visited with Alex Shliminoff and his family in Milwaukee. On Thanksgiving Day, 1982, Kailing invited Tom and Bob over to his family's home. "They were very polite," said Kailing. "Tom had said, 'Yes, Ma'am' to my mother, totally unlike his touring persona. They ate pumpkin pie and were so overwhelmed. It was like they'd had nothing greater. They gave my mom a big hug.

"Tom talked real highly of his mother. He missed his family. A couple of nights on the tour he cried because he didn't have the money to send his wife to pay some bill she needed it for."

The band eventually went back on the road, but found dates were falling through. It turned out Joey Molland had returned to the states and was, allegedly, causing problems for Tom's Badfinger bookings. Steve Craiter recalled, " . . . Joey had come to stay with me after he came back from England, planning to try and start his own tour here. . . he didn't think Tommy should be doing Badfinger gigs without him."

Bob Jackson recalls the band's perspective, "We'd been getting dates canceled because promoters were confused as to who could use the name Badfinger. Joey was telling them *he* was the 'original' Badfinger. Tom was really pissed off because we'd asked Joey to join before this whole thing even started. Joey even sent us a letter at one point claiming there could be any numbers of Badfinger bands out there. Then he goes and sabotages our gigs. He would deny it, but the promoters would tell us he had spoken to them."

On December 6, 1982, the band was in Newark, Delaware where they had a gig at a club called Cowboys. Kailing recalls, "We were backstage and Molland comes bursting into our dressing room. He had shaken up a beer bottle and he started spraying it around. Apparently this was some sort of ritual between him and Tommy. We had all our guitars set up on stands and he'd doused them. Donnie had about four really nice guitars. We were ready to kill.

"Eventually Joey started getting on Tom with some B.S. and I jumped in and said, 'Look Joey, as long as I'm going around with Badfinger, I'll be damned if you're going to screw with the band's name and reputation. 'Cause this is Badfinger – Tom, Mike, and Bob, three former members. We're on the road, doing it legit. Go and start your own thing!' He just got real sheepish and said, 'Well, I was part of the band too . . .' I said, 'Fine, if you and Tommy want to work something out, go ahead. But don't drag me into this. I'm out here breaking my ass to do it right. It's not my band, but once I devote myself, I'm into it!' "

The show was later reviewed in the paper *Fine Times*. Writer Steve Harvey commented it was a good performance, but also brought up rumors that a bogus Badfinger may have cut down the crowd. Then he stated: " . . . .*What really shook things up was the appearance of Joey Molland. His presence almost caused a fight backstage after the show. What a way to end the night!*"

The morning after the gig, Tom rushed off to the home of Steve Craiter, who now lived in New Castle, Delaware, some fifteen minutes from the Cowboys club. Craiter had brought Joey to the gig the night before. He says Tom's appearance at his home was a surprise, even though he remembers Joey and Tom had discussed the prospects of meeting up that day. Tom had taken down Steve's address at the club. "I halfway wanted to hang with them, but Joey hinted he wanted to talk to Tom alone . . . I know Joey wanted to settle the Apple money and get his share out if it. He told me the band's agreement was pretty straightforward . . . Joey went off to talk with him."

Tom's Badfinger continued on. The band was going over well. Rumors were floating that Radio Records had a renewed interest in doing a "Badfinger" album. Mike Lloyd of Curb Records was also sniffing around. Kailing recalls, "Tommy had this aura, a lot of people in the industry would come up to him. We were getting interest for major tour support. We had gigs at the Other End in New York that went on until four or five in the morning, with lines still around the block. The club owner was ecstatic. He said, 'When are you guys coming back?' I was telling Tom, 'See, you're doing it!' "

But the omnipresent Beatles ghost was still there and it bothered Tom. Nary an interview went by where related questions weren't asked. At one gig the band was billed as "The Fingers – George Harrison's backing band." "Tom didn't want to be called Badfinger," says Bob. "He would've been happy not to do 'Come and Get It' ever again."

Despite the encouraging prospects, all was far from well. Kailing remembers, "Tommy was drinking heavily and on a number of occasions it almost cost us. One night he disappeared and the next morning we couldn't find him. We had to take off for the next state. He had to be flown in. He said, 'I know I'm drunk, but I'm here, so let's play.' The gig hadn't drawn well and Tommy had no sleep. At the end of the gig this club owner comes up and says, 'I'm not paying you any more money. You guys didn't draw and the bass player showed up late.' So we argued that we'd done the two sets and fulfilled our contract. He said, 'I'm not paying you!' Rey Reneri, our road manager, who is five feet with his Cuban heels on, had to deal with this guy, a huge Irishman. Rey was very calm. He kept saying, 'We want our money.' Me and Donnie left.

"The next morning Donnie and I were having breakfast in the adjacent coffee shop, which this Irish guy owned, and we hear a woman pleading, *'Please don't hurt my husband. He's a good man. He doesn't know this business. Please don't hurt him!'* She was talking to Rey. We looked at each other and said, 'What?!' It turned out Rey had made a phone call and had some guys drive four or five hours up from New York. They had waken up this guy in the middle of the night telling him 'Pay up Badfinger, or you'll *have* a bad finger.' Needless to say, the money got paid, and Rey had this tiny little smile on his face the whole rest of that day."

On December 16, 1982, Badfinger were playing at a club called PR's in Alton, Illinois. Bob Jackson recalls, "There was a knock on the dressing room door. Some guy comes in says, 'Are Tommy Evans and Bob Jackson here?' We said, 'Yeah.' The guy walks in and holds out his hand like he's going to shake it. Instead he puts writs in our hands. John Cass had sued us!"

Cass had filed against Mike, Bob, and Tom for $302,933, claiming he wanted a return of expenses he'd put forth the previous summer, a remuneration for future gigs he claimed to have booked, attorney fees, and punitive damages. Mike Gibbins was furious, "This guy sues me for splitting, for starving six weeks in the middle of a strange country, in a house empty of furniture. Six weeks with hardly any gigs. It was a joke! Totally humiliating!"

Cass had first filed suit in August of '82, one week after the band originally bailed. But the case was dismissed by a judge in November. This time, Cass added a second cause of action against Tom Evans, regarding the management contract Tom signed. It stated:

> *As a proximate result of the defendant Tom Evans's breach of agreement, the plaintiff has sustained or will sustain in the future, loss of profits, remunerations, royalties and business opportunity . . . in the total amount of $5,000,000.*

Tom was stunned. Though the Cass suits were based on preposterous situations and ridiculous figures, Tom did not have a copy of the management contract. The serving of these papers also heightened the stress over the enlarging Apple kitty. Bob recalls, "Toward the end of that tour Tom and Mike had huge rows over the Apple money and who should get what share. There was a lot of bad feeling there."

Kailing adds, "On the bus Mike and Tom would sit with their calculators for hours. They'd be 'tick, tick, tick,' going at it really fast. Every once in awhile they would thrust out their arms and compare calculations. I asked Tom what was going on and he said, 'There's hundreds of thousands of pounds tied up with Apple from our previous work. We have to come up with a mutually agreeable division.' "

Mike: "Tommy came up to me one night in a bar and said that his lawyer had told him he was going to have to pay back all this money. He had already ripped a pile from the front and would have to give much of that back. That took him over the edge."

Tom had found that, if it was determined the others should have had shares in his ASCAP income of "Without You," he may have to pay back a portion of his earnings from the previous years. Bob recalls, "Tom was trying to think how he could work something out. He thought maybe he should side with somebody's position against somebody else. It seemed like that was the only way anything was ever going to get settled."

As the tour wound down, Reed Kailing says he got more insights into Tom. "I have an outgoing personality and it took awhile for Tom to be comfortable with me. We had the same likings and background in music. We talked about our mutual experiences with The Beatles. He thought McCartney had been inspirational. He said he was the most disciplined musician he'd ever seen. And he related to the anger of John Lennon. He liked the way he could channel it effectively into his music.

"The only time I ever got really pissed at him was one night when we played at this large-scale club for uppercrust kids. We were waiting to go on, in the restaurant kitchen, and Tommy wasn't around. I could sense something was wrong, because I asked Mike and Bob and they avoided the subject. Then Rey Reneri comes in dragging Tom. Tom was . . . I mean this guy gave a whole new meaning to 'drunk.' He couldn't walk. He couldn't stand. At first I thought he was kidding. To top it off, he had poured a bottle of shampoo on his head and it looked like it was coated in axle grease. I just freaked. I was yelling, *'I'm not going onstage with this guy! I'm not going to be seen with this guy!'* I had a tantrum.

"The club owner hears this commotion and he comes over and says, 'What's going on?' He takes one look at Tommy and says, 'Ohhhh dear!' I said, 'Sir, I respect your club too much to go onstage with that man.' He said, 'You have a contract. You better do it!' I was totally bummed out.

Tom's Badfinger, 1982

"So we go on to play in front of this squeaky-clean crowd of guys in polo shirts, and blonde, underage girls in white. And here's Tommy next to me with his Elvis jacket, heavy boots, long sideburns – with shampoo dripping from his hair!

"We start the set with 'Come And Get It' and Tom starts hitting his open 'E' string, 'Bum bum bum bum.' I can remember looking at him and his bass – which must've weighed forty pounds with those thick piano strings he had – and it was slowly pulling him down. He started lowering the mic, then back to the bass, back to the mic, back to the bass . . . He couldn't get himself together. Then I noticed his head was starting to foam up because the stage lights were really hot. I felt like I was in one of those dreams where you're trying to run away and your legs won't work.

"Tom starts to sing and he's just slurring all the words. The audience starts yelling, *'Do fucking Led Zeppelin, man!' 'Yeah, play 'Stairway To Heaven!''* I lost it. I unplugged, gave the roadie my guitar and said, 'Put that to sleep and put Tommy to sleep. I'm outta here!' I left the club and spent the rest of the night lying on the grass, cursing at the sky.

"The next day I got a hold of Tommy and I said, 'Look Tom, don't ever do that to me again!' I didn't yell at him in a malicious way. I did it in a very factual and honest way and he respected it. He said he was really sorry, he'd never do it again. It was as if he was testing me, 'How much can Reed take?' And when I still respected him, he really took to that."

Kailing says he felt brotherly to Tom, who often came across like a "wounded bird." "One night Tommy gave me the chills. He said, 'Yeah, Peter had the right idea.' I said, 'What was that?' He said, 'You know, leaving a note and hanging himself.' I said, 'That's not going to get you anywhere, Tom. Look where it got Peter. He'd give his right nut to be where you are today. He's not anywhere. He's in limbo somewhere. Do you wanna be there?' You had to be a little philosophical with Tommy. But I was scared, because he was literally contemplating suicide. I didn't leave his side much from that time on."

At Steve Craiter's insistence, Joey Molland finally decided to try and book gigs as Joey Molland & The Spare Parts, instead of Badfinger. But after awhile he found he couldn't get many shows lined up. Tommy's Badfinger tour was finishing up in late December. Says Craiter, "Joey just said 'fuck it' one day and went back to calling it Badfinger."

Joey brought in Bob Evans, the ex-Straight Up member. Craiter alleges it was because Joey felt he was good at scrounging up bookings. But Bob Evans was dropped after a few shows. Craiter, who was now drumming in Joey's band, claims some of the shows they received were originally meant for Tom's "Badfinger."

Joey's Badfinger:
Dave Simpson, Steve Craiter, Joey Molland, Skip Coverdale, Andrew Russell

Joey's "Badfinger" played mostly the southern part of the United States throughout January and the early part of February, 1983.

Tom spent January of that year writing new material. One day late in the month, he was interviewed at his home in Surrey by Glenn A. Baker, a prominent Australian journalist. Tom told him he was writing songs with Frankie Miller (for one of Miller's solo albums) and prospective tunes were also being aimed at Joe Cocker. As it was, producer Chris Thomas was impressed by Tom's material and he reportedly made some offers to help Tom around this time. Also, according to Spencer Davis of "Keep On Running" fame, Tom's material was being pushed to him by a publishing agent named Alan MacDougall.

A local Minneapolis musician named Al Wodtke had met Tom and Bob during their previous U.S. tour. They had complained to him about their situation and Wodtke wanted to help. Wodtke recalls, "I knew this guy in Minneapolis named Don Powell, who had once managed Stevie Wonder. He was successful in the auto industry and was still managing groups. I went to him and he turned out to be a big fan of Badfinger's music. He became quite interested in doing something. I contacted Tom and eventually Powell, a guy named Paul Moe, and I, all went over to London to meet with Tommy and Bob to discuss a deal."

Bob Jackson continues, "They came to meet at this hotel in London, this swanky hotel. They had brought over all these contracts. We were very wary. We really didn't want to sign the terms and conditions they had laid out. We went back and forth with them. It really wasn't getting sorted out and they left. But Tommy phoned me one day and said he'd signed his contract and sent it off. I think Tommy got a little desperate to get some money. He jumped the gun. That put me in a bad position. But like a lot of these situations, I gambled and signed my copy too."

The deal encompassed an advance, studio time, payment upon completion of demos, and a promotional video. All this was in line with getting a record deal. Tom and Bob had figured they could do the recordings in Minneapolis, and then go out for the Koshick tour that spring.

They came to the U.S. in February of 1983. Al Wodtke recalls, "Things started out innocently enough. We did the backing tracks for the recordings. Everything was going smoothly, the rapport with the producer was fine; he liked Tommy. But when it came time to do the solos we had a terrible time finding anyone to do them. No one had the feel."

Bob Jackson: "Powell and Moe had claimed to have these crack musicians. They brought this guitarist in, but he had no sense of melody. We'd already been through two others and Powell said, 'Wait 'til you hear this guy!' We told him we'd play the song a few times so he could get a feel for the track. As soon as we put it on the chap said, 'Turn it up! Turn It Up!' He looked into the sky and blew all over the track. We went through it again and he did the same thing. Powell said, 'This is going great, isn't it?'

"Then Powell brings in this guy to put on a string arrangement. He had been bragging about Quincy Jones and how he'd like to do the same quality of an arrangement. The guy he brings in starts holding down chords on some cheap synthesizer. It wasn't a sympathetic part. It was like, 'Damn, is this what we're stuck working with!?'

"We went out to this club after the session and had a couple of drinks. I said to Tommy, 'This is crap, Tom.' He agreed with me. The managers were in another corner of the bar and he went over to them and said, 'Did you hear what Bob said?' They said, 'What?' He said, 'Tell them what you said, Bob.' So I did. I said I wasn't happy with the production or the quality of the musicians they were bringing in. They had wanted to call the project Goodfinger and I said that was crap, too. I just laid it all out. Well, Don Powell said, 'I think you ought to go then, Bob.' I said, 'You're right. I think I should just go back to England.'

"We were in the car later and I broke down. With all we'd been going through, we had a lot banking on this, and it just hit me how it had all gone wrong again. I think my reaction was a cry for help. I was hoping they'd react, 'Well, lets talk about this and put it right.' Instead, they said, 'Fuck off and leave then.'

"They dropped Tom and I off, and Tom said to me, 'Bob, you made your bed. Now I don't know what to do. I need the money and you need the money and you blew it.' A little while later the managers came back and took Tom away. He didn't come back all night. In the morning the managers picked me up and took me to their office. I was in a terrible state.

Al Wodtke recalls, "I happened to be at Powell and Moe's office when they had Bob in there. They were saying, 'Look Bob, we'll give you your money and a plane ticket home. Just sign this release for all of your songs.' I grabbed the paper right out of Bob's hand and started screaming. I was beside myself because they were trying to rip him off. It was the most blatant thing I'd ever seen in my life. For them to steal his stuff for a plane ticket home. Let's just say it was a good thing I was there, because Bob looked like he was going to sign. He was not in a good state."

Jackson finishes, "They told me they were taking me to the airport. I called my wife and went and got my stuff at the apartment. I was hoping Tom would be there, but he wasn't. They dropped me off about ninety minutes before my flight was to take off. I sat there and thought to myself, 'Bob, you've been a fool.' I called Paul Moe, who I thought was more sympathetic, and I said, 'Look, I'm really sorry. I feel I can finish the tracks and do a good job. I'll do my best. I'll be a good boy. Can you give me a chance?' He talked to Powell, who wasn't very keen, but they did come minutes before I was getting on the plane. Later on I found out Tommy had been running all over the airport trying to find me."

The plan had been to finish five songs, but with things behind schedule, only four tracks were completed. Three weeks had been scheduled for rehearsal, pre-production, recording, mixing, and a video shoot. It was a hectic time and Tom was reportedly showing signs of great depression.

Wodtke recalls an incident, "Tom and Bob were staying at the Cedar Riverside Apartments, which is a thirty story building that houses a lot of college students. One time I was visiting them on the fourteenth floor and we were all talking about the good old days. Tom had been drinking and the conversation became more bitter and angry and despondent. Tom was talking about Pete. He said, 'That fucking cunt! Why did he do this? Why did he do this to me?' He was sobbing. He went over his last night with Pete. He thought Pete didn't really want to do it, that he might have changed his mind at the last moment, because of the way his body was found. He walked out to the balcony and I was frightened. There was no doubt in my mind he was contemplating jumping. I got this overwhelming feeling. I went outside and hugged him. The next day he had another bout, but after that he was fine. He apologized to everybody."

Goodfinger video shoot, 1983,
Bob Jackson, Dan Grenier, Al Wodtke, Greg Gehring, Tom Evans

Early in March, Bob and Tom came back to England. "We'd finished the tracks," says Bob, "but proper mixes weren't done. The packaging was terrible. We did this performance video; it was lousy. And they did call the project Goodfinger."

The demo package consisted of four songs. Despite pedestrian production, the strong melodies shine through. Bob's "I Won't Forget You" and Tom's "You And I," were the standout, commercially-oriented songs, yet they were placed third and fourth on the tapes.

All along, Reed Kailing had been standing by, hoping to get on the road again with Badfinger. "After our 1982 tour, Tommy and I had talked, and we'd agreed to try and do another one together. But I told him Donnie Dacus and I had compromised our wages before and we'd like to do it for more money this time. Tommy said, 'Fine, no problem.' He called me back later and said, 'Koshick says we lost money on the last tour and you're gonna have to do it again for *less* money.' I told him, 'Look, Jack's responsible for the money, not you. I can't do that.' Tommy told me there were some problems with some of the promoters who had wanted our band back. They were confused because Joey had been going around with pick-up bands, demeaning the name of Badfinger. . . ."

Tom was getting furious about Joey's actions. Towards the end of Tom's stay in Minnesota he had seen Joey, whose family had, coincidentally, relocated to Kathie's hometown of Minneapolis. Joey had come there after ending his Badfinger tour in late February, 1983. Wodtke recalls, "One day Tommy asked me to drive him over to see the Mollands. We got to their house and it was obvious there was great deal of tension between them. It wasn't a comfortable situation. They went off to talk." [Tom Evans/Steve Craiter phone call – May, 1983]

Eventually, Joey returned to Florida. He got in touch with one of the agents who had been booking some of his live dates, Hugh Rogers. "Rogers made a phone call," said Joey, "and this fellow named Don Perry flew down to meet me. He was just getting involved with a new label and he offered me a solo deal. I jumped at it."

The label was called Earthtone Records. Don Perry first asked Joey to produce a band he was involved with called Money. Almost immediately, Joey came to Columbus, Ohio to work on their album. After arriving he saw a poster for a Badfinger concert being promoted by Bent Back Records. Joey called the promoter of the show, a record store owner, and convinced him to cancel the gig, which was part of the tour being set up for Tommy's band. Shortly after, Jack Koshick decided to temporarily cancel Tom and Bob's prospective new Badfinger tour. It simply wasn't coming together.

That spring and summer the Goodfinger demo trickled around. Bob remembers his and Tom's discouragement, "Powell and Moe hadn't tried very hard to sell the project. Powell told us he would ring people up and if they didn't return the call, he wouldn't try a second time." Wodtke adds, "Powell gave Paul Moe the tapes to shop. I'd wanted Powell to do the legwork. He came across like a CEO. Moe is the one who called it Goodfinger. He liked to walk in offices and demand people listen to him. It turned them off."

While in Minnesota, Bob and Tom had come up with a lawyer to help with the Cass lawsuits, but he was let go around mid-summer. They had previously procured Mike Kulkoski, while they were in Wisconsin, and he was rehired in July. At one point, Mike Gibbins had found his own separate representative. All this maneuvering served to slow down the suit's progress.

Joey spent the spring, summer, and early fall of 1983 working on his solo album. He was now living with Kathie and their two sons in Westerville, Ohio. He recorded the LP in nearby Columbus. The eventual results of his self-produced proceedings turned out to have some weaknesses. Joey's vocals often have little strength behind them. A lot of the guitar performances and guitar sounds are surprisingly insubstantial. On the positive side, Joey continued his mastery of writing strong, tangible material, including one gem of a song, the beautiful "Inside My Heart." There's also some deft arranging by him; solid, professional backing from the

Columbus group, Money, and a well-programmed feel to the record. Overall, the resulting album, *After The Pearl*, does rate worth seeking.

Continuously during this time, Jack Koshick had been trying to get another tour going for Tom's Badfinger. Bob Jackson recalls, "Tommy told me he wanted Tony Kaye in. Tony plays keyboards like I do, so it was a bit weird. But Tommy said, 'I want him in. He's a really good guy.' "

Tom had occasionally been meeting up with Kaye, who was in England doing sessions for the Yes album *90125*. "There was a bit of 'faffing' going on there," said Kaye, "so I had time to go over and do this tour with Tommy." They recruited guitarist Glenn Sherba and he found them a drummer, Lenny Campanero.

On August 19, 1983, Tom had a phone conversation with Steve Craiter (who had played drums for Joey's "Badfinger" band earlier in the year). Craiter had recently sued Joey, as had several other musicians, for a number of unpaid debts. Craiter taped the call. Tom's venom is unrestrained:

> *I really have a vendetta against Joey Molland right now . . . Joey is following the agents and phoning the different gigs and saying this is not the real Badfinger . . . [Joey's] gone too far . . . He's done a lot of things . . . He broke the fucking Badfinger band up. . . .*

Craiter was caught off guard by Tom's intensity. He tried to be upbeat, but Tom constantly rambled:

> *It takes an awful lot to get me pissed off. He's pissed me off! . . . He's suing me for the Apple money from 'Without You . . .' Bastard! . . .They're all trying to sue me now . . . They want the money from 'Without You. . . .'*

Joey Molland, 1983

(Joey's) trying to stop me all of the time and he was a good friend of mine. I'm just trying to get a good road situation going . . . just trying to give people a good show . . . I don't believe what he's been doing . . . It's over between him and me . . . I'm gonna give him death from now on. Watch what happens. Watch how I do it . . . .

You can sense Tom's agony and confusion over what he perceives is betrayal from his one-time good mate, as he even compliments Joey at times. At a certain point, Tom says, "You know why Peter died? Kathie. Bill Collins . . ." before quickly pulling back. When Steve Craiter asks him if he was going to tour again, Tom's voice cracks, as he painfully exclaims, "No, I'm next to dying basically. Because this guy is giving me so much shit. . . ."

Tom Evans sounded a broken man. {Tom Evans/Steve Craiter phone call – August 19, 1983}

During the summer of 1983, Tom had been occasionally writing new songs. He'd also been spending a lot of time hanging out with friends and neighbors. Rod recalls, "Anyone who had a bit of character, Tom would hang with. It didn't matter if they were a plumber, or a postman, or a railway worker. Tom Evans liked regular people. He had a neighbor who owned an electric train and he would spend hours with that guy, playing with the trains. He was very happy just to do that."

Tom and Rod occasionally made demos. They had built up a solid collection over the years. "A Step From Heaven" was one of their more coverable tunes. They had other punchy numbers: "I Don't Know Why," "The Rain," and "Stolen Love," all of which sounded great with Tom singing them. Then came the exceptional, "Over You," a song which Tom wrote for his wife, Marianne.

Tom and Marianne had been together since the early 70s. They'd been through the highs and lows of Tom's career. They'd weathered rough financial times. They'd raised a child. But despite their many years of sharing and caring, their relationship had often been turbulent and troubled. Tom's mood swings, addictive nature, and careless spending habits made him very difficult at times. He would readily admit he was "impossible" to his friends, but he was more than defensive when dealing directly with Marianne.

Marianne: "Tom would say things like I was 'boring,' because I wouldn't party as much as he would . . ." Tom was also not faithful, and Marianne was well aware of it. But as Tom told many people, "All the songs I write are about her." Rod adds, "Tom's one true love in life *was* Marianne. And he was absolutely crazy about his kid, Stephen. But Tom's problems simply overwhelmed him. . . ."

On August 28, 1983, Tom went to see a doctor. The doctor's report stated that Tom was drinking heavily, sleeping poorly, and was extremely anxious because of marital problems. He was given a prescription for a sedative. Around this time, Tom picked up his acoustic guitar and wrote the song entitled "Over You."

Marianne, Tom, Stephen

The love we had, still my concern
Why did it die? How did it burn? . . .
I'll get you back, I think you know
It's not over yet, that's all I know . . .
I'm not over you, I'm not over you. . . .

Tom went to Rod's house and laid it down; his voice on edge. Rod was impressed. This song could make waves. It was heart-wrenching, clearly one of the most deeply-felt numbers Tom had ever written. But this rendition would be hard to top. Tom had captured his rawest, truest feelings, and put them down for posterity. But would anyone ever hear his outpouring? {Over You - demo}

Jack Koshick had finally been able to set-up a Badfinger tour for the fall of 1983. In September, Tom and four other musicians set out to play the U.S. They soon found they got along fantastically. Drummer Lenny Campanero said, "That was the most fun I ever had with a band on the road. It was the only band where within an hour of arriving at the hotel, everyone would get together in a room for a game of poker, or we'd all go out together. It was just great."

Audience tapes show them sounding decent, though occasionally loose. The gigs were hampered because guitarist Glenn Sherba had to play many of the dates with an injured hand. "I slammed it in a car door and had to play with two smashed fingers," he said.

Each member was given a chance to showcase. Bob sang his two songs from the Goodfinger demo. Sherba sang a new-wave number he'd written called "Modern Romance." Tony Kaye played a long keyboard introduction into "Crocadillo."

The gigs usually started with a tape played over the P.A. system of a bunch of drunken people singing along with a Frank Sinatra record. The jokes carried throughout. Sherba recalls, "One time we bought this inflatable Hulk suit and Bob put it on under his clothes. We inflated the suit while he was performing "I Won't Forget You." For the next number he was supposed to come out to play guitar and sing "No Matter What." But we couldn't get the suit deflated!"

The group talked about staying together. Tom even allowed for contemplation of an "oldies" tour, anything to gather some money for recording. "Tom was looking for an angle," recalls Bob. "He said, 'I have to get in touch with McCartney.' He thought maybe he would help us."

Tom's mood was described as good at times, but at some point he became worried about his throat. He was having trouble hitting high notes. "He felt he was letting the band down," says Bob. "Then he started coughing up blood. . . ." Tony

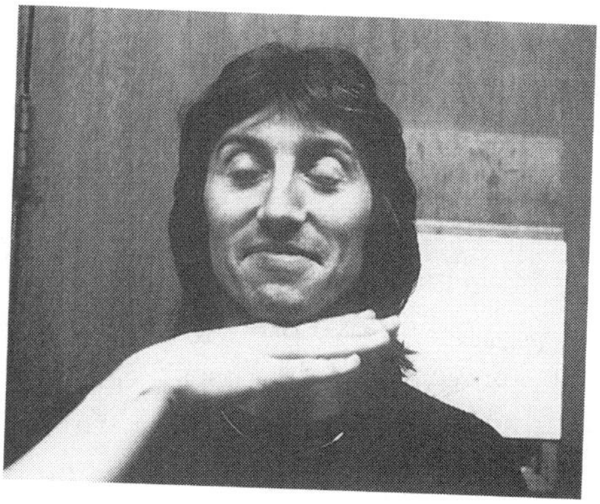

Badfinger on tour, 1983

Kaye says Tom eventually became "very depressed. Just depressed about a lot of things. Being away from his wife and little boy was adding to his general confusion. I remember one day we went to a bar and Tommy left his wallet on the counter. It totally bummed him out. . . ."

Glenn Sherba: "I knew how much money Tom had because I had the same amount and it was nothing to get upset over. We chipped in as best we could and gave him some money. But he couldn't replace the personal items. . . ."

Bob Jackson: "It was all the money in his pocket, a couple of cards, pictures of Marianne and Stephen and everything. He was really, really crying. To him it was the end of the line."

When the band played New York City in October of 1983, Tom became thrust into his past. At one gig, May Pang showed up. Someone had told her they'd seen an advertisement for a Badfinger gig and she went down to the club as a surprise. "Tom couldn't believe I'd come," she says. "My book *Loving John* had just come out and gotten a lot of publicity. He said, 'You're famous now.' I said, 'Tom, this is May, your friend.' He said, 'You're right. You're right. You are a friend.' " Tom also ran into ex-Polley client Lou Christie, "I ran into Tom somewhere in Greenwich Village. It was a pretty friendly get-together. The conversation was, 'How have *you* survived all of this insanity?' "

Tom called ex-Polley partner, Stan Poses. "Tommy called my house and my wife answered," said Poses. "She said, 'Who's this?' He said, 'It's Tommy, from Badfinger.' He told her, 'I just wanted to say I always loved you, Stan, and the kids. I'm going to England soon and I won't be able to visit, but we'll have to get together and have a barbecue when I come back.' My wife told me about this when I got home from work."

The tour deteriorated. Says Bob Jackson, "The last two weeks we didn't have that many dates." The last show was an October gig at Lupo's Heartbreak Hotel in Providence, Rhode Island.

Another Badfinger friend from the early days appeared, Wayne Treiber. "I was really impressed," he says. "Tommy seemed extremely happy to see me. He came running across the room to give me a big hug. After the gig I went back to Tommy's hotel and hung out 'til four or five in the morning. He talked about doing a new album and putting some stuff together. He seemed so optimistic. . . ."

But after the tour ended, Tom became disconsolate. Tony Kaye had told Tom he was definitely going back into the Yes fold. The Cass suit was also still lingering. The tax man was calling round Tom's home. There were bills to pay. No money was coming in. "Tom felt his only way out of all the impending financial problems was to recover the Apple profits being withheld," says Kaye.

Badfinger, Lupo's Heartbreak Hotel, Providence, Rhode Island, 1983
Tony Kaye, Tom Evans, Glenn Sherba, Lenny Campanero, Bob Jackson

When Tom first returned to England he was turned on to a factory job, which he took in desperation. Just days after he started working, the place burned to the ground. "He blamed himself," says Rod Roach. "He thought he'd jinxed the place."

Shortly after, a White Hart regular named Alan Williams was seated with Tom at the pub's bar. Williams recalls: "Tom was really depressed. I said, 'Why don't you come over to the house for a drink?' He came over and sat down on my couch and said, 'I'm gonna kill myself.' Just like that. I said, 'No you're not. That's ridiculous.' He said, 'No, I'm gonna kill myself. I've bought a rope.' He said he had gotten one from Chandlers, a yachting supply store. He'd sussed it out, the exact length and diameter. He described the whole scenario. I was thinking, 'I've got to keep him alive. . . .'

"We ended up talking the whole night. Finally the sun came up and I said, 'Look Tom, it's a beautiful day. Let's go for a walk.' We went out and he was laughing and joking with people. He seemed better. We came back and he started talking about his son. I said, 'Bring him over for a good old English breakfast.' He went and got him and we all ate a big meal. But when they left that day, I was still really worried.

"The following day was a Sunday and I saw Tom at the pub. I came up to him and he said, 'I've thrown the rope!' I said, *'Alright! Good man! Yeah!'* "

May Evans

Tom's mother, May, came to visit Tom that November. She recalls, "Marianne was visiting in South Wales at the time. I was watching Stephen, and David's son, Ben. One day Tom went off with his friends, Jackie and Tony. They came back and Tom was in a good mood. He put a record on, put headphones on, and started to dance with a chair. He didn't know the sound was off in the room. We just watched him and had a good chuckle. It was a good time. Then he put on John Lennon's 'Imagine' and he became very quiet."

Jackie Friend recalls Tom came back to her house later that evening. "He had gotten this film, "Elephant Man" on private video. I cooked a meal and we all sat down to watch it. It's a sad picture and I cried, but Tommy, he cried almost all the way through it. We went to the pub and he couldn't shake it. I couldn't believe how much it affected him."

The next day, Tom went to the zoo with his mother, son, and nephew. May Evans recalls, "We first went to the House of Mirrors. We didn't have much money, so we let the kids go in alone. After a while, I got worried and I started standing at the door. The man kept telling me to get away. I said, 'Those are my grandchildren. I'm worried about their safety!' They came out and Tommy snapped at the man.

"Then, we went over to this cafe and Stephen really wanted some chips so he went up to the counter, but the man threw the chips away, right in front of him. Tommy got mad and the chap just laughed at him. . . .

"Later on, we went over to this slide where you go down on a mat. When the kids were going up, Stephen looked back at Tom. I said, 'Tom, why don't you help him. He looks frightened.' It was a windy day. So Tom started going up the slide to help Stephen and this woman yells, 'Hey, what are you doing? You've got to pay!' I said, 'He's only going up to help his little boy and then he'll come down.' Tom came down and said, 'I just don't know people, mum.' He looked so sad. He walked over to where the elephants were and stared at them. I went over to him and I said, 'What is it Tom? Is it because you don't have any money?' He said, 'No mum, it's okay, it's okay . . .' He barely touched his stew that night. I fed it to the ducks out back."

About the second week of November, Tom traveled to Bournemouth, a city in southern England, to visit with his brother. Jan, David's wife, recalls, "When Tom first came over he seemed to be in a good mood. He liked our house. He said he liked getting a break from everything." David and Tom went out for a drink. "Tom talked a lot about this John Cass thing," said David. "He'd been trying to laugh it off, but the guy was persistent. Tom was worried. He said the guy had threatened him physically. He said Cass wanted a lot of money. . . ."

Tom commiserated with his brother for hours. Jan Evans: "They came back and after dinner we all sat down and talked. Tom talked about Marianne, about his future. He became despondent. He said he couldn't do anything, except maybe go back on the road, or make a record. I tried to encourage him about maybe trying record production, because he had a track record and it seemed like a logical step. I suggested opening a restaurant because Marianne was a good cook, she might like that. We were trying to be encouraging, but he was negative. He was obviously troubled by this contract he had signed.

"When he went to bed he had these white tablets and he told me he needed them to get to sleep. It struck me as strange because of all the alcohol he'd had that night. The next morning I was expecting him to look like death, but he came out smiling and said it was the best sleep he'd had in years. But David was deathly ill.

Tom Evans

He wasn't used to drinking that much. Tom was worried about him. He said, 'Is he always like this?' I don't think he could comprehend someone getting that sick from that much alcohol, at least not what he was used to. He wanted David to see a doctor, but we called and the doctor said it was just the drink, he'd be alright.

"Tom and I went to the beach with my son and on the way he started mentioning some phone call he had to make. Once we got there he seemed to enjoy the beach. He was joking with these German girls, saying things in German and they were laughing. He swam way out for a really long time. I remember thinking it was strange. I think it crossed my mind, 'I wonder if he's coming back?' When he finally came in I suggested he stay a few more days and he said, 'No, I've got to go back for this phone call.' I can't remember if he was the one making it, but there was some mention that he might have to go back to America. He came back to our house, but he didn't stay for dinner. He said he had to go home."

Tom was clearly obsessed with the Cass lawsuit. "Tom would always tell me this Cass was a very nasty character," said Marianne.

Jack Koshick called Tom in mid-November and he said they discussed the Cass situation. "I reassured Tom it was a totally groundless suit, but he was still worried about it. He thought if he lost, he lost everything, his whole life. He told me he had just sent his lawyer some money and a note regarding Cass."

In the Cass management contract, Tom had assigned certain financial rights, including publishing and recording royalties for much of Tom's music, dating back to his earliest days. But Tom told his lawyer, Mike Kulkoski, he didn't know what he'd signed, as he'd been well under the influence of alcohol and drugs at the time. He hoped this would be consideration for a rescinding of the agreement. Kulkoski states, "Unfortunately, a lot of judges don't take kindly to that excuse. It's an argument that can backfire."

Because of the lawsuit, and his failure to pay some taxes, Tom was getting more and more nervous. "He seemed to think everything was going against him," says Marianne. "He was saying, 'They're going to take my house away. They'll take everything away. He couldn't see a way out.'"

From the time Tom had returned to England in late October he was phoning numerous people late at night. Marianne says this pattern had actually occurred off and on for years, "Tom would call people at three, four in the morning. Then he might call them right back, forgetting he'd *just* called. He'd say, 'I'm going to kill myself. . . .'"

Many of Tom's friends and acquaintances related late night phone calls during October and November of 1983. Often they could hardly understand Tom, as he would slur, or speak in very cryptic terms. They might try to get him to come over, but rarely would he show up. Rod Roach: "Over the past few years Tom had phoned

The White Hart pub

me many times in the wee hours of the morning. He would say in a real finished voice, 'I can't do it anymore . . . it's no good . . . I can't go on . . .' He would give me the impression that he might do something. I'd come over sometimes, but after a while, it didn't seem like anything would happen. It got exhausting for me."

In mid-November, a benefit was held at the White Hart pub. Rod and Tom were enlisted; joined by BBC Radio One DJ Mike Read and several other local musicians. Ex-Apple publishing man Terry Doran happened to stroll in with some friends. He recalls, "They had a little gig going on in the garden and I remember Tommy on the lawn, playing and singing. He looked as happy as could be. He was on top of the world. . . ."

When Tom was in his element – playing music, hanging with fellow musicians, relaxing at the pub - he was in heaven. But Tom was quite distressed at this time. His closest mate, Rod Roach, was about to move away. Rod recalls, "I was only going to be about thirty miles down the road, but Tom had made it clear he didn't want me to go. He wanted to have someone he could call who was five minutes away. He didn't have many people who really understood him. Tom had been telling me for a couple of weeks now, that he would help me move. But when the day came he said, 'I can't bring myself to help you. I'm sorry.' "

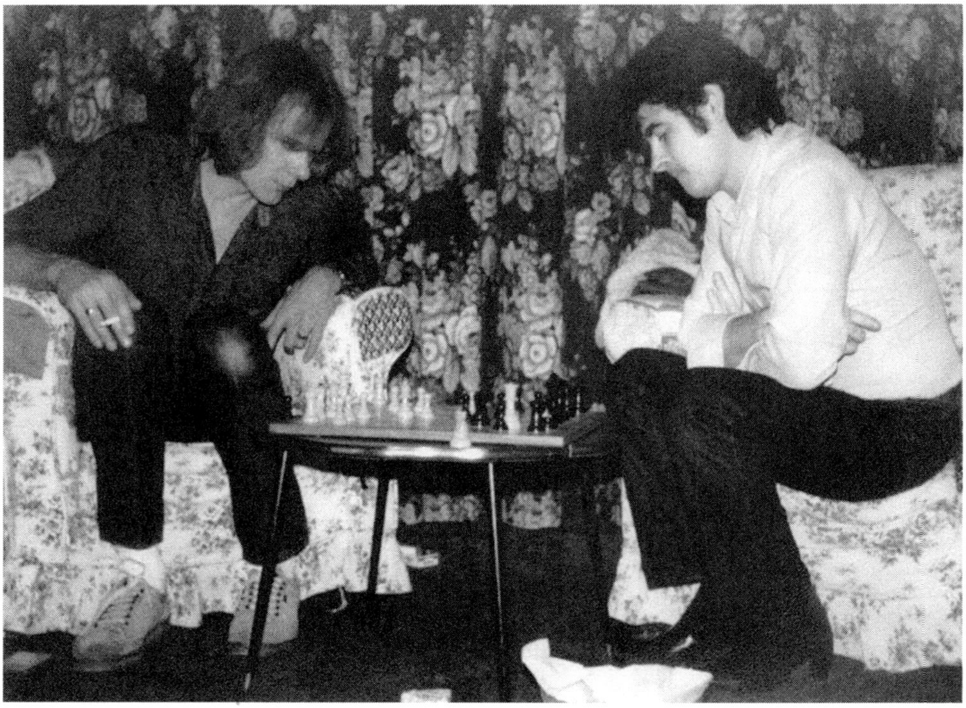

Rod Roach, Tom Evans, 1983

That same week, Wayne Treiber called Tom from the states to see how he was doing. "I was very surprised. Tom said everything had fallen apart. I asked him about Tony Kaye and he said he was doing his thing with Yes. He kept talking about Joey. . . ."

On November 17, 1983, Bob Jackson got a call from Tom, "He said to me, 'I want to carry on, but let's forget this Badfinger thing. It's not worth it anymore.' He started talking about working up something new through the clubs in England, and getting a deal. I said, 'That's all well and good Tom, but how are we going to get the P.A. together, the logistics of it, how are we gonna do it? The van, the roadies. We haven't got any money.' I remember he said, 'I'm going to get the money. I'll *get* the money.' I asked him if he wanted to stop by for a few days. He said, 'No, no. I've got to get this money together. I'll speak to you soon.' "

On November 18, 1983, Marianne had a friend coming over. Her name was Kerstin Lorenzen. Kerstin had known Marianne for over fifteen years. Kerstin arrived that afternoon, planning to stay for a few days. Tom greeted her warmly. That same evening, Tom and Marianne agreed to trade off watching Stephen, so each could go out to the pub. Tom went out first. Paul Wilson recalls seeing him at the White Hart. "Tom was sitting at a table with a bunch of regulars. They were playing a game with a *Who's Who Book of Hit Singles*. He was having a good old time. . . ."

After a couple of hours, Tom returned home. At one point, he and Marianne called Gaynor Gibbins, Mike's ex-wife. "It was my birthday," said Gaynor. "Tom comes on the phone singing 'Happy Birthday.' He said, 'Whatcha doin' tonight?' I said, 'Going out with my friends.' He said, 'I'll bet you look lovely.' I said, 'Of course I do . . .' He sounded really happy. He said, 'You go out and have a real good time. I'm telling you to.' "

Around 9:30 p.m., Tom, Marianne, and Kerstin, had a drink together. Marianne recalls, "We all shared a bottle of Cognac. I saw my friend slip Tom some pills, but I didn't say anything."

At 10:00 p.m. Tom called Joey in the states. Kerstin and Marianne went out to the pub, just as he was dialing. Joey recounted his conversation with Tom in *Beatlefan* magazine, *"Tommy called me from England. He was depressed that we couldn't sort the Apple thing out . . . I said, 'Tommy, there's nothing I can do about it, you know that.' And from that it went into this huge, long discussion about what was happening, and then we had a big fight. A massive argument on the phone. . . ."* In another interview, Joey expressed he told Tom the only way they were ever going to resolve this dispute was in court, and that's when the argument had really escalated.

Marianne and Kerstin got back from the pub about 11:00 p.m. and found Tom in a heated conversation. Around 11:30, Tom got off the phone, slamming it down. According to police statements taken from both women, Tom then declared, *'I'll be dead before I get the money!'*

Joey Molland,
Tom Evans

"It was a very nasty discussion they had," said Marianne. "I could hear Joey yelling all the way into the next room." She added that after the call was over, Tom stewed, then suddenly, ". . . he appeared more relaxed, more calm than he'd been in quite some time. He began playing his Everly Brothers records. He played his guitar. We sang songs. He even wrote the words down for me. He seemed to be having a great time. I went to bed at half past one. Tom was still downstairs playing his records."

The following morning, at 8:45 a.m., Marianne's friend, Kerstin Lorenzen, was awakened in her room by Stephen, then six years old. Kerstin recalled, "We both went down to the lounge and I happened to look out the French windows across to the rear garden. At first, I thought there was a man standing at the bottom of the garden. . . ."

In a panic, Kerstin raced into Marianne's bedroom. Marianne recalled, "Kerstin said, 'Where is Tommy?' I said, 'I don't know.' She said, 'I think he's hanging in the garden.' " Marianne ran downstairs to look. Recognizing Tom's clothing, she saw him, suspended from a backyard tree. . . .

Tony Kaye was in Los Angeles, "I had been sleeping and I woke in a cold sweat. I bolted upright. My wife was next to me and I said, 'Something terrible has happened and I think it's Tommy.' She said, 'No, no, you're just having a bad dream.' I said, 'No, I think something's happened.' Then Marianne called. . . ."

Marianne was in a frantic state. She told Tony what had happened. Kaye telephoned Joey, but Tony says he was so angry, he now can't remember what Joey and he discussed. According to Kathie Molland, Joey had "really let Tom have it" during the phone call, confronting Tom about many different issues from the past.

Kathie then called a few people herself. One of them was Beverley, Pete Ham's former girlfriend, who was now living in England. Beverley recalls, "Kathie comes on the phone saying, 'Tom's dead!' and I just freaked. I'd spoken to Tommy just a few days before. She said, 'Tom was shouting at us!' She was going on and on about money and contracts. Joey was in the background. 'Has she heard anything? Does she know anything?' She kept going on. I said, 'But Kathie, Tommy's dead!' Does any of that really matter? Tommy's dead!' She yelled, *'It was Tom's fault!'* I had to get off the phone. . . .' "

Al Wodtke was in Minneapolis. "Kathie called me and she was totally blase, like, 'Oh, by the way, Tommy's dead. . . .' " Wodtke contacted Bob Jackson, figuring he already knew. Said Bob, "I had woken up in the middle of the night in a panic. My wife, Christine, asked me what was wrong and I couldn't explain it. When I got that call from Al I was knocked for a six. I was very, very upset. . . ."

Tom's body was taken to a coroners office by mid-morning. That same afternoon, Marianne said she got a surprise visitor at her home. "It was Bill Collins. He said he had some money for me, but I had to sign something first. All those years he had been trying to get Tom to sign something. I refused to do it. . . ." (Bill Collins very strongly denies this ever happened).

By the afternoon, Marianne was being consoled by many people. The following day, Bob Jackson came down from Coventry. "I took the same train as I had when Pete died, took the same walk, down the same road, turning the other way at the final crossing. It was almost a total rerun. I can't tell you how much that upset me."

Marianne says there was quite a scene at her home, "People were coming in like leeches. I found out later I had some jewelry stolen. Some of Tom's tapes were taken. I lost a picture of Tom and Stephen. But I was in no condition to keep an eye on stuff. I was too heavily sedated."

Steve Craiter says he got a phone call at his home in Delaware. "It was Joey. He said, 'Tommy's dead' and I said, 'That's not a funny joke, Joey.' He said, 'Yeah, I was talking to him last night. We were talking about the Apple money and he was in great spirits. I don't understand it.' I asked him how he found out and he said Tony Kaye had called him. I called Tony Kaye and he said Marianne told him Joey and Tom had a terrible screaming fight on the telephone. It was nothing like Joey described it."

Drummer Pete Clarke (Clarkie) was informed of Tom's death by Tony Kaye. He said he was furious when he heard about Joey's conversation with Tom. He tried to reach the Mollands, but by now, their telephone had been disconnected. . . .

Kathie Molland, Joey Molland

Tom Evans body was cremated at the Woking crematorium in Surrey. There was a service held on November 25, 1983. Besides Tom's relatives and family, friends and acquaintances were there to pay their final respects. Beverley recalls, "Bill Collins was there. He was trying to talk to people and they were avoiding him. People were upset to see him. He stood away from the crowd. . . ."

Bob Jackson: "As I was leaving I heard these footsteps running at me. *'Bob! Bob!'* It was Bill Collins. He launched into this big thing, 'You know, Tom could be difficult. But it was nothing to do with me. I'm not saying we didn't have our disagreements, but I always looked out for what was best for him . . .' I wasn't saying anything. It was raining and we were getting soaked. He kept going on and on. I stood there for ten minutes while he went on this continuous monologue."

Afterwards, there was a gathering at Tom's house. "Music was being played," says Bob. "They played some of Tom's music. Marianne was doing pretty well, but near the end of the night she came over to me and began crying. I put my arms around her. . . ."

On December 1, 1983, an inquest was held in Chertsey, England. Marianne and her friend, Kerstin Lorenzen, had their previous police statements gone over, as did a reporting officer from the scene. Tom's alcohol levels were shown to be approximately three times the English legal driving limit. There was no suicide note left behind. Tim Boyle and Beverley's husband, Colin Tucker, did go through Tom's music notebooks to see if anything pertinent was written. Beverley says, "There was a lot of cryptic stuff, but nothing you could specifically tie to the event."

Tom's death did not get widely reported in the United States. Tom's local paper had a front page article, "Modest Star Mourned By Friends," in which several pub regulars were interviewed. Many British newspapers which did cover the story also made mention of Pete's suicide. But there were no statements from any of the record companies that had been affiliated with Badfinger. Weeks later, *Billboard* published a letter from Jeff Malack of Pennsylvania:

> *If anyone cares to flashback to early 1975 – when Pete Ham died at the end of a rope – they'll remember that this wonderful business we call rock'n'roll totally turned its back on the incident . . . In fact, the death of Ham produced nothing more than a single-column news item in Rolling Stone. I never saw a single line in Billboard mentioning his passing.*
>
> *Only a few brave souls dared to speak out against an insensitive music machine that's all too quick to hype its success stories, while sweeping its losses under the rug. Well, we lost another one and I'm mad as hell about it . . . Isn't it time that this industry begins to deal with artist burnout? It seems to me that the cost has become much too high.*

Former Stan Polley client, Al Kooper, said in 1994, "This issue is long overdue for the music business to address. They need to have their own Betty Ford type center for rock'n'roll. The new Hall Of Fame they're touting is full of people who are dead because no one would take care of them. There are a lot of Pete Hams and Tom Evans who could've been saved."

There were many factors bringing Tom Evans down near the end of his life. His bad throat condition was one. Many people theorized it could have been key in his decision. But Tom's mother, May Evans, says he'd had it checked. "I had told Tommy singers get nodules. I told him not to worry about it. He got tested and they weren't malignant." (The autopsy had reported a "white tumor mass seriously occluding the esophagus. . . .")

Marianne Evans still has a hard time believing Tom actually made the ultimate decision to take his own life. "After all the threats and years of depression I never really thought he'd do it. The doctor blamed it on his alcoholism. . . ." Rod Roach said he also remains surprised, "I always thought Tom's strength of character would carry him through. Just before he died he was calling everybody up. But he didn't call me. I had called him a few days after I moved and said, 'Hey, it's not all bad. I'll still come around,' but he barely responded."

One of the more unusual aspects surrounding Tom's death was the fact he was so happy shortly before taking his life. But Beverley wonders if there was a reason for this, "Some people say when a person finally decides to commit suicide they can become very blissful, because in their mind they've found the solution to their problems. It's ironic that Tom was like that, because when Pete died, Tom had made a point of Pete's great mood his last night. . . ."

Bob Jackson: "The thing that will always bother me is Tom knew suicide was so ridiculous and ineffective. He *knew* that from Pete's situation. He knew how difficult it was for those left behind"

Tom's brother, David, relates, "The night before Tom died I had phoned him. I had felt bad about his visit to my house a few weeks earlier, because at one point I'd gotten upset with him. I'd accused him of patronizing me. He used to give me this 'big brother' attitude, which I hated. But I wanted to be positive now and encourage him. He had been worried about Stephen. So I told him on the phone, 'Don't worry. Whatever happens, your boy is going to be fine.' I told him to do whatever he felt he needed to do. I was trying to give him confidence. He really seemed to appreciate the call. He said, 'Yeah, thanks man. Thanks.' I felt really good about it. When I was told that he had died I was absolutely devastated. I thought he had taken what I said literally, as an okay to do what he did. I blamed myself for a very long time. . . ."

Over the years, there have been varying comments from fellow Badfinger members Joey Molland and Mike Gibbins on Tom. Mike has expressed his anger of his former friend many times over, criticizing Tom in virtually every aspect of his being. In 1991, he softened slightly when he told journalist Conrad Atkin, "That man was sad, man. He was brain damaged . . . never happy and always left you with a sad feeling . . . The day before he died he was so sick I slammed the phone down on him. I can't remember what he said to me, but it must have been sad . . . He's like Keith Moon . . . If, if the band had kept going and made millions upon millions, Tommy would have died anyway. He would have partied himself into the ground. . . . But you've got to love him. He got into it 100 percent."

Joey Molland has often praised Tom for his musical abilities, but he has trouble resolving Tom's decision of suicide. In 1987, he discussed both Tom and Pete's deaths, "It is weird, man, that they just opted out like that. It really pisses me off. Those guys had everything to live for. Both of them. No excuses at all. I'm still very angry at them for doing it . . . These guys are making £25,000 a year in songwriting royalties without getting out of bed, you know what I mean? Give me a break."

Bill Collins came across as obsessed with Tom Evans, far more than the other Badfinger members. He definitely seemed to care for Tom – there was praise and a fatherly bond – but also a vividly apparent animosity, most of it relating to Bill's perception that Tom was continually plotting to have Bill let go.

Countless local residents of New Haw, Weybridge, and Addlestone commented on their great sadness over Tom's death. Jack and Marge Tidbury, who owned the local White Hart pub for over twenty-five years, praised him highly. Their two teenage sons grew up helping on the premises and were very close to Tom. One wrote a poem in remembrance, "*Many hours spent with you, extreme sadness and mirth . . .*" A tree was planted in Tom's honor near the pub's back patio. It still stands today.

Most people who knew Tom paid him a very positive tribute. Beverley spoke of Tom's true devotion as a friend. Producer David Malloy talked of Tom's great influence on his career, and their many enjoyable outings together. Joe Tansin related how he still misses Tom, despite the over-the-top loyalty tests he'd been put through.

Al Wodtke said that Tom made a deep impact on him, too, despite the short time they'd known each other. He recalls, "After Tom had left Minnesota in early

1983, he used to call me all the time from England. He was a big fan of 'Monty Python' and we'd talk about the show for hours. I really connected with Tom. I remember one time when we were rehearsing in Minneapolis, it was just the two of us in a rehearsal room, and I started playing his Iveys song "Maybe Tomorrow." I started singing it and he just took it over. He was singing it, putting his whole heart into it. And the whole time tears were streaming down his face. . . ."

Many musicians, friends, and acquaintances reminisced about Tom's sensitivity and talent. Tony Kaye summed him up best: "Tommy was that man on the cover of *Say No More*. That look in the distance, the poet or painter who suffers to do his masterpiece. It was all suffering for Tommy.

"When he stayed at my apartment, sleeping on my couch, I'd come out of my room at night and he'd be hunched over a strong pot of coffee, smoking countless cigarettes, working on lyrics – totally somewhere else. That was the real Tommy Evans. Tommy wasn't pretending to be an artist. He *was* an artist."

No doubt, Tom Evans' life had been strongly affected by his relationship with Pete Ham. Yet, Tom rarely discussed Pete in interviews, as he seemed to find the subject too painful. He could be heard breaking up on several occasions. He might describe Pete as "hardworking," "determined," "stubborn," "a hell of a nice bloke," but never in much detail.

During Tom's last touring in 1983, he began to bring up Pete's name onstage more often. He now had his band playing "Without You," but, instead of the earlier *No Dice* LP approach, the song was performed closer to Harry Nilsson's studio arrangement. Tom sang it with more melodrama and angst than he ever had before; his anguish seemed obvious.

Said Rod Roach, "Tom felt Pete had been his best friend in the world. But he also had some guilt about Pete's death. It would come out when he was drunk. He would go to pieces. I think the way he chose to do it was a symbol, a symbol of his grief for Peter."

As Pete had done, Tom would sometimes burn his hands with cigarettes. And Tom used to tell people he and Pete "loved each other;" that he was Pete's "silent partner." Tony Kaye remembers Tom being haunted by his memories, "In deeper, darker moments Tom would say, 'I was there. I saw it.' He'd keep repeating himself."

For Marianne, the deaths of Pete and Tom are doubly tragic. "It makes me so sad," she says, "how it all evolved. Tommy and Pete, such close friends. Pete half a mile away . . . two close friends. And then Pete died and Tommy didn't have anybody he could talk to, write songs, his other half was gone. He felt lost and lonely. Many times he said, 'I want to be where he is.' Many times. . . ."

Thomas Evans

June 5, 1947 – November 19, 1983

Afterword

On May 15, 1995, the twelfth annual ASCAP Pop Music Awards were scheduled to be held at the Beverly Hilton Hotel in Beverly Hills, California. It was now more than eleven and a half years since Tom Evans had died. His widow, Marianne Evans, was in one of the hotel suites, waiting for the affair to start. She had flown in from Germany with her son, Stephen, then nineteen years old. As heirs of Tom Evans, they were there to receive a special presentation.

In 1994, Mariah Carey had brought "Without You" renewed attention through her highly successful adaptation. As a result, it had become one of the fifty most played and performed songs of the past year by an ASCAP affiliated writer. Carey's version even outsold Harry Nilsson's smash hit of the early 70s. ASCAP was now giving out plaques acknowledging "songwriter" accomplishments. Others to receive similar honors were: Bruce Springsteen, Jackson Browne, Phil Collins, Bryan Adams, and Van Morrison.

As it was, Marianne and Stephen Evans were also due to attend the prestigious Ivor Novello Awards in London a few days later, as "Without You" had been nominated for "Song Of The Year," an award it had previously won in 1972. But neither Marianne nor Stephen were particularly enjoying themselves since arriving in California. Their anger had been burning for weeks now. For "Without You" was not being honored simply as an Evans/Ham co-write, five people were scheduled to receive composer acknowledgment: William Daniel Collins, Thomas Evans, Michael George Gibbins, Peter William Ham, and Joseph Charles Molland!

When Marianne had first been informed, she could not believe it. But "there it was" she was told, all five were listed in the ASCAP computers as "co-writers" of the song. This upset her. She became even more infuriated when Bill Collins and Joey Molland contacted her about their intentions to appear and accept their awards. She asked ASCAP to straighten out the situation, but an ASCAP representative said it was too late, "the show must go on."

On the Pete Ham side, his daughter Petera Ham, now twenty, had also been keen to attend. But when she got news of the others sharing in her father's accomplishment, she became disappointed. "It wasn't right," she explained, that these men were willing to take credit for co-composing her father's most renowned work, a number he'd written with Tom Evans. Petera chose not to attend.

But Marianne Evans was determined. She planned to step up to the podium and explain who had actually written the song. But the organizers from ASCAP had told her, "no speeches will be allowed."

Petera Ham, 1994

Eventually Marianne and Stephen came down from their hotel room on the evening of the ceremonies. "Bill Collins was there," explained Marianne. "He was going around telling people he did have a part in writing the song. It made me really angry. And Joey also insisted he had a part in writing the song, too. My son was furious, but what could he do?"

For Mike Gibbins, the situation was difficult. After all the pain of the group's past, he felt proud to share a positive moment with his wife, Ellie; and to celebrate the song's success. Said Marianne, "At least Mike admitted to me he didn't have anything to do with writing the song. And he was very nice to my son. I really did appreciate that."

After the serving of cocktails and dinner; live performances were done by Peter Frampton and the duo of Lieber & Stoller. Then, various ASCAP awards were handed out. Early on, "Without You" was acknowledged. Marianne: "When the big screen came on and it said the writers of 'Without You' are Bill Collins, Joey Molland . . . I nearly fainted. I had been hoping until the last minute they would get it right."

Harold Bronson, President of Rhino Records, was also attending that night. His company had put out a CD compilation of Badfinger in 1990, and he'd known all of the members and Bill Collins as far back as the early 70s. "I'd been thinking about going over to say 'Hello,' but when the two surviving members and Bill went up to collect awards for writing "Without You," I was taken aback. I was thinking, 'Are they robbing the grave here?' "

Marianne sent Stephen onstage to get Tom's award. With him were Collins, Gibbins, Molland, and representatives from the song's administrating publisher, Warner/Chappell. After Joey received his plaque he stepped forward from the pack and held up his award, drawing a big applause. Photographers flashed his picture. "I was incensed," said Marianne. "This was the only pride my son had, to go and pick up an award for his dad. They'd ruined it for the children. . . ."

ASCAP Pop Music Awards,
Beverly Hills, California, May 15, 1995
Bill Collins, Stephen Evans, Joey Molland, Mike Gibbins, ASCAP presenters

---

On September 24, 1985, almost ten years prior to the ASCAP awards show, and nearly two years after Tom Evans died, an interpleader proceeding had been held to sort out aspects of the ongoing financial controversy of Badfinger. Appearing at the London High Court of Justice, Queen's Bench Division, were a battery of lawyers, barristers, clients, and other interested parties. Marianne Evans showed on behalf of Tom Evans' estate. Anne was there representing Pete's side. Bill Collins, Joey Molland, and Mike Gibbins came for themselves. But there was no sign of Stan Polley. A lawyer for the Pete Ham estate, Tim Douglas-Jones, explains, "Polley got a settlement earlier, based on the Apple sales royalties that were left over. I don't think he was accounted for on any of the publishing or ASCAP shares which had built up over the years."

Polley had settled for £15,750, but his non-pursuit of any publishing money *is* very surprising. Bill Collins thinks it was because Polley could no longer pay his lawyer at that point. One may wonder why he hadn't been sued by the Badfinger members for money he'd kept. Tim Douglas-Jones explains, "It was decided on our part not to pursue Polley, because the unaudited accounts he provided seemed to be papering over a lot of very wide cracks. The feeling was, money had fallen deep inside the cracks."

Joey, Bill, and Mike had pushed to get these "interpleader" proceedings going after Tom died. Joey explained, "We tried to get a court date and Bill Collins was holding out and holding out. We finally convinced him that if we didn't do this, nobody was ever going to get any money."

Both Anne and Marianne had been given advice that they risked losing large amounts in litigation fees if they continued to fight the others. Marianne recalls, "I didn't want to give in, but I had Stephen to take care of. Joey had nothing to lose. He was using Bill's lawyer."

The major dispute concerned the division of "publishing" and "writers share" income of Badfinger songs. For example, when a song is released commercially on a CD, on vinyl, in a movie, etc., it is considered "published," and the different incomes it makes are accounted for between the"publisher shares" and the "writer shares."

The "writers share" was originally set up to secure benefits for the actual writer(s) of a song. Granted, it can become a negotiable point in business dealings. It covers earnings for every performance of a song, be it live, over the radio, on television, for commercials; any possible presentation from which a fee can be collected. ASCAP is an American organization which monitors and collects from the various income sources for its affiliated songwriters. They then distribute the money to the parties they are specified to.

In a 1992 interview, Joey gave his slant on what he felt Badfinger's songwriting agreement was, "If any of us wrote a song, the writer would get 25% right off the top, and the remaining 75% would be split five ways . . . This agreement was made before we had any hits . . . It was only stuff that Badfinger recorded though. Say somebody comes along and picks up a song that Badfinger hadn't recorded. Well, the writer would get all the royalties for that."

As it came down, the interpretations continually varied amongst the involved Badfinger parties. There were constant discrepancies over what songs were to be considered, under what time frames, and who should even *be* considered. For example, Ron Griffiths had been a member of The Iveys throughout their existence. And all of The Iveys published material was being included in this settlement. Yet Ron hadn't even been told about these proceedings. Bill Collins represented to the court that Ron had no current rights to anything being considered, that Joey Molland had legally accrued Ron's financial position on The Iveys material and all the songs on *Magic Christian Music*. Griffiths recalls, "When I left the band in 1969, I had been told by Bill that I would get royalties from 'Come And Get It,' because I was on it. Time went on and the record became a big hit. Bill came to me and said, 'Look, here's a check, but you have to sign something to buy yourself out of the group.' I assumed it meant I was officially not a member of the band anymore, so that I wouldn't get any of their future royalties. It was later when Bill claimed that I had signed a paper giving away my rights to everything I'd worked on in the past. Even my own song, 'Dear Angie!' " I never got a copy of that paper, but I finally saw it years later, and it said nothing of the kind!"

Tim Douglas-Jones recalls that while he was waiting for these interpleader proceedings to start, "Bill Collins came up to me looking like some retiree from Haight-Ashbury – which he'd been too old for in the first place – and he says *'Your client owes me for a phone bill!'* Eleven years later and he was still crossed up because Pete Ham hadn't paid him for some phone bill. . . ."

Eventually the day's discussions began. Douglas-Jones: "Molland, Gibbins, and Collins were all sitting in the back of the room. Each of them with a solicitor, barrister, and leading counsel – you're talking £1,000 an hour here – and while everyone's trying to hack out an agreement, they're playing guitars, drinking a bottle of whiskey, and reliving old times. They were being a bloody nuisance!"

Nick Kanaar, Marianne Evans' lawyer, who had worked for Tom Evans from the mid-70s until his death, recalled his discussions with Tom, "He had very strong feelings that Bill Collins had taken advantage of the band. He considered he was being ripped off by Collins, especially on the song publishing. He never wanted to give in . . . But when Tom died it definitely made it easier for the others to forge ahead."

The lawyers eventually conferred for about an hour in the hallway, "We ended up doing a form of compromise," adds Kanaar. "It was very much guesstimate and horse-trading."

Finally the results came in:

1. Recording royalties	*– 20% to each group member and Collins*
2. Publishing royalties	*– 32.5% to writer(s), 67.5% (split five ways)*
3. ASCAP royalties	*– 25% writer(s), 75% (split five ways)*

A list of songs was drawn up to distinguish what specifically fell under this settlement, and *who* the actual writers of each song were. Included were all of the previously Apple published songs, a portion of the band's Warner Brothers published tunes, and a few obscure Iveys songs which had never been released. Interestingly, none of Pete and Tom's material published by Warner Brothers was listed here. This seemed to clarify that Molland, Collins, and Gibbins were primarily concerned with getting their cuts out of the big Apple hits of the past, as they let this potentially important documentation slip by without due attention.

Many issues had now played out. The biggest conflict had been the ASCAP income. The resolution seemed to uphold the argument that Joey, Bill, and Mike had claimed – that the group and Bill had previously agreed everyone should share in each other's "songwriting" income. Yet the 1972 meeting's minutes showed possible precedence that – if this was a valid agreement – it was only meant to exist while the band was still together. And being that it was to end on April 11, 1974, any such agreement would have to be renegotiated.

The 1972 meeting's minutes, with Polley and Poses present, stated the group and Bill would share in *"advances of any kind from any "Performing Rights Society. . . ."* with the splits as *"50%"* to the writer(s), with the other *"50%"* divided amongst the four members and Bill.

So why did Bill Collins, Joey Molland, and Mike Gibbins assert 25% goes to the writer(s), and the remaining 75% is split five ways?

In 1997, Bill claimed that Joey had come up with this proposed "songwriting income" idea during that 1972 meeting, which was around the time "Without You" was evolving as a big hit. Yet Bill claims the discussion made that day was incorrectly documented by Stan Poses. Bill also noted any agreements which may have made, were never drawn up legitimately or signed, thus nullifying any notion of a 50/50 division. Bill stands by the premise of the alleged, earlier, "25/75 verbal agreement" as his proof of his stance.

In 1980, a lawyer for Bill Collins was documented in court papers promoting the 50/50 division, and he used the 1972 "minutes" as his basis, but the lawyer also stated it related only to songs written, not necessarily *recorded* by the group?!

In 1980, Stan Polley's lawyer alleged Joey Molland signed some sort of reverification of a 50/50 split in 1974. Bob Jackson remembered Joey reciting a group songwriting agreement to him in 1974 as 50/50. Beverley Tucker says her diaries from the late 60's indicate a 50/50 division. Mike's ex-wife, Gaynor Gibbins, said the issue was well-acknowledged around the Park Avenue house, "Look, everyone who lived at Park Avenue knew what the agreement was, 50% to the writer and the rest was split five ways. Everyone used to talk about it all the time, 'There's no need to put it in writing because we all love and trust one another.' *Mistake number one!*"

Neither Beverley Tucker, Gaynor Gibbins, Bob Jackson, nor Ron Griffiths were asked to testify regarding their potential corroborating evidence.

In 1998, Mike Gibbins strongly insisted it was a 25/75 split for both the ASCAP *and* publishing royalties. Joey and Kathie Molland have consistently asserted the same premise. Bill Collins has said his diary can prove this, but he hasn't made any particular entries available to the public.

This overall Badfinger money dispute was obviously influenced by factors of "weak documentation," "vague documentation," and, in some cases, "no documentation." The sad outcome of all this does portray some clear business lessons for one to heed.

The final court settlement that day dictated that Pete and Tom's estates had to pay back all the recoverable ASCAP royalties they'd received in the past, which otherwise would have gone to Molland, Collins, and Gibbins. As it ended, Joey, Mike, and Bill were awarded about £90,000 each. The Pete and Tom's estates; about half as much. All lost a good chunk through their lawyer bills, except Joey, who was using Bill's lawyer, and according to Bill, as of June 2000, has yet to pay Bill back.

The bottom-line results certainly bore testimony to the advantage Joey, Bill, and Mike had. They were a three-to-two majority over Marianne and Anne regarding each and every issue. They were considered "first-hand providers" of information. The final agreed resolution of 32.5% vs. 25% on the "publisher's share" income was the one compromise of their original position. But Bill Collins says even that decision was unjustified for him. "I really should have gotten an equal 20% split on all the songwriting," he said "I was an equal member of The Iveys, a part of the team. In fact, *I wrote the first song we ever did*! But I never wanted it said that I made as much as the members of the band."

Joey later made this argument in regards to why he felt he deserved to get a part of the "writers share" of Pete and Tom's "Without You." "It made a lot of money. But Badfinger recorded that. Nilsson had heard it on our album. If we hadn't recorded it, he never would've heard it. . . ."

On October 21, 1985, the John Cass five-million-dollar lawsuit against Tom Evans was settled in a judge's chambers at a Milwaukee, Wisconsin courthouse. American booking agent Jack Koshick, and Alex Shliminoff, had come to assist lawyer Glen Kulkoski. Glen had taken over from his brother, Mike, to represent the estate of Tom Evans and Bob Jackson's side. Marianne Evans had basically no involvement. She said John Cass put relentless pressure on her, which broke down her mental capacity to fight. Bob Jackson had sent his last £300 to Kulkoski.

The focus that day became the management contract Tom had signed. It dictated that a multitude of potential incomes go to Cass, including potential Apple royalties. But Tom had signed under suspicious circumstances – a possibly induced cocaine and alcohol high. Tom claimed he had no idea what he'd signed.

Despite the fact this lawsuit was ludicrous to begin with, it was settled in chambers that Cass be granted fifteen to twenty percent of any future gross publishing income, ASCAP income, and the sales royalties of all of Tom's compositions from Badfinger's *Airwaves* album, their *Say No More* album, and some of Tom's unreleased songs.

Koshick said he and lawyer Glen Kulkoski agreed to this because the judge was refusing to toss the case out, so they reached the settlement with the thinking that the albums these songs came from were "dead in the water" anyway; in essence, Cass was going to get nothing. "We were simply trying to save a friend's family from future aggravation," said Koshick. "This guy was a bloodsucker and we wanted to put an end to it." The other part of the lawsuit, involving Bob Jackson, Tom Evans, Mike Gibbins, and the Cass "agent contract," was dropped.

Stan Polley had been marginally operating in the music business ever since Pete Ham's death. In 1983, he dropped his last artist client. That same year, he came across a gentleman named Peter Brock.

Brock worked in the automotive industry. He had been involved in one of the Corvette engine designs and was greatly respected in manufacturing circles. But in 1983 he was looking to tackle something new – the development of a motor for very tiny airplanes which could operate at extremely high altitudes. These specialized aircraft would potentially be used for reconnaissance type duties by the military or secret service.

He started a company to develop his ideas called Ultra Light Products. At some point in 1983, he needed additional capital to expand. Brock was then situated in Temecula, California, and he was introduced to Stan Polley. Brock was very eager to get moving. Polley told him he could help. Polley didn't have the cash, but he suggested that, if Brock agreed to give him 50% of the stock in the Ultra Light company, he would see what he could do. An agreement was struck between Brock, Polley, and some minority partners.

After about six months, Polley had failed to come up with anything. But he had a new idea. Polley suggested that he and Brock start a joint company. Polley claimed that with his contacts in the music industry, he could scout talent who needed cash, and he and Brock could loan these artists money in exchange for their potentially-valuable music copyrights. Stan suggested calling the business The Polleybrock Corp.

But Polley had no start-up capital himself. He claimed his ex-wife's frequent attempts at civil actions kept him from having much money around. Polley tried to convince Brock to put up $350,000 in stocks and bonds Brock owned as the security for a line of credit. Polley wanted to draw from this credit to establish the Polleybrock company. Polley also suggested Brock be a "silent" partner. A deal was eventually struck. It was agreed Polley would take $2,500 a month for general business expenses.

After six months, however, Brock discovered that Polley had actually been taking out $5,000 a month, in addition to one lump sum of $25,000. Polley explained to Brock the business expenses were higher than he foresaw, and he'd fully intended to pay back the $25,000. Brock reminded him they had never had this type of consent between them.All along, Polley had been calling Brock about "other ventures." Brock was now irritated. He reminded Polley that he was only interested in the musical copyright angle, and if Stan couldn't get something happening soon, he was going to pull the plug.

Shortly after, on December 15, 1985, Brock received a letter from a First Credit Bank, thanking him for paying off a $250,000 loan. Brock had no knowledge of any such loan being made. When he asked Polley if he knew what this was about, Stan allegedly became evasive and irritable, stating the situation was too complicated to explain. He told Brock to contact their accountant to explain it. The accountant told Brock he had no idea what Polley was doing. Brock tried to obtain an accounting rundown of the Polleybrock Corp. He found it had to be done under another name. Polley had moved their company to be under the wing of a new "parent corporation" – Stan Polley Company Incorporated!

Brock was furious. He confronted Polley, demanding receipts. Polley claimed they were too voluminous and cumbersome to deal with. Polley began avoiding further calls. Shockingly, Brock soon found that his last $250,000 had been pulled out of his account.

Realizing he was now essentially broke, Brock could not even pay for a lawyer to go after Polley. He pleaded with the District Attorney's office in Riverside, California to take the case. They almost balked. However, after Brock did his own investigation, the D.A.'s office did a little preliminary work, and eventually, decided there was enough evidence to prosecute.

John Hansen, a detective for the Riverside D.A., started a serious investigation into Polley in late 1987. He was able to uncover a massive series of banking transactions. Polley had taken the $250,000 and maneuvered some loans, eventually routing all of the money into his Stan Polley Company Inc. Later, Polley branched part of the money into other certificates of deposit and a *new* company called White Bread. He followed that with the purchases of more certificates, all the while dispersing funds into many banks. Continually, he was co-mingling money from other sources. Hansen also found an FBI file on Polley.

At one point, Brock showed the D.A.'s office how Polley had taken Brock's signature and photocopied it onto a banking document he'd obtained. Brock had the original paper which did *not* have Polley's signature. This was very strong evidence. On September, 14, 1988 an arrest warrant was issued. Stan Polley was accused of "*. . . laundering stolen and embezzled money, through convoluted financial transactions . . . and grand theft of corporate funds.*" Shortly after Polley was put under arrest.

On February, 14, 1991, after delaying the trial for *two-and-one-half years* through pleas of ill health and lawyer finagling – and knowing there was overwhelming evidence staring him in the face – Stan Polley finally decided he had no choice but to plead guilty to all charges.

But Polley avoided a jail sentence. On his behalf, a doctor stated that incarceration would almost certainly cause Stan's premature death, due to a heart condition. On October 10, 1991, Stan Polley was put on five years probation and ordered to pay $250,000 in restitution.

A full year after the restitution judgment, Polley still had not paid a dime. Peter Brock was supposed to receive an initial $10,000 from Polley and $5,000 a month after that. Brock wrote a passionate letter to the Riverside court, pleading his hardship and disgust. He claimed that Polley had financed his defense through Brock's money, and was continuing to live in a beautiful home and drive a new Mercedes Benz, both of which Brock claimed were bought with his money. Nothing came of his plea.

Brock later commented, "Stan Polley destroyed my life. He destroyed my marriage. He destroyed my business. He destroyed my kid's education. He put me on the street – completely annihilated me financially . . . And he doesn't care. He has absolutely no feelings for what he did to me or my situation. . . ."

Eventually, Stan Polley had been forced into making minimal restitution; just $167 a month trickled to Peter Brock. Down the road that stopped, too. Whenever pursued about his assets, Polley claimed he was broke, suffers from very ill health, and is being persecuted. Allegedly, all his assets are in his new wife's name or company names, and he can not be legally attached.

The week following the 1995 ASCAP Awards ceremony, the event had been written up in *Billboard Magazine*. It featured the same credits of "five" writers for "Without You." Later, the publication acknowledged the error by placing a *For The Record* column which stated:

> ***The correct credit for "Without You" . . . should have read Peter William Ham and Thomas Evans . . . An incorrect credit appeared in the May 27 issue of Billboard due to inaccurate information provided by ASCAP."***

As of the year 2000, one can look up the ASCAP writer database on the Internet. It lists their affiliated songwriters, the writer's published songs, and the publishers of these songs. A disclaimer is shown which says the information *"has been supplied to ASCAP by various sources and ASCAP makes no representation as to its accuracy."*

In terms of the four main members of Badfinger, these records are a complete mess. For example, many of the Badfinger members' songs are credited as being composed collectively by "Collins, Evans, Gibbins, Ham, Molland." If you call ASCAP directly, to verify this, they will give you the same credits as listed in the database. And they will pretty much insist these are the correct songwriters, even if you bring up the discrepancies from the earlier Badfinger albums and 45s.

So how did the ASCAP writing credits for Badfinger get so fouled up? After the 1985 interpleader settlement hearing was completed, ASCAP asked for a clearer direction on how to pay out for each song affected by the settlement, and who actually wrote each song. Alas, who should be picked to supply the information on ASCAP forms? Bill Collins (according to Robert Press of Badfinger's English accounting firm, Goldblatt & Co.). The information Collins wrote in was either read exactly as he put it, or interpreted by ASCAP as changes from the previous songwriter credits. The other possibility is ASCAP have been negligent, and simply made errors in accounting for the songwriters. It is likely an audit will eventually be done to figure all this out.

This bureaucratic sloppiness has caused some "songwriter" credits to be documented incorrectly whenever Badfinger songs are covered by other artists. For example, the most common way for anyone covering a song, and needing to verify the writers – besides looking on vinyl, cassettes, CD's, or sheet music

– is to check with ASCAP or BMI (another performance rights organization). When the band, Lillian Axe, released their cover version of "No Matter What," in 1991, Bill Collins and the four Badfinger members were listed as the writers of the song, instead of just Pete Ham. There have been other errors on other CD titles – and probably more to come.

While the ASCAP organization was probably taken aback by the response to the "Without You" credits at their 1995 awards show, they have continued to wash their hands of any responsibility to rectify the situation, nor will they even acknowledge that this may be an issue which *should* be resolved. Yet ASCAP states in their World Wide Web site "*. . . our reason for being is to protect the rights of our members – their musical copyrights – and their right to be compensated. . . .* "

As of the year 2000, the publishing company Warner-Chappell works as the administrator of Badfinger's original Apple Music song copyrights. They, too, have passed the buck as far as straightening this situation out, basically taking the position this is not for them to take care of. They do have some very concerned employees, but no one seems to be able to do anything constructive.

Sometime in the early 90s, Mike Gibbins moved to Florida. He has found opportunities to play with other musicians, besides doing a little record production. In 1998, Mike released his first solo album, *A Place In Time*. The music was recorded at home. Mike's voice sounds somewhat Dylan-esque here. There are a lot of blues and early-70s progressive influences, but his melodic aspects are still intact, especially on the songs "Layaway" and "Time In." He intends to release another album of originals in the year 2000.

In the mid-90's, Kathie Molland published a "Badfinger" fan club newsletter. Kathie and Joey also disseminated information through *Good Day Sunshine*, a prominent Beatles fanzine. A "Badfinger" page in each issue explained what Joey was up to, kept notice to the Badfinger reissue product available, pushed Badfinger-related merchandise, and occasionally, Kathie editorialized.

In 1995, an "Official Badfinger" Internet Page was set-up on the World Wide Web. Joey and Kathie Molland contributed a lot of its material, thus the "Official" moniker. The Mollands encouraged people to E-mail in comments or questions. In early 1996, someone sent in an E-mail objecting to an "Official Badfinger" web page claim that Joey, Mike, and Bill had a part in writing "Without You." That claim (by Kathie) had been posted right after the uproar caused by Bill, Joey, and Mike appearing in Los Angeles to accept awards as co-writers of the song.

Through her "web page" response, Kathie Molland furthered her assertion. In her posted reply she had the e-mail portrayed, criticized the e-mailer, and then took unsolicited liberties to tear into the character of Tom Evans. Also, after hearing rumors that facts surrounding the 1985 settlement regarding Badfinger finances were going to be exposed, she discussed and defended the determined settlements. She stated the final publishing and ASCAP splits were what was originally agreed to by the band; that there was a "*signed agreement*" verifying these figures completed some time after Joey had joined.

Yet, through June of 2000, the only related "document" proven to have existed was the minutes taken of the 1972 band meeting in New York; the one which stated *different* percentage figures than what was eventually settled on, and one which cited a time limit – the agreement to end on April 11, 1974.

As far as any contentions that Bill, Mike, and Joey were actually involved in writing "Without You," there still exists Pete and Tom demos of the two songs which were joined together, plus Badfinger's band demo recorded prior to the group's first studio recording, not to mention Pete Ham's various lyric sheets portraying the germination of the song.

Kathie Molland, 1993

There is also a 1974 taped phone conversation featuring Pete Ham himself. Pete is asked who wrote "Without You." The topic was brought up because the *Son Of Dracula* soundtrack album had just been released. It included Nilsson's version of the song and it had songwriting credits listed as "Ham/Evans" on the rear jacket, but only "Evans" on the label copy (a misprint). Pete's reply to the query, "I wrote the verses, and Tommy wrote the chorus."

Usually, a song's "writer" determination is established as 50% of the content being the lyrics, and 50% being the prominent melody line. This criteria is often used to legally ascertain the credit. Sometimes contentions are made based on musical arrangements. Also, chord sequences or riffs made on keyboard, guitar, bass, or other instruments may be legally construed as part of the song's "writing." The considered split is sometimes 33.3% lyrics, 33.3% melody, and 33.3% chords.

When Badfinger recorded "Without You," Bill Collins said he helped Joey construct the "melody" of the intro guitar solo and lead break guitar solo. Bill uses this scenario to justify his claim to partial compositional credit for "Without You."

Since 1997, Joey has denied publicly that he had anything to do with writing the song, and says that he has never claimed he had any part in writing it. But he does consistently contend the song's studio creation was initiated by a brainstorming-together-by-the-band toward the end of the *No Dice* album sessions – when they needed something to fill out the record. However, Abbey Road Studio logs, master tapes, and personal diaries, show "Without You" was one of the first songs the group recorded for *No Dice*. Also, a version was demoed at 7 Park Avenue two months prior to the album being started. It was even recorded again, two weeks prior to the *No Dice* sessions, in a studio with Mal Evans producing.

As far as the concept of "communal group songwriting," the rock band REM are a good example of a collective unit which set out an early agreement to share equally in each others song credits and financial stake. But, obviously, some of REM's songs have parts written more by certain members than others. REM take it as far as listing every song as being written by "REM."

Badfinger, on the other hand, always listed who actually *wrote* each song on their albums and singles, except when Capitol Records credited "Badfinger" on the U.S. version of the *Ass* LP (presumably to cover a publishing conflict). Ultimately, REM's system has worked well in terms of their camaraderie. But for many groups, it simply does not, and the infighting and jealousies can destroy relationships. Semantic arguments can be made about songwriting. But, at some point, it often ends up going back to a legally defined position.

On January 16, 1997, a British primetime TV show called "Watchdog" put forward a six to seven minute vignette of what the producers considered to be an injustice, the acceptance of the ASCAP awards for "Without You" by Joey, Bill, and Mike. After some video shown of Mariah Carey, and a little sound excerpt of Nilsson singing the song, some background was given on Badfinger's history. Footage was shown of the actual ASCAP ceremonies, in which a beaming Molland gets his award and thrusts it in the air, followed by excerpts of an interview with him and Bill Collins. Beverley Tucker is then shown explaining the song's origins. Comments by Marianne Evans are also portrayed. Near the end, the narrator tells us Joey and Mike say they did not write the song, though Bill Collins still insists he and Mike were involved, somehow. According to the program's director, Jonathan Maitland, it was Kathie Molland who actually talked to him, not Joey, and she is the one who said that Joey admits to never having helped write the song.

In 1996, Kathie became involved with an Internet web site designer, Russ Anderson. He creates the "Official Badfinger" web site. Anderson stated on the page in May of 1997, *"We look forward to providing the Badfinger community a FORUM of TRUTH. Information on our pages is verified by Badfinger themselves and is CERTIFIED TRUE by those who were there in our history . . .,"* and he wrote in an email to this author in April of '97, *"I'm here to promote Badfinger . . . And to warn those that THIS IS the Badfinger site, with those who ARE Badfinger . . . WE have the proof, because WE ARE Badfinger. . . ."*

From 1998 through June of 2000, Kathie has put forth most of her "info" through another Badfinger website, whose webmaster states his major sources as "the Mollands." Kathie has also made occasional "guestbook" postings.

Joey Molland has continued playing gigs as "Badfinger" or "Joey Molland's Badfinger" since Tom Evans' death in 1983. Since 1991, he has led a rock trio. The performances have generally been Joey's solo work mixed with with varying amounts of Badfinger songs. He doesn't attempt to recreate Badfinger's signature sound, instead pushing an overall more taut, hard-rocking edge. Joey has made it clear he has desired to be a solo artist, but professed, as of the year 2000, he hasn't been able to get bookings under his own name. In May of 2000, one of Joey's handlers announced a five-piece "Badfinger" line-up was impending.

Joey did get a solo CD out in 1992, entitled *The Pilgrim*. His material again portrayed his consistent ability to write a gratifying rocker and skillful, plaintive ballad. Joey has always been a talented tunesmith. But in other aspects, *The Pilgrim*

Joey Molland onstage, 1991

CD fell frustratingly short. A strong negativity shows through on the first track, "You Make Me Sick," a message which defuses the good tune underneath. The guitar work, singing, and arranging often do not reach up to a majority of Joey's earlier efforts. It seems apparent Joey may need to team up with a strong-willed producer who can pry the depth and the great performances out of him. It is questionable if Joey's vocal chords are in good enough shape. In 1996, Crosstown Productions privately pressed a few hundred CD's and cassettes of some demos, labeling the package *Timeless*, by "Joey Molland's Badfinger." The melodies and hooky riffs are there, but Joey's voice sounded thrashed.

In 1995, a bizarre CD/cassette project was released by Eclipse Music Group entitled *Badfinger*. Included are ten versions of Badfinger songs sung by Joey Molland. The instruments are played by uncredited Nashville musicians. Featured are all of Badfinger's big hits and a further selection of, mostly, "Apple album" tracks. Joey admits he had no involvement with the music. The cover is Joey's face circa 1972.

In the late 90s, these songs were repackaged and reissued through two other CD labels, with the 1970-1974 version of the band represented each time on the cover. Thus, at times, this product is confused by potential buyers as a legitimate release of *original* Badfinger recordings. Joey stated this regarding the project in 1999, ". . . they offered me a chunk of change [$10,000], and said 'we'd like you to come and sing some Badfinger songs. Would you do it? I said 'no.' And then I thought for twenty-four hours. I said, 'okay, I'll do it.'. . . I flew down. I took the money and I sang the songs. I'm sorry if it offends anybody, but yes, I did it."

In 1999, the Mollands, through their Independent Artists company, put out *Basil: Demos Old And New*, a collection of various Joey recordings from the early 70s through the 90s. Though demos and roughs, and not mastered for uniform sound or levels, it is a good cross-section of Joey's various writing styles. He has a number of strong tunes on it, especially "Mirror" and "Isn't That A Dream." Joey has been working on a new solo album for release in the year 2000.

Badfinger's sterling albums of the 70s were finally reissued throughout the 1990's, after years of bureaucratic tie-ups. Other CD labels did pursue to license the Badfinger catalog throughout the late 80s, but Apple admitted to one particular company that they didn't want to chance upsetting EMI, who were almost certain to handle the Beatles reissues at the time, and who were expected to want the Apple artist catalog. Badfinger's first three Apple albums did get brought out by EMI/Capitol in 1991 and 1992 on CD, cassette, and vinyl. As it turned out, *Magic Christian Music*, *No Dice*, and the Iveys' *Maybe Tomorrow* all had fairly decent remastered sound, and each was complemented with numerous bonus tracks, but the packaging and attention to liner notes was a surprisingly mediocre effort at best.

In 1993, the "truly-faulty" release came out; the very important reissue of the much-adored *Straight Up*. The remastered sound was extremely bass-heavy and dull. And the bonus tracks are "alternate versions" of compositions that were already on the LP. These extra tracks may have been better served as a CD reissue of the complete album from which they came from. Still, the music transcends, and the reviews of the *Straight Up* reissue were consistently of the "rave" variety.

Thankfully, DCC Compact Classics in America put out a remastered audiophile "gold disc" CD of *Straight Up* in 1995. It received more brilliant reviews, including some from admitted earlier skeptics who now acknowledge that Badfinger's music had grown quite well over time. DCC did an additional remastering of *No Dice*; releasing it in 1997. These are highly-recommended.

An Apple *Best Of Badfinger* CD came out in 1995. The sound quality of the *Straight Up* tracks were only slightly improved and the selection and sequencing showed little forethought. Here was a chance to create a shining example of what made Badfinger great, a chance to put together a brisk sequence of superb songs that flowed, showed all sides of the band, and left you feeling exhilarated. It was not accomplished.

The year 2000 brings the new *The Very Best Of Badfinger* collection. The material includes both Apple & Warner Brothers tracks. All the considered "rarities" were eventually vetoed off the project, one-by-one (tunes such as "Baby Please," "No Good At All," "Do You Mind," "Sing For The Song," and a newly-mixed version of "Lay Me Down"). The CD material was remastered and the sound is generally much improved. Still, some important aspects of Badfinger's team chemistry are not well represented, especially the rock'n'roll side, and unfortunately, no tunes from Mike Gibbins. A broader Anthology release is truly needed to help this band's legacy be properly critiqued by the media and enjoyed by the public. All the core albums should be made available, too. A solid rarities package could also be put together.

Badfinger's last Apple album, *Ass*, was reissued in November of 1996, but only in Europe and Japan, as Capitol Records in America stated, at the time, they needed to re-evaluate their entire reissue campaign of Apple artists. The *Ass* CD, like *Straight Up*, suffers from inferior remastering. One bonus track was added, "Do You Mind," but instead of the superb version from the first unreleased edition of the album, an awkward, incomplete take was mixed and tacked on. "Piano Red," "Dreaming," "Regular," and "Rock'n'Roll," were other outtakes from that era which were left off. EMI representatives said they had felt they did not fit in well musically.

The two Warner Brothers Badfinger albums, *Badfinger* and *Wish You Were Here*, are available as Japanese, German, and U.K. CD's. Rhino Records licensed various tracks for a Warner Brothers/Elektra compilation in 1990, calling it *The Best Of Badfinger: Volume 2*. A similar U.K. compilation, called *Shine On*, was put out in 1990; discontinued in 1993.

In 1994, Gipsy Records, a London-based company, put out a CD of Tom Evans/Rod Roach demo recordings, calling it *Over You (The Final Tracks)*. It included refurbished and remixed four-track demos Tom and Rod had created during the years 1980 through 1983. Overall, a very viable project, now nearly impossible to find. A CD package of Evans demos is being planned for 2001.

The year 1999 saw the re-release of *Airwaves* on CD. Included is one session outtake, "One More Time." Other bonus tracks are various solo recordings done by Joe Tansin, plus Joey Molland's 1999 recording of a song he and Joe Tansin wrote during that era, "Love Can't Hide." Attempts to get the *Airwaves* demos on this CD were not successful, thus the CD company asked Joe Tansin for solo works from various stages of his career to fill it out. Badfinger's *Say No More* LP came out on CD in 2000, and it, too, is a valuable addition for one's collection.

In 1989, a CD entitled *Day After Day: Badfinger Live* came out on Rykodisc. This product is portrayed as Badfinger playing a March 4, 1974 gig at the Cleveland Agora rock club. Joey Molland had the sixteen-track master tapes in his possession. He stated in several interviews that when he had quit the band in November of 1974, his wife, Kathie, had snuck out these tapes from the band's Park Avenue house (by putting them under her coat). Later, his assertion in a court setting became – Kathie took the tapes out of a recording studio the band were working in (Air). A CD company, Rykodisc, approached Joey to put out the concert, promoting their potential worldwide distribution set-up.

Joey asserted to Rykodisc that he had rights to represent these tapes, and that any payments due to Mike, Tom's' estate, or Pete Ham's estate, would be handled by him, through his Independent Artists Company. Rykodisc went ahead and covered themselves by making sure, contractually, all liabilities fell on Joey.

The CD Joey and engineer/producer Mark Healey put together contains the re-recording of virtually all of Joey's original vocals, most of his guitar solos, many of the rhythm guitars, and all of Tom Evans' bass tracks. Re-sequencing of the tracks was also done (all of Pete Ham's songs were shifted to the end).

While live album post-production is somewhat common, the amount of work here is quite extreme. Joey had asserted there were considerable technical problems to overcome such as consistent feedback. And Kathie has stated Joey had to spend over "three hundred hours taking it apart and redoing most of the parts, because they were so rotten." But Pete's vocals are sometimes rendered "flat," by out-of-tune overdubs, and several of his guitar solos ended up buried. Also, some of the "effects" added are too obviously done after the fact. The most off-kilter aspect is Mike Gibbins snare drum. It triggers a very brash drum sample, mixed way upfront. The tom-toms are nearly non-existent. This overall production style was described by Joey as an effort to "plug into the 90s."

As of June 30, 1995, the *Day After Day: Badfinger Live* CD had earned sales royalties of $76,046, which Joey collected as the project's licensor. Allegedly, Joey's Independent Artists Co. was going to be collecting these sales royalties. In 1992, in the Badfinger fanzine *No Matter What*, a statement from Joey read "*. . . everybody in the band's gonna get a nice royalty check . . . and then next June, everybody will get a nice publishing check. . . .*"

As it turned out, for over six years, through the end of 1995, Pete's estate, Tom's estate, Mike Gibbins, and Bill Collins, did not get any portion of the sales royalties which Rykodisc had sent to Joey. Flemming Erik Carlson, who worked as Joey's manager for over a year (through late 1993), remembered, "Joey told me many times he had set up his Independent Artists company for himself, Mike Gibbins, and Pete Ham and Tom Evans estates, to collect money for the band members, to make sure all of them were paid for the Badfinger projects he was going to put out; that they would never be ripped off again. When I mentioned to Kathie we should let Marianne know about this, she told me, '*No, it's too complicated for her! Don't tell her.*'"

Marianne Evans – then living in Germany – was made aware of the *Day After Day* CD's existence shortly after it was released. She claimed she expected any sales royalties were being dealt with properly through the group's accountant, and for years, she never checked up on this. She had written Kathie in 1990 asking why the song "I Don't Mind" did not have Tommy credited as a co-writer on the CD booklet, and, was payment being correctly accounted on the publishing of that? But, she stated, no answer was ever given to her. Mike Gibbins alleged he was so fed up at getting no sales royalties that he threatened to sue Joey. Mike said he was sent $2,000 by Joey; Mike alleges, "to shut him up." Mike claimed he turned some of the money over to Badfinger's accountant for re-distribution to all the parties involved.

Based on the 1985 court settlement, any co-Badfinger-owned product, which includes the four main members, is supposed to have its sales royalties split five ways, with Bill Collins included. As it turned out, an investigation was done by Goldblatt & Co. in 1996, and steps were taken to subtract the CD's royalties Joey would allegedly owe the others via the settlement guidelines – by a massive deduction from his Apple publishing royalties. Joey had seemingly lost out. By not setting up a better personal division for himself early on – as he would have deserved for his production work and the money he spent in production costs – the court order was simply followed. Joey's moves backfired financially. He began litigation in 1997 to try and get back his "producer" costs and establish a "producer" royalty.

An offer was made to Joey early on in the case, according to a lawyer representing the Ham estate, for Joey's production expenses, but no continuing "producer royalty" was proposed. Joey declined, requesting a "6%-of-retail producer royalty." The Rykodisc sales royalty which Joey was being paid had been for 13%. With Joey's new desired arrangement, he would receive 7.2%; the other four parties, 1.2%.

In his 1997 affidavit for the case, Joey stated, *"I fully accept that the recording royalties from the album fall with [the Consent Order] and should be divided in accordance with it... I therefore ask that I should receive the production costs incurred by me and that I should receive a proper producer's royalty for the work done by me."* Also, in the affidavit, Joey asserted he had, at various stages, discussed with Bill and Mike what he was doing regarding the royalties for the project, and that they had never objected. Joey claimed this meant he felt they had been fine with how he was handling it.

In April of 2000, witness testimony was given in London for the case by Joey Molland, Kathie Molland, Robert Press (of Goldblatt & Co.), Bill Collins, Anne Collins, and Mike Gibbins. Mark Healey didn't show up. Marianne Evans also did not appear in court. She was ill at the time. The two technical recording expert witnesses did not appear (their affidavits were addressed). Joey had never turned over the 24 track tape he'd used for his studio overdubs to the experts, which they had wanted for closer examination of what was re-done from the show. Joey claimed the tape had been "lost."

The first day of testimony was entirely by Joey. The second day of the court proceedings everyone else available, including Joey, testified. Molland's lawyers worked hard to portray the other four parties and accountant Goldblatt & Co. had certain knowledge of the CD project at various stages, and never seemed to clearly show any objections; not until a lot of money had been accumulated. The Defendant's lawyer focused on contradictions by Joey, as related to evidence and previous statements. Extreme emotion came out from Bill Collins during his testimony.

The case ended on April 19, 2000. In his decision the U.K. judge wrote, *"The Claimant (Molland) then arranged, by an agreement dated 1st May 1990 with Rykodisc Inc. a record manufacturer in Minneapolis, for Rykodisc to manufacture and distribute the release under licence on a worldwide basis in return for a royalty rate escalating with sales effected from a base of 13% of net retail sales in the United States and half that amount for sales outside the United States. Under the written agreement the Claimant (Molland) warranted, amongst other things, that he was the sole and exclusive owner and proprietor of all rights in the recordings, that he had full right, power and authority to enter into the agreement and that he had secured the consent in writing of all artists including the musicians who performed. At least two of those warranties were not in fact justified: Mr. Molland was not the sole and exclusive owner of all rights on the recordings, and he had not secured the consent in writing of all artists including of the musicians who performed. As to the other warranty, he had not consulted any of the Defendants as to the terms of the Ryko deal before entering this agreement . . .*

"Mr. Molland is to be criticised for the way he dealt with the recording royalties. He told me that he had always intended that the group would share in the recording royalties. I do not accept this . . .

"He made no attempt to share any part of those royalties with any other members of the band or to account for them to Goldblatts, notwithstanding his knowledge of the Consent Order . . .

"I was pressed to consider whether that conduct amounted to dishonesty, but, in the absence of that issue being properly explored in cross-examination with Mr. Molland, I am not prepared to reach that conclusion. Rather, I consider that Mr. Molland (with his wife's encouragement) had persuaded himself that, given that they had been in possession of the tapes for over 15 years, that he had done all the work to produce a salable recording, and that the band members would be receiving publishing royalties. It was just that he should retain profits from the recording royalties . . .

"Overall, I regard Mr. Molland's conduct as open to serious criticism . . . However, given that I reject the allegation that he kept the whole project secret and reject the allegation of outright dishonesty, I do not regard his conduct as so egregious as to deprive him of any remuneration for the undoubted value he provided through his considerable and specialist efforts . . .

"I reject some of the conflicts suggested as being unrealistic and not related in any way to the commercial exploitation of this material, which is what the account of profit is about. For example, (Defendant's Barrister) suggested that other beneficiaries might have preferred that no commercial re-mix be made at all because the underlying tapes were poor and that they would prefer to retain the memory of the original group members intact. I regard this as unrealistic.

"I conclude, having regard to these factors, that this is one of those exceptional cases where the court is justified in awarding remuneration to the fiduciary notwithstanding the general rule . . .

"It is appropriate to adjust an allowance to Mr. Molland to take account of the fact that I do not regard it as right, in the circumstances, that he should have received the same amount as he would have received if he had openly consulted and agreed with other band members and Mr. Collins. . . .

Joey was awarded a one-time producer fee of $10,000, not a continuing producer royalty he desired (which would have given him $35,098 for the sales royalty earnings through June of 1995). Joey also was granted $14,000 for his production expenses. He'd sought $21,181. The biggest financial hit to all was the court costs. According to U.K. court proceedings, since it was Joey who was bringing up this argument that he deserved "producer" income, and since he was ultimately deemed worthy of some producer earnings; the judge used this pro-Joey-position-criteria to say he was making 4/5 of Joey's court costs accountable to the other four parties. According to one Ham estate lawyer, in the United States, this "cost" scenario would not have been a forced issue.

As of May 2000, an appeal of the decisions are being considered by the four defendants (according to lawyer Hugh Hitchcock, who worked on the case).

It almost seems as if Badfinger's name will continually bear this weight of a troubled, litigious history, but the primary focus should be on their music; that is their positive legacy; their major contribution. And many encouraging and exciting events have been developing since the start of 1997. That year brought the Rykodisc CD, *7 Park Avenue*, a collection of home demo recordings of Pete Ham's. A second Ham demo collection, *Golders Green*, was released in 1999.

There was also a 1997 Copper Records CD, *Come And Get It: A Tribute To Badfinger*, featuring twenty-two artists performing Badfinger tunes. Also, *Badfinger Live 72-73: BBC In Concert*, a 1997 U.K. CD, portrays fifteen live song performances. It was later released in America by Fuel 2000 Records.

On June 12, 2000, Pete Ham's hometown of Swansea launched a two-week tribute to Pete's accomplishments at their Central Library. Opening night was attended by many of his friends and family menbers, and a display was set-up of old photos, memorabilia, and video clips.

From the visual front, there has been a Badfinger documentary released by Pegasus Flight Productions. It has six full-length performance/promo films included. Primarily, the storyline is told through the perspectives of Joey Molland, Kathie Molland, and Mike Gibbins.

A prime-time British television show on "Top Ten Love Songs" aired in February of 2000. A segment profiled Badfinger, with the show rating the song "Without You" #3 all-time – for its overall impact in the U.K. market. A 1999 Welsh documentary on artists from Wales also featured Badfinger.

VH-1's *Behind The Music* cable TV program is intending to air a Badfinger documentary sometime in the year 2000.

The opportunity is still there for Badfinger's music to be much more widely discovered. Hopefully it can manifest to a level for which it is certainly justified. For Badfinger remains, arguably, the most impressive "British-born band" to have carried forward the Beatles melodic musical heritage utilizing the same exciting potential of a "full group" songwriting team. The reasons Badfinger succeeded more than most is the consistent quality of their compositions, their skilled, yet emotional playing, their impassioned singing, plus the fact they amalgamated four strongly-divergent individuals into a magical chemistry, just as The Beatles did. The extraordinary thing is, Badfinger had just begun to truly blossom their own special identity when they suffered their sudden collapse. Their quickly deleted LP, *Wish You Were Here*, is brilliant, even "progressive" as a pop-rock album, but even then these four talented men were still scratching the surface of what they might have accomplished as a unit.

Producer Chris Thomas certainly deserves kudos for *Wish You Were Here*, but – as The Beatles had George Martin – most rock groups need a superior studio director to bring their ideas to full-on fruition. In that respect, Badfinger were lucky. They worked with many highly-regarded icons of the rock'n'roll industry. But the question is, had this group been handled with a consistent degree of professionalism, respect, and kindness, would they have reached far greater heights? As it was, many of their classic songs *were* born from their painful arena, their art *was* driven by their emotions; and we were the ones blessed with the excruciating – yet exhilarating – musical scrapheap of their tormented lives.

In the long run, Badfinger may simply end up being regarded as one of many other accomplished rock'n'roll groups who traveled down the tortuous music entertainment road; ill-fated dreamers who expected the industry would embrace – and then wholly nurture – their own uniquely personal talents. But the conditions this particular band collapsed from meant some truly amazing abilities were never allowed to reach their full maturity. Under more compassionate circumstances, dealing with a few more altruistic hearts, there's no telling what could have been; we might have had yet one other, "Fab Four," rock'n'roll legend. Then again, maybe we really *did* have, all along. . . .

Badfinger

Joey Molland, Mike Gibbins, Tom Evans, Pete Ham

BIBLIOGRAPHY

I WOULD LIKE TO THANK the following publications for their material and reproductions therein: *Badfinger Connection, Badfinger File, Beatlefan, Beetle, Billboard, Cashbox, Chicago Sun Times, Chicago Tribune, Circus, Cleveland Plain Dealer, Cleveland Press, Columbus Dispatch, Creem, Daily Mirror, Disc and Music Echo, Discoveries, Fab 208, Free Press, Focus, Fusion, Gainesville Sun, Goldmine, Herald of Wales, High Fidelity, Los Angeles Times, Los Angeles Herald Examiner, Melody Maker, Mirabelle, New Musical Express, New York Daily News, People, Phonograph Magazine, Record Collector, Record Mirror, Record World, Sailor, Scene Magazine, Springfield Union, Sounds, South Wales Evening Post, Stereo Review, Teen Magazine, The 910, Trouser Press, Variety, Zoo World.*

DISCOGRAPHY

Iveys (45s & EP)

Year	Release	U.S.	U.K.	Japan
1968	Maybe Tomorrow/ Daddy's A Millionaire	Apple 1803	Apple 5	AR-2198
1969	*Walls Ice Cream EP* "Storm In A Teacup"	N/A	Apple CT-1	N/A
1969	Dear Angie/ No Escaping Your Love	N/A	N/A	AR-2354

Badfinger (45s)

Year	Release	U.S.	U.K.	Japan
1969	Come And Get It/ Rock Of All Ages	Apple 1815	Apple 20	AR-2444
1970	No Matter What/ Carry On Til Tomorrow	Apple 1822	N/A	N/A
1970	No Matter What/Better Days	N/A	Apple 31	AR 2701
1971	Day After Day/Money	Apple 1841	N/A	AR-2953
1971	Day After Day/ Sweet Tuesday Morning	N/A	Apple 40	N/A
1972	Carry On Til Tomorrow/ Without You	N/A	N/A	EAR-10151
1972	Baby Blue/Flying	Apple 1844	N/A	EAR-10046
1973	Apple Of My Eye/Blind Owl	Apple 1864	Apple 49	N/A
1973	Apple Of My Eye/Cowboy	N/A	N/A	EAR-10547
1973	Love Is Easy/My Heart Goes Out	N/A	WB 16323	N/A
1974	I Miss You/Shine On	WB 7801	N/A	P-1312W
1974	Know One Knows/ Your So Fine	N/A	N/A	P-1356W

1979	Lost Inside Your Love/ Come Down Hard	Elek E-46022	Elek K12345	P-452E
1979	Love Is Gonna Come At Last/Sail Away	Elek E-46025	N/A	P-397E
1981	Hold On/Passin' Time	RR 3793	N/A	N/A
1981	I Got You/ Rock'n'Roll Contract	RR 3815	N/A	N/A
1981	Because I Love You/ Too Hung Up On You	RR 3833	N/A	N/A
1993	Baby Blue/Day After Day (blue vinyl)	CEMA 57-19487	N/A	N/A
1993	Without You/ No Matter What (CD)	N/A	N/A	TODP-2406

Badfinger (original LPs & CDs)

Year	Release	U.S.	U.K.	Japan
1970	*Magic Christian Music*	Apple SW-3364	SAPCOR 12	AP-8914
1970	*The Magic Christian* (soundtrack)	Comm CU 6004	PYENSPL 28133	N/A
1970	*No Dice*	Apple ST-3367	SAPCOR 16	AP-80147
1971	*Straight Up*	Apple SW 3387	SAPCOR 19	AP 80432 ('72)
1973	*Ass*	Apple SW 3411	SAPCOR 27	EAP-80948
1974	*Badfinger*	WB BS 2762	WB K56023	P-8454W
1974	*Wish You Were Here*	WB BS 2827	WB K56076	P-8533W
1979	*Airwaves*	Elektra 6E-175	ELK 52129	P-10657E
1981	*Say No More*	RR 16030	N/A	N/A
1990	*Day After Day (live) LP, CD*	RykoRCD10189	RykoRCD10189	ALCB-181 ('91)
1997	*Badfinger BBC In Concert, CD*	N/A	SFRS(CD)-031	N/A

Badfinger (Reissues)

Year	Release	U.S.	U.K.	Japan
1990	*Shine On*	N/A	Edsel ED 302	N/A
1990	*The Best Of Badfinger, Volume 2*	Rhino R2 70978	N/A	N/A
1991	*Apple EP* "Come And Get It"	N/A	Apple LC 0542	N/A
1991	*Maybe Tomorrow (Iveys)*	Apple 7986922	CDSAPCOR 8	TOCP 7099 ('92)
1991	*Magic Christian Music*	Apple 7975792	CDSAPCOR 12	TOCP 6896
1992	*No Dice*	Apple 7986982	CDSAPCOR 16	TOCP 7098
1993	*Straight Up*	Apple 7814032	CDSAPCOR 19	TOCP 7681
1991	*Badfinger*	N/A	N/A	WPCP-4801
1991	*Wish You Were Here*	N/A	N/A	WPCP-4082
1994	*Day After Day (live) LP, CD*	N/A	N/A	VACK-1005 ('94)
1995	*The Best Of Badfinger*	Apple 8301292	Apple 8301292	TOCP 8306
1995	*Straight Up* (gold disc)	DCC GZS-1088	N/A	N/A
1996	*Ass*	N/A	CDSAPCOR 27	TOCP 50066 ('97)
1997	*No Dice* (gold disc)	DCC GZS-1095	N/A	N/A

1999	*Airwaves* CD	Perm Press 52712	N/A	N/A
2000	*Badfinger BBC In Concert 72-3*	Fuel61048(CD)	N/A	N/A
2000	*Badfinger BBC In Concert 72-3*	N/A	TPM-99201V(LP)	N/A
2000	*Badfinger*	N/A	7599-26539-2	N/A
2000	*Wish You Were Here*	N/A	7599-26540-2	N/A
2000	*Say No More* CD	Real Music 20001	N/A	N/A
2000	*The Very Best Of Badfinger*	Apple5269742	Apple5269742	N/A

Compilations

Year	Release	U.S.	U.K.	Japan
1973	*Rock Now '73* LP "Carry On Til Tomorrow"	N/A	N/A	Toshiba PRP-50
1974	*History Of British Rock Vol. 2* LP "Come And Get It"	SASH 3705-2	N/A	N/A
1975	*History Of British Rock Vol. 3* LP "Day After Day"	SASH 3712-2	N/A	N/A
1983	*Hits Reunion* LP, "Come And Get It" (1979 version)	BU 5900	BU 5904	N/A
1984	*Those Were The Hits of 1970* LP "Come And Get It"	N/A	N/A	IA002-1582931
1987	*Back To Rock'n'Roll* LP "Come And Get It" (1979 version)	BU 6243	N/A	N/A
1988	*British Pop Tea Bag Vol. 5* CD "No Matter What" and "Day After Day"	N/A	N/A	20PT-88Z35
1991	*Steal This Disc Vol. 3* CD "Sometimes" (live)	Rykodisc 00205	N/A	N/A
1994	*The Treasures Of Rock* CD "Know One Knows"	N/A	N/A	WEA WPCR-121
1996	*Now And Then* (soundtrack) CD "No Matter What"	Columbia 67380	N/A	SRCS 7955
1997	*Poptopia: Power Pop Classics of the 1970's* CD, "Just A Chance"	Rhino 72728	N/A	N/A
1998	*Hits Powerage Rock* CD "Just A Chance"	N/A	N/A	WPCR-2152
1999	*Outside Providence* CD, "No Matter What"	Giant 24271-2	N/A	N/A

Special Interest Items

Year	Release	
1972	*Four Smash Hits* EP (4 songs)	Apple AEP-3002 (Australia)
1972	I'd Die Babe/Take It All	Apple 35J (South Africa)
1991	*Apple Daze* (Tom Evans Interview)	Raven RVCD (Australia)
1992	*Come And Get It* (CD EP, 4 songs)	Apple 2046522 (Germany)
1997	*Badfinger* CD	WB 7599265392 (Germany)
1997	*Wish You Were Here* CD	WB 7599265402 (Germany)

Pete Ham

Year	Release
1970	*All Things Must Pass*: appeared on George Harrison LP, Apple STCH 639 (U.S.)
1971	It Don't Come Easy/Early 1970: appeared on Ringo Starr 45 (A-side), Apple 1831 (U.S.)
1971	*Concert For Bangla Desh*: appeared on benefit LP, Apple STCX 3385 (U.S.)
1971	Try Some Buy Some/Tandoori Chicken: appeared on Ronnie Spector 45 (A-side), Apple 1832 (U.S.)
1972	Back Off Boogaloo/Blindman: appeared on Ringo Starr 45 (B-side), Apple 1849 (U.S.), Apple 5944 (U.K.)
1972	*Tomorrow's Another Day:* appeared on Gothic Horizon LP, Argo Records 2DA150 (U.K.)
1972	*Lonely Man*: appeared on Splinter track for film *Little Malcolm And His Struggle Against The Eunuchs*
1973	*Living In The Material World*: appeared on George Harrison LP, (final use of Pete's tracks unconfirmed) Apple SMAS 3410 (U.S.), Apple PAS 10006 (U.K.)
1975	*Extra Texture*: appeared on George Harrison LP, (final use of Pete's tracks unconfirmed) Apple SW 3420 (U.S.), Apple PAS 1009 (U.K.)
1984	*Heavy Jelly* ("Take Me Down To The Water"): appeared on Heavy Jelly LP, (recorded 1969), Psycho 30 (U.K.)
1997	*7 Park Avenue* CD: as Pete Ham, Rykodisc RCD 10349, (U.S. & U.K.)
1997	*7 Park Avenue* CD (w/5 bonus tracks): as Pete Ham, Video Arts Music VACK-1122 (Japan)
1997	*Without You: The Tragic Story Of Badfinger*: as Pete Ham, (1000 limited edition CD of various demos)
1999	*Golders Green* CD: as Pete Ham, Rykodisc RCD 10481 (U.S.)
1999	*Golders Green* CD (w/2 bonus tracks): as Pete Ham, Video Arts Music VACK-1164 (Japan)
1999	*7 Park Avenue* CD remastered (w/5 bonus tracks): as Pete Ham, Video Arts Music VACK-1163 (Japan)

Tom Evans

Year	Release
1970	*All Things Must Pass*: appeared on George Harrison LP, Apple STCH 639 (U.S.)
1971	It Don't Come Easy/Early 1970: appeared on Ringo Starr 45 (A-side), Apple 1831 (U.S.)
1971	*Concert For Bangla Desh*: appeared on benefit LP, Apple STCX 3385 (U.S.)
1971	*Imagine* "I Don't Wanna Be A Soldier Mama, I Don't Wanna Die": appeared on John Lennon LP, Apple SW 3379 (U.S.)
1976	Don't Let Me Be Wrong/Get To You: with The Dodgers, Island IS-058 (U.S. 45)
1976	Don't Let Me Be Wrong/Get To You: with The Dodgers, Island WIP 6292 (U.K. 45)
1977	Just Wanna Love You/Don't Know What You're Doing: with The Dodgers, Island WIP 6342 (U.K. 45)
1977	Down/Don't Know What You're Doing: with The Dodgers, Island WIP 6361 (U.K. 45)
1978	*Innocent Bystander*: appeared on John Palumbo LP, Lifesong 35503 (U.S.)
1984	*Heavy Jelly* ("Take Me Down To The Water"): appeared on Heavy Jelly LP (recorded 1969), Psycho 30 (U.K.)
1991	*Apple Daze* (CD): Tom interviewed by Glenn A. Baker in 1982, Raven RVCD-25 (Australia)
1993	*Over You (The Final Tracks)* (CD): as Tom Evans w/Rod Roach, Gipsy BF1CD (U.K.)
1997	*Without You: The Tragic Story Of Badfinger*: as Tom Evans, (1000 limited edition CD of various demos

Mike Gibbins

Year	Release
1970	*All Things Must Pass*: appeared on George Harrison LP, Apple STCH 639 (U.S.)
1971	*Concert For Bangla Desh*: appeared on benefit LP, Apple STCX 3385 (U.S.)
1973	*Iceberg* "Nothing Is Happening": appeared on Deke Leonard LP track, United Artists LA150 (U.S.)
1977	It's A Heartache/Got So Used To Lovin' You: appeared on Bonnie Tyler 45, PB 5057 (U.K.)
1978	*It's A Heartache*: appeared on Bonnie Tyler LP, RCA AFL 1 2821 (U.S.)
1978	*Whiskey Sundown*: appeared on Digby Richards LP, RCA PL 25124 (U.K.)
1978	Dallas/Play Mama Play: appeared on Digby Richards 45, RCA PB 5037 (U.K.)
1978	Whiskey Sundown/ Too Long Gone: appeared on Digby Richards 45, RCA PB 5095 (U.K.)
1983	*Queen Of China*: appeared on Dave Tipton LP, Kicking Mule SNKF 174 (U.K.)
1996	*Young Savage Florida* (artist compilation) CD: as Mike Gibbins, "Dream Harder (Ballad Of The Red Coats)," "Lay Away," Rotten Sun 001 (U.S.)
1998	*A Place In Time*: as Mike Gibbins, Forbidden Records CD, FOR1962 (U.S.)

Joey Molland

Year	Release
1965	She Belongs To Me/Taken My Love: with The Masterminds, Immediate IM005 (U.K.)
1968	Spooky/I Can't Stand To Lose You: with Gary Walker & The Rain, Philips SLF1150 (Japan), Polydor 56237 (U.K.)
1969	The View/Thoughts Of An Old Man: with Gary Walker & The Rain, Philips SLF1174 (Japan)
1969	Magazine Woman/Take A Look: with Gary Walker & The Rain, Philips SLF1190 (Japan)
1969	*Magazine Woman* (EP): with Gary Walker & The Rain, Philips SLF3243 (Japan)
1969	*Album #1*: with Gary Walker & The Rain, Philips SPX7433 (Japan)
1969	Come In You'll Get Pneumonia/Francis: with Gary Walker & The Rain, Philips BF 1740 (U.K.)
1970	Don't Leave Me Now/So Lonely Without You: appeared on Jimmy Campbell 45, Fontana 6007025 (U.K.)
1970	*Half Baked* (uncredited): appeared on Jimmy Campbell LP, Vertigo VEL1000 (U.S.)
1970	*All Things Must Pass*: appeared on George Harrison LP, Apple STCH 639 (U.S.)
1971	*Concert for Bangla Desh*: appeared on benefit LP, Apple STCX 3385 (U.S.)
1971	*Imagine*: ("I Don't Wanna Be A Soldier Mama, I Don't Wanna Die"): appeared on John Lennon LP, Apple SW 3379 (U.S.)
1975	*Blue Goose*: appeared on Blue Goose LP, ANCL 2005 (U.K.)
1976	*Natural Gas*: with Natural Gas, Private Stock PS2011 (U.S.), PVLP 1007 (U.K.), EMS 80545 (Japan)
1976	Right Time/Dark Cloud: with Natural Gas, Private Stock PS45100 (U.S.), PS EMR-20084 (Japan)
1976	Right Time/Miracle Mile: with Natural Gas, Private Stock PVT 71 (U.K.)
1976	Once Again (A Love Song)/same: with Natural Gas, Private Stock PS 46116 (U.S.)
1978	*Innocent Bystander*: appeared on John Palumbo LP, Lifesong 35503 (U.S.)
1984	*Trust Me*: produced LP by Money, Earthtone ET-01001
1984	*After The Pearl*: as Joey Molland, Earthtone ET-1002 (U.S.)
1984	Here Comes Heartache/What Happened: as Joey Molland, Earthtone ET-7002 (U.S.)

1987 *The Best Of L.A.*: "Time Marches On" & "Back In The Shadows": appeared on various artists CD, tracks by Raz, MRR007 (U.S.)

1987 Time Marches On/Back In The Shadows: appeared with Raz, MRR021 (U.S.)

1992 *The Pilgrim*: as Joey Molland, Rykodisc RCD 10212 (U.S.), VACK-1006 (Japan)

1993 *Victory Gardens*: appeared on John & Mary CD, Rykodisc RCD 10203 (U.S.)

1993 *Missing Children Minnesota* (compilation), "Merry Christmas (Follow Your Star)": as Joey Molland, Zomax MN-Z10011, (U.S.)

1994 *The Immediate Singles Collection Vol. 1*, "She Belongs To Me" & "Taken My Love": with The Masterminds, Sony Special Products, AK47351 (U.S.)

1995 *Badfinger* (Joey Molland - lead vocals): as Badfinger (CD), Eclipse Music 64825-2 (U.S.)

1996 *Best Of The Walker Brothers CD:* with Gary Walker & The Rain, Merc PHCA-4121 (Japan) Spooky & The View

1996 *Timeless* (4 song CD EP): as Joey Molland's Badfinger, Crosstown Productions, no matrix

1997 *Badfinger* (Joey Molland - lead vocals): as Badfinger, Retro Music SLD 23492 (U.S.) same CD as Eclipse Music

1997 *Hey Cats, We're The Sandwiches*: produced CD by The Sandwiches (U.S.)

1997 *Hello Sunny Day*: appeared with Randy & The Wolfpack on CD, MIT 1001 (U.S.)

1997 *Hannah Cranna*: produced CD by Hannah Cranna, Big Deal 9039-2 (U.S.)

1998 *Rock On, Scubatron*: appeared on CD/LP with The Sandwiches (U.S.)

1998 *Re-Emerge*: appeared on and co-produced (with "Zip" Caplan and James Walsh) CD by The Litter, ArfArf80 (U.S.)

1998 *Basil (Demos Old and New)*: as Joey Molland, Independent Artist CD, IA 001 (U.S.)

1999 *Badfinger (featuring Joey Molland)*: as Badfinger, Excelsior 20362 (U.S.) same CD as Eclipse Music and Retro Music

1999 *Raz With Joey Molland:* appeared on Razfinger CD, MRR 102155 (U.S.)

In addition to this list, there are numerous promotional vinyl and promotional CD releases, bootlegs, 8-tracks, reel-to-reels, cassettes, and other Iveys/Badfinger items specific to certain countries. There are also sessions and recordings done by former Iveys/Badfinger members: Dai Jenkins, Ron Griffiths, Bob Jackson, Joe Tansin, Glenn Sherba, Tony Kaye, Kenny Harck, Richard Bryans, Rod Roach, Lenny Campanero, Mark Healey, John Richardson, Randy Anderson, and countless others. For more details, go to the internet website listed below; or write the author at:

Frances Glover Books
7 West 41st. Ave. #229
San Mateo, CA, 94403
U.S.A.

http://www.sirius.com/~crimson
email - crimson@sirius.com
phone & fax – 650 508-9585

Iveys Live

The following list is approximately 95% to 98% of all the gigs The Iveys ever played.

11-7-64 Sketty Hall, Swansea, S.WALES
11-14-64 Clyne Cellar Club, Swansea, S.WALES
12-1-64 The Ritz, Skewen, S.WALES w/The Jets, Misfits, Comancheroes
1-1-65 Langland Court Hotel, Swansea S.WALES
1-31-65 The Big T, Mumbles, S.WALES w/The Jets
2-6-65 The Big T, Mumbles, S.WALES w/The Jets
2-9-65 The Ritz, Skewen, S.WALES w/The Bystanders, Corncrackers
2-12-65 The Big T, Mumbles S.WALES
2-13-65 Memorial Hall, Burryport S.WALES w/The Corncrackers
2-27-65 The Ritz, Skewen, S.WALES w/Wild Ones
3-10-65 Lodge Cinema, Briton Ferry w/Wild Ones, The Jets, Blackjacks
3-13-65 The Big T, Mumbles, S.WALES w/The Bystanders
3-16-65 The Ritz, Skewen, S.WALES w/Eyes of Blue, Wild Ones, The Jets,
3-18-65 The Glen, Llanelli, S.WALES w/Corncrackers
3-20-65 The Ritz, Skewen, S.WALES w/The Fleetwoods
3-23-65 Patti Pavilion, Swansea S.WALES w/Eyes Of Blue, Echoretz
3-27-65 The Ritz, Skewen, S.WALES w/The Bystanders
4-1-65 The Ritz, Skewen, S.WALES w/Eyes Of Blue
4-3-65 The Ritz, Skewen, S.WALES w/Wild Ones
4-22-65 The Ritz, Skewen, S.WALES w/Corncrackers
4-26-65 Langland Court Hotel, S.WALES (Red Cross charity)
4-29-65 The Ritz, Skewen, S.WALES w/The Jets
5-8-65 The Ritz, Skewen, S.WALES w/The Kingpins
6-8-65 Afan Lido, Port Talbot S.WALES w/Echoretz
6-10-65 The Ritz, Skewen, S.WALES w/Blackjacks
6-17-65 Afan Lido, Port Talbot S.WALES
7-1-65 The Ritz, Skewen, S.WALES w/Nashville Teens, Kingpins
7-9-65 Seven Sisters Rugby Club, Swansea S.WALES
7-15-65 The Ritz, Skewen, S.WALES w/The Who, Eyes Of Blue
7-24-65 The Ritz, Skewen, S.WALES w/Kingpins
7-29-65 The Ritz, Skewen, S.WALES w/Geno Washington, Eyes Of Blue
8-5-65 The Ritz, Skewen, S.WALES w/Screaming Lord Sutch, Kingpins
8-14-65 The Ritz, Skewen, S.WALES w/Kingpins
8-19-65 The Ritz, Skewen, S.WALES w/Nashville Teens, Kingpins
8-22-65 The Ritz, Skewen, S.WALES
8-24-65 Haggars Ballroom, Pembroke S.WALES w/Wayne Fontana
9-1-65 Fountain's Disco, Tenby, S.WALES
9-2-65 The Ritz, Skewen, S.WALES w/Lulu & The Luvvers, Smokestacks
9-5-65 The Ritz, Skewen, S.WALES w/Lulu & The Luvvers, Smokestacks
9-12-65 The Ritz, Skewen, S.WALES w/Lulu & The Luvvers, Smokestacks
9-16-65 The Ritz, Skewen, S.WALES w/Kingpins, Herbie Goins
9-23-65 The Ritz, Skewen, S.WALES w/The Honeycombs, Eyes Of Blue
10-4-65 The Glen, Llanelli S.WALES w/Missing Links
10-9-65 The Ritz, Skewen, S.WALES w/The Smokestacks
10-14-65 The Ritz, Skewen, S.WALES w/The Hollies, Kingpins
11-11-65 The Ritz, Skewen, S.WALES w/The Merseybeats, The Smokestacks
11-20-65 Afan Lido, Port Talbot, S.WALES w/The Dekkas
11-25-65 The Ritz, Skewen, S.WALES w/The Rockin' Berries
11-30-65 The Ritz, Skewen, S.WALES w/E Of Blue, Smokestacks, Kingpins
12-3-65 Regal Ballroom, Ammanford, S.WALES w/ The Fireflies
12-4-65 Regal Ballroom, Ammanford, S.WALES w/Wayne & The Comets
12-10-65 Regal Ballroom, Ammanford, S.WALES w/W. Fontana, E Of Blue
12-11-65 Regal Ballroom, Ammanford, S.WALES w/The Smokestacks
12-12-65 The Ritz, Skewen S.WALES w/The Fleetwoods, Cheating Hearts
12-16-65 Regal Ballroom, Ammanford, S.WALES w/Comancheroes
12-16-65 The Ritz, Skewen, S.WALES w/Eyes Of Blue
12-23-65 The Ritz, Skewen, S.WALES w/Geno Washington, Eyes of Blue
12-27-65 The Ritz, Skewen, S.WALES w/Eyes Of Blue
1-1-66 The Ritz, Skewen, S.WALES w/The Smokestacks
1-8-66 Afan Lido, Port Talbot S.WALES w/The Sensational Sultans
1-13-66 Embassy Ballroom, Swansea S.WALES
1-22-66 The Ritz, Skewen, S.WALES w/The Jets
1-27-66 The Ritz, Skewen, S.WALES w/The Moody Blues, Eyes Of Blue
2-5-66 The Ritz, Skewen, S.WALES w/Echoretz
2-10-66 The Ritz, Skewen, S.WALES w/The Merseybeats, Eyes Of Blue
2-12-66 Afan Lido, Port Talbot, S.WALES w/Eyes Of Blue
3-5-66 The Ritz, Skewen, S.WALES w/Blues Organisation
3-10-66 Embassy Ballroom, Swansea, S.WALES
3-11-66 Regal Ballroom, Ammanford, S.WALES w/The Mojos (Bill Collins)
3-12-66 Charlton Ballroom, Kidwelly, S.WALES w/Agents 4
3-14-66 The Glen, Llanelli S.WALES
3-17-66 Afan Lido, Port Talbot, S.WALES w/Unit 4 Plus 2
3-21-66 The Glen, Llanelli, S.WALES w/Lott13, E of Blue, Swansea Drifters
3-23-66 Charlton Ballroom, Kidwelly, S.WALES
3-25-66 Craigcefn Parc Hall, Swansea, S.WALES
3-25-66 Regal Ballroom, Ammanford, S.WALES w/Eyes Of Blue, Kingbees
3-26-66 The Glen, Llanelli, S.WALES w/The Pimples
3-31-66 The Ritz, Skewen, S.WALES w/Spencer Davis Group, Eyes Of Blue
4-2-66 The Glen, Llanelli, S.WALES w/Swansea Drifters
4-7-66 The Ritz, Skewen, S.WALES
4-11-66 Afan Lido, Port Talbot, S.WALES w/The Dekkas
4-14-66 The Ritz, Skewen, S.WALES w/Manfred Mann
4-15-66 Regal Ballroom, Ammanford, S.WALES w/M. Mann, Blues Org
4-16-66 The Ritz, Skewen, S.WALES w/Eyes Of Blue
4-18-66 The Glen, Llanelli, S.WALES
4-23-66 The Ritz, Skewen, S.WALES w/Kingbees
4-25-66 Garnant Club, S.WALES
4-26-66 St. Benedicts Club, Swansea, S.WALES
4-29-66 Regal Ballroom, Ammanford, S.WALES w/Merseybeats, E Of Blue
4-30-66 The Ritz, Skewen, S.WALES w/Lott13
5-2-66 The Glen, Llanelli, S.WALES w/Swansea Drifters
5-12-66 The Ritz, Skewen, S.WALES w/Yardbirds, Eyes Of Blue
5-14-66 Afan Lido, Port Talbot, S.WALES w/Chicos
5-16-66 The Glen, Llanelli, S.WALES w/The Kelts
5-28-66 The Ritz, Skewen, S.WALES w/The Jug And Bottle Set
5-30-66 The Glen, Llanelli, S.WALES w/NMO
6-13-66 The Glen, Llanelli, S.WALES
6-18-66 The Ritz, Skewen, S.WALES w/The Kingbees
6-20-66 The Glen, Llanelli S.WALES
6-25-66 Seaside Pavilion, Port Talbot, S.WALES
6-25-66 Afan Lido, Port Talbot, S.WALES w/The Sect Maniacs
6-7-66 Empire, Neath, S.WALES (Bill Collins records Iveys)

6-24-66 Rehearsal club, Picadilly, ENG. (audition for Robert Wace)
7-8-66 7 Club, Shrewsbury, ENG. (D. Garrick) w/Karacters
7-9-66 Gaiety Ballroom, Ramsey, ENG. (D. Garrick) w/The Raging Sons
7-10-66 Olympia, Cromer, ENG. (D. Garrick) w/G. Freeman & The Contours
7-14-66 Dreamland, Margate, ENG. (D. Garrick)
7-15-66 Newmarket, ENG. (D. Garrick)
7-21-66 Cavalier Club, Golders Green, ENG. (first London gig)
7-24-66 Kimball's Ballroom, Portsmouth, ENG.
7-31-66 The Shoreline, Bognor, ENG.
8-1-66 Oasis Club, Portsmouth, ENG.
8-6-66 Boston, ENG. (D. Garrick) w/Solomon Burke
8-13-66 Espresso Continental, Eastbourne, ENG.
8-19-66 Axminster, ENG. (D. Garrick)
8-20-66 Exeter, ENG. (D. Garrick)
8-27-66 7 Club, Shrewsbury, ENG.
8-29-66 The Cavern, Liverpool, ENG.
9-3-66 The Glen, Llanelli, S.WALES
9-10-66 Flamingo Club, London, ENG. w/Zuyder Zee
9-11-66 Scotch St. James, London, ENG.
9-17-66 La Scala, Runcorn, ENG.
9-24-66 Flamingo Club, London, ENG.
9-24-66 Sybilla's, London, ENG.
9-30-66 Flamingo Club, London, ENG.
10-1-66 Corby, ENG.
10-7-66 7 Club, Shrewsbury, ENG.
10-8-66 La Scala, Runcorn, ENG.
10-14-66 Liverpool College, Liverpool, ENG.
10-15-66 Dudley College, Dudley, ENG.
10-16-66 The Sumner House, Kings Winsford, ENG.
10-17-66 Newcastle-u-Lynne, Astra, ENG.
10-18-66 Shenley Y. Centre, Birmingham, ENG.
10-19-66 Cleveland Arms, Wolverhampton, ENG.
10-20-66 Palais de Danse, Ashton-under-Lyne, ENG. (D. Garrick)
10-21-66 The Tabernacle, Stockport, ENG. (D. Garrick)
10-22-66 New Century Hall, Manchester, ENG. (D. Garrick)
10-28-66 Flamingo Club, London, ENG.
10-29-66 East Finchley Youth Club, London, ENG. (Brian Epstein attends)
10-30-66 Downbeat, Liverpool, ENG.
10-30-66 Mardi-Gras, Liverpool, ENG.
10-30-66 Blue Angel, Liverpool, ENG.
11-3-66 East Finchley Youth Club, London, ENG.
11-5-66 Arcadia, Bray, Ireland (D. Garrick)
11-6-66 Cork Town Hall, Cork, Ireland (D. Garrick)
11-7-66 Dublin Downtown, Dublin, Ireland (D. Garrick)
11-8-66 The PlayHouse, Walton-On-Thames, ENG. (D. Garrick)
11-9-66 The Ritz, Skewen, S.WALES
11-13-66 Mecca, Blackpool, ENG.
11-15-66 El Partido, Lewisham, ENG.
11-19-66 Le Carnaby Club, Loughborough, ENG.
11-21-66 Marquee, London, ENG.
11-22-66 Bethnal Green, Green Gate, ENG.
11-26-66 Alexander Hall, Halifax, ENG. (D. Garrick)
11-27-66 Las Vegas Club, Dewsbury, ENG. (D. Garrick)
12-2-66 Market Hall, Carlisle, ENG. (D. Garrick)
12-3-66 PlayHouse, Walton-On-Thames, ENG.
12-4-66 Bluesette Club, Leatherhead, ENG.
12-7-66 Top Rank Suite, Wolverhampton, ENG. (D. Garrick)
12-9-66 Marquee, London, ENG. w/The Sands
12-10-66 Adelphi, West Bromwich, ENG.
12-11-66 La Scala, Runcorn, ENG. w/Drifting Sands
12-15-66 Royal Ballet, Hammersmith, ENG.
12-16-66 Tabernacle Club, Stockport, ENG.
12-17-66 Il Rando, Leicester, ENG.
12-18-66 Welcome Inn, Eltham, ENG.
12-20-66 Whiskey-A-Go-Go, London, ENG.
12-21-66 Ludwick Youth Hall, Welwyn Garden City, ENG.
12-22-66 Marquee, London, ENG. w/Pink Floyd, The Question
12-23-66 Blaises Club, London, ENG.
12-26-66 Glen Ballroom, Llanelli, S.WALES w/New Mayfair Orchestra
12-30-66 Queen's Rink Ballroom, West Hartlepool, ENG. (D. Garrick)
12-31-66 The Tabernacle Club, Stockport, ENG. (D. Garrick)
1-2-67 The Staffordshire, Stafford, ENG.
1-3-67 The Green Gates, Bethnal Green, ENG.
1-14-67 Union Rowing Club, Nottingham, ENG.
1-19-67 Locarno, Burnley, ENG.
1-21-67 Tiles, London, ENG. w/The Twilights
1-24-67 Adelphi, Slough, ENG.
1-27-67 Victoria Hall, Oakham, ENG.
1-28-67 YMCA Herbert St., Gloucester, ENG.
2-3-67 Tabernacle Club, Stockport, ENG.
2-4-67 Dorothy Ballroom, Cambridge, ENG.
2-5-67 White Hart, Tottenham, ENG.
2-7-67 Green Gates, Bethnal Green, ENG.
2-10-67 Bluesette Club, Leatherhead, ENG.
2-11-67 Le Carnaby Club, Loughborough, ENG.
2-12-67 Starlight Ballroom, Wembley, ENG. w/The Who
2-14-67 The PlayHouse, Walton-On-Thames, ENG.
2-17-67 Claudette Club, Epson, ENG.
2-18-67 Queens Hall, Barnstaple, ENG. w/Wynder K. Frog
2-20-67 Community Centre, Welwyn, ENG.
2-22-67 Dreamland Ballroom, Margate, ENG.
2-23-67 Graves Grove Community Centre, Harlow, ENG.
2-24-67 The Tower, Blackpool, ENG. w/G. Bond, Easybeats, Cryin' Shames
2-25-67 La Scala, Runcorn, ENG.
2-26-67 Welcome Inn, Eltham, ENG.
3-2-67 Locarnos, Burnley, ENG.
3-3-67 Glenlyn Ballroom, Forest Hill, ENG.
3-4-67 Rub-A-Dub Club, Reading, ENG.
3-5-67 The New Yorker, Swindon, ENG. w/Jo Jo Gunne, The Inspiration
3-6-67 The Glen, Llanelli, S.WALES w/The Outer Limits
3-7-67 British Legion Club, Briton Ferry, S.WALES
3-9-67 Collos Cathedral Club, Newport, S.WALES
3-11-67 The Ritz Ballroom, Bournemouth, ENG.
3-16-67 Empire Ballroom, Neath, S.WALES
3-17-67 Koo-Koo Byrd Club, Cardiff, S.WALES
3-25-67 The Elm Hotel, Leigh-On-Sea, ENG.
3-26-67 Starlight Ballroom, Crawley, ENG.
3-27-67 Oakham Victoria Hall, Easter, ENG.
3-30-67 The Discotheque, Bristol, S.WALES
3-31-67 Starlight Ballroom, Crawley, ENG. w/Chris Farlowe
4-1-67 El Partido, Lewisham, ENG.
4-1-67 Glenlyn Ballroom, Forest Hill, ENG.
4-7-67 The Tabernacle, Stockport, ENG. w/Manchester Playboys
4-11-67 The PlayHouse, Walton-On-Thames, ENG.
4-14-67 Glenlyn Ballroom, Forest Hill, ENG.
4-15-67 Evington's Boys Club, Leicester, ENG.
4-16-67 Cooksferry Inn, Edmonton, ENG.
4-21-67 Temple Bar Hotel, London, ENG.
4-22-67 Temple Bar Hotel, London, ENG.
4-24-67 Glen Ballroom, Llanelli, S.WALES w/Headline News
4-26-67 Glanmor Jazz Club, Swansea, S.WALES
4-27-67 Empire Ballroom, Neath, S.WALES
4-28-67 The Kings Head, London, ENG.
4-29-67 The Kings Head, London, ENG.
4-30-67 The Kings Head, London, ENG.
5-4-67 Summer House Hotel, Kingswinford, ENG.
5-5-67 Koo Koo Byrd Club, Cardiff, S.WALES
5-6-67 Corn Exchange, Bristol, S.WALES
5-7-67 Gold Crest Club, Pembroke, S.WALES
5-8-67 The Robin Hood, Dagenham, ENG.
5-11-67 Blackpool Works, Worcester, ENG. w/The Corncrackers
5-12-67 Fiesta Ballroom, Andover, ENG.
5-13-67 The London Hotel, Southend-On-Sea, ENG.
5-14-67 Starlite Ballroom, Crawley, ENG.
5-18-67 Railway Hotel, Tilbury, ENG.
5-20-67 Princess Ballroom, Halifax, ENG.
5-21-67 Welcome Inn, Eltham, ENG.
5-22-67 Atlanta Ballroom, Woking, ENG.
5-26-67 Victoria Ballroom, Oakham, ENG.
5-27-67 Dorothy Ballroom, Cambridge, ENG.
5-28-67 The King Alfred, Catford, ENG.
5-29-67 Yeoman, Staffordshire, ENG.
6-1-67 Locarno Ballroom, Stevenage, ENG.
6-2-67 Kings College, Chesham, ENG.
6-3-67 Assembly Hall, Framlingham, ENG. w/Wild Oats
6-4-67 The Maids Head, Kings Lynn, ENG.
6-5-67 Starlite Ballroom, Herne Bay, ENG.
6-6-67 The Elms, Southend, ENG.
6-9-67 Ballroom Over Burtons, Uxbridge, ENG. w/Guy Darrel
6-10-67 Evington Boys Club, Leicester, ENG.
6-14-67 Glanmor Jazz Club, Swansea, S.WALES w/Eyes Of Blue
6-15-67 Empire Ballroom, Neath, S.WALES
6-16-67 Swansea Univ., Swansea, S.WALES w/S. Dupree, EOB, Jug & Bottle
6-17-67 The PlayHouse, Walton-On-Thames, ENG.
6-18-67 John's Children Club, Leatherhead, ENG.
6-20-67 Starlite Ballroom, Herne Bay, ENG.
6-22-67 SummerHouse Hotel, Kingsford, ENG.
6-23-67 Manchester University, Manchester, ENG.
6-24-67 The Catacombs, Eastbourne, ENG.
6-25-67 The Wheels Discotheque, Reading, ENG. w/Cream
6-26-67 The Watersplash Nite Club, Walsall, ENG.
6-27-67 The Watersplash Nite Club, Walsall, ENG.
6-28-67 The Watersplash Nite Club, Walsall, ENG. w/Montanas
6-29-67 The Watersplash Nite Club, Walsall, ENG.
6-30-67 The Watersplash Nite Club, Walsall, ENG.
7-1-67 The Watersplash Nite Club, Walsall, ENG.
7-2-67 Royal Oak, Leicester, ENG.
7-6-67 Whiskey-A-Go-Go, London, ENG.
7-7-67 Tigers Head, Catford, ENG.
7-8-67 London Hotel, Southend, ENG.

7-9-67 Golden Diamond, Sutton-In-Ashfield, ENG.
7-14-67 Glanmor Jazz Club, Swansea, S.WALES
7-15-67 U.S. Air Force Base, Ditton Priors, ENG.
7-16-67 Crown & Cushion, Birmingham, ENG.
7-17-67 Penny Farthing Club, Southend, ENG.
7-18-67 Chateau Imphey, Droitwich, ENG.
7-20-67 Marquee, London, ENG. w/Marmalade
7-21-67 Civic Hall, Wolverhampton, ENG.
7-22-67 Princess Ballroom, Halifax, ENG.
7-25-67 W.M. Club, Cannock, ENG.
7-27-67 Kingfisher Club, Kingswinford, ENG. w/The Fourmost
7-29-67 Town Hall, Walsall, ENG. w/The Exception
7-30-67 Summer House, Kingswinford, ENG.
8-4-67 The Witch Doctor, Catford, ENG. (Tom's first gig w/Iveys)
8-5-67 Adelphi Ballroom, Slough, ENG.
8-7-67 W.M. Club, Kettering, ENG.
8-10-67 Whiskey-A-G-Go, London, ENG.
8-11-67 Golden Diamond, Sutton-in-Ashfield, ENG.
8-12-67 Herbert YMCA, Gloucester, ENG.
8-20-67 Starlite Ballroom, Crawley, ENG.
8-21-67 The Astor Theatre, Deal, ENG.
8-24-67 Marquee, London, ENG.
8-25-67 Dorothy Ballroom, Cambridge, ENG.
8-26-67 Dorothy Ballroom, Cambridge, ENG.
8-27-67 Upperent Club, Forest Gate, ENG. w/The Kinks
8-28-67 Golden Torch Ballroom, Stoke-On-Trent, ENG.
8-30-67 Glanmor Jazz Club, Swansea, S.WALES
8-31-67 Adams Beach Ballroom, Merthyr Tydfil, S.WALES
9-1-67 The Harrows, Abbey Wood, ENG.
9-2-67 Temple Bar Hotel, London, ENG.
9-7-67 Palais de Danse, Nottingham, ENG. w/Frilly Gear
9-8-67 Pavilion Ballroom, Porthcawl, S.WALES w/Eyes Of Blue
9-9-67 Temple Bar Hotel, London, ENG.
9-10-67 Bluesette Club, Leatherhead, ENG.
9-11-67 Golden Torch Club, Stoke (Tunstall), ENG.
9-16-67 Marquee, London, ENG. w/The Dream
9-19-67 W.M. Club, Cannock, ENG.
9-21-67 Seahawk Club, Helston, ENG.
9-21-67 H.M.S. Culdrose, S.WALES
9-22-67 Concord Club, Bridport, ENG.
9-23-67 Princess Ballroom, Yeovil, ENG. w/West Coast Vision
9-24-67 Brett's Club, Oxford, ENG.
9-25-67 Redliffe Hotel, Swansea, S.WALES
9-26-67 Hen & Chicken, Langley, ENG.
9-28-67 Adams Beach Ballroom, Merthyr Tydfil, S.WALES
9-29-67 Glanmor Jazz Club, Swansea, S.WALES
9-30-67 Empire Ballroom, Neath, S.WALES w/Wedgewood Blues
10-2-67 Yeoman, Stafford, ENG.
10-5-67 Adams Beach Ballroom, Merthyr Tydfil, S.WALES (van crash)
10-13-67 Ship & Rainbow, Wolverhampton, ENG.
10-14-67 Marquee, London, ENG. w/Neat Change
10-16-67 The Scotsman Club, Cologne, GERM. w/Pinky & The Fellas
10-17-67 The Scotsman Club, Cologne, GERM. w/Pinky & The Fellas
10-18-67 The Scotsman Club, Cologne, GERM. w/Pinky & The Fellas
10-19-67 The Scotsman Club, Cologne, GERM. w/Pinky & The Fellas
10-20-67 The Scotsman Club, Cologne, GERM. w/Pinky & The Fellas
10-21-67 The Scotsman Club, Cologne, GERM. w/Pinky & The Fellas
10-22-67 The Scotsman Club, Cologne, GERM. w/Pinky & The Fellas
10-23-67 The Storyville Club, Cologne, GERM. w/The Fireballs
10-24-67 The Storyville Club, Cologne, GERM. w/The Fireballs
10-25-67 The Storyville Club, Cologne, GERM. w/The Fireballs
10-26-67 The Storyville Club, Cologne, GERM. w/The Fireballs
10-27-67 The Storyville Club, Cologne, GERM. w/The Fireballs
10-28-67 The Storyville Club, Cologne, GERM. w/The Fireballs
10-29-67 The Storyville Club, Cologne, GERM. w/The Fireballs
10-30-67 The Storyville Club, Cologne, GERM. w/The Fireballs
10-31-67 The Storyville Club, Cologne, GERM. w/The Fireballs
11-2-67 The Storyville Club, Cologne, GERM.
11-3-67 The Storyville Club, Cologne, GERM.
11-4-67 The Storyville Club, Cologne, GERM.
11-5-67 The Storyville Club, Cologne, GERM.
11-6-67 The Storyville Club, Cologne, GERM.
11-7-67 The Storyville Club, Cologne, GERM.
11-8-67 The Storyville Club, Cologne, GERM.
11-9-67 The Storyville Club, Cologne, GERM.
11-10-67 The Storyville Club, Cologne, GERM.
11-11-67 The Storyville Club, Cologne, GERM.
11-12-67 The Storyville Club, Cologne, GERM.
11-13-67 The Storyville Club, Cologne, GERM.
11-14-67 The Storyville Club, Cologne, GERM.
11-15-67 The Storyville Club, Cologne, GERM.
11-17-67 Thingamajig Club, Reading, ENG.
11-18-67 Flamingo Club, London, ENG.
11-23-67 Roundabout Club, Aldershot, ENG.
11-25-67 Prudential Sports Club, Reading, ENG.
11-30-67 Marquee, London, ENG.
12-1-67 The Golden Torch, Tunstall, ENG.
12-2-67 New Century Hall. Manchester, ENG. w/Temptations
12-6-67 Queens Hall, Burslem, ENG.
12-8-67 The Kiosk Club, Castleford, ENG.
12-10-67 Wagon And Horses, Stoke-On-Trent, ENG.
12-14-67 Queens Hall, Burslem, ENG.
12-15-67 Kobels Club, Prescot, ENG.
12-16-67 Civic Hall, Hednesford, ENG. w/The Living End
12-17-67 Bluesette Club, Leatherhead, ENG. w/Johns Children
12-19-67 Golden Torch, Tunstall, ENG.
12-20-67 St. Matthews Youth Club, Reading, ENG.
12-22-67 The Corn Hall Discotheque, ENG.
12-23-67 The Queens Hall, Burslem, ENG. w/Yaboos
12-26-67 Royal Lido, Prestatyn, Wales
12-27-67 Glanmor Jazz Club, Swansea, S.WALES
12-29-67 The Church Hall, Fishguard, S.WALES w/The Dream
12-30-67 Golden Torch, Tunstall, ENG.
12-31-67 Thingamajig Club, Reading, ENG.
1-6-68 Marquee, London, ENG. w/The Open Mind
1-11-68 Heburn W.M. Club, Newcastle-On-Tyne, ENG.
1-12-68 Technical College, Chelmsford, ENG. w/The Glass Opening
1-13-68 The Spa Lounge, Cheltenham, ENG.
1-14-68 Bank Hall Miners Club, Burnley, ENG.
1-19-68 The Queens Hall, Burslem, ENG. w/Geno Washington
1-20-68 Thingamajig Club, Reading, ENG.
1-21-68 SummerHouse, Kingswinford, ENG.
1-25-68 Marquee, London, ENG.
1-26-68 Youth Club, Peterborough, ENG.
1-27-68 Dorothy Ballroom, Cambridge, ENG.
2-2-68 Royal Art College, Kensington Grove, ENG. w/Black Cat Bones
2-3-68 Marquee, London, ENG. w/The Open Mind
2-8-68 Silver Horse Club, Arborfield, ENG.
2-10-68 Embassy Suite, Colchester, ENG.
2-14-68 Matthews Youth Club, Reading, ENG.
2-14-68 Thingamajig Club, Reading, ENG.
2-17-68 Top Spot Ballroom, Rhos-On-Wye, S.WALES
2-18-68 R.F. Club, Seven Sister, S.WALES
2-19-68 Langland Bay Hotel, Swansea, S.WALES
2-20-68 The Catholic Hall, Gorseinon, S.WALES
2-21-68 Glanmor Jazz Club, Swansea, S.WALES
2-22-68 RAF Club, St. Athens, S.WALES
2-23-68 W.M. Club, Swansea, S.WALES
2-24-68 The Ritz, Skewen, S.WALES w/The Powerstop
3-3-68 Palais-de-Danse, Asthon-under-Lyne, ENG.
3-7-68 Culdrose Sea Hawk Club, Cornwall, ENG.
3-8-68 Freshwater East Club, Pembroke, S.WALES
3-10-68 Wharf Hotel, Worcester, ENG.
3-11-68 The Yeoman, Stafford, ENG.
3-12-68 Memorial Hall, Aberdare, S.WALES
3-14-68 Comm. & Youth Centre, Milford Haven, S.WALES
3-15-68 Croesxyciliog Sec. School, Cwmbran, S.WALES
3-16-68 Caerlyon College, Newport, Monmouth, S.WALES
3-18-68 The Glen, Llanelli, S.WALES w/Eyes Of Blue
3-19-68 Top Rank Ballroom, Swansea, S.WALES
3-23-68 Marquee, London, ENG. w/The Gods
3-28-68 Thingamajig Club, Reading, ENG.
3-29-68 St. Benedicts, Swansea, S.WALES
3-30-68 The Castle Hotel, Llandovery, S.WALES
4-5-68 Thingamajig Club, Reading, ENG.
4-6-68 Queens Hall, Narbeth, S.WALES w/The Granny's Intentions
4-7-68 Woodpecker Club, Port Talbot, S.WALES w/Liquid Umbrella
4-11-68 Litherland Town Hall, Liverpool, ENG.
4-12-68 Kavels Club, Prescot, ENG.
4-13-68 The Harlequin Club, Liverpool, ENG.
4-14-68 Sandwich Country Club, Warmingham, ENG.
4-15-68 The Black Lion, Cardigan, S.WALES w/The Fawn Glass
4-17-68 St. Matthews Youth Club, Reading, ENG.
4-18-68 Marquee, London, ENG. w/Marmalade
4-20-68 Evington Boys Club, Leicester, ENG.
4-27-68 University Of Wales, Aberstwyth, S.WALES
4-29-68 The Glen, Llanelli, S.WALES
5-4-68 The Wellington Manor, Crowthorne, ENG.
5-10-68 Sport Centre, Brackley, ENG. w/The Maddening Crowd
5-11-68 The Cobweb Club, Hastings, ENG. w/The Lace
5-16-68 RAF Lythan, Chippenham, ENG.
5-17-68 Baronial Hall, Tottenham College Of Art, ENG.
5-23-68 The Cambridge Hotel, Camberley, ENG.
5-25-68 Atlantic College, Llantwitt Major, S.WALES
5-30-68 Thingamajig Club, Reading, ENG.
6-1-68 The Cavern, Liverpool, ENG.
6-3-68 The Ritz Ballroom, Rhyl, Wales
6-4-68 The Church Hall, Aberdare, S.WALES
6-5-68 The Pavilion, Hemel Hempstead, ENG. w/John Fred & The Playboys
6-6-68 The Roman Way, Luton ENG.

6-8-68 Dorothy Ballroom, Cambridge, ENG.
6-15-68 Ye Ye Club, Rimini, ITALY w/I Titani
6-16-68 Ye Ye Club, Rimini, ITALY w/The Casuals
6-17-68 Ye Ye Club, Rimini, ITALY
6-18-68 Ye Ye Club, Rimini, ITALY
6-19-68 Ye Ye Club, Rimini, ITALY
6-20-68 Ye Ye Club, Rimini, ITALY
6-21-68 Ye Ye Club, Rimini, ITALY
6-22-68 Ye Ye Club, Rimini, ITALY
6-23-68 Ye Ye Club, Rimini, ITALY
6-24-68 Ye Ye Club, Rimini, ITALY
6-25-68 Ye Ye Club, Rimini, ITALY
6-26-68 Ye Ye Club, Rimini, ITALY
6-27-68 Ye Ye Club, Rimini, ITALY
6-28-68 Ye Ye Club, Rimini, ITALY
6-29-68 Ye Ye Club, Rimini, ITALY w/The Cliffters
6-30-68 Ye Ye Club, Rimini, ITALY
7-4-68 Dreamland Ballroom, Margate, ENG. w/Geno Washington
7-5-68 Cavern Club, Margate, ENG.
7-6-68 Dreamland Ballroom, Margate, ENG. w/J. Jones & The Vagabonds
7-7-68 Dreamland Ballroom, Margate, ENG.
7-13-68 Marquee, London, ENG. w/The Neat Change
7-20-68 The Cavern, Liverpool, ENG.
7-21-68 Bowaters Club, Ellesmere Port, ENG.
7-28-68 Seven Sisters RF Club, S.WALES
7-29-68 Langland Bay Hotel, Swansea, S.WALES w/Eyes Of Blue
8-3-68 Dorothy Ballroom, Cambridge, ENG.
8-11-68 St. Patrick's Youth Centre, Walsall, ENG.
8-17-68 The Marquee, Baston, ENG. w/Flower Pot Men, Muffin Bank
8-23-68 Top Rank Suite, Swansea, S.WALES
8-24-68 The Sands Club, Merthyr Tydfil, S.WALES
8-29-68 The Hilltop Hotel, Hatfield, ENG.
9-6-68 Thingamajig, Reading, ENG.
9-13-68 Wellington Manor, Crowthorne, ENG.
9-20-68 Sybilla's Club, London, ENG.
9-21-68 Sybilla's Club, London, ENG.
9-23-68 Sybilla's Club, London, ENG.
9-28-68 Gliderdrome (Starlite Ballroom), Boston, ENG. w/Duster Epics
10-1-68 Del Arestusa, Chelsea, ENG.
10-3-68 The Cambridge Hotel, Camberly, ENG.
10-4-68 Sybilla's, London, ENG.
10-5-68 El Grotto Club, Ilford, ENG.
10-6-68 Fryern's Community Centre, Basildon, ENG.
10-7-68 Golden Torch, Stoke-On-Trent, ENG.
10-9-68 Sybilla's Club, London, ENG.
10-12-68 Faculty Of Technology, Manchester, ENG.
10-13-68 The Royal Naval Club, Widres (Lancs), ENG.
10-15-68 The Viadnet Club, Newton-le-Willows, ENG.
10-19-68 Town Hall, Abergavenny, S.WALES
10-20-68 Jewish Youth Club, Stanmore, ENG.
10-25-68 Wellington Manor, Crowthorne, ENG.
10-26-68 Wellington Manor, Crowthorne, ENG.
10-28-68 Sybilla's, London, ENG.
10-29-68 Sybilla's, London, ENG.
10-30-68 Sybilla's, London, ENG.
10-31-68 Sybilla's, London, ENG.
11-1-68 Sybilla's, London, ENG.
11-2-68 U.S.AF Club, Bentwaters, Ipswich, ENG.
11-3-68 Royal Pier Ballroom, Southampton, ENG.
11-9-68 County Home of Lord Banbury, Circester, ENG.
11-23-68 Hull University, ENG.
11-27-68 Hatchett's Club, London, ENG. w/the Playground
12-7-68 Wellington Manor, Crowthorne, ENG.
12-14-68 Rhodes Centre, Bishops Stortford, ENG. w/Clem Curtis
12-31-68 Alexander Palace, ENG. w/S. Faces, S. Tooth, A. Corner, J.Mayall
1-2-69 Mecca's Locarno, Portsmouth, ENG.
1-3-69 Lafayette Club, Wolverhampton, ENG.
1-6-69 Hatchett's Club, Picadilly, ENG.
1-10-69 Wellington Manor, Crowthorne, ENG.
1-17-69 College of Art, Cheltenham, ENG. w/Heaven
1-18-69 The Institute, Braintree, ENG.
1-24-69 Glanmor Jazz Club, Swansea, S.WALES
1-25-69 Market Hall, Haverfordwest, S.WALES w/Haverson Apricot
1-30-69 Brays Youth Club, Harlow, ENG.
1-31-69 Swaversy College, Cambridgeshire, ENG.
2-1-69 The Cavern, Liverpool, ENG.
2-2-69 The Spinning Disc, Leeds, ENG.
2-7-69 Odeon, Birmingham, ENG. (Gene Pitney tour) (no Pitney)
2-8-69 Odeon, Lewisham, ENG. (Gene Pitney tour) w/Marmalade, J. Cocker
2-9-69 Odeon, Gaumont, Southampton, ENG. (Gene Pitney tour)
2-11-69 Odeon, Wolverhampton, ENG. (Gene Pitney tour)
2-12-69 Fairfield Hall, Croydon, ENG. (Gene Pitney tour)
2-14-69 Colston Hall, Bristol, S.WALES (Gene Pitney tour)
2-15-69 The Capitol Theatre, Cardiff, S.WALES (Gene Pitney tour)
2-16-69 Coventry Theatre, Coventry, ENG. (Gene Pitney tour)
2-18-69 Adelphi, Slough, ENG. (Gene Pitney tour)
2-19-69 Gaumont, Doncaster, ENG. (Gene Pitney tour)
2-20-69 ABC, Peterborough, ENG. (Gene Pitney tour)
2-21-69 Astoria, Finsbury Park, ENG. (Gene Pitney tour)
2-22-69 Gaumont, Doncaster, ENG. (Gene Pitney tour)
2-23-69 Empire Theatre, Liverpool, ENG. (Gene Pitney tour)
2-25-69 Granada, East Ham, ENG. (Gene Pitney tour)
2-26-69 Regal Cinema. Cambridge, ENG. (Gene Pitney tour)
2-27-69 ABC Cinema, Lincoln, ENG. (Gene Pitney tour)
2-28-69 Hanley, Gaumont, Stoke-On-Trent, ENG. (Gene Pitney tour)
3-1-69 City Hall, Newcastle-Tyme, ENG. (Gene Pitney tour)
3-2-69 DeMontfort Hall, Leicester, ENG. (Gene Pitney tour)
3-4-69 Odeon Theatre, Glasgow, SCOT. (Gene Pitney tour)
3-5-69 ABC Cinema, Carlisle, SCOT. (Gene Pitney tour)
3-6-69 ABC Cinema, Stockton-On-Tees, SCOT. (Gene Pitney tour)
3-7-69 City Hall, Newcastle-upon-Tyme, SCOT. (Gene Pitney tour)
3-8-69 Odeon, Manchester, ENG. (Gene Pitney tour)
3-9-69 ABC Cinema, Blackpool, ENG. (Gene Pitney tour)
3-14-69 Wintergardens Pavilion, Penzance, S.WALES
3-15-69 The Blue Lagoon, New Quay, S.WALES
3-16-69 Top Rank Suite, Plymouth, ENG.
3-20-69 Town Hall, Reading, ENG. w/Move
3-21-69 Royal Lancaster Univ. Ballroom, London, ENG. w/Tremeloes
3-22-69 College of Technology, Wolverhampton, ENG.
3-29-69 Barn Club, Little Bardfield, ENG.
3-30-69 Tower Ballroom, Great Yarmouth, ENG. w/Lasto
5-1-69 Cavern, Liverpool, ENG.
6-5-69 Mecca Ballroom, Portsmouth, ENG. w/The Rainbow People
6-7-69 Rhodes Centre, Bishops Stortford, ENG. w/Mr. Lucifer
6-21-69 Rhodes Centre, Bishops Stortford, ENG.
6-28-69 Palais de Danse, Bridgend, ENG.
7-1-69 Fountain's Disco, Tenby, S.WALES
7-4-69 Top Rank Suite, Swansea, S.WALES
7-5-69 The Golden Ballroom, Llanelli, S.WALES
7-7-69 Hilton Hotel, London, ENG.
7-11-69 Parochic Huis, Hellendoorn, HOLLAND
7-12-69 Appolo Dansing Club, Renesse, HOLLAND
7-13-69 White Horse Club, Nootdorp, HOLLAND
7-13-69 Club Spiero, Nieuwdorp, HOLLAND
7-21-69 Narracott Hotel, Woolacombe, ENG.
7-22-69 Narracott Hotel, Woolacombe, ENG.
7-23-69 Narracott Hotel, Woolacombe, ENG.
7-24-69 Narracott Hotel, Woolacombe, ENG.
7-25-69 Narracott Hotel, Woolacombe, ENG.
7-26-69 Narracott Hotel, Woolacombe, ENG.
8-1-69 Dorothy Ballroom, Cambridge, ENG.
8-6-69 Park Juliana, Utrecht, HOLLAND
8-7-69 La Vigne Club, Tilburg, HOLLAND
8-8-69 Cartouche Disco, Apeldoorn, HOLLAND
8-9-69 Grote Tente, Lemmer, HOLLAND
8-10-69 Mr. Buutje's Club, Avenhorn, HOLLAND
8-10-69 Nieuwdorp, HOLLAND w/The Shoes
8-13-69 Langrove Club, Swansea, S.WALES
8-14-69 Tai Beach Club, Port Talbot, S.WALES
8-16-69 Palais de Danse, Bridgend, S.WALES
8-17-69 Blue Lagoon, New Quay, S.WALES
8-18-69 Blue Lagoon, New Quay, S.WALES
8-19-69 Blue Lagoon, New Quay, S.WALES
8-20-69 Blue Lagoon, New Quay, S.WALES
8-23-69 Blue Lagoon, New Quay, S.WALES
8-24-69 400 Club, Torquay, ENG.
8-25-69 400 Club, Torquay, ENG.
8-26-69 400 Club, Torquay, ENG. w/Foundations
8-27-69 400 Club, Torquay, ENG.
8-28-69 400 Club, Torquay, ENG.
8-29-69 400 Club, Torquay, ENG.
8-30-69 400 Club, Torquay, ENG.
9-5-69 Hanselheil, Zutphen, HOLLAND w/Grain Box & Soul Machine
9-6-69 City Hall, Wuppertall, GERM. w/New Yardbirds (Led Zeppelin)
9-7-69 Youth Club, Boskamp, GERM.
9-12-69 Spotlight, Brise Norton Air Base, Oxford, ENG.
10-4-69 Market Hall, Haverfordwest, S.WALES w/The J. Drummer B.Band
10-9-69 Cavern, Liverpool, ENG.
10-10-69 The Electric Garden, Glasgow, SCOT.
10-11-69 The Electric Garden, Glasgow, SCOT.
10-12-69 The Electric Garden, Glasgow, SCOT.
10-13-69 Cavern, Liverpool, ENG.
10-16-69 St. Paul's Crypt, London, ENG.
10-17-69 El Grotto, Ilford, ENG.
10-20-69 Youth Club, Chesham, ENG.
10-24-69 Town Hill, Pontypridd, S.WALES
10-25-69 The Glen, Llanelli, S.WALES
10-29-69 Glais, Clydach, S.WALES
10-30-69 Tai Beach, Port Talbot, S.WALES
10-31-69 Glanmor Jazz Club, Swansea, S.WALES
11-1-69 Palais de Danse, Bridgend, ENG. (Ron Griffiths last gig)

Badfinger Live

The following list is approximately 98% of the live shows the original Badfinger played.

12-8-69 Odeon, Haymarket, ENG. (three numbers for press)
12-12-69 Lambda party at college, ENG.
12-19-69 Apple Christmas party, London, ENG.
12-27-69 Civic Hall, Solihull, ENG. (first official gig w/Joey)
1-9-70 The Grand Hall, Kilmarnock, SCOT.
1-10-70 Glasgow University, Glasgow, SCOT.
1-12-70 Park Hotel, Golthorpe, ENG.
1-17-70 Baths Ballroom, Scunthorpe, ENG. w/Dear Mr. Time
1-26-70 The Belfry, Sutton Coalfield, ENG.
1-31-70 Starlite Ballroom, Boston, ENG. w/Midnight Express, Ricky Tee
2-1-70 Silver Blades Club, Bradford, ENG.
2-1-70 Lafayette Club, Wolverhampton, ENG.
2-2-70 Quaintways Cafe, Chester, ENG. w/Principals, Fairground
2-3-70 Rebecca's Club, Birmingham, ENG.
2-5-70 Cavern, Liverpool, ENG. w/Klubs, Robbie Rave & Gray Donna
2-7-70 Carousel Ballroom, Belfast, Ireland
2-8-70 The Count Down Club, Dublin, Ireland
2-10-70 Cardiff University, Cardiff, S.WALES w/The Rainbow People
2-11-70 Electric Garden, Glasgow, SCOT.
2-12-70 Salutation Hall, Perth, SCOT.
2-13-70 Community Hall, Bonnyrigg, SCOT.
2-13-70 Frisco's Club, Edinburgh, SCOT.
2-14-70 The Community Centre, Auchinleck, SCOT.
2-15-70 Cinema Ballroom, Dumfermline, SCOT.
2-18-70 Richmond Club, Manchester, ENG.
2-21-70 Royal Links Pavilion, Cromer, ENG.
2-26-70 The Glen, Llanelli, S.WALES w/Angelique, Quicksand
2-27-70 Up The Junction Club, Crewe, ENG. w/Staffords
2-28-70 Dreamland Ballroom, Margate, ENG.
3-1-70 Lyndon Sporting Club, Bournemouth, ENG.
3-6-70 Aviemore, SCOT.
3-20-70 Finsbury Park, Astoria, ENG. (Pitney tour w/C. Rodgers, J. Hackett)
3-21-70 Empire Theatre, Liverpool, ENG. (Gene Pitney tour)
3-22-70 Birmingham, ENG. (Gene Pitney tour)
3-24-70 Odeon Cinema, Wolverhampton, ENG. (Gene Pitney tour)
3-25-70 Odeon Theater, Doncaster, ENG. (Gene Pitney tour)
3-26-70 City Hall, Newcastle, ENG. (Gene Pitney tour)
3-27-70 ABC Cinema, Hull, ENG. (Gene Pitney tour)
3-28-70 ABC Cinema, Blackpool, ENG. (Gene Pitney tour)
3-29-70 ABC Cinema, Blackpool, ENG. (Gene Pitney tour)
3-30-70 ABC Cinema, Blackpool, ENG. (Gene Pitney tour)
4-1-70 ABC Cinema, Gloucester, ENG. (Gene Pitney tour)
4-2-70 Colston Hall, Bristol, S.WALES (Gene Pitney tour)
4-3-70 Capitol Cinema, Cardiff, S.WALES (Gene Pitney tour)
4-4-70 City Hall, Sheffield, ENG. (Gene Pitney tour)
4-5-70 Coventry Theatre, Coventry, ENG. (Gene Pitney tour)
4-7-70 Cambridge, ENG. (Gene Pitney tour)
4-8-70 Guild Hall, Portsmouth, ENG. (Gene Pitney tour)
4-9-70 Granada Sutton, Surrey, ENG. (Gene Pitney tour)
4-10-70 Granada, East Ham, ENG. (Gene Pitney tour)
4-11-70 Odeon, Lewisham, ENG. (Gene Pitney tour)
4-12-70 Winter Garden, Bournemouth, ENG. (Gene Pitney tour)
4-14-70 Gaumont, Ipswich, ENG. (Gene Pitney tour)
4-15-70 ABC Cinema, Northamptom, ENG. (Gene Pitney tour)
4-16-70 Shrewsbury, ENG. (Gene Pitney tour)
4-17-70 Bolton, ENG. (Gene Pitney tour)
4-18-70 Derby, ENG. (Gene Pitney tour)
6-8-70 Capitol Records Convention, Hawaii, U. States
6-20-70 Sports Stadium, Frankfurt, GERM.
6-24-70 Devalance Hall, Tenby, S.WALES w/Jackie Lomax, Byrds, Family
6-26-70 400 Ballroom, Torquay, ENG.
7-1-70 Headlands Pavilion, Bude, S.WALES
7-2-70 Blue Lagoon, S.WALES
7-3-70 Queens Ballroom, Barnstaple, S.WALES
7-10-70 Rutherford College, Canterbury, ENG.
7-11-70 Dreamland, Margate, ENG.
7-30-70 RNAS Station, Yeavilton, S.WALES
7-31-70 Club Camelot, Taunton, S.WALES
8-1-70 Club Camelot, Taunton, S.WALES
8-7-70 Park Hall Ballroom, Hereford, S.WALES
8-15-70 Groningen Festival, HOLLAND
8-22-70 Bilsen Festival, BELGIUM w/Cat Stevens, Screaming Lord Sutch
9-25-70 Univ. of North Dakota, Grand Forks, SD, U.S.
9-26-70 Pershing Auditorium, Lincoln, NB, U.S.
9-27-70 Bohler gym, Wash. State, Pullman, WA, U.S.
9-28-70 Field House, E. Wash State, Cheney, WA, U.S.
9-29-70 Gym, Central Oregon College, Bend, OR, U.S.
9-30-70 East Montana College, Billings, MT, U.S.
10-1-70 Valley City State, Valley City, SD, U.S.
10-2-70 Church hall, Central College, Pella, IA, U.S.
10-5-70 Armory, SD School of Mines, Rapid City, SD, U.S.
10-7-70 Dorman Gym, Upper IA Coll., Fayette, IA, U.S.
10-9-70 Morningside College, Sioux City, IA, U.S.
10-11-70 Gym, Sack Valley College, Dixon, IL, U.S.
10-14-70 Bemidji, MN, U.S.
10-15-70 Gym, University of Minnesota, Morris, MN, U.S.
10-16-70 St. Thomas Col., St. Pauls, MN, U.S.
10-17-70 Fort Collins, CO, U.S.
10-18-70 Palchy Hall, Adams St Col., Alamosa, CO, U.S. w/Exodus
10-20-70 Baptist Chapel, Shawnee, OK, U.S.
10-22-70 Fine Arts Auditorium, Texas Wesleyan, Ft.Worth, TX, U.S.
10-23-70 Gym, North Dakota State, Fargo, ND, U.S.
10-24-70 Las Vegas, NV, U.S.
10-25-70 Omaha, NB, U.S.
10-29-70 Clinton, MS, U.S.
10-30-70 Wilson Hall, Madison College, Harrisburg, VA, U.S.
10-31-70 Gym, Shepherds College, Sheperdstown, WV, U.S.
11-2-70 Knoxville, TN, U.S.

11-3-70 Gym, Emory University, Atlanta, GA, U.S.
11-4-70 Jacksonville, AL, U.S.
11-6-70 Louisiana State Univ., Baton Rouge, LA, U.S.
11-7-70 Portland, MA, U.S. w/Black Sabbath, Mungo Jerry
11-9-70 Ballroom, NY State Univ., Rochester, NY, U.S.
11-10-70 Depew High School, Depew, NY, U.S.
11-12-70 Bull & Heifer Club, Horseheads, NY, U.S.
11-13-70 War Memorial Auditorium, Syracuse, NY, U.S. w/The Rascals
11-14-70 The WareHouse, Ithaca, NY, U.S. w/Butch
11-20-70 Magical Mystery Tour Coliseum., Norfolk, VA, U.S.
11-21-70 War Mem. Aud., Chattanooga, TN, U.S. w/Nesmith, P.R. & Raiders
11-24-70 Ungano's, New York, NY, U.S. (George Harrison attends)
11-25-70 Ungano's, New York, NY, U.S.
11-26-70 Ungano's, New York, NY, U.S.
11-27-70 County Comm. Hall, White Plains, NY, U.S. w/Brooklyn Bridge
11-28-70 Palladium, Birmingham, MI, U.S. w/Julia, The Woolies
11-30-70 The Plato, Cleveland, OH, U.S. w/Raspberries, Freeport
12-2-70 Memorial Hall, Dayton, OH, U.S.
12-5-70 Bill Auditorium, Augusta, GA, U.S.
12-6-70 Castaways Club, Greensboro, NC, U.S.
3-5-71 University of Toledo, Toledo, OH, U.S.
3-6-71 Civic Aud., Wilmington, NC, U.S. w/Grassroots, McKendrie Spring
3-7-71 Civic Aud., Charleston, SC, U.S. w/Grassroots, McKendrie Spring
3-9-71 Appalachian State College, Boone, NC, U.S.
3-10-71 Erskine College, SC, U.S.
3-13-71 Virginia Theater, Arlington, VA, U.S.
3-19-71 East Town Ballroom, Detroit, MI, U.S. w/War, Wishbone Ash
3-20-71 The Draft House, Akron, OH, U.S.
3-25-71 Music Factory, Greenville, NC, U.S.
3-26-71 Civic Auditorium, Kingsport, TN, U.S.
3-27-71 Civic Auditorium, Knoxville, TN, U.S. w/Grassroots
3-28-71 Castaways Club, Greensboro, NC, U.S.
4-2-71 University of Alabama, Tuscaloosa, AL, U.S.
4-7-71 Cyrus Erie, Elyria, OH, U.S.
4-8-71 Sugar Shack, Columbus, OH, U.S.
4-10-71 Punchie's Club, Birmingham, AL, U.S. w/The Third Power, The Tea
4-11-71 Sherwood Forest Aud., Davidson, MI, U.S. w/Ormandy, Big Red
4-13-71 East Town Theater, Detroit, MI, U.S.
4-14-71 Cow Palace, Fondulac, WI, U.S.
4-17-71 Athletic field, NC State Univ., Raleigh, NC, U.S.
4-18-71 South Conn. State Univ., Newhaven, CT, U.S.
4-19-71 High School, Gloucester, MA, U.S.
4-20-71 Memorial Auditorium, Dallas, TX, U.S.
4-22-71 Sam Houston Coliseum, Houston, TX, U.S.
4-24-71 Fairgrounds, Oklahoma City, OK, U.S.
4-25-71 Field, Texas Christian University, Ft. Worth, TX, U.S.
4-26-71 Memorial Hall, Joplin, MO, U.S.
4-27-71 Central State Univ., Oklahoma City, OK, U.S.
4-28-71 Henry Levelle Arena, Wichita, KS, U.S.
4-30-71 Civic Auditorium, Pasadena, Ca, U.S. w/Pollution
5-1-71 St. Claire Fair, San Jose, CA, U.S. w/Tower Of Power, Lee Michaels
5-6-71 Salem State College, Salem, MA, U.S.
5-7-71 Rock Pile, Long Island, NY, U.S.
5-8-71 Rock Pile, Long Island, NY, U.S.
5-13-71 Lexington, KY, U.S.
5-16-71 Continental Safari Club, Chadsford, PA, U.S.
8-1-71 Madison Square Garden, New York, NY, U.S. (Bangla Desh concert)
9-18-71 Reykjavik, Iceland w/Man, Writing On The Wall
10-15-71 Polytechnic College, Huddersfield, ENG.
10-25-71 Top Rank Suite, Swansea, S.WALES w/Nashville Teens
10-30-71 Kings College, London, ENG.
11-6-71 Mecca Ballroom, Hull, ENG.
11-20-71 DeLaSalle College, Manchester, ENG.
11-25-71 Pandora's Club, Swansea, S.WALES
11-27-71 Loughborough University, ENG.
12-9-71 Sheffield Tech College, ENG.
12-10-71 Carmaethen University, S.WALES
1-22-72 Scene 1 & 2 Club, Scarborough, ENG.
2-2-72 Fenway Theater, Boston, MA, U.S. (2 shows)
2-3-72 Springfield, MA, U.S. w/Pure Prairie League
2-4-72 Loew's Theater, Prov., RI, U.S. (2 shows) w/PPLeague, Al Kooper
2-5-72 Palace Theater, Waterbury, CT, U.S. w/Pure Prairie League
2-9-72 Comack Arena, Long Island, NY, U.S. w/Cactus
2-10-72 The Armory, Rockford, IL, U.S. w/PPLeague, REO Speedwagon

2-11-72 Ford Auditorium, Detroit. MI, U.S. w/Pure Prairie League, Redbone
2-12-72 Franklin & Marshall Coll., Lancaster, PA, U.S.
2-13-72 Wheeling, VA, U.S.
2-15-72 Yosileny College, Detroit, MI, U.S. w/Pure Prairie League
2-17-72 Municipal Aud., Colorado Springs, CO, U.S.
2-18-72 The Draught House, Denver, CO, U.S. w/Pure Prairie League
2-19-72 The Draught House, Denver, CO, U.S. w/Pure Prairie League
2-20-72 Comm. Concorde, San Diego, CA, U.S. w/PPLeague, Alice Cooper
2-21-72 Whiskey A Go Go, Los Angeles, CA, U.S.
2-22-72 Whiskey A Go Go, Los Angeles, CA, U.S.
2-23-72 Whiskey A Go Go, Los Angeles, CA, U.S.
2-25-72 The Valley Theater, Van Nuys, CA, U.S. w/Billy Joel, PPLeague
2-26-72 Anaheim Convention Ctr., Anaheim, CA, U.S. w/War, Rare Earth
2-27-72 Berkeley Theater, Berkeley, CA, U.S. w/The Kinks
3-1-72 Carnegie Hall, New York, NY, U.S. w/Michael Gately, Al Kooper
3-2-72 C.W. Post College, Long Island, NY, U.S.
3-3-72 The Paper Mill Theater, Baltimore, MD, U.S. w/David Pomeranz
3-4-72 William & Mary Coll., Williamsburg, VA, U.S.
3-5-72 County Hall, Charleston, SC, U.S.
3-6-72 West Carolina University, Cullowee, SC, U.S.
3-8-72 The County Hall, Columbia, SC, U.S. w/The Doors, David Pomeranz
3-10-72 Pirates World, Miami, FL, U.S.
3-11-72 The Sports Ground, Tallahassee, FL, U.S.
3-12-72 Ft. Hesterley Armory, Tampa, FL, U.S. w/The Doors
3-14-72 Lincoln High School, Yonkers, NY, U.S.
3-15-72 La Coliseum, Quebec CAN.
3-17-72 Ritz Theater, Staten Island, NY, U.S.
3-18-72 Memorial Field House, Indiana Univ., IN, U.S.
3-19-72 Robert's Stadium, Evansville, IN, U.S. w/Canned Heat
3-22-72 Academy Bldg., Canandaigue, NY, U.S.
3-24-72 Auditorium Theater, Chicago, IL, U.S.
3-26-72 Auditorium Theater, Chicago, IL, U.S.
3-28-72 Coliseum, Indianapolis, IN, U.S. w/Curtis Muldoon, Sea Train
3-29-72 Field House, New Hampshire University, Durham, NH, U.S.
3-31-72 Mem. Aud., New Orleans, LA, U.S. w/K. Crimson, A, D. & Gardner
4-1-72 Municipal Auditorium, Birmingham, AL, U.S. w/King Crimson
4-2-72 Steel Pier, Atlantic City, NJ, U.S.
4-5-72 The Armory, Springfield, IL, U.S. w/Ashton, Dyke, & Gardner
4-7-72 Cowtown Ballroom, Kansas City, MO, U.S.
4-8-72 Kiel Auditorium, St. Louis, MO, U.S. w/Jo Jo Gunne, Lee Michaels
4-9-72 Robinson High School, Fairfax, VA, U.S.
5-5-72 Newcastle University, Newcastle, ENG.
5-14-72 Marquee, London, ENG.
5-27-72 U.S. Air Force Base, Lakenheath, Suffolk, ENG. w/Atomic Rooster
5-28-72 Coliseum, London, ENG. w/Faces
6-3-72 The Yate Entertainment Centre, Bristol, S.WALES
6-9-72 Birmingham College of Education, Birmingham, ENG.
6-10-72 Civic Centre, Whitchurch, ENG. (first gig w/Robbie Stawinsky)
6-11-72 Shaw Theatre, London, ENG.
6-19-72 Wollman Skat. Rink, C. Park, NY, U.S. w/B.B. King, J.Gang, TRex
6-21-72 Civic Center, Ottawa, CAN.
6-23-72 Isadora Ballroom, Youngstown, OH, U.S.
6-24-72 Ritz Theater, Staten Island, NY, U.S.
6-25-72 O'Keefe Center, Toronto, CAN.
6-27-72 Cin. Gardens, Cincinnati, OH, U.S. w/Kindred, McKendrie Spring
6-28-72 Elk Grove High School, Aurora, IL, U.S. w/Kindred
6-29-72 Lyons Township High School, LeGrange, IL, U.S. w/Kindred
7-1-72 Boston Gardens, Boston, MA, U.S. w/Faces, Cactus
7-2-72 Spectrum, Philadelphia, PA, U.S. w/Faces, Cactus
7-3-72 Akron Rubber Bowl, Akron, OH, U.S. w/Faces, Cactus
7-5-72 Chrysler Arena, Ann Arbor, MI, U.S. w/Faces
7-6-72 War Memorial Hall, Syracuse, NY, U.S.
7-8-72 Mount Pocono Raceway, PA, U.S. w/Faces, ELP, Cactus, Humble Pie
7-9-72 Civic Arena, Pittsburgh, PA, U.S. w/Faces
7-10-72 Dillon Stadium, Hartford, CT, U.S. w/Faces
7-12-72 Civic Arena, Duluth, MN, U.S. w/Sugarloaf, Cactus
7-14-72 San Antonio Mun. Aud., San Antonio, TX, U.S. w/Kindred, Cactus
7-15-72 Memorial Hall, Kansas City, MO, U.S. w/Kindred, Cactus
7-16-72 Tulsa Civic Center, Tulsa, OK, U.S.
7-17-72 Municipal Aud., Corpus Christie, TX, U.S. w/Cactus
7-19-72 Stadium, Albuquerque, NM, U.S.
7-21-72 Sioux Falls Arena, SD, U.S. w/Kindred, Cactus
7-22-72 JFK Center, Washington DC, U.S.
7-23-72 Boardwalk, Steel Pier, Atlantic City, NJ, U.S.
7-24-72 Boardwalk, Steel Pier, Atlantic City, NJ, U.S.
7-25-72 Boardwalk, Steel Pier, Atlantic City, NJ, U.S.
7-26-72 Boardwalk, Steel Pier, Atlantic City, NJ, U.S. (2 shows)
7-27-72 Boardwalk, Steel Pier, Atlantic City, NJ, U.S. (2 shows)
7-28-72 Boardwalk, Steel Pier, Atlantic City, NJ, U.S.
7-29-72 Boardwalk, Steel Pier, Atlantic City, NJ, U.S. w/Kindred, Cactus
8-1-72 Memorial Field House, Huntington, WV, U.S.
8-3-72 Atlanta Auditorium, Atlanta, GA, U.S.
8-4-72 Coliseum, Macon, GA, U.S.
8-5-72 Bell Auditorium, Augusta, GA, U.S.
8-6-72 Buffalo, NY, U.S.
8-7-72 Williamsport, PA, U.S.
8-9-72 O'Keefe Center, Toronto, CAN.
1-19-73 Aragon Ballroom, Chicago, IL, U.S.
1-20-73 Convocation Ctr, Athens, OH, U.S. w/Amazing Blondell, McK.Spring
1-21-73 Kiel Auditorium, St. Louis, MO, U.S. w/Rare Earth, Chi Coltrane
1-24-73 Furman College, Greenville, SC, U.S. w/REO Speedwagon
1-25-73 College Field House, Morehead, KY, U.S.
1-26-73 Georgia Southern College, Statesboro, GA, U.S.
1-27-73 Pirates World, Ft. Lauderdale, FL, U.S. w/Bloodrock
2-1-73 Northern University, Ada, OH, U.S.
2-2-73 St. Joseph's Auditorium, Hazelton, PA, U.S.
2-3-73 Towson, MD, U.S.
2-6-73 University Of Georgia, Athens, GA, U.S.
2-7-73 Mobile, AL, U.S.
2-9-73 Frostburg College, Frostburg, MD, U.S.
2-11-73 Frostburg College, Frostburg, MD, U.S. w/John Sebastian
2-16-73 Terrace Ballroom, Salt Lake, UT, U.S.
2-17-73 State College Gym, Boise, ID, U.S.
2-18-73 Aquarius Club, Seattle, WA, U.S.
2-23-73 Hara Arena, Dayton, OH, U.S. w/The Guess Who
2-24-73 Fredrich, MD, U.S.
3-3-73 Rag Ball, Reading University, Reading, ENG. w/Nazareth, Thin Lizzy
3-9-73 Salford University, Lancs, ENG.
3-10-73 NE Essex Tech College, Colchester, ENG.
3-14-73 Edge Hill College, Ormskirk, ENG.
3-16-73 Westfield College, Hampstead, ENG. w/Arthur Brown
3-17-73 Cambridge, ENG.
3-23-73 Bath University, ENG. w/Greenslade
4-14-73 Dudley Tech College, ENG.
8-22-73 Global Village, Charing Cross, London, ENG.
8-23-73 Global Village, Charing Cross, London, ENG.
8-24-73 Hare Krishna Party, Elstree, ENG.
9-2-73 Roundhouse, London, ENG. w/Colin Blunstone
9-14-73 Lyceum, London, ENG.
9-15-73 Golden Diamond, Sutton-In-Ashfield, ENG.
10-5-73 Salford University, Lancs, ENG.
10-6-73 London College Of Printing, London, ENG.
2-23-74 Palace Theater, Detroit, MI, U.S. w/McKendrie Spring
2-24-74 University of Wisconsin, Madison, WI, U.S. w/Flock, Status Quo
2-25-74 The Brewery, East Lansing, MI, U.S.
3-1-74 Painters Mill, Baltimore, MD, U.S.
3-2-74 VIP College, Blacksburg, VA, U.S. w/Marshall Tucker Band
3-4-74 Agora, Cleveland, OH, U.S.
3-5-74 Agora, Toledo, OH, U.S.
3-6-74 Agora, Columbus, OH, U.S.
3-8-74 Gardens Auditorium, Vancouver, CAN.
3-10-74 Stadium, Lethbridge, Alberta, CAN.
3-12-74 Jubilee Hall, Edmonton, CAN.
3-14-74 Thiel College, Greenville, PA, U.S. w/10CC
3-15-74 College, Lansdale, PA, U.S.
3-18-74 Cumberland College, Williamsburg, KY, U.S.
3-20-74 Alex Cookey's Ballroom, Atlanta, GA, U.S.
3-21-74 Alex Cookey's Ballroom, Atlanta, GA, U.S.
3-22-74 Alex Cookey's Ballroom, Atlanta, GA, U.S.
3-23-74 Alex Cookey's Ballroom, Atlanta, GA, U.S.
3-24-74 Robinson Center, Little Rock, AK, U.S.
3-26-74 The Bayer Club, Washington DC, U.S.
3-27-74 Joint In The Woods, Parsipenny, NJ, U.S.
3-28-74 Stratfield Hotel, Bridgeport, CT, U.S.
3-29-74 Victory Burlesque, Toronto, CAN.
3-31-74 Performance Center, Boston, MA, U.S.
4-5-74 Auditorium Theater, Chicago, IL, U.S. w/Grass Roots
9-27-74 Norwich, ENG.
10-2-74 Apollo Theater, Glasgow, SCOT. (Man tour starts)
10-3-74 The Usher Hall, Edinboro, SCOT.
10-4-74 University of Lancaster, Lancaster, ENG.
10-6-74 The Palace Theatre, Manchester, ENG.
10-7-74 The Civic Hall, Wolverhampton, ENG.
10-9-74 Town Hall, Greenwich, ENG.
10-11-74 Bath University, Bath, ENG.
10-12-74 Imperial College, London, ENG.
10-13-74 The Greyhound, Croydon, ENG.
10-14-74 Polytechnic Concert Hall, Oxford, ENG.
10-15-74 Town Hall, Birmingham, ENG.
10-16-74 Top Rank Suite, Swansea, S.WALES
10-17-74 The Guild Hall, Portsmouth, ENG.
10-18-74 Leas Cliff Hall, Folkestone,ENG.
10-19-74 The Town Hall, Cambridge, ENG.
10-23-74 Top Rank Suite, Swansea, S.WALES
10-24-74 Town Hall, Cheltenham, ENG.
10-25-74 Adelphi Theatre, London, ENG.
10-26-74 The Kursaal, Southend, ENG.

Iveys & Badfinger Studio Sessions

The following list portrays the date of the session, the studio, producer, and any songs which were verified to be worked on by documentation. This is approximately a 95% to 98% comprehensive list.

1-15-67 Maximum Sound, R. Davies, Sausage And Egg, I Believe, Taxi
9-18-67 Albrighton, Iveys, Black & White Rainbows, I Believe, Another Day
9-19-67 Albrighton, Iveys, I'll Kiss You Goodnight, Mr. Strangeways
4-2-68 Pan Studios, Mike Hurst, Angelique, Bittersweet Adieu
4-4-68 Pan Studios, Mike Hurst, Angelique, Bittersweet Adieu
7-23-68 Trident, Tony Visconti, Daddy's A Millionaire, No Escaping
7-24-68 Trident, Denny Cordell, Daddy's A Millionaire
7-24-68 Trident, Tony Visconti, Mrs. Jones
7-25-68 Trident, Denny Cordell, Daddy's A Millionaire
7-26-68 Trident, Tony Visconti, I'm In Love
8-9-68 Trident, Tony Visconti, Daddy's A Millionaire, Maybe Tomorrow
8-15-68 Trident, Tony Visconti, Maybe Tomorrow, Daddy's (new version)
8-22-68 Trident, Tony Visconti, Maybe Tomorrow, Mrs. Jones, I'm In Love
9-25-68 Trident, Tony Visconti, Dear Angie
9-30-68 Trident, Tony Visconti, Maybe Tomorrow, Dear Angie (strings)
10-6-68 Trident, Tony Visconti, Maybe Tomorrow (mixing)
10-17-68 Trident, Tony Visconti, Maybe Tomorrow (new mix)
10-25-68 Trident, Tony Visconti, Daddy's A Millionaire (mixing)
11-7-68 Olympic, Glyn Johns, I've Been Waiting
11-10-68 Olympic, Tony Visconti, Yesterday Ain't Coming Back, Sali Bloo
12-4-68 Olympic, Tony Visconti, Think About The Good Times, Angelique
12-13-68 Olympic, Tony Visconti, Think About The Good Times, (3 mixes)
12-21-68 Morgan, Mal Evans, Storm In A Teacup
12-22-68 Morgan, Mal Evans, Storm In A Teacup (mixing)
1-1-69 Olympic, Mal Evans, Maybe Tomorrow (backing track - Lulu Show)
2-6-69 Trident, Mal Evans, Sali Bloo (mixing)
2-10-69 Trident, Mal Evans, Beautiful And Blue, See Saw Grandpa
2-17-69 Trident, Mal Evans, Fisherman, Knocking Down Our Home
2-21-69 Trident, Mal Evans, See Saw Grandpa (Nicky Hopkins),
2-24-69 Trident, Mal Evans, (mixing)
3-4-69 Trident, Mal Evans, (mixing)
3-5-69 Wessex, Mal Evans, Knocking Down Our Home (Collins - piano)
3-6-69 Trident, Mal Evans, (mixing)
3-7-69 Trident, Mal Evans, (mixing)
3-12-69 Trident, group, See Saw Grandpa, I've Been Waiting (mixing)
4-1-69 Trident, Mal Evans, Give It A Try, Arthur
8-2-69 EMI, Paul McCartney, Come And Get It
8-22-69 EMI, Paul McCartney, Carry On Til Tomorrow
9-17-69 IBC, group, working on song ideas for film
9-18-69 IBC, Paul McCartney, Rock Of All Ages
9-25-69 IBC, group, (editing for single)
9-26-69 IBC, group, Crimson Ship
10-22-69 EMI, Mal Evans, (mixing)
10-28-69 EMI, Mal Evans, Give It A Try (mixing)
11-21-69 IBC, Mal Evans, I'm In Love, Midnight Sun, Walk Out In The Rain
11-24-69 EMI, Mal Evans, (mixing)
11-27-69 EMI, Mal Evans, (mixing)
12-4-69 EMI, Mal Evans, (mixing)
12-8-69 EMI, Mal Evans, (mixing)
3-8-70 Trident, George Harrison, Tom, Pete (It Don't Come Easy)
4-18-70 ? studio, Mal Evans, Without You, Get Down, I Can't Take It, NMW
4-27-70 EMI, Mal Evans, Carry On Til Tomorrow (editing)
5-13-70 EMI, Mal Evans, Get Down, Believe Me, Photograph, NMW
5-16-70 Trident, Mal Evans, No Matter What
5-20-70 Trident, Mal Evans, Believe Me
5-28-70 EMI, George Harrison, All Things Must Pass (Pete & Joey)
5-29-70 EMI, George Harrison, All Things Must Pass (Pete, Tom, Joey)
6-1-70 EMI, George Harrison, All Things Must Pass (Pete, Mike, Tom, Joey)
6-2-70 EMI, George Harrison, All Things Must Pass (Pete, Mike, Tom, Joey)
6-3-70 EMI, George Harrison, All Things Must Pass (Pete, Mike, Tom, Joey)
6-15-70 EMI, Mal Evans, No Matter What, Believe Me
6-22-70 EMI, George Harrison, (Pete, Tom – session work)
6-23-70 EMI, George Harrison, (Pete, Tom – session work)
6-27-70 EMI, Geoff Emerick, We're For The Dark, I Can't Take It
7-3-70 EMI, Geoff Emerick, We're For The Dark (strings)
7-15-70 EMI, Geoff Emerick, Without You, Better Days
7-16-70 EMI, Geoff Emerick, Watford John
7-18-70 EMI, Geoff Emerick, Watford John, Better Days
7-21-70 EMI, Geoff Emerick
7-22-70 EMI, Geoff Emerick
7-25-70 EMI, Geoff Emerick, It Had To Be, Get Down
7-27-70 EMI, Geoff Emerick
7-28-70 EMI, Geoff Emerick
7-29-70 EMI, Geoff Emerick
8-2-70 EMI, Geoff Emerick, Blodwyn
8-3-70 EMI, Geoff Emerick, Blodwyn
8-12-70 EMI, Geoff Emerick
8-18-70 EMI, Geoff Emerick, (mixing)
8-19-70 EMI, Geoff Emerick
8-25-70 EMI, Geoff Emerick, No Matter What, Believe Me
8-26-70 EMI, Geoff Emerick, No Matter What, Believe Me (mix)
1-9-71 EMI, Geoff Emerick
1-10-71 EMI, Geoff Emerick
1-16-71 EMI, Geoff Emerick
1-19-71 Command, Geoff Emerick
1-23-71 EMI, Geoff Emerick
1-27-71 EMI, Geoff Emerick
1-28-71 EMI, Geoff Emerick
2-3-71 Air, Geoff Emerick
2-4-71 Air, Geoff Emerick
2-5-71 Air, Geoff Emerick
2-8-71 EMI, Geoff Emerick
2-9-71 EMI, Harrison, Spector, (Pete – session work)
2-12-71 Air, Geoff Emerick, Loving You
2-13-71 Air, Geoff Emerick
2-14-71 Air, Geoff Emerick, Perfection (harmonica)
2-17-71 Air, Geoff Emerick
2-20-71 Air, Geoff Emerick
2-21-71 Air, Geoff Emerick
2-23-71 Air, Geoff Emerick, Sweet Tuesday Morning
2-25-71 Air, Geoff Emerick, Baby Please
2-26-71 Air, Pete Ham, Loving You
2-27-71 EMI, Geoff Emerick
2-28-71 EMI, Geoff Emerick
3-2-71 EMI, Geoff Emerick
3-23-71 Bell Sound, Al Kooper, Name Of The Game (mix)
4-1-71 Bell Sound, Al Steckler, Name Of The Game (mix)
4-23-71 EMI, Harrison, Spector, Name Of The Game (mix)
5-24-71 John Lennon home in Tittenhurst, (Tom, Joey - session work)
5-30-71 EMI, George Harrison, Name Of The Game
5-31-71 EMI, George Harrison, Suitcase
6-1-71 EMI, George Harrison, I'd Die Babe
6-3-71 EMI, George Harrison, I'd Die Babe
6-4-71 EMI, George Harrison, Day After Day
6-5-71 EMI, George Harrison
6-7-71 EMI, George Harrison, Suitcase (Leon Russell)
6-8-71 EMI, George Harrison, Day After Day (Leon Russell)
6-9-71 EMI, George Harrison, Name Of The Game
6-10-71 EMI, George Harrison, Name Of The Game
8-18-71 ? studio, George Harrison, (Pete on Ringo session)
8-19-71 ? studio, George Harrison, (Pete on Ringo session)
9-24-71 Air, group, Baby Blue
9-25-71 Air, group, Sometimes
9-26-71 Air, Todd Rundgren, Baby Blue, Sometimes
9-27-71 Air, Todd Rundgren
9-28-71 Command, Todd Rundgren
10-1-71 Air, Todd Rundgren
10-2-71 Morgan, Todd Rundgren
10-3-71 Morgan, Todd Rundgren, Perfection, Money
10-4-71 Command, Todd Rundgren, Money, I'd Die Babe
10-5-71 Morgan, Todd Rundgren, Baby Blue
10-6-71 Morgan, Todd Rundgren, Sweet Tuesday Morning (Bill - accordion)
10-7-71 Morgan, Todd Rundgren, (rough mixes)
1-17-72 Apple, Todd Rundgren, Winner, I Can Love you
1-18-72 Apple, Todd Rundgren
1-20-72 Apple, Todd Rundgren
1-21-72 Apple, Todd Rundgren
9-11-72 Apple, group, drummer - Jeff Sweetingham
9-12-72 Apple, group, drummer - Jeff Sweetingham
9-13-72 Apple, group, drummer - Jeff Sweetingham
9-14-72 Apple, group, arranger - Mike Liston
9-15-72 Apple, group, arranger - Mike Liston
9-16-72 Apple, group, Sandcastles
9-23-72 Apple, group, Timeless, drummer - Howard Burkett
9-24-72 Apple, group, drummer - Harry Rix
10-4-72 ? studio, George Harrison, (Pete & Tom – session work)
10-11-72 ? studio, George Harrison, (Pete & Tom – session work)
10-17-72 Morgan, group, Do You Mind
10-18-72 Morgan, group
10-20-72 Morgan, group, Cowboy (Joey not present)
10-21-72 Morgan, group, Timeless, Do You Mind, When I Say
10-26-72 Morgan, group
10-27-72 Morgan, group
10-28-72 Morgan, group
10-29-72 Morgan, group
11-7-72 ? studio, (Pete, Tom - Keith Moon session)
11-12-72 The Manor, group, (Joey not present)
11-13-72 The Manor, group
11-14-72 The Manor, group
11-15-72 The Manor, group
11-16-72 The Manor, group
11-17-72 The Manor, group
11-18-72 The Manor, group
11-19-72 The Manor, group
11-20-72 The Manor, group
11-29-72 Apple, group, Cowboy (violin)
11-30-72 The Manor, group
12-1-72 The Manor, group, (Beresford-Cooke filming)

12-3-72 The Manor, group
12-4-72 The Manor, group
12-5-72 The Manor, group
12-7-72 The Manor, group
12-8-72 The Manor, group
12-9-72 The Manor, group
12-10-72 The Manor, group
12-11-72 The Manor, group
12-28-72 The Manor, group
12-29-72 The Manor, group
12-30-72 The Manor, group
12-31-72 The Manor, group
1-2-73 Trident, group, (mixing)
1-3-73 Trident, group, Apple Of My Eye, Winner (mixing)
1-5-73 Air, group, I Can Love You
1-14-73 Air, group, (mixing)
4-2-73 Olympic, Chris Thomas
4-3-73 Olympic, Chris Thomas
4-4-73 Olympic, Chris Thomas
4-5-73 Olympic, Chris Thomas, Constitution
4-6-73 Olympic, Chris Thomas
4-7-73 Olympic, Chris Thomas
4-8-73 Olympic, Chris Thomas
4-9-73 Olympic, Chris Thomas
4-10-73 Olympic, Chris Thomas
4-11-73 Olympic, Chris Thomas
4-12-73 Olympic, Chris Thomas
4-19-73 Olympic, Chris Thomas
4-21-73 Olympic, Chris Thomas
4-22-73 Olympic, Chris Thomas, Blind Owl, Get Away (mixing)
4-23-73 Olympic, Chris Thomas, (mixing)
4-24-73 Olympic, Chris Thomas
4-25-73 Olympic, Chris Thomas
4-26-73 Olympic, Chris Thomas
4-27-73 Olympic, Chris Thomas
6-21-73 Olympic, Chris Thomas
6-22-73 Olympic, Chris Thomas
6-25-73 Olympic, Chris Thomas
6-26-73 Olympic, Chris Thomas
6-27-73 Olympic, Chris Thomas
6-28-73 Olympic, Chris Thomas
6-29-73 Olympic, Chris Thomas
7-2-73 Olympic, Chris Thomas
7-3-73 Olympic, Chris Thomas, Matted Spam (horn session)
7-4-73 Olympic, Chris Thomas
7-5-73 Olympic, Chris Thomas
7-6-73 Olympic, Chris Thomas
7-9-73 Olympic, Chris Thomas
7-10-73 Olympic, Chris Thomas
7-11-73 Olympic, Chris Thomas
7-12-73 Olympic, Chris Thomas
7-13-73 Olympic, Chris Thomas
7-15-73 Air, Chris Thomas, (mixing)
7-16-73 Air, Chris Thomas
7-17-73 Air, Chris Thomas
7-18-73 Air, Chris Thomas
7-19-73 Air, Chris Thomas
7-20-73 Air, Chris Thomas
7-27-73 ? studio, Tom Evans, Tom producing Fatgrapple
8-14-73 ? studio, Tom Evans, Tom producing Fatgrapple
8-30-73 Olympic, Chris Thomas, Shine On
8-31-73 Olympic, Chris Thomas, Shine On
9-7-73 Air, Chris Thomas, Shine On, Love Is Easy (mixing)
10-17-73 EMI, Chris Thomas, Love Is Easy (mixing)
10-18-73 Olympic, Chris Thomas
10-19-73 Olympic, Chris Thomas
10-22-73 Olympic, Chris Thomas
10-23-73 Olympic, Chris Thomas
10-24-73 Olympic, Chris Thomas
10-25-73 Olympic, Chris Thomas
10-26-73 Olympic, Chris Thomas
10-29-73 Olympic, Chris Thomas, Give It Up
10-30-73 Olympic, Chris Thomas, Give It Up
10-31-73 Olympic, Chris Thomas
11-1-73 Olympic, Chris Thomas, Give It Up
11-2-73 EMI, Chris Thomas, Love Is Easy (mixing)
11-2-73 Air, Chris Thomas, (mixing)
11-5-73 Olympic, Chris Thomas
11-6-73 Olympic, Chris Thomas, Where Do We Go From Here
11-7-73 Olympic, Chris Thomas
11-8-73 Olympic, Chris Thomas
11-9-73 Olympic, Chris Thomas
11-12-73 Olympic, Chris Thomas, (mixing)
11-13-73 Olympic, Chris Thomas
11-14-73 Olympic, Chris Thomas
11-15-73 Olympic, Chris Thomas, Andy Norris
11-16-73 Olympic, Chris Thomas, Lonely You
11-19-73 Olympic, Chris Thomas, (mixing)
11-20-73 Olympic, Chris Thomas, (mixing)
11-21-73 Olympic, Chris Thomas
4-9-74 Caribou Ranch, Chris Thomas
4-10-74 Caribou Ranch, Chris Thomas
4-11-74 Caribou Ranch, Chris Thomas
4-12-74 Caribou Ranch, Chris Thomas
4-13-74 Caribou Ranch, Chris Thomas
4-14-74 Caribou Ranch, Chris Thomas
4-15-74 Caribou Ranch, Chris Thomas
4-16-74 Caribou Ranch, Chris Thomas
4-17-74 Caribou Ranch, Chris Thomas
4-18-74 Caribou Ranch, Chris Thomas
4-19-74 Caribou Ranch, Chris Thomas
4-20-74 Caribou Ranch, Chris Thomas
4-21-74 Caribou Ranch, Chris Thomas
4-23-74 Caribou Ranch, Chris Thomas
4-24-74 Caribou Ranch, Chris Thomas
4-25-74 Caribou Ranch, Chris Thomas
4-26-74 Caribou Ranch, Chris Thomas
4-27-74 Caribou Ranch, Chris Thomas
4-28-74 Caribou Ranch, Chris Thomas
4-29-74 Caribou Ranch, Chris Thomas
4-30-74 Caribou Ranch, Chris Thomas
5-1-74 Caribou Ranch, Chris Thomas
5-2-74 Caribou Ranch, Chris Thomas
5-3-74 Caribou Ranch, Chris Thomas
5-4-74 Caribou Ranch, Chris Thomas
5-5-74 Caribou Ranch, Chris Thomas
5-6-74 Caribou Ranch, Chris Thomas
5-7-74 Caribou Ranch, Chris Thomas
6-3-74 Air, Chris Thomas
6-4-74 Air, Chris Thomas
6-5-74 Air, Chris Thomas
6-6-74 Air, Chris Thomas
6-7-74 Air, Chris Thomas
6-10-74 Air, Chris Thomas
6-11-74 Air, Chris Thomas
6-12-74 Air, Chris Thomas
6-13-74 Air, Chris Thomas
6-14-74 Air, Chris Thomas
6-17-74 Air, Chris Thomas
6-18-74 Air, Chris Thomas
6-19-74 Air, Chris Thomas
6-20-74 Air, Chris Thomas
6-21-74 Air, Chris Thomas
6-24-74 Air, Chris Thomas
6-25-74 Air, Chris Thomas
6-26-74 Air, Chris Thomas
6-27-74 Air, Chris Thomas
6-28-74 Air, Chris Thomas
6-29-74 Air, Chris Thomas
6-30-74 Air, Chris Thomas
7-2-74 Air, Chris Thomas, orchestra and brass overdubs
7-3-74 Air, Chris Thomas
7-5-74 Air, Chris Thomas
7-8-74 Air, Chris Thomas
7-9-74 Air, Chris Thomas, Know One Knows (mixing)
7-10-74 Air, Chris Thomas
7-11-74 Air, Chris Thomas
7-12-74 Air, Chris Thomas
7-13-74 Air, Chris Thomas
7-14-74 Air, Chris Thomas
7-15-74 Air, Chris Thomas
7-16-74 Air, Chris Thomas
7-17-74 Air, Chris Thomas
7-18-74 Air, Chris Thomas
7-21-74 Air, Chris Thomas
7-23-74 Air, Chris Thomas
7-24-74 Air, Chris Thomas
12-1-74 Apple, Kerner/Wise
12-2-74 Apple, Kerner/Wise
12-3-74 Apple, Kerner/Wise
12-4-74 Apple, Kerner/Wise
12-5-74 Apple, Kerner/Wise
12-6-74 Apple, Kerner/Wise
12-7-74 Apple, Kerner/Wise
12-9-74 Apple, Kerner/Wise
12-10-74 Apple, Kerner/Wise
12-11-74 Apple, Kerner/Wise
12-12-74 Apple, Kerner/Wise
12-13-74 Apple, Kerner/Wise
12-14-74 Apple, Kerner/Wise
12-15-74 Apple, Kerner/Wise, (rough mixes)
1-16-75 Record Plant, Kerner/Wise, (mixing)
1-17-75 Record Plant, Kerner/Wise, (mixing)
1-18-75 Record Plant, Kerner/Wise, (mixing)
1-19-75 Record Plant, Kerner/Wise, (mixing)
1-20-75 Record Plant, Kerner/Wise, (mixing)
1-21-75 Record Plant, Kerner/Wise, (mixing)

Photo Credits

The photographs and reproductions in this book have been gathered from many collections and are used with the kind permission of the photographers or owners that are indicated. While every attempt has been made to trace and credit proper owners, holders of some historic, publicity, and other photographs are not known. I wish to extend our apologies to any copyright holder whose photograph may be uncredited or inadvertently miscredited. If any are perceived, please contact the Publisher for rectification in any future editions. The book's pictures are listed left to right, or clockwise (starting at top left) for pages with three or more photos. The owner of the photo is listed first. The photographer, if known, is listed second, in parentheses.

page VII	(1) Dan Matovina (Dan Matovina)
	(2) Farrell Grehan (Farrell Grehan)
	(3) Farrell Grehan (Farrell Grehan)
page VIII	(1) Dan Matovina (Dan Matovina)
	(2) Farrell Grehan (Farrell Grehan)
page IX	(1) Farrell Grehan (Farrell Grehan)
	(2) Dan Matovina (Dan Matovina)
page X	(1) unknown
	(2) Farrell Grehan (Farrell Grehan)
page XI	(1) BBC Wales
	(2) Dan Matovina (Dan Matovina)
page 2	(1) John Ham
	(2) John Ham
page 3	Beverley Tucker
page 5	(1) Alwyne Jenkins
	(2) Alwyne Jenkins
page 9	Ron Griffiths
page 11	Conrad Atkin
page 12	Ron Griffiths (Spiv Morris)
page 13	Alwyne Jenkins
page 15	Ron Griffiths (Boscobel)
page 16	(1) Geoff Kebbell (Geoff Kebbell)
	(2) Geoff Kebbell (Geoff Kebbell)
page 17	(1) Geoff Kebbell (Geoff Kebbell)
	(2) Geoff Kebbell (Geoff Kebbell)
page 19	Ron Griffiths (R. Greenwich)
page 24	Geoff Kebbell (Geoff Kebbell)
page 25	David Evans
page 27	David Evans
page 28	Beverley Tucker
page 30	unknown
page 32	(1) Conrad Atkin
	(2) Conrad Atkin
page 33	(1) Conrad Atkin
	(2) Conrad Atkin
page 38	Beverley Tucker
page 40	Ron Griffiths
page 45	Beverley Tucker
page 46	Apple Corps. Ltd.
	unknown
page 49	Ron Griffiths
page 50	Beverley Tucker
page 53	Apple Corps. Ltd.
page 57	Tom Hanley (Tom Hanley)
page 59	Apple Corps. Ltd.
page 62	Gaynor Gibbins
page 67	Tom Hanley (Tom Hanley)
page 69	unknown
page 73	Brian Slater (Brian Slater)
page 74	Barry Plummer (Barry Plummer)
page 75	Apple Corps. Ltd.
page 77	Barry Plummer (Barry Plummer)
page 78	Apple Corps. Ltd.
page 79	Shepard Sherbell (Shepard Sherbell)
page 80	Richard DiLello (Richard DiLello)
page 82	Richard DiLello (Richard DiLello)
page 85	(1) Gaynor Gibbins
	(2) Gaynor Gibbins
	(3) Gaynor Gibbins
page 86	Lou Christie
page 87	Lou Christie
page 89	Gaynor Gibbins
page 90	Gaynor Gibbins
page 92	Marianne Evans
page 94	(1) Gaynor Gibbins
	(2) Gaynor Gibbins
	(3) Wayne Christian Treiber (Wayne Christian Treiber)
page 97	Gaynor Gibbins
page 99	Beverley Tucker
page 100	Shepard Sherbell (Shepard Sherbell)
page 102	Gaynor Gibbins
page 103	Estate of Peter William Ham
page 104	(1) Wayne Christian Treiber (Wayne Christian Treiber)
	(2) Wayne Christian Treiber (Wayne Christian Treiber)
page 105	(1) Wayne Christian Treiber (Wayne Christian Treiber)
	(2) Wayne Christian Treiber (Wayne Christian Treiber)
page 108	Wayne Christian Treiber (Wayne Christian Treiber)
page 109	Wayne Christian Treiber (Wayne Christian Treiber)
page 110	unknown
page 112	Apple Corps. Ltd. (Richard DiLello)
page 114	Beverley Tucker
page 115	Ardith Polley
page 117	(1) Apple Corps. Ltd.
	(2) Apple Corps. Ltd.
	(3) Apple Corps. Ltd.
page 118	(1) Gaynor Gibbins
	(2) Gaynor Gibbins
page 119	Gaynor Gibbins
page 120	Wayne Christian Treiber (Wayne Christian Treiber)
page 123	John Ham (Pete Ham home movies)
page 125	Marianne Evans
page 126	(1) Wayne Christian Treiber (Wayne Christian Treiber)
	(2) Wayne Christian Treiber (Wayne Christian Treiber)
page 127	(1) Dixie Butz
	(2) John Ham (Pete Ham home movies)
page 128	(1) Wayne Christian Treiber (Wayne Christian Treiber)
	(2) Wayne Christian Treiber (Wayne Christian Treiber)
page 129	(1) Wayne Christian Treiber (Wayne Christian Treiber)
	(2) Wayne Christian Treiber (Wayne Christian Treiber)
page 132	(1) John Ham (Pete Ham home movies)
	(2) John Ham (Pete Ham home movies)
	(3) John Ham (Pete Ham home movies)
	(4) John Ham (Pete Ham home movies)
page 133	John Ham (Pete Ham home movies)
page 134	Retna Ltd. Pictures (Michael Putland)
page 136	Tim Boxer (Tim Boxer)
page 137	unknown
page 140	Apple Corps. Ltd. (Tom Hanley)
page 141	Beverley Tucker
page 142	Wayne Christian Treiber (Wayne Christian Treiber)
page 144	Richard DiLello (Richard DiLello)
page 146	Apple Corps. Ltd.
page 147	unknown
page 148	unknown
page 150	Trouser Press
page 154	Apple Corps. Ltd. (Richard DiLello)
page 156	John Ham (Pete Ham home movies)
page 158	Trouser Press
page 160	Wayne Christian Treiber (Wayne Christian Treiber)
page 162	Wayne Christian Treiber (Wayne Christian Treiber)
page 164	Al Steckler
page 167	Al Steckler
page 168	Apple Corps. Ltd.
page 169	Estate of Peter William Ham
page 173	(1) Gaynor Gibbins
	(2) David Evans
page 174	New Musical Express
page 175	(1) John Ham (Pete Ham home movies)
	(2) BBC Wales
page 176	John Ham (Pete Ham home movies)
page 177	Wayne Christian Treiber (Wayne Christian Treiber)
page 179	(1) David Evans
	(2) David Evans
	(3) David Evans
page 181	Wayne Christian Treiber (Wayne Christian Treiber)
page 183	unknown
page 184	John Ham (Pete Ham home movies)
page 186	Marianne Evans
page 189	Billboard Magazine
page 191	Japanese documentary
page 193	Tom Hanley (Tom Hanley)
page 195	(1) Estate of Tony Beresford-Cooke (Tony Beresford-Cooke)
	(2) Estate of Tony Beresford-Cooke (Tony Beresford-Cooke)
	(3) Estate of Tony Beresford-Cooke (Tony Beresford-Cooke)
	(4) Estate of Tony Beresford-Cooke (Tony Beresford-Cooke)
page 196	John Ham (Pete Ham home movies)

page 197 Gaynor Gibbins
page 200 Estate of Pete Ham
page 202 (1) Midnight Special
(2) Midnight Special
(3) Midnight Special
(4) Midnight Special
page 204 Barry Plummer (Barry Plummer)
page 205 (1) John Ham (Pete Ham home movies)
(2) Marianne Evans
(3) Wayne Christian Treiber (Wayne Christian Treiber)
(4) Estate of Tony Beresford-Cooke
page 208 (1) John Ham (Pete Ham home movies)
(2) John Ham (Pete Ham home movies)
page 210 (1) Estate of Tony Beresford-Cooke (Tony Beresford-Cooke)
(2) Estate of Tony Beresford-Cooke (Tony Beresford-Cooke)
page 211 (1) Estate of Tony Beresford-Cooke (Tony Beresford-Cooke)
(2) Estate of Tony Beresford-Cooke (Tony Beresford-Cooke)
page 214 Apple Corps. Ltd.
page 216 Marianne Evans
page 221 (1) Japanese Documentary
(2) Japanese Documentary
(3) Japanese Documentary
(4) Japanese Documentary
page 223 Japanese Documentary
page 225 (1) Japanese documentary
(2) John Ham (Pete Ham home movies)
(3) Gaynor Gibbins
(4) John Ham (Pete Ham home movies)
(5) Japanese documentary
page 226 Retna Pictures Ltd. (Michael Putland)
page 230 Estate of Peter William Ham
page 232 (1) John Ham (Pete Ham home movies)
(2) Wayne Christian Treiber (Wayne Christian Treiber)
page 235 Warner Brothers Records
page 237 (1) Wayne Christian Treiber (Wayne Christian Treiber)
(2) Wayne Christian Treiber (Wayne Christian Treiber)
(3) Wayne Christian Treiber (Wayne Christian Treiber)
(4) Wayne Christian Treiber (Wayne Christian Treiber)
page 239 (1) Janet Macoska (Janet Macoska)
(2) Janet Macoska (Janet Macoska)
(3) Janet Macoska (Janet Macoska)
page 241 (1) John Ham (Pete Ham home movies)
(2) John Ham (Pete Ham home movies)
(3) John Ham (Pete Ham home movies)
(4) John Ham (Pete Ham home movies)
page 243 John Ham (Pete Ham home movies)
page 244 Estate of Peter William Ham
page 245 John Ham (Pete Ham home movies)
page 247 (1) Estate of Peter William Ham
(2) Estate of Peter William Ham
page 252 Anton Corbijn (Anton Corbijn)
page 253 Estate of Peter William Ham
page 255 Warner Brothers Records
page 256 John Ham (Pete Ham home movies)
page 258 (1) John Ham (Pete Ham home movies)
(2) John Ham (Pete Ham home movies)
(3) John Ham (Pete Ham home movies)
page 260 Ian Murray (Ian Murray)
page 262 Estate of Tony Beresford-Cooke (Tony Beresford Cooke)
page 264 unknown
page 266 (1) Christopher Makris
(2) Christopher Makris
(3) Christopher Makris
(4) Christopher Makris
(5) Christopher Makris
(6) Christopher Makris
(7) Christopher Makris
page 268 Tom Hanley (Tom Hanley)
page 272 (1) Wayne Christian Treiber (Wayne Christian Treiber)
(2) Wayne Christian Treiber (Wayne Christian Treiber)
page 273 unknown
page 274 Retna Pictures Ltd. (Michael Putland)
page 276 Estate of Peter William Ham
page 279 (1) Japanese documentary
(2) John Ham (Pete Ham home movies)
(3) Japanese documentary
page 282 John Ham (Pete Ham home movies)
page 285 unknown
page 286 John Ham (Pete Ham home movies)
page 288 (1)Tom Hanley (Tom Hanley)
(2) John Ham (Pete Ham home movies)
page 292 Estate of Peter William Ham
page 300 Beverley Tucker
page 302 Tom Hanley (Tom Hanley)
page 307 Island Records
page 308 Private Stock
page 309 (1) Janet Macoska (Janet Macoska)
(2) Janet Macoska (Janet Macoska)
page 313 Cindy Tansin (Cindy Tansin)
page 316 (1) Kenny Harck
(2) Cindy Tansin (Cindy Tansin)
page 321 (1) Liz Hays (Liz Hays)
(2) Liz Hays (Liz Hays)
(3) Liz Hays (Liz Hays)
(4) Liz Hays (Liz Hays)
page 322 Cindy Tansin (Cindy Tansin)
page 323 Cindy Tansin (Cindy Tansin)
page 324 (1) Cindy Tansin (Cindy Tansin)
(2) Cindy Tansin (Cindy Tansin)
page 326 Liz Hays (Liz Hays)
page 328 Estate of Peter William Ham
page 331 Cindy Tansin (Cindy Tansin)
page 332 Cindy Tansin (Cindy Tansin)
page 333 Liz Hays (Liz Hays)
page 334 (1) Elektra Records
(2) Elektra Records (Jim Shea)
page 337 (1) Elektra Records
(2) Elektra Records
(3) Elektra Records
(4) Elektra Records
page 339 (1) Liz Hays (Liz Hays)
(2) Liz Hays (Liz Hays)
(3) Liz Hays (Liz Hays)
(4) Liz Hays (Liz Hays)
page 342 Estate of Tony Beresford-Cooke
page 346 Radio Records
page 347 Cindy Tansin (Cindy Tansin)
page 349 Radio Records
page 350 (1) Solid Gold
(2) Solid Gold
page 353 Cindy Tansin (Cindy Tansin)
page 358 (1) Shock Theater
(2) Shock Theater
(3) Shock Theater
(4) Shock Theater
page 360 Alex Shliminoff
page 363 Reed Kailing
page 364 Steve Donahue
page 369 (1) John Weber (John Weber)
(2) John Weber (John Weber)
(3) John Weber (John Weber)
(4) unknown
page 371 Steve Craiter
page 374 Michael Holm
Page 376 Earthtone Records (Roman Sapecki)
page 378 (1) Marianne Evans
(2) Marianne Evans
page 379 (1) John Weber (John Weber)
(2) unknown
(3) John Weber (John Weber)
page 381 Wayne Christian Treiber (Wayne Christian Treiber)
page 382 Japanese documentary
page 383 Rod Roach
page 385 Dan Matovina
page 386 Rod Roach
page 385 John Weber (John Weber)
page 387 (1) John Esselman
(2) John Weber (John Weber)
page 389 unknown
page 394 Tim Boyle (Tim Boyle)
page 396 Dan Matovina (Dan Matovina)
page 397 Lester Cohen (Lester Cohen)
page 407 Flemming Eric Carlson (Flemming Eric Carlson)
page 410 Paul Nyman (Paul Nyman)
page 418 Barry Plummer (Barry Plummer)
page 425 (1) unknown
(2) unknown)
page 429 (1) Wayne Christian Treiber (Wayne Christian Treiber)
(2) Wayne Christian Treiber (Wayne Christian Treiber)
page 430 (1) Wayne Christian Treiber (Wayne Christian Treiber)
(2) Wayne Christian Treiber (Wayne Christian Treiber)
(3) Wayne Christian Treiber (Wayne Christian Treiber)

INDEX

"A Lonely Day," 192
A Place In Time (Mike Gibbins), 406
"A Simple Song," 35
"A Step From Heaven" (Evans and Roach), 377
Abbey Road album (The Beatles), 62, 64, 95, 143
Abbey Road Studios, 63, 64, 89, 93, 94, 118, 136, 137, 408
Aberbach Music, 23
Ace, Martin, 10, 11, 22, 148, 185, 187, 325
Adams, Beau, 9, 10, 11
Adams Beach club, 28
Adams, Bryan, 395
Adcock, Bob, 74, 176
After The Pearl album (Molland), 376
AGI Graphics, 213
Agora nightclub (Cleveland), 236, 239, 412
Aharoni, Danny, 177, 180, 201-203, 206, 208
Air Studios,122, 151, 199, 209, 251, 413
Airwaves album, 335, 336, 347, 350, 402, 412
Airwaves band, 314
Airwaves LP cover, 334
Alcoholics Anonymous, 280
Alice Cooper, 161
Allen, Adam, 356, 357, 359
Allen, Maureen, 121
Allman, Duane, 105
All Things Must Pass LP, 142
All Things Must Pass sessions, 90, 91
Amen Corner, 7, 32, 33
American Bandstand (TV), 338
American Talent International (ATI), 86, 103, 166, 171, 177, 200, 219
Anderson, Roy, 2, 4, 5
Anderson, Russ, 409
"Andy Norris," 223, 260
"Angelique," 40, 54, 68
the Angry Samoans, 156
"Apple, et. al. v. Badfinger Music," 253, 254, 261
Apple Music, 37, 43, 45
"Apple Of My Eye," 194, 199, 231, 233, 238
Apple Records
 Badfinger's contract expires with, 180, 182
 BEI files suit against, 231
 continues to hold Badfinger's income, 318
 financial difficulties of, 227
 first employee Christmas party of, 49, 50
 growth of, 45
 the Iveys' sign with, 41-43
 Melody Maker on, 31
 Molland's copyrights and, 217, 231, 234
 new atmosphere of, 81
 Pete's musical tribute to, 194
 the press criticism of, 47, 75
 rejects Badfinger's album, 135
 reorganizations of, 58, 99
Apple royalties, 318, 341, 342, 361, 363, 368
Apple royalties settlement, 398
Aragon Theater (Chicago), 201
Argent, 188
Argent, Rod, 188
Arthur Howes Agency Ltd., 51, 78, 86
ASCAP Pop Music Awards (1995), 395, 405, 409
ASCAP royalties settlement, 400, 401
ASCAP shares, 318, 361, 362, 368
ASCAP songwriting credits, 405
Asher, Peter, 37, 40, 41, 56, 58
Aspinall, Neil, 58, 67, 101, 217, 296
the Assassins, 69
Ass LP (Badfinger), 213, 214, 217, 227, 231, 233, 234, 238, 408, 412
Atkin, Conrad, 6, 10, 392
Atlantic Records, 343
Atomic Rooster, 119
Average White Band, 68, 254
"Baby Blue," 152, 153, 165, 201, 203
"Baby Please," 122, 409
"Back Again," 275
"Back Off Boogaloo" (Ringo Starr) 143
"Badfinger At The Crossroads" (Leviton), 161, 162, 163
"Bad Finger Boogie" ("With A Little Help From My Friends"), 66, 68
Badfinger Enterprises Inc. (BEI), 114, 168-170, 206, 227, 231, 245, 327, 329
"Badfinger" fan club newsletter, 406
Badfinger (Joey's), 351, 352, 354, 370, 371
Badfinger Live 72-73: BBC In Concert, 417
Badfinger LP, 412
Badfinger LP cover, 235
Badfinger LP recording of, 219-224, 228-231
Badfinger Music, 231
"Badfinger Music v. Apple, et. al.," 253, 254, 261
Badfinger (original)
 at Manor Studios, 194, 195
 attempts to ease out Collins of, 206-207
 compared to The Beatles, 103, 104, 111, 116, 131-133, 233, 234
 confusion over songwriter credits of, 406, 407
 criticism of *Straight Up* album of, 155, 156
 democratic system used by, 126
 documents on 50/50 division agreement, 400, 401
 financial pressures on, 218
 Iceland gig, 147, 148
 increasing financial frustration of, 280-286
 Japanese documentary film (1973) on, 221, 222-224, 241
 Joey quits, 265, 267, 268
 Joey on songwriting agreement of, 399
 Mal Evans separated from, 93
 meeting at Polley's office (1972), 168-170
 Mike leaves, 174-176
 Mike returns to, 188
 musical legacy of, 411, 414
 musical struggles of, 90, 97-99, 119-122
 new dynamics of, 76
 personalities within, 133
 Pete quits, 257-259
 Pete rejoins, 262, 263
 Pete, Tom, advised by Poses to distrust Polley, 183, 184
 plays at Bangla Desh concert, 142-144
 reaction to Pete's suicide by, 293-296
 releases "Come And Get It," 78
 Rob Stawinsky joins, 176
 Rolling Stone article on, 80-81
 Rundgren's reflections on, 149, 150
 sent to Capitol Records Convention, 91
 signs stockholders agreements, 115
 signs with Warner Brothers Records, 188
 the Iveys renamed, 67, 68
 Treiber's relationship with, 95, 96
 TV appearances by, 79, 80
 U.S. tour #1 (1970) by, 102-111
 U.S. tour #2 (1971) by, 124-133
 U.S. tour #3 (1972) by, 158-168
 U.S. tour #4 (1972) by, 176-184
 U.S. tour #5 (1973) by, 200-203, 206, 207
 U.S. tour #6 (1974) by, 236-242
 Warner Brothers Records terminates contract with, 302
 Warner Brothers Music's termination with, 248
 works with Harrison, 135-139
 See also The Iveys
"Badfinger" page (Good Day Sunshine), 406
Badfinger (the second)
 disadvantages against, 350, 351
 dropped by Elektra, 340
 formation of, 317-319
 Gibbins joins/quits, 325, 326
 Malloy's musical influence on, 329-331
 musical reviews of, 335
 rehearsals of (1979), 322
 signs with Radio Records, 343, 344
 U.S. tour (1979), 336-339
 works on a first album, 323-326
Badfinger (Tom's), 362-370, 378-380
Badfinger (under Cass management), 355-360
Badfinger/WB Music publishing contract, 189, 190, 327, 329
Badger band, 333
Bailey, David, 153
Baker, Glenn A., 64, 371
Balaban, Sigmund, 170, 256
The Band, 79, 101, 106, 132, 149, 151, 199
Bangla Desh concert (1971), 142-145
Bankers Life Of Iowa, 302
Banks, Clive, 311
Barnes, Ken, 270
Barrett, Syd, 35
Barton, Dick, 341
Basil: Demos Old And New (Molland), 411
Bauman, Arnold, 234, 252
BBC Radio, 79, 174
Beach Boys, 217, 219
Beaterama column, 6-9, 21, 47
Beatlefan magazine, 335, 387
The Beatles, 3, 23, 26, 55, 75, 77, 81, 95, 100, 101, 103, 111, 131-133, 190, 233, 234
The Beatles Recording Sessions (Lewisohn), 62
"Beautiful and Blue," 52, 68
"Because I Love You," 340, 345, 349
Bedford, Piers, 102
Behind The Music (VH-1), 417
BEI meeting (1972), 168-170
"BEI stockholders agreement," 115
"Believe Me," 89, 90, 101, 107, 124
Bell, Nicky, 78, 103, 105, 107, 113, 124, 125, 139, 148-149, 151, 153, 161, 167, 178, 180, 187, 192, 205, 207-208

Bell, Tony, 226
Bennett, Al, 111
Bent Back Records, 375
Beresford-Cooke, Carola, 278
Beresford-Cooke, Tony, 226, 227, 278, 297
Berry, Mike, 30, 37, 40, 43
The Best of Badfinger: Volume 2, 412
The Best of Badfinger (Apple), 411
"Better Days," 96, 105, 107, 164
"Beverley," 44
Bierstadt, Peter, 231, 234
Big Star, 238, 296
Big Three, 119
Billboard, 52, 55, 113, 116, 154, 157, 165,166, 171, 231, 296, 405
Billboard Top 100, 81
"Birthday," (Beatles), 56
Bishop, Robert, 1
"Bittersweet Adieu" (demo), 39, 40
Black Horse pub, 315
Black Sabbath, 108, 188
the Black Velvets, 4, 5
Blacker, Ira, 251
"Blame The Devils," 102
"Blindman" (Ringo Starr), 143
"Blind Owl," 191, 199, 201, 211, 212, 231, 236, 260
"Blodwyn," 96, 106, 107, 126
Blood Brothers (Russell), 26
The Blue Angel (Liverpool), 70
the Bluesbreakers, 43
Bogart, Neil, 171, 271
Bon-y-Maen Rugby Club (Swansea), 6
Bowie, David, 333
Boyd, Franklyn, 23
Boyle, Tim, 23, 124, 139, 145, 155, 156, 176, 187, 255, 258, 259, 311, 390,
Bramwell, Tony, 59, 75, 116, 125
Braun, David, 227, 231
The Brewery (Michigan State University), 236
Bright Tunes, 250
Brock, Peter, 402-405
Bronson, Harold, 128, 396
"Brother Louie," 271
Brown, Bernard, 217
Browne, Jackson, 319, 395
Brown, Larry, 88, 116, 130, 171, 248, 249
Brown, Peter, 58
Bryans, Richard, 344
Bryn Hall, 3
Bryson, Wally, 201
Buddah Records, 171
Burkett, Howard, 187
"By Order Of The Fuhrer," 273
the Bystanders, 7, 10, 32
Cactus, 177
Caldwell, Jordan, 88
Cale, John, 209
Calello, Charlie, 87, 88, 115, 130, 145, 171, 249
Cameron, Bill, 304-306, 308, 310, 313, 315
Campanero, Lenny, 376, 378, 381
Campbell, Junior, 39
"Candida" (Dawn), 116
Canned Heat, 161
Capitol Records, 52, 231
Capitol Records Convention (Hawaii), 91, 92
Cardiff, 7
Carey, Mariah, 395, 409
Caribou Ranch, 242-249
Carlson, Flemming Eric, 413
Carmen, Eric, 201, 289, 290
Carnegie Hall, 163-165
"Carry On Til Tomorrow," 64, 68, 104
the Cars, 320, 338
Casablanca Records, 271
Cassidy, George, 70
Cass, John, 354-357, 359, 360, 367, 368, 383
Cass lawsuit, 367, 368, 383, 384, 401
"Catherine Cares," 38
Cavalier Club (London), 16, 20
Cavern Club (Liverpool), 19, 26, 41, 69, 73, 78, 79
CBS Records, 23, 40, 182
Cellar Club (Swansea), 7
Charles, Dave, 187
Charlesworth, Chris, 163, 165
Cheetah, 352, 353
Chicago, 219, 242, 323
Chicago Tribune, 160, 161, 201
Chieffo, Vincent, 327, 329
Christie, Lou, 86-88, 101, 115, 130, 131, 171, 172, 218, 297, 380
Circus magazine, 110, 111, 157, 240
Clapton, Eric, 143, 259
Clarke, Mark, 301, 304, 305, 311
Clarke, Pete "Clarkie," 69, 332, 333, 336, 338, 343, 389
Clearwell Castle, 139, 140, 146, 147, 153-155
Clemens, Michael, 327
Climax Blues Band, 209
"The Clown Of The Party," 50
the Club Four (Club Foot), 8
Cocker, Joe, 51, 73, 371
Coffey, Brian, 2, 3
Collier, Anne, 280, 303, 312, 414
Collins, Phil, 395
Collins, Sylvia, 37
Collins, Lewis (Lew), 13, 16, 23, 36, 78, 84, 198
Collins, Toni, 224, 241,242, 269
Collins, William Daniel "Bill"
  alleged trying to get Marianne to sign papers (1983), 389
  Apple/ASCAP royalties settlement with, 398-401
  Apple royalty check dispute and, 261
  at the ASCAP Pop Music Awards, 395-397
  at the December 16, 1974, celebration, 275, 276
  attempts to sell Badfinger equipment by, 303
  attends Beatles' recording session, 23
  attends Tom's funeral, 390
  Badfinger's attempts to ease out, 206, 207
  Beryl Green leaves, 197, 198, 207
  challenges Polley's "statement of claim," 341, 342
  claims that he gave Pete money, 268, 269
  comments on Tom by, 392
  on community phone bill, 277
  concerns expressed by, 160
  control over The Iveys by, 21, 23, 36, 45, 46
  defense of Polley by, 285
  dislike of Tim Boyle by, 155
  dispute with Tom over ASCAP shares, 361, 362
  early life of, 12
  on Emerick, 135
  finishes music room, 117
  gets married to Toni, 224
  growing rebellion against, 83, 84
  hears about Pete's suicide, 293
  on Joey's resemblance to McCartney, 76
  marital problems of, 241
  meeting on band status of, 168-170
  meets Beryl Green, 168
  meets and joins with The Iveys, 12-18
  musical influence of, 54
  personality of, 36, 56
  photographs of, 46, 85
  plays piano on Iveys recording, 54
  on Polley, 108
  pursues Tom Evans for The Iveys, 27, 28
  searches for American connections, 88-90
  separates Mal Evans from Badfinger, 92, 93
  signs contract with Joey, 92
  signs contracts with The Iveys, 21, 46
  signs release to Polley, 312
  signs stockholders agreement, 115
  on suspicions against Polley, 251
  travels to Hawaii (1970), 91
  on Warner Brothers contract, 189
Come And Get It: A Tribute To Badfinger, 417
"Come And Get It," 62-64, 68, 76, 78, 79, 81, 103, 106, 111, 124, 131, 340, 353, 370, 399
"Come And Get It" ad (1969), 75
"Come Down Hard," 338
"Come In You'll Get Pneumonia" (Walker Brothers), 73
"Come On," 344
"Come On Back" (The Crying Shames), 71
Commonwealth United Films, 63, 65
Commonwealth United Records, 68
"Constitution," 211, 234, 236
Cooper, Alice, 344
Cooper, Tommy, 263
Coote, Mal, 361
Copper Records CD, 417
Cordell, Denny, 42
the Corncrackers, 7, 11
Cornick, Glenn, 163
Corriston, Peter, 213, 214
Coverdale, Skip, 371
"Cowboy," 190, 199, 211
Cowboys club, 365, 366
Craiter, Steve, 267, 352, 361, 365, 366, 371, 376, 389
Crane, Charlie (Paul Crane), 71, 72, 73
Crane, Tony, 70, 71
"Crawling Up a Hill" (The Bluesbreakers), 43
Cream, 74
Creedence Clearwater Revival, 55
Creem magazine, 270, 335
"Crimson Ship," 5, 66, 68, 79, 106, 111, 112, 124
"Crippled Inside" (Lennon), 198

"Crocadillo," 344, 378
Crosstown Productions, 410
Crouch, Nicky, 21
the Crying Shames, 71
Crystal Sound Recording, 306
Curb Records, 366
Dacus, Donnie, 362-365, 367, 374
"Daddy's A Millionaire," 42, 44, 51, 131
Dalby, Dave, 68
Daly, George, 320, 330
"Dancing Girls," 35
Dark Side Of The Moon LP (Pink Floyd), 209
Davies, Dave, 16, 20
Davies, Ray, 20
Davis, Clive, 130, 182
Davis, Jesse Ed, 143
Davis, Spencer, 4, 371
"Dawn," 80
Dawn, 116
Day After Day: Badfinger Live CD, 410-414
"Day After Day," 136, 137, 141, 153-155, 157-159, 163-166, 187
DCC Compact Classics, 411
"Dead End Street" (The Kinks), 20
"Dear Angie," 54, 60, 68, 399
"Dear Father," 80
Decca Records, 23
DaCosta, Danny, 68
Deep Purple, 161, 188
Delaney & Bonnie, 79, 106
DeMontfort Hall, 73
"Dennis," 252, 253
Detective, 333
DiLello, Richard, 55, 101, 102, 116, 126, 153, 164, 297, 298, 303
DiMartino, Dave, 236
Dire Straits, 10
Disc & Music Echo magazine, 47, 60, 62, 76, 116, 240
Discoveries magazine interview w/Joey, 249, 250, 261
Disks A Go Go, 7
Dixie, 126-128, 135, 152, 178, 180-185, 193, 195-197, 203
the Dodgers, 306, 307, 311, 314, 315
the Dolphin, 6
"Don't Let It Go," 311
"Don't Let Me Be Misunderstood" (Animals), 31
"Don't Let Me Be Wrong" (Dodgers), 307
the Doors, 161
Doran, Terry, 37, 385
Doud, Mike, 254, 255
Douglas-Jones, Tim, 396, 397
"Down" (Dodgers), 311
"Do You Mind," 187, 199, 213, 234, 411, 412
"The Dreamer," 329
"Dreaming," 35, 187, 412
drugs
  Badfinger during the U.S. tour #1 (1970), 106, 107, 111
  used around Natural Gas, 310
  used by Joey, 322
Duffield, Dave, 15, 20, 22, 36
Dunbar, Aynsley, 21, 175
Duryea, Richard, 219, 242, 245, 248, 256, 271, 275-277, 291, 293-295
Dylan, Bob, 143, 340
the Eagles, 222, 319
Eagles club (Milwaukee), 358
Earthtone Records, 375
Eclipse Music Group, 410
the Easybeats, 73
Edmunds, Dave, 7, 32, 317, 318
Educating Rita (film), 26
Elektra-Asylum, 319, 320, 340
Elektra, Films, 88
Elephant Man (movie), 382
Ellis (Tucker), Beverley
  on Bill Collins, 36, 37
  breaks off with Pete, 121, 122
  comments on Tom by, 29, 390, 391
  on the early Iveys, 16, 17
  engagement to Colin Tucker, 228, 229
  hard times suffered by, 141
  informed about Pete's suicide, 294
  on Kathie Molland, 192
  moves into Sunshine Cottage, 173
  on Pete's life, 299
  on Pete's moods, 50, 51
  on Pete's premonition dreams, 34
  on Pete's songwriting, 34
  on Pete's split with Badfinger, 259
  on Pete's stressful condition, 283, 284
  on Pete and Tom, 35
  relationship with Pete, 18
  renews friendship with Pete, 212, 213
  on roadside accident of The Iveys, 29
  "Sille Veb" written for, 114
  told of Tom's suicide, 388
Embassy Ballroom (Swansea), 5
Emerick, Geoff, 68, 93-95, 98, 118, 119, 122, 133-135
EMI/Capitol, 411
the Empire, 70
Epstein, Brian, 19
the Escorts, 69
Etcetera, Etcetera (TV), 45
Evans, Barrie, 18, 35, 102, 283
Evans, Bob, 351, 354, 370
Evans, David, 25, 173, 174, 198, 383, 384, 391
Evans, Grace, 25
Evans, Jan, 173, 174, 215, 383
Evans, Mal, 23, 37, 40, 41, 48, 49, 54-56, 58, 68, 83, 89, 91-93, 100, 305, 306, 408
Evans, Marianne
  accepts Tom's marriage proposal, 215, 216
  on Clearwell Castle, 154
  during Apple royalties settlement, 398
  during ASCAP Pop Music Awards (1994), 395-397
  financial problems, 347, 348
  gives birth to son, Stephen, 313
  marital problems with Tom, 377
  moves in with Badfinger, 121
  on new house, 186
  returns to Germany, 203
  on Tom's death, 386-388, 391
  on Tom's discomfort around business, 323
  on Tom's new Porsche, 185
  worries about Tom's drinking, 352
Evans, May, 25, 214, 215, 382
Evans, Stephen, 313, 378, 380, 387, 388, 391, 395-398
Evans, Thomas (Tom's father), 25, 85
Evans, Tom
  anger at Joey's sabotage of gigs, 365, 375-377
  antics by, 178, 203, 341, 345-347
  ASCAP income of, 318, 361, 362, 368
  asked to leave Dodgers, 314, 315
  at MIDEM festival, 352
  at Pete's home following suicide, 292
  attempts to form new band, 305-307
  birth of child to, 313
  brings Patsy to England, 214, 215
  complaints about third U.S. tour, 162
  conflict between roadie/driver and, 364
  dispute over "Without You" royalties 361, 362
  early life of, 25-27
  emotional state of, 357, 359, 360, 361, 377, 379-386
  fixes RV, 363, 364
  forms own Badfinger, 362-370
  goes to U.S. at Mike's invitation, 354
  helps form new Badfinger, 317-319
  on Iveys sessions with Paul McCartney, 64
  joins The Iveys, 27-28,
  Kailing on behavior of, 368, 370
  late night phone calls of, 384, 385
  leaves Marianne, 202, 203
  on legality of Badfinger identity, 352
  Malloy on personality of, 336
  marital problems of, 377
  marries Marianne, 215, 216
  meets Rod Roach, 340, 341
  moody personality of, 311, 312
  musical insecurities of, 119
  on Pete's changing personality, 283, 284
  phone argument with Joey, 387, 388
  pictured, 204, 205
  purchases house, 185, 186
  reaction to John Lennon's death by, 348
  reaction to Pete's death by, 302, 303, 342, 348, 370, 373, 393
  relationship between Bill Collins and, 84, 85
  resists signing with Polley, 108, 113
  Rolling Stone interview of, 129, 130
  signs Cass agreement, 355, 356
  signs with Don Powell, 371-373
  signs release to Polley, 312, 313
  smashes his Porsche, 198
  songwriting by, 35
  sued by John Cass, 367, 368, 383, 384, 402
  suspicions about Polley by, 185, 186, 245, 246
  switches to bass, 68
  throat condition of, 391
  trip to zoo with family, 382, 383
  on the U.S., 107
  See also Badfinger; The Iveys
Everly Brothers, 25, 45, 55
"Everybody's Talkin' " (Nilsson), 152
"Everything's Alright" (The Mojos), 13
Eyeline, 102
the Eyes of Blue, 8, 10, 11, 31, 32, 163, 187
Ezrin, Bob, 320

F&M College (Pennsylvania), 160
the Faces, 172, 173, 177, 188, 219
Faded Glory, 354
Fairweather-Lowe, Andy, 7, 32
"Feelin' Alright" (Mason), 102, 106, 159, 165
"Feel Like I'm Flying," 123
Feliciano, Jose, 305
Fenway Theater (Boston), 159
Ferguson, Anne
 asked to exonerate Polley, 301
 during Apple settlement, 396
 Fergie confronts, 265
 finds new home with Pete, 269
 finds Pete's body, 291, 292
 friendship with Pete, 233
 on her life with Pete, 242-243, 246, 255, 256, 278, 279
 on Kathie, 138
 on Pete and her son, Blair 252, 253
 on Pete's death, 299
 on Pete's depression, 289, 290
 Toni attack on, 269
Ferguson, Blair, 121, 229, 253, 253, 255, 277-279, 292
Ferguson, Ian "Fergie," 52, 76, 78, 90, 91, 103, 117, 124, 125, 145, 146, 150, 151, 153, 162, 194, 197, 199, 203, 206, 218-220, 222, 226, 228, 256, 265
Finley, Chris, 70
the Fireflies, 4
Finch, Peter, 71
"Fisherman," 58, 68
Five Arts, 88, 115, 130, 131, 145, 171
Flamingo Club (London), 30
"Flying," 122, 123, 151, 165
the Flying Aces, 325
"(Call on Me) For My Sympathy," 34
"For The Record" (Billboard Magazine), 405
41st Floor Associates, 100
"For You Blue" (Beatles), 90
the Four Pennies, 72
Frampton Comes Alive! album, 308
Frampton, Peter, 308, 396
Francis, Richie, 8
Franklin, Aretha, 55, 65
Franklin, David, 2, 4
Franklin, Jeff, 86, 88, 166, 172, 182, 219, 251
"Fresh," 35
Friend, Jackie, 315, 383
"Friends Are Hard To Find," 101
Friend, Tony, 315
the Fruit Eating Bears, 70, 71
Fryer, Fritz, 72
Fuel 2000 Records, 417
Gaff, Billy, 281
Garrick, David, 14, 16, 19, 20
Gary Walker & The Rain Album #1, 72
Gately, Michael, 164
George, Jack, 4
"Get Away," 194, 199, 211, 260
"Get Back" (Beatles), 47
"Get Down," 83, 89, 101
"Get To You" (Dodgers), 307
Gibbins, Ellie, 396
Gibbins, Gaynor, 97, 99, 124, 139, 141, 154, 172, 173, 175, 176, 192, 197, 202, 203, 206, 215, 218-220, 224, 232, 247, 299, 387
Gibbins, Mike "Mickey"
 left in New York City, 111
 left in St. Louis, 166
 Apple/ASCAP royalties settlement with, 396-399
 at ASCAP Pop Music Awards, 396, 397
 at Cavalier Club, 16
 comments on Tom by, 392
 decides to leave Badfinger, 174-176
 "disappearing acts" by, 166-167
 does English T.V. spot with Badfinger, 185
 invites Tom to form 4th version of Badfinger, 354
 joins the Iveys, 8, 9
 joins/fired from, the second Badfinger, 325, 326
 on Mal Evans, 93
 marriage of, 99, 100
 on possible first American tour, 89
 reaction to Pete's suicide by, 294
 returns to Badfinger, 188
 Ringo and, 96
 roadside accident injuries of, 29, 30
 Rolling Stones interview of, 129
 signs Cass agreement, 356
 signs release to Polley, 312, 313
 songwriting by, 35
 with Tom's Badfinger, 364
 on the U.S., 109
 See also Badfinger; The Iveys
Gibbins, Owen, 172, 175, 247
Gipsy Records, 412
"Give It A Try," 56, 68
"Give It Up," 223, 260
Glanmor Jazz Club, 4, 7, 24
Gleason, Terry, 5, 8
the Glen, 7, 14, 18
"Go All The Way" (the Raspberries), 201
Goldblatt & Co., 256, 405, 414
Golders Green (London), 15, 184
Golders Green CD, 416
Golove, Len, 188
"Goodbye John Frost," 102
Good Day Sunshine, 406
Goodfinger video shoot (1983), 374, 375
Goodless, Kenny (Kenny Tuesday), 70
"Good Times Together," 28
Gors Junior School, 1
"Got To Get Out Of Here," 247, 260
Gothic Horizon, 200
Grand Funk, 161
Grand Hotel LP (Procol Harum), 209
the Grassroots, 128
Green, Beryl, 168, 185, 186, 197, 198, 206, 207
Griffiths, Jason, 48
Griffiths, Maureen, 39, 40
Griffiths, Phil, 55
Griffiths, Ronald Llewellyn
 Apple settlement and, 399
 at Cavalier Club, 16
 Disc & Music Echo interview of, 60
 early life of, 6
 early musical experiences of, 6
 marriage of, 409
 on meeting Mike Gibbins, 8
 on Pete's life and talent, 299
 resigns from The Iveys, 66
 on roadside accident, 29
 songwriting by, 36
 on meeting Bill Collins, 12
 on songwriting agreement with Collins, 46
 records "Come And Get It," 63
 stressful relationship with The Iveys, 61, 62, 64, 65
 on The Eyes of Blue, 8
 See also The Iveys
Grossman, Albert, 130, 149
Guercio, Jimmy, 242
the Guess Who, 344
Gustafson, Johnny, 119
Hackett, Johnny, 78
Hafferkamp, Jack, 201
"(If Paradise Is) Half As Nice" (Amen Corner), 32
Hall, David "Tag," 199, 224, 243, 266, 278, 282, 298
Ham, Bernard John, 1
Ham, Catherine, 1, 38-39
Ham, Irene, 1, 37, 264
Ham, John, 4, 14, 37, 51,113, 198, 259, 261, 262, 265, 282, 293-295, 302
Hammersmith Odeon, 281
Ham, Maureen, 37
Ham, Petera, 393, 394
Ham, Peter William
 asked to work on George Harrison's album, 199
 at Cavalier Club, 17
 autopsy report on, 295
 blues fascination of, 102
 breaks off with Beverley, 121-124
 breaks up with Dixie, 195-197
 business personality of, 180
 comments on life and death of, 298, 299
 commits suicide, 291, 292
 continual trust in Polley by, 218, 219
 depressed state of, 289-291
 during U.S. tour (1970), 106, 107
 early life of, 1, 2
 early musical experiences of, 2-7
 emotional expression through music by, 50, 51
 financial problems of, 278, 280, 282, 289
 friendship between Gaynor and, 172, 173
 frustration with Kathie by, 192, 193, 212, 213, 257, 258
 generosity of, 147
 invites Dixie to come live with him, 185
 involvement with Anne, 242, 243, 246
 lack of publicity about death of, 296-298
 list of concerns by, 209
 marriage plans by, 39, 44, 45
 meets Dixie, 126, 127
 musical creations by, 82
 near auto accident of, 146
 New Musical Express magazine interview by, 79, 80
 performance personality of, 133
 "Piggy" nickname for, 10
 plays with George Harrison, 143, 190
 quits Badfinger, 257-259

reaction to Beverley's engagement by, 228, 229
reaction to Sue Wing's death by, 232
receives £6000, 268, 269
rejoins Badfinger, 262, 263
relationship with Beverley, 18, 19
relationship with family, 37-39
religious beliefs of, 212
roadside accident of, 29-30
Rolling Stone interview of, 129-130
on Ron Griffiths' resignation, 66
songwriting by, 17-18, 34
suicide note of, 292, 297
throws guitar, 273
tirade against Bill Collins by, 84
tribute by hometown of Swansea, 417
on Toni Collins' "knife incident," 269
on Trident Studios recording, 91
on the U.S., 107
writes "Sille Veb" for Beverley, 114
See also Badfinger; The Iveys
Ham, William, 1, 293
"Hand In Hand," 80
Hansen, John, 404
Harck, Kenny, 316-325, 331
Hare Krishna, 228
Harold Davidson agency, 14
Harrison, George, 23, 41, 63, 83, 90, 91, 96, 100, 109, 110, 111, 120, 133, 135-139, 142, 143, 149, 158, 182, 190, 192, 199, 228, 298
Harrison, Patti, 109, 110
Harris, Rolf, 190
Harvey, Steve, 366
Harvey, Terry, 130, 145, 188, 201, 251
"Has Apple Gone Rotten?" (Melody Maker), 47
Head First multitracks, 278
Healey, Mark, 411, 412
"Helping Hand," 284, 286
Hell's Angels, 56
Hemel Hampstead, 66
Hendrix, Jimi, 51
Herald of Wales (newspaper), 6, 21
Herbert, Twyla, 131
the Herd, 71
"Here Comes The Sun," 143
"Hey Jude" (Beatles), 42, 45, 52
"Hey, Mr. Manager," 274
"Hi Fli" (demo), 40
Hofer, Walter, 182, 188, 217, 227, 231, 233, 235, 250, 256, 327
"Hold On," 345, 348
the Hollies, 6, 7, 55
Hollis, Tony, 10, 11
Hooper, Paul, 311, 312, 314, 315
Hopkin, Mary, 41, 45, 47, 49, 56, 59, 152
Hopkins, Nicky, 58, 135, 319, 320
Horrel, John, 3, 4, 5
Hurowitz, Scott, 343-348, 350, 351
Hurst, Mike, 36
"I Am Myself," 35
"I Believe In You," 311
"I Believe In You Girl" (Ron Griffiths), 21
"I Can Love You," 157, 199, 210
"I Can't Live," 98, 99
"I Can't Take It," 83, 95, 107, 180
"Icicles," 211, 234
Iceland gigs, 147-149
"I'd Die Babe," 136, 201
"I Don't Know Why" (Evans and Roach), 377
"I Don't Mind," 107, 260, 414
"I Don't Want To Be A Soldier, Mama, I Don't Wanna Die" (Lennon), 135
Ienner, Donnie, 290
"I Feel Bad Today," 35
"If I Loved You" (Carousel), 6
"If It's Love," 98
"If You Don't Come Back" (Gary Walker & The Rain), 72
"I Got You," 344, 349
"I'll Be The One," 118
"Imagine" (Lennon), 341, 382
"I'm A Joker," 50
"I'm Alone," 56
"I'm Gonna Make You Mine" (Christie), 171
"I'm In Love," 42, 58, 68
"I Miss You," 229, 230, 240
Immediate Records, 70
"I'm Only Human," 82
"I'm Too Shy," 56
the Inbeatweens, 27
In Concert (TV show), 336, 338
Independent Artists company, 411
"Inside My Heart" (Molland), 375
"In The Meantime," 244, 254, 260
the Iron Door, 73
"Island," 223
"Island" (Ham), 39
Island Records, 311
Isley Brothers, 116
"Isn't It A Dream" (Molland), 411
"It Doesn't Really Matter," 253, 286
"It Don't Come Easy" (Starr), 83, 125
It's A Heartache album (Bonnie Tyler), 325
"It's Over," 152
"I've Been There Once Before," 34
"I've Been Waiting," 48
"I've Waited So Long To Be Free," 213
The Iveys
coffin incident, 20
contract between Collins and, 21, 45, 46
controlled by Collins, 22, 23
Dai leaves the, 24
Dublin trip with Garrick, 19, 20
early origins of, 6, 8, 9
introduction to LSD, 48
join with Bill Collins, 12-18
the Kinks and, 20-21
pictured 1966, 19
renamed Badfinger, 66-68
in roadway accident, 29, 30
sign with Apple, 41
signs contract with Collins, 21
stage act/musical talents of, 31, 33, 34
Tom joins the, 27-29
work on *The Magic Christian* sound track, 63-68
See also Badfinger (original)
Ivor Novello Awards, 209, 395
The Ivy League, 66
I Was A Teenage Sex Pistol (Matlock), 303
"I Won't Forget You," 357, 374, 379
Jackson, Alwyne, 1
Jackson, Bob
with the Badfinger group, 363, 364
Cass lawsuit and, 400
contacted for Cheetah situation, 352
during Badfinger tour (1983), 381
during U.S. tour (1974), 265
on financial problems of the band, 270, 283, 303, 304
invited to U.S. by Evans, 354, 355
joins Badfinger, 259, 260
music written by, 311
on Pat Moran producing The Dodgers, 314
on Pete's death, 295, 296, 299
on Pete's return to the band, 263
on signing with Don Powell, 371-373
signs Cass agreement, 356
on Tom's funeral, 390
on Tom's suicide, 388, 389
on Tom's wallet being lost, 380
the Jaguars, 5, 6
James, Stuart, 21
Japanese documentary film (1973), 221-224, 241
Jayvee Entertainments, 9, 14
"Jealous Guy" (Lennon), 135
Jenkins, Alwyne, 4, 5, 8, 11-14, 18, 24
Jenkins, David 'Dai,' 4, 5, 8, 16, 19-21, 23-24, 97, 141
Jethro Tull, 188
the Jets, 7, 10, 11
Joey Molland & The Spare Parts, 370, 371
John, Clive, 10
"John Forgot To Sing," 82
"Johnny B. Goode," 125, 131, 160, 336
John, Paul, George, Ringo... & Bert (musical), 26
John, Robert, 171
Johns, Glyn, 48, 320
Johnson, Ginger, 191
Johnson, Jon, 249
Jones, Kenny, 178
Jones, Mickey, 263
Jones, Stella, 37
Journey, 320
"Just A Chance," 246
"Just One Look" (Hollies), 31
"Just Wanna Love You" (Dodgers), 311
Kaffinetti, David, 304
Kailing, Reed, 362-370, 374
Kanaar, Nick, 397, 398
Kansas City Star, 157
Kass, Ron, 41, 56, 58, 59, 220
Kaye, Tony, 333, 336, 338, 344, 347, 348, 350-352, 376, 380, 386, 388, 389, 393
"Keep Believing," 271
Keltner, Jim, 135, 143
Kerner, Kenny, 271, 273, 275, 278
Khachaturian, Aram, 32
King, David, 77
"King of the Load," 254, 260

King, Tony, 182, 208, 209, 217, 293
King Crimson, 161
the Kinks, 13, 16, 20-21, 48, 71
Kinsley, Billy, 70, 71, 73, 74
Klein, Allen, 57, 59, 81, 82, 86, 88, 91, 93, 99, 100, 134, 149, 163, 164, 182, 190
Kline, Dick, 343
the Knack, 338
"Knocking Down Our Home," 41, 54
"Knock Three Times" (Dawn), 116
"Know One Knows," 246, 251, 254
Kooper, Al, 88, 124, 125, 133, 164, 250, 281, 297, 301, 302, 327, 391
Koshick, Jack, 362, 374, 375, 378, 402
Kowinski, William, 159
Kramer, Eddie, 165
K-Tel Records, 340, 353
Kulkoski, Glen, 402
Kulkoski, Mike, 375, 384, 402
Lambert, Chris, 236, 238
Lambert, Kit, 70
Lane, Ossie, 37
Lawson, John, 71, 73
"Lay Me Down," 273, 411
"Lawaway" (Gibbins), 406
LSD (acid), 48
Leather, Joyce, 37
"Leaving On A Midnight Train," 102
Led Zeppelin, 48, 132, 147
Leeds, Gary (Gary Walker), 71-73
Lee, Larry, 351
Leiber & Stoller, 72, 396
Lennon, John, 41, 42, 58, 63, 75, 76, 123, 134, 135, 198, 210, 249, 348
Leonard, Deke, 7, 84, 147-149, 187, 263, 281
Let It Be album, (The Beatles), 56
Levenson, Maurice "Schmoo," 7, 8
Levensen, Vivien, 16, 22
Levine, Charlie, 130, 201
Levine, Irwin, 88, 116, 130, 248
Leviton, Mark, 161-163
Lewis, Bob, 88, 172
Lewisohn, Mark, 62
Ley, Vernie, 7
Life magazine, 45
"Lightning Strikes" (Christie), 87
Lillian Axe, 406
Lindbergh, Charles, 130
Linzer, Sandy, 88, 115, 116
Liquid Umbrella, 11
"Lion Sleeps Tonight" (Robert John), 171
"Little Mary," 82
Little Switzerland, 358
"Live, Love All Of Your Days," 80
Living In The Material World LP (George Harrison), 120, 199
Lloyd, Mike, 366
Lockwood, Joseph, 81
Lomas, Roger, 315
Lomax, Jackie, 41, 49, 56, 333
London Colosseum, 173
London Records, 99, 100
"Lonely Man" (Splinter), 199
"Lonely You," 222, 223, 230, 240
The Longest Cocktail Party (DiLello), 55
"Long Tall Sally" (The Beatles), 43, 65, 125
"Look Out California," 330
"Look What You've Done," 273
"Looking For My Baby," 40
Lorenzen, Kerstin, 386-388, 390
"Lost Inside Your Love," 317, 330, 335, 336, 338
"Love Can't Hide" (Molland), 412
"Love Is Easy," 219, 220, 226, 227, 230, 260
"Love Is Gonna Come At Last," 329, 330, 335
"Love Me Do," 95, 125
Love Sculpture, 32, 33
"Love Time," 247
"Love Will Be," 192
Lovin' Spoonful, 55
Loving John (Pang), 380
"Loving You," 122
Lucas & The Mike Cotton Sound, 51
"Lucille," 125
Lulu and the Luvvers, 9
Lulu Show (TV), 51, 73
Lupo's Heartbreak Hotel, 380, 381
Lush, Richard, 137
Macabre (Swansea), 7
McCartney, Jim, 23
McCartney LP, 82
McCartney, Mike, 23
McCartney, Paul,23, 37, 40-42, 44, 45, 51, 77, 81, 82, 132, 227, 298, 319, 320
McDonald, Phil, 62, 68, 271, 273
MacDougall, Alan, 371
McGaughey, Scott, 127, 160, 180
McKay, Duke, 7
McKendrie Spring, 128
McLaren, Malcolm, 303
"Magazine Woman" (Gary Walker & The Rain), 72
Magdoff, Sam, 88
The Magic Christian (film), 62, 63-68, 75, 76
Magic Christian Music LP, 76, 78, 80, 81, 106, 111, 399, 411
Magnet, 311
Mahon, Gene, 101, 102, 153
Maida Vale studios, 55
Maitland, Jonathan, 409
Make Your Own Kind Of Music (TV show), 79, 80
Makris, Christopher, 238
Malack, Jeff, 390
Malloy, David, 320, 322, 324, 326, 329, 330, 336, 392
Mama Cass show (TV), 79, 80
Man, 32, 146-149, 254, 263-265
Manfred Mann, 7
Manor Studios, 194, 195, 199, 226
Mansfield, Ken, 52, 59
"Man Without A Heart," 18
Marcucci, Bob, 87, 88
the Mardi Gras (Liverpool), 25, 27
Marino, Rose, 130
"Market Tavern" (Gary Walker & The Rain), 72
Marmalade, 39, 51, 52, 68
Marquee Club, 37, 39
Marshall, Barrie, 86, 255, 257, 278, 311
Martin Ace All-Stars, 354
Martin, George, 64, 95, 122, 123, 209, 417
"Mary Anne With The Shaky Hands" (Townshend), 43
Mason, Dave, 102, 106, 177
the Masterminds, 70, 71
Matlock, Glen, 303
"Matted Spam," 222
Maxie's Nightspot (Swansea), 7
Max, Peter, 348
"May Blues," 123
Mayall, John, 43
"Maybe Tomorrow," 44, 47-49, 51-53, 55, 56, 59, 60, 68, 80, 393
Maybe Tomorrow LP, 58, 59, 411
"Maybe Tomorrow" sheet music, 53
"Mean Mean Jamima," 122
"Meanwhile Back At The Ranch," 246
Medress, Hank, 88, 116, 171, 250
Melanie, 114
Melody Maker, 20, 31, 47, 72, 73, 76, 112, 116, 155, 163, 165, 227, 295
"Memories," 18
Mendelsohn, John, 80, 81
The Merseybeats, 70
The Merseys, 70, 71
The Merv Griffin Show (TV), 349
The Meteorites, 7
Michaels, Lee, 127
MIDEM festival, 352
"Midnight Caller," 97, 236
Midnight Special (TV), 202
"Midnight Sun," 66, 68, 79, 106, 164
Miller, Frankie, 371
Miller, Steve, 102, 106
Mills, John, 187
"Mirror" (Molland), 411
The Misfits, 8
Modern Jazz Quartet, 41
"Modern Romance", 378
"Modest Star Mourned By Friends" article, 390
Moe, Paul, 372, 373, 375
The Mojos, 13, 14, 15, 16, 21, 22, 23
Molland, Joseph, 342,344, 375
Molland, Joseph Charles "Joey"
  Apple/ASCAP royalties settlement with, 398-401
  Apple and copyrights of, 217, 231, 234
  on Apple royalties check, 261
  arrives at Badfinger Cowboy engagement, 365, 366
  at the ASCAP Pop Music Awards, 396, 397
  Badfinger contract release of, 304, 305
  "Badfinger" fan club newsletter by, 406
  "Badfinger" gigs since Tom's death, 409
  on Badfinger's song-writing agreement, 399
  books as Joey Molland & The Spare Parts, 370, 371
  break arm, 178
  comments on Tom by, 392
  Day After Day: Badfinger Live CD put out by, 413-416
  early life of, 69, 70
  early musical career of, 70-74
  forms new Badfinger (2nd), 317-319
  forms new Badfinger (3rd), 351, 352
  on George Harrison, 138
  goes to work with Mark Clarke, 301
  goes to work with Pete Clarke, 343

has child, 344
informed about Pete's suicide, 293
joins Badfinger, 74
on Mal, 93
marries Kathie, 176
new band (Natural Gas) of, 303, 304
partnership with Cameron ends, 315
personality traits of, 224
on Pete rejoining the band, 262, 263
on Pete's life and death, 299
phone argument with Tom, 387, 388
pictured with Kathie, 389
on Polley and Tom's "deals," 184, 185
on possible American tour, 89
quits Badfinger, 265, 267, 268
refused reentry into U.S., 313
Rolling Stone interview of, 130
sabotage of Badfinger bookings by, 365, 375-377
signs contract with Collins, 92
solo album by, 375, 376
on Trident Studios recording, 89, 90
on working with Harrison and Rundgren, 158
See also Badfinger
Molland, Kathie (Wiggins)
arguments/conflicts with, 133, 138, 139, 191-193, 220, 247, 257, 258
attends Pete's funeral, 295, 296
"Badfinger" fan club newsletter by, 406
Harck on, 322, 323
in Miami Beach, 344
on her control over Joey, 184, 212, 213
marries Joey, 176
meeting with Seider claimed by, 249
meets Joey (in U.S.) (in London), 105, 120, 121
moves into Sunshine Cottage with Joey, 173
on phone argument between Joey and Tom, 388
pictured with Joey, 389
resentment by Natural Gas members against, 310
sneaks out master tapes under coat, 412
"Without You" credits claim by, 406, 407
"Monday Morning Blues," 56
"Money," 122, 151
the Monkees, 152
the Moody Blues, 9
Moon, Keith, 9, 143, 161, 199
"Moonshine," 273
Moran, Pat, 314
Morgan Studios, 49, 190
Morris, Andy, 223
Morrison, Van, 7, 395
Morris, Vyvan "Spiv," 7, 11, 263- 265, 268
Mothers Of Invention, 128
the Move, 42
Mozian, Paul, 149
"Mr. Strangeways" (Ron Griffiths), 36
Mundy, Kenny, 70
"My Dark Hour" (Miller), 102, 106, 160
"My Head's Like Lead," 35
"My Heart Goes Out," 220, 227, 240
"My Sweet Lord" (Harrison), 143
"Name Of The Game," 121-122, 124, 133, 136, 139, 153
Natural Gas, 303, 305, 308-310
Natural Gas LP, 308, 310
Natural Gas LP cover, 308
Nevison, Ron, 320
Newman, Beverley, 251
Newmark, Andy, 329
New Musical Express, 47, 79, 80, 116, 238, 335
New York Times, 144, 145, 165
nicknames, 10
Nilsson, Harry, 151, 152, 174, 201, 202, 209, 409
No Dice LP, 106, 107, 111-113, 116, 118, 125, 151, 156, 408, 411
No Dice LP cover, 112
"No, Don't Let It Go," 286, 287
"No Escaping Your Love," 42, 60
Noe, Tim, 156
"No Good At All," 122, 411
"No Matter What," 82, 83, 89, 90, 100, 101-104, 107, 111, 113, 116, 118, 156, 379, 406
No Matter What (Badfinger fanzine), 413
"No Matter What" (Lillian Axe), 406
"No More," 344, 345
"No More" (Ham demo), 287
"No One Knows Me," 246
the Nomads, 69
Norris, Andy, 223
Northern Dance Orchestra, 55
Oakley, Vic, 32
Odell, Anne, 254
"Official Badfinger" Internet Page, 406, 407, 409
"Oh Wow", 221
Oldham, Andrew Loog, 70, 100
Oliver, Jack, 44, 56, 58, 59, 60, 76, 81, 83
Oliver, Nigel, 199
Olympic Studios, 52, 210, 219, 222
"One" (Three Dog Night), 152
"One More Time," 412
"Only You Know And I Know" (Mason), 159
Ono, Yoko, 41, 63, 182
Orange Amplifiers, 78
Orbison, Roy, 32, 71
The Orient (Swansea), 7
Orlando, Tony, 116
Other End (New York), 366
Outer Limits, 18
"Over You," 377, 378
Over You: The Final Tracks (Evans/Roach), 412
Pacific Steam Navigation Company, 69
Pamalan Management, 254
Pang, May, 120, 123, 126, 182, 249, 250, 288, 293, 380
the Panthers, 3
Pappalardi, Felix, 306, 308
Paramount Theater (Massachusetts), 159
Parker, Will, 282
Parton, Stella, 322
Pasadena Civic Auditorium, 127
"Passed Fast," 273
"Passin' Time," 344, 348
Patsy, 202, 214, 215
Paul Revere and The Raiders, 108
Pegasus Flight Productions, 417
Pellinera, 11
People magazine, 349
"Perfection," 107, 108, 120, 151, 201
"performance rights," 400
Perry, Don, 375
Perry, Richard, 152
Philips Records, 23
Phonograph Record magazine, 161-163, 240, 270, 307
"Photograph" ("Friends Are Hard To Find"), 89, 101
"Piano Red," 187, 199, 213, 412
Pickford-Hopkins (Hopkins) , Gary, 8, 12, 22, 23, 163
The Pilgrim (Molland), 409-410
Pinder, Mike, 135
Pink Floyd, 161, 209
Pinkett, Nick, 68
Pitney, Gene, 51, 79
P.J. Proby, 9
the Planet, 8
"Please Stay" (The Crying Shames), 71
Poco, 128
"Poison Ivy", 6
Polleybrock Corp., 403
Polley, Stan
accused in Schweitzer matter, 145
Apple settlement with, 398
arranges recording dates with Warners, 217, 218
attempts to claim Apple royalties, 341, 342
attempts to salvage Badfinger contract, 304
Badfinger's discussions on, 285, 286
brings new contract on BEI accounts, 245
concerns about impact of Pete's suicide, 301, 302
files lawsuit on behalf of Badfinger, 231
financial control kept by, 171
gets releases from Badfinger former members, 312
goes in for heart surgery, 327
impresses the band, 101
increasing distrust against, 249, 250
initial contacts between band and, 86-88, 91
meeting with Badfinger (1972), 168-170
meets with Badfinger in NYC (1971), 124-125
organizes Badfinger's finances, 114-116
Peter Brock and, 402-405
Pete's suicide note on, 292, 297
pleads guilty to grand theft, 404
pushes *Head First* album be recorded, 278
settles WB Music lawsuit, 327-329
taking Badfinger ASCAP shares, 318
treatment of Al Kooper by, 281
tries to sign Badfinger, 108
unprofessional behavior of, 130, 131
Warner Brother's letter to, 301
Polydor Records, 72
Polygram, 314
"A Portrait Of Someone We Knew," 273
Poses, Stan, 114, 115, 124, 130, 131, 133, 168, 183, 184, 289, 293, 380, 400
Powell, Dave, 305, 311
Powell, Don, 371-373, 375
Presley, Reg, 63
Press, Robert, 405, 414
Preston, Billy, 59, 90, 142
Price, Bill, 149, 251
Price, Jim, 143

Princess Margaret, 76
Private Stock, 305, 310
Procol Harum, 209
The Profiles, 70
PR's (Illinois), 367
"publisher's share," 401
Pure Prairie League, 164
"Purple Haze," (Hendrix), 43
Pye Records, 23, 32, 68
Pye Studios, 72
Pylot Promotions, 9
Pylot Records, 10
Queen, 320
"Queen of Darkness," 254
Quinn, Mike, 51
Rabbitt, Eddie, 322
Radd, Gary (Conrad Atkin), 6
Radio One (BBC), 255
Radio Records, 343-345, 348-351, 366
"The Rain," 377
Ramsey, John, 354
Rare Earth, 161, 315
the Rascals, 108
the Raspberries, 201, 296
Raymond, Michael, 145
Read, Mike, 385
Ready, Steady, Go, 70
Record Collector magazine, 60
Reddy, Helen, 323
Red's Grate On The 88 nightclub, 187
Red Shadow management team, 314
Rees, Wyndham, 8, 12
Regal Ammanford Ballroom, 11, 12
Regal-Zonophone, 42
Regent Sound, 40, 70
"Regular," 190, 199 234, 412
REM, 406
Reneri, Rey, 365, 367, 368
"Respect" (Aretha Franklin), 55, 65
"Revolution" (Beatles), 56
Revolver album (The Beatles), 95
Revox "sound-on-sound" tape machine, 17, 18, 28, 43, 82
Rhino Records, 396
Richards, Digby, 325
Richardson, Jack, 344, 345, 347, 351
Riley, Tommy, 187
"Ringside," 286, 287
"Rip It Up," 125
Ritz Entertainments, 7
The Ritz (Skewen), 7
"River Deep, Mountain High" (Supremes), 56
Roach, Rod, 340, 343-345, 347, 348, 352, 360, 361, 377, 378, 381, 384, 385, 391, 393, 412
Robinson, Harry, 97
Rock & Fountain Pub, 4
"Rock'n'Roll Contract," 187, 274, 340, 344, 345, 349
"Rock Of All Ages," 65, 68, 79, 106, 124, 131
"Rockin' Machine," 273
Rockpile, 10, 319
Rodgers, Clodagh, 79
Rogers, Hugh, 375
Rolling Stone magazine, 80, 112, 128, 129, 155, 156, 234, 240, 270, 296, 335, 338
the Rolling Stones, 48, 70, 99, 100
"Roll Over Beethoven," 125, 131
Rosenfeld, Michael, 317
Ross, 259
Roxy Music, 119, 209
Roxy Theater (L.A.), 337, 338
Rundgren, Todd, 149-153, 156-158, 162, 165, 175
Russell, Andrew, 371
Russell, Leon, 106, 128, 132, 136-138, 143
Russell, Willy, 26
Ryan, John, 317, 319
Ryan, Phil, 8, 12, 187
Rykodisc, 412-416
"Sabre Dance" (Khachaturian), 32
Sadistic Mika Band, 254
"Sail Away," 317, 329, 335, 336
"Sali Bloo," 58
Satisfaction, 79
Saunders, Mike, 155, 156
"Sausage And Eggs," 21
"Savile Row," 275
Saville, Les, 4, 17, 22
Say No More LP, 348-350, 402, 412
Say No More LP cover, 349
"Scarlet Willow," 192
Scene Magazine, 157, 236
Schacht, Janis, 110, 111
Schaefer Music Festival (Central Park), 176
Schroeder, John, 23
Schweitzer, Mitchell D., 144, 145, 170, 171
Scott, David, 7
Screaming Lord Sutch, 96
"See Saw Granpa," 58
Seider, Harold, 249, 250
Sellers, Peter, 64
7 Park Avenue CD, 416
Seven Club (Shrewsbury), 15
Seventeen Magazine, 349
the Sex Pistols, 303
Sgro, Tony, 356
Sgt. Pepper LP (The Beatles), 95, 101
Shadow, 177
the Shadows, 2, 6
Shankar, Ravi, 142
Shaper, Hal, 30, 45
Sharp, Ken, 158
Shaw, Greg, 307
"She Belongs To Me" (The Masterminds), 70
"She Came Out Of The Cold," 35
Shell, Bob, 335
Sherba, Glenn, 344-347, 349, 351, 376, 378, 380, 381
"Shine On," 221, 222, 230
Shirley, Jerry, 303-306, 308, 310
Shliminoff, Alex, 355, 356, 359, 360, 365, 402
Shneidman, Edwin S., 297
Shock Theater (TV), 357, 358
"Should I Smoke," 251, 254
Sigmund Balaban & Co., 170
"Sille Veb," 114
Silvers, Ed, 182, 188, 233, 234, 248, 250, 256, 277, 327, 329
Simon, Carly, 319
Simpson, Dave, 371
"Sing For The Song," 118, 119, 409
"Sitting Down, Wasting Time," 35
Sky, 176
Slater, Brian, 70, 72, 73, 99, 116, 119, 121, 138, 198, 212, 288, 289, 295, 303
Small Faces, 14
Smith, Joe, 182, 188, 189, 217, 258, 275, 277, 281, 323, 331
Smith, Mike, 40
Smith, Norman, 95
Solid Gold (TV), 349, 350
"Someday" (Delaney and Bonnie), 79
"Some Other Guy" (The Beatles), 26
"Some Other Time," 244, 254, 260
"Sometimes," 159
"Song For A Lost Friend," 229
Son Of Dracula soundtrack album, 408
"Sorrow" (The Merseys), 71
Soul, David, 305
Sounds magazine, 116, 227, 297
Sparta Music Ltd., 30, 37, 43
Special Merit Spotlight (Billboard), 52
Spector, Phil, 90, 91, 133, 143
Spector, Ronnie, 120
the Spencer Davis Group, 9
Splinter, 199
"Spooky" (Walker Brothers), 71, 72
Springfield Union, 112
Stage Fright LP (The Band), 149
Stallone, Sylvester, 323
Stamp, Chris, 70
Stan Polley Company Incorporated, 403
Starr, Ringo, 49, 64, 75, 83, 90, 96, 125, 142, 143, 298
Stawinsky, Rob, 176, 177, 187
Steckler, Al, 99-101, 125, 133, 135, 149, 164, 165, 180, 182, 183, 206, 298
Steel Pier (New Jersey), 167, 180
Stereo Review magazine, 157
Stewart, Mike, 250
Stewart, Rod, 173, 177, 178, 210, 281
"Stolen Love" (Evans and Roach), 377
"Stop Waiting For The Sun To Shine," 34
"Storm In A Teacup," 49, 60
Straight Up (band), 351, 354, 370
Straight Up LP, 153-159, 174, 175, 178, 192, 351, 411, 412
Straight Up LP cover, 154
Strawbs, 42
Stuart, Hamish, 68
Styx, 317
suicide note (Pete), 292, 297
"Suitcase," 119, 120, 124, 133, 136, 138, 159, 236, 260, 362
"Summertime" (Gershwin), 43
Sunshine Cottage, 173
Swansea Central Library, 417
Swansea rock'n'roll scene, 6, 7
Swansea Top Rank, 265
"Sweet Tuesday Morning," 122, 152, 160, 164
Sweetingham, Jeff, 187
Szymczyk, Bill, 320
"Take Good Care Of My Baby," 34

"Take It All," 144, 151, 159, 161, 165, 180
"Take Me Back," 82
Talent Associates, 357, 359
Tansin, Joe, 316, 317, 319, 325, 331, 332, 345, 351, 354, 392, 412
"Taxi," 21
Taylor, Derek, 40, 43, 47, 56, 58, 60, 76, 77, 93, 116, 182, 226, 279, 280
Taylor, James, 41, 56, 188
Teddy Bear's Picnic, 215
Terry Oates Productions, 23
"That's The End" b/w "This Time" (Pylot Records), 10
Them Calderstones, 25, 27
"Things Are Really Getting Tight," 102
"Think About The Good Times," 58
"Think Twice," 34
"This Time," 187
Thomas-Baker, Roy, 320
Thomas, Chris, 209, 211, 213, 214, 219, 220, 223, 228-230, 244, 246, 249, 251, 252, 254, 280, 295, 318, 320, 371, 417
"Those Were The Days" (Hopkins), 45, 52
Three Dimension Management, 116
Three Dog Night, 152
"Three Time Loser," 340, 345
Thunderbird Artists, 343
Thunderclap Newman, 68
Tidbury, Jack, 315, 392
Tidbury, Marge, 315, 392
"Tie A Yellow Ribbon Round The Old Oak Tree," 130, 248
"Tie Me Kangaroo Down Sport" (Harris), 190
"Time In" (Gibbins), 411
"Timeless," 187, 191, 199, 201, 212, 236, 238
Timeless (Joey Molland's Badfinger), 410
Tin Pan Alley, 259
Title, Julius, 329
the Tivoli, 7, 11
"To Love Somebody" (Bee Gees), 34
"Tomorrow Never Comes," 35
"Too Hung Up On You," 345, 349
Top Of The Pops (TV show), 78, 116, 155
Toulouse No-Neck, 357
The Tower, 4
Tower of Power, 127
Townshend, Pete, 43
Traffic, 55
"Traffic" (Molland), 71
Treiber, Wayne, 95, 96, 110, 113, 131, 166, 177, 272, 380, 386
Trident Studios, 42, 44, 89, 90, 199
the Troggs, 305
Trouser Press magazine, 335, 349, 354
"Try Some Buy Some" (Spector), 120
"Tube Train," 36
Tucker, Beverley. See Beverley Ellis (Tucker)
Tucker, Colin, 228, 229, 390
"Tulip," 82
"Turn Around," 273
"Turn On Your Loving Mood," 18
Turtles, 152
"Twelve Days Of Christmas," 49, 50
Twiggy, 47
Tyler, Bonnie, 325, 326
Tyranosaurus Rex, 42
Ultra Light Products, 402
"Uncle C," 85
Undertakers, 69
Ungano's (New York City), 109-111, 143
U.S. tour #1 (1970), 103-113
U.S. tour #2 (1971), 124-133
U.S. tour #3 (1972), 159-168
U.S. tour #4 (1972), 176-185
U.S. tour #5 (1973), 200-203, 206-207
U.S. tour #6 (1974), 236-243
Universals, 71
"Up On Cripple Creek" (The Band), 79
Uttal, Larry, 305, 306
Valli, Frankie, 305
Variety, 165, 176
the Ventures, 6
Vernon, Deke, 21, 22
Visconti, Tony, 42-44, 48, 54-56
The Very Best Of Badfinger, 411
Voloshen, Nathan, 144-145
van Eaton, Derek, 182
van Eaton, Lon, 182
Voorman, Klaus, 135, 136, 142, 143
Wace, Robert, 14, 16
Wakeman, Rick, 152
Wald, Jeff, 323
"Walk Away Renee" (Left Banke), 43
the Walker Brothers, 71, 72
Walker, Gary, 71, 72
Walker, Rob, 343
Walker, Scott, 72
"Walk Out In The Rain," 57, 68
Wallace, Ian, 340
"wall-of-sound" technique, 90
Walls Ice Cream EP, 60
Walt, 124, 125
War, 161
Warm Records, 36
Warner Brothers Records, 182, 188, 261, 301, 304
Warner-Chappell, 406
Wash, Peter, 68
"Watchdog" (TV), 409
"Watford John," 95
Wax, Steve, 319, 320, 323, 331
WB Music, 188, 189, 233, 248, 256, 258, 274, 327-329
WB Music/Badfinger publishing contract, 328
Weathers, John,8, 10, 12, 22
Webber, Joel, 308
"Weep Baby," 34
"We Gotta Get You A Woman" (Rundgren), 149
Welch, Chris, 72
Welch, Raquel, 64
Welsh music scene, 10, 11
"We're For The Dark," 97, 107, 126, 128, 160, 161, 165
West, Ed, 304
Whaley, Ken, 263-265
"When I Say," 194, 199
"When Will I Be Loved" (Everly Brothers), 55, 56
"Where Do We Go From Here," 221
Whiskey-A-Go-Go (LA), 161
Whiskey Sundown LP (Richards), 325
White, Alan, 90
White Album (The Beatles), 59, 209
White Bread, 404
White Hart pub,315, 340, 381, 385, 387, 392
the Who, 7, 9, 43, 70, 143
The Who Sell Out LP (The Who), 43
"Why Don't We Talk," 220
Wickland, Bobby, 351
Wiggins, Kathie. See Kathie Molland
Wiggins, Peter, 70
Wild Horses, 241
the Wild Ones, 4, 5, 6
Wild Turkey, 163
Williams, Alan, 381
Williams, Taff, 8, 12
Williams, Terry, 7, 10, 148, 263-265, 311
Wilson, Flip, 323
Wilson, John, 307, 311, 314
Wilson, Paul, 387
Wing, Sue, 23, 24, 97, 141, 185, 232
"The Winner," 157, 199, 210, 260
"Winner" 329
Winwood, Muff, 305, 307
Winwood, Steve, 12, 273
Wisconsin Summerfest, 357
Wise, Richie, 271, 273, 275, 278
Wish You Were Here LP, 254-256, 265, 267-270, 274, 275, 279, 329, 412, 415
Wish You Were Here LP cover, 255
"With A Little Help From My Friends," 67, 68
"Within You Without You" (George Harrison), 23
"Without You," 83, 98, 99, 151, 152, 157, 161, 163, 169, 174, 187, 188, 296, 361, 362, 368, 393, 395, 396, 400, 401, 405-409, 417
"Without You" (Carey version), 395
"Without You" (Nilsson version), 151, 152, 157, 163, 201, 209, 393, 395
"wobble board" rhythm, 190, 211
Wodtke, Al, 371-374, 388, 392, 393
Wonder, Stevie, 166, 371
Wood, Peter, 304, 306
Wood, Ron, 178
Wright, Gary, 90, 139, 152
Writing On The Wall, 147
"writers share" issue, 398, 400
Wyn-David, Tony, 10
the Yardbirds, 9
Yes, 333, 376, 380, 386
"Yesterday Ain't Coming Back," 54
"Yesterday" (Beatles), 44
Yoko Ono, 41, 63, 123, 182
"You And I" (Goodfinger), 374
"You Can All Join In" (Traffic), 56
"You Can't Always Get What You Want" (Rolling Stones), 107
"You Didn't Know Each Other Very Well," 34
"You Had A Dream," 229
"You Know," 17
"You Make Me Sick" (Molland), 410
Young Fresh Fellows, 127, 160
"You're So Fine," 247
"You're Such A Good Woman," 192
Zoe, 222, 223
Zombies, 188
Zoo World magazine, 240